Andy B
18 TO 11 86

THE ROCK YEARBOOK

VOLUME VII

EDITED BY
TOM HIBBERT

Virgin

VIRGIN BOOKS
LONDON

In-house editor
JANE CHARTERIS

Picture researcher
DILL ANSTEY

Interior designed by
SUE WALLIKER with **URSULA SHAW,
FRASER McDERMOTT** and **CHRIS McCOWAN**

Cover design by
KEN ANSELL and **DAVE DRAGON, THE DESIGN CLINIC**

First published in Great Britain in 1986 by
Virgin Books, 328 Kensal Road, London W10 5XJ

Copyright © 1986 Virgin Books

ISBN 0 86369 169 2

Printed in Great Britain by The Thetford Press, Thetford

Bound by D R Skinner & Co, Cambridge

Typeset by Capital Setters, London SW1

Distributed by Arrow Books

● CONTRIBUTORS

● **Lloyd Bradley's** writing has been called a joke for years; now he earns a better than average living writing jokes for stage, screen and comic strips. He only reverts to journalism for *really* worthy causes such as this one.

● **Brian Chin** loves to run around saying, "I heard this *fabulous* record . . ." It is one of his primary joys in life and he indulges it so regularly in *Billboard*, the *New York Post*, *Music Week*, *International Musician and Recording World* and the *Village Voice*.

● **Pete Clark** lives and occasionally works in London.

● **Mark Coleman's** articles have appeared in *Rolling Stone*, the *Village Voice*, and *Star Hits* in America, and in *Smash Hits* and *Melody Maker* in England. Currently, he is at work on unauthorised biographies of both Lionel Richie and the Mentors.

● **Richard Cook** is editor of *Wire*, Britain's jazz and new music magazine. He has studied and discussed music all his life and thinks he has a few more things to say yet. Besides regular broadcasting and contributions to the national press and *Sounds*, he also hopes to complete at least two of the three books he's working on this year. He lives as calmly as possible somewhere in North London.

● **Ian Cranna** is a former contributor to *NME* from his home town of Edinburgh and pioneering editor of *Smash Hits*. He no longer wants to be rich and famous – just rich will do. These days, when not managing obscure and troublesome pop groups, he has two remaining ambitions: to record Sparks' 'Rockin' Girls' with OMD, and to grow old disgracefully. (There now – I didn't mention XTC or the Blue Nile once!)

● **Fred Dellar** claims to have been into rock since Pete Frame's *Family Trees* were mere acorns. A regular contributor to *NME* since 1972, he's responsible for the infamous 'Fred Fact' column where you can find mention of such classic songs as 'We're Going To Hire A Wino To Decorate Our Home' and 'In The Woodshed She Said She Would'.

● **Dessa Fox** is video editor of *NME* and contributes to *Time Out*.

● **Pete Frame** lives in remotest Buckinghamshire, isolated from reality. There he continues to convince himself that the world of rock is still exciting enough to write about and is *still* bashing together a third volume of *Rock Family Trees*.

● **John Gill** has been music editor of *Time Out* for three years, having been disgracefully abandoned by Geoff Brown who had shared the burden for the previous two years. Earlier he had spent five years as *Sounds'* captive pseud.

● **Loyd Grossman** as an undergraduate wrote extensively about pop music for a number of publications including *Fusion*, *Vibrations*, *Rolling Stone*, the *Cambridge Phoenix* and *Boston After Dark*. His book, *A Social History of Rock Music* was published in 1975.
  After a brief fling as a rock guitarist which took him to the dizzying heights of number 49 in the hit parade, Grossman joined *Harpers & Queen* as design editor. He was contributing editor to the *Sunday Times Magazine* from 1984-85 and has written about food, architecture and sports for *Geo*, *The Times*, the *Financial Times*, *Harpers & Queen* and the *Mail on Sunday*.

● **Brian Harrigan** is deputy editor of *Video Business* and *was* news editor at *Melody Maker* and a contributor to *Smash Hits*, *Record Mirror*, *Time Out* and so on. He has written several books and has never once got his copy in on time. His contribution here was no exception.

● **Chris Heath** is a *Smash Hits* 'journalist', and is 'famous' for his disgusting clothes, his appalling taste in pop music, and for his annoying habit of not talking loud enough.

● **Tom Hibbert** is apparently the 'voice' of *Smash Hits*, and sometime contributor to the *Observer*, *Time Out*, *Company*, *Just Seventeen* (cry-baby comic), *Skateboard Dealer*, um, *What Buy?* and, ahem, other 'fine' titles. So bloody what? His wife is far more impressive, having once kissed Elvis Presley on the lips and having been born just round the corner from Eric Brann of Iron Butterfly. (Eats toast.)

● **David A Keeps** hates writing about himself when he could be talking about himself. A typical Gemini, both of him collect state map memorabilia, watches, boxer shorts and 'monkey' things, which are stored in his New York City apartment. Still the editor of *Star Hits*, he visited Disneyworld with Joan Rivers and lived to tell the tale.

● **Dave Laing's** recent study of punk, *One Chord Wonders'* was compared by one reviewer to Princess Anne. Other books written or edited by him have covered electric folk music, Buddy Holly and rock aesthetics. In 1987 he will publish a Popular Music Encyclopedia which he has co-edited with Phil Hardy. A writer and journalist, he has now taken refuge from the hurly burly of the freelance life by becoming Information Officer of IFPI.

● **James Manning** is the editor of *Smash Hits* in Australia. When not thinking up some way of floging the latest English 'craze' to his readers he can be found behind the counter of his bookshop selling 'rock' books and associated memorabilia. He also provides a weekly on-line news service and listens to lots of black music.

● **Simon Mills** is the impeccably mannered 'stylist' for *Just Seventeen* (the cry-baby comic) and is much given to saying things like "Word up man!" in a phoney American accent. But do not be fooled – this is the man who really knows the stars and his articulate profiles of Marie Osmond, a man who thinks he's a refigerator, and ten thousand highly famous soul stars that no one's ever heard of have fairly startled the known publishing world. A 'free-wheeling' 'diamond in the rough', Mills drives a car with plastic hubcaps and occasionally wears plaid shorts. Such is his incredible style.

● **Tony Parsons** a professional sportswriter at the age of ten, was educated at Nick Logan's *NME* and has published three novels – *Platinum Logic*, *Winners & Losers* and *Limelight Blues* (soon to be a minor motion picture).

● **Penny Reel** has been writing about reggae for some fifteen years, and for *Echoes* and the *NME* for ten.

● **Paul Rider** takes photographs of Five Star's lawn, Prince's bottom, Tony James' boots, Nik Kershaw's fluffy toys and Bogshed. And why not?

● **William Shaw** was born in Newton Abbot in 1959. He has been a petrol pump attendant, a council labourer and a university student. Before his current job of editing the newly launched *Mix Magazine*, he wrote for *Zigzag*, *Smash Hits* and *Blitz*.

● **David Sinclair** is rock critic of *The Times*, drummer in the Riding Hoods and has been researcher on BBC TV's *The Rock 'n' Roll Years* and *Rockschool*. His book *Tres Hombres – The Story of ZZ Top* is published in September.

● **Phil Sutcliffe** contributes to *Time Out*, *Mizz* and *Q*. 64:50 for ten miles at 38!

● **Steve Taylor** was the first assistant editor of *The Face* and moved into television with the advent of Channel 4, devising, producing and presenting the innovative live chat show, *Loose Talk*. He now works as a freelance TV producer and production consultant, specialising in subjects such as fashion, product design, music, film and video, for ITV and Channel 4, government bodies, arts centres and commercial companies.

● **Allyce Tessier** is a freelance writer and picture researcher phenomenon who once kissed Elvis Presley on the lips and was born just around the corner from Eric Brann of Iron Butterfly. An American person with a pathetic devotion to Bob Dylan and Carl Yastrzemski of the Boston Red Sox, she once bought an oscillating fan in a hardware store with her mother's credit card. (Perfect ankles.)

● **John Tobler** has written over twenty published books on music of the rock era and has worked on several successful series for BBC Radio One. He is currently contributing to *Music Week*, *Billboard*, *Folk Roots* and *Which Compact Disc?*

● **David Toop** once saw the Ronettes in concert and is still alive to tell the story. Additionally author of *The Rap Attack*, musician/record producer and music columnist for *The Face*.

● **Paul Vernon** has been a fly in the ointment of the blues world for over twenty years now, contributing to and publishing assorted specialist publications, hacking out sleeve notes, compiling albums and appearing on radio shows both in the UK and US as guest speaker. Currently, he can be found in the plush editorial garret of *Blues & Rhythm*, a monthly magazine devoted to blues, R&B, gospel, cajun and tex mex.

● **Hank Wangford** from Intercourse, Pennsylvania, is the radical godfather of anarchistic British country music and the leader of its finest band. Often described as eccentric, Hank is in fact a loony and has been known to contribute to such world-famous country music publications as the *NME*.

ACKNOWLEDGEMENTS

Tom 'Tom' Hibbert and Jane 'Jane' Charteris would like to thank the many people who helped to put this the *seventh* volume of opinion, information and prejudice together. The absence of any single one of them would undoubtedly have meant the end of the endeavour, so in no particular order here they are:

All the long-suffering persons who staff the publicity offices of record companies large and small: without their co-operation there would be no pictures in the book, and what a dull book that would be! Unfortunately, they are just too many to mention by name, but they know who they are.

For photographs not otherwise available: Associated Press; Bartle, Bogle & Hegarty; *Blues Unlimited*; Channel 4; David Corio; Dick James Organisation; Robert Ellis; Jak Kilby; Denis Lewis; London Features International; Loose Tubes/ Colin Mazarini; Modern Publicity; Photo Source; Steve Rapport; Retna Pictures; Michael Putland/Adrian Boot; *Sid And Nancy*: An Alex Cox Film/Palace Pictures; Ashley Slater; Sterns; TVS; Champion Doug Veitch; Stella Whalley.

Ian Cranna, Pete Clark and Steve Taylor for emergency services.
Chris Ledger for long hours spent on the telephone checking and updating the Rock Reference.
Jane Carr for help above and beyond her job description.
'Ginger Fringe' Sue, Ursie Baby of the seriously black barnet, 'Billy Idol' McDermott and 'Zodiac' McCowan for long hours, flexibility and inventiveness with scalpel, hair-dye and blades.
Dill 'Bill' Anstey for, among other things, persuading John Blake to give us a pic of himself.

Tracey Waite, possibly the most important person in our world, if not *the* world, for the last two months, for without her dexterity at the keyboard and her unflagging spirit you would not be reading this or anything else in the book. She is Typesetter of the Year.

And Paul Barton, who knows a lot of shortcuts (which he doesn't use) and quite a few quotations from *Twelfth Night* (which he does) and without whom we would have had no strawberry cakes for tea . . . whoops, nothing would have been delivered. There, Paul, you are, as you wished, 'mentioned in despatches' (ugh) . . .
If anyone is smarting because his/her name is not here, please forgive the omission and considered yourself thanked.

CONTENTS

THE YEAR

AUGUST 1985

3 'Into The Groove' becomes Madonna's first UK number one, but she's sold more singles than any other act this year. In America, 'Shout' brings Tears For Fears their second chart-topping single, while *Songs From the Big Chair* maintains its position at the top of the album chart.

8 Escalating riots in South Africa leave sixty-five dead. America warns that sanctions will be applied unless reforms in the apartheid law are swiftly implemented.

10 Simon Le Bon cheats death when his sloop *Drum* capsizes in storm-tossed seas off the Cornish coast during the Fastnet Race.

15 *With a new Atlantic crossing record in sight, Richard Branson's powerboat* Virgin Atlantic Challenger *capsizes and sinks only 100 miles from home.*

● DEXY'S MIDNIGHT RUNNERS

18 Michael Jackson forks out $40 million for the extensive ATV Music catalogue, with rights to some 5000 songs, including many by Lennon and McCartney.

31 Exactly twenty years after carrying Sonny & Cher to the top of the UK singles chart, 'I Got You Babe' does the same for the unlikely combination of UB 40 and Chrissie Hynde. On the US album chart, Dire Straits' *Brothers in Arms* finally rises to number one.

■ Simon Le Bon, Nick Rhodes and Roger Taylor temporarily desert Duran Duran to launch Arcadia.

■ Kate Bush, Madness and Dexy's Midnight Runners return to the fray after long regenerative absences.

■ Saul Zaentz, boss of Fantasy Records – once home of Creedence Clearwater Revival – sues John Fogerty for a reported $144 million, claiming that two tracks on the hit album *Centerfield* portray him in a less than favourable light.

SEPTEMBER 1985

3 *Divers locate the* Titanic, *lying in 13,000 feet of Atlantic, some 550 miles off Newfoundland.*

7 Top US single is 'St Elmo's Fire' by Englishman John Parr – all but unknown in his homeland. 'Dancing in the Streets' by David Bowie and Mick Jagger, zooms to the top of the UK chart, where it stays for the whole month. Meanwhile, Mick Jagger becomes a dad for the fourth time – his first boy, James Leroy Augustine Jagger.

9 *Forty-five shops are destroyed and two brothers burned to death during riots in the Handsworth district of Birmingham.*

10 *Britain blocks EEC proposals to impose sanctions on South Africa. President Reagan announces limited US sanctions.*

19 *Two massive earthquakes leave Mexico City devastated. Over 5000 die, over 30,000 are injured.*

21 'Money For Nothing' takes Dire Straits to the top in America, where they now head both charts. In Britain, Madonna's *Like a Virgin* outsells all other albums.

28 *After a black woman is accidentally shot by police searching her home in Brixton, property is looted and set alight, police are attacked and a police station petrol-bombed.*

28 *Hounds of Love* by Kate Bush enters the UK album chart at number one.

● KATE BUSH

■ Sigue Sigue Sputnik become the hottest unsigned band since Spandau Ballet. Record companies clamour.

■ Elton John, Stevie Wonder, Gladys Knight and Dionne Warwick join forces on 'That's What Friends Are For', proceeds of which will go to AIDS research; Iron Maiden donate royalties from their new single to anti-heroin organisations; and Pete Townshend forms a new band, Deep End, specifically to play benefit gigs, the profits of which will help finance drug rehabilitation centres.

OCTOBER 1985

1 Britain's Frank Bruno knocks out Anders Eklund to take the European heavyweight boxing title.

2 Film star Rock Hudson dies at his Hollywood home, aged 59, of AIDS. Public awareness is concentrated on the escalation and spread of the disease.

5 Midge Ure's solo single 'If I Was' tops the UK chart – a feat he previously achieved in 1976, as a member of Slik, and in 1984, as an instigator of Band Aid.

6 After the collapse and death of a black woman during a police search of her home, severe riots break out in Tottenham, North London, during which a policeman is stabbed to death.

7 Four PLO guerillas hijack the Italian cruise ship Achille Lauro, killing an American passenger. After giving themselves up to Egyptian authorities, the plane carrying them home is intercepted by US fighters and they are arrested in Sicily after a forced landing.

10 Actor, writer, director and 'misunderstood genius' Orson Welles dies, aged 70; film star and 'enigma' Yul Brynner also moves on, aged 65.

19 A-ha have the number one single in the States, 'Take On Me'. In Britain, 'Gambler' provides Madonna with her seventh Top Ten hit this year. On the indie scene, the Smiths have top single, 'The Boy With The Thorn In His Side', the June Brides top album, There Are Eight Million Stories.

25 Actor Gary Holton, once leader of the Heavy Metal Kids and famed for his role in the TV series Auf Wiedersehen, Pet, dies in bed at a friend's Wembley home, aged 33. An inquest hears that he died from a mixture of heroin and alcohol on top of doses of valium and cannabis.

■ John Foster joins Bronski Beat as replacement for recently departed vocalist Jimmy Somerville.

■ Former Clash stalwart Mick Jones denies seeking to prevent the latest line-up from trading under the name.

■ Madness tour for the first time in over two years; Simple Minds return after an 18-month hiatus.

■ The Thompson Twins' UK tour collapses after the promoter, Paul Loasby, goes into liquidation, claiming poor advance sales as the major reason for his bankruptcy.

NOVEMBER 1985

2 Stevie Wonder's 'Part Time Lover' is the best-selling single in America, where the Miami Vice soundtrack heads the album list. Simple Minds have the number one album in Britain, Once Upon a Time.

2 The South African government bans media reporting of civil unrest. Journalists and cameramen face long prison sentences should they infringe the new law.

8 475 people go on trial in Palermo, Sicily, charged with mafia complicity.

9 Jan Hammer's title theme single gives Miami Vice supremacy over both US charts. The Cult rule both UK indie charts, with 'Rain' and Love.

10 Jerry Lee Lewis, hospitalised in Memphis with a bleeding ulcer, is given only a 50/50 chance of survival after emergency surgery. The 50-year-old rocker pulls through.

14 The Nevado Del Ruiz volcano in Colombia erupts, burying a town and three villages. After typhoid ravages the area, the death toll rises to over 25,000.

16 Still going strong after nineteen years of changes, the former Jefferson Airplane/Jefferson Starship, now plain Starship, tops the US singles chart with 'We Built This City'. In Britain, Sade heads the album chart with Promise, while former Undertone and Assembly man Feargal Sharkey confirms his solo arrival with the number one single 'A Good Heart'.

● BRONSKI BEAT

● GEORGE MICHAEL: WHAM!

19 Reagan and Gorbachev start the first summit conference between America and Russia for six years. They fail to overcome major policy differences.

29 After a protracted court battle, Elton John and Bernie Taupin fail to recover the copyright of 169 songs published by DJM Music under an agreement signed in 1967. However, the judge rules that Dick James must stump up as much as £5 million in unpaid royalties due to the pair. A few days earlier, James had dropped his High Court action, alleging that George Michael had nicked the melody of 'Last Christmas' from the 1975 Barry Manilow song 'Can't Smile Without You'. DJM were ordered to pay costs.

30 Wham! return to the top of the UK singles chart with 'I'm Your Man', while yet another TV promoted compilation, Greatest Hits of 1985, tops the album chart. Phil Collins and Marilyn Martin have America's best-selling single, 'Separate Lives'.

■ Under ringleader Miami Steve Vandt, Artists United Against Apartheid cut 'Sun City', deploring South Africa's apartheid system and the cosmetic integration visible at Sun City, where large financial inducements have lured many top showbiz names. Among the thirty-six singers and musicians on the record are Hall and Oates, Bob Dylan, Bruce Springsteen, Peter Gabriel and Ringo Starr.

■ The American Immigration Department deny New Model Army a work permit on grounds of "no artistic merit". A few days later, the Blow Monkeys also have visa applications turned down.

● VINCE NEIL: MÖTLEY CRÜE

■ Mötley Crüe singer Vince Neil, over the legal alcohol limit when the car he was driving in December 1984 went out of control, killing Hanoi Rocks drummer Razzle and seriously injuring two others, is given a one month jail sentence and five years probation by a California court. He is also ordered to do 200 hours community service and to pay $2.6 million dollars compensation to the accident victims.

■ The Clash lose three members, leaving only Joe Strummer and Paul Simenon holding the name; Kaja, formerly chart-topping band Kaja-GooGoo, split up.

■ A good month for Phil Collins: as he tops the US singles chart for the third time this year, his album No Jacket Required becomes the first to sell one million copies in Britain alone in 1985.

■ The end of the line for Laser 558, the offshore pirate radio station, which goes off the air and limps into Harwich Harbour accompanied by a government patrol vessel.

DECEMBER 1985

4 A verdict of accidental death is returned at the inquest on Cynthia Jarrett, whose death had instigated the Tottenham riot in October.

7 Generic rock group Mr Mister head the US singles chart with 'Broken Wings'. Now That's What I Call Music 6 is the latest compilation to top the UK album chart.

11 Meteors' guitarist Paul Fenech is given a nine months' prison sentence, suspended for two years, and fined £1000 for causing an affray and carrying an offensive weapon at a gig in Walsall.

12 Ian Stewart, who, together with Brian Jones, founded the Rolling Stones, dies of a heart attack, aged 47.

17 Northern Ireland's fifteen Unionist MPs resign their seats over the recent Anglo-Irish Agreement.

21 Lionel Richie's latest, 'Say You Say Me', becomes the best-selling US single, while Heart's eponymous offering climbs to the top of the album chart. Yet another hits compilation, Now; The Christmas Album, tops the UK chart.

● LIONEL RICHIE

21 Winnie Mandela is arrested for returning to her home in Soweto, an area she had been officially prohibited from entering.

22 D Boon, guitarist and singer with the acclaimed San Pedro, California, group the Minutemen, dies in a road accident in the Arizona desert, aged 27.

28 Shakin' Stevens enjoys his fourth number one UK single 'Merry Christmas Everyone'.

31 Fifties rock star Rick Nelson, his fiancée and his band all die when his private plane crashes en route to a gig in North East Texas.

■ Bob Geldof meets the Indonesian Ambassador to protest about the immorality of bootleg Live Aid records and tapes originating in his country, which is not a party to any international copyright agreements.

■ David Crosby, on the run from Texas police after being found guilty of drug and gun possession charges, gives himself up in Florida. He faces up to ten years in prison.

JANUARY 1986

4 Former Thin Lizzy leader Phil Lynott, one of the biggest rock stars of the seventies, dies in Salisbury General Infirmary of "heart failure and pneumonia following septicaemia". 34-year-old Lynott had collapsed on Christmas Day, suffering from a combination of blood poisoning and liver and kidney failure.

● PET SHOP BOYS

11 The Pet Shop Boys see their debut, 'West End Girls', rise to number one on the UK singles chart.

16 The Sex Pistols are awarded around one million pounds after a court ruling against their former manager Malcolm McLaren.

18 In the indie album chart, *Back in the DHSS* by Half Man Half Biscuit deposes *Frankenchrist* by the Dead Kennedys. 'Echoes In A Shallow Bay' keeps the Cocteau Twins at the top of the indie singles chart all month.

20 *Britain and France authorise a channel rail tunnel to link the two countries. It is expected to be operational by 1993.*

25 Under the banner Red Wedge, several rock stars committed to the Labour Party set out on a UK tour designed to bring young people and politics closer together. Among those participating are Paul Weller, Billy Bragg, the Communards, Junior Giscombe and Jerry Dammers.

25 Albert Grossman, once manager of several illustrious rock stars including Bob Dylan and Janis Joplin, dies on a flight from the States to Britain.

27 In the American Music Awards ceremony in Los Angeles, Bruce Springsteen takes the Male Vocalist, Best Album and Male Video Star categories. Other winners include Tina Turner, Huey Lewis and the News, Pat Benatar, Wham! and Chicago. Chicago?

28 *The space shuttle Challenger explodes soon after take-off. All seven astronauts are killed. Millions witness the tragedy on a live TV broadcast.*

30 *Unemployment in Britain reaches a new record: over 3.4 million, representing 14.4 per cent of the workforce.*

■ Ozzy Osbourne denies newspaper reports that he is being sued by the parents of a California boy who killed himself after listening to one of his songs, 'Suicide Solution'.

■ Spandau Ballet part from Chrysalis Records after months of legal dispute and acrimony.

■ Bob Geldof, voted Man Of The Year by Radio 4 listeners and every compassionate human being in the world, is snubbed in the New Year Honours List – despite the Live Aid concert having generated over £60 million for Ethiopian famine relief.

FEBRUARY 1986

1 Erstwhile singer, music publisher, record company boss and litigant Dick James dies of a heart attack at his London home.

3 Radio Caroline, the original pirate station, snaps its anchor chain in heavy seas, but resumes broadcasting. Since Laser's departure, Caroline has been using the 558 MW frequency, despite its having been allocated to BBC's Radio Essex, due on the air soon.

7 Haitian dictator Jean-Claude Duvalier flees the country, setting up temporary residence in France.

8 'When The Going Gets Tough' hoists Billy Ocean to the top of the UK singles chart.

9 Pete Townshend, Chrissie Hynde, the Communards and Working Week are among those teaming up for a Royal Albert Hall concert to raise money for the Colombian Volcano appeal.

10 At the annual BPI awards ceremony, Phil Collins is declared Best Male Artist and his *No Jacket Required* Best Album. Other winners include Dire Straits, Paul Young, Go West, Tears For Fears, Bruce Springsteen and Annie Lennox. A special BPI Award goes to Bob Geldof.

15 *After bare-faced manipulation in the Philippines Presidential election, Ferdinand Marcos is ousted by overwhelming public support for Mrs Corazon Aquino.*

15 'Whistling In The Dark' by Easterhouse becomes Britain's best selling indie single.

● HALF MAN HALF BISCUIT

23 News of a national payola scandal breaks in the States. Several major labels sever ties with independent record promoters, some of whom are suspected of buying radio time with drugs, prostitutes and cash pay-offs.

Wham! announce plans for "an amicable split". Jo Boxers split up, blaming the "abominable pressures of the music business mafia"; Echo and the Bunnymen lose their drummer, Pete de Freitas; and Steve Strange launches Strange Cruise, in which he will be partnered by former Photos singer Wendy Wu, now Wendy Cruise.

● JAMES BROWN

Sigue Sigue Sputnik make their vinyl debut; John Lydon releases his first album for two years; the Damned make the Top Ten for the first time; and James Brown has his biggest hit for twenty years.

The Indonesian Government orders the withdrawal of all Live Aid bootlegs following international pressure.

The Thompson Twins, having been forced to cancel their British tour the previous October, keep good their promise to reimburse disappointed fans. The band records a limited-issue live album to be offered free to all ticket-holders.

MARCH 1986

1 Mr Mister rule both US charts – with 'Kyrie' and *Welcome to the Real World.*

3 *A pay settlement is reached between the teaching unions and local authorities, ending a year-long dispute.*

4 *Today, Eddy Shah's new national newspaper, begins publication.*

4 Richard Manuel, 42-year-old keyboard player and founder member of the Band, hangs himself in his hotel room following a gig in Florida.

8 Whitney Houston's eponymous album tops the US chart. Diana Ross has the number one UK single, 'Chain Reaction' – more than twenty years after first achieving the position with 'Baby Love', when she led the Supremes. The Cramps enter the UK indie album chart at number one with *A Date With Elvis.*

15 Starship continue their renaissance as 'Sara' heads the US singles chart. On the UK indie album chart, King Kurt's *Big Cock* deposes the Cramps.

19 *Buckingham Palace announces the engagement of Prince Andrew to 26-year-old Sarah Ferguson.*

22 *The United States explodes a nuclear device in the Nevada desert. Days later, Reagan rejects Gorbachev's proposal to convene a summit meeting to end nuclear tests.*

24 *After Libyan objections to American warships exercising in the Gulf of Sirte, US fighters attack Libyan patrol boats.*

● THE CRAMPS

29 The fourth new US number one single in as many weeks is Falco's 'Rock Me Amadeus'. The best-selling UK single is 'Living Doll' by the unlikely combination of Cliff Richard and the Young Ones. Cliff and the Shadows originally took the song to number one in 1959. Top indie single is by Half Man Half Biscuit – 'The Trumpton Riots'.

31 O'Kelly Isley, at 48 the oldest of the Isley Brothers, dies of a heart attack at his home in Alpine, New Jersey.

Big Country play their first UK dates for over a year; ELO return to the fray after a three-year absence; and former Ace singer Paul Carrack returns to the US Top Ten for the first time in eleven years – as frontman with Mike & The Mechanics.

Two of London's most historic rock venues, Dingwalls and the Marquee, close for extensive facelifts.

Gary Glitter finds himself in hospital after taking too many sleeping pills.

Two of Prince's bodyguards are sentenced to two years' probation, fined $500 and ordered to do 100 hours of community work for assaulting photographers attempting to snap the singer.

Following an incident at a Reading University concert, Sigue Sigue Sputnik drummer Ray Mayhew faces three charges of wounding.

At the Grammy Awards ceremony in Los Angeles, winners include Phil Collins, Sade, Whitney Houston, Don Henley, Dire Straits and Aretha Franklin. 'We Are The World' is declared Record Of The Year, Song Of The Year, Best Pop Vocal Group Performance, and Best Music Video.

Alan Lancaster fails to prevent former partners Francis Rossi and Rick Parfitt from resurrecting Status Quo without his participation.

PRT Records, once the powerful Pye label, and Bronze Records both go under.

APRIL 1986

2 A terrorist bomb concealed in an Athens-bound TWA Boeing 727 kills four, but the plane lands safely. Three days later, an American soldier is among casualties of a bomb planted in a crowded West Berlin disco.

5 'Shellshock' by New Order enters the UK indie singles chart at number one. Best-selling indie album is Depeche Mode's *Black Celebration*. Both records maintain their position all month.

● DEPECHE MODE

8 Film star Clint Eastwood is elected Mayor of Carmel, his Californian hometown.

10 The US explodes another underground nuclear device in Nevada. The following day, the Soviet Union announce the end of their eight-month self-imposed weapon test ban.

15 British-based US bombers attack targets in Tripoli and Benghazi in retaliation for increased Libyan terrorist activity. Colonel Gadaffi's baby daughter is among the thirty-nine known to have died.

15 Jean Genet – poet, playwright, novelist and film-maker – dies in Paris.

16 England's cricket team maintain their unbroken run by losing the final test match against the West Indies.

17 Hüsker Dü and Stevie Ray Vaughan are the first of several US rock acts reported to be pulling out of European tours for fear of being seen as potential reprisal targets by Libyan terrorists.

19 More than sixty are arrested at an Oxford Street demo protesting against British complicity in the bombing of Libya.

19 The compilation album *Hits 4* fends off Dire Straits from the top of the UK album chart for the fourth week. George Michael's 'A Different Corner' is best-selling UK single, while Prince's 'Kiss' tops the US chart.

21 Kim Wilde and Nik Kershaw headline the first of five Green-peace benefit nights at the Royal Albert Hall. Lloyd Cole, Echo and the Bunnymen and the Cure are among others lending support.

23 Rock stars cram into London's Donmar Warehouse to establish Artists Against Apartheid, under the leadership of Jerry Dammers.

26 An explosion at the Chernobyl nuclear power plant causes a massive radiation leak, which subsequently affects much of Europe. Soviet authorities are slow to disclose the news and the potential dangers.

■ Thanks to the Art of Noise, Duane Eddy finds himself back in the Top Ten for the first time since 1975, while another fifties star, Sam Cooke, shot dead in 1964, has his biggest ever UK hit with 'Wonderful World' – resuscitated by a Levis 501 TV advert.

● PETER GABRIEL

■ David Bowie returns to the screen in *Absolute Beginners*. Panned by critics, the movie is a box-office smash nevertheless. Also opening to less than enthusiastic reviews is *Time*, the Dave Clark-backed stage musical starring Cliff Richard.

■ PiL and Pete Wylie return to the fray, as does Peter Gabriel, whose 'Sledgehammer' is his first single since 1982.

■ Drummer Roger Taylor leaves Duran Duran for "an indefinite sabbatical"; Blair Cunningham, once of Haircut 100, replaces Pete de Freitas as Echo and the Bunnymen drummer; Craig Gannon, ex-Aztec Camera, replaces bassist Andy Rourke in the Smiths; and guitarist Craig Goldie replaces Vivian Campbell in Dio.

MAY 1986

3 After monopolising the position for forty-nine weeks, Dire Straits are removed from the top of the UK CD chart by Bryan Ferry's *Streetlife*. *Dirty Work* is the thirtieth Rolling Stones album to reach the US Top Ten – a total exceeded only by Frank Sinatra and Bing Crosby!

3 All change on the UK indie chart: *Victorialand* by the Cocteau Twins becomes best-selling album, 'A Question Of Lust' by Depeche Mode the top-selling single. In America, Island's long-term faith is vindicated as Robert Palmer's 'Addicted To Love' reaches the top of the singles chart.

3 *175 policemen and 150 pickets are injured in the worst violence yet seen at News International's new plant in Wapping.*

10 Nigeria's Afro-Beat king Fela Kuti is released from a Lagos prison after serving twenty months of a five-year sentence for currency violations.

10 With 'West End Girls', the Pet Shop Boys are the latest British invaders to top the US singles chart. We've Got A Fuzzbox And We're Gonna Use It have the best-selling UK indie single, 'Rules and Regulations'.

14 *Soviet leader Gorbachev speaks about the Chernobyl disaster after eighteen days' silence . . . he appeals for an international early-warning system for nuclear accidents.*

17 Dublin is the setting for Self Aid: fourteen hours of music by twenty-eight acts, in aid of Ireland's unemployed.

19 *South African forces attack suspected African National Congress bases in Zimbabwe, Botswana and Zambia.*

20 *Ian Botham is dropped from the England cricket team and banned from first-class cricket for two months after admitting having smoked cannabis.*

25 Band Aid and Unicef combine to organise the 'Race Against Time'. In one hundred cities worldwide, millions of sponsored runners undertake a ten kilometre run to raise money for famine relief in Africa.

31 *The Government announces a 'Clean Up Britain' scheme, planned to provide jobs for the young unemployed as well as tidying up the environment.*

● JOE STRUMMER

■ Joe Strummer of the Clash is fined £200 and banned for eighteen months for driving under the influence of alcohol.

■ Hugo Peretti, producer (Sam Cooke, Stylistics, etc) and songwriter ('Can't Help Falling In Love With You', 'The Lion Sleeps Tonight'), dies in Englewood, New Jersey, aged 68.

JUNE 1986

7 Madonna has the best-selling US single, 'Live To Tell', while in Britain, Doctor and the Medics' revival of Norman Greenbaum's 1970 hit 'Spirit In The Sky' is the new number one.

12 *In South Africa, several hundred anti-apartheid activists are arrested after new government measures give virtually unlimited powers to the security forces, as well as imposing severe restraints on the media.*

13 Jazz clarinettist Benny Goodman, 'the King of Swing', dies aged 77.

14 Queen's *A Kind of Magic* is the fifth of their fourteen albums to top the UK chart.

● TOM WAITS

15 U2 and Sting headline an Amnesty International concert in New Jersey, celebrating the organisation's 25th anniversary.

20 Glastonbury CND festival is a three-day affair featuring the Psychedelic Furs, Madness and Level 42 among others.

20 Paul Young, Howard Jones, Tina Turner, Elton John, David Bowie and Mick Jagger are among a throng of stars playing the tenth Prince's Trust Charity Show at Wembley Arena.

21 *Invisible Touch* returns Genesis to the top of the UK album chart.

22 *England are knocked out of the World Cup when Argentina win the Mexico City quarter final 2-1.*

24 *Ireland's Barry McGuigan loses his WBA featherweight title to Texan Steve Cruz in Las Vegas.*

28 'The Edge Of Heaven', Wham's tenth and last single, hits the top of the UK chart – coinciding with their final concert at Wembley Stadium.

28 A 70,000-strong anti-apartheid rally in Hyde Park is followed by a Clapham Common concert featuring Sting, the Communards, Billy Bragg and Boy George.

29 *Richard Branson's Virgin Atlantic Challenger II sets a record for the fastest Atlantic crossing – three days, eight hours and 31 minutes.*

■ Tom Waits' play *Frank's Wild Years* opens in Chicago, with Waits playing the lead role.

■ British sales of Michael Jackson's *Thriller* now exceed 2.5 million, making it the best UK seller of all time.

■ Fifty-three-year-old Little Richard returns to the chart with 'Great Gosh A Mighty', thirty years after his first British hit, 'Rip It Up'.

JULY 1986

5 Billy Ocean reaches the top of the US singles chart with 'There'll Be Sad Songs', while Janet Jackson's *Control* is the best-selling album. On the UK indie charts, the Smiths head the album list with *The Queen Is Dead* and the Housemartins the singles list with 'Happy Hour'.

6 *Two Australians are hanged in Malaysia for transgressing drug trafficking laws.*

6 *Boris Becker and Martina Navratilova retain their Wimbledon titles.*

7 *Pessimism about the US economy causes the biggest one-day drop ever recorded on New York Stock Exchange share prices.*

11 Queen fill Wembley Stadium for the first of two nights.

12 'Holding Back The Years' by Simply Red has the British flag flying at the top of the US singles chart – but in the UK Madonna rules both charts, with 'Papa Don't Preach' and *True Blue*.

12 After much press hounding and speculation, Boy George is arrested and charged with heroin possession. Later in the month, he is found guilty and fined £250.

14 A concert by Durutti Column kicks off Manchester's week-long festival to celebrate the tenth anniversary of the punk explosion. The Damned also celebrate their tenth anniversary.

15 *Zola Budd is banned from the Commonwealth Games, but over half the participating countries withdraw their teams in protest at the British stance on South African sanctions.*

16 Dolly Parton opens Dollywood, a 400-acre theme park glorifying her folksy Tennessee background.

18 This year's WOMAD Festival features Siouxsie and the Banshees, Gil Scott-Heron, and the Housemartins.

19 With 'Invisible Touch', Genesis hold the top spot on the US singles chart, with erstwhile member Peter Gabriel's 'Sledgehammer' replacing them a week later. Patti LaBelle, who first charted in 1963, has the best-selling US album, *Winner In You*.

20 *Frank Bruno fails to take the World Heavyweight boxing crown from America's Tim Witherspoon at Wembley Stadium.*

23 *A worldwide audience of 500 million watches the royal wedding of Prince Andrew and Sarah Ferguson.*

24 Bob Geldof, in morning suit and top hat, receives his honorary knighthood from the Queen at Buckingham Palace. He is also immortalised in wax at Madame Tussaud's.

26 The soundtrack album from *Top Gun* is America's best-seller.

31 *President Reagan and Margaret Thatcher refuse to yield on South African sanctions, despite heavy international pressure and the failure of Geoffrey Howe's persuasion mission.*

31 Chris De Burgh finds himself with the best-selling UK single, 'The Lady In Red'. In America, Chicago veteran Pete Cetera takes 'The Glory Of Love' to number one.

■ Joe Strummer (Clash), Daryl Hall (Hall & Oates) and Peter Case (the Plimsouls) all release debut solo singles.

■ The Sid Vicious movie *Sid and Nancy* is released.

■ The producers of the original Monkees television shows of twenty years ago advertise for new Monkees to star in a 1986 series.

■ Rod Stewart plays British dates for the first time in three years; Spandau Ballet release their first single for eighteen months; Edwyn Collins returns to the stage after a year's absence.

■ Dave Alvin and Gene Taylor leave the Blasters; guitarist John McGeoch joins PiL full time (after temporary affiliation) and is replaced in the Armory Show by former Professional and Duellist Ray McVeigh.

■ The June Brides call it a day.

● SID AND NANCY

● DURUTTI COLUMN

● THE JUNE BRIDES

THE YEAR IN ROCK

"Last night I sat down and tried to make a list of the truly great British bands of the 1980s, bands whose recordings and influence would endure," said Andy Kershaw in a *Whistle Test* programme last May. "After nearly an hour I was staring at a sheet of paper with only one name on it: the Smiths."

As the morose sound of the Smiths playing 'Vicar In A Tutu' came to an end Kershaw and fellow presenter Mark Ellen prepared to announce the winner of that week's 'Video Vote'; the contenders were Culture Club (not fashionable), the Pet Shop Boys (flavour of the month), Little Richard (archive corner) and W.A.S.P. (extremely unfashionable).

"The smart money's on the Pet Shop Boys" Ellen said confidently just before the winning video was revealed. And there on the screen, with chainsaw arm-pieces, awkwardly shaped, big-knobbed guitars and explosions all around, were the daft HM band W.A.S.P. playing a song called 'Wild Child'.

● W.A.S.P.

Earlier in the year the readers of *NME* voted *Whistle Test* the number one TV show, well ahead of *The Tube*, never mind *Top of the Pops* which failed to register at all. Could this mean that *NME* readers were secretly phoning in to vote for W.A.S.P.? And what would all those W.A.S.P. voters make of Kershaw's remarks about the Smiths?

In other words, it was again a year in which the now well-advanced process of fragmentation of the rock market into many quite contradictory themes and strands proceeded apace. Never before has such a disparity of audiences and even generations been found huddling together under the multi-faceted umbrella. To use 'rock' as a rubric has become almost impossible.

Sigue Sigue Sputnik foolishly declared themselves to be the "fifth generation of rock 'n' roll", but what a lonely generation it turned out to be. There they were, a bright spearhead badly in need of a good shaft, but nobody joined them, no new movement emerged, and by the time their second single, '21st Century Boy' peaked at number 20, it looked as though they were going to have their work cut out to last as long as Adam Ant.

The fact is that the fifth generation of rock 'n' roll has so far failed to emerge, and the rock world is currently in a state of undefined flux where you don't have to *be* anything in particular to join up as

● BOB GELDOF

part of the 'movement'. You could be cool soul boys like Simply Red, or cool pop strategists like the Pet Shop Boys, or gloomy, angst-ridden, avant-garde arrivistes like the Jesus And Mary chain or a reincarnated punk like Mick Jones of Big Audio Dynamite, or an all-girl band playing sixties beat like the Bangles, or a bland Genesis/Police rip-off like Go West, or even an ersatz Mozart of an Austrian rap artist; if you

were reasonably good at whatever you did you got a fair crack. All the new acts were one-offs, bearing absolutely no relation to one another, and any *musical* movements in rock were being made on too many fronts to indicate any hint of direction, cohesion or advance.

But in the absence of any stylistic coherence, and in the aftermath of Live Aid, rock in 1985/6 became organised and motivated instead by The Cause. Having been something of a spoilt and unruly child in the sixties, and then experiencing a painful adolescence and coming of age in the seventies, rock has now reached the age and stage of the second-year University student. It is still loud and raucous, preserves a yobbish veneer and has a lot of energy to expend, but it has found positive practical aiming-points for its previously unfocused idealism. It wants to make an impact on the real adult world, and has just begun to realise that it is now big enough and strong enough to challenge the grown-ups at their own games.

Having got used to the sight of dear Bob Geldof casually chatting with Prince Charles or belligerently arguing the toss with Margaret Thatcher over EEC food surpluses, it came as no surprise to find his reactions to political developments in the wake of *Sport Aid* widely covered in the quality press. In a front page story, *The Observer* reported that: "The Band Aid founder, waving a copy of [Foreign Secretary] Sir Geoffrey [Howe]'s speech, marched up to British ambassador to the UN, Sir John Thomson, in New York, and said bluntly: 'This is crap'."

Two weeks later, Geldof was made a Knight Commander of the Most Excellent Order of the British Empire. The award of the KBE star and ribbon was formally presented by Sir Geoffrey Howe.

If any proof were needed that rock has now long abandoned its original function as an anti-establishment instrument of teenage rebellion, in favour of an attitude of social and moral responsibility, look no further than the new work and words of Pete

● PETE TOWNSHEND

Townshend. Townshend, once the personification of wild-eyed nihilism, now reckons to spend a third of his time working for charity. In November he put on a lively old codgers' show at Brixton Academy in aid of his Double O organisation, which helps the victims of heroin addiction, and in February joined stars like Annie Lennox, Chrissie Hynde and David Gilmour in an Albert Hall concert to raise funds for the victims of the volcano disaster in Colombia. Speaking about Little Steven's Artists United Against Apartheid record, 'Sun City', Townshend summed up the new mood in rock when he said: "People have realised that the early idealism, the idea that the spiritual uplift of music itself would effect change in society, was very naïve. The only way you effect change is by seizing the opportunity to influence people who control what happens in the world."

Nothing could have underlined the difference between the old and new attitudes more succinctly than the coincidental arrival in London on the same night in March of Yoko Ono's Starpeace tour and the Red Wedge Labour campaign collective. Ono chose to play at Wembley Arena, which she had difficulty in half-filling, while Bragg and Weller presided over a standing-room-only gig at the Hammersmith

● YOKO ONO

Odeon. The *Guardian*'s venerable critic, Robin Denselow, somehow managed to get to both concerts. He noted the difference between the two concerts, portentously describing the contrast as "historic": Ono wandered around the Wembley stage accepting countless bunches of flowers and delivering

● PAUL WELLER   ● BILLY BRAGG

vague peace homilies such as "We are all sixtieth cousins", while at the Red Wedge gig the message was hammered across in specifically party political terms while Labour MPs and luminaries of the left, like the copper's chum Bernie Grant, loomed in the foyer to buttonhole members of the audience on their way out.

Significantly, not much was said about the actual music that was performed at either concert, which was in both cases, no doubt, a motley appendage to the figurative banner waving. But there was some great political music around. Stan Ridgway produced

● PETER GABRIEL

the perfect political pop album, *The Big Heat*, while Andy White's 4-track EP, 'Religious Persuasion' revived the kind of stinging, barbed folk message not heard in rock since Dylan was in his prime. Peter Gabriel's album, *So*, with its deep forlorn cry on behalf of so many haplessly unemployed people, 'Don't Give Up', went straight to number one.

But if Live Aid was the catalyst that set rock to work on behalf of worldwide causes as diverse as the Nicaraguan government, American farmers with a cash-flow problem and Russian victims of the Chernobyl disaster, it also instated a new rock aristocracy, far more static and monolithic than the old order that punk was supposed to have swept away in 1977. Indeed, many of this new ruling class emerged in the late seventies – Sting, Dire Straits, U2, Midge Ure, Phil Collins – while others like Queen, Elton John and Paul McCartney had simply never noticed any change. *Live Aid* redefined and bolstered their pre-eminence. *Queen Greatest Hits* has not been out of the album charts since Live Aid, and Dire Straits' *Brothers in Arms*, as well as yielding five hit singles, has been at or near the top of the album and compact disc charts in both Britain and America for the entire year. Their world tour, which began in Jerusalem on 30 April 1985 and ended in Perth, Australia, on 26 April 1986, confirmed

● PHIL COLLINS

their position as the most commercially successful international rock act of the year.

Sting made an effortless transition from leader of a supergroup to super solo star, though it was in America that his *Dream of the Blue Turtles* album did the best business, and Phil Collins was absolutely everywhere, picking up armfuls of Grammy awards, appearing in *Miami Vice,* and even finding time to play in his old rock group Genesis, which now sounded like the Phil Collins Band.

Mick Jagger and David Bowie, their pert bottoms wiggling at the camera, picked up a number one hit with their Live Aid video 'Dancing In The Street', and as the baby bulge generation reached their middle-to-late thirties, rock became more of a mainstream global entertainment than ever before.

But what of the punks who had said goodbye to all that, the angry young tearaways who had gobbed on the grave of such bloated excess? 1986, we were frequently reminded, was the tenth anniversary of the punk rock explosion. And what was left? John Lydon brought out *Album,* with songs that sounded similar to old Led Zeppelin records; he even started his live shows with a version of Zeppelin's 'Kashmir' but ended his gig at the Brixton Academy prematurely, objecting to being spat upon by a minority at the front. Even without Captain Sensible, the Damned made complete clowns of themselves, and picked up their biggest hit in years with an inconsequential version of Barry Ryan's baroque melo-drama from 1968, 'Eloise'. The Clash made a feeble album called *Cut the Crap,* which the critics and the record-buying public wisely washed their hands of, whereupon Joe Strummer disband-ed what was left of the group. The Ramones were still good value to watch but seemed dated and reaction-ary, while Bob Geldof K.B.E. and the Boomtown Rats were about the only act not to get a hit from Live Aid.

● FEARGAL SHARKEY

Alone from the Class of '76, Siouxsie and the Banshees continued to be relevant. In October they struck out on a British tour, without any new record to promote, but on stage at Hammersmith Odeon Siouxsie wrenched her knee so badly that she had to be hospitalised. She carried on touring with the aid of a black cane, a high chair and several long dresses. Her positive spirit, integrity and regard for her fans are perhaps those qualities that have sustained her progress where most of her punk contemporaries have fallen by the wayside.

Given the benefit of a decade of hindsight, it appeared that very little had changed as the result of punk. The fate of the Undertones was a perfect allegory for what had become of rock by 1986. Feargal Sharkey signed to Virgin Records and stepped into a solo career which was as well groomed as his gorgeous flowing locks. A string of hits including the number one 'A Good Heart' preceded a tour on which he

was backed by a superbly drilled ten-piece soul revue band.

Other members of the Undertones formed That Petrol Emotion, who got a deal with the independent label Demon, and, joining the likes of Easterhouse and the Redskins, released a harsh, politically motivated album *Manic Pop Thrill.* The album's success in the independent charts led to considerable interest from the major labels, and it will be interesting to see what happens to them when they do sign a major con-tract. They may go the way of the Red Guitars – whose debut recording for Virgin, *Tales of the Expected,* was a terrible disappointment compared with their previous independent releases – or, if successful, they will sooner or later find themselves on *Wogan.*

If there was one sure indicator that rock as a potent instrument of rebellion and subversion has had its day, it was the number and nature of acts that found their way on to the grinning Irishman's talk show: It's Immaterial,

● THAT PETROL EMOTION ● SIOUXSIE

Brilliant, Fine Young Cannibals, the Blow Monkeys and Echo and the Bunnymen all made appearances, *before* being on *Top of the Pops.* Billy Bragg and the Style Council both appeared twice on Wogan. But whereas Bill Grundy put the Sex Pistols on TV to expose them as filthy degenerates and an outrage to moral decency, Wogan's guests were there to entertain and give his programme 'youth credibility'. Pop stars, whether smooth careerists or radical activists, were all part of one happy, showbiz family.

In the absence of any genuine rock 'n' roll outrage, the tabloid papers manufactured their own stories by mounting organised campaigns of harassment against the biggest pop stars. Madonna arrived in Britain in March to work on the film *Shanghai Surprise* and was set upon by a rabid horde of journalists who reported her generally gracious and dignified be-haviour in the most distorted and sen-sational way possible. George Michael,

and particularly Andrew Ridgeley (seen as the weaker target) were treated no less scandalously, especially once the news of their imminent split became known. Garry Bushell of the *Sun* wrote a singularly despicable front-page piece, spuriously attempting to link Suggs of Madness with members of a right-wing rascist organisation.

On a broader scale, all this interest indicated just how much pop stars since Boy George have become part of the fabric of the entertainment world; largely thanks to Live Aid they are now on a par with politicians, the Royal Family and sport and TV personalities.

While no one, except for a few cranks like the Redskins, would wish to criticise the intentions and practical humanitarian results that Live Aid achieved, the respectability which that event bestowed on rock has changed its nature for ever, and a lot of people may have found themselves agreeing with Tony James when he said: "I'm desperately looking for something that's a bit EXCITING or DANGEROUS or SUBVERSIVE and I can't find anything."

The Americans, on the other hand, could see nothing *but* danger in coming to Britain, and having valiantly set out from their air bases over here to strike a blow for the free world against Libya, promptly cancelled plans to come anywhere near Europe for fear of possible reprisals (of which, incident-ally, there have been none). Neil Young, Stan Ridgway, Lionel Richie, Starship, Prince, Manhattan Transfer, Wynton Marsalis, Stevie Ray Vaughan and Lone Justice were just some of the acts who suddenly found it an inconvenient time to undertake previously announced visits. The Ramones came to Britain but baulked at going to play in Berlin. Asked about Libya, Dee Dee could only endorse his President's view of the situation: "We'll blow 'em up if we have to, send the Bomb right on over there." Meanwhile, in the wake of Sylvester Stallone's refusal to attend the Cannes film festival, a French DJ invented a dance called the Rambo Rhumba, a simple step which required only that the dancer should constantly move timidly backwards.

The year's sharpest dancers, by a mile, were Prince and Janet Jackson, though James Brown, nearly three times older than Ms Jackson, gave a good run for the money at his Wembley shows in April.

While videos undoubtedly maintained Prince and introduced Janet Jackson to audiences in the absence of the stars themselves, the age of the video star was drawing to a close. The video for Kate Bush's 'The Big Sky' was reputed to have cost £100,000, yet the song only reached number 37; the ailing Culture Club's 'God Thank You Woman' was a similarly extravagant outlay for a very poor chart showing.

Instead, the best money went on simple, good-quality videos that didn't require vast location or special effects budgets. Wham! ('I'm Your Man'), Madonna ('Live To Tell'), and George Michael ('A Different Corner') all produced videos that were straightforward substitutes for having the act in the studio. With not a peep from Frankie

● DEXY'S MIDNIGHT RUNNERS

Goes To Hollywood or Michael Jackson all year, Duran Duran lying low, Culture Club on the wane, and Adam Ant ancient history, the beneficiaries of large-budget video production values seemed thin on the ground. There were exceptions: A-ha broke through entirely on the strength of the video for 'Take On Me' while Peter Gabriel and Robert Palmer produced extraordinarily memorable (if, for some, infuriating) videos for 'Sledgehammer' and 'Addicted To Love', which both reached the Top Five. But by and large the record companies and their acts were beginning to look a little more closely at their balance sheets.

After the initial excitement, videos have ceased to be such a dominant factor in determining what sort of acts become successful. In America CBS announced they were cutting back on making videos, while Van Halen (5150) and Journey (Raised on Radio) announced their intention not to make videos to support their albums, both of which were spectacular chart successes, regardless.

Dexy's Midnight Runners chose to cock a snook at traditional marketing strategies by initially not releasing a single to promote their album Don't Stand Me Down. The album stiffed, and their poorly-attended tour was an embarrassing disaster with Kevin Rowland spending much of his time on stage abusing the audience for not paying due respect to his latest James Thurber-like flights of pantomime fancy.

The Thompson Twins had a miserable year too: their tour promoter, Paul Loasby, went bankrupt before they'd even played a gig, and Joe Leeway left

the trio shortly afterwards. In fact, as the year wore on, such tales of woe became quite common. PiL's tour sold badly and Yoko Ono and Julian Lennon both cancelled gigs. Chart acts like the Communards, Bronski Beat and Blancmange (who subsequently split up) all suffered similarly, while non-chart acts like Maze and Tom Waits sold out nine nights at Hammersmith Odeon and eight nights at the Dominion respectively. No great insight was needed to

● RAMONES

divine that the people who bought singles were not necessarily the people who went to live concerts, and that acts could do big business in one area without having to cover all the bases.

One extraordinary group to tour Britain was Cameo, the American 'soul' band who scored a chart breakthrough with 'Single Life'. Those expecting to hear the mellifluous jazzy sounds and airy vocals of their album produced live suffered a rude jolt when they were confronted by a show that was noisier, gaudier and heavier than any of the heavy metal acts such as AC/DC, Mötley Crüe and Ozzy Osbourne who passed through in the early months of 1986.

While heavy metal continued to be denied access to the rock mainstream, there was still plenty of scope for the original rock unit – the guitar-based band – to flourish. Big Country made a welcome comeback, trailing around behind Queen on a tour that delighted the fans and left all the critics chosen to cover the show wondering why they had been unlucky enough to draw the short straw.

Hüsker Dü and the Screaming Blue Messiahs showed that power guitar trios could still come up with something new and vigorous, while both the Robert Cray Band and the Beat Farmers secured major recording contracts. The American blues guitarist Cray really had an exceptional year, starting at Dingwalls, later selling out Hammersmith Odeon and finally appearing near the top of the bill at Glastonbury. His album False Accusations followed its predecessor, Bad Influence, to the top of the independent charts (the first

blues act ever to do this) and even made the lower reaches of the national American Billboard chart.

Not since rock audiences belatedly discovered the work of first generation electric blues singers like Muddy Waters and BB King has a similar performer made such critical and commercial inroads on the rock mainstream, and at thirty-three years of age he may be poised to become one of the greatest bluesmen yet.

It was frequently said by those in the know that in the wake of Live Aid, rock was as good as dead. The lack of what Tony James called exciting, dangerous or subversive music as a dominant trend had rendered rock an impotent middle-aged variety show. What seems strange is that this should come as a surprise to anyone. After all if you seek to judge a middle-aged person by the proficiency of his skate-boarding technique, it is not likely that he will shape up to much. The criteria by which the "rock is dead" judgement is made is now similarly unsuitable, and the continuing decline in influence of those music papers which adopt this yardstick for judging rock acts only underlines the irrelevance of such proclamations to the great majority of rock fans, young or old.

Rock is now catering to a vastly disparate audience. The average age of the Rolling Stones is forty-five, and yet they still turned out an album, Dirty Work, which picked up good reviews in NME and Melody Maker. ZZ Top, a band who have been together for sixteen years, were continuing to enjoy their first flush of success in the teenage pop market and proving to be America's top grossing act on the road in 1986.

Simple Minds graduated to the stadia. The Cure and Echo and the Bunnymen were celebrating long periods of success with Greatest Hits albums, the Pogues had a stunning hit with Rum, Sodomy and the Lash, and We've Got A Fuzzbox went to the top of the independent charts with 'Spirit In The Sky', an old Norman Greenbaum song, which curiously enough also took the witless Dr and the Medics to the top of the national chart.

In one sense rock has never flourished more on so many fronts. But its success as a mass media entertainment has inevitably led to a dissipation of the original outrage that fuelled it during its most passionate moments.

The smart money may be on the Smiths just now but there is bigger money than ever backing good old rock 'n' roll for another year or so. At least the successors of Live Aid are channelling a small amount of it in more useful directions than in the past.

David Sinclair

THE YEAR IN
REGGAE

The dispossessed dirt track district of Waterhouse in Kingston 11, known locally as Firehouse after the frequent gun warfare for which the area is notorious, remains also the epicentre of the reggae dancehall sound in the mid-eighties. It is here at the beginning of 1985 in the one Jammys studio down St Lucia way where that which subsequently comes to be celebrated as the 'Sleng Ten' rhythm after Wayne Smith's opening salvo 'Under Me Sleng Ten' is first computed via a Casio electronic keyboard. It goes on to become the dancehall hit of the year, spawning some few hundred versions, scores on the Jammys imprint alone, including among them his epochal 'Put It By Number One' call and response with Johnny Osbourne; but it is the second Jammys cut 'Pumpkin Belly' which heralds the single most influential new voice of the year, that of Tenor Saw.

Emerging on the Youth Promotion sound system set run by Sugar Minott, Tenor Saw soon establishes himself as its principal entertainer on the mike at dances. His gospel-inflected vocal style echoed in the singing of other contemporary newcomers such as Nitty Gritty and King Kong. His debut recording 'Roll Is Called', for George Phang's Powerhouse label, based partly on a church lyric long popular in Jamaica, while the theme of 'Pumpkin Belly' reiterates a local folk phrase. In addition to the Jammys version, Tenor Saw cut this a second time for the Youth Promotion team, with whom he also had another acclaimed title in 'Lots Of Sign', but it was 'Ring The Alarm' for Techniques over Chancery Lane which really set the seal on his success. Utilising the vintage Techniques 'Stalag' rhythm, 'Ring The Alarm' dealt in dancehall preoccupations regarding the claims and merits of respective sound systems and was inevitably the yardstick by which one set would measure itself against another at sound contests. Such was its popularity that Techniques issued a whole album of 'Stalag' adaptations with emergent dancehall contenders like Yammie Bolo, Admiral Tibett and Little Kirk featured alongside more established names such as Michael Prophet and Sugar Minott. Jammys responded with a computerised pastiche of the same rhythm and a compilation album of similar conception to Techniques'.

If Jammys never had a monopoly on Tenor Saw, he did have in Nitty Gritty one who would seriously challenge the other's supremacy towards the end of 1985 and maintain Jammys' profile after 'Sleng Ten' had lost much of its impetus. Favouring a relaxed, highly idiosyncratic delivery, Nitty Gritty came to prominence with 'Trials And Crosses' for Phang on Powerhouse before stirring things up with digital compositions for Jammys 'Hog In A Minty' and 'Run Down The World' and going on with the producer to have one of the most enduring titles in the early months of 1986 with 'Sweet Reggae Music', followed by the similarly popular 'Gimme Some Of Your Something'. And Jammys kept things simmering with such as Admiral Tibett's 'Feel The Vibes', Little John's 'Understand Me' and 'Clarks Booty', King Everald's 'Bad Girls', Don Angelo's 'Gigantic' and 'Reggae Music We Want' rumpus, Peter Metro's 'Police In A England' and the well-received Dennis Brown and Leroy Sibbles coupling 'All For One'.

● NITTY GRITTY

● TENOR SAW

What really fires Waterhouse towards the latter part of 1985, though, is the return to producing on a regular basis, after a decade or so lay-off, of King Tubby, with a newly installed 32-track mixing desk replacing the pioneering four-track studio at his headquarters in Drumille Avenue. It is here that King Tubby experiments with the earliest dub techniques in the late sixties effectively changing the course of reggae for the next decade, and here too that Jammys starts out as Tubby's engineer. Now ploughing the same pastures the rivalry between the two studios is particularly keen, with in recent months King Tubby perhaps stealing some of Jammys' thunder.

His return is announced in certain terms in the autumn of 1985 when, with Jammys still in the ascendant with 'Sleng Teng' and its variations, King Tubby issues an even more digitally eccentric construction when Anthony Red Rose marks 'Tempo' for the producer's Firehouse label, the singer having previously made his Drumille Avenue debut on 'Under Me Fat Thing', itself a 'Sleng Teng' derivative adapted by Tubby. As with Tenor Saw's 'Ring The Alarm', the subject matter of 'Tempo' is the sound system contest runnings and the badmouthing that often ensues. Red Rose has a string of releases for Tubby: 'Bangarang', 'Can't Knock Me', 'Canta', and one 'Pension' on his own Temper Rose label, all with the stylised mannerisms of his hit.

And the tempo inside Tubby's studio seemed to gather pace as well, with engineers Peego and Fatman firing on all cylinders for titles ranging from the mean skanking of Little John with 'A We Rule', his denunciatory 'Love A Kill Me' version of 'Tempo' and the stop-start 'Me No Response', to the comparatively more pastoral reflections of Lilly Melody wailing 'Ghost Buster' and 'Pressure Me'. Other interesting sides on Tubby's Firehouse, Waterhouse and Kingston 11 labels included King Everald's 'Automatic', Lloyd Hemmings with 'Rude Boy' and of course King Kong's pertinent comments on the year's scare in 'AIDS'.

After Tenor Saw and Nitty Gritty and with something in the style of both of them, King Kong was another singer brought forward by Tubby towards the end of 1985, and who began to establish himself a favourable reputation during the following year. Before making a stir with 'AIDS' around Christmas, Kong had already adapted 'Magic Moment' for Tubby and had followed this with the studio's own workout of the 'Stalag' rhythm for the abrasive 'Step On Me Corn'. Now there appeared a stream of titles for various producers bearing the King Kong soubriquet: 'Niceness' for Black Scor-

● ANTHONY RED ROSE

● KING KONG

● FRANKIE PAUL

pio, 'Progress' for John Holt and Dennis Brown, 'Reggae My Litis' and 'Ninja' for Harry J's Sunset enterprise among many. It was the singer's next work for Jammys, however, that was to give King Kong his big summer 1986 hits 'Legal' and 'Trouble Again'. "*Gadaffi lick a shot and Reagan lick it back,*" he sang on the latter, "*Trouble again and the world is getting nervous.*"

Another Waterhouse sound which made its mark during the year was Black Scorpio, previously best known for its associations with DJs Sassafras and General Tree. On the label bearing its familiar scorpion logo Bobby Melody borrowed a current reggae catchphrase 'Live Stock' for a song on the subject and Echo Minott did likewise on his 'Lazy Body' skank for the label, with whom he also cut 'Bubbling Style' although his finest moment of the year came with a scathing 'Uncle Sam Country' for Harry J. Also upfront from Scorpio's Headly Avenue base in Waterhouse was General Tree with 'Mini Bus' and 'Peanut Man' and Mikey Melody declaring 'Jambo We Jambo' in response to the Hollywood motion picture industry. Earlier than this there had been a side from Frankie Paul crooning 'Midnight Lover'.

That had been one of the last singles in some time from an uncharacteristically inactive Frankie Paul at this time, then taking it easy after his busy schedule of the previous couple of years. "*After that I took a break,*" he sang on his return, on the autobiographical 'Hits Song' for Vena shortly before Christmas. "*Now I'm gonna change my style, go in a crucial style.*" Since when he has voiced a strong collection, *Ripe Mango*, for Blacker Dread of the Sir Coxsone Outernational massive and made singles like 'Play With Me' for Aqua, stirring polemic on 'Ghettoman Skank' for Phang and another comeback tune 'Deh Pon Street Again' for the Corner Stone triumvirate, with whom he has also recorded an album yet to be issued.

Frankie Jones, on the other hand, was busier than ever. The author of Leroy Smart's 'Ballistic Affair' hit from the mid-seventies had now entered the dancehall. His early efforts during 1984 such as 'Baby Come Back' for Tasha and 'Chase Them Jah' for Tony Shabazz were in more tentative traditional vein, but wholly in the current vogue were Mini Bus releases like the 'Love Me Forever' reworking, 'Cool Profile' and 'Settle Fe Me', as was 'Back Off' for Chiney Burro and Jimmy Dread. He followed this with another forward item for the same partnership in 1985 with 'War And Crime'. Much of his more recent material favours revamped rock steady rhythms, further evidence of the dictates of the dancehall: 'Old Fire

Stick' riding the 'Never Let Go' rave and 'No Touch The Riddim' over 'Shank I Sheck', both for Phang; 'Nah Look No Body' for Aqua over the sleazy insidious 'Queen Of The Minstrels' melody; 'Mix Up' for Village on 'I'm Just A Guy'; and his sinister 'Watch The Jeep', very much in the vocal style of Sugar Minott, over a Bunny Lee cut of 'You Don't Care'. Also bubbling of late has been a latest Mini Bus issue 'Dance Cork'.

Perhaps the most influential producer of them all this year though has been Winston Riley, who's been putting out music from Chancery Lane on his Techniques logo for more than a decade now and is at last striking the right chord in this present iwah. *"Room full, all full, you can't get a spoonful. Tell me which one o' them a trouble are the good Techniques – are the general now,"* as Michael Prophet sang on his own version of the producer's 'Stalag' rhythm 'Room Full', from a singer who went on to record further winsome Techniques sides, 'Who Control Them' and 'Easy Squeeze', and subsequent developments would seem to have borne out Prophet's claims. Following the 'Stalag' revival referred to earlier, Techniques was in the vanguard of promoting rekindled interest in both the Wailing Souls' 'Back Out' rhythm and that famous loping rock steady which numbers the Maytals' '54-46', the Ethiopians' 'The Ship' and Marcia Griffiths' 'Feel Like Jumping' among its many components.

Properly the first of the Techniques 'Back Out' adaptations to make any impact was Admiral Tibett's 'Leave People Business', a song appropriate to the runnings of its time and a follow-up to the singer's own 'Stalag' reading, 'A Trouble To A Man'. A succession of versions swiftly followed from Chancery Lane: young Yammi Bolo gospelling 'Jah Made Them All', Little John imploring 'Run For Cover', Cutty Ranks on the 'Gunman Lyric', Ernest Wilson's lovelorn 'Every Day With You', and most significantly Super Cat uttering his heartfelt 'Cry For The Youth', one of two new Techniques titles with the Cat. The other was 'Boops'.

As told by Super Cat the expression 'boops' – Jamaican slang for a sugar daddy – was the reggae catchphrase of 1986 and thrust into the limelight the self-styled *"wild Apache"* from Cockburn Pen, who had in any case been forging for himself a lively reputation with the current rave sound Stero Mas. Super Cat had started out in the dancehalls with the Soul Imperial set before going on to gain wider recognition with Killimanjaro. It was then that he cut his first record 'Mr Walker' for Techniques and in 1985 he voiced a couple more shots with Jammys, 'Trash

● SUGAR MINOTT

● SUPER CAT

And Ready' and 'Ride And Shut Off'. He was on his first visit to Britain in the company of Stero Mas sidekick Nicodemus when 'Boops' broke and the record achieved the rare distinction of being a simultaneous number one hit in both Jamaica and the UK reggae charts. 'The Whip' rhythm has been a rock steady perennial and Super Cat invested it with an expedient currency for his reading of 'Boops'. His 'Vineyard Party' on Skeng Don, released around the same time as 'Boops' and 'Cry For The Youth', personified various vegetables as dancehall participants, while his later 'Jah Paradise' for Tuff Gong confirmed, like 'Cry For The Youth' before it, that Super Cat is adept at handling a serious message lyric as well. But none of them had such an impact as 'Boops'.

Due to its controversial subject matter the song prompts immediate retort from citizens keen to defend themselves from any implications detrimental to their standing in the community. Particularly sharp off the mark is Sugar Minott, a man noted for his indiscriminate largesse, who stutters his angry indignation on 'John Boops' for the Corner Stone collective. There are further mixes of 'The Whip' rhythm as used on 'Boops' from Techniques who cuts Michael Prophet once again, this time pleading 'Nuh Call Mi John Boops', and from the less disinterested distaff point of view for the same outlet Junie Ranks with 'Cry Fi Mi Boops'. There are also many versions utilising the 'Feel Like Jumping' variation of the same rhythm: Little John's 'Boopsie', the one Lyrical on a Harry J cut with 'No Try No Boops' among them. There is yet a further King Kong response on 'Toots Boops' for Java. In addition, Anthony Red Rose wails 'Me No Want No Boops' over a digital delay rhythm from Tubby, rock stone toaster Pampiedoo claims 'I Love My Boops' for Striker Lee, there is Pappa San with 'Scandalising Boops', Super Dad's 'See Boops Ya', Horace Martin 'Talkin' 'Bout Boops' and dozens more in similar vein, as well as titles pertinent to the same theme like Sister Maureen's 'Toots Fe Man' and Shadowman's 'The Don'. Even an old head like Bunny Wailer, a man not usually noted for dealing with dancehall runnings, feels obliged to cut his own interpretation of 'The Ship' for his Solomonic label and comment on the phenomenon with 'Old Time Sing Ting'. And the list awaits its conclusion yet.

But perhaps the last word on the subject proper is already said by Super Cat himself, who now identifies himself as 'Pops' on his latest Skeng Don release.

Penny Reel

● THE YEAR IN
SOUL

It's probably fair to assume that most of you will have erased the existence of the artists responsible for the following hit records from your memories: 'I Can't Wait', 'All And All', 'Jump Back (Set Me Free)' and 'Magic Man', which all enjoyed respectable placings on the national pop and soul charts during the past year. Even the most blinkered, dyed-in-the-wool soul fan (the wool being pale yellow and knitted into a fashionable, zip-necked Pringle sweater, by the way) would admit that the undeniable talents of Nu Shooz, Joyce Simms, Dhar Braxton and Rochelle (respectively) are unlikely to pose any real threats to the more established soul heavyweights. Nevertheless, it's the likes of Miss Braxton who, perhaps unwittingly, are shaping soul music, imbuing the movement with glorious fluidity: every hit lasts a comparatively short time, only to be replaced by another, even harder tune that somehow renders the previous cut obsolete, yet simultaneously ensures it cult status by virtue of the fact that each record has its own particular merits, such as an original and distinctive percussive breakdown or a new bass sound, that go on to be highly influential in later recordings.

It is this ever-changing, ever-evolving, 24-hour shiftworking soul-funk factory which has given us another year of the *real* deal; definitive black music. That's the genius of soul.

It was the year that Larry Blackmon and Cameo adopted a new, abrasive, bump 'n' grinding sound for their *Single Life* album, the title track of which was voted single of the year by just about every respectable music publication on the market. Cameo took the bare elements of minimalist, ferocious funkers like the Gap Band and stripped them down even further, adding one of Blackmon's blistering rap-attacks for good measure. Indeed, Larry Blackmon proved his talents indisputably this year when he took on production duties for Barbara Mitchell's 'High On Love' (which had a similar feel to that of the superb Arthur Baker-produced 'Hard Times For Lovers' by Jennifer Holliday) and for Cameo's adopted little

brothers, Cashflow, soul's American Expressives, who kept out of the red with floor-fillers like the wicked house rocker 'Party Freak' and 'Mine All Mine', which scored highly despite the fact that it was a deadringer for Fatback's 'I Found Lovin'. Nevertheless, Cameo blotted their copybook when Blackmon

● CAMEO

● DHAR BRAXTON

stood stage centre at Hammersmith Odeon, his glistening, chisel-cut afro quiff wobbling, and pronounced defiantly, "It's only black rock 'n' roll," before launching into the kind of metallic powerchord onslaught that even Iron Maiden would've been proud of. He had to listen carefully for the muted response that followed.

This year, as in all years, the soul audience proved to be a largely curious and anachronistic phenomenon. It hurtled around suburbia in its now typecast, but truly omnipresent Mk II Cortina with bare bottoms more often than not mooning from the windows and black music blaring from the graphic equalised in-car entertainment module. But what kind of black music? The puerile, beer-swill beat of the Beastie Boys perhaps, or maybe even the blubber blast of the Fat Boys? Wrong. The average soul boy thrives on overtly mature masters of the midnight mood like Freddie Jackson, the Womacks, Alexander O'Neal and Atlantic Starr. One would assume, however, that no 19-year-old could truly relate to the soul-warring, marital problems of Bobby Womack's beautiful 'I Wish He Didn't Trust Me So Much' (which dealt with the problems of fancying your best mate's wife, for heaven's sake!) from *So Many Rivers*, the follow-up album to *The Poet II*; or, indeed, to designer-clothed, designer-heartache merchants like Freddie Jackson, who crooned in a vintage Marvin Gaye style on 'Rock Me Tonight (For Old Times Sake)', and Alexander O'Neal who sang the delicious 'If You Were Here Tonight', unashamedly exploiting every screw metaphor and groan cliché in the soul book.

But c'mon, you'd look a bit silly, wouldn't you, asking 'Do You Wanna Like I Do?' or declaring that 'You Were Meant To Be My Lady, Not My Girl' (both titles of O'Neal album tracks) to your girlfriend if you lived in Peckham and were barely old enough to buy a pint of Miller Lite? Of course the appeal of such music has nothing to do with such trivial details. The attraction of these artists is their sheer class and vocal quality and the way that listening to their songs makes one feel wealthy and fulfilled. Corny but true.

This past year saw many a talented vocalist straining to live up to the ridiculous media pressure of being labelled the natural successor to any one of a number of more established singers. Anita Baker whose *Rapture* was a lusciously warm bed of ballads was immediately called "the new Aretha Franklin"; Colonel Abrams, yet another person who was "once in a group with Prince", packed dancefloors around the world with the insistent 'Trapped' but was probably only called "the new Michael Jackson" because of his taste in garish Sgt Pepper-style jackets. Then there was Whitney Houston, "the new Dionne Warwick" (!), who, with the help of no less than four very expensive and experienced producers and not least a wonderfully powerful and sensual voice, dished up an album of delightful smaltzy slush which positively dripped with pedigree.

Despite being a newcomer, Whitney Houston did not belong to the new breed of bad-girl vocalists who decided to start slamming a few doors in a few faces and get all tough with their men friends. Shirley Murdoch, for example, the ex Zapp-er who asked, almost in

a lady devastator with the big drum beater.

Comebacks came back in the form of Aretha Franklin, who emerged bravely from her agoraphobic existence to record the rather disappointing *Freeway of Love*, with Narada Michael Walden at the desk in favour of the more suitable Luther Vandross. Although this big production job was choc-a-bloc with memorable, good time tunes it contained only one really crucial track in 'Another Night', a superbly crafted song, superbly sung. More of the same, please. James Brown finally landed himself a decent recording contract, but found himself compromising with the gritty *Rocky IV* anthem 'Living in America' which, though flawed, still cut it on the dancefloor – and anyway he's still wearing those tasteful, stack-heeled Italian shoes so he can't be all washed up yet.

Purple Rain or *Around the World in a Day* and a second single released from the album, 'Mountains', failed even to dent the Top 40. But, hey, sometimes it snows in April, right? Curiouser and curiouser. Fabber and fabber.

This was the year that soul music went truly public. It began to record charity records like 'That's What Friends Are For' (for AIDS research), and politically aware records like 'King Holiday' (about Martin Luther King) and 'Sun City' (which referred to Apartheid in South Africa). Soul was never out of the pop charts and nearly always on *Top of the Pops* (American paranoia about terrorist reprisals permitting). Soul even got it's own TV programme with Channel 4's *Solid Soul* (né *Soul Train*) where British soul fans danced badly to rotten British soul bands and occasionally watched video clips of wickedly brilliant American soul

● WHITNEY HOUSTON

● ALEXANDER O'NEAL

● JANET JACKSON

disgust, "*Are you really sleeping with that girl?*" on her 'Billie Jean' beat single 'Truth or Dare', and Gwen Guthrie who trashed her previous, rather weak 'Just For You' set with 'The Rent', an uncompromising rap much in the mould of her work with Sly and Robbie which warned, "*You've got to have a J.O.B. if you wanna be with me*", so putting 3½ million Brits out of the running straightaway!

But the biggest surprise of all came from Janet Jackson with the staggering Jimmy Jam and Terry Lewis produced (aren't we all, dear) album *Control* which really set the roof on fire with its relentless techno attack and massive beat. *Control* found Michael's kid sister punching, kicking and spitting out spiteful lyrics like "*No, my first name ain't baby, it's Janet, Miss Jackson if you're nasty*", on killer cuts like 'Nasty' and 'What Have You Done For Me Lately' as well as reverting to more cutesy but irresistible material like 'When I Think Of You'. *Control* is the album of the year from the newly crowned Dominique Devereux of soul,

George Clinton, whose tastes veer more to the synthetic day-glo dreadlock side of things, bounced back after his rather patchy *Some of My Best Jokes Are Friends* with the mad but bad 'Do Fries Go With That Shake', an incredible slice of fast food junk funk that incorporated as a bassline a space shuttle ignition sound played backwards . . . well it sure sounds like that. The self-explanatory *R 'n' B Skeletons in the Closet* album which followed saw the Funkadelic Mothership locked back on course and Captain Clinton back on the bridge.

Prince's Paisley Park pop party machine continued to churn out some groovy and blissfully bizarre vinyl, the best being Sheila E's teasing jazzy, funk work-out 'A Love Bizarre', while Prince provided the video single party freak of the year with the brilliant George Macrae soundalike 'Kiss'. Prince kissed more ass, sorry, kicked more ass on his weird LP *Parade*, though, in Britain at least, nobody seemed to be particularly interested anymore. *Parade* sold less copies than

dancers grooving along to the music of superb American soul bands. But nobody ever said life was fair, did they?

Your favourite soul records of the year are probably the ones you've already forgotten about like the Loony Tunes/Hanna Barbara funk of Zapp's 'It Doesn't Really Matter' (which is probably the only record ever made which employs a sneezed "At-choo! At-choo!" intro), 'Chief Inspector' by Wally Badarou, the man responsible for producing all those dreary Level 42 songs, 'The Finest', the finest song to date by the SOS Band, Morris Day's dance sensation 'The Oak Tree', the soaring soul gospel of the Winans' (God bless them) 'Let My People Go', Betty Wright's 'Pain' and the fantastic 'Saturday Love' by Cherelle.

And my personal favourite? Well, it's that one they're playing on the radio right now. It's quite new so I haven't managed to find out who it's by or what it's called yet but as soon as I do I'll let you know.

Simon Mills

THE YEAR IN
HIP HOP

"Ladies and gentlemen – the most exciting stage show you've ever witnessed. Appearing live . . ."

Dressed like forties' bebop vocalist Babs Gonzalez, grand wizard Slick Rick the bible scholar, the Harlem hipster born in England of Jamaican parents, addresses 20,000 New York teenagers on the subject of his Gucci underwear.

"Yo!" says Doug E Fresh, "Everybody here tonight who's got the herpes be quiet."

"Whaaaaaaaaaah!"

Seems nobody has the herpes. This, I suspect, is not quite the whole truth and nothing but. What *is* the whole truth is that rap, hip hop, call it what you like, was once again consigned and condemned to the graveyard of 'we're tired of that shit' phenomena, but made it from summer '85 to summer '86 in the naked city with as many success stories as any other kind of music.

Whatever rap was once thought to be – headspins, sportswear and paint jobs – hardly matters. It's a music that continues to discover and recycle its past in order to create its future.

Rap is the art of drums. It is the art of a (New York) city in which the buildings are canyons of reverberation and echo; the subways are the loudest in the world – the noise loud enough to be heard in the street. It comes up through the grills mixed with steam; fire-escapes clank; people shout to be friendly. Roxanne Shanté's 'Bite This': music of colliding klaxons, steam horns, metal industry scissoring its way across town. The Boogie Boys' 'You Ain't Fresh': electric surges in Times Square *Playland*. "Polyester pants with the big bell bottoms… oh no, don't step on my toe with the platform shoes from the Flashback store," sneer the Boogie Boys over a backing track of collapsing civilisation.

"*Walking down the street to the hardcore beat/while my JVC vibrates the concrete/I'm sorry if you can't understand/why I need a radio inside my hand/don't mean to offend other citizens/but I kick my volume way past ten*" says L L Cool J.

"*He would terrorise the neighbours with the heavy bass/but now his radios gone and look at his face/I took his*

● LL COOL J

radio just the other day/snatched it out of his hand and ran down the subway" answered back Steady B from the mean streets. 1985-86 was a year of biting (this meaning theft). Roxanne Shanté defied the biters in her usual kiss-my-ass way but they swarmed all over Doug E Fresh and Slick Rick, the *Inspector Gadget* theme, the Peter Gunn theme, Washington DC go-go rhythms, old breaks and beats from back in the days (especially the intro from Bob James' 'Mardi Gras' which turned up on Run-DMC's 'Peter Piper' and Grandmaster Flash's 'Freelance'). The white boys' pop got bitten, too. MC Craig 'G' took Tears For Fears' 'Shout', already a favourite B boy record, and made a soundscape of urban warfare out of it – tribal chants, rockets and machine-gun fire in the distance.

For perhaps the first time since 1979 when rap went into record production, undiluted B boy music became com-

mercial. Despite radio resistance hardcore beats were moving large numbers. Even crossover sounded tough. Whodini's sweetened R&B, the Fat Boys' bubblegum, Kurtis Blow's pop rap – the big successes stopped sounding like skimmed milk. The market that was opened up by Run-DMC with their early tracks like 'It's Like That' and 'Hard Times' was developed into an arena of industrial post-computer game noise by releases in the manic manner of DJ Cheese & Word Of Mouth's 'King Kut'. Drum machines were no longer mechanical; they had become hammer blows from machinery in overdrive.

Hip hop's big moment came soon after Christmas: the Krush Groove Christmas Party at Madison Square Garden. *Krush Groove* was aiming to be *the* feature film of B boy culture – the rap film that would lay waste to the misconceptions created by *Breakin' 1*, *Breakin' 2*, *Rapping* (or was that *Rappin'*?) and *Beat Street*. Masterminded by Russell Simmons and Rick Rubin of Rush Management-Def Jam Recordings fame, with music production by Kurtis Blow and direction by Michael Schultz, the film – I was told by Russell – would have the hardest music and the most def, the *deffest*, expressions. It would set new trends.

As usual, major league film budgeting turned out to be the Godzilla that can defeat the highest ideals. *Krush Groove* was crushed. One new street word materialised – the mysterious *illin'* (a derivation of chilling, one must assume) and a whole lot of half-assed and illin'ly familiar clichés. As Russell Simmons correctly pointed out – in a condition of being retrospectively chastened but not bowed by the teen movie experience – it was at least a film with which young blacks could identify. They may only have been moments of identification but they were important moments. Important enough for the film to stand tall at the box office and for a wave of moral panic to sweep the nation as excitable youth got fractious in the vicinity of a cinema or two.

The Christmas Party was a whole 'nother thing. A black rap show filling the Garden. Impossible. Doug E Fresh

● DOUG E FRESH

makes a speech about it from the stage – proud of the fact that the show contradicted every expectation of the music business, the Mayor, the subway vigilantes, the ladies looking to clean up lyrics for a pure America, Rambo and probably just about everybody else. With one of the hottest records of the year under his belt – 'The Show' – Doug, Slick Ricky D and DJs Chill Will and Barry B tore up. 'The Show' was typical of the new-breed hip hop: atmosphere, gimmicks, cartoon themes, catch-phrases ("*six minutes, six minutes, Dougie Fresh you're on*", "*Is it real?*" and "*'scuse me Dougie*"), human beat box, famous pop tunes like the Beatles' 'Michelle' and an irresistible shuffling beat. No intrusive bass lines, guitar riffs or over-elaborate synth chords and fills. Just beats.

The other great success of the Krush Groove party was L L Cool J. The young L L is Def Jam's teenage heart-throb with the body. Sweet love songs are his speciality. However, they are spoken to the accompaniment of a concrete crusher beat. They are not all sugar 'n' spice. L L's album, called *Radio*, was a hugely popular record in America. Good job really, since Def Jam had just signed a reported seven-figure deal with Columbia Records. The label, lock stock and barrel, complete with rap brats the Beastie Boys, L L the-milk-and-donuts boy, not to mention plans for Californian speed metal, some go-go, some B Boy ballads and some rap.

The vital labels in rap are still the small ones. In the second half of '85 it was still companies like Pop Art, Select, Reality and Sleeping Bag that made the running. Def Jam, started by college boy Rick Rubin, had forged the sound of the year. To move into the arms of Columbia was a big swing to mainstream.

This was not unsupported by the flakier figures of rock. Madonna showed where her sympathies lay by having the Beastie Boys as support on her tour. Lou Reed couldn't praise Run-DMC enough and when Little Steven figured on doing something about apartheid he called on Afrika Bambaataa, Kurtis Blow, the Fat Boys, Melle Mel, Scorpio and Run-DMC to join with everybody else in declaring "*ain't gonna play Sun City*". Rap was in line with the rest of rawk 'n' roll when it came to throwing down the gauntlet for a cause or two. The trend continued with the Tommy Boy label's *Master of the Beat* album – pure beats from luminaries like Keith LeBlanc and The Latin Rascals – and all writers' royalties donated to The Coalition for the Homeless. A lot of the 'Sun City' contributors showed up again in early '86 for King Holiday, an anti-racism tribute to Martin Luther King.

● BEASTIE BOYS

● REAL ROXANNE

● LOVEBUG STARSKI

● KURTIS BLOW

● LISA LISA AND CULT JAM

● FULL FORCE

Meanwhile, back in the land of dollars, the mainstream hits were happening. In August '85 the Fat Boys were pushing the title track from their second album. Though still graced with a Kurtis Blow production (and Kurt is one of rap's best producers), *The Fat Boys Are Back* was weak by comparison with their debut LP. Never mind – their 'All You Can Eat' sequence in *Krush Groove* (a case of stuff yourself dizzy) was one of the film's highspots. Other hits included Run-DMC's *King of Rock*, still lingering in the US charts, the Boogie Boys, Rock Master Scott, the Force MDs and the Brooklyn family of UFTO, Lisa Lisa and Full Force.

Full Force get busy one time. Full Force in the place to be. Lisa Lisa's 'I Wonder If I Take You Home' was the record everybody hated except for the hordes of teenagers who took it home. By November, producer/musicians Full Force had their own hooky little number. 'Alice, I Want You Just For Me', following in a tradition of convoluted titles that ate the pop-buyer, was climbing the American charts and about to do the same thing with a vengeance in the UK. The UK had been half awake to hip hop for years but suddenly the penny seemed to drop with the full clang. July '86 saw Street Sounds presenting the first big deal rap show at Wembley to Brits of both B boy and pop persuasion, not to mention the merely curious.

Full Force were obviously finding a fresh balance of pop hip hop. Pop hooks were set against a bare bass 'n' drums backdrop. The new rhythms, from Full Force, Def Jam and Mantronix, you could describe as 'lightly swinging'. Not that they would be confused with Herb Alpert or Ray Conniff, but there was a jazzy shuffle in there that contrasted with the marching rhythms of snare drum salvoes and bass drum depth charges that could leave you pinned up against a club wall. That Washington go-go was having its effect. The Beastie Boys' 'Hold It, Now Hit It', Kurtis Blow's 'If I Ruled The World', Lovebug Starski's 'House Rocker', Run-DMC's 'My Adidas' and the Real Roxanne's 'Bang Zoom Let's Go-Go!' all had more than a touch of that go-go syncopation.

Of course, there were whispers that rap was last decade's thing. Disco was on its way back, or the electro pop of TKA and Information Society that Tommy Boy were moving into, or the Chicago garage funk from DJ International Records. Maybe, maybe. All I know is that when I hear 'You Be Illin'' by Run-DMC I'm hearing the new Coasters. This is Leiber and Stoller all over again and that is music that will run and run. Excuse the pun.

David Toop

● THE YEAR IN
JAZZ

The cats, at last, are no longer napping. This last year, jazz re-awoke to an audience hungry for the sound and the style, eager for the first *real* time in nearly three decades to lock into the spirit of the music. It doesn't matter that there's an awful long way to go before jazz outplays Madonna and Dire Straits on the global stand – it breathes and it lives, genuinely strong again.

British media coverage of a jazz 'revival' has been a useful misdemeanour. Of course, it's not a revival – the music's never been away. But it *is* something of a reaffirmation. The causes are complex and manifold. Last year, jazz in the UK still looked like a club phenomenon, an occasional distraction from the usual business of dancefloor music. But as rock has gorged itself on pop stars and dance has sold itself to electronic drums, the casting around for fresh human avenues has led inevitably to jazz, the most human music.

It's been a slow movement through the eighties, a flavouring of the mainstream that led finally to Sade and Alison Moyet, where 'jazz' is the merest wisp of atmosphere in a pop setting. But suddenly, in London, Sheffield, Edinburgh, Glasgow and dozens of other points of purchase, musicans of sterner stuff have come forward. Jazz in Britain is strong again because its team of players has marched out of the shadows. They're insisting on dismissing the mass of neglect, bad organisation and bad reputation that spoils jazz's public profile here.

As recently as a year ago, it might have been difficult to find traces of Iain Ballamy, Tommy Smith, Phil Bent, Nigel Hitchcock, Django Bates, Steve Arguelles and Ashley Slater in a fan's notebook. But it's cool to be a cat again. Saxophones and trumpets sound better than guitars, anyway.

The style of this new scene fits perfectly with the sound. It's not quite the zoot-suit obsession hashed together by the likes of Blue Rondo A La Turk – more a sense of sharpness without actually having to dress *up*. The presence of *Absolute Beginners* (a jazz film without the jazz) has had little

● ASHLEY SLATER

● DJANGO BATES (seated)

effect. The muted quality of old Blue Note album covers is the emotional pitch of the style, something that the music itself uses as a lift-off point. The sound of modern jazz in Britain now is a hard, boppish vocabulary powered into places where funk and free styles can inform the muse too. Bands like Clark Tracey's Quintet and Iain Ballamy's Quartet blend sources in ways which would be mushy if it weren't for the crackling, single-minded skill of the playing itself. A new excitement has been bred. The music has a firmer heartbeat than it did under the cloud of fusion/jazz-rock.

If the focus for all this activity has to fall on one man, the gentleman in question has to be Courtney Pine. In the summer of 1985 he was a well-kept secret on the verge of breaking out; a year later, this London tenorman was

the strongest face in British jazz. He is only 22, a brimming, volatile performer on tenor and soprano saxes and bass clarinet. He leads an impassioned young quartet and a remarkable all-black big band called the Jazz Warriors. British blacks have normally opted for soul as a musical course; jazz is finally making waves as a viable alternative, and Pine is more than a token proof. (Much the same can be claimed for jazz women – a notoriously macho music is having its barriers undermined by a force of fine female musicans like Gail Thompson, Annie Whitehead, Louis Elliott, Angele Veltmeijer, Anita Carmichael and the Guest Stars.)

Pine's reign as our leading face may be comparatively short-lived: he has been asked to join Art Blakey's Jazz Messengers, one of the most sought-after gigs in jazz, and in June this year he was still trying to make up his mind. But Island Records have signed his quartet, the first contract for an all-out acoustic jazz group from a major British label for a decade. He's a very fine player in need of steady, intelligent development – his furious amalgam of Coltrane licks and more personal ideas is exciting but as yet incomplete. From Pine's own viewpoint, he'll have to hope that the biz will let him mature at his

● ANNIE WHITEHEAD

● COURTNEY PINE

● LOOSE TUBES

● BRANFORD MARSALIS

own pace. But the attention on him, and on jazz too, can be nothing but vital for the general health of the music. Courtney and his young peers are proving that jazz can look good, sound thrilling and *be popular* all at once.

In a wider sense, jazz's fortunes have been set fair but mixed. It's still a music to go out and hear, in clubs and pubs – jazz groups have more gigs than ever, but they seldom get the chance to broadcast or make records. Jazz still doesn't attack the charts. Reissues are as plentiful as last year but the fortunes of Blue Note and the other programmes have fluctuated – there are simply too many old records for everyone to buy.

The National Jazz Centre took on a semi-humorous status as it advanced not one brick further towards completion. The BBC happily dug some old jazz television out of their archives, but weren't so quick to sponsor new broadcasts. The radio hid the usual tiny outposts for this music in obscure corners of the schedule. The establishment is still resisting; another year may surrender more ground.

With all this activity on our own shores, the Americans have reaped less attention than usual. The Marsalis Brothers split apart, with Wynton sacking Branford from his band because of the saxophonist's dalliance with Sting,

and both worked without sensation at their music. There was rather more interest in the serious young men of the Messengers, Terence Blanchard and Donald Harrison, who left Blakey this May and have signed to CBS. But by and large the American industry still sees jazz marketing in tasteful terms. Instead of jazz-funk, it was the doubtful jazz associations of so-called New Age Music that appealed to US executives – pretty, vapid, ideal for cucumber sandwiches, cool rooms and watercolours.

Miles Davis turned 60 in May, and was reported to be working on a record with Prince, whom he once described as "a funky little dude". Sonny Rollins proved his appetite for playing was undiminished by releasing the first solo saxophone record. Generally, though, it was an undistinguished year for jazz albums, a lot of solid LPs and very few to galvanise the ears. Incus Records chalked up its 50th issue: this label for improvised music run by Evan Parker and Derek Bailey is a monument to the integrity of enterprises organised by the players themselves. Improvising musicians struggled again to impose some standing on their music in the face of the customary corporate indifference: they survive.

New York's Kool Festival, one of the traditional highlights of the jazz calendar, finally found itself a new sponsor.

We now call it the JVC Festival. British festivals have this year decided to be small and beautiful on their own terms: US visitors are fewer this summer, for familiar diplomatic reasons. But one astonishing quartet paid a fleeting visit to London this May: Last Exit, an alternative supergroup of Bill Laswell, Peter Brotzmann, Sonny Sharrock and Ronald Shannon Jackson, shook the deepest foundations of improvising with electro-acoustic music so loud and violent that audiences were stunned into acclaim. They did not play at Ronnie Scott's Club, although that establishment joined Max Gordon's New York Village Vanguard in having its biography published.

Most unlikely of all was the reappearance of a jazz creature that experts had long deemed dead of economic starvation: the big band. The great composer George Russell paid his first visit to Britain (a mere thirty years overdue) and assembled a fine Anglo-American ensemble; Charlie Watts, a jazz fan all his life, put together "the world's biggest big band", a 30-strong entourage of literally dozens of British stars; and 22 young turks of the home scene called themselves Loose Tubes and stirred up a heady mixture of serious blowing and intellectual vaudeville. Everywhere, the cats are smokin'.

Richard Cook

THE YEAR IN HEAVY METAL

Maybe it was the fact that the two events happened on the same day that made such an impact. Looking in the mirror in the morning the first grey hairs of impending old age were discovered in the previously jet black barnet. Nasty shock.

Then, half an hour later, while idly glancing at the record section in Woolworths I saw, among the Max Bygraves, Bruce Forsyth and Slim Whitman bargain albums, several slightly more familiar covers. Like Whitesnake's *Ready 'n' Willing*, the Scorpions' *Lovedrive* and, God help us all, Iron Maiden's *Killers*. They were priced at £3.25 apiece so I figured it was worth a tenner just to save them from the ignominy of being in there with

● SCORPIONS

Maxie and Brucie. Anyway, my old copies were practically worn out.

There was an oldist air to the past year of heavy metal. Reformations seemed to be the order of the day – reformations of bands who had seemed long gone and most definitely part of HM history.

Knebworth Festival, traditionally the biggest event of the metallic year, had a pensioner's look about it. Meat Loaf was rated by many as embarrassing, especially since his idea of a good show seemed to be shouting "fuck" at every conceivable opportunity.

UFO, who in my book had always been one of the absolute greats of HM

● MOTORHEAD

but who, I also reckoned, were now consigned to the mists of time for ever and ever, reformed and showed the massive crowd that they still knew how to do it.

The Scorpions, meanwhile, showed that they'd *never* forgotten how to do it. It still astounds me that they can generate so much enthusiasm, so much honest-to-Jesus *passion*.

And then there was Deep Purple. I was mildly surprised when I'd heard previously that the old stagers were going to get back together again. Having followed them for years and then followed the myriad offshoot bands for even more years, having heard what individual members had said about each other, having predicted

● DEEP PURPLE

quite firmly that they'd never team up again – well, imagine my surprise, dear Doctor. (Incidentally, could you double my usual supply of tonic wine – I find I get tired so much more easily these days.)

Passion is not a word that could be aimed at the 'new' Deep Purple. Going through the motions has become a speciality and Ian Gillan's scream, once so blood-curdling, is a sad old imitation of itself. To heighten matters even further 'Black Night' was re-released. Oh, those classic chords; ah, that drive and drama; oh, what a shame.

And this was the year Motorhead celebrated their tenth anniversary. Who said they wouldn't last? Practically anyone who's ever had a taste of

● MEATLOAF

Lemmy's social life, I should reckon.

In traditional fashion the Lemmy Legion celebrated Motorhead's anniversary at Hammersmith Odeon. It was somehow fitting that Wendy O Williams should join them on stage as another rabble-rousing gesture, considering she had been the cause of one of the splits in the band's history because she and Lemmy had announced their intention to record a daft version of 'Stand By Your Man'.

And talking of age and tradition, Reading Festival was mooted to make a return appearance in 1985, before the whole notion was knocked quickly and firmly on the head. "Local council problems" people muttered, "licence problems" they mumbled, "local residents" they moaned.

By the middle of 1986 Reading Festival was definitely making a comeback. The press releases started flowing and the list of bands taking part started growing and growing as it always had done in the 200-year (or however long it's been going) history of the annual mud, blood and booze gathering.

But you had to *see* the list of bands to believe it. Headlining the Sunday night were Hawkwind, for God's sake. All it needed was a return appearance of Stacia – the only woman I've ever heard a heavy metal audience encourage to keep her clothes *on* – to put the icing on the mouldy old biscuit. And then there was Saxon lined up for Saturday night.

That was a band that I loved up to a point – the point was when they did their *Eagle Has Landed* tour and all of a sudden Biff had developed an American accent.

Earlier in the year – well, towards the end of '85 actually – Saxon had wheeled out the *Innocence Is No Excuse* album. I welcomed it as an old fan but I couldn't help feeling that here was another band entering a pale shadowland.

Van Halen cheered me up no end by dumping David Lee Roth and then

● SAXON

● WAYSTED

● VAN HALEN

entering into the kind of public slanging match that makes a hack rejoice. Eddie Van Halen revealed, to my even greater delight, that he hadn't been able to stick Roth at any price for some years. I know how he felt.

Lee Aaron was the main woman in the world of HM, proving once again that looks could well be everything. She's got her followers, music-wise, and I doff my titfer to them; but anyone with even a single eyeball in his head has to recognise that she's the latest purveyor of sex 'n' rock 'n' roll. In this most sexist of musical forms foxy chicks make it.

At Castle Donington ZZ Top con-

● LEE AARON

tinued their extraordinary world domination plan. How the band has grown from a minority interest to one of the biggest on the planet is a story in itself. Longevity explains some of it, brilliant videos a bit more – but out and out class turns out to be the final clincher.

Whoops! – that was Waysted dumping singer Fin Moore and replacing him with Danny Vaughan. The wheels and the merry-go-rounds keep on turning among the second division bands and never show any signs of stopping.

There were new(ish) people to be thoroughly welcomed in this essential old person's year. Bon Jovi blitzed and razed us with a vengeance – what a fabulous crew they are. Contender for album of the year was Marionette's *Blade Secrets and Dark Bombshells* – rated by many as an out and out classic and who would argue with that.

There were golden oldies to cherish, too. Ozzy Osbourne remains a dizbusting winner of a wildman – long may he run (and reign).

Status Quo point – blank refused to lie down thus contending with the Crazy Gang and Frank Sinatra in the world-record stakes for greatest number of final farewell/reunion announcements. No matter what form they take, no matter how old they get they remain truly great.

● ZZ TOP

Robert Plant remains truly wonderful, Randy California as bizarre and impenetrable as he ever was and, my personal favourites (these days), Iron Maiden gave us more and more pleasure.

What did it all mean? I guess, it means heavy metal remains alive and kicking as it does every year. It means the flow of good new bands lessened. There are always plenty of contenders but the good ones get scarcer. It means some old contenders should shove off this mortal coil. It means good old contenders should stay for ever. Long live Ozzy and fellow titans, and cobblers to the rest. **Brian Harrigan**

THE YEAR IN BLUES & GOSPEL

"The Blues never die, no sir; just like the world, they gonna stand long after you and me and everybody else has gone."

● SONNY BOY WILLIAMSON

● MUDDY WATERS

● SKIP JAMES

Furry Lewis spoke these words to a film crew in Memphis eight years ago, his aged and bony fingers wrapping themselves around a blue-smoke cigarette. Repeated out loud to oneself in a non-blues-hero voice they might sound impossibly trite, but this last year has proved once again the inherent value of the philosophy behind them.

Certainly the music continues to be documented with care and attention; the flood of vinyl that nearly submerged the blues punter during the previous year has not abated. Indeed, it has turned into a steadily flowing river which has, in itself, produced some interesting tributaries. One of these has been the emergence of the box set. Charly Records has issued two fine and lovingly constructed extravaganzas. *Sun Records – The Blues Years 1950-1956* gave us a nine-album summary of early post-war blues as it was performed in and around the Memphis area. For what seems like a relatively modest sum (around £38) you can now avail yourself of a handy footstool-sized box containing the sounds, words, pictures and information that paint a pretty accurate portrait of that city's musical activities before Elvis turned up and changed it all for ever. Established legends and satisfyingly obscure cult figures jostle one another in a crowd of 150 musical performances, all carefully selected to reflect the individual pieces that went to make up a complex jigsaw.

Some six months later Charly jumped in with both boots again and presented us with a six-album box set of Sonny Boy Williamson's career at the Chess studios in Chicago. There are relatively few blues musicians who can undergo this kind of intense scrutiny and emerge untarnished; Rice Miller, Sonny Boy No.2, Foots, call him what you will, is one of those people. Other obvious candidates would be Muddy Waters, Howlin' Wolf and Little Walter, all of whom are apparently under consideration. In fact, if you want to go prospecting and don't mind forking out in excess of £100 you can already indulge yourself in the complete Muddy Waters on a Japanese import.

Future historians might therefore see this as the year in which the box set gained its first real foothold, but for the more impecunious I'm happy to report that the traditional pay-no-more-than-a-fiver album is far from dead. The companies you would expect (Charly, Ace, Demon, Krazy Kat, Red Lightnin', Mr R&B, Edsel, Flyright) have continued to feed us absorbing cross-sections of music that range from solid down home blues through R&B of all persuasions and out beyond those boundaries to such esoteric ground as Cajun, Zydeco, vocal groups and even Chicano R&B.

Ace Records has adhered unerringly to its chosen course of plundering the West Coast record company vaults, and the treasures they have emerged with have been both exciting and enlightening. Sets by Gene Phillips, Percy Mayfield, Don & Dewey, BB King and anthologies of more obscure artists have all helped to add to our ever growing knowledge. Recently they have looked south, to Houston and the Peacock label, to bring the story of urban Texas blues into the homes of European listeners. More of this will follow in the next twelve months, laying a foundation not only for new perspectives awaiting the chance to emerge, but also for someone to be able to say, this time next year, that yes, the music is still alive and well.

The pre-war roots of all this activity have not been ignored either. The American Yazoo company has provided us with the opportunity to hear every single recording by a key figure – Skip James – at the height of his powers – 1931 – in the finest possible sound quality. This does *not* mean a completely noise-free experience but it does mean that we can hear enough to confirm suspicions long held; that Skip's rhythmic foot-stomping really did propel his piano technique the way we thought and that he really did sing *"If I ever get off this shit-house floor"* fifty-five years ago on a commercially released 78rpm record.

Matchbox and Travellin' Man Records in England, Wolf and Earl Records in Austria and Bluestime Records in France have also offered us interesting

● BB KING

● ROBERT CRAY

● SON SEALS

music from that pre-nuclear period, serving long-overlooked areas such as mid-to-late-thirties urban blues with thoughtful releases by the likes of Big Bill Broonzy, Washboard Sam, Jazz Gillum and Walter Davis as well as singers from an earlier generation like Julius Daniels and the Mississippi Shieks. Esoteric perhaps, but enjoyable and fascinating, nevertheless.

Plenty of vinyl then, even for the deepest pocket. What of live music you may rightly ask? Not such a rosy picture, I'm afraid, but there has been some activity. Robert Cray has been here more than once – with a new album to promote, too – and has filled increasingly large venues, including the Hammersmith Odeon. He's younger than your Average Blues Person of course, and we suffer little from the fear of his dying in mid-performance as a result of years spent working a cotton field. Given their track record during the last few visits to the UK, however, the less charitable among us might be found sticking pins in Junior Wells and Buddy Guy dolls hoping to bring about just such a conclusion to what has become a travesty of a powerful and moving music – Chicago blues. You get about as much value from this pair nowadays as you would expect from a dodgy second-hand car dealer in a reject camelhair coat and thin moustache. However, Lowell Fulson, Little Willie Littlefield, Eddie Vinson, Ray Charles and Memphis Slim all performed as one would expect them to (more so in a couple of cases) and accepting that the choice of artists was safe to the point of being unadventurous, what they offered was satisfying enough. Where, though, were the likes of James Cotton, Son Seals, Albert Collins, Earl King, Snooks Eaglin et al – all still performing regularly and surely all willing to play here if the circumstances were right? Ultimately, the blame must lay squarely at the feet of promoters in this country, who seem unwilling to go about their business properly. Perhaps time will turn things around and in twelve months a quite different report could be written. Perhaps. I doubt it, though.

If, given all that, you had chosen instead to have a quiet evening at home curled around a good book, what would have been available to you? Surprisingly little. Only one book of major importance has emerged in the last year but it is certainly one worthy of attention. *I Hear You Knocking – The Sound Of New Orleans Rhythm & Blues* by Almost Slim (a soubriquet that hides the identity of native journalist Jeff Hannusch) supplies the reader with a relevant and handsomely crafted impression of one of the most vital areas in contemporary R&B. Unfortunately

not published here, it is nevertheless available as an import from bookshops that care.

Broadcasting, viewed by some as a sleeping giant in blues terms, woke up long enough to provide a five-hour gourmet dinner in July. Co-hosted by John Walters and BB King (good kudos, that...), BBC-2 served its public with an *hors d'oeuvre* of vintage Sonny Boy Williamson and Lightnin' Hopkins, then launched into a main course that included BB King, Muddy Waters, Bessie Smith, Louis Jordan and other heroes and heroines that the capricious whims of film history had decided to preserve. The problem with providing an overview of blues history through the medium of film is the appalling gaps that were created by key figures never getting a chance at achieving celluloid immortality. Nevertheless, given these obvious shortcomings, the *Arena* team did a worthwhile job for which we must be genuinely grateful. Radio, for those who remember the halcyon pirate days of Mike Raven and Radio 390, also sat bolt upright in its bed and spewed forth an ectoplasm that it called *Rhythm & Blues*, thirteen consecutive weeks on Radio 2 hosted by Paul Jones. It ran a huge gamut from sixties British bands to pre-war and all points above and beyond, which has naturally left some listeners feeling less than satisfied with the format – but it was a nationally broadcast programme and in my view any media attention is welcome.

On the obituary scene, I'm pained to report that the Grim Reaper had a field day. We lost Big Joe Turner, Eddie Taylor, Pee Wee Crayton, Piano Red and Sonny Terry. It could, I suppose, have been worse, but not a lot.

The predicted Gospel Explosion didn't quite happen this year either; perhaps the fuse is a little longer than some of us imagined. The Rev James Cleveland did a prestige gig at the Albert Hall but – if you'll excuse the rather obvious metaphor – ended up preaching to the converted. Vintage reissue albums trickled rather than poured out. There was one stunner, *New Orleans Gospel Quartets 1947-55*, on Gospel Heritage and more are promised for the next twelve months but one swallow of a tasty morsel does not a banquet make. Please, let's have more very soon.

Looking over my shoulder at this last year induces the usual mixture of emotions that any given twelve-month period might produce. The one sure thing that I can safely predict about the coming year is that there will be activity worthy of chronicle. In essence, that is the key to the music's staying power. Like politics, summer, rain or *The Times* crossword, it's here to stay.

Paul Vernon

THE YEAR IN
COUNTRY & WESTERN

We all see it from different eyes, don't we, friends? For us the Year in Country started with our final alienation from the Mervyn Conn establishment; not that the Wangfords and the Conns were ever Big Buddies, but after we were unable to accept Mervyn's kind offer to appear unpaid on his Fine Stage it felt like our last effort for a while to play to the straight country audience.

And it's a pity, because through the year there's been progress in an alternative country scene, outside the mums' and dads' C&W bingo world and embracing more and more rock fans. Not just the older world of pubrock, either; younger folks are looking to country roots. Good country is being listened to, and in spite of it being about as hip as Leon Brittan more people are seeing beyond the schmaltz and feeling, just as Gram Parsons did all those years ago, to the rough and jagged edges of hard country. This is no sudden fad, the scent has been on the wind for a couple of years now; some of the Class of '84, Yip Yip Coyote and the Boothills, have left us, but the Pogues and the Men They Couldn't Hang carry on, country cousins all. Throughout Britain young musicians are feeling the bloody heart and dark fire burning in country roots as it does in rock and blues. Country is being plundered shamelessly in Dundee and Darlington by bands with more chance of creating a living music than many on the C&W circuit, where bands with dead eyes play to people they despise. It shouldn't be that way. I know everyone has the right to bad music, but even country fans don't deserve to be treated this way . . . no more than HM fans deserve Ozzy Osbourne.

Which takes me back to Mervyn Conn; for, hard to believe though it is, friends, he too is guilty of short-changing the fans, and it ain't right. He is not the Saviour but the Undertaker of C&W, though he's doing no more than laying to rest wraiths from the Nashville Nursing Home, wheeled out for their ritual twenty minutes on his attractive stage. And though there is always a nod to 'progressive' country music, Mervyn relies on C&W greats like the Osmond Brothers (actually only SOME, not THE Osmonds) and Bobby Ewing to give the fans what he knows they want . . .

In the meantime, through this year there has been a fair flow of good country-based music from the States, and a lot of it I've been pleased to see in the Mean Fiddler in London's Harlesden, the best Honky Tonk in Britain.

The Long Ryders were exciting, carrying Gram's torch; Los Lobos, too, with pokey Tex-Mex flavoured Cantina rock; Flaco Jiminez is a regular and welcome visitor, often with the eerie yodelling but soppy songs of Peter Rowan. Jason and the Scorchers are stayers and personal favourites, good Nashville boys. And we've been well serviced by the Texas scene with Jerry Jeff Waler's and Butch Hancock's fine music and Terry Allen's high plains madness – universal country music breathing Beefheart fire.

The Wangfords have been gigging so much I'm bound to have left your favourite out and it's hard to say whether the biggies like Waylon and Willie *did* come this year or last; Waylon was okay, but Willie was stunning. Ricky Skaggs, a great player, a fine high harmony singer and a brill haircut, arrived staggering under the weight of Nashville's Great Traditional White Hope, and to give the bloke his due it's not his fault that it's too heavy a responsibility. But his Dick van Dyke cockney routine did not endear him to the cynical British audience. Back in the States, Ricky's loved by many, especially the CMA who voted him Entertainer and Instrumental Group of the year. Over on the West Coast they've gone for the even less radical choice of Alabama for Entertainer of the Year: these boys are like Eagles with beards, massively successful doing patronising nonsense like '40 Hour Week', a sincere Hi! to the working men of America. Their video has lots of shots of the Als, hammers in hand, sweating beside some steelworker, driving a Big Rig, out on a combine with a farmer on the prairies; the only woman to be saluted in it is a waitress . . .

Country videos this year have continued to be sensationally bad, typically featuring drips with hair perms like Earl Thomas Conley singing to model girls floating in a bubble over his head. They are so *literal*. Two welcome exceptions were the CMA best vid 'All My Rowdy Friends Are Coming Over Tonight', a stompingly fine piece of deeply sexist fun from Hank Williams Jr, with guest appearances by famous country fun-lovers – most famously George Jones coming to the party on his lawnmower, just as he went to Nashville to get booze once when Tammy had cleaned

● JASON AND THE SCORCHERS

● THE LONG RYDERS

● MERLE HAGGARD

the house of drink and taken all the car keys. My personal favourite video was Merle Haggard's 'Are The Good Times Over For Good?' which, like the song, could have been another bit of nostalgic rubbish, but is sweet and hard, Merle in great form. But then Merle didn't get any awards. No, the Country Establishment wants to appear forward and modern but is still very conservative in their choices. Both the CMA and the Californian Academy of C&W go for the same Male and Female Singer and Album of the Year. Yer man is George Strait, a big hunka instant cheesecake, country's first big sex symbol, they say, since Hank Williams; bosoms are heaving for George and saddles are moistening. He's a fair singer, a nice voice and has made a pleasant but unremarkable Album of the Year, *Does Fort Worth Ever Cross Your Mind?* Reba McIntyre, a redhead from Oklahoma with a folksy voice a little warmer than Emmylou's took it for the women. The Judds are the Mother-Daughter Duo who have taken all the awards for Vocal Group; they do sing sweet and everybody wants them . . . The most exciting and indicative award is Song of the Year, in case you were in any doubt as to where Nashville is coming from, for Lee Greenwood's 'God Bless The USA'. There's no more to say, really, except that the Wangfords should cover it.

In a year when Nashville offered us Ricky Skaggs as their Traditional face and George Strait as their Honkytonker, there is still the overwhelming desire to produce FM blandouts like the Heavy Pop of Rosanne Cash. Sales is all, and many music businessmen dismiss the term C&W as archaic; in their de-specialising frenzy they don't even want to call it country, but AMERICAN MUSIC, for God's sake. In parts of Nashville the pedal steel spells Shame; they are trying to hide their roots like

some preposterous old tart and their peroxide is called New Country . . . So the formula for a top-heavy organisation like the Nashville record company giants is to search for a music that OFFENDS NO ONE; this sells to the great mass of people searching desperately for the Inoffensive.

And it *does* sell. But this is nothing new, just a final slide towards the Terminal. It's not middle- but end-of-the-road music, so I can only hope in these dark times that independent talent will blast its way through the smoking ruins of country. Heart music, passion, it's all there, so let's see it again; country always was white soul music . . . black people yodel, too, you know . . .

There is something stirring down among the golfers, still glossy but with something fine inside like the Judds or the Louvin tradition, carried on by the Whitstein Brothers who do a wonderful country rendition of one of my least favourite songs, the awkward and pretentious 'Bridge Over Troubled Water'. I'm a sucker for the Brother duets, which have the Dark Fire we crave; it's this fire that lives in hard country that kids are stumbling over now and then, moving through punk to rockabilly to honkytonk, sorting the True Grit from the Rhinestones. So we have two movements, rock 'n' rollers moving towards country roots, while the country establishment is coy and uneasy about the whole thing. American music, indeed. But there is hope with people like Dwight Yoakam leading a good honkytonk band in LA, very straight strong country, going down well in the sixties/Byrds/country revival, Rickenbackers ringing from the West Coast, country music much stronger than the dreaded Californian 'country rock' which at its worst could out-pap even Nashville's worst excesses. But up in Alberta something stirs. A young Canadian, KD Lang, a punk Patsy Cline, is on her way with a big voice and sawn-off cowboy boots. I think Hank 'n' old KD could get along just fine.

Back here in Peterborough, England, Jed Ford, a promoter cast firmly in the Sincere Products No Regard To Quality tradition, has been trashed by Jeffrey Kruger who is putting on this year's

Fest. It promises some good acts and also at last MU fees guaranteed for the musicians, a new and unprecedented move in the world of British C&W.

Meantime, I've been going backwards, way past George Jones, because there's been nothing that's made my spine crumble like Joe Ely did in '77. So I've been listening to all the old Brothers, the Delmores, the Monroes, the Blue Sky Boys, the Louvins; listening to Jimmie Rodgers, Ernest Tubb, Webb Pierce, and most of all to Lefty Frizzell; listening to Karl and Harty, Darby and Tarlton, the Girls of the Golden West, lots more Hank Williams of course, but most of all to the voice of Lefty Frizzell. Right now he's the One. And there has been nothing around this year to make me change my mind.

Hank Wangford

● WAYLON JENNINGS

● WILLIE NELSON

● DWIGHT YOAKAM

● THE JUDDS

● THE YEAR IN
FOLK

It was a year when everyone did their charity record for Africa, and the British folk world was no exception. Apart from its altruism, the album *Feed the Folk* symbolised two important aspects of the current scene. With one exception the artists taking part belonged to the roll-call of success stories of the sixties and seventies. There was Lindisfarne, whose first album summed up life on the dole in 1972 and who still provide Geordie anthems. There was Steeleye Span and Fairport Convention, giants of British folk-rock a decade ago. There, too, were the most famous ex-members of those groups, two great guitar stylists, Martin Carthy and Richard Thompson. The Celtic connection was represented by two Scottish and two Irish acts. Billy Connolly acknowledged his musical roots in the folk world, while ex-Planxty guitarist/singer Paul Brady took a step back from his current electric music to provide one of his dramatic performances of a big traditional ballad. These soloists were complemented by two bands who have found new ways with old tunes – the Chieftains and the Battlefield Band.

Rounding off *Feed the Folk* were three American acts who have become firm favourites in the British scene; Kate and Anna McGarrigle, the Roches and Loudon Wainwright III. The album had it all: English, Irish, Scots, American; singer-songwriters and interpreters of traditional material. There was only one interloper from the eighties – the harsher, unrefined tones of Billy Bragg. But even he was singing a song with a proper seventies pedigree – Leon Rosselson's tribute to the radicals of the English Civil War, 'The World Turned Upside Down'.

Now, Bragg in the last couple of years has become the focus of much excited debate in both the rock and folk worlds. In rock, the argument is about the politics of his music – whether it's proper to mix politics and music and (in some cases) whether his socialist views are left-wing enough. Among folk commentators the political issue was less vital – for various historical reasons, left politics have been a

● THE POGUES

flavour of folk since the earliest revivals of the forties. For folk ideologues, the key question has been: what does the emergence of Billy Bragg and other 'rogue folk' such as the Pogues mean for the established structure of folk clubs and festivals and more basically, for the identity of 'folk' itself.

Folk has a permanent identity crisis, which has a lot to do with its ambivalent relationship to the commercial mainstream of popular music. Folk doesn't know whether it wants to become part of pop or if it should keep its distance. This in turn reflects the double nature of rock and pop – they are at once 'commercial' (and therefore can be seen as the source of insincerity and of the corruption of artistic integrity) and 'popular' (their audience is precisely that mass of ordinary people which any folk music worthy of the name should be communicating with).

The last two decades have been full of attempts to resolve this dilemma. There was electric folk, the folk comedians (Jasper Carrott, Billy Connolly, et al), chamber folk from the Chieftains, MOR folk from Mary O'Hara and the Spinners, and so on. In many ways, the current rogue folk affair is very similar: the denizens of the folk scene are once again split between those who applaud

the chart success of Bragg and the Pogues and those who condemn it. There is even a strong whiff of the sixties, when there were passionate arguments about whether electric music could ever be folk, in the attacks on the Pogues for their cartoon versions of traditional songs. A more appropriate criticism is surely that their models among earlier folk performers seem to come from such superficial operators as the Dubliners.

But, while the folk revival currently being hailed has more than a little in common with earlier failed revolutions, there is another, less obvious, way in which the scene is radically changing.

Feed the Folk is released on a label called Temple (and is still available by post from them at Shillinghall, Temple, Midlothian, Scotland). The company was formed by Robin Morton to record and distribute the music of his own group, the Boys of the Lough, as well as other Scottish folk artists. Temple is just one of up to a hundred folk labels which between them now release around 500 albums a year in Britain.

There is an established tradition among folk club artists that they produce and release their own records to sell at gigs. But these have been

● BILLY BRAGG

seldom conceived as anything more than a souvenir of a live performance – to be bought much as anyone would buy a concert programme. As such, they have sometimes been of a lamentably low technical standard, recorded in haste in a poorly equipped studio by an engineer with no feel for acoustic music and its special qualities.

Apart from the sheer numbers, one thing that is different about the new folk records is that for the most part they are made as recordings, not just as adjuncts to performances. They can stand on their own without any need for a listener to have seen the artist in person. This has much to do with two factors. First, many of the people behind the new independent folk record labels come from bands who have formerly been signed to orthodox record companies, dedicated to the production values of the modern studio. Thus, Robin Morton recorded for Transatlantic, the company whose mixture of inspiration and sleaze did much to mould the folk revival in the sixties. The Woodworm label is run by Fairport Convention's Dave Pegg, who spent many years with Island and Phonogram before the big labels decided folk-rock was dead.

The second factor relates to one of the essential advantages of recording over other musical media. It can enable you to experience music that you could never hear in live performance either because of the age of the music or the geographic distance separating artist from listener. Folk, with its built-in sense of the past, has always understood to some degree the importance of archive material. But the last few years has seen an explosion of releases documenting the past glories of such varied musics as bluegrass, calypso and country blues. All these are in addition to the re-releases of British folk records of past years. 1985

saw the welcome return of *Anthems in Eden*, a remarkable 1969 collaboration between the singers Shirley and Dolly Collins and the master of early music styles David Munrow. Although the mixture of traditional English songs and medieval instruments may seem a very precious idea, *Anthems in Eden* is unusually effective. The strangeness of the instrumental sound serves to bring out the elemental qualities of the songs and the singing. The availability of past glories has its other side, though. There is even a label (Awareness) which exists primarily to reissue the early recordings of singer-songwriter Roy Harper, the hippie bard of the sixties.

The importance of this extensive programme of reissues is not limited to the folk music audience. It also has the potential to influence what music is produced in the future, since it provides a remarkably rich and varied source for any young performer to draw on. And if it provokes a Roy Harper or Al Stewart revival, that seems a small price to pay if the authentic bluegrass sounds of early Bill Monroe or Flatt and Scruggs inspire some spirited British folk music. Already, Britain has an impressively large number of bands reproducing the sounds of most styles of American music of the last fifty years, from cajun to Western Swing. There are also artists like Champion Doug Veitch dedicated to blending reggae with country music, highlife with cajun.

Mention of this range of musical styles and forms brings up another important feature of the current British folk scene. There has been a decisive shift away from the nationalistic insularity which has always been one of its prominent features. There are good historical reasons for that narrow nationalism, since the whole idea of preserving folk cultures developed with the rise of nationalist feeling at the end of the nineteenth century. In England it has taken various, often ludicrous forms such as debates over

● LOUDON WAINWRIGHT III

● CHAMPION DOUG VEITCH

whether women should perform morris dances or whether English singers should include Scottish songs in their repertoire. Now, however, the vast international range of the recorded folk music on offer is a sign that the folk scene has embraced the fact that Britain itself is a multi-cultural society.

There is tangible evidence of this shift in the pages of *Folk Roots*, the lively and informative national monthly magazine. In the last year features have been published on Thomas Mapfumo from Zimbabwe, on the Gou Brothers from China, on Asian music in Britain, on the blues guitarist Lowell Fulson and on traditional music from Tanzania. Meanwhile, the magazine's record review section sings the praises of new music from Sweden and Italy.

Of course, not all these musics belong exclusively to folk. African music of all kinds is enjoyed by rock audiences, for instance. But it is only in the folk context that they can all be found in one place. For one of the functions of the folk scene has always been to provide a space for the unusual and unfashionable in music to develop. It is free of the competitive pressures of the rock world – there is no folk hit parade – which means that while it tolerates some awful club singers, it also nurtures valuable new music which sometimes goes on to influence the wider popular music scene. In the sixties it was singer-songwriters with acoustic guitars, in the seventies the entertainment-comedians. There is no guarantee that folk will provide another new style of such impact in the eighties – especially since rock has another research and development department now in the independent labels. But if it does, it may not come from the now-favoured Pogues and rogues.

Far more promising for the late eighties is the ferment of international fusion music typified by Champion Doug Veitch, the self-proclaimed "king of Caledonian cajun swing".

Dave Laing

THE YEAR IN
EUROPOP

No European artist had ever had the success that A-ha had this year. Somehow three unremarkable blokes who'd spent their youth humming tunes as they strolled round Norwegian fjords in comfy thick sweaters had managed to come up with a handful of songs which the whole world liked (or bought, anyway). The conclusion was obvious. If they could do it, why, surely hundreds of other Norwegian youths, could too? Bags were packed and off went Britain's A&R men as one, Filofaxes in hand, to catch the next flight to Oslo, to scour the rugged Norwegian countryside and offer a small fortune in cash upfront to any Norwegian youth who showed reasonable competence in shaking a tambourine. Because, they now all knew, the Next Big Thing, after rock'n'roll, psychedelia, glam, punk and new romanticism, was going to be the Norwegian Sound . . .

That, at least, is what you might believe had happened from all the snide comments in British magazines whenever Norway or A&R men were mentioned. If it had been true it would have been the most interesting large-scale musical development in Europe for years. But sadly it was a fanciful fib. Only four Norwegian bands in total are signed to British record companies and all were either signed or under negotiation before A-ha's success. A-ha themselves rather liked the theory that they'd inspired a rash of copycat signings, but, in so much as they encouraged it, they were suffering from false vanity. "If we ran an A&R department along those lines," said Ronnie Gurr, the Virgin A&R man who signed Fra Lippo Lippi, "it'd be a complete disaster. It's as silly as saying 'oh look, Wham! are big, let's go and find ourselves an act from Bushey'." Fra Lippo Lippi, he said proudly, were signed on merit and "the fact that they're Norwegian is neither here nor there. They're singing in English, they're writing intelligent English lyrics . . . they're just another band to me. They could just as easily be from Glasgow or Dublin or Yugoslavia."

Or *Yugoslavia*? Maybe. I'll come back to that. Whatever, Fra Lippo Lippi

● THE MONROES

● FRA LIPPO LIPPI

released one beautifully wispy single, 'Shouldn't Have To Be Like That', which was nearly a hit, and an album *Songs* (actually their third) which wasn't, and being Norwegian didn't seem to help them one bit. Nor did it help the nearest thing there was to A-ha clones: 2 Brave, two strikingly good-looking teenagers who believed in God and made deliberately poppy records – which also flopped. And the Monroes – the band who were at least until recently bigger in Norway than A-ha, their *Face Another Day* album selling quarter of a million

copies at home (the equivalent of a British group selling over three million here) – found that their appallingly pleasant pop/rock had no fans at all. The idea that Norwegian pop had finally come of age was every bit as ridiculous as it sounds.

Nor had, as some tried to suggest, the rest of Europe really come of age as a producer, rather than simply one of the most important consumers of pop music. While nearly every European countries' pop charts were continuously packed with English and American records, only nine European records made the British charts in the year up to the summer of 1986 – four by A-ha, two by Austria's Falco ('Rock Me Amadeus' and 'Vienna Calling') and one each by Holland's Mai Tai ('Body And Soul'), Switzerland's Double ('The Captain Of Her Heart') and Greece's Nana Mouskouri ('Only Love'). And of these only Mai Tai (with 'History' the previous year) and Nana Mouskouri (some solid success years ago) had previous hits, and only A-ha and Falco didn't follow their success with some resounding flops. From a commercial point of view Europe was as irrelevant as ever. What *was* going on?

Germany, usually the one bright spot, probably produced less interesting music than it had done for years. The long-promised new Kraftwerk album was postponed once again. The specialists in avant-garde noises congregating around Einstruzende Neubauten carried on banging and boring away. As for Propaganda, who, after the 'Dr Mabusi' and 'Duel/Jewel' singles, had looked like they might be the most exciting German export for years . . . they just fizzled out. Their album *A Secret Wish* was good, though not the masterpiece people had hoped for, but the next (and still rather fine) single, 'p-Machinery', flopped even after two releases on a British public fed to the teeth with anything to do with ZTT records; and the dance remix album *Wishful Thinking* was a sloppy mess.

Slightly more exciting were the antics of Berlin's Exile Records, a small enthusiastic operation whose releases sparkled with the vitality that so many

European records lack – perhaps because, instead of clumsily hiding it, the groups involved make no secret of the fact that their music is second-hand and borrowed. They even rather rejoice in the fact. The Nirvana Devils, the Legendary Golden Vampires and the A-Bones all play different varieties of rattly, energetic rock'n'roll pop, at its best a sort of Cramps meet Abba.

The only near-triumph that Germany had was in exporting their sultry, pouting, sub-Madonna sex-bomb Sandra. Most of her work was dire, but '(I'll Never Be) Mary Magdalena' was exactly the sort of brilliantly trashy and tacky Eurodisco that we've come to rely on Europe for. Its failure here was quite puzzling.

And then there was Falco. Falco was interesting for several reasons. Firstly he appeared to be completely and utterly bonkers. At various times he was reported as claiming to hang around in bars with Mozart, going on insane shopping sprees for gold watches and plying a teddy bear with champagne and cakes on a transatlantic flight, having bought it a first class ticket in the seat next to his. Secondly he actually dared to sing in German (well, a bizarre fusion of German and English). "I think that's the special secret of my success," he boasted as 'Vienna Calling' followed 'Rock Me Amadeus' into the Top Ten. These hits – remarkably similar, cleverly edited cut-ups of speech and song dropped on top of a relentless rhythm – only hinted at a fraction of his capabilities. On the accompanying album, *Falco 3*, he slid through a bewildering amount of styles – from the raunchy American rock of 'Jeanny' (which sold 1½ million copies as a single in Germany despite its references to drug-taking and prostitution) to an indescribably abominable version of Bob Dylan's 'It's All Over Now Baby Blue' – suggesting either he's an extremely versatile talent or, alternatively, not the slightest bit serious about any of it.

Next door in Switzerland Double found nothing in this pop star lark that could liven their long faces. Never mind that 'The Captain Of Her Heart' was a hit because of its nice, dippy lyrics and the romantic sub-Shakatak cocktail-jazz atmosphere it conjured up – all this making music was a serious matter. They wanted people to know that this was art. But, like Falco and Mai Tai (who seemed not to care) and A-ha (who did), they found themselves having to contend with British journalists who know a good angle when they think of one and who rained down endless questions about *lederhosen*, cuckoo clocks and yodelling. All Double wanted to talk about was "music for the soul". No chance. "Swiss rolls? What are *they*?...

Toblerone? Er, yes, I like the shape...St Bernard dogs? Er, I'd rather be rescued by a beautiful nurse..." They had a hard time of it.

Still, better to suffer like that than be ignored altogether. In France Princess Stephanie of Monaco's decision to enter the pop world automatically guaranteed her a number one; in Britain, where, to be honest, most people wouldn't be able to tell you where Monaco is, her single 'Irresistible', a flimsy, breezy but rather endearing piece of rubbish, was re-

● SANDRA

sisted with unnatural ease. Likewise Denmark's De Film's album of stunning average synth pop was received almost totally without comment. Anno Domino, a singer who's actually "from America by way of Tokyo", but who lives half the year in and works from Belgium, released some beautiful soft dance records, 'Take That' being particularly good, but also without result. True Belgians La Muerte droned away on their grotesquely loud and distorted guitars, and compatriots Front 242 played their hard funk (or "hip hop without the clever bits" as one 'fan' described it), all to greater or lesser degrees of indifference.

No, it must be said, Europe has been a fairly useless place to live this year if you want to sell records in Britain. But why? Because lyrics have to be in English? Well, yes, but so many European groups do sing in English and *still* fail. Because there is no tradition of pop stars to emulate? Maybe, except that so many British and American pop stars spend half their lives in Europe these days, either touring or recording (or, if they're Brits, just avoiding tax). No facilities? Maybe, on a small scale; but on the professional level there are far more big studios in Europe than its home pop stars ever need.

Perhaps, as different areas of Europe have insisted frantically over the years, the same level of talent *is* there, latent, waiting to be sprung upon by those A&R men with their Filofaxes.

Certainly, the latter is the opinion of Yugoslavian journalist Peter Lukovic, who this spring, took it upon himself to educate the West about Yugoslavian pop, convinced that though it has for so long been "the backward infant of European rock'n'roll" it "could soon be headed for world recognition". With a stack of records and a handful of photos he makes his case for likely success stories. There's the national megastar Lepa Brena (Beautiful Brena) and her band Slatki Greh (Sweet Sin), apparently "familiar sounding Yugo-pop with a non-stop rhythm orgy of folkish memorable tunes" (actually rather dodgy, souped-up Greek folk music – but never mind). There's teen pop idols Plavi Orkestar (Blue Orchestra) whose singer Sasha 'Loshi' Losic drives the girls wild (they play rather dodgy seventies pop and their "best" song is a terrible number with English lyrics called 'Goodbye Teens' – but never mind). There's Riblja Corba (Fish Soup) with their "unrestrained raucous sounds and memorable melodies" who have somehow roped in Eddie Grant to appear on their album (which isn't very good – but never mind). There's socially conscious Johnny Stulic, apparently "Yugoslavia's Billy Bragg" (except that he's just done a very un-Billy Bragg-like thing and gone into tax exile in Holland – but never mind). And there's Oliver Mandic, he of the "outrageously sensual lyrics", who is "the natural successor to Michael Jackson", has actually had one of Prince's managers, Joe Ruffalo, over to see him, apparently

● DOUBLE

on the orders of the Purple One himself, and whose sparse old-fashioned slow disco is really rather good (though even in Yugoslavia they manage to have tastelessly sexist album covers – but never mind). Yugoslavia! There you have it. Maybe soon, bags will be packed and off will go Britain's A&R men as one, Filofaxes in hand, to catch the next flight to Dubrovnik to scour the rugged Balkan scenery...

Chris Heath

THE YEAR IN
AFRICAN RHYTHMS

Whem 'primitive' became the buzzword among London's smart set some three years ago, it was natural that African music be invited along for the ride. In spite of what many people believe, it was not that a discovery of Africa's rhythms triggered off the surge of designer ethnicity that rampaged through clothing, jewellery and graphic art, but that a small amount of such music put the final touches to 'style's' confused notions of the noble savage. In 1983's summer, any DJ worth his space at a strictly-by-word-of-mouth function 'threw in a couple of African' for the young blades of the day to sweat up their new shirts to. Naturally, when a music's acceptability is based on anything as (literally) flimsy as a freak hot summer's chic print pattern, it is doomed. As the threads changed, so did the soundtrack. Your average fad will leave behind a residue of support which, when combined with major record labels, delayed reactions, ensures at least survival. Although UK consumer interest in African affairs has dropped to the point where in recent months around 90 per cent of all sales made were to Africans living in Britain and buying a piece of their respective motherlands, and 95 per cent of all titles available in this country were on import, African music has not gone away.

Of these expats keen to continue enjoying the music of their native area, the overall picture is impossible to define in terms of trends. Between twenty and thirty new titles find their way on to specialist shop shelves every month, with sales ranging from five to five thousand depending on the artist's standing back home and the size of the particular community on these shores (which usually means London, as there is still no effective distribution network for African music outside the capital).

Hits, so to speak, rely largely on who has a record out, but with sales of just five hundred reckoned to be healthy, the large numbers of Nigerians and Ghanains make sure that Ju Ju and Hi Life styles are better than averagely represented, with Segun Adewale, Chief Ebenezer Obey, King Sunny Ade

and George Darke being among the leaders.

Much how things stood prior to the events of 1983.

The British African music buyer, however, has no such blood ties, and can therefore afford the luxury of travelling round the continent seeking undiscovered sounds. In terms of sales patterns, all but a few are cultural gypsies, hitching their caravans and cheque books to whatever region sounds good.

Many UK devotees openly welcomed the media spotlight being removed from what they saw as their scene. They had heard Africa calling long before the British music machine did, and although previously bleating about

● SEGUN ADEWALE

● KING SUNNY ADE

lack of exposure were anxious to preserve their own sense of elitism. There has never been a sight quite so twitchy as a cultist watching his back, so naturally the beat shifted in the calm after the African awareness storm.

Nigeria was by and large abandoned. It had unwittingly become this country's sole conception of Africa, and Adewale, Obey and Ade became a media focal point. When they emerged from this fame clutching UK recording contracts, for the first time they tailored their approach to an alien market. Fine, if to succeed you must get Top Of The Pops, but it removed the very spark that attracted interest in the first place and once the circus had left town these erstwhile champions were sounding distinctly soggy to the remaining band of hardened purists.

Other Ju Ju artists who had not left Africa had noticed this main chance across the seas, and followed suit, resulting in a generation of afro-pop that, like most hybrids, failed to satisfy either camp.

Maybe Fela could have stopped the rot, as his radical politics, injustices suffered at the hands of Nigerian authorities and outlandish public presentation are spot on for the romanticism of the British market, but he was in jail until April 1986. His son Femi Anikulapo-Kuti kept his beat going in Africa, but successful export needed the man himself back at the mixing desk. Hopefully, he will have completed some new studio work by the time this is published.

The music of Zimbabwe and Zaire has dominated the British-bought African albums. The traditional styles of the two countries – Chimurenga and Soukous respectively – have become increasingly mixed as many Zairean musicians now base themselves in Zimbabwe, where the best studios in Africa are reckoned to be found.

Harare, the capital, is now producing a very unurbanised African sound – the best recent example of which was displayed by the Real Sounds' spring concert appearances. It is essentially a rumba-based dance music, heavy on guitar, ethnic enough to be interesting but falling easily on Western ears and feet. It appeals greatly to the floating punter – the 'I want to buy some African music, what's a good album?' bracket – who, much to the chagrin of the purist, is the major force in the sales figures.

The biggest sellers from this area are Mabu Ley, Franco, Sam Mangwana, Kanda Bongo Man, Brit-based Somo Somo and Thomas Mapfumo. Mapfumo and his band, the Blacks Unlimited, enjoyed summertime exposure with the album *Chimurenga for Justice*. It featured UK reggae band Misty In Roots, and proved that Mapfumo's admitted admiration for Bob Marley goes beyond his hairstyle. This may be a way of getting to BIGGER THINGS.

The sounds of Senegal drew critical acclaim, and consequently consumer interest, through leading exponents Toure Kunda and Youssou N'Dour. The latter's *Nelson Mandela* album is one I would recommend to anyone contemplating a journey into African music; it stands as the best and most complete example of the year.

In the awareness backwash that followed the apalling situation in South Africa, its music increasingly trod the international stage. Such luminaries as Hugh Masekela, Leta Mbulo, Miriam Makeba, Dudu Pukwana and Abdulla Ibrahim who have long been part of the Western scene were joined by a number of acts, usually in compilation albums, who represented more traditional township music. The demand for this sharply increased after the absolute success of Amandla's (the cultural wing of the outlawed African National Congress) UK tour in the autumn of 1985.

These shows were THE highlights of the year in African music. The thirty performers, who came together in exile in Angola after the Soweto uprising ten years ago, told through music, dance and theatre the story of their people's freedom struggle from the advent of colonialism to 16 June 1976 (Soweto). To see and hear the music and song as part of their struggle's tradition, and now with such a powerful sense of purpose, gave it dimensions that could never be achieved by listening to a record or even watching a conventional concert.

The regret engendered by the fact that such a rich musical source needed such terrifying circumstances to bring it to Britain is immeasurable.

Overall, during the last year, total sales of African music in the UK have declined. Independent labels Sterns, Earthworks, Celluloid and Globe Star now monopolise the domestic output, Oval having put themselves on what they assure is temporary hold, but these companies do not have the promotional resource to match their commitment and enthusiasm.

● THOMAS MAPFUMO

● YOUSSOU N'DOUR

● HUGH MASEKELA

An act can hope to sell a few more albums to the casual buyer after live appearances, but the abolition of the GLC has led to these becoming fewer. Their marvellously varied arts policy underwrote many promoters willing to risk bringing groups over, and it is honestly difficult to imagine whatever central government committee is responsible for contemporary entertainment putting up the money to fund African music events, when their head office diligently imposed VAT on the Band Aid single and Live Aid concert. The Africa Centre in Covent Garden,

Club O'Mankind and Dougie's Night Spot in Hackney are keeping the fire burning thanks to a strong regular clientele, but wider publicity for shows away from this circle seems to be a problem, especially if they try larger halls. When Thomas Mapfumo played the Town and Country Club – the venue with the most adventurous booking policy in London – even in the wake of a much talked about album, the 'crowd' numbered less than a couple of hundred.

The annual WOMAD Festival (The World Of Music And Dance) always lives up to its name, presenting artists from all areas of the African continent, often in their only British appearance. Unfortunately WOMAD is only one weekend out of fifty-two, and the attendant music media tend to concentrate on the bill's bigger names.

The music press's willingness to swim in the African sea has diminished too. On the specialist black music side, *Echoes* devotes increasing energies to seemingly endless club charts, while *Blues & Soul* never pretended to have any interest in this field. With this year's demise of *Black Beat International*, the authoritative and long-departed *Black Music and Jazz Review* is more keenly mourned. It is impossible to expect the pop glossies to save any space for anything as theoretically unappealing to a female caucasian teenager as an almost middle-aged black man who may well sing in a foreign language, does not make videos and whose idea of image is probably a new pair of flares; but the so-called serious rock press is shamefully remiss in this area.

The constantly boiling circulation war has ruled much of their previous indulgences to be unaffordable luxuries, and since Neil Spencer – a true African enthusiast with a thirst for further knowledge – departed the *NME* last summer, many of his empathetic scribes have also left, and the paper's once innovative coverage has shrunk to a response from press officer cajoling. It is doubtful that African music will ever rise much beyond its present status in British record shops. Unlike other intitially alarming styles – R&B, reggae, funk, rap – it does not have enough single-minded musicians and one-man labels constantly pushing themselves, it is much too broad a spectrum to throw up one or two clearly defined, dynamic figureheads and, perhaps most importantly, it is never, ever, likely to find a white, British exponent who is acceptable to national radio.

Perhaps none of this matters. Without relying on international trade agreements, African music remains undiminished, self-satisfying and vital. It's just a pity so few people realise.

Lloyd Bradley

●THE YEAR IN AUSTRALIAN ROCK

The past year will be best remembered, at least in Australia, as the year when local music achieved, at long last, substantial success overseas. International success for an Australian act is not just needed to satisfy some inbred cultural inferiority. It is an important part of a band's need for financial security: in a country with a population of only 15 million a hit single doesn't really mean much money in your pocket. In the days of flashy videos, the contribution from an overseas record company is just about essential.

Leading the way internationally, and holding the Australian flag aloft quite aggressively (unlike some former success stories, like Air Supply – yes, these American 'megastars' are from Australia), is INXS. Originally known as the Farriss Brothers, this Perth-based band changed their name and headed west to Sydney in 1980.

It has taken the proverbial 'long time' to get to the top but now INXS are easily Australian's most popular act. And, with a Top Five single in the United States, 'What You Need', and a Top Ten album, *Listen Like Thieves*, it seems that a few 'foreigners' are in agreement.

The savaging they have received from a number of English critics is unlikely to stop them. They already have a strong following elsewhere in Europe, in Japan and, of all places, South America. INXS played one memorable concert there in 1985 where the stage was ringed by gun-toting soliders!

Lead singer Michael Hutchence is the group's focal point. INXS, in fact, tend to play down their rock star 'image' by trying to cultivate some sort of mystery about themselves which, of course, only inflames their audience's desire to know what the guys are really like. Hutchence has recently completed a locally produced movie called *Dogs in Space* which will be screened early in 1987 and should be doing the rounds at the Cannes Film Festival. It was directed by Richard Lowenstein, who has worked on many of the band's more memorable videos (in particular the extravagant 'Listen Like Thieves' clip) as well as directing Pete Townshend's *White City* and his own feature film *Strikebound*.

The world, or at least part of it, is also likely to be set on fire by the Models. This former Melbourne band (who now reside in 'fashionable' Sydney) have been around in various forms for nearly ten years. They now boast two rather charismatic front men, Sean Kelly and former pop 'idol' James Freud. Both write strong songs and both have fine voices. As former 'cult' favourites, the Models have crossed over into the mainstream in a big way with their album *Out of Mind Out of Sight*, while still managing to keep their credibility intact.

If anything, Australia's convict background should help to provide us with our fair share of rockers. The most successful birth from this environment over the last ten years is the Easybeats' bastard son, AC/DC (so successful, in fact, that they now only seem to holiday here). Carrying on the tradition in the eighties is Jimmy Barnes, the Scottish-born former lead singer of Cold Chisel. He topped the local charts for ages with his most recent album, *For the Working Class Man*, and 1986 saw him spending most of the year in the US as

● INXS

opening act for ZZ Top. That probably gives as good an indication as any as to the style of his music.

Another outfit not scared of crunching guitars is the Divinyls. Although their biggest hit at home to date has been 'Boys In Town' (their first ever release, too), they have steadily built up a loyal following in the US. They, too, spent most of 1986 there, largely touring with English group the Cult.

The only other metal act around of any international stature seems to be the Angels (once known internationally as Angel City). Although they still record, the music contained thereon is a pale shadow of what the band was capable of some five or six years ago.

The most exciting thing to happen here in recent memory is the emergence of some truly invigorating 'dance' bands. Leader of the pack is undoubtedly I'm Talking, who only recently released their debut album *Bear Witness*. They have developed an indigenous funk style which is whipped into a frenzy by their talented and stylish lead singer Kate Ceberano. Their powerful singles, 'Lead The Way', 'Trust Me', and 'Do You Wanna Be', sound best on the radio – they have yet to excite live. So far their records have gone unreleased outside Australia. Wisely enough it would seem to be a conscious effort on their own part to be successful at home first. Wham!'s management, Nomis, and in particular Jaz Sumner, liked what he saw on a 1985 tour and expressed interest in managing the band overseas.

Kate has also recorded a superb live album, the cover of which features her, clad only in the merest of leotards, in a champagne glass.

Both the Triffids and the Go-Betweens have released new albums, *Born Sandy Devotional* and *Liberty Belle and the Black Diamond Express* respectively in the past twelve months, although both acts remain largely unrecognised in their own lands. Although the Triffids have actually been featured on the cover of English magazines it is hard to imagine them gracing the cover of anything important at home. Likewise the Go-Betweens, whose relatively short tours here seem to be interspersed with interviews in which they complain about their lack of acceptance in Australia. They shuffle from record company to record company and move about the world as if in search of a home.

Of the other acts nestled in what is generally known as the 'indie' scene, Hunters And Collectors have fared the best. Once signed to Virgin Records, but now based back in Melbourne, the band released an album, *Human Frailty*, and actually had a hit single with 'Say Goodbye'. They also seem to have managed to shed their weighty pretentiousness. When a visiting international 'star' is asked what local music he likes best it is a fair bet, for some unexplained reason, that he'll nominate Hunters And Collectors.

Of the old-timers still around the Saints have staged a rather remarkable career revitalisation. They too had a

● THE MODELS

● THE GO-BETWEENS

● HUNTERS AND COLLECTORS

● IVA DAVIES

● MENTAL AS ANYTHING

new album, *All Fools Day*, and a hit single with 'Just Like Fire Would' – both of which presumably outsold their previous success, the punk anthem 'I'm Stranded', now all of ten years old. It's nice to have leader Chris Bailey around, if only for his cynical 'stuff you all' attitude.

Although not strictly old-timers, the Hoodoo Gurus have been around for five years now. From humble beginnings in Perth (when the band boasted the word 'Le' in front of their name), Dave Faulkner remains the only original member. The group's two successful albums, *Stoneage Romeos* and *Mars Needs Guitars*, owe much to American trash culture, which has blossomed so much over the past couple of years. They have had much chart success even though they still appear on the relatively small Big Time label. They spend a lot of time in the United States playing the lucrative college circuit.

Another Perth group who have had several successful tours of America are the Eurogliders. Although not being able to repeat the international success of the single 'Heaven', the band have filled the charts at home with various singles culled from their latest album, *Absolutely*. And if you ever wondered what happened to Ron François from Teardrop Explodes . . . he plays bass in the Eurogliders!

An Australian-based band, originally from New Zealand, called Dragon didn't really get up to much this year. They did record an album with Todd Rundgren in his Woodstock studios but at the time of writing it has yet to appear. Part of the delay could be because their keyboard player, Alan Mansfield, has been touring the US as a member of Robert Palmer's band.

One 'old-timer', Iva Davies, and his band Icehouse, came back from one of their prolonged lay-offs with some very

tough music and initial signs of an overseas hit. The song that started it for them, this time around, was 'No Promises', which was followed up by a very glam-rock 'Baby, You're So Strange', and a strong album, *Measure for Measure*.

Icehouse have always been linked, perhaps a little unfairly, with the synthesiser movement in Australia. Keyboard-based acts have gone through a tremendous resurgence in the past few years. This has been spearheaded by Melbourne-based Pseudo Echo who have scored hit after hit with a strong vocal and a catchy keyboard 'riff'. The fact that all the lads in the band are rather cute has not hindered their cause, either! They, too, are hopeful of international success, but they realise the costs involved in overseas promotion and so are waiting until the right 'deals' are in place. They still have youth on their side (one is still 18); there's no hurry. Pseudo Echo are being managed by Glenn Wheatley, the man who saw the Little River Band on their way to fame and fortune.

Other acts following in their footsteps include the Venetians and two Sydney duos, one very young called Wa Wa Nee, the other older and more experienced called Koo De Tah.

Kids In The Kitchen could also be said to fall into this category. They have had their first, and to date only, album, *Shine*, released worldwide. 'The Kids' have spent quite a bit of time away from home promoting the record. They, perhaps to a certain extent like Duran Duran, depend on a look and, more recently, the slash of a guitar chord.

Additionally, of course, there is a wide range of acts that refuse to be classified in any particular mould. Varying degrees of success have been achieved in the local market by groups such as Mental As Anything. 'The

Mentals' are peculiarly Australian – perhaps hindering them in their quest for international sales. The band's most recent album, *Fundamental*, brought them their biggest ever chart success to date in the single 'Live It Up'. They, too, toured the US and Europe in 1986 (there are literally times when it seems that there are no local acts left in the country – the standing joke being "Will the last one out turn off the lights"!). One member of the Mentals, Martin Plaza, also released a solo album, *Plaza Suite*, which leapt up the charts and supplied the hit 'Concrete And Clay'.

While on the subject of solo artists we should not forget former Split Enz member Tim Finn. After seemingly ages since his last recording, and a farewell Split Enz tour, Tim returned to the charts and Australia (he lives in England with girlfriend Greta Scaachi) with his new album *Big Canoe*.

Relative newcomers who had early career successes were Do Re Mi, with the album *Domestic Harmony*, and Boom Crash Opera, with the single 'Great Wall'. It's still far too early even to guess how long these aggressive acts will be around but they've certainly had a good start.

A good example of an extremely Australian act is the Uncanny X-Men. Led by a very loud, brash, yet somewhat cute singer called Brian Mannix, the band, with their irreverent behaviour and very rowdy music, have managed to capture the imagination of the country's younger followers of fashion. The group has recently signed to CBS records for the whole world but it would surely be a puzzled 'overseas' audience who chanced upon them at a concert. One particularly has trouble imagining what the English music press would make of them. We have enough trouble out here!

James Manning

ALBUMS

ABC
How To Be A Zillionaire
(Neutron)
The words are almost exactly as you might expect, although Martin is beginning to topple on the tightrope between smart words and dumb mouthings.
Melody Maker

. . . *Zillionaire* is simply not a very good record.
NME

AC/DC
Original Soundtrack –
Who Made Who (Atlantic)
Seldom in their painfully protracted career have AC/DC been any good . . . strictly for collectors only and even then for the sort who'd frame Angus Young's used bog paper.
Melody Maker

A-HA
Hunting High And Low
(Warner Bros)
These Scandinavians have come a long way since the last Eurovision song contest . . .
Sounds

Keep the cutesome foreigners coming.
Record Mirror

. . . A-ha are Norwegian and they have very fine trousers indeed.
Smash Hits

● THE ALARM

THE ALARM
Strength (IRS)
Strength is an exciting and honest LP, and if that's a crime – then the musical law, under which we often cower, is an ass!
Record Mirror

. . . numerous 'O' levels will be failed because of it, but that doesn't stop this record being an overwrought, plodding thing, redundant and pretty stupid.
NME

An album for fireside revolutionaries, for soft-focus tough guys, a stifled scream of cushioned pain. A good pop record, in fact.
Sounds

ALEEM
Casually Formal (Atlantic)
This is the usual sound from the Aleem twins, who obviously got so involved fiddling with their new Yamaha DX-21 with eight module MIDI rack that they forgot to write

any songs for lead vocalist Leroy Burgess.
Melody Maker

● MARC ALMOND
Stories of Johnny (Virgin)
. . . a collection of proper, grown-up, passionate songs . . .
Smash Hits

. . . the warmer, more mellow side of Marc Almond has at long last been fully allowed to come out from under the covers.
Record Mirror

. . . his most amiable record . . .
NME

Be wilder, please.
Sounds

A Woman's Story:
Compilation 1
(Some Bizarre)

This boy is a major talent . . .
Record Mirror

. . . he's now almost befriended the compact disc – albeit one that's slipped into the sewer of deprivation, of course.
Melody Maker

ANIMAL NIGHTLIFE
Shangri-La (Island)
Things have come to a pretty pass when the best thing about a record is the bassist's shoes.
Sounds

. . . the title is profoundly old hat, the sleeve is a masterpiece of cliché, the songs dither on and on mercilessly . . .
NME

ANNABELLA
Fever (RCA)
It's executed here with less vision and zest than a doped-up bumblebee; it's to punk what Elvis' Vegas paunch was to jailhouse riots . . .
Sounds

It isn't a BAD record as such, merely an over-made-up, indecisive indentikit version of 1986 pop.
Melody Maker

. . . an album of quite staggering monotony
Record Mirror

ADAM ANT
Vive Le Rock (CBS)
. . . just what does Adam mean by *"diddy bopping", "crish crish in rinky dink", "wha-la-ba-loomba", "doop-de-boop civilian",* or indeed *"crinkum crankum"*? Infantilism in such a grown man is a distinctly nauseating sound.
NME

. . . six *"wah-la-ba-loomba"*'s do not make you less contrived, young man, than the lustreless Italiano Fabian, replete for years with similarly plastic dreams.
Sounds

"Wah-la-ba-woomba/Wah la ba loom. Well it's dopey mopey doop do boop" . . . That's right, boys and girls, after all this strain, his mind has been reduced to sour mash, and his songs, a mish-mash of cradle rock and pensioner pomp – the disturbing result of advanced senility.
Melody Maker

Why isn't Adam Ant a hugely famous pop star anymore? It's a monstrous swizzle if you ask me . . . he sings things like this all the

time: *"wah-la-ba-loomba dopey mopey doop-de-boop crinkum crankum mop-mop ubangi yabba-yabba yippee-ya chipmunk-full-of-beatlenuts cha cha . . ."* If you were a bit snooty you might think it idiotic rubbish – but actually it's just brilliant and timeless (?) pop music.
Smash Hits

ARCADIA
So Red The Rose (Parlophone)
This doesn't sound like good business, but at least it's human nature.
Melody Maker

You can't help but admire these boys for their smart business sense.
Beat

A warmer and less clinical collection than anything yet attempted by . . . dare I say it? (No, I daren't.)
Smash Hits

. . . these contrived over-indulgences say nothing.
NME

● RICHARD JOBSON: THE ARMOURY SHOW

THE ARMOURY SHOW
Waiting For The Floods (Parlophone)
At the risk of sounding sexist, this is more of a boys' album . . .
Record Mirror

Waiting for the Floods is an album striving to be cinema.
Melody Maker

But then, this is a musician's album . . .
Sounds

The only not v. good aspect of this *'oeuvre'* is the grandiose lyrics about mountains – but you can't hear most of those anyway.
Smash Hits

THE ART OF NOISE
In Visible Silence (China)
Horrible.
Beat

As wallpaper goes, this is nicely textured.
Record Mirror

The Art of Noise has become nothing more than a pop paint-by-numbers.
Melody Maker

B

PHILIP BAILEY
Inside Out (CBS)
... like cling-filmed cucumber sandwiches with the crusts cut off – ready to slap in the microwave should George Clinton drop in to tea.
NME

● ANITA BAKER

ANITA BAKER
Rapture (Elektra)
Anita turns out a class of performance so rare, it's collectable.
Record Mirror

Anita Baker appeals to a type of Sanatogen soul sensibility that's too old to get down but too young to lie down.
Melody Maker

BANANARAMA
True Confessions (London)
There's something sooo heart-warming and touching about Bananarama ... Is it the fact that they don't dare try to harmonise and so all sing exactly the same notes at the same time *all* the time? ... Convincingly listenable. A proper 'pop' album.
Smash Hits

Yet another slab of formula Bananas sees the girls executing cooing harmonies and fey story lines ...
Record Mirror

... a vapid piece of work from any angle and typical of their candied tra-la-la nonsense ...
Melody Maker

These songs, then, are good fun to listen to and significant ...
NME

THE BANGLES
In A Different Light (CBS)
With their urbane harmony singing and spangling guitars, the girls make a *wonderful* noise.
Smash Hits

... with *A Different Light* they ride on the back of a big wave that's always about to break but somehow never quite does. Mind you, if it did I'd probably be dead from ecstasy.
NME

"Just another maaaa-nic Monday". Wrung from Susanna Hoff's glottis like the mewling whine of a ewe in heavy labour ...
Sounds

THE BATFISH BOYS
The Gods Hate Kansas
(Batfish Incorporated)
Worth the price for the wonderful frog on the cover alone
NME

THEREZA BAZAR
Big Kiss (MCA)
Ah me, the world just hasn't been the same since Dollar split up. The way Thereza used to glance at partner David Van Day whenever they were on telly was *heart-rending* – "I know he's a bit of a bimbo, viewers, but he *needs* me!" her eyes seemed to say. Without a straight man to bounce her comic ideas off, however, Thereza is stranded.
Smash Hits

She sounds at best like Madonna and at worst like a baby seal.
NME

Thereza Bazar certainly isn't as pea-brained as this album suggests, so we can only assume she's taken to believing all that Morley nonsense (if she ever *understood* it) and systematically set out making this collection as shallow, flighty, vacuous and disposable as possible.
Melody Maker

● THE BANGLES

● BLOW MONKEYS

BLOW MONKEYS
Animal Magic (RCA)
... I can't see myself ever carving Blow Monkeys on bus shelters.
Beat

Out of order music for all hours.
Record Mirror

Animal Magic pulls off what the Style Council can't – an exuberant, full-bodied soul sound which seems *effortless.*
Melody Maker

... one rather excellent record.
NME

BODEANS
Love & Hope & Sex & Dreams (Slash/London)
... solidly conventional rather than plainly mediocre.
NME

... out of its superficially predictable mix of eclectic influences crafts something undefinably special, ingeniously memorable.
Melody Maker

THE BEAT FARMERS
Glad 'N' Greasy (Demon)
If this is the 'Beat Generation' then I, like Richard Hell, can take it or leave it each time. Let me out of here.
Sounds

Van Go (MCA)
The Beat Farmers are in their musical element – swill.
Sounds

BIG COUNTRY
Seer (Phonogram)
... the acceptable face of rock to the beer 'n' football crowd.
Kerrang!

For a lads' night out, they're the business alongside a case of ale and a few dodgy videos.
NME

BLACK UHURU
Brutal (Real Authentic)
One day Uhuru will make the definitive reggae record, but until then ... kiss this.
Sounds

Slight return of the living dreads!
NME

● BODEANS

THE BOMB PARTY
Drugs (Abstract)
. . . this particular species of stupidity is rarely found outside the swamps and bayous of large North American cities.
NME

. . . so gormless, so utterly bereft of self-awareness that it takes on a charm and life all of its own.
Melody Maker

BRONSKI BEAT
Hundreds And Thousands (London)
A poor tribute to a great band
Smash Hits

If you are a committed consumer of Bronski product then more fool you if you let yourself be conned into parting with a fiver for this glorified 12″ remix single.
NME

At some point we were always going to get sick to death of Jimmy's voice and being worthy clearly wouldn't be enough. This record proves there was a future for this band and gives us a glimpse of where it might have lain.
Melody Maker

Truthdare Doubledare (London)
The maturing of the Beat Boy comes over again in the progression from their electro-synth past to a new-found Feargal Sharkeyish breadth of pastiche.
Record Mirror

. . . worse than Black Lace or Tight Fit
Sounds

A very safe and careerist LP . . . Bronski Beat, as of now, are up there with the Thompson Twins.
NME

It's all a bit sub-Depeche Mode . . .
Melody Maker

KATE BUSH
Hounds Of Love (EMI)
. . . the only possible drawback is that it's the sort of record your parents will probably like too and pinch off you to play.
Smash Hits

A howling success? I think so.
Record Mirror

The company's daughter has truly screwed the system and produced the best album of the year doing it.
NME

BUTTHOLE SURFERS
Rembrandt/Pussyhorse (Red Rhino Europe)
Since the Buttholes have arrived at Absurdity's terminus via hardcore's tunnel vision of indignation, denial and nihilism, they are schooled in the art of discord and disquiet.
NME

The soundtrack for the madhouse . . .
Melody Maker

. . . there's something alien and darkly brilliant at play here that's more than the result of too many bad drugs. Whatever it was that addled the Buttholes' minds to produce this erratic masterpiece should be kept under lock and key.
Sounds

● CACTUS WORLD NEWS

DAVID BYRNE
Music For The Knee Plays (EMI)
. . . casualty-of-too-many-intense-discussions-over-black-coffee-in-the-design-school-refectory . . .
Melody Maker

. . . an LP that shows off a fertile, and distinctly mischievous, imagination.
NME

CABARET VOLTAIRE
The Covenant, The Sword, And The Arm Of The Lord (Virgin)
The Cabs' real problem is that after three albums with Virgin they aren't much further forward than they were with the first.
Sounds

With their ever-unchanging moods they have become Rolling Stones for people who detest Jagger . . .
Melody Maker

CACTUS WORLD NEWS
Urban Beaches (MCA)

. . . *Urban Beaches* is a place for your emotions to sunbathe, from which they'll return refreshed but with the grit still lodged between the toes. This is a holiday, but this is no picnic. Leave no litter.
Sounds

● LLOYD COLE AND THE COMMOTIONS

JOHN CALE
Artificial Intelligence
(Beggars Banquet)
In his hands and voice love, the
subject of most of the songs, lies
limp with huge bruises around its
mendacious throat.
Sounds

. . . if he hasn't got his heart on his
sleeve, he's usually got his foot in
his mouth.
Melody Maker

Include me out.
NME

GLEN CAMPBELL
It's Just A Matter Of Time
(Atlantic America)
You'll probably listen to this a lot if
you live in Dakota and you're
going through a messy divorce . . .
Sounds

THE CANNIBALS
Please Do Not Feed The . . .
(Scarface)
The Cannibals take time out to
show us what a good time they

had in making this album, which is
a subtle way of making us feel
guilty when we yawn.
Sounds

CLUBLAND
Pojken Pa Bilden (Alexpop)
. . . like A-ha, the three pout
lusciously.
Melody Maker

JOE COCKER
Cocker (Capitol)
. . . if he was a horse they'd have
stuck him away in a field long ago.
Sounds

This sad, ungrateful little man has
gone and groaned his way into the
eighties.
Melody Maker

THE COCTEAU TWINS
Victorialand (4AD)
If you've ever heard a Cocteau
Twins album before, you'll have a

good idea what to expect – high
fragile whispery vocals,
'shimmering' and 'sparkling'
instruments and songs with titles
like 'Fluffy Tufts' . . .
Smash Hits

Victorialand is just what you'd
expect a Cocteau Twins album to
sound like – ambient sounds;
beautiful vocals.
Record Mirror

LLOYD COLE AND THE COMMOTIONS
Easy Pieces (Polydor)
Now there's no need to be
famous, because you can figure in
a Lloyd song if your name begins
with a J. We have Jesus, Jane,
Jesse, James . . . wot, no Jesse
James?
Beat

But taken on its own terms, it's
that most simultaneously fine and
useless of creations, a very good
pop record.
NME

Most of all, *Easy Pieces* is a
lesson on how to write a good
pop song . . .
Record Mirror

COLOURBOX
Colourbox (4AD)
. . . a selection of the finest pop
songs in a long time.
Smash Hits

If there were prizes for plagiarism,
Colourbox's dexterity would allow
no competition. Not so much
petty crime as grand theft.
Record Mirror

In theory, the LP might come
across too clever and plagiarist
but it doesn't sound that way.
NME

Buy, dance and be merry.
Sounds

COMMUNARDS
Communards (London)
... this is a little sneeze of a record
... Communards are remorselessly
right-on ... [they] want to be
clever, shy, soft, sincere and
loving; they're glad to be
wimps. Okay, for sure. The pop
music still stinks.
Sounds

Their hearts are in the right place,
but the songwriting still leaves a
lot to be desired.
Melody Maker

All in all, however, I would say that
it is now all right to like the
Communards.
NME

One of most joyous and
celebratory records ... This fine
musical article is quite simply a
cracker.
Record Mirror

An inspirational record.
Smash Hits

SAM COOKE
The Man And His Music (RCA)
... unzip that sound.
Record Mirror

Flabbergasting. (Lots out of 10).
Smash Hits

... this album has absolutely the
best work of Sam Cooke collected
on it ...
Sounds

As a double album of 28 digitally
remastered tracks it does nothing
but retrace old ground ...
Melody Maker

It just can't be said, however, that
this collection covers either the
man or his music in anything like a
representative manner.
NME

● COMMUNARDS

THE COSTELLO SHOW
King Of America (F-Beat)
... probably enough to make his
fans happy though I doubt it will
win him any new ones.
Smash Hits

I don't know if I should forgive at
once or mourn the longer.
Sounds

King Of America ... remains the
only album in a coon's age that
I can – without hesitation –
recommend even the most
poverty-stricken among you to
purchase.
Melody Maker

THE CRAMPS
A Date With Elvis (Big Beat)
Like all their other albums, *A Date
With Elvis* sounds like it was
recorded in the garden shed.
Smash Hits

It's the same old Cramps, snarling
for Jesus to spit down on them.
Sounds

Most of the tracks are so rude that
I was left gasping at the wondrous
filth of it all.
Record Mirror

This LP in fact consists mainly of
originals, and perhaps suffers for
it. A neat, over-clean production
adds to the feeling that the
Cramps are really a bit tame,
a bit muted.
Melody Maker

CROCODILE TEARS
Crocodile Tears
(Dodgey Ticket)
This record is adorned by a sleeve
so complete in its awfulness that
I'd like to believe it's a very
personal form of in-joke designed
to put off potential purchasers
from intruding upon a closely-
guarded form of self-expression.
Sounds

● THE CRAMPS

● THE CURE

THE CULT
Love (Beggar's Banquet)
The Cult provide a tonic for the eighties!
Beat

Love is a terrible, horrible, witless and conniving *abortion* . . . The wind cries hairy, and a guitar mistakes plagiarism and pomposity for poetry.
Sounds

Musically, it's the old classic shrinker – songs you like less the more you hear them.
NME

Anyone asking you, in 1985, to swallow kitsch spiritualism delivered with pseudo-Morrison melodrama over Led Zeppelin riffs and Hendrix guitar solos must be aware of the joke.
Record Mirror

It sounds like a 45 playing at 33. In fact it's '69 playing in '85.
Melody Maker

Maybe it's as if punk never . . . but who cares?
Smash Hits

CULTURE CLUB
From Luxury To Heartache
(Virgin)
. . . this is comprised largely of the cluelessly 'jolly' soul/pop fluff that made the last LP so wretched.
Smash Hits

The lazy lyrics are as illuminating as a night in a coal-hole with David Attenborough and about as interesting . . .
Sounds

A necessarily dismal record.
Melody Maker

Is George losing his grip on the realities of romance, rumpo, funny clothes and world domination?
NME

● THE CURE
The Head On The Door
(Fiction)
. . . Robert Smith *does* tend to go on about things like screaming babies and the blood of Christ, but don't let that put you off.
Smash Hits

It makes you wish *more* pop stars were hip enough to stay in bed all day.
Sounds

● Standing On A Beach (Fiction)
The only thing better than owning this compilation is owning everything they've ever recorded.
Beat

. . . testifies to the longevity and continued originality of everyone's favourite loo brush.
Record Mirror

You've probably heard them all before. And here they are again. Hurrah!
Smash Hits

● THE CULT

D

ROGER DALTREY
Under A Raging Moon
(10 Records)
Roger Who? Why don't you all f-f-find something better to blow your dosh on?
Sounds

THE DAMNED
Damned But Not Forgotten
(Castle)
Only a mother of a Damned fan could want this LP.
NME

. . . the Captain's 'Nice Cup Of Tea' still sounds like a damaged Robyn Hitchcock.
Melody Maker

Phantasmagoria (MC)
The Damned are actually just a rather breezy pop group – and losing the good Cap'n has done them little harm.
Smash Hits

Yep, the old boys have delivered a corker!
Record Mirror

This really is the brave new face of post punk.
Kerrang!

DEATH OF SAMANTHA
Strungout On Jargon
(Homestead)
. . . very tame, essentially harmless and almost quaintly old-fashioned.
Melody Maker

DEXY'S MIDNIGHT RUNNERS
Don't Stand Me Down
(Mercury)
A lot of people will probably dismiss it as pretentious tuneless rubbish . . . but others will find these tortured songs about Kevin's loves, Kevin's past and Kevin's this-and-that quite captivating.
Smash Hits

This one will run and run, brave and brazen.
Sounds

. . . only Kevin Rowland could make a record like this, as fussy, as unfocused, as irritatingly compelling as this.
NME

He's not to be trusted with your life but he's worth a fiver of your money any day.
Melody Maker

● KEVIN ROWLAND

DIVINYLS
What A Life! (Chrysalis)
Christina Amphlett and the Divs are Australian. It's a pity they live so near to Britain.
Sounds

All Divinyls songs deal with what they deem to be the important aspects of life, namely sex and power.
NME

The Divinyls are an over-rehearsed bunch of axe heroes who want to rock out every chance they get . . .
Melody Maker

THE DREAM ACADEMY
The Dream Academy
(blanco y negro)
Drips.
Sounds

. . . a study in cold-blooded calculation, a papier-maché concoction so liberally plastered in hundreds and thousands that you'd swear there's a gooey cake inside.
NME

If this is hippy music, then pass the joss sticks.
Melody Maker

● THE DREAM ACADEMY

DREAM SYNDICATE
Out Of The Grey (Chrysalis)
What an astounding gang of dullards Dream Syndicate are! .. I hope their visas get cancelled and their guitars stolen . . .
NME

STEPHEN DUFFY
Because We Love You
(10 Records)
You never quite believe Mr Duffy's lovelorn tales, you never quite believe in the people of his songs.
Record Mirror

. . . [his] cataloguing of romantic entanglements has some way to go before it reaches even post-adolescent cynicism.
NME

. . . this album floats and drifts and even pleases, but never stings or hurts or twists or hurts your guts. Which is, after all, what love is supposed to do.
Sounds

. . . it's rather good.
Smash Hits

E

SHEILA E
Sheila E (Warner Bros)
. . . this is either a complete mess or an 'intoxicating', 'heady' 'brew' of 'saucy' summer 'fun'. 'Chick', eh?
Smash Hits

Ah, to be so hot, and yet so cool!
Sounds

. . . unbelievably fine.
Melody Maker

EASTERHOUSE
Contenders (Rough Trade)
What we have here is a serious lack of talent.
Record Mirror

Worth investigation, but watch for falling clichés.
Beat

● ECHO AND THE BUNNYMEN

ECHO AND THE BUNNYMEN
Songs To Learn And Sing (The Singles) (Korova)
A pretty damn fab collection if you ask me.
Smash Hits

. . . decadent pop classicism.
Record Mirror

● SHEILA E

Stellar and statuesque
Sounds

. . . charts the progress of Echo from dour rock group to Laurie Latham-produced dour rock group.
NME

. . . damned splendid listening whether you're sitting, standing or comatose.
Melody Maker

ED GEIN'S CAR
Making Dick Dance
(Ed Gein's Car)
. . . *Ed Gein's Car* leaves a curiously addictive, acid taste on the gums, making no false claims to camouflage all this welling, crack-brained obsession streaming from the urban pockets. Sickly seductive, check it out.
Sounds

EMERSON, LAKE AND POWELL
Emerson, Lake and Powell
(Polydor)
Elephantiasis. Needs a swift prick. As a sagging moussaka it makes a neat unhealthy sealion.
Sounds

EMPTY QUARTER
Delirium (Illuminated)
... has its own appropriateness and a vaguely snake-charmer appeal.
Melody Maker

A balance of ultra-contemporary contrivance and relaxed rusticity. Coolly good.
Sounds

... unsuitable even for its designated purpose.
NME

ENGLAND WORLD CUP SQUAD
World Cup Party
(Columbia EMI)
... their record is the vinyl holocaust: a crime against humanity.
NME

Still, what do you expect from grown men who willingly *bath* together?
Melody Maker

ROCKY ERICKSON
Don't Slander Me
(Pink Dust –US Import)
... once this new blood gets into your system you'll hunger for no other type.
Sounds

EURYTHMICS
Revenge (RCA)
... the triumph of the mediocre art thief over the sources that arouse his envy more than they inspire him.
NME

FAITH
Eventide (Siren)
... inaccessible prose that heads straight for Pseuds Corner, adding a few chords as an afterthought.
Beat

Choruses full of corny chords and vapid vacillations ... Self-righteous *squares*, basically.
Sounds

Franks tends to whine rather than exalt, his lyrics a print-out of pity, lacking either the venom or acidity of his more practised peers.
Record Mirror

● FALCO

... its more memorable moments do confirm Franks' emergence as an interesting and perceptive rock lyricist.
NME

FALCO
Falco (A&M)
... histrionic warbling grows rapidly *intolerable* ...
Beat

'Europop' they call this ... oh dear, oh dear, oh dear ...
Smash Hits

I'm sure he *is* singing in German ...
Record Mirror

Falco achieves the rare feat of being wildly talentless and almost unbearably arrogant in the space of one record.
NME

It takes trash to new extremes well below sewer level and if this is album number three, it's already given me nightmares that the postman will turn up on my doorstep tomorrow morning and present me with the first two.
Melody Maker

● ENGLAND WORLD CUP SQUAD

● THE FALL

THE FALL
This Nation's Saving Grace
(Beggars Banquet)
As always it's hard to be quite sure
what he's on about . . .
Smash Hits

. . . this is a cracking LP which
never compromises the Fall we all
know and love, despite its new
found accessibility.
Record Mirror

It's easier to lose a sprint to a
turtle than to categorise this.
Sounds

. . . they have made a record that's
infinitely more peculiar than
almost anything else released
this year.
NME

THE FAMILY
The Family (Warner Bros)
. . . v. weak songs that sound like
David Cassidy and Samantha Fox
sharing a packet of crisps and
imitating Prince. A swindle.
Smash Hits

THE FAMOUS B BROTHERS
The Four Horsemen Of The Apocalypse (Charly)
It gets worse when he starts to
impersonate Jagger.
NME

It's an album of such gigantic
proportion, such monumental
magnificence, such colossal
unimportance.
Melody Maker

FAT BOYS
Fat Boys Are Back (WEA)
. . . it comes as something of a
surprise to learn that they're a
middling-skilled hip hop crew,
afflicted by the same tendency
toward grandiosity as their smaller
cousins. But there's a difference:
these guys are obsessed by
calories, not Valeries . . .
Melody Maker

The Fat Boys are a one-gag band,
and that gag is *fat*. And once the
gag wears thin those lips aren't fat
enough to carry the weight – or is
the assumption that fat *must* be
funny a pathetic example of
stoutism on my part?
NME

Big And Beautiful
(Sutra Records)
Be there or be skinny!
Sounds

The Fat Boys . . . give fat loving . . .
a gristle free Big Mac to their
previous vegeburgers . . . A
takeaway must!
NME

FELT
Ignite The Seven Cannons
(Cherry Red)
Likeable, in a disgusting way.
Sounds

Let The Snakes Crinkle Their Heads To Death
(Creation)
Snakes is as breathtaking and
beautiful and blank as can be.
Melody Maker

. . . a massive step backwards and
an unforgiveable waste of
Lawrence's talents.
Record Mirror

BRYAN FERRY AND ROXY MUSIC
Street Life – 20 Great Hits
(EG)
. . . as neatly packaged and finely
presented as a box of Lessiters'
chocolates.
Record Mirror

● THE FAMILY

... there's enough here to warm the jaded heart of the most cynical Roxy relic...
NME

... ultimately a redundant purchase.
Melody Maker

52ND STREET
Children Of The Night
(Virgin 10)
A good debut album by the best and most likely to succeed of British soul bands I've heard in donkey's years!
Sounds

All this hedonistic mooning and swooning drains the spirit... A depressing night out.
NME

FINE YOUNG CANNIBALS
Fine Young Cannibals
(London)
Buy it!
Beat

... a vibrant wholesome piece of vinyl.
Record Mirror

● 52nd STREET

The Cannibals are up there, helping to make delightful sow's ears from the silken gentility of pop.
Sounds

This is not great pop.
NME

THE FIRM
Mean Business (Atlantic)
The Firm have dug their own grave and they must rot in it.
Melody Maker

FIVE STAR
Luxury Of Live (RCA)
... like a black Buck's Fizz really!
Beat

... professional but entirely featherweight stuff that makes Shakatak sound like Motorhead. Have these people nothing of their *own* to offer?
Smash Hits

... the slickest kids this side of *Fame*.
Melody Maker

THE FLAMING MUSSOLINIS
Watching The Film (Portrait)
The best career move here would be for the Mussolinis to board some airline without engine and at least ensure their rock immortality.
Sounds

In a perfect world, the Flaming Mussolinis would never have made this record. In a perfect world, *Swallow Glass* would have been an enormous worldwide hit and the band would have celebrated by taking off to monasteries pronto.
Melody Maker

● FINE YOUNG CANNIBALS

THE FLESHTONES
Speed Concoction II – The Final Chapter (IRS – US Import)
The Fleshtones are pretty much due for mass acclaim. True talent surely can't remain an impediment for too much longer?
Sounds

A FLOCK OF SEAGULLS
Dream Come True (Jive)
None of the songs stray very far from a 'safe' dance tempo, while Mike Score blethers on and on about lovely girls, heartbeats, crying over yoo-hoo, blah blah.
Smash Hits

It wasn't so bad when I could laugh at their silly haircuts, but now they're utterly depressing.
Record Mirror

Had he still borne that ridiculous winged hairstyle, at least you'd have something to concentrate on to take your mind off the music.
Sounds

FLOY JOY
Weak In The Presence Of Beauty (Virgin)
This is an album whose ingenuity, sweat and striving are about as useful as a pair of sunglasses in the Ukraine.
Record Mirror

● A FLOCK OF SEAGULLS

I still can't see why anyone would want to go weak in the presence of Floy Joy.
Melody Maker

THE FORCE MDs
Tender Love (Island)
. . . the music you'd expect to come drifting out of a Golf GTI soft-top . . .
Sounds

Drippy!
Melody Maker

SAMANTHA FOX
Touch Me (Jive)
The chick who 'invented' ripped jeans has a serviceable voice . . .
Sounds

Sam's arse hangs or busts out of her jeans on the cover . . . but let's remember this is a record, and as such it stinks.
Record Mirror

Pull yer socks up, little lady, why don'tcher? You could be the next Meat Loaf.
Smash Hits

. . . Sam (comes) on like a female Shakin' Stevens.
NME

In years to come someone will glean a certain podgy absurdity to it all. But not yet.
Melody Maker

FRA LIPPO LIPPI
Songs (Virgin)
Pure unadulterated mush, this.
Smash Hits

It's a delight to hear music which rests solely on strength of voice, strength of melody and strength of sentiment.
Record Mirror

. . . a proficient, sometimes joyful collection of European pop . . . it does the new tune thing rather well.
Melody Maker

FULL FORCE
Full Force (CBS)
. . . the dodgiest dressers around . . .
Smash Hits

Awesomely unpleasant haircuts . . . My only advice is to get some decent shirts.
Melody Maker

. . . they can't wear all the hats all the time.
Record Mirror

There haven't been so many medallion men on one album cover since the last *Top of the Pops* DJ compilation.
Sounds

● FLOY JOY

G

PETER GABRIEL
So (Virgin)
If you're looking for bawdy humour and a bit of a rave-up, you won't find either here.
Melody Maker

There's a chill of death about the material, as if he'd worked all the life out of it. What's left is a collection of spooks... A nice fellow and his obsessions.
Sounds

There is the odd duff track – 'That Voice Again'... but what we are left with is an album that has class and originality seeping out of its immaculate grooves.
Record Mirror

... 'That Voice Again' [is] probably the only song to represent the more inventive side of Gabriel's peculiarly rhythmic approach...
Kerrang!

All the songs ooze sincerity and passion... Here, if you dare let it in, dare to listen closer, is music as exorcism, music to tear your fears out, music to drown inside and still come up feeling better for it. Beautiful! Champion!
Beat

THE GAP BAND
Best Of (Phonogram)
The music itself is hard, catchy and full of lots of instruments going 'boing' and 'chink'.
Beat

The Gap Band's most important contribution to the whole business of making your body twitch appears to have been the introduction of a noise that sounds something like 'boing'... You always start off thinking that they *can't* be putting that sound on a record again but once it jams its foot in the door you have to ask it in for a coffee or show it the bedroom.
Melody Maker

Gap Band at their best will throw the dedicated into uncontrollable spasms of rump-shaking.
NME

Of course there's a few snoresome *lurve* songs which spoil things a bit, but when these boys groove, they *groove* (maaan!).
Smash Hits

MARVIN GAYE
Romantically Yours (CBS)
'Too Busy Thinking About My Baby' really is one of the hundred greatest records ever made –some kind of wonderful – probably always will be. But this is not.
Sounds

GENE LOVES JEZEBEL
Discover (Beggars Banquet)
I'm all for freedom of speech and all that, but really, some people just shouldn't be given an LP's worth of mouthspace.
NME

The really bad news is that the first 20,000 copies are accompanied by a free live album...
Smash Hits

The bad things about *Discover*? It comes with full breasts but has duffel-string for nerve endings.
Sounds

Discover wasn't quite the onerous torture I'd anticipated.
Record Mirror

GENERATION X
The Best Of (Chrysalis)
The best thing about Generation X were always their T-shirts anyway.
Smash Hits

... Billy's haircut was one of the best things about punk...
Record Mirror

● GENE LOVES JEZEBEL

GENESIS
Invisible Touch (Virgin)
. . . more like rejects from Phil's solo work.
Smash Hits

. . . a super collection of mid-eighties Genesis songs.
Kerrang!

VIC GODARD
T.R.O.U.B.L.E. (Rough Trade)
A good album, and a must for young lovers everywhere.
Record Mirror

Music to don those shades, click those fingers and go watch *Absolute Beginners* to.
NME

. . . the whole album could be the theme track for *Absolute Beginners*.
Sounds

THE GO-BETWEENS
Liberty Belle And The Black Diamond Express
(Beggars Banquet)
The struggle ends here with pop perfection!
Beat

. . . this *is* rather good, even if one of the songs is called 'Palm Sunday' . . .
Smash Hits

Go-Betweens detractors, your apologies are now being accepted.
Record Mirror

. . . such is the Go-Betweens' mastery of atmosphere and aching melody, that they can entrance the listener even when you don't know why you're being moved.
Melody Maker

You can't want more.
Sounds

. . . unbearably twee lines . . .
NME

MARK GOULDTHORPE AND SIMON HINKLER
Flight Commander Solitude And The Snake (Golden Dawn)
I wouldn't listen to it on acid. In fact I wouldn't listen to it alone.
Sounds

● GRANDMASTER FLASH

. . . after half an hour, just a touch nauseating.
Melody Maker

GRANDMASTER FLASH
The Source (Elektra)
. . . a record so inferior to previous Flash that some merciless mixer scratched the record before we could.
NME

. . . a hot fashion tip on the back cover where the Grandmaster crew can be seen wearing plastic shower caps to keep their jerri-curls moist.
Melody Maker

. . . all bump! and clap! and boring.
Smash Hits

More jerking irrepressible rap attack, another appallingly tasteless cover and more dubious lyricism.
Sounds

AL GREEN
Full Of Fire (Hi)
. . . the perfect marriage of corn and porn.
Melody Maker

GREEN ON RED
No Free Lunch (Mercury)
An *hors d'oeuvre*, not without taste.
Sounds

Indeed, the only thing wrong with *No Free Lunch* is that there isn't enough of it.
Melody Maker

Green On Red hoist their flag somewhere between a sturdy homage to the Parsons legacy and a virtual fetish with Neil Young's mid-seventies approach.
NME

HACKNEY FIVE-O
Between The Floors
(Midnight Music)
Hackney Five-O are primed to surf into your heart. Book it, Danno!
NME

● **HALF MAN, HALF BISCUIT**
Back In The DHSS (Probe Plus)
This fantastically absurd record must be the fruit of minds deranged by having sod all else to do all day but watch diabolical programmes on the telly and wish they had more money to spend on drugs.
Sounds

. . . essential listening for viewers . . . a dire warning to Mrs T of what happens to a generation condemned to a lifetime of *Watch With Mother*.
Melody Maker

DARYL HALL AND JOHN OATES

Live At The Apollo With David Ruffin And Eddie Kendrick (RCA)
Phew, rock 'n' soul!
Smash Hits

A major disappointment perhaps, but it's still the first half-decent album that the duo have managed to date.
Record Mirror

PETER HAMMILL

Skin (Foundry)
This is respectable adult music, music with ideologically sound barmy edges.
NME

HANOI ROCKS

The Best Of Hanoi Rocks (Lick)
Oh, Jesus wept! It's Hanoi Rocks! I could have sworn it was the Stones/Dolls/Church Wardens/Stooges/Heartbreakers etc etc. File under Hollow Cheekbones.
Sounds

PAUL HARDCASTLE

Paul Hardcastle (Chrysalis)
Frankly this offering is too dull even for supermarkets.
Record Mirror

Strictly for the bods from Squaresville.
Sounds

Paul Hardcastle is b-b-b-b-b-be-be-be-boring!
NME

● PAUL HARDCASTLE

. . . as dreary as a speech by Sir Geoffrey Howe . . .
Melody Maker

SCREAMIN' JAY HAWKINS AND THE FUZZTONES

Live (Midnight Music)
Culled from a benefit gig for the record company, at Irving Plaza, Screamin' Jay is actually the *guest* although the Fuzztones must be paying tribute to a huge influence as they take a discreet, not to say sedate, passenger role while Jay throttles them with the seat belts.
Melody Maker

HEAVEN 17

Endless (Virgin)
Eighty-five minutes of cassette, 68 of compact disc and no record . . . This collection is a cock-up.
NME

JIMI HENDRIX

Jimi Plays Monterey (Polydor)
Pop music that kisses the sky.
Sounds

. . . without Jimi Hendrix there wouldn't be a *Kerrang!* It bears thinking about.
Kerrang!

Here he is, conquering (not to mention blowing) the hearts, minds and hips of young America, grooving on his moment of triumph, and earning every decibel of his triumph.
NME

● DARYL HALL AND JOHN OATES

● HOODOO GURUS

THE HIGH FIVE
Down In The No Go
(Rainbow/No Go)
. . . this is a sparkling offering . . . what more can you ask from a debut album?
Melody Maker

More ambition please.
NME

HIPSWAY
Hipsway (Mercury)
It hit the turntable with sprightly vigour and left it with a dull thud.
Record Mirror

Hipsway is affectation rather than affirmation, lukewarm where it should have been cool.
Melody Maker

Hipsway are pop's essence and I don't want a word said against them . . .
Sounds

Hipsway is a worthless record . . . a hollow sham . . .
NME

ROBYN HITCHCOCK AND THE EGYPTIANS
Gotta Get This Hen Out
(Midnight Music)
There is nothing faintly second-hand about Hitchcock and if you've never discovered him . . . you should do it.
Sounds

Perfection is not a word normally applicable to live albums, but this time around . . . what other word is there?
Melody Maker

HITLIST
Good Evening Yugoslavia
(Virgin)
One or two good songs, six or seven excellent songs, and one of the best of the year to date.
Sounds

. . . the only surprise on this album is how Japan producer John Punter stayed awake long enough to record it.
Smash Hits

Hitlist are in fact Quality Rock Music and they are abysmal.
NME

● HIPSWAY

HOODOO GURUS
Mars Needs Guitars (Chrysalis)
Yes, a bit of R&B, C&W, psychedelia and stuff that sounds vaguely like all those mouth-organ puffing old fogeys at Live Aid is filtered through the brain of Skippy the Bush Kangaroo to wind up as *wonderful*.
Smash Hits

If the Martians want guitars, these are the boys for the next space mission.
Beat

The Hoodoo Gurus write from *life*. And if that life happens to have been spent entirely in front of the telly or at schlock-horrors all-niters, then who am I to cast the first stone?
NME

The fact that three out of four Gurus wear paisley shirts... shouldn't distract anyone from the main event.
Melody Maker

The Gurus are like now, like wow!
Sounds

THE HOUSEMARTINS
London 0 Hull 4 (Go! Discs)
Quite possibly the brightest band in Britain.
Smash Hits

... this one's a cracker.
Record Mirror

This is an exceptionally attractive debut album.
Melody Maker

The Fish City Four are already more than *quite* good. The best, however, is yet to come.
NME

HÜSKER DÜ
Candy Apple Grey (WEA)
The most salacious hard metal since MC5 shuffles the cards, changes its grimy underpants and mutates into a streak of some of the best tidal pop that we own.
Sounds

There's never been anything cultish or difficult about Hüsker Dü – please don't deny yourself this beauty any longer.
Melody Maker

Incidentally, Hüsker Dü ('ere, use my hankie) really means 'do you remember?' in Scandinavian though what *that's* got to do with anything, heaven only knows.
Smash Hits

● THE HOUSEMARTINS

I

ICEHOUSE
Measure For Measure
(Chrysalis)
If you've got a fast car, live near a craggy coast road and have just finished a passionate romance, this LP is perfect. Otherwise it's boring.
Smash Hits

THE ICICLE WORKS
The Small Price Of A Bicycle
(Beggars Banquet)
Is this *really* what turns Mike Read on? What a spooky person he must be.
Smash Hits

It's not their fault Mike Read likes them (the debauched ignoramus) so let's not bypass a band as good as this for fashion's sake.
Melody Maker

● THE ICICLE WORKS

THE IDLES
Agroculture (Upright Records)
Agroculture boasts one studio side and a live set from Auckland's Mainstreet. The latter is instantly larger, looser, more flamboyant against the close attention of the recorded tracks . . .
Melody Maker

The studio side is far superior . . . Lesson one: more time at the mixing desk.
Sounds

INXS
Listen Like Thieves (Mercury)
Listen Like Thieves is a depressingly definitive example of excruciatingly boring, incredibly unimaginative MTV rock.
NME

INXS are prime exponents of the INXplicable Antipodean predeliction for emulating US arena-sized bands so adeptly that they end up on MTV right beside them.
Melody Maker

The late, late Australian entry in this year's contest for the Americas Cup for boring, bland, transatlantic pop-rock twaddle.
Sounds

A really sound investment!
Record Mirror

IRON MAIDEN
Live After Death (EMI)
. . . a thoroughly worthwhile piece of vinyl.
Record Mirror

The free tour booklet with the album gives value for money, and there is a wide range of Iron Maiden merchandise available by post . . . More I cannot say because I only played one track.
NME

The music? Magic! Old and new; *déjà-vu*. Come on, you don't need *me* to give you a clue.
Sounds

● ICEHOUSE

J

JANET JACKSON
Control (A&M)
Far from startling but quite nice all the same.
Smash Hits

Control is JJ's self-explanatory, conscious step out of the shadow of the Pepsi Cola Kid, a step that plonks her firmly in the shadow of the monarch of Paisley Park.
Sounds

JERMAINE JACKSON
Precious Moments (Arista)
. . . do we really need all these horrible, gooey, lumpy, sugary ballads that make up half the songs on the LP?
Smash Hits

Another lousy record, Jerms.
Sounds

MICHAEL JACKSON
Looking Back To Yesterday (Motown)
Michael cheerfully massacres a few Motown 'classics' and squeals his way through some of the sickliest, soppiest nonsense ever to be unearthed from the Motown musical vaults.
Smash Hits

WANDA JACKSON
Let's Have A Party (Charly)
Obviously she's got her head screwed on right and this is a perfect soundtrack for opening the party fours and chucking up in a stranger's bathroom.
Melody Maker

● THE JESUS AND MARY CHAIN

THE JESUS AND MARY CHAIN
Psycho Candy (blanco y negro)
Psycho Candy is one of those records that makes you want to just lie back and HOWL.
Beat

Follow them back down the garden psycho-path to the future.
Record Mirror

The Jesus And Mary Chain are the spottiest group in rock (true). *Psycho Candy* is a wonderful LP which should bring the Scottish brats the success they've missed out on so far (true).
Smash Hits

An immaculate conception of *love* songs, and one of the finest debut albums *ever*.
Sounds

. . . sounded exactly like they were coming through the wall with a Black & Decker. Bloody frightening.
Melody Maker

An innocent little sugar cube, just waiting for a tongue.
NME

JIMMY JIMMY
Here In The Light (Epic)
Oh, and that's a twat of a voice you've got, Jimmy.
NME

This abominable 'commercial' sound induces stomach cramps . . .
Sounds

Till I heard this record I never knew there were so many different kinds of old-fashioned.
Melody Maker

ELTON JOHN
Ice On Fire (Rocket)
... even the 'host' of 'guest artistes' can't stop them from sounding disappointingly old-fashioned.
Smash Hits

It's all too safe by half, Reg.
Record Mirror

'Taupin' should take note that Nikita is in fact a boy's name, as in Kruschev.
NME

... the LP reaffirms Elton's position as top British pop performer and master interpreter of songs.
Sounds

And it's really awful.
Beat

ALED JONES
Where E'er You Walk
(10 Records)
It's all very 'nice' – not nearly as fearful as Bonnie Langford singing 'Good Ship Lollipop' at the age of four, for instance – but rather 'creepy' all the same.
Smash Hits

JOURNEY
Raised On Radio (CBS)
Journey '86 is all about wimphem. Fast wimphem, slow wimphem, mid-paced wimphem ... but wimphem all the same!
Kerrang!

They're no softer than Marillion. And they're only as American as Springsteen or the Blasters. Nobody's perfect, after all ...
Sounds

For its sense of vision alone, this must be the most essential album released in the last two years.
NME

JUNIOR
Acquired Taste (London)
... despite ... the South Molton Street togs on the front cover, this is still well within the realm of the depressingly familiar.
Melody Maker

... more South Molton Street than Streatham High.
NME

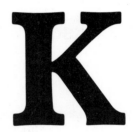

KAJA
Crazy People's Right To Speak (EMI)
A band that even supplies its own put-downs.
NME

I doubt if we will be hearing from them again.
Melody Maker

They are doomed.
Sounds

● JUNIOR

JESSE JOHNSON'S REVUE
Jesse Johnson's Revue (A&M)
JJ's Revue are definitely a purple-stained crew, but less musically extravagant than His Paisleyness.
Beat

... the fact that America laps up the relaxed Revue is mere confirmation, were it needed, of the maudlin romantic indulgence that tolerates the raising to its own desperate monarchy of a diseased, pumpkin-headed ham.
Sounds

THE JUNE BRIDES
There Are Eight Million Stories ... (The Pink Label)
... a mish-mash of a record that suffers from a lack of time and money and perhaps a little bit of thought.
Record Mirror

Ah, to be in England, where they celebrate the eccentric, accentuate the common man and still make records like this.
Sounds

All good boys deserve a June Brides album.
Melody Maker

● KAJA

● KATRINA AND THE WAVES

KATRINA AND THE WAVES

Waves (Capitol)
She has a big girl's voice . . .
Efficient AOR . . .
Beat

Dumb but quite endearing in its child-like way.
Smash Hits

The boyish Katrina has only a so-so pair of lungs . . . Let's just wave goodbye.
Sounds

KEEP IT DARK

First Down And Ten (Charisma)
Keep It Dark . . . lose themselves in textures that whimper to be shaped into songs.
Sounds

. . . and they wrote it all themselves! I wish they hadn't.
Melody Maker

KING

Bitter Sweet (CBS)
The songs, me dears, are still completely limp . . .
Record Mirror

When it was all over, I didn't die, I didn't feel hot . . .
Sounds

In other words, it's perfect.
NME

. . . he's imbued this set of lust songs with quasi-mystical, stream-of-consciousness rambling designed to befuddle the listener into believing he's *not* saying 'let's schtup'.
Melody Maker

KING KURT

Big Cock (Stiff)
I think I'd rather run around the office 200 times carrying my typewriter above my head, or leap naked from the window on the third floor, than defile my ears with this.
Record Mirror

. . . the prevailing tone of biological schoolboy humour which makes Benny Hill look like Noel Coward is so harmlessly dim (barely more sophisticated than the Sun) . . .
Sounds

Offal, just plain offal.
NME

KISS

Asylum (Vertigo)
Asylum continues to display Kiss's ability to flog hapless consumers a product they don't need and which has no intrinsic value whatsoever. This is marketing at its best. And music at its worst.
NME

Possibly the worst album of all time!
Sounds

● KING KURT

ED KUEPPER
Electrical Storm (Hot Records)
Beguiling. Thrilling. Sad. Honest . . .
What more could you want?
Sounds

Electrical Storm is the sound of
one desperate man and his
garage . . . it takes a touch of
brilliance to be this unremittingly
morose and still compel . . .
NME

Kuepper makes personal
statements near perfectly.
Melody Maker

LAIBACH
Nova Acropola (Cherry Red)
. . . a highly recommended antidote
to silence.
NME

. . . a strange, but almost wonderful
piece of vinyl.
Record Mirror

Bleak, hostile and deeply
evocative . . . Laibach's debut LP is
full of mystery and madness.
Sounds

Laibach have produced the first
dangerous album of the eighties.
A triumph of the will.
Melody Maker

DENISE LASALLE
My Toot Toot (Epic)
Think of Millie Jackson, only twice
the size . . .
Smash Hits

Sharp, punchy backings and horns
zesty just the way they should be,
and the percentage of statutory
US soul slop kept to an
acceptable minimum.
NME

JAMES LAST
Leave The Best To Last
(Polydor)
Since when has a cover version

of 'Hooray, Hooray, It's a
Holi-Holiday' been the best unless
you're lying pissed on a beach
near Palma? If you're a Scottish
cowboy just back from the sea
who wears white tuxedos and
swoons to 'Moon River' then vote
SDP and follow your leader.
NME

THE LEATHER NUN
Alive (Wire)
. . . a group that delivers almost
everything.
Sounds

A Jesus And Mary Chain for Lou
Reed fans, a Lou Reed for Mary
Chain fans . . .
Melody Maker

A few more bands like this and the
eighties could be saved from
being a wonderland for fakers and
fifth-raters.
NME

THE LEN BRIGHT COMBO
**The Len Bright Combo
Presents . . .** (Empire)
The real world starts here.
Melody Maker

The 'wacky pub rock' tag has
never fitted so snugly.
NME

Combo offer you the works. From
the ridiculous to the ridiculous.
Sounds

● JULIAN LENNON

● LAIBACH

JULIAN LENNON
The Secret Value Of Daydreaming (Virgin)
Julian Lennon wouldn't know a great pop song if it jumped up and bit him on the nose.
Smash Hits

Why is it that good taste has no real flavour?
Record Mirror

He could not excite a knee into movement if he struck it with a hammer.
NME

Heavy. Dull. Worried over.
Sounds

Now, then, when are we gonna hear from Sean?
Melody Maker

● LEVEL 42

LEVEL 42
World Machine (Polydor)
More vacuous funk from the Isle of Wight lads who seem content to carry on in the tradition of making pleasant, unassuming dance music.
Smash Hits

A repetitive, dull skid-along...
Sounds

Bet it sounds great in Chelsea Girl...
Melody Maker

LOVE AND ROCKETS
Seventh Dream Of Teenage Heaven (Beggars Banquet)
... it's the kind of record to sit in your bedroom with as the long winter nights draw in...
Smash Hits

From strength comes forth sweetness
Sounds

● LOVE AND ROCKETS

I simply don't see the point of recycling a dozen obscure old psychedelic albums...
Record Mirror

This is jolly catchy, colourful, spruce and eight yards too long...
NME

... compelling and mystifying and almost totally unique.
Kerrang!

LOVEBUG STARSKI
House Rocker (Epic)
... the man might be a mouth and a half but he's got a sense of humour, right there on 'Amityville (The House On The Hill)' which has the tongue firmly in the cheek of the mock-horror mask.
Record Mirror

Judging by his manly newscaster tones, Lovebug was raised on tongue sandwiches...
Sounds

MICHAEL McDONALD
No Lookin' Back (Warner Bros)
Be selective, and this is for feeling good and bad to.
Sounds

Feels good to me.
NME

He may look like a cheeseburger but he sure don't sing like one.
Melody Maker

MALCOLM McLAREN
Swamp Thing (Charisma)
Malcolm's wicked sense of humour is uppermost again, harking back to the eclectic style of the first album . . . Don't expect to understand it, just open up, duck in and enjoy.
Beat

And it's all mega-mixed together with hip hop rhythms, ethnic beats and Malcolm's inimitable sense of humour. Trick or treat? Both actually.
Smash Hits

MADNESS
Mad Not Mad (Zarjazz)
. . . what we are offered here is a sort of mixed pop/soul style which suits Suggs and Co down to the ground.
Smash Hits

Mad Not Mad, where slippers replace dancing shoes, and the boys grow old gracefully but lose none of their eccentric charm.
Sounds

Most of all *Mad Not Mad* manages the impressive shuffle of being revealing – and therefore bleak – and lightfooted both at once.
NME

Grim, but grinning, they come to the surface clutching an album of ten sparkling, black diamonds.
Record Mirror

● MALCOLM McLAREN

MADONNA
True Blue (Sire)
. . . a collection of pleasant, even-paced tunes . . . some of them good ('White Heat', 'Where's The Party'), some less so . . . I doubt it will do her long term reputation much good at all.
Smash Hits

On 'Where's The Party' (did it really take three people to write this?), she behaves like an overexcited kid who's had one too many jelly trifles.
Record Mirror

. . . 'Where's The Party' is as empty as a toilet roll toob . . .
Sounds

'Where's The Party?' . . . is a hedonist tantrum . . .
Melody Maker

'Where's The Party' sounds like a formula . . . Madonna has long transcended the realms of mere music. She is the Reproducible Girl. And the poster campaign is inspired.
NME

YNGWIE MALMSTEEN'S RISING FORCE
Marching Out (Polydor)
Someone ought to tell him how ordinary he really is.
Sounds

. . . no words can describe what this 22-year-old wiz kid can do to an axe on a good night.
Circus

MANFRED MANN'S EARTH BAND
Criminal Tango (10 Records)
Danger! Digital mastering at work! Men in studios with headless guitars, chipboard hairstyles and floppy jackets.
Melody Maker

Talk about barking up the wrong tree . . .
Sounds

● MADNESS

MATT BIANCO
Matt Bianco (WEA)
... the initial impression is of a Manhattan Transfer LP...
Melody Maker

... totally frivolous and throwaway but at the same time undeniably catchy and irresistible, employing instruments like a washing-up bottle full of dried peas and a keyboard that sounds like Star Wars' CP30 giggling.
Smash Hits

Matt Bianco are having a flirtation with your feet; an affair with your wardrobe...
Sounds

WYNTON MARSALIS
Black Codes – From The Underground (CBS)
What's it like? It's like dazzling, of course...
Beat

Wynton Marsalis proves knowledge to be the opiate for Woganised jazz musak.
Melody Maker

... there is a consistently excellent outpouring of ideas, an interlocking musical imagination and fire power, and to crown the achievement, a spirit of mischief...
NME

THE MEAT PUPPETS
Out My Way (SST)
His gibberish lyrics and out-of-it singing are a kind of worship; his guitar kisses the sky. The Meat Puppets are far out.
Melody Maker

THE MEMBRANES
Gift Of Life (Creation)
Ignore the awful sleeve and check out the weird and wonderful world within.
Melody Maker

The best thing to do with it is just put it on and watch it go round while those horrible noises come out of it.
NME

● MICRODISNEY

● WYNTON MARSALIS

MICRODISNEY
The Clock Comes Down The Stairs (Rough Trade)
... there's a darkness, depth and detail to 'The Clock...' that makes it one of the albums of the year.
NME

Conventionally twee songs and verbiage which narrowly fails to be interesting.
Sounds

It is a breath of fresh air among the putrid stench of most current releases.
Melody Maker

They do a lovely line in classy cover versions, to boot.
Record Mirror

JOHN MILES
Transition (Warner Bros)
I was going to say this horrible assemblage of old man transatlantic clichéd bozorock might appeal to a deaf person, but then the cover's so appalling you'd have to be blind as well.
Sounds

... he's come up with a deliciously mature bunch of immaculate AOR tunes... seeping class and distinction.
Kerrang!

MINIMAL COMPACT
Raging Souls (Crammed Discs)
... it's certainly the best record to have come out of Israel this year.
Sounds

● GARY MOORE

● JONI MITCHELL

MINIMAL MAN
Slave Lullabyes
(Play It Again Sam)
I don't know about you, but when I see a flugelhorn listed in the credits I begin to doubt the worth of even playing the record in the first place.
Sounds

MINISTRY
Twitch (Sire)
... by golly (as we say now), it has the potential to really slam 'em in the clubs, or anywhere else where throbbing bass lines and blasting percussion rules the day.
Sounds

... it's hard to believe that anyone will have *fun* dancing to this soul-less product.
Melody Maker

JONI MITCHELL
Dog Eat Dog (Geffen)
Forgive her a few clichés, and wonder what holds her fast to the principles most of her generation abandoned.
Beat

... the melodies and lyrics are as picturesque, enigmatic and demanding as ever.
Sounds

But don't worry all you purists, she hasn't gone electrobop ...
Melody Maker

THE MODELS
Out Of Mind Out Of Sight
(Geffen)
Give me a char sui chow mein any day.
Sounds

... has about as much actual substance as a tub of margarine.
Melody Maker

MOMUS
Circus Maximus
(El/Cherry Red)
This is a huge, gentle music, half a step away from pop ... probably the most stimulating thing you'll hear all year.
Melody Maker

... throw this to the lions, though I have a feeling they would choke on it.
Sounds

GARY MOORE
Run For Cover (10 Records)
... yet more mediocre metal ... Completely unspoiled by failure, the boys are back with everything you might expect.
Record Mirror

... a pompous load of old twaddle.
Smash Hits

If this is the best heavy metal can offer in 1985, pity today's spotty teenager.
Melody Maker

... a very fine record in the classy manner you'd expect from the multi-talented guitarist.
Kerrang!

Rockin' Every Night
(10 Records)
... is packed to the max with The Man's devastating digital displays.
Kerrang!

MOTORHEAD
Orgasmatron (GWR Records)
... Lemmy has ordered forth noise, filth and fury in *Sun* front page proportions ... The highest compliment I can give is that *Orgasmatron* makes you *want* to be a scumbag! Here's to the lowlifes!
Kerrang!

There are nine good reasons why Motorhead *must* exist, nine burning, churning wedges of sound nurtured with a sledgehammer ...
Sounds

... it's all speed and reactionary signals, one great single and eight puny blood-brothers.
NME

NANA MOUSKOURI
Alone (Philips)
Her most 'commercial' album . . .
Get back on the balalaika, little
lady, why don'tcher?
Smash Hits

EDDIE MURPHY
How Could It Be (CBS)
Avoid at all costs.
NME

Is this some kind of joke?
Beat

Eddie, Eddie, stick to your side of
the tracks. What would it be like if
Lionel Richie decided to try his
hand at comedy . . ?
Sounds

PETER MURPHY
Should The World Fall Apart
(Beggars Banquet)
. . . he still has a tendency to sound
as if he's choking on his own arty
pomposity . . . the fact remains that
this album, complete with flaws, is
practically transcendental.
Record Mirror

. . . probably best remembered for
being the poseur with the amazing
cheekbones on the *Maxell*
advert . . .
Smash Hits

Lothe [sic] as I am to state the
obvious, that's precisely what
Murphy masters in . . . a charlatan
best standing still and staring
inside those white eyes and
cheekbones.
Melody Maker

You only have to look at this man
to know he was born to be a star . . .
an unpretentious album.
NME

N

NAKED RAYGUN
All Rise (Homestead)
Naked Raygun present the
smuttier side of the all-American
nightmare. *All Rise* is a gutsy
series of venomous sentences laid
bare over a sea of rampant noise.
Sounds

Roar power, bringing a lump to
your throat, and if it isn't the devil's
erection then it can only be
cancer.
Melody Maker

NASTY SAVAGE
Nasty Savage (Roadrunner)
Complete and utter guttural
rubbish. Has about as much
musical ability as a stuffed
hedgehog . . .
Sounds

NEW EDITION
All For Love (MCA)
Anyone who includes Almighty
God, their lawyers, their wardrobe
director and Nancy Reagan on
their inner sleeve can't really be
living in the real world.
NME

. . . so teen angst it positively
oozes with acne. Mmm . . .
Melody Maker

STEVIE NICKS
Rock A Little
(Modern Records/Parlophone)
. . . this 'new' Stevie Nicks album is
much like any other 'new' Stevie
Nicks album . . .
Kerrang!

● NANA MOUSKOURI

● TED NUGENT

. . . Stevie should come out of the
studio and take up flower-
arranging immediately . . . I'd rather
listen to Nana Mouskouri.
Record Mirror

The sound of California crumbling
into the sea.
NME

TED NUGENT
Little Miss Dangerous (WEA)
Little Miss Dangerous is no more
than the latest low point in the
continuing decline of a one-time
folk hero.
Sounds

You're too old Ted. Piss off.
Melody Maker

GARY NUMAN
The Fury (Numa)
Musically, this LP is the same old boring keyboard plod and slurred vocals as ever, lovingly put together for Gary's own pleasure – but who else's?
Record Mirror

Gaz boy, this is almost as furious as Val Doonican on valium.
Sounds

Lyrically the thin white puke sets himself up for ridicule so often, I hardly know where to begin . . .
NME

O

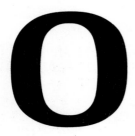

PHILIP OAKEY AND GIORGIO MORODER
Philip Oakey And Giorgio Moroder (Virgin)
The only way you could, like, *dance* to this would be to impersonate Muffin the Mule on springs.
Sounds

This ain't rock 'n' roll – this is aural euthanasia! . . . probably the most boring and worthless album of the year?
Record Mirror

PO&GM is actually godlike . . . Impeccable.
Melody Maker

BILLY OCEAN
Love Zone (Jive)
Love Zone? Pah! More like *Woman's Own* . . .
Sounds

I've thrown the pathetic thing away.
NME

Stick to the singles.
Melody Maker

MIKE OLDFIELD
The Complete . . . (Virgin)
All in all, a good musical compilation with fine sleeve notes.
Kerrang!

YOKO ONO
Starpeace (Polydor)
Oh Yoko, oh Yoko, oh Yoko, No-No . . .
Sounds

. . . for a woman who's taken out full page ads in the world's leading newspapers preaching for love and peace, this must be an end in itself. But for the rest of us? I suspect that it won't do nicely, thank you.
NME

OPPOSITION
Empire Days (Charisma)
. . . powerful, thoughtful, melodic . . .
Beat

Having traded in their electric piano for a polyphonic synthesiser, that grubby pub-bashed Fender for an incontinent fretless bass . . . Opposition set about making a sausage dog from a bag of grey balloons . . .
NME

Cold, calculated and decidedly colourless in its mediocrity, this album will sentence the Opposition to the hi-fi's of unadventurous middle-aged rock pundits.
Melody Maker

OPUS
Live Is Life (Polydor)
Forget 'Live Is Life' (na, na, na, na, na), Opus are **not** jaunty Europeans with cheesy grins and rather awful trousers after all. They are something infinitely more terrible. Yes, it's true, I'm afraid: Opus, Austria's top rock attraction, are suffering from the disastrous delusion that they are actually Supertramp circa 1974 . . . (I tell a lie – their trousers *are* rather awful).
Smash Hits

MARIE OSMOND
There's No Stopping Your Heart (Capitol)
. . . Marie's brand of country rock is tame, seamless and determinedly aimed at transatlantic aeroplane headphone exposure.
Beat

. . . this girl and her voice are so characterless she can't even *whine* properly.
Melody Maker

OZZY OSBOURNE
The Ultimate Sin (Epic)
. . . Ozzy has produced his most accessible selection of songs so far. But at the same time, he hasn't diluted the awesome power which has kept him going . . .
Record Mirror

I'd sooner listen to *The Ultimate Sin* daily than eat a bat, but it's a pretty near thing.
Melody Maker

● OZZY OSBOURNE

. . . if *The Ultimate Sin* doesn't deliver the crazy-house antics of yore, that's probably because it just doesn't need to. Buy it and I promise you won't be disappointed.
Sounds

● MARIE OSMOND

P

PALLAS
The Wedge (EMI)
By turns hyperbolic and 'atmospheric', Pallas' music is honestly too boring to talk about.
NME

Pallas are a tiresome anachronism trying to breathe life into a symphonic soft-rock genre which should have been left to rest in peace ages ago.
Melody Maker

ROBERT PALMER
Riptide (Island)
. . . he brings all his craft to bear on the kind of lively, sophisticated white soul that is his hallmark. His quest for perfection took him to five different mixing studios . . .
Sounds

The unbelievably tedious funk arrangements bury his voice at the bottom of the mix – another case of white boy with soul aspirations and pop capabilities.
Melody Maker

It sounds vile.
NME

RAY PARKER JUNIOR
Sex And The Single Man (Arista)
. . . an enormous load of banal, derivative twaddle – Lionel Richie, Kraftwerk, Billy Joel and Prince all have grounds to sue.
Sounds

It's like finding out Colonel Sanders is a vegetarian, isn't it? What a let down.
Melody Maker

JOHN PARR
John Parr (London)
This kind of formula rock – all glossy guitars and growled cliché – is designed entirely for the soundtracks of films about American teenagers cruising about in automobiles and snogging and expressing themselves through wild pranks because they're young and rebellious . . .
Smash Hits

This sort of tripe really is the most loathsome, worthless sort of cop-out, of no musical value whatsoever, bursting at the seams with manufactured energy and sham emotion.
Sounds

GRAM PARSONS' INTERNATIONAL SUBMARINE BAND
Safe At Home (Statik)
That the album sounds like it could have been cut in 1985 is a reflection on how little country rock has changed.
Sounds

. . . the fan will find an invaluable outline of the shape of things to come; twenty years on he still sounds like no other.
NME

It's a measure of his greatness that the little he left us remains so uniquely enduring.
Melody Maker

ANNETTE PEACOCK
I Have No Feelings (Ironic Records)
. . . don't be afraid when your lover comes in just as Annette shrieks sonically *"We're all sandwiches!"*
Sounds

. . . there's that sound that comes out of her mouth, half voice, half instrument. Warm, evocative, soulful . . . Peacock lady both floats and flies. Catch her, one fine bluesday.
NME

● ROBERT PALMER

● TEDDY PENDERGRASS

TEDDY PENDERGRASS
Workin' It Back (Asylum)
Workin' It Back is a black Barry Manilow vehicle which reverses the rules of the genre with six slow mattress manifestos and a brace of dancefloor concessions.
NME

Handsome man, handsome music.
Sounds

PENDRAGON
The Jewel (Elusive)
. . . if you wear long lank hair, have a dropping 'tache, wear grubby jeans and swear the early Genesis/late Marillion cause, then this one's for you.
Sounds

PERSON TO PERSON
Stranger Than Reason (Epic)
. . . greasy ballads of the dreariest kind.
NME

A poppy, cruising disco funk struts and sways and flickers and flows.
Sounds

TOM PETTY AND THE HEARTBREAKERS
Pack Up The Plantation Live! (MCA)
. . . a turgid four-sided video soundtrack . . .
Sounds

. . . sounds like a high octane adrenalin hit on a dry summer freeway, radio on, cool with the promise of hot, if you know what I mean.
Melody Maker

A sonic masterpiece!
Kerrang!

PET SHOP BOYS
Please (Parlophone)
Here the Pet Shop Boys romp through ten thoroughly catchy songs . . . all about dark mysterious love affairs and whispered crimes, all crammed with wonderfully tacky atmospheric sound effects.
Smash Hits

. . . just when you least expect it, belated passion comes kerbcrawling round your eardrums.
NME

. . . the acceptable face of modern thinking pop . . . a technological band for all reasons and it sounds wonderful.
Melody Maker

To the Pet Shop Boys we say: no more! Please.
Sounds

PHANTOM, ROCKER & SLICK
Phantom, Rocker & Slick (EMI)
. . . better than a poke in the eye with a sharp stick.
Sounds

PHRANC
Folksinger (Rhino/Stiff)
Still, it's a friendly record . . .
Beat
. . . she is set apart by her wit, her deadpan liberalism and the conversational quality of her writing, a virtue enhanced by her loose, smartarse vocal delivery.
NME

For the very first time in the eighties, here's a case where 'worthy' isn't prefaced by the usual 'dull but . . .' Hear it.
Melody Maker

Phranc hits that perfect beat.
Sounds

ANNE PIGALLE
Everything Could Be So Perfect (ZTT)
She still does her sleazy French Sade impression but the complicated mysterious songs . . . are really rather good.
Smash Hits

Imagine a cheerless Cilla Black singing of men in bowler hats, body-poppers and suitcase salesmen on the streets of Liverpool and you'd have a rough idea of the disservice Anne Pigalle does to France and more specifically, Paris, with her cluttered red-light cartoons.
NME

Her breathy accent, dramatic phrasing and orchestral fairground swirl conjure up more than just nostalgic re-creation.
Sounds

Words come to mind . . . Harsh words. French words. Words for Anne Pigalle . . . Give up.
Melody Maker

● ANNE PIGALLE

PRINCE AND THE REVOLUTION
Parade
(Warner Bros/Paisley Park)
Parade is simply magnificent. From the winking horns and lemonade of 'Christopher Tracy's Parade' through some chundering, weepful ballads and turbulent sex-outs, to the completely unstoppable romperama 'Anotherloverholenyhead', this whole creation is shiveringly compelling.
Smash Hits

Parade is a world of its own... When it's over you wonder if it can really exist. If life was ever this real. After this it seems it must be, mustn't it?
Beat

PRINCE JAMMY
Computerised Dub
(Greensleeves)
Computerised Dub is a record that needs to be played at foundation-shaking volume – then it provides an adequate backdrop to the most menial household tasks.
NME

... the album chugs along in a pleasant, hi-tech easy-listening mode that makes me think that *Computerised Dub* could be the first reggae exercise record. Dub aerobics, you could call it.
Melody Maker

PRINCESS
Princess (Supreme)
Stock, Aitken and Waterman (whose names merit the boldest print among the sleeve credits) have produced, written and arranged Princess into just another chip off the block.
Sounds

Princess' success... has perhaps less to do with her than the production team, Stock/Aitken/Waterman.
Smash Hits

PUBLIC IMAGE LTD
Album (Virgin)
Complacent, sluggish and apathetic... If *Album* had been released by anyone else it is unlikely it would ever have been reviewed.
Melody Maker

If there's fire in your veins you won't want to miss out on this. Buy it, there's nothing more I can say.
Kerrang!

Yus, it's John Lydon, sounding as unsettling as ever and as mad as hell... he reminds one that punk actually *did* happen after all.
Smash Hits

Lydon has always been less interested in the music than in the spectacle of a credulous public rising to the bait... it's good to see that the perverse old grouch is still in love with showbiz. Gross, lazy and occasionally magnificent.
Record Mirror

The man has extracted the false phallus from rock's trouserfront and is smashing it over our heads.
Sounds

QUEEN
A Kind Of Magic (EMI)
The only strong emotion Queen now evoke in me is a fervent wish that Brian May would cut his hair.
Melody Maker

To dismiss this out of hand would be as thoughtless as giving a cigarette to a man dying of cancer... Fancy a fag your majesties?
Sounds

... we never needed Queen more than we need them now.
Record Mirror

● QUEEN

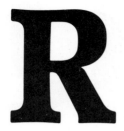

R

RAIN PARADE
Crashing Dream (Island)
Crashing Dream is an unobtrusively mild, lazily satisfying complement to sounds which are categorised clumsily, on both old and new records, as 'dreamy psychedelia'.
NME

If you're contemplating buying this record on the strength of their past, make sure you hear it first.
Melody Maker

Beyond The Sunset
(Restless – Import)
. . . constant, insistent and unbearably annoying.
NME

RAMONES
Animal Boy (Sire)
If they can just keep going, they'll become *Status Quo for the punk generation.*
Beat

. . . you can't help thinking how wonderful the Ramones might have seemed if they'd been arrested in 1976.
NME

. . . pristine goofball ramoning at its best.
Record Mirror

THE RATTLERS
Take A Ride (Lost Moment)
Listenable, but essentially uninspiring.
Sounds

They're not quite mean or cool enough to make out as straight rockabillies.
NME

Perhaps the biggest disappointment, however, is in finding the Rattlers still playing straight rockabilly without having given much consideration to progression.
Melody Maker

RED GUITARS
Tales Of The Expected (Virgin)
Yes – guitars. Lots of them. A-flinging and a-flanging and a-squaking and a-squonking all over the shop . . . and it's brilliant.
Smash Hits

This is AOR disguised as drugs . . .
Sounds

Tales of the Expected is such a pleasant listen, it leaves an indelible blank on my mind.
NME

It's guitar music, chords and words, patterned, random tales of human nature, all slipping finely into place.
Melody Maker

RED HOT 'N' BLUE
Wait 'n' See
(Northwood Records)
If Brilliantine is your style, don't wait 'n' see, go out 'n' get it.
Beat

Essential listening for all you cats out there, dig!
Record Mirror

RED LORRY YELLOW LORRY
Paint Your Wagon (Red Rhino)
. . . like British Rail's sordid fantasies, they're getting there.
Beat

It's grim, brutal, almost a celebration of life's uglier aspects; you could even call it irresponsible. Funny thing is, it's joy-making at the same time . . . *Paint Your Wagon* is a crushing success.
Sounds

THE REDSKINS
Neither Washington Nor Moscow (Delta)
. . . if agitpop, getting down, or even posing by the bedroom mirror is your bag, then this record is the best you're likely to hear for a long time.
Record Mirror

. . . you can dance yourself stupid to large parts of it and, indeed, frugging to a mixed lyrical backdrop of the speeches of Karl Marx and Chris Dean's bleatings on the miners' strike is a lot more fun than it sounds.
Melody Maker

The Redskins' new album is a surprisingly light-and-shade record, full of deft, soulful, hi-power anthems . . . Trouble is, the songs all have titles such as 'Kick Over The Statues' and 'Take No Heroes'.
Sounds

LOU REED
Mistrial (RCA)
Mistrial will probably be a tough one to prise off your turntable.
Sounds

Way to go, Lou . . .
Melody Maker

Poor old Lou Reed now resembles a toothless vampire with the sun at his back.
Record Mirror

RENALDO AND THE LOAF
Olleh, Olleh Rotcod
(Rotcod Productions)
Against all the odds, a pop record.
Sounds

● THE REDSKINS

● STAN RIDGWAY

RENE AND ANGELA
Street Called Desire (Club)
. . . this is third-rate, graceless disco sludge.
Sounds

THE RESIDENTS
Pal TV LP (Doublevision)
. . . as musicians, these studio moles have outlived their moment.
NME

The best word to describe this meagre offering of quirks by jerks is *acceptable* – probably the most damning word in their limited vocabulary.
Melody Maker

RIP STRIP & F . . . IT
A Month In Bohemia Is Worth Two In The Bush (Disposable Discs)
They are, in short, tremendous wankers.
NME

STAN RIDGWAY
The Big Heat (IRS)
Time to surrender your crown, Harry Chapin.
NME

Tom Waits, eat your heart out.
Sounds

ROCKY IV
Original Soundtrack
(Scotti Bros)
If this package of reactionary right wing ideology is what you need to live in America these days, then I'll take Albania.
Sounds

. . . a very dull LP.
Smash Hits

THE ROLLING STONES
Dirty Work
(Rolling Stone Records)
'Hey kids!' these men seem to be saying, 'it's 1976!' But actually, it *isn't*, and . . . the whole thing is monstrously absurd.
Smash Hits

. . . every prejudice you ever had about the Rolling Stones applies to this maggoty heap of dead flesh on record.
Record Mirror

The thirty-fifth Stones album is a rocking reaffirmation of their best qualities.
Kerrang!

● JENNIFER RUSH

Dirty Work is a bona fide rock 'n' roll album, a difficult thing to pull off in 1986.
Melody Maker

For rock to grow up doesn't mean it has to be pompous, toothless or cowardly and the *Dirty Work*-era Rolling Stones are none of those things.
NME

RUN DMC
Raising Hell (London)
I don't like Run DMC, I don't enjoy *Raising Hell* . . . I don't like their clenched fist egotism. I don't like their seemingly utter lack of humour. But their sound slams me up against the wall, kicks my teeth in and leaves me demanding more.
Record Mirror

Yet Run DMC's self-directed gaze is more than mere narcissism. They see in themselves an end to passive consumerism.
NME

In terms of sexual politics . . . they've just crawled out of the primordial ooze.
Melody Maker

. . . an aggressive, sexist, abusive and extremely *loud* LP.
Smash Hits

JENNIFER RUSH
Movin' (CBS)
I cannot imagine *anybody* wanting this record.
Smash Hits

S

SADE
Promise (Epic)
Worth buying if you're a fan.
Beat

Here is a luxury you can afford...
Sounds

I'd go and buy it if I were you.
Melody Maker

You'll be happier and healthier without it...
NME

RYUICHI SAKAMOTO
Illustrated Musical Encyclopedia (10 Records)
... neat and tidy, perfectly constructed musak...
NME

Sakamoto is busy creating warm, intelligent *new* music that knows no boundaries.
Melody Maker

East meets west, swift and turbulent, serene and sensual, this is a mesmerizing collection.
Beat

... to say it's disappointingly lightweight is the understatement of the month.
Sounds

ALEXEI SAYLE
Panic (CBS)
Alexei Sayle – the perfect Alternative Comedian – has produced the perfect Alternative Comedy record. It isn't even funny the first time.
Sounds

So you think someone's head being knocked off in a motorcycle accident is not funny? It is. But it's not alternative.
NME

SAVATAGE
Power Of The Night (Atlantic)
... there is actually some intelligence behind this metal glove.
Sounds

There are so many of this kind of release, perpetuating this kind of male-propagated idiot-rhetoric, that adjectives begin to fail me.
Melody Maker

SAXON
Innocence Is No Excuse
(Parlophone)
I wouldn't be so foolish as to suggest that Saxon no longer have a role to play in the modern heavy rock genre, but it's that of a rock Rambo, storming through a career laying waste to subtlety and good taste...
Melody Maker

... all I can recommend is that you give this album some equally serious attention and that Saxon find themselves a serious rock 'n' roll producer and climb back up to Division One where they belong.
Kerrang!

SCRAPING FOETUS OFF THE WHEEL
Nail (Some Bizarre)
... grating, mock-American vocals wrap themselves around six schlock-horror mini operas, to create a macabre Gilbert and Sullivan for Birthday Party goers.
Record Mirror

Is it alright if I approve of this record more than I enjoy it? Is that the done thing? The statement?
Sounds

... it bears a caravan of conceits camouflaged as concepts...
NME

SCREAMING BLUE MESSIAHS
Gun Shy (WEA)
Oh yes. This hits hard and direct, but it's not unduly loud or distorted.
Beat

They've swapped the bludgeon for the stiletto, and they're cutting up a treat.
NME

... these bar-stool meanies make a sound like a howitzer.
Record Mirror

... the Messiahs are ugly brutes who don't pansy around with pretty production techniques or shrinking pretensions of art – they have the primitive basics of rock music in sharp focus and they don't take any detours in delivering it.
Melody Maker

● SCREAMING BLUE MESSIAHS

BOB SEGER AND THE SILVER BULLET BAND
Like A Rock (Capitol)
... the remarkable thing about this album is that, as soon as it hits the turntable, you begin, almost unconsciously, to read the paper. Then you leave the room, make a cup of tea, do the washing up, come back, turn the album over ... tidy your bedroom and basically do all those little jobs you never seem to get around to.
Melody Maker

This perfectly adequate LP, full of surging moans like 'Tightrope', will undoubtedly satisfy the tastes of party-mad LA dentists ...
Sounds

SEX GANG CHILDREN
Re-Enter The Abyss (The 1985 Remixes) (Dojo)
Tuneless, monotonous listening. For music lovers everywhere – a personal insult.
NME

It's a revamp of their nine best-loved tracks ...
Sounds

... remixed, reshuffled, remorselessly redundant for 1985.
Melody Maker

SEX PISTOLS
Live Worldwide (Konexion)
Many songs here sound as though they were taped off a radio that was not quite tuned in properly. Also, the LP has been pressed on newspaper, and sounds like one's dinner is being fried on it ...
NME

... what you have here is a record I would not necessarily cross the street to pick out of the gutter.
Sounds

For fans – indispensable; for the rest of us – at best a cheerio, at worst avoidable.
Kerrang!

CHARLIE SEXTON
Pictures For Pleasure (MCA)
... one minute your eyes are glazing over and you're getting that awful my-name-is-Bryan-Adams-and-I-jus'-wanna-rock feeling, the next you're being shaken awake by the husky mooning and scintillatingly subliminal geetah tweaking.
Smash Hits

This is the age of the teenage bland-out.
Record Mirror

... colourless, unfocused grunge.
Melody Maker

The Kid's going all the way, just watch him now, there's not a star like this born every minute of the day.
Kerrang!

● SHAKATAK

SHAKATAK
Day By Day (Polydor)
Shakatak have regressed into the cosiest of Wogan muzak. Tesco superstars.
Sounds

SHAKIN' STEVENS
Lipstick, Powder And Paint (Epic)
Flimsy rubbish in a party hat.
Smash Hits

SHANNON
Do You Wanna Get Away (Club)
... this is an OK sort of album, really ...
Smash Hits

... a mushy mixture of mundane melodies.
Melody Maker

FEARGAL SHARKEY
Feargal Sharkey (Virgin)
This is an album full of armchair soul music, text book jazz, boardroom pop and rock 'n' roll by number. Worst of all, though, it's not even the right characters he's nicking from.
Melody Maker

This is sweet-tooth rock. No wonder Feargal is looking so bilious on the sleeve
NME

A pleasure to listen to and a well-deserved hit.
Beat

● CHARLIE SEXTON

SHOCKABILLY
Vietnam (Fundamental Music)
This record is full of wacky falsetto voices, twanging wacky fuzztone guitars, playing wacky cover versions . . . and generally being bloody annoying. Even the Flying Pickets were more entertaining than this . . .
Melody Maker

Not a group for every mood, but when dem old Top 50 blooz get me down, mama, I know to which pills I'll be returning.
NME

SIGUE SIGUE SPUTNIK
Flaunt It (Parlophone)
. . . once you've got the joke, it's really quite enjoyable: not as good as Adam Ant but a birrovalaff anyway . . .
Smash Hits

This album makes my day. It has done *every* day since I got it, because this group make me smile . . . they are entertainers par excellence. This album is great, great fun . . .
Melody Maker

The sequencer riff that powers this sound is the riff of our collective heart, pumping fast, faster, faster still. We are listening to ourselves. We love it.
Sounds

. . . it was a mistake to put out 'the album' at all. A singing hologram of a male stripper, simulating sex with a cashpoint machine, maybe, but just another floppy old disc is hardly hard-on software warfare.
Record Mirror

. . . they bark and bark, like blue-rinsed poodles . . . [they] aren't really in it for the music, so they won't mind me pointing out the fact that it's the biggest heap of garbage since the last heap of garbage . . . [they] are a microcosm of the modern world and the modern world is plastic, expendable, disposable, finite and forgettable . . .
NME

● SIGUE SIGUE SPUTNIK

THE SILOS
About Her Steps
(Record Collect)
The Silos sound fresh, stylish and invigorating. Essential.
Sounds

. . . the result of obvious care and affection. I like it.
NME

SIMPLE MINDS
Once Upon A Time (Virgin)
I still love it, but only just.
Beat

Simple Minds simply sound too comfortable, and the music grand but not great.
Smash Hits

After the last course, the lingering taste is infuriatingly pleasant, laid-back and inoffensive.
Record Mirror

. . . Simple Minds are slowly sinking in the West under the awful weight of their own destiny . . . and *Once Upon A Time* is really the end of the story.
Melody Maker

SIMPLY RED
Picture Book (Elektra)
. . . it's nowhere near as funny as Paul Weller.
Sounds

Picture Book's soul-by-numbers is as cliché-ridden as the ugliest offspring of Gothic interbreeding.
NME

Forget the *soul* stuff, and you've got one of the better debuts of the year.
Melody Maker

● FRANK SINATRA

FRANK SINATRA
Greatest Hits (Reprise)
Still cool, but just beginning to verge on the ridiculous. Doo bee doo bee do indeed.
Record Mirror

SIOUXSIE AND THE BANSHEES
Tinderbox (Wonderland/Polydor)
The main problem is Sioux herself; her miserable obsession with death . . .
Beat

The Banshees should be writing film scores for thriller movies . . .
Record Mirror

Really this accord is the sound of nothing going nowhere.
Melody Maker

SLY AND ROBBIE
Language Barrier (Island)
A monochrome if beefy album . . .
Sounds

. . . this is industrial strength technovoodoo . . .
NME

THE SMITHS
The Queen Is Dead
(Rough Trade)
The Smiths *aren't* like anybody else. The Smiths are quite good.
Smash Hits

SONIC YOUTH
E. V. O. L (Blast First)
Sonic Youth is advanced noise, a pretty goddam sophisticated cultural signpost . . .
Beat

● SOS BAND

SOS BAND
Sands Of Time (Tabu)
. . . for people not looking for the future of rock 'n' roll.
Smash Hits

No shocks, no unsigned valentines, just lovey-dovey drippery . . .
Melody Maker

This group . . . are big, broad, massive and dull.
NME

A sense of hot mysteries in icy castles and that heaven-sent undercurrent of yearning. Mostly magnificent.
Sounds

THE SOUND
In The Hothouse (Statik)
In The Hothouse grinds tediously through four sides of torpid rock. Average rather than terrible, worthy rather than offensive, this is still a hopeless record.
NME

And this *is* a wonderful sound.
Sounds

SPEAR OF DESTINY
World Service (Epic)
. . . there's a lot of barking and bravado but not a great deal to back it up.
Record Mirror

This is a record which aspires to grandeur; unfortunately it doesn't really make it.
Smash Hits

In the end, though, the whole thing proves that if Brandon wants to stop being a prep-school antichrist, he'd better start being something more, rather than less, interesting instead.
NME

. . . people will be suspicious of this record because it is not one-dimensional.
Sounds

SQUEEZE
Cosi Fan Tutti Frutti (A&M)
This is by no stretch of the imagination a 'happy' record – unless, that is, one is perverse enough to take delight from alcoholism, poverty, marital breakdown, unrequited love and drug addiction.
NME

Perfectly detailed council house pain. A big hand, ladies and gents.
Sounds

● SQUEEZE

STARSHIP
Knee Deep In The Hoopla
(RCA)
A very long time ago, Starship's singer Grace Slick used to go on about how wonderful it would be if there was no money in the world and everybody had to live on berries but she grew out of *that* pretty sharpish and these days feeds her several love children on fine delicacies bought out of the vast profits she makes by singing in a disgustingly dreary rock band who sound like Toto (except on 'We Built This City' where they sound like a very wonky Abba).
Smash Hits

A tasteful, interesting piece of US chart-rock vinyl.
Sounds

Tight, lively and brilliantly good.
Kerrang!

CANDI STATON & BETTYE SWANN
Tell It Like It Is (Stateside)
... you'd have to be virtually dead not to love this record.
NME

Brill album. Gorgeous cover. Fab sleeve notes. What more do you want?
Melody Maker

STEEL PULSE
Babylon The Bandit (Elektra)
If you've lost touch with reggae, here's the front door. Superb.
Beat

Actually, one of the highlights is the cover which represents a variety of historical and contemporary items which the West has thieved from Africa (for instance, pyramids and the lion on a 10p piece, respectively) ...
Record Mirror

STING
Bring On The Night (A&M)
Like someone telling you about their dreams, it's probably a lot of fun for them, but dull as turtle talk for you.
Record Mirror

... forgoes any sense of challenge or risk-taking.
NME

● STYLE COUNCIL

ROD STEWART
Rod Stewart (WEA)
With this album, Rod Stewart takes the piss out of himself as well as us, and that I admire. Brilliant.
Melody Maker

His voice is wonderful, his songs are terrible. His singing is immortal, his lyrics are mortal and mouldy ... Rod Stewart – the cipher not the song – has always been First Division, but on this performance, his comeback at Wembley could be a lonely affair.
NME

STRATUS
Throwing Shapes (Steel Trax)
I can hardly believe that they're serious.
Sounds

BARBRA STREISAND
The Broadway Album (CBS)
A million miles from Broadway.
NME

STRYPER
Soldiers Under Control
(Enigma)
Each and every one of the album's ten toons gets The Word across in a way which renders Billy Graham positively restrained in his approach!
Kerrang!

... a band pledging 'special thanks' to God on the sleeve can't be *all* that bad, can they?
Sounds

STYLE COUNCIL
Home And Abroad (Polydor)
Weller's loathing of dirt and rough edges has led him to make a live recording that is dead from the waist down.
NME

It sounds as if the rough edges have been filed off this with an iron rasp ...
Record Mirror

The minimally informative sleeve makes one thing clear: "The Style Council are anti-apartheid" ...
Melody Maker

This is a very enjoyable record, and if there's a point to the sheer fun of everyday meaninglessness then it's not pointless.
Sounds

DONNA SUMMER
The Greatest Hits Collection
(Mercury)
Most of these songs can be bought for 40p in a good secondhand record shop in fair condition; and that way the ageing session bigot won't get any of your money. Ha! ha!
NME

SURFIN' DAVE AND THE ABSENT LEGENDS
In Search Of A Decent Haircut (Crammed)
The last of the big-time milksops, Dave wipes the sand from a tear-stained eye to whine these 'Twelve Tales Of Teen Angst' ... Drab, flab and utterly unfunny ...
NME

Surfin' Dave is essentially an affectionate joke incarnate ...
Sounds

SWANS
Greed (K 422)
Swans with oil on their wings.
Melody Maker

Greed the sound of the Swans in love and the most appealing sound to these ears for many months. I want *more*.
NME

● 10,000 MANIACS

T

TAKA BOOM
Middle Of The Night (Polydor)
Middle of the Night is like eating Miss Ellie's macadamia nut cookies in a jacuzzi full of warm, bubbling Lindt chocolate – more a matter of swoon or puke, than sink or swim.
NME

● TALK TALK
The Colour Of Spring (EMI)
... straightforward ace pop music here to prove that Talk Talk have matured excellently away from the spotlight. Okay, so they still don't go for the jugular but that's because they take their music too seriously to stamp 'hit' and 'hook' all over the place.
Record Mirror

Its quality lies in the night and day of each track, Hollis's voice surging up from a velvety purr...
Beat

... they have the straining despair and moribund conventional approach that passes for rigorous intellect and challenging pop in some quarters.
NME

TARZEN
Tarzen (Valentino/Atco)
Tarzen is the perfect record to play very loud whilst immensely drunk and savour the jokes.
Kerrang!

... it's enough to bore yer loincloth off...
Sounds

TENOR SAW
Fever (Blue Mountain)
Like having your ears massaged by a velvet glove...
Sounds

10,000 MANIACS
The Wishing Chair (Elektra)
Like an aural sepia print, 10,000 Maniacs are tainted by memory...
Melody Maker

... the Maniacs' music harks back to an international sepia past... Not bad at all for hippy American folk-rockers.
Record Mirror

● TALK TALK

● THAT PETROL EMOTION

TERRAPLANE
Black And White (Epic)
Competently played but innocuous, Terraplane's songs just don't have enough class to leave an indelible mark.
Record Mirror

Terraplane are the band to remind us all that 'rock music' doesn't have to mean tedium, cliché and all the other things that have come to be associated with it. It can be tasteful too.
Melody Maker

TERRY AND GERRY
From Lubbock To Clintwood East (In Tape)
Perhaps the band is just a little too narrow in their scope to attract popular recognition as yet, but that will surely come in time.
Record Mirror

... to have to wait at all to warm to an album is a sign of weakness, especially in a band who can create such an instant reaction when they play live. Maybe next time they'll get it right.
Sounds

... remarkably wearying.
NME

TEX AND THE HORSEHEADS
Life's So Cool (Enigma)
... they're sprawling, anarchic; a firestorm of punk guitar riffs and bone-breaking rhythms, over which Tex declaims her psycho-babble lyrics, like an asthmatic hyena barking at a neon moon.
Melody Maker

Tex sports holed fishnets and her hobby is unprintable.
Sounds

THAT PETROL EMOTION
Manic Pop Thrill (Demon)
Left-over punk rockers from Ireland ... have finally defied pop logic and produced an LP of unseemly guitar-fuelled brilliance.
Smash Hits

Drop the needle and breathe in some unadulterated, untethered, manic pop music ...
Record Mirror

... is to jaded pop palates what babies' blood is to complexion-conscious 500-year-old vampirines.
NME

It's pop.
Sounds

For every track of genuine potency here ... there are even more that collapse in a discordant mess, stripped of all melody and sense of direction.
Melody Maker

THEATRE OF HATE
Original Sin Live (Dojo)
Buy it and hear something that shows a lot of these third-rate rock bands up as the fakes they really are.
Sounds

This is a worthless artifact. We are virtually positive even Kirk Brandon himself wouldn't want you to buy it.
Melody Maker

THESE TENDER VIRTUES
The Continuing Saga . . .
(Carousel)
... majestic in meaning and poignant in principal [sic]. It's all the fun of the fairground, or Friday nights down at the old Bull and Bush, with a rousing piano player giving the ivories a going-over in one corner.
Record Mirror

Show them the door.
NME

THEY MUST BE RUSSIANS
They Must Be Russians And Other Groundless Accusations (Native)
So much for the cynics that proclaimed for so long that the Russians have never had an eye to world domination; the invasion starts here.
Sounds

DAVID THOMAS
Monster Walks The Winter Lake (Rough Trade)
We don't understand it but are convinced. It's quite unique. Brilliant.
Melody Maker

On this record David Thomas is a *"city Crow"*, a *"crazy bus driver"*, he feels, by turns "fuzzy", "weird", "abstract", "abstracted", "desperate" ... mostly he feels like a Martian. Marooned. Like the rest of us, only more so.
NME

I can't handle this one at all ... If David Thomas is an inventive genius, I'm a bit styoopid ...
Sounds

● DAVID THOMAS

● PETE TOWNSHEND

THE THOMPSON TWINS
Here's To Future Days (Arista)

Future Days is pop for the football terraces . . .
Record Mirror

The Twins probably regard their new-found sophistication as burning with a cool flame.
Melody Maker

And they have the gall to include a piece of paper asking me to join their *fan club.*
NME

THE THREE JOHNS
The World By Storm (Abstract)
Ignore at your peril.
Record Mirror

The Three Johns have gutted rock music with their obnoxious wit and excellent songs.
Sounds

Fruitcakes still, but with a little sugar now added in all the right places.
Melody Maker

JOHNNY THUNDERS
Que Sera, Sera (Jungle Freud)
You could have been the champ, Johnny, but now you're just a washed-up has-been.
Record Mirror

Why Johnny Thunders has done this is a complete mystery . . . maybe he's done it for the money and surely he deserves some, but it's a shame because poverty always seemed to suit him.
Melody Maker

PETE TOWNSHEND
White City (Atco)
I rather think my multi-media project 'Penguins In West Wimbledon' will be far more exciting.
Record Mirror

White City – the album – is a pitiful specimen, it really is.
Melody Maker

It's almost as if he's learned how to avoid enjoying himself.
NME

SIMON TOWNSHEND'S MOVING TARGET
Simon Townshend's Moving Target (Polydor)
Is this really Pete Townshend's little brother? Well, if so, why does he sound so like Roger Daltrey? . .
Sounds

Musically Simon's more of a Keef than a Pete . . .
Melody Maker

THE TURBINES
Last Dance Before Highway (Bigtime America)
. . . not music for sissies. No sir! These boys are buddies for the Blasters and their hardy ilk, four men with the guts of six and just enough humour to make a traffic cop grimace. It's American, it's all been done before somewhere else and just drove to this rendezvous with destiny by itself.
Sounds

TUXEDOMOON
Ship Of Fools (Cramboy)
I might call it elevator music if elevators were elevating.
Sounds

Tuxedomoon make modern furniture music . . .
Melody Maker

TWISTED SISTER
Come Out And Play (Atlantic)
Surely only the year's most boring album would dare instruct you, writ large on its inner sleeve, to 'PLAY IT LOUD MUTHA!'
NME

Never let it be said that Twisted Sister are boring. Why there are as many as two interesting things about this LP . . . If [they] keep up this rate of improvement they may make a halfway decent LP before the century is out.
Smash Hits

Most of the songs might easily have been dashed off by the average ten-year-old lout in a spare lunchbreak after his football's been punctured.
Sounds

The Twisteds' best bit of plastic for ages, if *ever* . . . menopausal but magnficently, gloriously, contagiously sick . . .
Kerrang!

● TUXEDOMOON

BONNIE TYLER
Dreams In A Forbidden Fire
(Columbia)
. . . she's turned into a raunchy songstress who belts out pompous over-the-top rock 'epics' . . .
Smash Hits

What a little treasure Bonita was when she pumped out unpretentious pop schlock singles . . . And what a terminal bore she's become since she discovered Cock Rock.
Melody Maker

Bonnie Tyler is 90.
Sounds

UB40
Little Baggariddim (A&M)
. . . a vibrant pulsating reggae record which by virtue of clever production avoids the usual reggae trap of becoming repetitive and boring.
Smash Hits

. . . a good idea poorly executed.
Record Mirror

By aiming to be more Kingston Jamaica than Kingston-Upon-Thames, UB40 have slipped on a whopping great banana skin.
Sounds

UFO
Misdemeanor (Chrysalis)
Misdemeanor is a mogadon ramble through fields already tilled to death by Foreigner et al, shallow stabs at AOR acceptance which fall flat not through lack of effort, but because effort is all you can hear.
Melody Maker

UFO manage to be romantic without being gooey, heavy without being mindless, and the result is devastating; a total reaffirmation of their power and prestige as one of rock's finest and most intelligent exponents.
Kerrang!

MIDGE URE
The Gift (Chrysalis)
If he cut his nose off it would make no difference, the album would still smell bad, if not actually *reeking* of Ultravox . . .
NME

I always think this kind of stuff is music for people who don't really *like* music at all. Zzzzzzzzz . . .
Smash Hits

I spent my birthday gift token on *this*? Let's see . . . no, proceeds aren't even going to Africa . . .
Sounds

. . . it's practically useless, a record with clinical rhyme but no reason, a record – for all its expertise, poise and textured pleasure – that's a sin, a self-indulgence, a useless, needless artefact that wastes rather than *fills* our precious time.
Melody Maker

Midge emerges head high, with a truly worthwhile album.
Record Mirror

VAN HALEN
5150 (Warner Bros)
5105 is a very creditable album, but the next one will be even better.
Record Mirror

Neat album, then. But the next one should be the goods.
NME

But 5150 isn't bad, just *different*. The outrider for a new era in Van Halen music.
Sounds

● UFO

● SUZANNE VEGA

● STEVIE RAY VAUGHAN

STEVIE RAY VAUGHAN & DOUBLE TROUBLE
Soul To Soul (Epic)
There can be no denying that Stevie Ray *is* heavily into Hendrix and on this ... you can hear the influences clearly ...
Kerrang!

The addition of keyboards and tenor saxophone to Vaughan's pumping-iron Hendrixy power trio has added richness and dimension to his music, as has his greatly improved singing.
NME

Accusations that the man has a Hendrix fixation are, however, ludicrous.
Record Mirror

ALAN VEGA
Just A Million Dreams
(Elektra)
This is much too nice. It's all plasma, no blood.
NME

Billy Idol is much, much funnier.
Record Mirror

By the end of the second side ... one finds oneself not so much begging for mercy as meditating idly on shopping, sex, fixing the fanbelt or dodging the Gas Board.
Melody Maker

SUZANNE VEGA
Suzanne Vega (A&M)
It's comforting, warm and intrinsically female ... rural values seen through urban eyes, sad, broody and wise.
Melody Maker

THE VELVET UNDERGROUND
Velvet Underground Boxed Set (Polydor)
They are essential listening to anyone at all interested in the shape of modern music and remind us of the immense debt owed by virtually anyone worth listening to today to these wracked visionaries.
Melody Maker

All in all, an educative voyage of intense pleasure and equally intense pain.
Beat

Some, if not all, of human life is here.
NME

The trip starts here.
Record Mirror

THE VIBES
What's Inside? (Chainsaw)
... whatever uncharted hinterlands they're patrolling, *What's Inside?* is

a more than adequate statement from a surging, urgent beat combo.
Sounds

... I can well see this sneaking back onto the turntable in the dead of night when no one's watching ...
NME

SID VICIOUS
Love Kills NYC
(Konexion)
... it doesn't matter that the entire band sound like they've swallowed a drug factory; this is the grot that legends are made of.
Sounds

VICTOR VICK
Komputer Kid
(Jones Records – Import)
Victor Vick may sound like a throat lozenge but believe me we're talking future funk.
NME

VIOLENT FEMMES
The Blind Leading The Naked (Slash – Import)
It's just that now the Femmes sound like a band, no longer a force of nature.
Melody Maker

... the music roars with a gale one second only to subside into a cool breeze the next ... Hallelujah and pass the meat cleaver.
Sounds

THE VIRGIN PRUNES
The Moon Looked Down And Laughed (Baby)
The Prunes have been lost so long that lost has become home. And where do they go from there?
NME

● GAVIN FRIDAY: THE VIRGIN PRUNES

W

LOUDON WAINWRIGHT III
I'm Alright (Demon)
He's alright.
Sounds

Loudon? He's alright.
NME

I'm Alright is simply okay, when it should have been just fine.
Melody Maker

JOHN WAITE
Mask of Smiles (EMI America)
Mask Of Smiles is essentially average AOR fodder . . .
Sounds

New Jersey rock 'n' roll. In other words, guitars squeal fearsomely, but everyone wears straight-leg pants, so it's not rockist, it's the New Pop.
Melody Maker

TOM WAITS
Rain Dogs (Island)
Ultimately, the lasting achievement of *Rain Dogs* is that Waits had to sacrifice none of his poetry in pursuit of new musical languages to meets its demands.
NME

. . . an addictive reminder of how special things are.
Beat

His music wraps itself around every American street form there is – jazz, honky tonk, blues, country and so on – while his voice is white-faced Robeson from the bottom of a bottle.
Record Mirror

There used to be a time when it was said that the Devil had all the best tunes. With the releases of *Rain Dogs* he's got some heavy competition.
Sounds

● TOM WAITS

THE WAKE
Here Comes Everybody
(Factory)
This album is, almost without doubt, more interesting than a chicken Oxo Cube but has the disadvantage of being very difficult to crumble into a saucepan . . .
Melody Maker

WALL OF VOODOO
Seven Days In Sammystown
(IRS)
Personally, I can hardly bear to listen to it.
Melody Maker

. . . unlike the people in their songs they take no risks. Perhaps they should.
NME

HANK WANGFORD BAND
Rodeo Radio (Situation Two)
. . . Russ Abbot's skits could have done this just as well. If not better.
Sounds

Don't give up your day job, Hank.
NME

If you find the idea of a sinful, rollerskating Hank being saved by Pentecostal jogging funny – then this album is for you.
Melody Maker

WASP
The Last Command (Capitol)
. . . misanthropic vulgarity.
Melody Maker

I swear fealty to WASP. I am not taking the piss.
Sounds

. . . about as intellectually demanding as belching.
Kerrang!

● STEVE WINWOOD

THE WATERBOYS
This Is The Sea (Ensign)
... it boasts the stolid thump of moral conviction ...
NME

... calming panoramas of tranquillity or stormy crescendos of nightmare. This is the sea and this is the one.
Melody Maker

THE WATERMELON MEN
Past, Present And Future
(What Goes On)
An LP of variety and splendour.
NME

JON WAYNE
Texas Funeral (Hybrid)
Texas Funeral gets worse with every listen ...
NME

It's prime stuff, warts and whiskey notwithstanding.
Sounds

WHAM!
The Final (Epic)
Andrew may be rather terrible at driving and George may be completely *useless* at shaving but these songs ... show just how good they were at being pop stars.
Smash Hits

Fake pop and fake soul; the perfect end to Wham! ... Completely meaningless, but well ... something to do, I s'pose.
NME

Wham! – God bless 'em – were like kissing with your eyes open; a fantasy that wasn't embarrassed by the contradictions of the real world.
Sounds

... four sides that put the full stop on the first half of the Eighties.
Record Mirror

MAURICE WHITE
Maurice White (CBS)
Maurice could be *the* 1985 dental hygiene poster model ... but listening to this is like having teeth pulled.
Sounds

I hereby sentence you to languish in the obscurity of the chart's lower regions until you get your act together.
NME

THE WHO
The Who Collection
(Impression)
This is what would happen if Giorgio Moroder remixed the Sex Pistols' Greatest Hits – stick with the originals.
Record Mirror

The Who *did not make* great records, and a double album is an unnecessary waste of petrochemical by-products.
Sounds

THE WHO SHOULD NOT SOUND LIKE this.
NME

JANE WIEDLIN
Jane Wiedlin (IRS)
Jane is not a super-relevant being or a wonderfully great performer ... but for mindless seaside sand-dancing she's just got to be tops.
Sounds

... she has the oestrogen and the haircut and the chirpiness to give herself an appeal.
NME

THE WINANS
Let My People Go (Quest)
Righteously righteous robust boys ... water down gospel, tailoring it to fit the requirements of some American Christian broadcasting network.
Sounds

... often this is just a lick of gospel varnish sprucing up old soul and pop ideas.
Record Mirror

When you're thoroughly fed up of being told what a decidedly fine fellow The Almighty is, they then start on about your parents, and *their* parents and so on. *"Everybody's granny must be a special lady,"* they tell you as you're reaching for the sickbag.
NME

STEVE WINWOOD
Back In The High Life (Island)
... a collection of cook-as-you-listen songs: ideal American rock background for perfecting paella or getting the rigatoni to separate properly.
Smash Hits

You can appreciate it without caring about it.
Record Mirror

... there's something rather effortless and unthinking about this collection.
NME

... this album's not half bad either.
Sounds

WIRE
Wire Play Pop (Pink)
Big fat fuzz guitars the way the good Lord intended.
Record Mirror

Songs like these should have been the foundation that contemporary pop music was built tall and strong upon. All that was best about the *new wave*.
Melody Maker

WIRE TRAIN
Between Two Words (CBS)
While at heart Wire Train have a certain soul to offer, the gauge seems to have been set firmly towards those . . . oh dear . . . U2 theatrics, and it's steaming up the more enticing Cole holes. Yes, a certain Lloyd-like lyricism leans over the tracks and waves, but Wire Train are too busy drowning in stadium mire to notice.
Sounds

Sometimes it feels like you're in church.
NME

THE WOLFGANG PRESS
The Legendary Wolfgang Press And Other Tall Stories (4AD)
The Wolfgang Press are a shaved Psychedelic Furs for the independent charts, too world weary to be bothered . . .
Record Mirror

● THE WOODENTOPS

The way it moves like a sick, horrible insect – croaks and flurries and nasty, incisive movements – makes it a strangely playful experience.
NME

A matter-of-fact record, as a matter-of-fact, fluent and fierce.
Sounds

BOBBY WOMACK
So Many Rivers (MCA)
A record to turn down the lights, hold hands and get smoochy to.
Beat

If Al Green is intimate, Marvyn Gaye breathless, then Womack's is a large, friendly hug . . .
NME

So what's wrong? Well, er, actually it's the songs. They're not really that good.
Record Mirror

STEVIE WONDER
In Square Circle (Motown)
. . . *In Square Circle* would not be an album to attract new admirers. But then again, it's not as if he needs any.
Record Mirror

. . . Stevie Wonder can be so much better than this.
Smash Hits

. . . positive proof that one of the truly great talents has crumbled to dust and that the blind boy born Steveland Morris must no longer be venerated as the ninth Wonder of the world.
NME

● THE WOODENTOPS
Giant (Rough Trade)
A year ago . . . the Woodentops were pushing and shoving in strange directions, putting a ragged, frayed, playful hand of intent on the child of pop and taking it for a stroll to a netherworld of (a)ghastly delights.
Sounds

. . . is an irreversibly homogenised sound.
NME

. . . make you want to shout words like magic and adorable and glorious.
Melody Maker

● ROBERT WYATT

ROBERT WYATT
Old Rotten Hat (Rough Trade)
The sounds of a man with the weight of the world on his shoulders, wandering through the cloisters, paying penance for who knows what?
Beat

Old Rotten Hat is not an album to listen to in a large group with the lights on and the laughter flowing.
Record Mirror

I can take it or leave it . . .
Melody Maker

By the way, a great record.
NME

X
Ain't Love Grand (Elektra)
X no longer mark the spot.
NME

Exene and John's harmonies are spot-on throughout, while the rest of the band have never sounded so good.
Melody Maker

Y

YEAH YEAH NOH
Cutting The Heavenly Lawn Of Greatness . . . The Last Rites For The God Of Love (In Tape)
They have absolutely no claim to originality, their music is rooted in the worst of the sixties, they even cover a Beatles track.
Melody Maker

. . . this marvy band turn the trivia of pop's past into comments for tomorrow.
Sounds

Fun On The Lawn (Vuggum)
Being the perfect pop group, their demise was inevitable.
NME

YIP YIP COYOTE
Fifi (Illegal)
There is no evidence from this wretched affair that Yip Yip Coyote are even capable of going anywhere but into oblivion.
Melody Maker

They just reek of insincerity.
NME

DWIGHT YOAKAM
Guitars, Cadillacs, Etc Etc (Reprise)
. . . a cut above the 'cripple and trucking' country acts.
Record Mirror

If it's careening kick-start country, a whisky-wise distillation of old forms you need, come round here.
NME

Unlike the bland whimperings of mainstream Nashville, Yoakam's vision of country has its roots in the primitive yelp of Appalachian hillbilly, bluegrass, rockabilly and the vintage honkytonk twang of Buck Owens and Merle Haggard.
Melody Maker

NEIL YOUNG
Old Ways (Geffen)
Let's face it. Neil's a nice guy but he always did sound as though he's played too much grid-iron football with his helmet off.
Record Mirror

. . . in Neil's fingers, rock 'n' roll is dead and gone, pushin' up those daisies bubba!
Kerrang!

Listen here to find out how the West was Young.
Sounds

Landing On Water (Geffen)
He can't be well, and this record mustn't be encouraged. A shocking business really.
Melody Maker

. . . the same old drivel really . . . Neil Young (who used not to support Ronald Reagan) as a born-again Popular Artist isn't going to wash.
NME

Tradition walks hand in hand in the future through emotional sidestreets heavy with moist emotions. A work shaped with genuine skill and vision out of an imagination scarcely eroded by the passing of the years.
Sounds

● ZODIAC MINDWARP

Z

ZENO
Zeno (Parlophone)
And here it is: guitar riffs of our ancestors inlaid with vocals by Aled Jones' younger brother.
Sounds

ZODIAC MINDWARP AND THE LOVE REACTION
High Priest Of Love (Food)
. . . another LP of adequately turgid cock-rock . . . a ridiculously mannered, mildly funny and ultimately useless piece of rock product. Avoid.
NME

. . . over-the-top boyish cock-rock . . . hugely, vainly and hilariously sexist . . . Zodiac Mindwarp and The Love Reaction are crucial and superfluous.
Melody Maker

Zodiac Mindwarp and The Love Reaction are smooth-talking bastards to a man. And their lascivious leers and wicked wit mean they're destined to zap the charts . . . all Zodiac wants to do is put his love gun in your mouth and blow your head off. Your finger is on the trigger.
Sounds

ZZ TOP
Afterburner (Warner Bros)
An album for the most dedicated fans only.
Beat

This album should never be too far out of your reach.
Record Mirror

Afterburner will get you in its clutches and lead you to highway heaven . . .
Sounds

Did you know you can dance to every track on this album? All of 'em. Even the slow one . . .
Kerrang!

SINGLES

One could be forgiven for thinking that any twelve months that started with the dreary and uninspired 'Axel F' and ended with a dreary and uninspired cover of a dreary and uninspired sixties sedative were, er, ... well, the words dreary and uninspired spring to mind. Not so, pop fans. The charts provided overwhelming evidence that the body pop is alive and well and still cocking a snook at its undertakers, 'Spirit In The Sky' notwithstanding. Nor is it necessary to penetrate the realms of obscure club hits from the Soho preen scene (heard by the only six people and an azure poodle who happened not to be in the loo at the time) or the equally obscure sub-indie backwoods (enthusiasm, 50p and an electric cheese grater) to prove the point. Honours were shared by a remarkably democratic bunch of toilers, chancers, fifteen-second merchants, stars, dead stars and lively newcomers. Similarly, the basic tunes were served up in a variety of guises throughout the pop/rock/soul/electro spectrum, with the occasional dash of reggae and (whisper it) modern folk to vary the tone. And just to prove that Satan was in his chariot and all was right with the world, one could usually catch the distant echo of honest headbanging from the lower depths of the charts.

The two artist(e)s who perhaps enjoyed the greatest success of the period shared no other similarities. Madonna carried on where she left off, only more so. August '85 saw her keeping herself away from the top spot with 'Into The Groove' and 'Holiday', while 'Crazy For You' was still loitering in the Top Twenty. Subsequently, 'Angel', 'Gambler', 'Dress You Up', 'Borderline', 'Live To Tell' and 'Papa Don't Preach' were all major hits. It appeared not to matter that some of this material was rank album filler stuff: show the public a Madonna single and they showed you their money. Slick marketing apart, the major reason for this state of affairs was that Madonna achieved a peak of media saturation which has rarely been equalled: the Marriage, the Film Star (of sorts) and (permanently out of sorts) Husband, the Rows, the Nude Photographs, the Film, the Jogging, the Sunglasses, the Other Film, the Colour of Nail Varnish. Faced with a steady diet of this sort, the average punter had to go out and buy a few of her singles just to retain a small grip on reality. It is also possible that they simply couldn't remember anyone else's name.

None of which should detract from the fact that Madonna produced some great music over the period. Using material from several different writers (even some that was, how shall one say, self-penned) and a string of producers (yes, Nile included), she retained a firm identity based on sound choice of songs and, mostly, her voice. Originally derided as the owner of a less than perfect set of pipes (much in the same way as Diana Ross during her early career), Madonna once more demonstrated that good voices obey only one rule: that they be appealing and distinctive. (The virgin/whore theory of Madonna appears in some other publication.) Whether or not the records arrived on a tidal wave of bullshit, they were, in the main, well worth that initial discomfort.

The Pet Shop Boys came in smaller and different doses.

Whereas Madonna had the outrageous allure of someone who takes stardom for granted, Chris Lowe and Neil Tennant exuded all the confidence and charm of a pair of instant passport snapshots. Their early TV appearances redefined the word 'diffidence': if the medium was the message, then the message was, 'We're in the wrong medium'. Which indeed they were. The Pet Shop Boys were an aural experience, whether it be listening to their music or the rumours which multiplied as to the derivation of their name (hamsters *where*?!). Bounding in on a bed of springy synth-pop, the tunes walked a giddy tightrope between the wistful and the cheeky and finally achieved an effect of suburban

● MADONNA

exhilaration. We were not in the presence of Something New, merely some good old chords with a surpassingly neat twist. The Pet Shop Boys, and in particular Neil Tennant, knew far too much about the pop process to go in for the big splash in the press, and in this sense were obviously pre-Madonna. And may well be post, to boot. Whatever, 'West End Girls', 'Love Comes Quickly' and 'Opportunities (Let's Make Lots Of Money)' were specific enough to be universal (ie they went down well in America, too).

While Madonna's appeal was ubiquitous and the Pet Shop Boys' was musical (let's face it, boys, the visages are an acquired taste), the true teeny pleasers had a less than convincing year. A-ha were the faces on everyone's lips in the last twelve months, a fashionably cadaverous trio from Norway (to the right and up a bit) who settled in London to get a better view of our beautiful music business. Their first single – 'Take On Me' – was released three times, before, with the aid of the obligatory clever video, it gave them the desired result. At this point, Mags, Morten and Pål really hit their stride with headlining appearances at every newsagents in the country, personal appearances on many bedroom walls and a fan club in every playground. All this and more records too . . . 'The Sun Always Shines On TV' was a surprisingly noisy follow-up success while 'Train Of Thought' pursued a more downbeat approach, which was unfortunately reflected in its chart placing. At the time of writing, 'Hunting High And Low', the title ballad from the group's debut album, is going much the same way. Much depends on the next batch of new videos, sorry, songs. While A-ha are obviously visually suited to the role of teen idol, their material seems to sit a little uncomfortably in the teeny lap.

Certainly A-ha have got a lot of grinning and nodding to do before they threaten the achievements of the Wham! dynasty, which came to a ritual end in June. George 'n' George 'n' Andy maintained an effortless grip on the charts whenever they deigned to release a record. 'I'm Your Man' took care of the jolly Christmas period, while the cruel month of April gave us 'A Different Corner', notable on two counts: it was the first chart-topper in living memory to have no trace whatsoever of a melody or a hook; it was accompanied by a video which gave the most complete performance to date of active vulnerability. Finally (some hope), 'Edge Of Heaven'

● WHAM!

has kept a low profile. King were overthrown. And what of that golden-throated, swivel-hipped warbler from the Valleys? I refer, of course, to Shakin' Stevens who kicked off the year in sprightly style with 'Lipstick, Powder And Paint', pushed out the obligatory Christmas single and then . . . nothing. Which also sums up the output of last year's bright young things, Go West. Is this, one wonders, the perfect time for a Roaring Boys comeback?

Two British male artists who did make an impression on the charts shared a similar background in the second wave of punk, but chose diametrically opposite ways of relaunching themselves. Feargal Sharkey was the distinctive vibrato voice of the Undertones, an obdurately anti-style outfit whose increasingly irresistible music was increasingly re-sisted by the public at large. Finally, teamed with fashionably bearded Dave Stewart of the Eurythmics as producer, the clean-shaven Feargal eased into a smoother style and was immediately rewarded by a monster hit in the shape of 'A Good Heart', a song written by Lone Justice vocalist Maria McKee. 'You Little Thief' consolidated his position, but further alarmed the traditionalists who feared yer man was sliding down to the West Coast. At the other extreme, Billy Idol swapped his career as a sneering punk with Generation X for a career as a sneering punk without them. Both his hits, 'White Wedding' and 'Rebel Yell', were old potatoes by the time they reached the charts, but Billy and, in particular, Billy's feelthy videos, have made black leather/blonde sex

● FALCO

gave Andy his chance to reprise some of that zen guitar frenzy which made his name, while giving George time to ponder his next step: full beard or just stubble? At the very least, Wham! deserve our respect for being able to shake their booty and count it simultaneously without being too obnoxious.

Elsewhere, the teen dreams of yesterdays had something of a thin time of it. Duran Duran appeared content to remain inert, leaving the chore of making records to the Power Station and Arcadia, about either of whom it is quite impossible to find anything to say. Spandau Ballet, having been locked in legal tussles, had more excuse for the leisurewear life, and the threatened comeback had not materialised at press time. Nik Kershaw made an early showing with 'Don Quixote', since when the diminutive one

indispensable to the modern household.

Which leads us neatly into Europop. Time was when that meant Abba and the occasional bunch of nutters from Holland, but no more. The last year has witnessed a growth in the species which can only be put down to some Brussels edict forcing us to have a certain amount in the charts at any given time. Austria began and ended the year in some style, first giving us Opus with their unfathomable (and unlisten-able) 'Live Is Life' and then Falco with 'Rock Me Amadeus' and 'Vienna Calling'. Holland chipped in with Mai Tai and their uncanny Chic impersonations, 'History' and 'Body And Soul', while Nana Mouskouri harked back to earlier Euro-days on 'Only Love'. As well as A-ha, Norway gave us Fra Lippo Lippi, while Switzerland roused itself from centuries-old indifference (Yello excepted) to provide 'The Captain Of Her Heart' by the

● ANNIE LENNOX ● ARETHA FRANKLIN

● KATE BUSH ● COLONEL ABRAMS

Swiss Navy. Sorry, by Double. The expected comeback by Plastic Bertrand did not take place.

Alongside the phenomenon of Europop, which naturally tends to ape its sources, was the phenomenon of the cover version which instinctively cannibalises its own history. The cover version falls into three categories: first and most rare is the one which brings to light a good song that had otherwise been lost or ignored; second is the one which treats a known song to an effective new arrangement or depth of performance; third is the one which leaves less than it found and should therefore be destroyed. There were no examples of the first, plenty of the second (notably Simply Red's 'Money's Too Tight (To Mention)' and the Damned's 'Eloise') and too many of the last (but a mention to the Far Corporation for managing to inject new death into 'Stairway To Heaven'). There should also be a mention for Sigue Sigue Sputnik, media darlings, for issuing a cover version of their first single under another title as their second. Straight reissues are another matter altogether: if it's good and you don't have it, buy it; if it's not and you don't, then don't; if it is and you have, don't; etc etc. The fact is that 'Wonderful World' and 'Heard It Through The Grapevine' hardly fouled up the charts and one would rather have the originals anyway than wait for Bananarama to get round to them.

The genuine upwardly-mobile chanteuse, meanwhile, was performing her own material, or at least that composed

● WHITNEY HOUSTON

specifically with her in mind. Proving that sometimes there is simply no substitute for class and pedigree, Diana Ross swept magisterially to the top of the charts with the excellent 'Chain Reaction', a song written by the venerable Brothers Gibb. A true diva for the eighties appeared in the shape of Whitney Houston coolly inflating decent ballads like 'Saving All My Love For You' to levels of teeth-grinding emotion. Unfortunately, the emotion thus far has been self-love. Sometime Queen of Soul Aretha Franklin showed distinctly regal touches both on her own with 'Who's Zoomin Who' and with Annie Lennox on 'Sisters Are Doing It For Themselves'. (The Eurythmics themselves had a solid but not startling year with the likes of 'There Must Be An Angel' and 'It's Alright'.) Down at the sharp end of the singles bar, Janet Jackson, a more life-like version of absent brother Michael, snarled fetchingly through a couple of disco dramas – 'What Have You Done For Me Lately' and 'Nasty' – without giving any indication of a third dimension. Kate Bush gave every indication of a fifth dimension and once more proved that there is life in a musical vacuum with a trio of singles from her *Hounds of Love* album, including the blissfully quirky 'Running Up That Hill'.

Male solo artists, particularly on the soul side of the tracks, had a somewhat thinner time of it. Stevie Wonder managed a decent hit with 'Part-Time Lover', which had a marvellously lazy rhythm, an infectious tune and was indubitably second-rate Wonder. Colonel Abrams' 'Trapped' juddered along in an endearingly old-fashioned manner and came emblazoned with the legend 'One Hit Wonder' (no relation). In a similarly old-fashioned vein, Billy Ocean continued to find a huge audience for his lime-green flared pop soul. 'Suddenly', 'When The Going Gets Tough, The Tough Get Going' and 'There'll Be Sad Songs (To Make You Cry)' proved the benefits of being unfashionably non-aligned. Lionel Richie speeded up his decline into mawkish balladry with 'Say You, Say Me': the man who used to be a Commodore now plays music for yacht clubs. The all-singing, all-dancing (and that's just his trousers) James Brown made a welcome reappearance, albeit with a sliver of watery gong-beating from *Rocky IV* – 'Living In America'. Alexander O'Neal made his chart debut courtesy of 'If You Were Here Tonight', faintly reminiscent of late period Marvin Gaye and faintly okay. The best shot by far came from Simply Red and 'Holding Back The Years', a ballad of effortless class which gave new meaning to the term 'Northern Soul'. The fact remained, however, that the likes of Teddy Pendergrass and Michael Lovesmith who ought to be delivering smoothly powerful soul classics at this stage in their careers, simply do not have strong enough material to work with, now that the heyday of the great songwriting factories is well and truly over. Thank heavens that some chaps are still content to remain in groups: best tingly moments by far came from Kool & the Gang – 'Cherish' – and the SOS Band – 'The Finest'.

It would appear that the advertising industry has taken out a patent on the public performance of anything in the rap/scratch/break/hip hop/electro/funk/DJ school of tough, black (mostly), urban noise. The sad little mutant strain that accompanies ads for almost anything is just about all most people hear. It does not help that daytime radio offers little or no exposure to the sounds of young New York going apeshit. The records which did make the charts tended towards the overtly humorous end of the genre: 'The Show' by Doug E Fresh and the Get Fresh Crew (not to be confused with the 'Theme From Connie'); '(Nothing Serious) Just Buggin'' from Whistle; 'Amityville (The House On The Hill)' by Lovebug Starski. The best of the lot came late in the year in the shape of the Real Roxanne's '(Bang Zoom) Let's Go-Go' which

● BILLY OCEAN

● IT'S IMMATERIAL

● JANET JACKSON

● SIMPLY RED

● SAMANTHA FOX

● JOHN LYDON

boasted a list of ingredients that included the kitchen sink. Perhaps in the next twelve months, the likes of Run DMC, LL Cool J, the Beastie Boys, Mantronix (who had a near hit with 'Bassline') and the Fat Boys will make the break and the charts will get lethal.

It was a good solid year for AOR. It always is a good solid year for AOR. Bruce Springsteen saved rock 'n' roll thirty-three times, aided by a relentlessly plodding beat, hoarse vocals and one song with many titles. Dire Straits continued to work that seam with a series of mogadon-flavoured ditties, including one (with the added attraction of Sting in its tail) called 'Money For Nothing' which kicked off with the riff from 'Jumpin' Jack Flash', played flat. Virtuoso stuff. Speaking of which, Sting brought extra jazz probity to his output for the year and didn't sell nearly as many records. In comedy corner, Starship gave us 'We Built This City (On Rock 'n' Roll)', which had recklessly exceeded its sell-by date by about fifteen years. Not to be outdone, Marillion whacked out a couple of slow belters – 'Kayleigh' and 'Lavender' – which had the denim hordes blubbing in their light 'n' bitters. Not a pretty sight, but then neither were Mr Mister, who were doing the same sort of thing even more lugubriously.

On the plus side, Talking Heads reaped the rewards of their best album in ages, while the late lamented B52s scored with their first single, seven years after its initial release. Robert Palmer and Peter Gabriel each proved the value of good production on 'Addicted To Love' and 'Sledgehammer', the latter making clever use of the guitar line from 'Superstition'. Van Halen, minus David Lee Roth, made a welcome return with their sparky metal pop, although 'Why Can't This Be Love' was hardly vintage. Iron Maiden's 'Running Free' was so good it doesn't bear talking about. And before we leave the AOR arena, a mystery. Someone out there is buying Queen records by the truckload. The question is, who are they?

The basis for a good year in singles, however, is in the one-offs: three minutes of the right stuff from whatever quarter. The last twelve months was packed with them and here's a few in no particular order: Propaganda's resonant 'Duel'; Cameo's 'Single Life' (dodgy lyrics, though); Grace Jones' insistent 'Slave To The Rhythm; 'Just Like Honey' from the cuddly Jesus And Mary Chain; Sophia George's 'Girlie Girlie'; 'Rise' by Public Image; 'Love Missile F1-11' by Sigue Sigue Sputnik; Prince and the Revolution's extraordinary 'Kiss'; the whimsically evocative 'Driving Away From Home' by It's Immaterial; 'Brilliant Mind' from Furniture. There were others.

It was, finally, a successful year for British artists. Solid performers such as Level 42, UB40, Big Country, Simple Minds, Midge Ure and anyone who was ever in Genesis all scored consistently. Five Star showed the world that America does not have a monopoly on slick family routines via the spectacular success of 'System Addict' and 'Can't Wait Another Minute'. Bronski Beat enjoyed life after Somerville and the Art of Noise demonstrated how to make novelty records without sending folk screaming for the toolbox. Late in the year, the Housemartins proved that it is still possible for indiepop to go right to the top.

This homegrown success was by no means insular: at the time of writing, Simply Red, Howard Jones, Genesis, Peter Gabriel and the Moody Blues (?!) were all lodged high in the US charts. Perhaps the most significant breakthrough, however, was achieved by a diminutive, ex-topless model, who combined all the finest elements of Madonna, early-period Donna Summer and Wendy O Williams. Samantha Fox donned a pair of tattered jeans and unleashed a massive pair of hits on an unsuspecting populace. 'Touch Me (I Want Your Body)' and 'Do Ya Do Ya (Wanna Please Me)' may not, in the strictest sense, be touched with genius, but trash just doesn't come any finer.

Pete Clark

BRUCE SPRINGSTEEN

Look, this is difficult. Bruce Springsteen has been designated an Act of the Year again. He's the first to make it twice. That's fine in itself. Let Bruce's joy be unconfined, you know. He's the Greatest Pop Artist In The World as far as I'm concerned, which means a bit greater than people and bands like Aretha Franklin, Little Feat, Randy Newman, Ian Dury and Talking Heads. But not only that: I think Springsteen is one of the Greatest Anykindof Artists In The World (alive, active, that I know of . . . not an over-extravagant claim, is it?), along with Woody Allen, Marlon Brando, John Cleese, Miles Davis, Torville & Dean, Saul Bellow, Billy Connolly... but my problem, loving his work and unable to make any very convincing distinction in my perceptions between that and his character, is a tendency to revere my heroes. Probably the downside of atheism. Anyway, I come to praise Springsteen, not to bury him under a pile of crap. These are some of the reasons why I hold him in such high regard.

Not for being called 'The Boss'
Which half-wit thought that one up? Which lame-brained conspiracy between the marketing men, the media and we-the-fans perpetuated it? In fact, does anybody who really likes Springsteen call him 'The Boss'? I only call people I detest 'The Boss', and then it's when they're not listening – otherwise they might get notions.

For being called Springsteen
'Springsteen' is good. A-hiss and a-clatter with sibilants and plosives. 'Jump' and 'stone', I'd imagine, in his dad's ancestral Dutch. Names do have their place in the way you respond to people, irrational as that may be. 'Bruce' I suppose I've got used to despite the associations with joke Australians and nasty Bruce King, the school bully who tore me apart out on the street when I was 14.

Not for his guitar playing
Because I can never tell which bit's him. For instance, the lovely Old Testament kerrang-a-twang in 'Adam Raised A Cain' – is that Springsteen or Miami Steve? Gawd knows.

For his words
Nearly always and profoundly. To start at the top, 'Racing In The Street' is the most powerful song lyric I know. The development from the opening auto-nut patter, *"I got a '69 Chevy with a 396/ Fuelie heads and a Hurst on the floor"*, to the final longed-for purgation of disappointed lives and love, *"Tonight my baby and me, we're gonna ride to the sea/and wash these sins off our hands"*, there isn't a false syllable. It's both raw and highly wrought, utterly beautiful.

Springsteen has always reached for such heights. Even on *Born in the USA*, which is generally thought of as more straight-ahead and even contrived as a row of hit singles, the key metaphor is "dancing in the *dark*". It's got closer than the edge of town. The whole world is out there just trying to score. Cover me, cover me, cover me . . . now if Robert Smith would forget about fright haircuts perhaps he'd be able to let that much fear loose in a chartbuster too.

On the other hand, Springsteen is quite capable of lyrical clangers, the 'simple' man rattling. 'Drive All Night' is magnificent, one of my favourite tracks, but the words of the chorus are conspicuously naff: *"I swear I'll drive all night/just to buy you some shoes/and to taste your tender charms"*. Cripes. Most of the time though he doesn't let his vast knowledge of and fondness for rock 'n' roll cliché take him by the throat like that.

Not for being born in the USA
I've always loved America (as in the heart rather than on the T-shirt), but being born there would seem to be as much bane as blessing. Despite wilful or pea-brained misinterpretations, that's what Springsteen was acknowledging in the title song and overall drift of *Born in the USA* and he is very unusual among current American pop artists in doing so. At 37 on 23 September 1986, there is not the slightest hint of Reagan-era intellectual and emotional torpor settling on him.

For being born in Freehold, New Jersey
Certainly! Freehold! The right stuff from the right place!

Not because he counts Van Morrison a major influence
It's odd. Nearly everyone I like thinks Van Morrison is wonderful. He strikes me as a stylist with nothing to say. This must be A Matter Of Taste. Difference of opinion makes horse-racing and doesn't do any harm at all to the arts crit industry.

For his singing
Perhaps more than anything else. His direct way, without mannerism, driven by passion, guided by deep honesty, is encapsulated in the half-minute of 'Drive All Night' that it takes him to sing the perfectly apt phrase *"heart and soul"* four times. It's naked and this makes some people ashamed. Their great-grandmothers blushed at table legs.

It's hard (and barely fruitful) to try to distinguish your responses to voice and word, but sometimes Springsteen clarifies matters because he's a great whooper and wailer (a male counterpart to Aretha). The lifeblood *"Yeah!"* at the start of 'Hungry Heart' or the black *"Hoooooo"* at the end of 'Something In The Night' are pure sound-as-emotion. The sound of joy, the sound of pain, the very essence.

Not for the holes in the knees of his jeans
That's for sure. A *Born in the USA* period aberration I expect. Torn jeans are *very* dubious chic. Nobody but the Ramones can carry it off for real these days and that's only because they're cartoon characters. For rock 'n' roll millionaires holey knees should be a definite no-no. Or, indeed, for anyone who can afford a decent pair of trousers. A generation of hippies proved there's something undignified, if not plain silly, about wearing out clothes before you wear them. Blue-collar people don't do it. They want value for their money. But maybe that's what Springsteen was worried about, his blue-collar connection, and he was looking for a sign to give them and got it wrong.

For his looks
Mm, somewhat. I wouldn't mind looking like Springsteen. My girlfriend wouldn't mind me looking like Springsteen. I do have the 7¾" hat size to be going on with. But really these days he's a bit too Italian for me (his mother coming out in him) – and young. I'd rather look like Clint Eastwood. That would see me out.

Not for his 'raps'
Or not recently at any rate. They sounded good on seventies live bootlegs, very funny, the natural tale-teller's enchantment. In '85 though, when I saw him in London and Newcastle, they had acquired the mannerism of embarrassment, a peppering of little false-note chuckles. Not as if he *was* embarrassed, you understand, but as if he felt he *ought* to be. It might have been the stadia that did it. When playing he handles them perfectly, not intimidated in the slightest, but perhaps when he talks there's a tic of uneasy humility nagging at him, saying it's just *too* godlike to chat comfortably to such a mass of people – leading him to the

mistaken and, for Springsteen, uniquely untypical conclusion that it might be effective to do your job badly.

For his live shows
Very much, because I like troupers. The quality, of course, is extraordinary. But I'm still impressed by feeling the width. Six till ten. Good grief. I paid for my tickets, yet it felt like a gift. This reminds me that, contrary to pop tradition, he's never had a degenerate streak, still less any leaning to self-destruction. Contrast: Keith Richards making legend out of staying up for four days, Springsteen out of playing for four hours (both work, I do realise).

Not for 'Nebraska'
By all means it's very brave to undertake such a 'radical departure' from what's expected and I do 'respect' him for it. I never play the record though, ergo I can't truly like it except in a professional-critic way.

For his dancing
Bravo! Encore! This man is not a natural mover but he *likes* to dance. He's determined to dance. He is Everyman dancing in front of 70,000, and if he can do that he makes me feel more confident about, ahem, cutting a rug.

Not for his production
Despite pseudo-erudite comments I may have made on the subject over the several years I earned much of my living as a record reviewer I still have no real idea of what difference a producer makes. It's the orchestra/conductor conundrum, made all the more impenetrable with Landau, Plotkin and Van Zandt co-credited as well as Springsteen.

For his music
It appears that the E Street Band play to the beat of my bloodstream. Scientifically proven by elaborate checks on pulse rate, volume of sweat shed, hairs stood on end. A very physical experience whether in their flat-out wall-of-sound vein or ruminating around piano and sax. Fellow journos who've spent time backstage at Springsteen shows have told me awestruck anecdotes of the road crew's efficiency and how this gives them time to be polite and considerate to one another and to outsiders. A touch Nissan perhaps, but the band's performance may be the ultimate company hymn, collective great art. The dedication, including Springsteen's, is not to the star but to the music. Eye-on-the-ball. Very unusual.

Not for his thing about cars
Though I don't mind it. They're just a vehicle, aren't they? I'm more interested in the drivers, but then so is Springsteen. The Car Factor is something anti-Brucers use to rationalise what they find hard to take about him – such as gut emotion, I'd suggest.

For his politics
Unimpeachably. Rock is one of the popular arts that makes you rich if you succeed. For a person with a worldview such as Springsteen expresses in his music this is both a pleasure (he never romanticises poverty) and a trial of conscience (his songs refer to the wealthy, mostly factory owners, only as faceless, heartless exploiters and thieves of life). He has set about finding his own answer with a clear head and considerable energy. At most concerts on his '85 international tour he gave large sums to *local* political causes. He's backed No Nukes Music, USA For Africa, Live Aid and Miami Steve's 'Ain't Gonna Play Sun City' campaign. More recently he's been involved with the launch of Jersey Artists For Mankind and perhaps that will be the cause to really fill the bill for him.

I can't think that, in making his choices, he's even flipped through anybody's manifesto. Nothing about himself that he's made public even hints at dogmatic inclinations. But I take 'My Hometown' as his fundamental political statement. Sorrow for what is lost, every day, ordinarily. It's a bad time. Hope, because he believes what we have had once can and should be regained. The 'regained' would apply equally to Freehold and Ethiopia. That 'darkness' at the edge of his songs implies he is philosophically a pessimist. But he seems to fight back against his own bleakest perspectives with political optimism, politically optimistic action. His effect on his audience, rather like Geldof's, is inspirational precisely because he doesn't pull any punches. Think: while Stallone was Ramboing around Vietnam to revamp history in the American mass consciousness, Springsteen's *Born in the USA* was drawing lines between Khe Sahn, unemployment, wasted life, and generally bringing Kurtz's apocalyptic *"The horror, the horror"* all back home.

That's enough reasons. Except to say that the aggregate of all this is reliability, trustworthiness. This doesn't necessarily mean I'm going to like his next record. It means much more than that.
Phil Sutcliffe

A-HA

Suddenly last summer, there appeared a pop group who captured the imagination of the world's youth in a way unheard of since... well, who? The Beatles? The Monkees? The Osmonds? A-ha were suddenly the biggest pop group *ever*, conjured up as if out of nowhere.

They weren't from nowhere of course, just Norway. Pål (pronounced Paul) Waaktaar and Magne (Mags for short) Furuholmen grew up in the Oslo suburb of Manglerud and, shortly after their tenth birthdays, started playing music together. It was probably Pål's idea – he was after all already a dab hand at the recorder and the one who decided to build his own drum kit because he wanted to write a musical like *Hair* (clearly a *confused* youngster).

They started writing together, swapping their favourite records – by Deep Purple, Jimi Hendrix, the Beatles and the Doors – and being very adolescent. Once they quarrelled while travelling through Europe and communicated with each other only through song lyrics. Another time, in an interview with a local paper when they were 16, they announced they'd soon be "hugely famous rock stars", something that Norway, by tradition, simply doesn't produce. "They laughed us out of school," remembers Mags.

Presumably, then, they got laughed at some more when they formed their first serious band, Bridges. Their one self-financed LP, with its *Revolver*-esque cover of a black-and-white collage, awful haircuts and lots of Norwegian scribbling, and its "almost symphonic" sub-Doors music, hardly set Norway, let alone the rest of the world, on fire. But instead of giving up they resolved to seek fame and fortune in London, dumping the other, rather more reluctant members, Viggo and Oystein, on the way. On arrival they quickly discovered that the streets are hardly paved with gold for *any* unknown band, let alone a 'pop group' made up of two Norwegians without work permits who'd demonstrate their songs by Mags plonking away on a cheap synthesiser, Pål strumming an acoustic guitar and the two of them humming the melodies. After six months of this folly the £2,000 they had saved was gone and they hitched home through the rain . . .

Back in Norway they met up with Morten Harket, a singer who had spent his childhood living a bizarre fantasy life and lying constantly, and who had discovered music when he was three after weeing on the shoulder of the conductor of the local Kongsberg brass band, an experience that was doubtless amplified by an adolescence filled with Uriah Heep albums. Mags had more or less asked him to join the group the year before but Morten was enjoying the soul/blues band he was in, Souldier Blue, too much. Now, however, he changed his mind, they retreated to Pål's parents' summer cabin in Asker to write songs and live off stolen plums (which the deeply religious Morten refused on principle) and then set back out for England with their new name, A-ha (the title of one of the songs spotted by Morten in Pål's notebook).

Convinced they'd have a hit "by the summer", they bought the *Melody Maker Yearbook* and Virgin's *Rock Yearbook* and phoned up every record company they could find. "When we used to tell people we were from Norway," said Pål later, with considerable resentment, "they just laughed." But, of course, they were getting used to that and just persevered all the more. Finally, they got a management contract with a company called Lionheart, but they were useless and A-ha soon retreated to their squalid flat – to stray cats, a pet mouse, a sole lightbulb and the remains of sandwiches filled with spaghetti, cabbage or just salt and pepper – until, after a row, Mags shoved Morten's head through a window.

Morten left and moved in with the bizarre–nightlife-entrepreneur-in-very-daft-clothes, Steve Strange, until the tiff blew over.

And then things started going right. They booked into a place called Rendezvous studios to record some demos and the owner John Ratcliff called up his mate, Terry Slater. Suddenly they had a manager. Before long they had a record contract too, with Warner Bros, their advance of £125,000 reputedly upped in stages from £25,000 because Slater got his friends in other companies (who *weren't* impressed by A-ha) to feign interest. They recorded a whole album with Tony Mansfield (the synthesiser specialist producer who had masterminded New Musik) and released their catchiest song, 'Take On Me', as a single, doubtless confident it would go to number one all round the world. It sold 30+ copies.

Unperturbed, they tried again, re-recording the song with Alan Tarney (the producer famous for his work with Cliff Richard and Leo Sayer who was also a mate of Slater's and who had been their original choice) and shooting a £30,000 video with naked girls in, doubtless confident that *now* it would go to number one all round the world. But it didn't. It flopped disastrously. Again. Disconsolate, they split up and Pål flew off to stay with his neuroscience student girlfriend, Lauren, in America. While there he phoned the Warner Bros head office, expecting to hear confirmation that A-ha had been dropped. Except that they hadn't been. In fact, the man on the other end of the line couldn't stop saying how they "loved A-ha". "You're our top priority group," Pål was told. "We're going to have a new video made of 'Take On Me' and it's going to be fantastic."

And so it was. Four months of editing and over £100,000 later the Steve Barron-directed semi-animated video in which A-ha (who had conveniently forgotten about splitting up) appeared and disappeared from the pages of a girl's comic, gave them the boost they needed. Three weeks before the American release of 'Take On Me', MTV was given the video – by the time it was in the shops there was an audience waiting for them. A few weeks later it was number one.

Unbelievably, things still didn't run so smoothly in the UK. The record still tottered precariously at the edge of the charts for weeks – until Radio 1 intervened. Then it shot to number two for three weeks (kept off the top spot by the year's biggest-selling record, Jennifer Rush's 'The Power Of Love'), and magazines like *Smash Hits* were besieged with letters about this group who, on the strength of one record, were voted Best New Act, Best Video and Second Best Single in the end of year polls. A-ha had finally made it. How could they fail to be anything but pleased?

Quite easily, as it happens. "We want to be as big as possible," muttered Pål that December, the three of them seemingly unimpressed by the fact that 'Take On Me' had finally gone to number one all round the world. That, their attitude suggested, was the very least they could expect. "We're going to take it as far as we can. Would we like to be the biggest band in the world? Yes. And we'll do everything we can to get there."

"We've always modelled ourselves on the Beatles," explained Mags, who had the previous month boasted that when Decca turned down A-ha it was "their second biggest mistake ever", their rejection of the Beatles being the first. "They had tremendous commercial success initially so that whatever they did afterwards they had the whole world listening to them. That's the path we would like to try."

If that sounded impossibly arrogant after just one hit, it at least sounded a tiny bit more reasonable after three more: 'The Sun Always Shines On TV', 'Train Of Thought' and 'Hunting High And Low'. And if someone had protested that these were not particularly timeless or brilliant works, A-ha could have pointed to 'Love Me Do' and 'Please Please Me' and asked whether that was really a handicap.

Whatever, the national press, who had been waiting years and years for a story as good as Beatlemania, eagerly jumped on the idea, even if they couldn't quite decide who was John, who was Paul and so on, and even if "A-ha Gaga", as one paper feebly suggested, didn't quite have the right ring to it. At least A-ha had *characters:* Morten, the singer with the dreamy eyes who supposedly makes everyone (of both sexes) swoon, but who claims to prefer climbing trees, growing orchids and reading the Bible; Mags, the 'lad', who is always dressed in denim, clowns around, makes the 'wisecracks' and tnrows the bangers under the table; and Pål, the musical mastermind, the pale, quiet, serious one who'd never kissed a girl until he was 18 (and even then it was Mags' girlfriend).

Maybe it was these qualities that made A-ha so popular with their audience as well. After all it surely couldn't just have been the *songs?*

Not that they were at all bad, but few even of the fans seemed to harp on about them; and as for Pål's lyrics ... His confession that they're "all about being in love for the first time in my life ... all the songs on the album were written in an attempt to secure a place in Lauren's heart for me ... every single song is a prayer for attention" definitely seemed to ring true. Certainly lines like *"Stumbling away/slowly learning that life is okay"* or *"Oh the*

things that you say/is it life or just a play" from 'Take On Me' might have been better left in the privacy of his transatlantic love letters.

And if their appeal was partly down to Morten's rich operatic voice – just about A-ha's only distinctive feature – it's unlikely that that was as important as the way their personalities were sold individually (each fan can have a favourite) and the fact that they're all quite good-looking (though not as good-looking as many new bands, and old pictures, especially Morten's long-haired Neanderthal passport photo, rather belie his claim that "we can't change the way we look"). What *they* want, however, explained Mags, at the press conference they rather grandiosely held to announce their world tour, is respect – "we have to gain

respect and respect gains you longevity."

It's presumably to this end that, since the first single, they've done no interviews with any of the pop magazines their fans read (manager Terry Slater constantly reiterating his theory that less press is better as though he'd just carelessly skimmed through a guide to the Michael Jackson/Prince/Madonna school of generating publicity via unavailability); they prefer the odd appearance on *Wogan*, Morten chatting amiably with Terry about Norwegian culinary delicacies (quite how *this* swells 'respect' ...). Admittedly, for the moment, it's working – A-ha are selling records (though not yet in truly huge amounts), filling concerts and driving the post office bonkers. But they also seem to be fooling themselves if they really think they're heading for this strange, rather serious 'respect' as purposefully as they pretend.

"I think it's a credit to Warner Brothers," said Morten at that world tour press conference, "that they did not exploit us with our faces plastered all over magazines until it was a hit ... "

... 'Take On Me' was widely advertised with pictures of the band on all three releases and finally packaged in a deluxe poster-book pin-up sleeve – A-ha did so many photo sessions before it was a hit that even today they're still surfacing ...

" ... they could have done it the safe way ... "

... 'The Sun Always Shines On TV' was released in two different 12" forms, one with a free poster, and also as a sun-shaped picture disc ...

" ... and got their hit ... "

... 'Train Of Thought' was available as a limited edition 12" single with a free poster and as a train-shaped picture disc with A-ha's faces on one side ...

" ... but that would have caused a lot of problems for us ... "... 'Hunting High And Low' could be bought in the shops in three 12" versions, one with a Pål poster, one with a Mags poster and one with a Morten poster. Fans who wanted all three posters had to buy three copies of the record ...

" ... we have been told that we have pin-up potential and that can be a big problem if you're serious about the music ... "

Hmmmm ...

Chris Heath

WHITNEY HOUSTON

There aren't many stories in pop music where Big Hits dovetail with All The Right Reasons. But in Whitney Houston's case, they do. That puts on awful lot of extra pressure on all the other players – but, after all, at stake was the making of the *première* female pop vocalist of the mid-eighties.

The what?! In point of fact, the five-million-and-counting sales of *Whitney Houston* do quantify a magnitude of success that will likely be greater than any single album by the multi-platinum competition: Tina Turner, Cyndi Lauper, Sade, and, yeah, even Madonna. But in other important ways, Whitney Houston is proving herself to be *the* class of the field.

It's not a terrible thing to say that Whitney was sold brilliantly, or that, like Lionel Richie, she is the perfect yuppie product. It would be terrible to say that the phenomenon was a sham, but there have been no false steps so far. The first Arista ads appearing in *Billboard* allowed the consumer press to predict that Houston would be a star. They didn't have her show vast amounts of skin, though she'd been a model. In a sadly atypical case (for the record business) of allowing a woman's merit to speak for itself, the industry, the critics, the public, were told in a low-key, dignified way: Hey, listen to this. And just see if you don't find it fine and genuine.

Arista has had lots of experience with classy women: *both* of Houston's much-noted relatives, cousin Dionne Warwick and "Aunt Ree", Aretha Franklin, staged stunning contemporary comebacks with Arista. But Whitney seems to have had a date with destiny.

Late in 1985, America's National Academy of Recording Arts and Sciences indicated that she would not be considered eligible to be nominated for the Best New Artist Grammy because of her duet work with Jermaine Jackson and Teddy Pendergrass prior to the spring 1985 release of her full album. She made the occasion an undiluted triumph anyway, receiving the best female pop vocalist Grammy from the very hand of cousin Dionne, and turning in a performance on the televised ceremony that shot the album to number one after a year on the charts, adding three million to the two million already sold.

Still, just for the record: Whitney Houston was first heard on the second Michael Zager Band album, *Life's a Party*, in 1979. With her mother, session legend Cissy Houston, in the chorus, she sang a two-line solo that appeared twice: *"Lift your head up when life looks dreary/let your wishes climb to the sky."* It was not a hit, but she delivered the lines with all the élan she would bring to her Arista album, six years later: she sang simply, with pronounced gospel implication and with vocal command that seemed to enable her to zero in on her notes like a heat-seeking missile. It felt as if you could learn perfect pitch just by listening to her.

Zager wanted to sign the 14-year-old Whitney to a contract, but her mother vetoed the idea as premature. Over the early eighties, therefore, she's heard in backups and cameo appearances, stepping out for just a couple of 1982 solo spots. With Material, on *One Down* (Elektra), she sang 'Memories', a jazz ballad with almost nothing on the track but her own voice and Archie Shepp's horn solo. The effect was like discovering a huge, beautiful rock formation in an empty desert. Houston's cut on *Paul Jabara and Friends*, 'Eternal Love', written by Grammy and Oscar-winner Jabara (Columbia), foreshadowed the pop ballads that would dominate her own album.

On her 1983 signing to Arista, Houston underwent a remarkable two-year gestation period, apparently under the direct guidance of Arista chief Clive Davis himself. No music was rushed out; instead, she continued singing at cabaret with her mother, while Davis made such significant gestures as personally introducing her on the *Merv Griffin* talk show. Somewhere, there is videotape of Whitney Houston singing 'Ain't No Way', with Cissy Houston on her left – adding the famous soaring obligato she had created on the Aretha Franklin version fifteen years previously! Back to the future, indeed: in the video clip of 'The Greatest Love Of All', Cissy is seen hovering supportively and lovingly near Whitney, and in a moving freeze-frame conclusion, they embrace.

The appearance, finally, of *Whitney Houston* on 14 February 1985 – St Valentine's Day – set in motion the campaign that would put Houston's voice, seemingly, on every radio in the world. The first single, 'You Give Good Love', was an R&B natural, hitting number one on the black chart just at the time of her initial live New York dates at Sweetwater's and the Bottom Line. It was also number three pop: successful, certainly, though not massive.

Careful exploitation of the remainder of the album did create a heavyweight: 'Saving All My Love For You' went all the way to the top of the US and UK pop charts, and Arista released the uptempo 'Thinking About You' as a single for US R&B radio and dance-clubs while preparing another major pop push for the second number one single, 'How Will I Know'. By that time, Houston was a Grammy winner, and a three-week number one run for 'The Greatest Love Of All' followed.

The repeated confirmation of her across-the-board appeal transferred the respect with which she was greeted in black music to the general pop market: by mid-1986, she was voted top new star in a *People Magazine* poll representing the most conservative of middle American tastes. Where, say, the Pointer Sisters have been at the mercy of their last hit single, Houston's identically-conceived album – just one album! – became far more of a real platform, a stepping-off point because of the ideals and standards of artistry she upheld. Never *mind* Madonna, honey. We're talking Streisand, Aretha, Diana Ross: the real paragons of high standards, inherent brilliance, sustained dazzlement. Anita Baker, among other peers, credited Houston with proving that a class act could succeed in trend-ridden pop.

Part of Houston's astonishing gift is her feel for alternately spotlighting herself or the song: she delivers the tongue-in-cheek suggestive 'You Give Good Love' with real torchiness, accentuating the youthful mix of innocence and awakening passion that also sparks the neo-girl-group 'How Will I Know'. Contrastingly, in her gimmickless 'Saving All My Love For You', Houston acts more as a vehicle for the purest possible expression of the song itself.

The more R&B songs – 'Thinking About You', a modified Chaka Khan/Evelyn King number, and the pop/R&B 'Someone For Me' – are almost tokens for the niche market, though Houston dots them with occasional sudden flights of fervour. The duets with Jermaine Jackson are the undiscovered gems of the album: 'Take Good Care Of My Heart' is neat as a pin and quite blissful; and on 'Nobody Loves Me Like You Do', they transform country into warm pop/soul puppy love.

But the most impressive performance is 'The Greatest Love Of All', a thoroughly underrated song, except to those in whom it inspired church-like reaction at George Benson's concerts. Here, Houston proves herself the master of the resonant line: she gives the mounting refrain, containing three of the finest couplets in pop, multifold symbolism. As an individual, as a black woman, and

as the fulfilment of the family and professional background that went into her breakthrough, Houston delivers Linda Creed's lyrics as a philosophy of the absolute:

"I decided long ago
Never to walk in anyone's shadow:
If I fail, if I succeed,
At least I'll live as I believe.
No matter what they take from me,
They can't take away my dignity."

'Greatest Love' is one of the few songs on the album that stands up to her live delivery of it, and it's in this single regard that Whitney Houston has ever been other than perfect. With her improvisational gifts and gospel intensity, Houston's probing causes otherwise adequate album cuts to implode – she herself betrays the slightness of a 'How Will I Know,' or an 'All At Once', for example, the way a magnifying glass burns a hole through paper with its focus.

Houston herself, by the way, isn't a woman of steel: in her first headlining appearance in New York, at the too-small Carnegie Hall (in essence a prestige booking), she missed entirely the easy warmth of her club showcases. Possibly, the symbolism of it all caught up with her; the performance was forced, overly stagy. This was no clinker: to the contrary, the rub was that she poured it on in each and every song, as if she needed to hit a brilliant note with every breath. Audience hysteria was high and the mood erratic, over-the-top, all evening long. The lack of resolution in the air at the end of the night was an indication – inevitable, really – that Whitney Houston did in fact need seasoning as a performer to bring off a live performance as consistently satisfying as the gems she'd been dropping episodically as pop radio singles.

This all supposes that Houston will have the time to develop greatness without burning out her audience – the way high-pressure marketing usually does, in careers built on the basis of a gimmick or an image. This career, however, seems based on an idea, well on its way to being universally accepted: as long as there is a first rank of excellence in pop, Whitney Houston is bound to claim a place there.
Brian Chin

SIGUE SIGUE SPUTNIK

A man called Tony James had a dream. It involved thin people with prominent cheek-bones dressed up as a gay street gang. They played the least number of songs with the least number of words and chords, and hard currency in high denominations poured down on their funny heads. All the money was invested in an exploding helicopter factory and the thin people died laughing. Tony James woke up, put on his sun specs and wrote the whole thing down. After the dream, the rest was child's play.

When Generation X subsided in 1981, doomed by their dismal showing in the punk credibility stakes, Tony James locked himself in a room with his first-class maths degree and did some concentrated thinking on those timeless equations of success and failure. Meanwhile, ex-Gen X alumnus Billy Idol packed peroxide and sneer and took himself off to New York. He sold some records and appeared semi-starkers on the cover of *Rolling Stone*. All this was probably less than thrilling for Tony James, but like a good mathematician, he fed in the data and sat back to await the big print-out.

It duly arrived four years later. Tony James had perceived that the ultimate 'rock 'n' roll' band would have as little as possible to do with music, so his ideal group were essentially amusical: they could make noise if necessary, but that was a rather curt nod to an outdated convention. Tony James explained it thus: "It's much easier to teach someone to play the drums than it is to teach them to be thin." The dietary inadequacy of this argument aside, it is clear that what he had in mind were style-monsters of the most livid stripe, rather than any half-baked or burnt-out specimens from the desperate musos section of *MM*. And this is just what we got – four youngish men with a deep commitment to extreme posturing and acne-free faces, plus a gaggle of rather fierce boilers fulfilling the ancillary tasks of mixing, bouncing and roadying. Not to mention Mr James himself, sporting a fetching feather duster on his head.

The choice of name presented no problems. The wildly cosmopolitan pages of the *International Herald Tribune* threw up Sigue Sigue Sputnik, allegedly the name of a Russian street gang. This was very much a perfect name, containing alliteration so that people could remember it, providing fertile ground for the yapping puns of furious journalists and suggesting by its very sound the hissing of the uncool. For Tony James had conceived Sigue Sigue Sputnik as a form of orbiting irritation. The group's image is, in a sense, the sum total of every offensive slogan, symbol, fashion imbecility, facial tic and rude noise that he could come up with. In most senses actually. This group *will* say taboo to a goose. They urgently want to wipe their noses on your sleeve. And if you don't like it, you just don't understand.

Tony James understood that making enemies in the world of pop showbiz is just as important as making friends. Thus he has propelled Sigue Sigue Sputnik right up the collective nose of the DJ fraternity. Most of these intrepid jocks would sooner get a proper job than play one of their records, but few can resist any opportunity for a cheap jibe or even a little session of on-air disc snapping. The jocks sniff a scam and the last thing they want is the unwelcome intrusion of a bunch of shameless scoundrels, who might just possibly be more brazenly cynical than themselves in their pursuit of brass.

In truth, Sigue Sigue Sputnik do seem to have a slight image problem, when viewed from certain angles. The intention was to take elements from all the really bad boys and girls who have contributed to rock's rich tapestry, throw in a hefty dose of the old ultra-violence, courtesy of the *Clockwork Orange/Mad Max/ Blade Runner* school of stylish termination, and top up with a liberal dose of porno. The drawback with such an accretion of styles is that it is hard to beat on the system, create meaningful rock 'n' roll mayhem or even take a pee when your outfit has you in a hammerlock. Sigue Sigue Sputnik can look to the jaundiced eye like a tetchy collection of topiarised tarts suffering aggravated wardrobe confusion. The fact that Tony James, by day, runs eight miles, is seriously in touch with the properties of vegetables and deplores the smack 'n' bourbon diet of rock wastrels merely raises the eyebrow a notch further.

This proved no drawback with the record companies, however. Tony James knew all about coming on down when the price is right. He had watched the merry development of the deal in rock 'n' roll, from the legendary management rip-offs of the golden era, through the outrageous supremacy of fat superstars and even porkier record companies, to the fleeting cackle of punk chutzpah. If Sigue Sigue Sputnik were the fifth generation of rock 'n' roll, then they were going for a deal five times better than anyone else. Tony James assembled a package so complete, a look so total, that it virtually excluded music – at least, their own. A video was the natural tool. A quick-fire collage of fantasy gore and porn set to the strains of *A Clockwork Orange*. Oh yes, and a glimpse of the Sputniks giving their all, should anyone at the record company forget who the cheque was to be made out to. Having perfectly defined his group in the terms of A&R, Tony James had only to count the money. The preferred moneybags belonged to EMI, those perennial navigators in the deep end, and while talk of millions was just another facet of the masterplan, it was undeniably true that never had so much been given so willingly for so little.

The Sigue Sigue Sputnik rhythm was now augmented by the hammering of journalists upon their door. Cover stories in both the music and popular press produced violent reactions from the public to music which they had never heard. Scripted pronouncements from the band (principally, bony Tony and boutique maestro Martin Degville) abounded, and while they fell somewhat short of Wildean waggishness, they did at least inject a note of arrogant vitality into a somewhat servile Scene. "The higher the hair, the higher the heel, the higher the income," screeched Martin. "The bigger the prat," roared the uncool in response, and a dialogue (which would later take a nasty twist or two) was born. Next, those hoary old campaigners, the controversial T-shirts were wheeled out. Rude words in gold! Girls with appendages! Fleece The World! Rambo Child! Sigue Sigue Sputnik Spanky Botty!!!

It must have saddened Tony James that, at this point, he had to get round to releasing a record. But Tony knew that T-shirts, interviews and gossip were not enough to pay for calculator batteries: the golden goosing took place at the record store.

Sigue Sigue Sputnik released their first single on 17 February 1986, almost five months after having signed to EMI. It was called 'Love Missile F1-11' and that title told you quite a lot about the record: it was about a man with an exploding fighter plane strapped to his groin. It was, however, the first chance most people had had to hear the group 'play'. Two drums, bass and guitar provided a sparse backdrop for the treated snarlings of Martin Degville, the man who was just too much for Walsall. A variety of taped noises announced the alternative title of the song as 'Love Missile 111 FX'. But there was something else. The Sigue Sigue Concept of Arrogant Self-Sufficiency obviously did not extend to the rather important chore of production. Tony James' breathtaking vision of ten million Pak-Men on a binge had instead been entrusted to Giorgio Moroder, whose interior-sprung Eurodisco (patents pending) has supported the weight of dozens of rock/pop bloaters. Strangely enough, this unholy mélange of venerable rock chords, disco rhythm and sub-dub noises works, particularly if it's played extremely loud and accompanied by the video with its fast-cutting images of . . .

Despite the fact that he had by and large avoided the more odious necessities of trainee rock superstardom, Tony James felt he had to take Sigue Sigue Sputnik on tour to promote the single (man). The dates were dotted around rock's provincial back-waters, where Martin Degville's beauty, uncertain sexuality and clueless stage presence aroused mindless enthusiasm, mindless antipathy and even a bit of good old mindless apathy. Bottles were thrown, as were tantrums. Tony James reaped the rewards of his punk heritage by getting covered in spit from time to time. The real point of the exercise was the presence (official) of the *Sun* on the tour, thus ensuring a stream-of-unconscious headlines. The single got to No. 2.

There ensued a period of calm while Tony James rummaged through his song-bag, the videos were rewound and replaced at Sputnik HQ and a lot of people wondered how Sigue Sigue Sputnik failed to hit the top spot while riding a publicity wave of such titanic (sic) proportions. The fact is that, even with Moroder, the sound was a touch too harsh for the milkpop eighties. It didn't work for Alan Vega, either. The soundalike follow-up '21st Century Boy' looks like proving the point even more forcibly. Much depends on the first album, provisionally titled *Flaunt It*, which will be the first to carry advertising. If Tony James insists on laying bare the connections between rock and commerce, he may well become merely a cult figure for sociologists. If he hasn't got half-a-dozen good songs under his wig, then he may not attain even those giddy heights, because soundtracks for videos won't do.

It would be something of a pity if the much-vaunted 'Fifth Generation' of rock 'n' roll had its antecedents revealed as The Rocking Vicars, Kim Fowley, Sailor and Ed Banger and the Nosebleeds. Just a follicle on the grand scale.

Pete Clark

PET SHOP BOYS

"Neil attends when he chooses and writes what he wishes – on what does he base his claim to superiority?" Thus did a certain English teacher (who had better remain nameless) sum up in a school report the life and works of the adolescent Neil Tennant. Now Neil Tennant is much too astute to let himself be caught making any claims to superiority (not in public, anyway) but his erstwhile educator's remarks, while not entirely free of bitchiness, are not without perception either. For it is precisely these qualities of insouciant detachment and discerning selectivity that sets the Pet Shop Boys apart from their peers and makes them such a fascinating phenomenon. (And, of course, a modicum of arrogance never went amiss in the make-up of a true star . . .)

As has been well documented, the Pet Shop Boys formed in London in August 1981 when Neil Tennant (effortlessly witty, stylish dresser, organised, generous, keeps Action Man in combat gear on his bookshelves) encountered Chris Lowe (funny, jeans and Italian training shoes, down to earth, untidy, paranoid about being burgled) in an electrical goods shop in London's Kings Road. The two got chatting about synthesisers – still relatively unusual at this point – became friends and a songwriting partnership followed. (The name? "One of the newspapers said that it's New York slang for rent boys who are into S&M," Tennant told *Melody Maker*, "but if it is, it's news to me. We did genuinely call ourselves after some friends we had who worked in a pet shop in Ealing. We wanted something with that kind of hip New York Peech Boys ring to it. If it has got that slightly dubious connotation then it's quite amusing but it's certainly not deliberate.")

Tennant had come down to London from Newcastle Upon Tyne (where he had played cello in the school orchestra and been involved in youth theatre) after gaining a college degree in history and was then pursuing a career in publishing. This included being a London editor for *Marvel* comics, where his job was to anglicise American spellings, and latterly assistant editor at *Smash Hits*, where his irreverent humour and confident, suitably theatrical proclamations on who was or wasn't currently "down the dumper" were an invaluable asset to the magazine. Meanwhile Lowe, a native of Blackpool, was studying architecture at Liverpool University – turning up in London on a job study programme – and can claim to have designed what has now become an almost legendary staircase in the new town of Milton Keynes.

Both had musical backgrounds of a kind. Tennant, having acquired a guitar in his teens, had been in an Incredible String Band-type group called Dust who specialised in deeply meaningful songs like 'Can You Hear The Dawn Break?' Lowe, by contrast, had been a trombone player but latterly a pianist for One Under The Eight, a seven-piece band (geddit?) who played standards such as 'My Way' and 'La Bamba' for social gatherings at the local Conservative Club and such like. At the time of meeting, Tennant inclined towards David Bowie and Elvis Costello but was introduced by Lowe to the dubious delights of Eurodisco and, more particularly, the entire recorded output of New York producer Bobby 'O' Orlando. By all accounts it was a formative experience . . .

And so the partnership developed, with Lowe commuting from Liverpool and the pair recording a song-per-weekend in a friend's studio in Camden, all in pursuit of the Holy Grail of the perfect New York disco record. The turning point came in August 1983 when *Smash Hits* sent Tennant to New York to interview the Police, whom he'd never liked. "So," he later recalled to the same

paper, "I thought 'well, if I've got to go and see the Police pl[...] some *horrible* concert and then do a *fantastically* bori[...] interview with Sting, I'm *also* going to have lunch with Bobby [...] The eccentric producer, bowled over by this odd journalis[...] encyclopedic knowledge of his work, duly responded in tr[...] fairy-tale fashion by offering to make a record on his own lab[...] without even hearing the Pet Shop Boys' demos. And so t[...] original version of 'West End Girls' was born.

It all ended in tears, of course. The record was a success [...] sorts but only in curious places like Belgium, while the contractu[...] side was not always strictly adhered to. (Bit of a euphemism he[...] readers.) Meanwhile, the frustrated Pet Shop Boys yearned [...] something bigger and better; several months of legal letters lat[...] they signed to EMI. Another single, 'Opportunities', creat[...] further interest, but it was a newer, subtler version of 'West E[...] Girls' (re-recorded with Stephen Hague of 'Madame Butterf[...] 'Hey DJ' fame) that climbed slowly but steadily to claim the Briti[...] No. 1 slot shortly after the beginning of 1986. It then proceed[...] to repeat the feat in America, where the ambiguities and atmospherics of the record, together with the refusal of the duo [...] play the part of traditional show-off rock stars, combined to gi[...] them a very English 'mystique'.

In fact, there's precious little mystique about the Pet Sh[...] Boys at all. There is no 'masterplan' as is often assumed, thou[...] this state of affairs should not be interpreted as their not knowi[...] what they're doing. As is clearly discernible in their first albu[...] *Please* – so called, according to Tennant, "because it's got [...] many implications: it's pleading, polite, subservient, it's sarcas[...] and petulant, and also looks good written down" (not to menti[...] providing a ready joke whereby punters can ask for "the Pet Sh[...] Boys' album, *please*") – the pair complement each other musica[...] as well as in terms of personality.

The Pet Shop Boys' grasp of what constitutes intelligent pop [...] almost uncanny. Neil Tennant's lyrics are incisive and succin[...] both as a recorder of what he sees around him – *"I only want [...] something else to do but hang around"* (from 'Suburbia') sa[...] more in terms of understanding and speaking for the frustratio[...] of urban youth than a whole roomful of albums by the likes of Pa[...] Weller, the Redskins and their grimly politically-correct kind – a[...] in matters of the heart. The strong gay undertones provide a th[...] of recognition and delight for those who are, while remaini[...] universal enough – *"Put your arms around me, it doesn't mean y[...] love me/Just that you want me and you need my company"* (fro[...] Want A Lover') – not to exclude those who aren't. Yet this is a m[...] who describes his solo compositions as "a bit wet" and choos[...] to leave most of the musical decisions to the moodier, brash[...] Lowe, who supplies most of the hooks and punches.

Together they produce a music that's melodic and poigna[...] and yet fuelled by enthusiasm, something which appeals to th[...] heart as much to the head or the feet. Nor does it try to [...] something else, which is quite rare these days. "I know it's a bit [...] a cliché," offers Tennant almost apologetically, "but I think we'[...] honest. We don't sing like we're black or pretend we're the Isl[...] Brothers. We deal with music that's inherent to us." And th[...] music, because it set out to be disco (a realm where no on[...] suspects intelligent life) and because it is fantastically tuneful [...] remains one of the last great unfortunate hangovers from th[...] hippy seventies that anyone who has a gift for a good melody [...] automatically deemed stupid and witless) has managed [...] establish itself by catching off-guard a musical establishme[...]

which, while reluctant now to make claims about art for fear of being branded a hippy, has yet to come to terms with enjoying pop music again for fear of being labelled mindless.

The Pet Shop Boys have no such reservations and are not in the slightest bit intimidated about openly enjoying the shiny baubles that their contemporaries would love to enjoy as well, were they not so preoccupied with peer pressure not to do so. With no pretences to keep up, the Pet Shop Boys revel in the transient joys of pop and unashamedly delight in its trivia, enthusing over the unfashionable and the unhip with words like "fab" and "naff" and, of course, "*tragic*".

"Pop music is rubbish in a good way," Tennant enthused to *Melody Maker*. "It sets out to be a tune which is sexy, memorable, you can wear it almost, you can fall in love with the singer and it's not lasting. You can't ask where a good pop group will be in five

debunking the pretentious whilst at the same time refusing to attach any great meaning or significance to what they do and refusing to give themselves airs and graces as 'stars' by constantly mocking the whole process.

When asked to consider the Pet Shop Boys' future after their autumn tour, Neil Tennant only half-joked with his former colleagues at *Smash Hits*: "We're not exactly thinking of retiring, but we've got this *plan*. Everyone thinks it's a joke but actually it's serious. The Pet Shop Boys will carry on but we'll stop being the front men. Instead we'll change the line-up in a year or so – suddenly there'll be four 16-year-old boys as the Pet Shop Boys and then the next thing you know they'll have been replaced by two 35-year-old Elaine Paige types. We'll be fed up with it all by then so we'll just write the music.

"We'll be able to spend our time doing nice things like going to

years time, because they'll have broken up. Pop is of the moment, like a newspaper only better. It doesn't aim to have lasting quality whereas rock aims to be a part of a body of work and to last.

"The irony is, of course, that when you look back over the sixties and seventies, everyone has to hide their Grateful Dead albums and say how much they liked the Monkees whereas, if they'd been honest at the time, they'd have really just liked the Monkees anyway. Rock music is about that kind of bullshit, it's about walking around school pretending you like the most dreadful old rubbish when you really don't like it at all."

Not that this enthusiasm is indiscriminate – the Pet Shop Boys understand the importance of ideas. They will cheerfully sling mud with the best of them, poking fun at the clichés and

bed early. We won't have to have our photograph taken or be asked why we're called the Pet Shop Boys. We can just make the records. And make *lots* of money."

It is this refusal to join the rock 'n' roll circus, to follow the set patterns and submit to the usual debilitating pressures, that helps set the witty, understated Pet Shop Boys above the dreary and the routine. It is those very qualities of selectivity and detachment that the irritable academic detected in the schoolboy Tennant which, allied to their natural gifts, are now the very base upon which the Pet Shop Boys can stake their claim to superiority. Not that you'd catch them making any such claim, of course – not in public, anyway.

Ian Cranna

PHIL COLLINS

It's no coincidence that the Year-In-Which-It-Was-Nice-To-Be-Nice has also been the year of Phil Collins' pre-eminence. Because Collins is a thoroughly nice and decent chap. I say this without ever having met him and with no knowledge whatsoever about his private life and proclivities, but you can bet your bippy that he is a loving husband (I believe that he's married), devoted father (providing he has children), good sport, dog lover and absolutely pukka fella to have a drink with. In short the sort of man who twenty-five or even five years ago would not have been a multi-national megastar.

To begin with he doesn't look the part. After all, in 1986 pop stars are meant to be lean, taut-bodied, high-cheekboned teenagers with what gossip columnists used to call 'smouldering good looks'. Now, smouldering, teenage, high-cheekboned, taut-bodied and lean, Collins ain't. He is chubby and balding and jovial, like one of those old-fashioned milkmen who was on first name terms with everyone on his route. But coupled with his bloke-in-the-street looks is this irresistible charm, and charm – which is, I regret to say, a rare commodity in the pop world – is a Collins forte: not the clichéd fixed-grin charm of showbiz, but the real warmth and desire-to-be-pleasant that is the most necessary lubricant of civilised living. Collins is interested in you and isn't afraid to show it. He has that newly refound bravery which I feel he shares with Mark Knopfler and Elton John: he's not afraid to respect his audience. Old-style pop ethics, as practised since the sixties, said treat the punters with contempt: after all, you're the star and they are there merely to be puked on, ripped off and turned out of the auditorium after a few grudgingly performed encores.

So Collins is a gentleman-performer, in the sense that gentility and a sense of fair play is part of his act. This well-mannered pop music recognises the fact that the audience, or at least a large part of the audience, has grown up both in years and expectations; that's why Collins has been unfairly and often savagely maligned by those music journalists and fans who take Peter Pan as a role model. "It's just music for yuppies" they sneer – a sometimes effective, if perhaps idiotic taunt sullied by the sixties/early seventies idea that pop music, in order to be good, must be both disturbing and performed by someone who looks as if he's been dragged out of a tweeny.

Collins is caught between a rock and a hard place – not glamorous enough for the weeny-boppers who like their pop delivered by male models and not 'relevant' enough for the old ideological brigade. Unfortunately a secure grip on the middle ground is always viewed with derision. Not that Collins or his fans should care – after all there are more of us than of the them who don't like Collins or his music.

It is tempting but, alas, misleading to see Collins as the performer who merely satisfies the demographics of an ageing pop audience, as he is anything but a marketing phenomenon. He is a success – a huge, global success – for the simple reason that he is a frightfully talented musician, songwriter and performer. This isn't dull reductionism: it is a musical fact of life. If you want to be successful and enduring you need more than a big wanger and a pair of tight jeans.

I admit that I haven't always appreciated the Collins talent. As an early non-fan of Genesis I loathed that band's art-schooly pretensions and Peter Gabriel's ludicrous baroque posturing. The first time I realised that Collins had something special to offer was when I heard him drumming with his part-time jazz-rock band, Brand X. Even at a time when American artists like Stanley Clarke and the Meters were making records with orgasmic drumming, Phil Collins stood out as someone who could be one of the finest percussionists in pop: a man with both sensitivity and a killer sense of rhythm – a lyrical and powerful player as good as any drummer who's ever made a pop record. Even when Collins took over as the Genesis front man – I remember seeing him perform at the Rainbow in 1976 – I was distinctly unimpressed, although I grudgingly admitted that for someone who couldn't sing he did try hard.

Brand X faded away and I forgot about Collins until he began to crop up on my radio with a string of hit singles starting with 'In The

Air Tonight' and continuing until now. Slowly I began to realise that this guy could sing – not, that is, for the lead in *Don Giovanni*, but in a moving and understanding way that has made him one of the best and most convincing vocalists of the eighties.

And as Collins developed his solo performances he began to introduce more and more of the elements of post R&B black American popular music which I so enjoy: he is in many ways the 'fusion' artist par excellence. Long before Sting, Collins was making a different and very musically sophisticated form of transatlantic pop that was much more intense than his pastiche of 'You Can't Hurry Love'. He has almost become a white James Brown, powerful and capable enough to master a big and funky brass section. His lyrics have sometimes been a problem – he can write a convincing and touching love song like 'One More Night', but I still haven't a clue what 'Sussudio' is about. It doesn't particularly bother me, though, as I've always inclined towards the form-over-content school of pop music.

The real revelation came last year. After a trip to America to see Prince, giving his 'last concert' in Miami, and Madonna, fetchingly flaunting her belly button in San Diego, I was lucky enough to be in Paris when Collins was performing at the huge Palais Omnisport halfway through his world tour. Of any performer I've ever seen in concert – and that runs a pretty wide gamut from Bo Diddley to Bruce Springsteen – Collins had the surest, easiest command of the stage and the crowd that I've ever seen. People who think that Collins' music is safe and complacent have obviously never been in a concert hall with him. He bantered with the audience in pidgin French and moved from the high-energied good-humour of songs like 'Only You Know And I Know' to the gloomy intensity of 'In The Air Tonight' with nary a hitch. He is one of those exceedingly rare performers in his field who is able to couple high emotionalism with sheer professionalism. "Je voudrai introduire l'équipe", he said towards the close of the show. "Sur le saxophone Monsieur Don Myrick, un homme qui est né à Paris." Thunderous applause. "Sur le trombone Monsieur

Louis Satterfield, merveilleusement né à Paris aussi." More thunderous applause. 'Et sur le trumpet Monsieur Rahmlee Michael Davis, un homme qui est etonnant né à Paris aussi!" Collapse of stout audience with laughter and an astonishingly effective performance of 'Take Me Home'. How many other pop stars are good enough to be so unpompous and to tease the conventions? From that concert on, Collins has had my dedicated devotion. His energy as a performer can be in no doubt: his transatlantic hop for Live Aid was not just a master-stroke of publicity but a fine example of his tirelessness and relentless desire to do things better than anyone else.

His mastery in the recording studio is undeniable as well; not only in his own recordings but in the work he's done for other artists, particularly *Chinese Wall* which he produced for Philip Bailey. Confident, crisp and ungimmicky, he must be one of the best producers working in pop music today. I doubt that his perfectionism has much to do with egotism though: he certainly acts and performs as very much an equal – obviously the first among equals – with his band. You can't exactly be a shrinking violet and perform for tens of thousands of fans every year, but I don't sense any overpowering conceit in Collins' make-up.

The pop audience has become more fragmented than ever before, and there are always going to be Sigue Sigue Sputniks and Duran Durans for those pop fans who demand and deserve them. The age of revolutionary rock may be over and done with or perhaps just resting. Phil Collins is a mature rock star, not just in terms of his own age or the age of his audience but as a representative of a rock music that has grown up, become more sophisticated and civilised. Perhaps rock should remain forever young and this gentrification of the genre will produce an arid music in the hands of someone less talented than Collins. But that in no way diminishes Collins' stature and ability. I admire his talent, energy, professionalism AND niceness. And I must say that I'm grateful for his success.

Loyd Grossman

107

TEARS FOR FEARS

"Good evening, New York," Roland Orzabal roars. "We're Tears For Fears and we come from England, that place where you store your Cruise missiles!"

Well, shout, shout and let it *all* out, brothers, you've surely earned it! A couple of years ago Roland and Curt Smith (with long-time band members Ian Stanley and Manny Elias) were nothing more than yet another synth duo, not particularly flashy and a bit too much on the brainy side. Copping their name and a good dose of lyrical inspiration from *The Primal Scream*, the bible of catharsis written by psychologist Arthur Janov (who recently thanked them

for a sudden increase in sales), they first assaulted the British consciousness in 1983 with odd haircuts, baggy sweaters and an angsty album called, appropriately enough, *The Hurting*.

Then they disappeared to the arty, antiquey confines of their native Bath for a while and returned with the eclectic, accomplished funk, chants, and jazzy easy-listening music of *Songs From the Big Chair* (the "big chair" coming from another pop-psych fave, *Sybil*, the story of a woman with multiple personalities). Number ones, magazine covers, international celebrity, sell-out tours and the opportunity to comment on foreign policy soon ollowed. A "totally calculated" song was written "to have an American hit," and while we Yanks sang 'Everybody Wants To Rule The World' Tears For Fears spent a few months doing just that – racking up over four million album sales in the US, and nearly duplicating Wham!'s feat of three consecutive chart-toppers ('Head Over Heels' reached number three after 'Everybody' and 'Shout').

"I find it good because we've done this under our own terms," Curt explains. "We haven't had to be seen in all the right places. When we go back to Bath we live our happy lives and keep away from the kind of musical atmosphere where being competitive comes before doing anything of worth and quality." "I think we deserve our success," Roland concurs. "We've succeeded because of good songs, not because we've discovered a new way of wearing clothes."

Too true, mate. Amongst pop's vast panorama, Tears For Fears are a certified anomaly: long-acquainted, happily married young men who look and dress no better than thousands of university students with the kind of average amiable personalities that give Fleet Street the willies. They met eleven years ago on the brink of teenagerhood. Each thought the other was a foreign exchange student. "He had a very sarcastic sense of humour and I did too," Curt recalls, "so we got on immediately." They also shared a passion for music and formed a 'kid band' with the bloke who'd introduced them. "We used to be mad on Led Zeppelin and played 'Stairway To Heaven' an awful lot," Roland confesses.

They were something of a study in opposites. Roland was studious and, according to Curt, "not a very scandalous person, he's been too bloody good." Yet it was Curt, who Roland describes as "a little criminal actually, he used to steal cameras and violins from school", who went on to college. Both shared typical lads' obsessions: "We tried to lose our virginity for a long time – both of us – before we managed to do it," Curt remembers. "Then one time we had this drinking race to see if he could drink a bottle of sherry faster than I could drink four bottles of beer. The first thing he did when he won was say he didn't feel any effect at all. And the next thing he did was fall over and spend the whole afternoon throwing up while Caroline watched him. That was his first date with her and now they're married."

The duo separated for a year "when Roland decided he wanted to go off and do folk music and I didn't," Curt says. "And he became very serious – we both did – when we were 16-18, but we've certainly lightened up over the last few years." "It wasn't until we were 19 or 20," Roland confesses, "that we decided to do something serious and started listening to Talking Heads and Peter Gabriel and just took it from there."

As Graduate, they released a Two-Toney ska single on an independent label, their first and last attempt at jumping on any kind of commercial bandwagon. The next leap proved more

difficult and frustrating. "Only one company wanted us," Curt told Star Hits, "because the rest didn't like our pictures. I used to argue with them. I wasn't going to take any of it. I'd say 'One of these songs is going to be a hit and you'll be sorry.' One of those songs was 'Pale Shelter' and I felt really good when it was a hit."

Before you could say 'long grey mac' the press had tagged Curt and Roland as very serious young men. "They didn't want to know that we might have a sense of humour," Curt explains in a tone consistent with the TFF style of sarcasm. With the snipping

of Curt's skinny plaits (still kept in a box at home) and an avoidance of anything remotely rockstar-chic, they've now achieved the rare distinction of being proper pop stars whilst remaining effortlessly imageless creatures who script their own videos, use their own snapshots on record sleeves and let the music do the talking. But, Curt demurs, "the last thing I want to do is preach to people. Our music does have a meaning but it doesn't necessarily have a message. The main thing is to encourage people to think a lot more and stand up for their rights. I'm not one for politics myself, but we do have a lot to communicate."

Sometimes, even that's a battle. However improbable in the face of pop peacocks like Duran Duran, Wham! and Spandau Ballet, Tears For Fears reached well beyond the expected following of music-loving deep-thinking college kids and emerged as bona fide teen idols. "I find it odd, and at times frightening,"

Curt shivers, "when fans decide they're going to take the shirt off your neck. I mean they don't even know me. I could be a complete and utter bastard for all they know and yet they think you're God. I mean I could understand why they would want to meet you, but when they scream at you when they've never even met you . . . When they scream during a song like 'I Believe' I just want to tell them to shut up. And Roland has done on occasion!"

If that doesn't prove deterrent enough, there's always Mr Orzabal's dry, sardonic views (and disregard for diplomacy) to annoy fickle Anglophile girlies. They were roundly criticised for cancelling an appearance at Live Aid, which they had termed "emotional blackmail", even though they donated money from concerts in London, Sydney, Tokyo and New York to the cause. "That's our part," Roland told Smash Hits. "We weren't into the whole event. We didn't get to play in front of billions of people which is the reason why an awful lot of groups appeared."

Still, they took the time and trouble to re-record 'Everybody Wants To Rule The World' as the musical theme for Sport Aid –not surprising, considering Curt's passion for footballing on tour. That's about the only sport the lads get up to. Their highly successful 1985 jaunt across America featured such un-rockstar-like activities as fixing blender cocktails and toasted sandwiches on a coach that once hauled Van Halen. "There's absolutely no affection, that's what I miss the most," Roland complained to Smash Hits. "You can meet a girl and go to bed with her – but how can you just have a cuddle? They'd just think you were weird."

It's obvious that home life is as important for Curt and Lynne (and their five cats: Treasure, Garp, Ben, Charlie and Enny) and Roland and Caroline (and their puss Zero Algebra Waldorf Churchill) as living out the jetsetter pop star clichés is to other performers, and certainly sheds light on Tears' contemplative lyrics and defiantly trendless music. Certainly such seclusion and stability augurs well for the partnership, though both concede "we're bound to split up one day." It's not likely to be over one or the other's sudden decision to become a film star, chat-show host, yachtsman or clothing designer, though. "When I die," Curt decides, "I want to be buried in New Orleans where they make a big party out of it. And I shall have a jazz funeral."

"And by the time I'm 50," Roland ripostes, tongue firmly in cheek, "I intend to be in the gutter. The idea is to be very successful when you're very young and then just do a looooooooong slide."

David Keeps

THE BANGLES

It was a bizarre, curiously winning combination. The first guitarist wore black, flared trews with golden spanglettes swishing about the ankles – very Suzi Quatro/class of '73; the second guitarist wore a sparkly silver mini-skirt and off-white sneakers – very High School cheerleader/class of '68; the bass player sported a Laura Ashley-type, pseudo-paisley, pseudo-maternity smock – very genteel hippie/class of God knows when; the drummer: black singlet, sweat-teased hair, bish-bash-bosh on the tubs – very proto-punk . . . They played a deranged song by sixties' high prophet of mad flower children, Sky Saxon ('Pushin' Too Hard'); they played a chiming number by seventies' low prophet of power-pop, Alex Chilton ('September Gurls'); they did something "especially" written for them by eighties' sage of sex style pop-cool, Prince ('Manic Monday'); and a wonderfully barmy song of their own ('Angels Don't Fall In Love'). Their harmonies were impeccably quavery, their guitars jangled trillingly; they were . . . quite good. The Bangles on tour in 1986, sucking up inspiration (Americana of three decades + the Beatles) and turning it out as the properest all-girl pop group (they actually play their own instruments – gaasp!) . . . ever . . .

Although the late seventies and eighties had seen the emergence of more and more and better and better female rock performers, all-girl rock groups were still viewed with scepticism and suspicion by consumers and music-business-persons alike.

Not surprising, really. Casting a glance across thirty years, bands of girlie twangsters scarcely get a look in. Fanny? Dire, pedestrian 'hard' rock produced, directed, arranged, etc etc by blokes (Richard Perry, George Harrison, Todd Rundgren); couldn't do it on stage anyway, so were forced to wear frocks of a vulgar cut to outlast novelty interest. The Runaways? Soft-porn, punky trash, loud and snotty 'nasty' girls in poutlicious lingerie, invented by a man (Kim Fowley) to make a bit of quick money; weren't nearly as 'outrageous' as they pretended to be anyway, so had to give up as soon as the 'authentic' punks appeared. The Slits? Left-over, would-be brats who made such a truly disgusting racket they had to resort to swathing their bosoms in mud on LP sleeves to engender any sales at all. The Raincoats? Boring. The Belle Stars? Too chirpily gormless by several miles. The Go-Gos? Glossy, MTV fodder with California beach tans, damp swimsuits, cocktails, designer deck chairs, etc. And who else was there? Can't think of hardly anyone . . . Perhaps the only successful democratic and artistically 'valid' female rocksters *before* the Bangles had been Josie and the Pussycats. And *they* were a US TV cartoon group. Created by fellows. In 1986, it seemed, if you wanted to be a member of a girl group, your best chance was to stick whitewash and tulip lipstick on your face, slip into a jet black skirt and slink around like a droid pretending to play an 'axe' behind Robert Palmer in some ghastly video. Or be a Bangle.

This girl group 'thing' was, initially at least, to the Bangles' advantage: what a wheeze of a gimmick – they played guitars and they were *actually not men!!* It got them noticed, but it rapidly became monumentally tiresome. "There is a sort of performing flea aspect to it," said Bangles bass player Michael Steele. "Let's go and see these weird girls jump up and down . . ." ". . . And make assholes of themselves . . ." added guitarist Vicki Peterson, acidly. "What's the difference between men making rock and *women* making rock?" Michael again: "It's a STUPID way to make a living either way . . ."

But to critics and the entire musicological world there *was* a difference – history 'proved' this. And so the press patronised: "For *girls*," they said, "the Bangles are quite good." For *girls*, the Bangles *were* quite good. For *people*, the Bangles were quite good, with their bizarre and curiously winning combination of 'fashion' and musical styles and pop purity. How *ever* had this occurred? . . .

American boy tots of the sixties who dreamt of growing up pop stars were supposed to pose in front of the bedroom mirror twanging invisibly along to 'Perfidia' by the Ventures, or some-such. But what were American *girl* tots of the sixties (who dreamt of growing up pop stars) supposed to do? Put Beatles records on at 78 rpm, make their Troll Dolls dance along to them – *and* charge admission to their friends to watch the rock happening? Of course! Well, that's what Debbi and Vicki Peterson spent quite a lot of time doing during their middle-class LA childhood(s), anyway. They learnt all the words to *A Hard Day's Night*, too – not just the song, but the entire movie: dialogue, train noises, Wilfrid Brambell whinings, *everything*.

The sisters, as you can see, were pretty thoroughly obsessed with the Beatles. So were the other two girls who would grow up Bangles – Michael Steele ("When I was in school, we used to dress up in Beatle wigs and do skits . . ."), and Susanna Hoffs ("I remember staring at the album covers and having daydreams about Paul McCartney . . ."). "We just went *mad* over the Beatles," Vicki would confess. "Except as we grew up, instead of wanting to *marry* Paul McCartney, we wanted to *BE* that. With the Bangles, we want to give back that intensity you feel in your childhood when you ascribe a turning point in your life to a particular song you heard on the radio . . ."

Intensity of childhood. Troll Dolls, daydreams, frightwigs, and all the things that reasonably well-heeled all-American girls are supposed to do: eat Milky Way bars in the shower, tell ghost stories at slumber parties, yell on the school football team with your pom-poms, cruise and snog at drive-ins. Listen to the radio: the Leaves, the Byrds, Sky Saxon and the Seeds, the Electric Prunes (and their brilliant song 'Bangles' in particular), Paul Revere and the Raiders, the Mamas and the Papas, and, naturally, the Beatles – inspirational elements to be scooped up years later into Bangleonia (*their* word). Then TV – a tubeful of 'influences' to stick into songs, style and general chatter in years to come:

Gidget ("*such* a cool character" – S Hoffs), *The Monkees* ("the first cartoon with real people – weird! CRISPY!" – M Steele), *The Partridge Family* ("always inspirational" – S Hoffs), *The Brady Bunch* ("here's the storeee of a lovely laydeee" – D & V Peterson; "it's very scary at the end where all those heads are looking at you" – M Steele), *Man From U.N.C.L.E*, etc etc etc . . .

Meanwhile, Vicki was hiding in the closet with her crappy plastic guitar from Sears, writing useless little 'pop' songs like 'I Think It's Love', trying to figure out the chords (all two of them) to 'Hang Down Your Head Tom Dooley', and wondering when she'd get to be Paul McCartney. Much later, after her obligatory Simon & Garfunkel phase, she formed a college 'female fab four' combo called the Fans. The Fans became the Muse became Those Girls became the Colors and got absolutely nowhere until 1981, when they found a good guitarist – Susanna Hoffs (itinerant folkie and Beatles maniac) – and bass player – Annette Zilinksas (itinerant C&W buff and Beatles maniac). As the Bangs, the new band began playing sleazy joints in LA and soon became part of the so-called Paisley Underground (alongside psychedelic revivalists the Dream Syndicate, the Salvation Army, the Rain Parade and a hundred others), graduating to performing their shimmeresque harmonies and sixties-tinged punky-slam in hippier locales of the city. They released their first single, the fuzzy, grungy garageland stuff of 'Getting Out Of Hand', on their own Downkiddie label; in 1983 they signed to Miles Copeland's LAPD management (Copeland, coincidentally – or was it? – also managed LA's *other* all-girl group the Go-Gos); they changed their name to the Bangles (when a New Jersey band also called the Bangs saw bucks in the Copeland name and threatened to sue) and put out an EP, 'The Bangles', on Faulty Products. After that, Annette Zilinksas departed for cowpoke boogie band Blood On The Saddle and was replaced by Michael Steele (a woman – real name 'unknown' – who knew all about girl-group pitfalls having been the original singer in Fowley's Runaways).

With a grown-up recording contract from CBS, the Bangles left the Paisley Underground world of chic biker bars and cult in-crowds behind and went on to mini-stadiums – where boys went ape and girls smiled from a distance – in jig time. The singles, 'Hero Takes A Fall' and Kimberley Rew's 'Going Down To Liverpool' got them big-time television exposure in America and beyond, while their first album, *All Over the Place*, an irresistible collection of sixties-tousled harmonies, guitars akimbo, Beatley bits and songs about girls being not in love and not wanting to have much fun in particular, was a critical success almost everywhere. Hurrah! Diamanté earrings of gi-normous proportions. Then onto 1986: 'Manic Monday' – dippy-doppy *Nutrasweet* melodies courtesy of Mr Christopher (Prince) – was by no means the best thing they'd ever done, but it established them for perpetuity (or the foreseeable future, at any rate), going Top Five almost everywhere; and the second album, *Different Light* (same as the first only prettier and, this time, songs about girls falling in love all over again and wanting to have fun after all . . .), a *hit* graduating to CD. Avanti!

The Bangles. The first proper sixties band of the eighties (even though they did hate being called revivalists: "We listen to all different kinds of stuff," said Michael, "and it goes in here and comes out in some other, strange, mutilated form. We don't really sit down and say 'We want this to sound like an Ultimate Spinach song'. We *tried* once to sound like Ultimate Spinach and couldn't *do* it . . !"). The first 'decent' all-girl, all-playing, all-singing (all four have supreme voices) group *ever* ("We're writing songs from a female point of view, which hasn't been the case throughout history," said Vicki. "We're not political about it because that would be soooo dull, but even the Shangri-Las' viewpoint was male. It's always been a male-dominated scene . . ."). Witty and deliberately 'innocent' (Susanna: "We're all going to get the Honey Bees and the Mosquitos back together – they were on *Gilligan's Island*." Michael: "And perhaps Rock Roll from *The Flintstones*." Susanna: "Or Pebbles and Bamm Bamm singing 'Let The Sun Shine In' . . . but it's all about LSD . . ."). Two Catholics, a Jew and a WASP, (Vicki: "We are a microcosm of America.") 'Pure' pop entertainment – for the moment. Tra la!

Tom 'Tom' Hibbert

BRYAN ADAMS

He keeps good company, Bryan Adams. The highlight of his year must have been a concert in April in his home country, Canada, attended by his illustrious fan Princess Diana. Shamefully, Bryan was sternly instructed not to perform his song 'Diana' on this occasion (since it implores the Princess to leave her present old man for this blond fireball). But he was at least granted a backstage audience. The Princess joshed him about his age ("I'm only 26!") and must have raised his hopes by asking if he was, in fact, married. "No," replied the hero, "but I do have an English girlfriend!"

Diana's reply was something in the order of "How super!" Gee whiz. What a life.

Bryan Adams is a personable fellow. He's a buddy to anyone who's prepared to crack a grin, stretch out a hand, stomp a foot to a rockin' beat. Adams' particular appeal isn't that he's not special, in the bland, eighties' not-special fashion of Nik Kershaw and Howard Jones, dismal creatures who make a virtue out of their smooth mediocrity. Adams likes a bit of style, a little flash. But he doesn't indulge it by stepping on some Olympian rock pedestal and gazing down on us. He insists that he *pulls us up there with him*. All of us or nothing, with Bryan. You say the kids wanna rock? Well, hell, they sure can rock with *me*!

The formula is one of those winning no-formulas that rock throws up every so often, a retreat from the meanest channels of the music but a very sweet piece of escapism. In Bryan Adams and his rock, the music bubbles up on generosity, on blind emotion. Each song has its arrow to the heart – love, rejection, nostalgia, hope, it's all delivered the same thunderous way. And it takes a strong heart to resist all those arrows. Bryan Adams is terribly good at his job.

He was born in Ontario in 1959, and spent his adolescence in Vancouver. Not exactly a prime spawning ground for a chart Hercules of the eighties – one still thinks of Canada as the birthplace of sensitive souls like Neil Young and Joni Mitchell – but there's an embattled tradition of Canadian hard rock which persists to this day. Adams isn't of the lineage that brought about crypto-hoodlums like Rush, but he *is* very close to the sort of music produced by Loverboy, one of the more interesting late-seventies Canadian exports.

Loverboy's ferociously playable *Get Lucky* LP took on American hard rock and beat it at its own game in 1981. Their viciously efficient blend of pop tunes and pump-iron beat was the real prototype of Adams' own music (maybe he can also learn another lesson from them – the eager cubs of that band now look like exhausted old men).

In fact, Adams was writing songs for bands like Loverboy when he was still in his teens. Inevitably, it fed little more than a desire for a more pocketable slice of the cake. So he took the usual route, toiling through demos and the calamitous false start (A&M whacked out a ridiculous single that set him up as a blow-dried, white disco boy).

It's a terrible apprenticeship, this USA rock. Americans love the gleaming matter they call AOR: it's an apparently simple format to Xerox, and because there are so many contenders its elite of champions is very small indeed. A musician can spend a rock 'n' roll lifetime on a gruelling gig and college radio circuit and never see a record go higher than 99 in the charts. The airwaves are so stuffed with the music that it all comes to resemble one album, played over and over.

Here, where there's no such constancy, it might be easier for a strong slug of hard rock to swipe the attention. But we like our tunes very simple. Our favourite hard rockers are the softest of them all, Status Quo. Bryan Adams stood a miserable chance on both sides of the water, and in 1980, '81 and '82 he trudged through a diary of second-string engagements as support to major acts in largely indifferent cities. Two solo albums earned about as much sensation as a dry spell in the Sahara. His idea of calling the second record 'Bryan Adams Hasn't Heard Of You Either' must have caused wry amusement in the A&M offices (it was eventually titled, even more snottily, *You Want It – You Got It*).

Hard work, though, sometimes reaps rewards. Exhaustive touring must have imprinted more of Adams on to the rock public's memory than many thought. Either that, or it was just one of those breaks when his third LP *Cuts Like a Knife* stormed the US charts. Three very respectable, if not quite massive singles kept shoving the album a little further forward, along with Adams' now almost continuous live work. By September the LP had gone platinum. By December's end, he had played 283 days on the road in a single year. No wonder a hard worker like Princess Diana admires him.

It was the follow-up *Reckless* which really soaked Adams into the bread and butter of rock. *Reckless* punches out everything in its mainstream path: where there are frills, they're always there for a purpose. The music is defiantly one-paced – as soon as one thumping tune is gone, the next one kick-starts up. Guitar and drums are massive in the manner of all this music, but no time is

wasted. Solo passages are swift and bloody and the music always lurches back into line for the next glory-glory chorus. Adams has a brawny voice with an agreeable trace of hoarseness – a hungrier, more boyish Rod Stewart. It should be monotonous, but something in the mix keeps working. He must have already played these songs to death on the road, yet he sings them all with an amazingly infectious spirit.

What a perfectly judged set of rousing clichés! There is 'Run To You', the perennial rewrite of 'Stand By Me'; 'She's Only Happy When She's Dancin'', which needs no elaboration (Adams usually rocks out at the dance, not in the bedroom); and the howling nostalgia of 'Summer of '69', which tells of the ten-year-old Bryan plunking guitar and pulling his first band together.

Truly, this boy was born to rock. There's no *time* for smooching, so it's all 'One Night Love Affair', 'Long Gone' and 'Ain't Gonna Cry'. 'It's Only Love' he declaims, with guest star Tina Turner (Adams' appearances on Turner's own tour were irresistible – the ancient goddess of raunch and a beaming young gigolo).

The keynote of the whole record is 'Kids Wanna Rock'. "*I've seen it all from the bottom to the top/Everywhere I go, the kids wanna rock*". No idle boast. The rock of Adams is hearty without

being slobbish, handsome without growing too beautiful. He's a hunk – a broad face with curt blond hair, framing a look like a slightly haggard puppy – but not a distant, untouchable one. He's not a maverick but he's not a bland fool, either.

This past year has been, if anything, a comparatively quiet one for him. By the summer of '85 he'd already seen *Reckless* through eight straight months in the US Top 20 and it had cracked our own charts, too. Since then he has been through another concert trek, done his bit for the Canadian part of Band Aid and worked his way up to the meeting with our royalty. Once they've cracked the highest ceiling of the business – and it seems that Adams has certainly done that much – things grow peculiarly calm for the rock superstar. The business is demanding a sequel to *Reckless*, but there's no special reason why Adams should hurry. He has no need to change his act, and what comes naturally to him is pleasing people.

He's a particular part of the back-to-basics trend fired by the likes of Bruce Springsteen and John Cougar Mellencamp. Adams is like a kid brother to such men, but his approach is even earthier: he has no cause to celebrate except rock itself.

Richard Cook

113

THE JESUS AND MARY CHAIN

December 1984: in a disgustingly unkempt venue in South London, hundreds of disgustingly unkempt people are gathered. They've come to a semi-derelict squatted ambulance station on the Old Kent Road to see a group called the Jesus And Mary Chain.

The Jesus And Mary Chain are three youths plus a borrowed friend/drummer, from East Kilbride in Scotland, who have just returned from a shambolic small-time tour in Germany to find that somehow in their absence they've gained themselves something of a reputation. What happened was this: just before they'd set out for Germany they'd played a support slot for a die-hard, worthy, but largely unremarkable independent label group called the Three Johns, and for some reason or other their appearance has provoked a set of remarkably hyperbolic sentiments from the 'rock press'. The NME has described them as the new Sex Pistols; Sounds says something to the effect that they're the worst group in the world. And then, to round it off nicely, a couple of nights before the Old Kent Road concert Radio 1's 'alternative' DJ has broadcast a session by the group, an intriguingly vivacious bunch of songs submerged under voluminous layers of noisy feedback. Amongst the crowd awaiting them at the disgustingly unkempt venue expectations are high.

In the throng lurks a ginger-haired Scot called Alan McGee, who's looking very pleased. Alan is an ex-member of MOR group H2O who has more recently earned himself a more credible reputation by running a little club in London called The Living Room which specialises in putting on new and largely unsigned groups. For the last few months he's been running around trying to get some recognition for his Creation record label and now, all of a sudden, it's here in the form of this group he once booked at his club. Alan's just released their debut single 'Upside Down'. Faced by a couple of journalists Alan grabs this black-clad figure with a thatch of hair who is weaving through the crowd and introduces him to them as Jim Reid from the Jesus And Mary Chain. Jim looks very drunk. Jim says hello and then stumbles off with unsteady gait.

Maybe an hour later the group finally make it onto stage. They are atrocious. By now Jim is so drunk that his sense of balance has almost totally evaporated. He has a tendency to fall backwards onto drummer Bobby Gillespie's meagre kit. Bobby smirks from behind dark glasses. On each side bass player Douglas Hart and guitarist William Reid – Jim's older brother – emit a barrage of noise from their reluctant amplifiers. It's a bit of a disgrace really. After fifteen minutes peppered with the odd bout of Jim's swearing at a drunken audience's attempt to pogo on stage, the Jesus And Mary Chain disappear and don't re-emerge. The crowd, who like an 'event', loved it all. But this is *not* the future of rock 'n' roll.

"Two years ago," remembers Jim Reid now, "the ideal gig was to be drunk, lying on your back. But things change . . . "

Things certainly do change. In last year's Virgin *Rock Yearbook* the Jesus And Mary Chain were dismissed in an aside as "preposterous"; now they're acknowledged as an Act of the Year. Now their reputation extends far beyond the independent record ghetto that that early concert represented. Their first album *Psycho Candy* has been one of the best critically received LPs of recent years and topped the 'rock press' polls. And they've turned up on the pin-up pages of *Smash Hits*, looking as if they belonged there all along. It's a considerable achievement for a group whom many saw as a passing gimmick based on volume, drunkenness and concert violence.

The Jesus And Mary Chain emerged from an independent record 'scene' which had lost all the creativity that had been the original reason for its existence. The only 'indie' group to capture the public's imagination in recent times had been the Smiths: the rest of the small labels' output had degenerated into shamefully unimaginative and self-conscious songs that sold in only meagre quantities. The Jesus And Mary Chain came along, sold 30,000 copies of 'Upside Down' and announced that they wanted nothing to do with the independent scene, they wanted to be pop stars. As soon as they could they signed to major label WEA through its subsidiary blanco y negro.

Of course it wasn't as simple as that. The "new Sex Pistols" tag was a millstone, and it wasn't helped by manager McGee fuelling rumours of goings-on at their concerts. Some of the stories were even partly true. There *was* some violence when they played. There was the odd fight. There was the time when the group locked themselves in the dressing-room to avoid physical complaints from dissatisfied members of the audience. There was, apparently, a spot of bother over the original B-side to 'You Trip Me Up', 'Jesus Suck'. But as a whole these minor outrages weren't going to impress people in the 1980s. We'd heard all this before. It just overshadowed the fact that the Jesus And Mary Chain were rather a good pop group.

"The people who were writing about us put us in this pigeon-hole," says Jim. "They'd say 'What have you been doing recently?' and we'd say, oh we've been reading Dostoyevsky and drinking a pint of beer. They'd go 'Pint of beer. Drunken idiots.'

"You'd get some guy in an interview and he goes 'Do you want some vodka?' No. 'Some speed?' No, it's okay. Can we have some sandwiches and some orange juice. The thing comes out and we're lying in the office pissed out of our brains and puking over each other.

"For too long people had been talking about the Jesus And Mary Chain but they didn't talk about the songs or whatever. 'Jesus And Mary Chain – what a bloody racket. How long will they last?'"

The thing that changed people's minds was last year's splendid single 'Just Like Honey' and the gorgeously self-assured *Psycho Candy*; the title alone was marvellous enough. Critically it was a total success. In terms of sales, however, it was more than a little disappointing, but then as Jim said cockily before it came out, "Everyone will buy this in 1990 and say I've had this for years."

Part of the problem was that WEA were never sure of what to do with the Jesus And Mary Chain and so the album lacked the promotion that would normally go with such a poll-topping record.

"Ah well," acknowledges Jim, "the record company did absolutely nothing for it. Look at it from their point of view. We had this record which is as extreme sounding as anything you're likely to hear. They're expecting it to sell 300 copies and then die. I think it took the record company by surprise. It was pretty appalling though."

The thing about the Jesus And Mary Chain is that they actually take their music very seriously. Jim *is* genuinely disgusted at the state of modern pop. He'll talk for hours about pop. And at the same time they have a complete innocence about the music.

For example, the Jesus And Mary Chain were *convinced* that their initial trilogy of feedback singles 'Never Understand', 'Upside Down' and 'You Trip Me Up' were *all* potential chart singles. "'You Trip Me Up' is pure summer," Jim said just before its release. "It should be number one for about forty-two weeks and then we'll take it to the United States of America and it'll be number one there." Wrong. The song was actually the noisiest of all three singles: a hit in the independent charts yes, but in the pop charts absolutely not.

"Every single that comes along we think this is going to be a huge hit. This is it. Surefire hit. Steve Wright says he doesn't play the Smiths, they're not daytime radio. We thought he'd play 'You Trip Me Up'! How naive can you get?"

The Jesus And Mary Chain's innocence is something they

preserve by being a very self-contained group. They don't mix with people from 'independent' groups; they never meet other pop stars. "I'm not against it," says Jim. "It's just that I don't go out much. I don't really like nightclubs or whatever so I don't really see many pop stars."

Jim Reid stays in a lot. He likes watching videos. He goes out to the cinema a lot too. "I got followed home by four Japanese girls the other day. I don't know why. They didn't even talk to me."

1986 has been the year when the Jesus And Mary Chain learned how to cope with pop; how to get ahead. Until the release of the luscious 'Some Candy Talking' EP the group had deliberately kept their heads down in the UK, just playing the odd concert, and removing themselves to the US for a couple of small tours. (Even there, the ghost of the Sex Pistols still traipsed around after them. "Everybody dragged up the past. A lot of Americans have chips on their shoulders about the British press. They were always talking about what they'd said. Hardly anyone talked about the record. They all talked about the 'reputation'.")

"It was deliberate, us keeping a low profile over here. We'd released *Psycho Candy* and we knew that would keep up interest We didn't like the way things were going. We could afford to take a rest."

They started out all wrong. They spent a year making mistakes, getting saddled with what Jim admits was a "stupid image". They spent a year getting compared with twenty-year-old groups ("The Velvet Underground would never have written a song like 'In A Hole'," protests Jim. "It's really quite annoying.") But they've overcome all that now. Because the Jesus And Mary Chain want to be, quite simply, a pop group. And now they are.

"What's next? We might use synthesisers. We might use drum machines. We might use an orchestra. Anything's possible!"

William Shaw

THE DEVIL MAY CARE

Or at least his musicians do. John Gill reports on the unprecedented success of rock 'n' roll as fund-raiser extraordinaire

This is being written the day after Sport Aid, the last of the numerous spin-off events from Band/Live Aid. Sport Aid involved an estimated thirty million people in 266 cities in seventy-five countries running ten kilometres each, at the same time all around the world. This resulted in the Australian races starting in torchlight at 0200 hrs. The New York race began at 1100 local time, London at 1600. 200,000 ran in London. The Kenyan runners braved a monsoon. The President of Burkina Faso (formerly Upper Volta) in Africa ordered his Cabinet to join the run. The people of Mali staged a camel race, and British troops in the Malvinas (aka the Falklands) staged a 'penguin run'.

Even prior to Sport Aid, the charity had amassed over one hundred million US dollars. It is taking care that the great bulk of that money goes direct to the needy, with back-up support being asked for as a donation, and even though the Band Aid organisation is now able to respond to crises within a matter of days it will still take a long time before all the money is distributed.

Even Bob Geldof is lost for words to explain just how, and why, the original 'Feed The World' single blossomed into the most enormous act of humanitarianism on and in the history of the planet. The eighties were meant to be the decade of Thatcherism in Britain, and of Reaganism tainting the world economy. In the West it was meant to be the decade of economic decline, unemployment, the arms race and a clawback of civil liberties won in the previous two generations. It was meant to be the decade of cocktails, nightclubs, fashion and the denial of politics in favour of vacant 'style'. All of this has indeed happened, at times nudging the 'nuclear clock' a few more minutes on through the few left before 'midnight'.

But, inexplicably, the decade of the survivalists sees the West, indeed the World, in an incredibly giving mood. And the action was instigated by musicians, the profession which a decade ago not only lost a revolution but then proceeded to betray it. The, or perhaps a, lowly pop musician has achieved what governments could but would not do.

The images coming out of Africa were appalling, although a sophisticated world media can be thanked for giving them greater impact than those from Cambodia, Vietnam, Biafra, Belfast, even Belsen. What makes the era of Live Aid so extraordinary is that people should respond so massively, without the safety net of the post-WWII boom and without the fashionable radicalism which inspired the sixties. It may be that the current explosion in 'cause pop' – for Band Aid is not alone in its campaigning fervour – is actually a sign that people think things have got so bad that there is no risk in giving a helping hand, or indeed that they may soon be reaching for a helping hand themselves.

In a sense the decade had been primed: by the shortlived Rock Against Racism in '76, the growth of CND, the dashing antics of Greenpeace, the miners' strike, and in continental Europe by diverse events such as the rise of the Green Party in Germany, Italian feminist action after the chemical disaster at Seveso, even the 'hands off' campaign in France, which saw masses of people donning the badge-of-the-slogan to combat the rise of racism, and fascism in general.

But this still does not fully explain what the last year has seen. After the

● RED WEDGE

● DIONNE WARWICK

116

inspirational monument of Live Aid, American stars clubbed together for Farm Aid, to help the beleaguered agricultural community. Inspired by Peter Gabriel's 'Biko', guitarist Little Steven bullied friends in the US and UK into the 'Sun City' anti-apartheid project, producing a single, album, book and video. The pro-Labour Red Wedge swept through Britain on a sold-out tour, grabbed the front pages and is still proliferating out into the worlds of theatre, sport, cabaret and elsewhere. The close of London's worst winter in decades saw a week of packed-out benefits for Greenpeace at the Royal Albert Hall. Amnesty International, for years the reserve of middle-class comedy benefits such as the *Secret Policeman's Ball*, is once again a hot issue, with U2, Simple Minds, Sting and Peter Gabriel staging mass benefits in America and Britain. Queen recently announced that Save The Children will receive profits from part of their 1986 tour. The Colombian volcano disaster and, external to Band Aid, Central Africa, have been the subjects of massed events in London. CND is currently being groomed by a trendy London publicity specialist. And even though Reagan's salute to the dying Rock Hudson brought about a public thaw on the subject, Dionne Warwick and Friends still risked media backlash when they released 'That's What Friends Are For' to help raise funds for AIDS research. (In Britain, while Coil donated royalties from their cover of Soft Cell's 'Tainted Love' – an unfortunate choice, that –AIDS is still too controversial for pop support; in the arts, only the theatre and film communities have put their money where their sympathies, indeed proclivities, are.)

The world has gone benefit-crazy, and it would be easy, if wrong, to become cynical in the face of such generosity. The explosion of care could be dismissed simply as pop music discovering its conscience *and* discovering that conscience sells. Given that the media were demanding the equivalent of sick notes from bands who did not play Live Aid, it would not be unreasonable to question the motives of those bands who now choose to rock against racism, militarism, famine, pollution or the HTLV-3 virus. Such suspicions are, however, both graceless and pointless. The only relevant consideration is whether any good is done, and it invariably is, even if it is only to increase public awareness. It might also have an unexpectedly pleasant side-effect; proving, perhaps, that humanitarianism and caring remain more or less constant regardless of what width of trouser-leg or length of frock is in current fashion, and regard-

● REDSKINS

● EASTERHOUSE

● NEW ORDER

less of whether the synthesiser or acoustic guitar dominate the charts. (This is not to suggest we relax our vigilance over Frockism; pop stars are crafty bastards.)

In Britain, it has left us in the position where politics are, if not exactly fashionable again, then at least no longer unfashionable, the condition in which it was left by the punks and the nightclubbers. Red Wedge – a genuine, grassroots socialist marvel, of which I'm sure Orwell would have been proud – started a heated media debate. The rock press, as always, merely stood on the sidelines and sneered, but politics, and socialist politics at that, are now back at issue. Chris Dean's Redskins and Rough Trade's Easterhouse espouse the far left, and their disagreements with Red Wedge's centrist politics filled the papers for weeks. Bands such as New Order and numerous other Liverpool and Manchester

● SPORT AID

bands recently played a controversial benefit for the radical Militant Tendency council in Liverpool, who were being witchhunted by the Labour leadership. Even the crassly manipulative Sigue Sigue Sputnik, who fully admit to foisting off a second-hand stew of *Rambo, Escape From New York, Star Wars* technology and glam-rock survivalism, take on political hues (of the irresponsible right, to be precise).

There is, on reflection, a further reason for the growth in cause pop. There is nothing of the rock *right* wing in this piece. Apart from the short-lived Oi! skinhead movement and the muddled controversy over Rush in the mid-seventies, they do not need to organise, agitate and militate. The current situation suits them – and the majority of uncommitted pop stars – quite well, thank you.

And it is this situation which impelled Bob Geldof into the brilliant, world-changing desperation of Band Aid.

Whatever has caused the growth in caring pop – and I still suspect it might be a desperate act of atonement done under the sign of the Bomb – it is doing undeniable good. Not least, it vindicates those Jonahs and Ancient Mariners among us, the musicians, writers, fans, who insisted that pop music was far more than a rhythmic noise accompanied by vague aerobic notions, and that it could – as Geldof has proved – change the world. And after the disastrous flop of the last revolution, it proved it could be changed to the accompaniment of much nicer music, too. Eat your heart out, Abbie Hoffman.

THEY SHALL BE RE-RELEASED

Covers and reissues everywhere – is there a creativity crisis in pop-writing? On the whole Lloyd Bradley thinks not

'Give us one of the old songs!'

It's a shout that goes up in the average Camden Town pub should the house band move into anything as radical as a Nik Kershaw medley.

It's a cry that has spread through the music industry, too. Over the past year, moguls and musos alike discovered looking back as a way of looking forward and over fifty of the songs that entered the Top 50 had, in some shape or form, been there before.

Not exactly an enormous figure when presented as a proportion of the total records charted, but the sharp end of a fast-rising curve – an average of one a week, which is more than twice last year's figure and over four times that of 1983/84.

True, an ever-growing number of so-called 'new' hits also owe their everything to times gone by; the issue of derivative tunes, however, is so contentious that it is impossible to discuss accurately.

But turning the musical clock back *is* cause for discussion. Any trend that leads to an event such as the Monkees (or three-quarters of them) regrouping for a vast tour should not be ignored.

Unfortunately, this fad that has become such a big commercial deal usually gets a bad deal when up for debate. Collectively revivalism is treated as a malignant tumour, poised to destroy POP MUSIC AS WE KNOW IT. Unless you find yourself trapped in the 1986 Monkee House there is no need for such fear and loathing; to take each aspect individually is the best way to dispel it.

Reissues: numerically, these made up about a quarter of this year's re-appearances, but in terms of success counted for a lot more. Unlike cover versions which tend to run in chronologically ordered packs, two-time hits vary in age from mere months to thirty years old. The reasons behind their resurfacing can be equally diverse: Band Aid and Tears For Fears came back to help the hungry, 'New York, New York' probably to make someone's mum happy, but scored a surprise hit anyway; a string of Grace Jones singles were reactivated after her big screen appearances, while Sam Cooke and Marvin Gaye prospered posthumously thanks to a groovy commercial for re-released jeans.

Most reissues (including the ones that didn't make it into the charts) were fairly recent soul records. Something which, strangely, didn't fit in with the fad for mid-seventies street funk (Fatback style) that is currently burning up the best-dressed dancefloors. Only Phonogram, who even as we speak are getting together a seminal Parliament collection, seem to be aware that a huge amount of people pursue their musical pleasures beyond the realms of legal radio.

Legal radio is a big factor in these soul stakes. While the Tavares, vintage

● MARVIN GAYE　　● SAM COOKE

Shalamar and the Real Thing are each strong enough to dump on today's pretenders they are all the soft side of eras that produced some well hard tunes. They are soft enough to make the playlists of such prominent 'soul' DJs as Tony Blackburn and Robbie Vincent, something any A&R man worth his expenses would take into account when flicking through his dancing days' memories for songs his company owns.

Shows such as Tony's and Robbie's have bolted their doors so securely against progressions, deviations or contemporary, gut-felt ghetto nastiness, that soul in this country has become hopelessly retarded. The underground club network and old sounds flourish because, in its attempts to recreate a lost age of innocence through all-round wetness, the soul establishment has lost sight of the endless quest for the perfect beat.

It is small wonder that the Real Thing can score again with two ten-year-old songs: all they are up against is a supreme limpness that rules out practically anything other than unconvincing love songs wailed by equally unbelievable singers – lovers' rock for Escort XR3 cassette decks. They also show that Brit soul might've grown into something pretty splendid had it not been hijacked by this obnoxious gang.

Unfortunately, this Re-al Thing won't last long enough to point the way anywhere. Their next release is 'Can You Feel The Force', sub-*Saturday Night Fever* shenanigans at its worst, first recorded about the time funk UK began to go wrong.

● THE DAMNED

Reissues as a whole are seldom learned from. When the records or the artists are examined, they are all too often placed to one side of the mainstream as a quaint but meaningless curio. Shame, because to put them into today's context would benefit both lively debate and music in general.

Cover versions are a different matter entirely. Everyone takes them much more seriously than re-releases, presumably because they begin as the idea of whoever is doing the covering. He or she will expect, in every area, the kind of treatment that befits their status, so the record company will treat it like any other new single, whereas a re-release is likely to be the result of a few in-house memos and a couple of meetings, and therefore could live or die very cheaply.

Because of this seriousness, many covers do much better than they deserve to on musical merit alone. Artists who gain the important column inches, and thus 'credibility', are those that come across like they're on a divine mission to salvage a song from its original ruins, or benevolently to educate a public to it and so, by immediate association, claim it as their own. Such self-obsessed behaviour has produced some notable musical disasters, in some cases only overshadowed by the sheer arrogance of the performer when given the chance to spout off to scribes eagerly lapping up their hero's every word.

The present lack of objectivity in the music media has more to answer for than just dull reading.

Among the worst offenders covering out of sheer selfishness were the new-look Matt Bianco who, without the input of Danny White, put out 'Yeh, Yeh' with a complete lack of concern for anyone who knew the Georgie Fame original, Grace Jones who might've been having a joke with Roxy Music's 'Love Is The Drug', but probably wasn't (she should've left it alone anyway), Chrissie Hynde and UB40 who totally missed the simpering naffness of 'I've Got You, Babe' that made Sonny and Cher icons of their era when they did it in the sixties and Working Week who, although they mercifully didn't have a hit

● SIMPLY RED

with it, shouldn't be allowed to have their version of Marvin Gaye's 'Inner City Blues' pass unnoticed – they might do it again.

The grandest of all this larceny though, was Simply Red. Mick Hucknall told me, without a trace of a smile, that he believed they had improved on the Valentine Bros, 'Money's Too Tight'!! I can only assume he had not heard the original, simply read about its critical and club acclaim, thus helping him find a name for his band.

It is a far better long-term career prospect to approach the cover with a breezy gait, free from this intensity of purpose. To celebrate a good song and not feel the need continually to justify your actions – this greatly expands your options for your next release.

Memorable sorties into this territory last year were Amazulu's airy styling of 'Too Good To Be Forgotten', Owen Paul

reviving the Marshall Crenshaw B side 'Waste Of Time', the Damned causing a few raised eyebrows but doing themselves no harm at all with 'Eloise' and the Stones' witty video version of 'Harlem Shuffle'.

Paul Young is a master of this class. As a celebrationist he picks his songs carefully, ones he can do justice to rather than using them as proficiency tests, records them with the care that comes of a long-standing empathy and, above all, enjoys singing them – pleasure that cannot be lost in the mix. This attitude often comes across as the singer being a vehicle for the song and not the other way round, and is frequently misinterpreted as a lack in the creativity department. Young did not release last year, but his crown is in good hands. LA band the Untouchables took it for their joyous cover of 'I Spy For The FBI' and a show at the Camden Palace that was a festival of old style given the benefit of modern technology. The Blues Brothers met a laser machine at the grass roots of dub and everyone went home with a broad smile.

Smile? Some of the best cover versions are jokes. Jokes that illustrate the huge gap between critic and buyer. The former will po-facedly analyse and usually arrive at glaringly irrelevant

● GRACE JONES

● MATT BIANCO

conclusions, while the latter will show their appreciation of a good wind-up by putting it in the charts. Even in the case of Cliff and the Young Ones most writers missed the joke; it was not the expected antics of the alternative quartet, but His Holiness's automatic-pilot smoothness that was really funny.

The best musical pranks came at the beginning and end of the year. Both spent a few weeks at number one and together proved that the harder you try to make yourself look silly, the less likely you are to end up looking stupid.

First was Bowie and Jagger who camped it up dazzlingly to 'Dancin' In The Street'. Not only was this in a good cause, but it also provided the best example in living memory of two fabulously wealthy old blokes acting like prats. A year later, Dr and the Medics showed that you don't need to be as well established as Dave and Mick to

make a fool of yourself on television, when they topped the charts with the utter ridiculousness that was 'Spirit In The Sky'. Don't try and judge this record by the original, or indeed anything to do with psychedelia; the yardstick is twenty years later. 'Spirit's' closest living relative is 'The Chicken Song'. Both shovelled on every cliché imaginable, plus a few that weren't, until the whole heap spilled gloriously over the top of the serious business called pop music.

With the Doctor, this came out more in interviews than performance. On demand he would stick his tongue so far into his cheek he risked internal bleeding, and give any scribe interested his carefully thought out and rather pleasant trip through anything they expected to hear. To show what a superb piss-taker he is, the Doctor should now wash his face and slip back into oblivion while everyone is still enjoying the joke. To try it again would be just plain tedious.

Some jokes didn't go far enough to get the BIG LAFF. Close to the chuckles were the Fine Young Cannibals with 'Suspicious Minds' who found that it took more than Andy Cox's dancing to undermine Roland Gift's posturing, and while 'Venus' must've had Bananarama rolling about, private jokes don't often go public too well, even when helped by a funny video.

It is worth noting that Keith Harris and Orville the Duck singing 'White Christmas' didn't even raise a smile.

So, in spite of 'thinking' pop journalists and tap-room intellectuals speculating about the creativity crisis in British pop, there is really nothing to worry about, as you can see. Really divvy reissues never get too far, the intense coverists self-destruct by setting themselves higher and higher mountains to climb and the others are usually quite enjoyable.

It's simply a matter of the past helping the present out of a fallow period between the just-gone and soon-to-come BIG THINGS, and in the wake of Samantha Fox and Stryper (an American heavy metal band that's got God – honest!) it's surely a good thing. It will only become a problem if it becomes a way of life. Not too far fetched a notion.

Motown UK, famed for their compilation sets that get released under a different name each year – presumably to fool, momentarily, seriously dyslexic record buyers – have now extended their reissue policy to the singles side. 'You Keep Me Hanging On' and 'My Girl' are all set to follow 'Grapevine' by reappearing in original form. When questioned about this, a company spokesperson replied: "We want to have hits!".

YOUNG, GIFTED AND BRITISH

Traditional US resistance to British black music is being worn down by a posse of UK producers and artists. Brian Chin reports

Quick, now: where was the largest-selling rap album of all time recorded? Wrong – not at SugarHill's Sweet Mountain studio, not at Shakedown, Unique, Green Street, INS, PowerPlay or any of the New York studio bastions of rap. Whodini's near million-seller *Escape* was recorded in London's Battery Studios.

Phonogram A&R man and former mobile DJ Nigel Grainge, when asked

● 52nd STREET

in 1975 whether he saw a future in UK-originated black music, was unsentimental: "Not really; there's rather a lack of feel that comes from British musicians working that type of material. It's been tried . . . I worry when probably 60 or 70 per cent of the tapes sent in are by British R&B acts."

Nigel Grainge, meet Billy Ocean, Loose Ends, 52nd Street, Princess, Five Star, Junior, O'Chi Brown, Precious Wilson, Wally Badarou and Total Contrast – and, *please*, stop that worrying. British-based black artists are now making regular stops on the black, pop and club charts of America, cradle of soul music.

Sometimes, British presence in the US has gone hand in hand with American producers or, quite often, an American studio mixer. To say that a record "sounded American" has generally been a sincere compliment. But more recently, there has been an identifiably British approach to pro-

duction and/or writing that, on occasion, made such records as Princess's 'Say I'm Your Number One', Precious Wilson's 'I'll Be Your Friend' and Loose Ends' 'Hangin' On A String (Contemplating)' sound not merely 'as good', but *more* elegant and well-crafted than the US item.

American club DJs and hipper black radio programmers are into a six-year-old love-affair with the British. When Billy Ocean's 'Nights (Feel Like Getting Down)' reached America on a UK GTO import late in 1980, pre-release club

● LOOSE ENDS

and even radio play made imports sell like a US release. By mid-1981, 'Nights', on US Epic, was a Top Five black hit and a pop charter. Karma was building (especially for Ocean): this was the first record to fly out of the import shops and eventually hit the official charts.

Following in that post-disco path were the mainstream pop/R&B of Junior's 'Mama Used To Say' (Top 30 pop in spring 1982), Central Line's serene and eloquent 'Walking Into Sunshine', and several of the underground cult grooves of that period: Eddy Grant's 'Time Warp', Powerline's jazz-funk 'Double Journey', Imagination's 'Just An Illusion' and 'Changes' and, especially, Bo Kool and Funkmasters' dubwise Garage hit, 'Love Money'.

Even the flukes – Modern Romance's 'Salsa Rappsody' and the Evasions' 'Wikka Wrap' – possessed a winning sense of style that tickled the interest of US listeners. Human League's 'Don't

You Want Me?', Yazoo's 'Situation' and Soft Cell's 'Tainted Love' were also perceived as an integral progressive aspect of the phenomenon (lumped in, simply, as more 'imports'), as were later, more radical records, such as Malcolm McLaren's 'Buffalo Gals', Art Of Noise's 'Beat Box', and West India Company's 'Ave Maria'. (Sade's two albums were also seen as being in the group, and added inestimable credibility to im-

● JUNIOR

ported British music although, strictly speaking, they weren't coming from the same place.)

The emerging question, by now, was: could the British *soul* community come up with something that rivalled the depth of feeling, the assurance, atmosphere and authenticity of, say, 'D Train, Kashif, or the Jimmy Jam/Terry Lewis productions?

The answers have come from several places. There is an Anglo-American approach: the fruitful collaborations of Billy Ocean and New York's Keith Diamond, and of Loose Ends and Philadelphia's Nick Martinelli put 'Caribbean Queen' and the gorgeously lush, jazzy 'Hangin' On a String' at the top of the US black charts in summer 1984 and 1985, respectively. In 1986, Martinelli, reteamed with writer/arrangers Loose Ends (Carl McIntosh, Jane Eugene, Steve Nichol), scored another Top Three US R&B hit in Five Star's sophisticated teenybop 'All Fall

Down', and while the follow-up (produced in Holland and Britain by Oattes/Van Schaik) 'Love Take Over' was going Top Five R&B, Martinelli and 52nd Street had a melodic soft-soul hit with 'Tell Me (How It Feels)'.

Ocean's second Jive album, *Love Zone*, matched him with a team of American producers, Barry Eastmond (Freddie Jackson) and Wayne Braithwaite (Glenn Jones). Co-written by the three, recorded in London and mixed in New York, the album was classy and soulful, with beautifully-developed ballads that underscored Ocean's accomplishment as a vocalist.

Clear centres of creativity have emerged in Britain: at Battery Studios, the production facility of Jive Records; at PWL Studios, in London's Borough, where former DJ Pete Waterman, hi-NRG and dance-rock producer of Divine and Dead Or Alive, launched the Brit-soul Supreme label; and in the diverse, clearly British-identified work of many others.

bass-heavy feel of Full Force's 'Alice, I Want You Just For Me', was an obvious afterthought; but a remix of O'Chi Brown's uptempo disco-soul 'Whenever You Need Somebody' overlaid with the driving electronic drum pattern of Harlequin Fours' cult hit 'Set It Off', sent Brown to the top of the US dance chart late in April 1986.

Jive Records was well on its way to becoming an international conglomerate of record production, music publishing, book publishing and producer management, operating out of a complex in the London suburb of Willesden and centred around Battery Studios. Its Motown-like staff of producers, engineers and keyboard players, under the collective tag 'Willesden Dodgers', created a patchwork of pop, soul, jazz and electro hits, from the crass yet undeniably interesting Samantha Fox hit, 'Touch Me (I Want Your Body)', to Ruby Turner's lovely revival of 'If You're Ready (Come Go With Me)', Mark Shreeve's 'Legion' and Precious Wilson's US sleeper beat-ballad, 'I'll Be Your Friend', not to mention the mega-selling Whodini, who far overshadowed

with a bigger hit (though not as big as at home), '19', both with wide black support: his vocal track featuring Carol Kenyon, 'Don't Waste My Time' was indistinguishable from a good American record. Junior Giscombe, still recovering from the dazzle of 'Mama Used To Say', scored a Top Fifteen US R&B hit with 'Oh, Louise', an arrestingly melodic combination of pop, soul, go-go and gospel that stiffed appallingly in Britain.

By 1986, Britain had also become an important pop outlet for black American artists frozen out of segregated US pop radio: Colonel Abrams (sharing production with Briton Richard James Burges), Mantronix, Joyce Sims, SOS Band, Aurra, Thomas and Taylor, and Whistle were just some of the artists enjoying greater pop success abroad than at home.

As black music became hotter on a pop level in the UK, though, it remained unclear whether artists and producers would tailor records more to pop to

● O'CHI BROWN

● 5-STAR

● PAUL HARDCASTLE

Most interesting was PWL, thanks to the cogent songwriting of Waterman, guitarist Mike Stock and keyboardist Matt Aitken, and to Waterman's ingenuity as a remix conceptualist. He was given to actually re-*producing* his hits, moulding rhythms and instrumentation from other current club items on to the original vocal tracks and somehow saving all the hooks.

Waterman pulled his most outrageous stunt in November 1985 when Princess's second single 'After The Love Has Gone', (like 'Number One', a near-clone of Jam/Lewis' SOS Band low-tempo funk) reappeared with a totally re-recorded backing track – patterned exactly after Wally Badarou's third world/electro/go-go 'Chief Inspector', another of the British productions to hit America's R&B Top 40 in early 1986. The execution was perfect, and highly amusing, too.

The third mix of 'After The Love Has Gone', mutated again, this time with the

Jive's other rap artists, all of them Americans produced by Britons. Key among the Dodgers: engineer-producers Bryan 'Chuck' New and Nigel Green; Fairlight programmer Pete O Harris; and writer/producer (and former Gang Of Four bassist) Jon Astrop.

Jive's productions mirrored the polyglot make-up of the British pop chart and, therefore, always seemed to have potential for a UK breakthrough, while in America, Whodini and Billy Ocean held the standard. But the company's fearless eclecticism extended to the signing of two more Americans: Millie Jackson and the tremendous gospel singer Vanessa Bell Armstrong.

Other active producers and artists existed between the underground and the mainstream, or were mainstream artists sporadically making hits in the UK or US: electronics whiz Paul Hardcastle followed his 1985 US pop chart debut 'Rain Forest', a UK sleeper,

take advantage of the real opportunities or whether they could take a more uncompromising attitude about their creative identity.

And while some excellent albums were appearing – Princess's debut; Haywoode's *Arrival*; 52nd Street's *Children of the Night*; *Total Contrast*; and Five Star's inexhaustible singles machine *Luxury of Life* – it was a fact that the best of them were basically producers' records, with the exception of Loose Ends' *So Where Are You?* Bottom line: in 1986, Stock/Aitken/Waterman, Steve Harvey, the Willesden Dodgers and Nick Martinelli were the movers and shakers; in 1987, it will be up to the artists and budding do-it-yourselfers to make more of an impression as individuals if they are to take the next step, from being makers of occasional hit singles in the US marketplace to taking a place among the biggest established American stars.

WALLPAPER FOR LIFTS

John Gill deplores the glorification of 'mood muzak' into New Age Music

Anyone around here remember the term 'Soft Rock'? It was common currency in the early seventies, alongside such linguistic gems as 'Progressive Rock', which took on darkly ironic properties after the third Genesis album. As the term suggests, 'Soft Rock' was the least offensive item in a lexicon which, re-read now, will curl your hair faster than anything manufactured by Braun.

While often inaccurate, even meaningless, these terms are not used lightly. Soft Rock was the music your parents would allow into the lounge. Soft Rock was trendiness for people fearful of four hairy Midlanders riffing through black magic anthems. Crucially, Soft Rock was also a sop to timid radio and television producers. It may have been lame and spineless, but Soft Rock was entirely innocuous, unlike its mid-eighties equivalent, New Age Music, currently rolling in on a wave from the West Coast. No mere musical genre, NAM – a telling, if accidental, acronym – is a *lifestyle*: a cereal, a Nautilus exercise, a jogging sweatband, a well-stocked bunker in the Rockies for when the balloon goes up. The men and women who produce this music want nothing less than your minds.

Or so current myth would have it. The genre is in fact confounded by its own diversity; it is almost defined by default. In America, it has come to symbolise something approaching libertarianism, but in Britain it seems to be a reaction against rowdy, improper and oversexed noise. Coda, the leading BritNAM label, defines its area as 'from Elgar to Eno', although few would place its two main acts, singer Claire Hammill

and keyboard clown Rick Wakeman, inside that spectrum. Equally unusual names in the Coda catalogue are those of one-time sideman to the likes of Mike Oldfield, rocker Tom Newman, jazzer John Themis, and Incantation who had a major success with 'Cacharpaya' which employed the sounds of Peruvian native pipes.

Next in line, the new Pan East label, specialises in hi-tech Japanese synth-pop in the Yellow Magic Orchestra vein, with artists such as Ichiko Yashimoto, Seigen Ono, Yoshio Suzuki and Masahide Sakuma. The genre is meant to appeal to a market lost to the current pop scene; those to whom even the mass-appeal MOR bands seem alien and impudent. This will seem bizarre to anyone with good reason for having this yearbook in their hands, but the NAM market seems so lucrative to businesspeople that Virgin and at least two other major labels are champing at the bit to jump. Everyone is now denying that the genre even exists, but, as in the manner of Washington protocols, it's leaked and then denied, leaving the journalists holding the baby. But I think we have more than enough to make this one stand up in court.

When NAM began to slip into Britain, in the form of imports from the highly successful American market-leader Windham Hill, which produces jazz-classical ear candy, stories began to circulate of a whole new US underground movement. It mixed eighties pragmatism with sixties idealism, and was said to buy most of its records in wholefood stores and alternative

bookshops. It even had its own magazine, incriminatingly called New Age, which promoted the missing link between muesli and monetarism, solar panels and survivalism. It was as fundamentally American as Thoreau at Walden Pond.

You couldn't give that away down the Mile End Road, of course. In any case, Britain had had its own brand of post-Aquarian mood muzak for over a decade. We might even claim it as our own invention, having given the world that NAM monument, *Tubular Bells*. In Europe, the electronic strain of NAM had been oozing out of studios in Berlin and Munich ever since Tangerine Dream inspired legions of imitators. France had made numerous forays into the area, and aptly enough the eighties saw Japan in the ascendant with the massively popular Kitaro and others. The style then had a much lower public profile, but worked in the same manner as NAM: offering a background hum – and not without a certain schoolboyish snobbery – to those who did not care to drink, dance, fight or fuck to the beat. Indeed, the notion of 'beat' was kindly shown the door.

In its original, anonymous, form, NAM was not without its charm. Mike Oldfield records are banned from my Dansette, but *Tubular Bells* invaded the globe to the extent that it is probably still the news signature theme on Radio People's Angkor Wat. Tangerine Dream, parents of the synthesiser drone school, were themselves at least original in

● KITARO

● JOHN THEMIS

● TANGERINE DREAM

forging the string compositions of Gyorgy Ligeti on electronic instruments. Brian Eno – widely touted as an elder statesman of the genre by NAMsters, but in a talismanic way, as though hoping some of his status will rub off on them – has produced some excellent albums, 'ambient' and otherwise. Forgetting the mind-rot produced by America's Muzak Inc and the countless 'library music' studios which produce background music for commercial venues, we all know and love records, bands and composers whose music we frequently use for background to work and play. (The radio, in fact, only survives as a commodity because it is used in a secondary function; that is, apart from actually sitting down and concentrating on what it is playing.)

NAM, however, committed to a name, a market and a function – almost as though it were a service industry – is fundamentally wrongheaded. The genre opens itself up to so much criticism; primarily, of using a disguise to palm off shoddy, substandard and unoriginal music which would never have got onto a 'real' record label. We may not always want to breakdance to Mantronix or headbang to Rush, but if we want music which works on a secondary level what's wrong – to pluck a few off the top of the head – with Chopin, Ravel, Gershwin, Porter, Gil Evans, Antonio Carlos Jobim, Keith Jarrett, Sandy Denny, Cluster, Michael Nyman, Joni Mitchell, Steve Reich, Suzanne Vega, Roedelius, Eberhard Weber, the Durutti Column? This is not to belittle 'noble' music – it's strong enough to survive any context – nor is it snobbery, although it may take a little effort to obtain. In promoting an arbitrary list of alternatives to brand-name NAM, I am less effective than the NAMsters, who have advertising budgets, distributors, shops and the persuaders of the media on their side. I may, however, be risking the boast that the Quality is on my side.

NAM hides its lack of originality, vision and muscle behind the modesty of its intentions; it is, after all, only pleading to be allowed in to sort of slither around the walls for a bit before humbly sneaking off. I actually wonder about the self-image of those involved in the music. Imagine a conversation in a trendy Soho, or indeed SoHo, bar: Ordinary Composer: "Hi. Robert Wilson's asked me to collaborate with David Byrne and Laurie Anderson on this new 12-hour multi-media piece he's staging for a week on a gigantic raft in the middle of Lake Titicaca. It's got a million's-worth of pyrotechnics. Twyla Tharp's choreographing two hundred dancers, the sets are by Keith Haring and it also involves seventy-five hot air balloons. I get to conduct two gamelan orchestras, the London Philharmonic, the Stuttgard Opera company, and the Vatican choir. Coppola's filming it."
NAM Composer: "Oooh er, well, at the moment I'm running up a few rolls of pink flock for a Chinese restaurant."

You wouldn't ask it of your dog.

We might also ask ourselves just where all these dazzling new talents are coming from. Perhaps, as the Was Brothers had it, woodwork squeaks. It is highly suspicious that at the drop of a convenient tag, all this talent should suddenly erupt on both sides of the Atlantic. Where *were* they hiding all this time? Personally, I haven't seen that many brilliant, undiscovered composers and musicians lounging on street corners waiting to importune the next passing record company executive.

What I *have* seen, however, is countless numbers of original and adventurous musicians and composers rolling up their sleeves and attempting to dismantle the barricades of disinterest themselves. This is no romantic ideal of the poet in his garret, starving for his art. These musicians, working in experimental rock, contemporary jazz, electronics and the avant-garde, all deserve more than they are getting. Having lived for a decade with a composer who is more or less happily Unfashionable, I also know a thing or two about garrets myself. But in this light, the so-called pioneers and frontiersmen of NAM look more like dole queue scroungers compared to those who, in the face of general antipathy, have decided to struggle on with their own bands, labels, clubs and magazines. It should also be noted that these people, even if they're *minimalists*, want to confront and provoke the listener, not put you to sleep.

And just what are we left with at the end of a typical NAM day? Another, far more insidious sop to timid radio and television producers. Cynically, we might also be left with a number of people whose eyes are rolling like fruit machines at the thought of all those lovely royalties from their soundtracks to a million natural history documentaries.

I also suspect that NAM merely panders further to people's laziness, and the careless, unthinking way we consume culture. As if Sade, Sting and Dire Straits weren't inoffensive enough to accompany their dinner parties and impress the boss's wife. Is this really why we dressed up in all those ridiculous clothes, spent all that money, danced, fell in love, got drunk? If you ask me, squire, they all need a bloody good dose of Einsturzende Neubauten.

● CLAIRE HAMILL

● TOM NEWMAN

● MIKE OLDFIELD

EXCLUSIVE!! POP STARS ARE EGO MANIACS

And that is why they make front page news, according to Fleet Street's pop gossip king John Blake. Tom Hibbert is unconvinced.

"The Sun are utter bastards but they don't try and cover it up. Everybody knows they're bastards. You ask anybody – every person who reads the Sun – they don't believe it. They don't believe a word that's written."
David O'Dowd, brother of Boy George, July 1986.

"God, I hate that man. He's so evil. It really freaks me out that someone like that has so much power. All he asked about was drugs but he does it in a way where he makes out he's being my friend, trying to do me a favour. I knew I shouldn't have talked to him."
Boy George, minutes after being interviewed by John Blade of the *Daily Mirror* (in May '86 – a few weeks before the Boy George junkie headlines broke).

"I know all the pop stars sit down and probably say 'John Blake! What a bastard!' But they all want to do interviews because they're all bleeding ego maniacs. They all want to see their mush staring out of the paper. They all think they're wonderful and they all want to be very, very famous."
John Blake.

The first few days of July had been dream-time for the pop music journalists of the British tabloids. After months of trying they had finally nailed Boy George. They'd found him out – a heroin addict – a juice-rich pop scandal; and, for once, they hadn't made it all up (well, not all of it, anyway). The *Sun* had got the whole story from no less a source than Boy George's own brother and the Boy George junkie headlines stretched across front pages for ever, forcing all 'proper' news within . . .

Before the eighties pop music-related stories rarely made Fleet Street front page news, give or take a Sid Vicious hotel 'incident' or two. But by 1986 it had become an almost daily occurrence. In relentless pursuit of new, young readers – 24 and under – the low-brow popular press had seized on pop gossip and tittle-tattle with an unpalatably desperate

glee, and treated it like major hard-line news. A nuclear reactor might be melting down in Russia but what made the front page of the *Sun* in letters eight miles high? Some inconsequential scoop about Simon le Bon visiting his "AIDS PAL" in hospital (Duran Duran publicist Nick Underwood who has since died of leukemia). Pop music tenuously linked with the "gay plague" – hey presto! a perfect story. Of course, the Royal Family remained the most newsworthy figures and the favoured targets of the 'street of shame', but pop stars now ran them a close second (with characters from TV soap operas – the sexy secrets of Dirty Den, etc etc – a poor third).

The gentlemen of the press had come to a reasonably simple conclusion: the average reader was no longer startled by or interested in the drinking and/or sexual habits of the toffs with fancy names who had previously provided Fleet Street with its gossip diet. As for film stars, those of the eighties were all American, boring and identical-looking – and no one went to the cinema anymore, anyway. Politicians? Too powerful and too *dull* (in surveys, only one in a million people have even heard of Geoffrey Howe but *everyone* knows Paul "big nose" King). And so Fleet Street turned feverishly to the world of pop music. It was so obvious, really. Rock persons were, by tradition, *supposed* to be ill-behaved – hence a rich source of 'juicy' stories, personalities falling down drunk in swanky nightclubs with no clothes on, etc etc. And rock persons were, by profession, *supposed* to welcome publicity of any kind – anything to sell their name and a few more musical units. The press and the pop stars (or, rather, the pop stars' publicists) entered into an unwritten pact of co-operation. As Dave Rimmer put it in his treatise on new youth culture *Like Punk Never Happened*: "The kind of fame the new pop stars wanted was no longer the youth culture or cult appeal that could be granted by the ailing traditional music press. They

wanted to be as famous as Princess Diana . . . So straight out of the window went anything more than a passing interest in the *NME, Melody Maker* etc. Fleet Street was much more exciting: uncharted territory and read by millions too."

But although on most days the press's pop coverage was harmless and innocuous enough – a blurry photo of Belouis Some (who?) flanked by a pair of "foxy" "chicks" here, a sensationally dull snippet concerning Annie from Amazulu's tattoo there – it was fully fledged 'scandal' that the editors wanted. And when their hounds went sniffing it out, the relationship twixt popsters and journalists turned less than cosy. The kind of paper that splashes a headline like "FREDDIE STARR ATE MY HAMSTER" across its front page would appear to be less interested in 'truth' than a cheap guffaw and an easy sale, and when David O'Dowd

● SEAN PENN AND MADONNA

called one paper "bastards", he was just repeating what a lot of pop folk had been thinking for ages.

John Blake is the king, the instigator, of the modern pop music gossip column. The first man to be employed by Fleet Street to serve up a daily diet of pop pap and ersatz high-life (youth/rock) gossip. It was Blake who started the 'Ad Lib' column on the *London Evening News* – a bitty mixture of rock things, trendy restaurants and cinema – moving it to the

Standard when the papers merged. In 1983, he was poached by Kelvin McKenzie, editor of the "soaraway" *Sun*, and began 'Bizarre' – a whole page of pop guff and nonsense every day. Blake did not, however, enjoy working for the *Sun* overmuch – or so he says – because "there was a lot of pressure to exaggerate and distort. If I wrote stories that I liked, the editor would come back and say 'this is a load of bollocks, I want something decent'. [For 'decent' read *its opposite*.] So you've got this tremendous pressure on you five days a week to come up with something sensational."

These days Blake works for the *Mirror* – his is the daily column called 'The White Hot Club' – having been through a battle of the giants, Robert Maxwell vs. Rupert Murdoch, for his services. Murdoch had Blake so Maxwell, when he took over the *Mirror, wanted* him. And so Murdoch, in his turn, wanted to *keep* him, flying Blake and his wife out to New York and enticing them with Porsches and outlandish salaries in his attempts to do so. "I was very aware," says Blake, "that Murdoch and Maxwell had probably never read a word of mine in their lives. I was like some painting they were both bidding for, two guys' egos on the go."

Maxwell was the victor but the *Sun* would counter with a team that would bestride the competition like a colossus ... the 'Bizarre' column fell into the hands of Nick Ferrari and

● JOHN BLAKE

Martin Dunn. The *Star*, too, would begin filling its pages with rock 'n' roll gibber-jabber and the *Mail* was not far behind. The past year has seen this cauldron of pop filth and fury bubbling more furiously than ever before. 'Great journalistic scoops' have included:

!! A front page "exclusive" based around Sade who, if the story was to be believed, burst into tears on stage in Germany and fled, blubbing "Hold onto your love – I lost mine". (In fact, she did nothing of the sort. She left the stage because she was ill.)

!! A front page "exclusive" based around Simon le Bon, who'd just married Yasmin, being unfaithful to his bride by having amazing rumpo with "glamorous" and "leggy" model Maree Herbert in Australia. (In fact, he did nothing of the sort. He was just *seen* in an Australian club with Maree with whom he happened to be filming a jeans commercial. Yasmin subsequently miscarried their baby and Simon's mum blamed *that* on these scurrilous press reports.)

!! Lots of front page "exclusives" about Madonna and Sean Penn being sulky egomaniacs. So miffed was the popular press that Madonna and Sean hadn't paused for a 'chat', when they arrived in England for the shooting of *Shanghai Surprise*, that it transformed the couple in reports into "The Poison Penns", a "crummy couple" whose behaviour was either "snooty" or like that of "animals" or like that of "the Gestapo", depending on which paper you happened to be reading. *Shanghai Surprise*'s executive producer, George Harrison, was incensed by the press's treatment of his two stars, saying "Everything in the press has been started *by* the press – either a photographer sitting on the bonnet of the car or the appalling behaviour of one newspaper who stole photographs from the film set." Well!

● BOY GEORGE

!! Lots of front page "exclusives" about Andrew Ridgeley being a drunken idiot. Poor old Andrew. Never a dull moment, what with his continual car accidents and enormous headlines like "OH ANDY! What *Were* You Doing With The Girl In Green Knickers?" (not very much at all, as it turned out) and "DRUNK WHAM! STAR IN SEX ROW" (in letters so jumbo that there was, fortunately, very little room left on the page for the stultifying non-story).

!! Lots of front page "exclusives" about the violence and "Nazi outrage" of Sigue Sigue Sputnik. With a bit of a kerfuffle at the band's first gig, the press thought they'd sniffed the new Sex Pistols and followed them on their mini-tour, almost *willing* Ray "menace" Mayhew to bottle someone else and Martin Degville to shout remarks of a racist nature. (But they didn't and so SSS became yesterday's news.)

!! And . . . 'Hop Off You Frogs': a soaring achievement by the *Sun*'s 'Bizarre' team – outdoing even their 'exposure' of the Red Wedge tour artists as "loony lefties" and their front page splash revealing that Suggs of Madness had once been friendly with a member of the National Front (this last story devised by new *Sun* recruit Gary Bushell, ex of *Sounds* and 'pioneer' of Oi). Their very own pop record. This was their reply to a song called 'Miss Maggie' by French singer Renaud which was less than complimentary about Mrs Thatcher and had thus caused a bit of a furore in the British media. 'Hop Off You Frogs' performed by The Bizarre Boy's (*sic*), a piece of jaunty xenophobia accusing the entire French race of being homosexual (*"even the bridges are bent"*) haw haw – sung all gruntily and out of tune. What a lark! How pathetic.

So it goes . . .

At the other end of the market, the "serious" newspapers had also latched onto rock music as never before, hoping to capture the loyalty and attention of the compact disc-buying generations (those youthful, upwardly mobile people with a taste for the sophisticated doings of Sade, Phil Collins, Dire Straits etc) with articulate but ultimately tedious star-at-home type profiles all over the shop. On 22 June 1986, each of the three so-called quality Sundays – the *Observer, Sunday Times* and *Sunday Telegraph* – carried glossy photographs of rock personalities –Eurythmics, Wham! and David Bowie respectively – on the front pages of their colour supplements. A decade before, great railways of Burma had vied with Third World refugees for supplement space, but now stars of film and music were the norm.

Meanwhile, down in the gutter, Wapping and Fleet Street were busy killing Boy George with their pea shooters... "I am quite amazed," the "bemused" victim was quoted as saying, once they'd tracked him down, "that all this has caused so much fuss. I can't believe everyone is so interested..." What a fool. If, that is, he ever spoke those words at all. It's so hard to tell, isn't it?

WHAT YOU SEE IS WHAT YOU HEAR

Robert Elms argues that the look IS the sound and always has been

As far as I'm concerned Zodiac Mindwarp and the Love Reaction had it the most this year. As soon as that picture appeared, so pretty, so perfectly wildly right, the phone began ringing. "That is the best group I've never seen" said the sages who speak deep and considered tones on these topics. Details, such attention to details, such a powerful emotional élan, such ludicrous names. There, in one deliciously grave and groovy psychedelic snapshot, was the perfect pop moment of the past twelve months. Some few special things make this life so exciting.

Good things look good. That is what you must tell the dour doubters who ask redundant questions like 'what about the music?' As if a trained eye cannot tell from looking what the listening will be like. Popular music has always looked like it sounds. It is inevitable, making a lousy lie of all that form and content dichotomy stuff. Were Elvis' sideburns form or content? And didn't he sing just like he swaggered? Pop is what it appears to be, and always has been; what you see is what you get. Muse, if you will, on those crazy mixed-up Sigue Sigue kids: wasn't their music just like you imagined? Now that is another story.

Sigue Sigue Sputnik and their silly clothes have certainly caused a fuss this year, but it's almost not a story any more. Every now and then a new band emerges in which a mind or two has very definitely been at work, and a good mind is a delight to behold. The intelligence involved in creating *one of those bands* is where the entertainment lies. And do not think for a moment that the corporate, mediocre minds of the record companies could ever come up with an original idea. It always comes from down there in the creative swamp of British street culture. That is why the hyped stuff is so often the right stuff. The Sex Pistols, Spandau Ballet, Frankie Goes To Hollywood, Sade, now Sigue Sigue Sputnik. Think what you will about the musical careers of the above mentioned, they've all played their part in stirring up the pop firmament. And that's what pop is, as it sounds: a perfect piece of onomat-

● ZODIAC MINDWARP
AND THE LOVE REACTION

● SIGUE SIGUE SPUTNIK

opoeia for something which goes bang but doesn't hurt anybody.

It's a serious business playing the pop game, but it isn't something to get serious about. The real joy of pop is rarely to be found in the mire of mediocre music that sweeps out of daytime radio, and never in the worthy 'Peeltime', polytechnic angst and humour of the real rock brigade. Its essence is in its stances and styles, the wonderful wind-ups, the clothes and the clamour, the twist and the shout;

the ephemera *is* the real thing. Some times, of course, you get the bonus of music, too – and far rather 'Relax' an 'F1 11' than Money For Nothing and Heaven Knows I'm Boring Now.

But if you want music, and Go knows it's a wonderful thing, listen t John Coltrane or Paco De Lucia Smokey Robinson or Eric Satie. If yo want music there's a whole world of wonderful, timeless talents to b soothed and inspired by. Pop, though is consumed in an entirely differen way. You might, or more probably migh not, buy a piece of vinyl, but even if yo choose not to pay you still see the pla It's a drama of style acted out i glorious techno-colour for all to enjo From every video juke-box to ever daily paper, from *Top of the Pops* to TV am we're a nation obsessed by th wonderful soap opera of pop. An thankfully, now and then, a new charac tor introduces himself and rewrites th script. Of course Sigue Sigue Sputni look terrible, it's trash of the lowes order. But through all the high heel and high hair has shone a wonderfu sense of the possibilities of pop. Fro the perfectly executed wind-up and th brilliantly constructed videos to th sharp cinematic steals, from the perfec press manipulation to the sleeve credit for their attorney. Tony James ha played the pop game like a master, an it is always worth watching a master a work. Sigue Sigue Sputnik don't loo good, but they've been well wort looking at. BAD have looked just fine but then Mick Jones is a style vetera too.

One of the great lies of our age i that punk was not about style: it was a about style. Based around Malcolr McLaren and Vivienne Westwood' designer clothes shop, and fuelled by bunch of over-educated art student punk was a trouser revolution. An Mick Jones, who, as a founder of th Clash first became famous as much fc his customised fatigues as for his guita playing, has taken many of the stylisti ideas of '76 and translated them int one of the best of the new bands of '8 Big Audio Dynamite.

Again the way they look and soun

have been a reflection of each other. Mixing up elements of classic Americana, English street style and rasta imagery, the blend of baseball caps and Dr Martens, Levi jackets and dreadlocks has been the perfect visual accompaniment to their aural mix of hip hop, funk, rock and reggae. The joyful style piracy of BAD has been one of the most refreshing inputs into a pop scene where the drabbies have been fighting back. The don't-give-a-damn dullards of the Dire Strai(gh)ts, Bryan Adams, Huey Lewis, John Parr school of ugly musos playing the turgid rock of ages have had a pretty successful year. But it isn't just the Jones gang with their engaging album and exciting gigs who've stood up for the right stuff.

At the other end of the sound spectrum from the irreverent dance pop of Big Audio Dynamite and as far removed as you can possibly get from the over-the-top glam outrage of Sigue Sigue Sputnik has been Sade and her boys. Inevitably, in the pedantically crafted Sade package sound and style are inextricably and naturally linked. They are also so finely, fluently honed that they've become seamlessly absorbed into the culture, as if they were always there. Yet with *Promise*, their second album, topping the charts throughout the world, they've been remarkable ambassadors for a genuinely radical British aesthetic.

The dramatically pared down and understated, but always meticulously styled Sade and her band have been the most successful sartorial and musical representatives of the vastly

influential *Face* ethic. Mixing the penthouse with the pavement, cowboy boots and Levis with Gaultier and Yamamoto, it is the unique chic of the London club world where low-life and high fashion are fused in the drive for perfect styling. The girl and the music are like that too; not cool, but passionately committed to perfection, the pursuit of fine things. And in that search they've added a subtlety and true sophistication to the pop vocabulary that was rarely there before.

Seventies soul, fifties jazz, contem-

● SADE

porary technology and the timeless elements of rhythm and melody all rolled together to create something new and now. That's the musical side of the Sade story and it's the same with the way they look, a thoroughly contemporary whole created out of strands of past and present. *Absolute Beginners* did that too.

In many respects Julien Temple's movie of Colin MacInnes' novel was the pop and style event of the year and about the year. Nominally set in 1958, *Beginners* was really an essay on swinging London now. The late fifties, which has long been an era of fascination for those who care about the culture, was a neat stylistic hook to hang the film on; the clothes and the cars looked good. But starring contemporary pop icons from Bowie to Patsy, using a soundtrack that included Sade, Style Council and Working Week, and full of extras dragged in from London's clubland, it was really set in the teaming Soho home of today's British film, pop and fashion industries.

Charting young England's continuing obsession with style, *Absolute Beginners* was loud, brash, bright, bold and young: it was almost a definition of pop. Visually it was stunning, it was great fun and it caused a hell of a fuss; what more do you want? The fact that it also managed to raise some pretty pertinent questions about racism, exploitation and youth was a bonus added to all the Italian cut suits. Pop ain't meant to change the world, that's what politicians do.

But it must be said that pop and style have made their move into the political arena this year. The Red Wedge, the Labour party's young cred committee, realising the power of the currency of style, got itself designed by *Face* man Neville Brody and recruited the likes of Paul Weller's sartorially sharp Style Council, Sade, Madness, DC Lee, Gary Kemp, the Blow Monkeys . . . For Britain's traditionally downbeat left to ally itself with so many committed stylists shows just how far it has all come. You simply cannot escape the importance of the look in a profoundly visual age.

And pop is a profoundly visual medium to watch. Here in ravaged, battered old Britain we still produce the most watchable acts in the world with remarkable regularity. We do so because we have mastered the complex vocabulary of style as no one else has done, and style is the motor behind the music. Its role cannot be denied; the lust for the look is what first makes a kid stand in front of a mirror and strike a pose, it's what drives the culture forward. My only worry is what kind of mirror was the young Mr Zodiac Mindwarp looking into.

BIG AUDIO DYNAMITE

QUOTES

What you really want to know is whether I lick pussy and stuff like that. 'Course I do. STING

All I ever wanted to do was sin and make a lot of money as well. MICK JAGGER, ROLLING STONES

We want to be phalluses ramming in the butthole of pop. We already are, even if we're small time at the moment. GIBBY HAINES, THE BUTTHOLE SURFERS

The only person I've met recently who lived up to my expectations was John Lydon. I think that was because he was drunk.
SUZANNE FREYTAG, PROPAGANDA

My idea of working out is getting from my bed into a car. I could be a lot firmer than I am, but I'm not willing to give up being a slob for being firm.
GRACE SLICK, STARSHIP

You go to a supermarket and you see a faggot behind the fucking cash register, you don't want him to handle your potatoes. It's true. It's paranoid, but that's the way it is. There's a lotta religious people, of course, who feel that this is God's work. God's saying "No more butt fucking or we're gonna getcha!"
NEIL YOUNG on AIDS

In the late sixties, a certain group of people got so far up their own asses, they shit all over themselves.
IAN ASTBURY, THE CULT

Whenever my girlfriend wears tights, I refuse to see her. I put her on the first train back to Hornchurch and tell her to come back wearing suspenders.
WILLIAM REID, JESUS AND MARY CHAIN

I've had a lot of dead weight around me over the years. Now I come to think of it, most of the people I've worked with have done nothing since. I've destroyed their lives! JOHN LYDON, PI

I didn't realise before how important a haircut actually is. Before, I just used to have hair. Now, it's in a style that relates to something. I get treated differently. It's like a statement. I'm not just kind of anybody.
MARILY

I've looked out into the crowd and seen some of them wanking. Some of the girls also fondle their breasts because they get so excited. I like watching them – it makes me feel real horny.
MARTIN DEGVILLE, SIGUE SIGUE SPUTNI

I think a lot of people have started to realise that it is time to stop fiddling while Rome burns. There is a chance to do something, to make people think through music. BILLY BRAG

What's Billy Bragg gonna change? He ain't doing nothing. All he's doing is telling people that Thatcher's a cow. Well, I think most people know that, don't they
RAT SCABIES, THE DAMNE

I can't do anything else. I can't put a fucking plug on an iron! This is what I've done since I was a kid.
JIM KERR, SIMPLE MIND

If we were devastatingly handsome and actually liked one another, we'd probably be the biggest band on earth. As it is, I'm actually quite a decent chap and the rest of the group are wankers.
JOOLS HOLLAND, SQUEEZ

I've just made the best album I have ever done. I am in the early stages of my career, I'm only just beginning to develop as a singer. I'm 32 years old and I'm not a pop star. KEVIN ROWLAND, DEXY'S MIDNIGHT RUNNERS

I've got no time for nuclear technology. It's obvious that capitalism and nuclear power work hand in hand. It's futile, it's immoral, it's inhumane, it's fuckin' wrong, and it's everything I don't agree with. It makes me fuckin' puke. CUSH, THE MEN THEY COULDN'T HANG

No one buys my records for the disco remix.
BILLY BRAGG

I don't feel any compulsion to pander to them [audiences]. I don't see the point. Most of them are real cunts; they shout at yer, they scream at yer, they spit at yer, they throw bottles at yer.
PETER HOOK, NEW ORDER

There were elements to Led Zeppelin I've always liked. JOHN LYDON, PiL

The Fun Boy Three were just totally geared to money-making. It was a pop group – that's why we had silly haircuts. TERRY HALL, THE COLOUR FIELD

I remember when Jimmy was arrested in the park and he came round the next morning and said "That's it, I'm gonna be dead political from now on" – and me and Steve just looked at each other . . . like whaaat? I mean, just because people want to fuck like bunny rabbits in the park at midnight doesn't make you political! LARRY STEINBACHEK, BRONSKI BEAT

If you're in this business for more than five years, you become a boring old fart. These days, I actually don't care one bit if someone likes what we do – I don't care that much about pleasing people. BRIAN TRAVERS, UB40

To be honest, there are a lot of boring old farts in the States, but I'm not one of them. I like music that makes you drop the crockery when you're doing the washing up. JOHN PARR

A lot of the reason I was able to do something on my own was that I stopped comparing myself to Green and started comparing myself to Howard Jones.
TOM MORLEY

I'm really fed up with royalty, to tell you the truth.
MARILYN

We got attacked by a religious maniac on this plane from Denver – a fucking loony in cowboy boots and sunglasses that only had one lens. He kept screaming at us, and then a bible came sailing over and hit the Captain on his head. Then he came over to me and started kicking my ankles and shouting "Hey, what about the Lord?" I said "Listen, fuck-face, you kick me again and you're dead!" RAT SCABIES, THE DAMNED

Andrew does have a lot to do with the filthy content of the Wham! stuff. When I'm writing, he walks in and goes, "oh, don't put that . . . put cock".
GEORGE MICHAEL, WHAM!

I think Paddy McAloon is the best songwriter in Britain, but probably a bit too left-field for most people. I think I'm in the top five, at least. STEPHEN DUFFY

It's really exciting! It's great! I'm really knocked out! It's wonderful! KATE BUSH

When I look back on what I've done, it seems a lot – but there are huge lumps of time in between each bit. Quite rightly so. Quality not quantity, that's my motto.
JOHN LYDON, PiL

We're really sort of normal. Getting a cat was the most dangerous thing we've done in a long time.
ELIZABETH FRAZER, COCTEAU TWINS

He [Pete Burns] sent me twenty-six roses when it was my birthday – and I sent him forty-eight naked sailors. MORRISSEY, THE SMITHS

My wife accepts that I'm not a monk.
BRUCE DICKINSON, IRON MAIDEN

If Spitting Image did me, I know full well that they'd either do some sexual thing or send up my religious beliefs in some outrageous way. They don't really care. When they do it, I bet they don't think "Oh crumbs, if Cliff and his family and friends are watching this, they're really going to be upset". CLIFF RICHARD

The biggest misconception people have about me is that I'm stupid. BILLY IDOL

We went over there [the US] with quite a humble nature, and we didn't expect any fanatical fervour or uncontrollable hysteria. Therefore, when it happened, I was rendered speechless for months.
MORRISSEY, THE SMITHS

For a dare, I took all my clothes off and walked naked through a Berlin restaurant. I had only my belt on. If you have a Scottish accent and you're big, there's a lot you can get away with, anywhere in the world.
FISH, MARILLION

I tried to curb my drinking but, to tell you the truth, I'm boring without a drink... so I'm a drinker. What's the fucking point of living miserably?
OZZY OSBOURNE

People know more about King Tut than what happened in the fifties. To me, rock 'n' roll is so great that everyone in the world should think it's the greatest thing that's happening. If they don't, they're turds.
LUX INTERIOR, THE CRAMPS

I've never been a bullshitter. I've always liked bands who had as little bullshit about them as possible.
SHANE MacGOWAN, THE POGUES

I don't go in for drugs. I think the only thing that will kill me is too much wanking.
BILLY BRAGG

You now have a nation of kids who don't read. The bulk of information that enters their brains comes from television or records... so control over those sources of information is rather attractive to an authoritarian mentality.
FRANK ZAPPA

I'm living the American Dream! You can start from rags and go to riches and walk with Kings and Queens and Presidents.
JAMES BROWN

There's a certain satisfaction in being a star, but anyone who's in this just to see their name in lights is doing it for the wrong reasons. I want to be remembered for my songs, not for having the glitziest blonde on my arm.
NEVILLE KEIGHLEY, BELOUIS SOME

People would like to see us crushed and killed. The British love you on the way up, but take greater pleasure in knocking you down once you've arrived at the top.
MIKE CRAIG, CULTURE CLUB

I can't do simple things like finding a flat. I just don't seem to be able to focus on those kinds of things, so a lot of my time is spent in less than ideal conditions.
BRIAN ENO

I don't buy things. If I can't wear it or put it in my mouth, I'm not interested. My only excess is that I don't look after my contact lenses properly. When they get too dirty to wear, I buy another pair.
GEORGE MICHAEL, WHAM!

I think God has warned me enough on the booze and pills and things. I'm a sober man, straight as an arrow right now.
JERRY LEE LEWIS

Mentally, I've got this huge pair of scissors – God, that sounds like Julian Cope – with which I cut and shape the world and share it with people. Usually, a good songwriter's got something to share.
PADDY McALOON, PREFAB SPROUT

I never thought I was wasted, but I probably was.
KEITH RICHARDS, ROLLING STONES

In my line of work, if you drank all the drinks, and took all the drugs you were offered, you would die. Simple as that.
ELVIS COSTELLO

Because it's such a desperate, dirty sort of place, we resisted the temptation to start singing about politics and how bad it was to be in Birmingham. We were a sort of escapism.
ROGER TAYLOR, DURAN DURAN

To be quite honest, I feel incredibly lucky to have a second chance.
MICK JONES, BIG AUDIO DYNAMITE

Each time I come back to England, it hits me how revolting and ridiculous it is. England really is a shit hole... and that hurts.
ALI CAMPBELL, UB40

I used to come to this place [the Savoy Hotel] to get thrown out, to get a picture in the paper, right? Now they fucking welcome me with open arms!
KEITH RICHARDS, ROLLING STONES

The whole thing about music for me is that I've always felt futuristic – the mood of tomorrow rather than today. I see WINNING the fight against apartheid . . . I don't see preaching about it, it's seeing beyond that.   STEVIE WONDER

On my gravestone, I want it to say "I told you I was sick". Achievement is for the senators and scholars. At one time I had ambitions but I had them removed by a doctor in Buffalo.   TOM WAITS

I am a ham. I've no business being in rock 'n' roll. I've said over and over again that I'm a classical composer, dishevelling my musical personality by dabbling in rock 'n' roll. I'm more interested in symphonic music.
                                    JOHN CALE

When I write love songs, people think they're really soppy – but I see love as a consolation for the boredom of life.   MARTIN GORE, DEPECHE MODE

It's so much more of a public life than that of a short-story writer. They tend to confuse the artist with the art more in this idiom than any other.   JONI MITCHELL

Politicians will fuck you up whoever they are. They never keep their promises.   LEMMY, MOTORHEAD

I like Madonna, she's doing it right. Using her image to gather terrific fire. You've got these kids of nine, who are totally virginal, running around like they've slept with everyone from Timbuktu to Brighton.
                                    MALCOLM McLAREN

That look I had around *Ready Steady Go!* developed by mistake. It was a bad copy of something I'd seen in French *Vogue* magazine. I couldn't do it properly, so I did it my own way.   DUSTY SPRINGFIELD

I use my songs as a way to awaken myself. It's like sticking a needle in your leg after it has gone to sleep.
                                    BONO, U2

I've listened to the Communards and I think it's just a load of self-indulgent crap.   STEVE, BRONSKI BEAT

What do bands like Tears For Fears and Spandau Ballet feel when they see programmes on Orgreave or Nicaragua or South Africa? I don't see how anybody can see things like that and not be affected in some way.   DAVID STEELE, FINE YOUNG CANNIBALS

I still go shopping a lot. I spent about £15,000 on clothes in Japan.   PETE BURNS, DEAD OR ALIVE

Since I was four or five, I've dreamt I was in the Beatles. First I played banjo with them, but recently I dreamt I was touring Japan and there were millions of flowers everywhere, and I'd hang out with John Lennon.   NICK LAIRD-CLOWES, DREAM ACADEMY

Most of my memories of sexual intercourse are quite pleasant. I'm not an aggressive lover at all.
                                    FEARGAL SHARKEY

I don't pretend to give a message of any kind, except enjoy yourself and get laid.   LEMMY, MOTORHEAD

When you're in my position of being an ex-pop journalist, it's simply an embarrassment trying to describe what you're doing, because you start saying all the really naff and ridiculous things pop stars used to say to you in interviews!
                         NEIL TENNANT, THE PET SHOP BOYS

Racing? I just like getting dressed up in the stuff and pretending I'm Alain Prost.   ANDREW RIDGELEY, WHAM!

I hate modern design houses – couldn't live in a Barratt home no matter what incentive they gave me!
                                    FEARGAL SHARKEY

It's like a corner grocery store, thirty years in the same location, we're still churning it out. If you like it, it's here and you know where to get it.
                         KEITH RICHARDS, ROLLING STONES

I don't think there's anything wrong with a little sherry before retiring . . . read a little Balzac and then lay out. I don't drink and drive. I enjoy a little cocktail before supper, who doesn't?   TOM WAITS

131

Where angels fear to tread, Geldof will go. At the meeting last week, he was on the phone to the White House – he just phoned them up and said "what about this bloody grain?" He's definitely cornered the market in being a spokesman for a generation.　　MIDGE URE

Perhaps it's time to think of putting the brakes on because I don't want to end up like some mad recluse in a mansion surrounded by barbed wire, guard dogs and bodyguards. And yet, when I'm not working, I lead a very normal life at home.　　STING

A lot of top recording artists are a pile of shit. I don't think I'm that bad, but I'm not brilliant either. I think I'm averagely listenable.　　DEE C LEE

All the stuff around now is a load of old pap. It's all suited to Terry Wogan and *Top of the Pops* and Thatcher and all those things that go hand in hand.　　MICK JONES, BIG AUDIO DYNAMITE

We're more a Boy Scout troop than a street gang.　　JON, THE JUNE BRIDES

A Dublin paper reviewed our last single and said "yet another gem from the Lord Lucans of pop". I think that was a fair comment.　　PAUL BURGESS, RUEFREX

The majority of pop stars are complete idiots in every aspect.　　SADE

If MTV isn't racist and sexist, then I'm a monkey's uncle.　　SID GRIFFIN, THE LONG RYDERS

I think we've been overlooked for a while because we were slightly out of sync – but I think that in 1986, people are going to be pleased to have us around. Unless somebody else comes along. Oh, what AM I saying?　　MARTIN FRY, ABC

Having your own studio means you can slip off to watch *Brookside* without financial worry.　　BRIAN TRAVERS, UB40

Most of the pop stars today seem to be too yuppie-orientated. They're too much to do with prefects and not enough to do with causing trouble.　　MALCOLM McLAREN

We don't want every record to become a bulletin of how England's doing. The next release won't be about the Common Market or the Channel Tunnel.　　DAVID STEELE, FINE YOUNG CANNIBALS

I'm not blowing my own trumpet, but I really do have a great sense of humour. I woke up from my nose job and the first thing I did was crack a joke. Put a machete through my head, and I still would.　　PETE BURNS, DEAD OR ALIVE

It's hard to be anonymous when you've got this huge neon sign above your head saying "Hey, look at me!"　　CURT SMITH, TEARS FOR FEARS

He [Jimmy Somerville] thinks I should do more for the gay community, and he's right . . . I should strangle him! That's the best thing anyone could do for them!　　MARC ALMOND

The editor [of the *Sun*] phoned up and asked for an interview . . . so I asked for a Ferrari Daytona Convertible – and they agreed! Then they sent me a contract saying I couldn't have total copy approval, which basically gave them a licence to write whatever they wanted. In the end, I decided against it. It just wasn't worth it . . . and anyway, I know what angle they'd take: "Andrew Talks Frankly About The Size Of His Willy".　　ANDREW RIDGELEY, WHAM!

There's no glory in overdosing on morphine like Gram Parsons, in a hotel room with a girl sticking ice-cubes up your rear end to keep you alive and jacking you off to stop you going comatose.　　SID GRIFFIN, LONG RYDERS

The Tories are shitbags and I've got nothing to say to them. They've destroyed this country and I hate them with every fibre of my fucking body.　　CHRIS DEAN, THE REDSKINS

Ten years ago, the US was starting to really drag ass, way behind the Soviets in build-up. I stand behind Reagan when it comes to build-up – to stand, be able to play hardball with powers aggressive towards free countries.　　NEIL YOUNG

We're a symbiotic doodah. It's a relationship where, if A relates to B, then B is dependent on A. It's anthropology, you see, and neuropsychology.

JJ, THE ART OF NOISE

I'm sure if there's a new fascism, it won't come from skinheads and punks. It will come from people who eat granola and believe they know how the world should be.

ENO

We weren't into any heavy drugs, like heroin or coke. I got totally into acid. I did fry my brain somewhat – went right over the edge.

YOUTH, BRILLIANT

Elvis's problem was that he needed the love of people around him, people who'd say "Elvis, don't eat those eight hamburgers, don't take those pills, Elvis, you're making a big mistake".

CLIFF RICHARD

We have sex whenever we can . . . and when we can't, we masturbate.

FLEA, RED HOT CHILLI PEPPERS

Every morning, I walk into the toilet, look in the mirror, and tell myself I'm the baddest motherfucker alive!

GEORGE CLINTON

I looked at the Top Ten and thought "I don't want to be in there with those people anyway". I've never seen such a dreadful mire of crap in all my life!

MICK HUCKNALL, SIMPLY RED

If it means leather sofas, shagpile carpets, holding your little finger out when you drink, and wearing lots of false finger nails, then I'm not sophisticated.

SADE

There has never been a riot at any of our gigs. You get the odd clown who thinks he's Rambo, doing tap dances on the mixing desk. I hate it, I despise it. We're trying to present ourselves as serious, not a Cockney Rejects Oi Oi type of group.

WILLIAM REID, THE JESUS AND MARY CHAIN

My music is designed to make you vibrate internally until the top of your head comes off and all this quick drying foam gushes out. I'd like to make people feel like toothpaste under unbearable pressure.

ROBYN HITCHCOCK

It's like these artists who say home taping is killing music. Duff music is killing music, it's as easy as that. Home taping encourages music, so does bootlegging. Enthusiasm encourages.

JIM KERR, SIMPLE MINDS

It used to be that we'd put LSD on our tongues when we started playing, and we'd swallow the hit after the first number. Really though, it's best taken half an hour before a gig so the furze and lights and shit are all revolving when you pick up your instrument.

PAUL WALTHALL, THE BUTTHOLE SURFERS

Anybody who takes a twenty-minute guitar solo should be shot, and I mean that. If it takes you twenty minutes to say something, then don't bother.

ROBERT CRAY

Sex is like water. You should always boil it before you drink it. Make sure everyone is totally clean or else you get really horrible diseases.

JAYNE COUNTY

He [Malcolm McLaren] stuck us on a Queen tour of Europe once – just because he wanted us out of the way. Every night we were bombarded with bottles.

ANNABELLA LWIN

Sometimes speed makes me feel like I could walk on water.

WILLIAM REID, THE JESUS AND MARY CHAIN

We're skimming the surface of something quite spiritual.

IAN ASTBURY, THE CULT

Because I don't make my sex life public, there's a section of Fleet Street desperate to know who I'm fucking. They're certainly not going to find out.

GEORGE MICHAEL, WHAM!

I never thought of myself so much as a confessional songwriter, but in order that my work should have vitality, I felt that I should write in my own blood.

JONI MITCHELL

I've had my nose done three times. Nose jobs are rife in this business – it's just like buying a new jacket. I haven't had anything else lifted.

PETE BURNS, DEAD OR ALIVE

Have you noticed the front of Paul King's trousers? Jeeeesus, it looks like he's holding a zeppelin down there!

MICHAEL MORAN, 5TA

Big tits on page three are really damaging to our society.

SIOBAHN, BANANARAMA

I don't want to sound too cosmic, but I'd really like to do my bit at bringing the world a little bit closer together. It's a wonderful feeling. HUEY LEWIS

I don't like people who say they fall in love every week. It's shit. What's the point in it? They're not in love. HARRY TRAVERS, HIPSWAY

I used heroin for a couple of years. I dunno whether I was addicted or not. I stopped, so I couldn't have been. HUGH CORNWELL, THE STRANGLERS

I'm becoming the Liberace of heavy metal. I wore a lime green dress once, with a blonde wig and a German helmet, just for a giggle. OZZY OSBOURNE

We called ourselves the Housemartins because it was a really safe name. If we'd given ourselves a really elaborate or silly name we could have regretted it. PAUL HEATON, THE HOUSEMARTINS

When you're young, you want to be a footballer. When you're older, you want to be in a pop band – it takes less talent! GRAHAM SKINNER, HIPSWAY

All the criticism is water off a duck's back. It doesn't worry me in the slightest. I laugh at the music press. I think you're hilarious. KEVIN ROWLAND, DEXY'S MIDNIGHT RUNNERS

When I was a teenager, I became immune to certain strains of NSU. Since all these killer ones have come into the scene, I don't put it about so much. YOUTH, BRILLIANT

The eighties began with Live Aid. You know the way that most decades peak in the middle . . . well, the eighties began with Live Aid. MIKE SCOTT, THE WATER BOYS

What is my life? Nothing. Boring, that's what it is. It's an absolutely terrible life. God, I've done nothing. LAWRENCE, FELT

Nobody complains that you put paintings on your wall and they don't change. My reply is to treat music in the same way. It becomes a condition of your environment without demanding that you concentrate on it intensely. ENO

Who wants to change the bloody world? SIMON LE BON, DURAN DURAN

Racists make me so sick. I just want to shit on their faces. FLEA, RED HOT CHILLI PEPPERS

Dexy's Midnight Runners, in its short history, has been more political than any other group ever, any of them. Just by the force of our actions. KEVIN ROWLAND, DEXY'S MIDNIGHT RUNNERS

I actually got rid of my television because of this sort of thing. CAPTAIN SENSIBLE on the TV show *Bullseye*

The drugs I've done have been the more traditional drugs. The ones I've had the most problems with have been cigarettes, caffeine and alcohol. I've had penicillin on a number of occasions. That's my favourite drug. I really get off on a good stiff jolt of penicillin. LOUDON WAINWRIGHT III

We almost used to apologise for our existence when we started because we didn't feel we were Supertramp. BILLY DUFFY, THE CULT

I'd still like to see a Labour government, but without Neil Kinnock and without Denis Healey at the top. I dunno about a leader . . . maybe Mick McGahey. RICHARD JOBSON, THE ARMOURY SHOW

All I ever do is listen to the little voices inside me. I don't want to disappoint the little voices that have been so good to me. KATE BUSH

When Led Zeppelin made it so big I was as jealous as hell – but I'm glad I carried on as I did . . . I personally couldn't have put up with that mass adulation.

JEFF BECK

In New York, punk was rich middle-class kids ripping their shirts and making a lot of noise about nothing. In Britain, I saw it as a means of personal expression.

SUZANNE VEGA

We always consider our greatest strength to be our taste in Vietnamese food. ROLO, THE WOODENTOPS

At the moment in Britain, you've got to be either this week's new band or a revered antique like Phil Collins. Bands which have been around for a few years seem to be falling down a hole in the middle.

ANDY McCLUSKEY, OMITD

I've noticed they do have a certain respect for me, some of these young pop stars. When I was young, there were no pop stars over thirty . . . it was a quick in-and-out thing. MICK JAGGER, ROLLING STONES

I applied to become a bulldozer, but nothing happened. I remained me. I am this thing.

ROBYN HITCHCOCK

I think the whole concept of interpreting dreams is the biggest wank really. My dreams are very straight-forward – very much like my life.

ROBERT SMITH, THE CURE

I'm not at all vain. I used to be. I don't care now if I get spots all over my face, although if you're going to a party where people like John Travolta and Cyndi Lauper are going to be, you do try to make yourself more attractive.

MARILYN

We've gotten this far just being ourselves. Four boring personalities. It doesn't make sense to me!

PAUL WESTERBERG, THE REPLACEMENTS

I get drunk, drinking Guinness with Creme de Menthe in it. It's really bad for you.

SHANE MacGOWAN, THE POGUES

I have no plans for an early retirement. I couldn't afford to do it. BRYAN FERRY

If anyone saw me nude, I think they'd be sick. I just don't have the sort of body that should be seen without clothes.

PATSY KENSIT

I'd like to portray a positive image of the lesbian. I want to portray that lesbians are just your basic, average person. I go to work, I'm happy, I'm sad, I eat and I drink and I shit just like everyone else. PHRANC

Music papers? I don't think about them. To me, they're just a waste of time – boring and full of shit. DEE C LEE

Would someone tell Jim Kerr how bad he looks in that hat and those trousers? The guy looks pathetic, sickening. Does his wife love him? I can't believe it! There you have this man singing "Sanctify yourself" – whatever that means! SHANE O'NEILL, BLUE IN HEAVEN

I was always dodging punches from jerks at school who didn't like me. I had my nose broken, and they'd pull knives on me. I had some pretty bad fights – but I wasn't a poofter. I gave as good as I got and beat the fuck out of them. I don't like to fight, but when they piss me off, I kill them! CHARLIE SEXTON

With that voice, Prince can do anything he wants. I haven't got that, so my armour is the English language; I'm forced to go for the accumulated effect of a line. PADDY McALOON, PREFAB SPROUT

Recording should be a pure process of thought to tape, without any outside interference from record moguls or trends. But I can't look my record company in the face if I'm not playing some commercial role.

JEFF BECK

Music paper interviews? I hate to tell ya, but two days after they're printed they're lining the trashcan.

TOM WAITS

THE THOUGHTS OF
TONY JAMES

I think we're all intelligent enough to make it last five or ten years. There's definitely enough hi-tec energy and sex in us to do that.

The great thing about Sigue Sigue Sputnik was that nobody could play.

I think that old rock 'n' roll lifestyle of drink and drugs should die. I'm amazed that rock stars still insist on swallowing bottles of bourbon and marrying models with big tits but nothing between the ears.

I find powerful women incredibly sexy. She [Janet Street Porter] is one of the only people who can make me forget about Sigue Sigue Sputnik. I think about the group from the first moment I open my eyes until five minutes before we have sex.

In ten years time, I want to be sitting on a beach somewhere, answering three telephones and making corporate decisions.

We're stars; we're strong and vital entertainment. Music is only a small part of what we're capable of.

The Fine Young Cannibals sound like the contents of Elvis Presley's draining board.

Billy Idol has made two or three good records, but when he opens his mouth he's still a prat.

The Smiths? Drab music for drab people.

I like what Billy Bragg says; at least he's articulate and good at interviews. Perhaps he'd even make a good game show host.

Nothing is new, so we'll be playing the same old three chords. But they've never been played like this before, and that's the difference!

Never let your wife design your dresses or the type of codpiece you want to wear. It only ends in trouble.

Our concept goes far beyond music. Sigue Sigue Sputnik is going to be the biggest corporation in the world. We're going to make *Dallas* seem like *Coronation Street*.

We'd like to see anyone be as smart, thin and good-looking as us.

Everything we said we were going to do, we've done. The best video, the best looking group, the best scams. If you've any intelligence, you have to believe that we will do it.

BUT ACCORDING TO OTHERS:

They're squawking, talentless, brainless morons. I'd be doing the public a great favour if I was to bite their heads off.   OZZY OSBOURNE on SIGUE SIGUE SPUTNIK

The quicker we get rid of – what are they bloody called? – Sigue Sigue Sputnik, the better. They're a joke, they're like something out of Boots the Chemists!
                                          JOHN LYDON

LADIES, HOW DARE YOU?

Mark Coleman charts the progress of the PMRC and talks to an outraged Frank Zappa about the implications of rock 'n' roll censorship.

● PRINCE

For all the ensuing furore and foolishness, the American media debate over pop lyrics started rather innocuously. In mid-1984, a father in Cincinnati, Ohio, brought Prince's *1999* home for his prepubescent daughters and didn't think much else about it. Overhearing side three a while later, he was shocked: 'Little Red Corvette' was one thing but 'Let's Pretend We're Married' another matter entirely. His complaint to the local Parent Teachers Association struck a chord: it was passed along to the group's national office, ultimately triggering a public statement urging a rating system for records. More a protest than a detailed proposal, the PTA's statement drew scant attention from the media and something less than that from the record industry. But it didn't go completely unnoticed.

In Washington DC, one mother's eyebrows had been raised ever since Prince's 'Darling Nikki' had violated the family stereo: *"I met her in a hotel lobby/masturbating with a magazine"*. A friend of hers had a similar experience with her seven-year-old, a clock radio

and Madonna's 'Like A Virgin', while another acquaintance "nearly drove off the road" when Sheena Easton's 'Sugar Walls' came up on radio rotation. Like the disgruntled viewers in *Network*, they were mad as . . . ah, heck and they weren't going to take it anymore. So they organised.

In May 1985, four Washington DC women founded the Parents Music Resource Center; yet another publicity-hungry 'non-profit group' in a city full of them. What set the PMRC apart were the names on its stationery. PMRC co-founders Mrs Tipper Gore and Mrs Susan Baker are married to prominent, conservative politicians: respectively a Republican Senator (Albert Gore Jr) and the Secretary of the Treasury (James A Baker). The flurry of publicity surrounding the

> *". . . sure love to ball"*
> 'Good Golly Miss Molly',
> Little Richard, 1958

> *"c'mon baby let's ball"*
> 'Let's Pretend We're Married',
> Prince, 1983

Washington Wives, as they came to be known, turned into a blizzard by the end of summer.

"Our purpose is to promote ethical boundaries in rock music, provide and disseminate information on rock culture and refer parents to sources of help . . . our principal objective at this point is to encourage people in the rock music world to CLEAN UP THEIR ACT!" – from the first PMRC press release, 13 May 1985.

That euphemistic tone didn't last long; within two months the PMRC had proposed a detailed system of ratings. And theirs were a good deal more specific than Hollywood's twenty-year-old guidelines. 'X' on the front jacket would indicate a record had profane, violent or sexually explicit references, 'O' references to the 'Occult', and 'D/A'

● MADONNA

glorification of drug and/or alcohol use. Of course, a panel of experts from both outside and within the record industry (and presumably, the PMRC) would administer the ratings. In response, record company representatives muttered about 'infeasibility' and basically waited for things to blow over.

But this was something more than the usual, periodic outcry against obscenity. Encouraged by supposedly 'middle-of-the-road' commentators (*Parents Are Finally Waking Up To The Dangers of Porno-Rock*), the PMRC was soon bandying about ideas like obliging retailers to rack offending records separately – or sell them in brown paper jackets. There was talk of rating concerts and even of pressurising record companies to 'reassess' the contracts of offending artists. The Washington Wives, it seemed, became a little more strident with each newspaper editorial and on-camera interview. You could almost imagine the President himself nodding his head in approval: "Well, gosh, you know back in Hollywood we didn't need sex to sell ourselves. I mean . . . "

By late summer, rock song lyrics had become a 'hot' issue. Debating it on the respected news/interview programme *Nightline*, the PMRC entered the ring against an unlikely tag-team of pop stars. Frank Zappa, who'd eventually emerge as rock's most outspoken defender, came as no surprise: he'd spent much of his twenty-year career violating standards of good taste as well as musical preconceptions. But Donny Osmond? The nation's best-known Mormon came down squarely against the ratings, reasoning that since he wouldn't want to be induced to record paeans to sex 'n' drugs why should Mötley Crüe be forced not to? This dramatic moment raised some interesting questions about the PMRC's actual base of support; but the Washington Wives had barely begun to fight. They were just saving their artillery for a more influential audience.

"Some rock artists actually seem to encourage teen suicide . . . Just last week in a small Texas town, a young man took his life while listening to AC/DC. He was not the first." From Susan Baker's statement before the Senate Commerce Committee, 19 September 1985.

"Taken as a whole, the complete list of PMRC demands reads like an instruction manual for some sinister kind of 'toilet training program' to house-break ALL composers and performers because of the lyrics of a few. Ladies, how dare you?" From Frank Zappa's statement before the Senate Commerce Committee, 19 September 1985.

That day's commerce hearing was far from dry discussion of export/import quotas, that's for sure. It's hard to pick a highlight: conservative Senator Paula Hawkins gingerly holding up a blown-up facsimile of WASP's *Animal (F**k Like a Beast)* sleeve as if it were radioactive; John Denver citing the furore over alleged drug references in 'Rocky Mountain High' in a statement denouncing ratings as Nazi-style tactics; Twisted Sister's Dee Snider striding to the stand in full denim regalia; Frank Zappa and Tipper Gore going out for a drink afterwards. Most entertaining was the testimony of one Jeff Ling, a born-again Christian "minister and youth counsellor" who's also one of the PMRC's hired 'experts' on rock 'n' roll raunch. He showed the august Senators a slide show which mixed examples of 'rock porn' from Sheena Easton and Morris Day with non-hits by deservedly obscure metal bands like Bitch and Impaler. Ling's presentation climaxed with a quotation from 'Golden Showers' by the now-infamous Mentors: *"Bend up and smell my anal vapor/Your face is my toilet paper."* Thirty years on, this is what rock 'n' roll had come to.

Since no actual legislation was pending, the Senate hearing was really just a media event (albeit a damned captivating one). Yet the message to the recording industry was not subliminal.

● FRANK ZAPPA

As Senator Donald Riele of Michigan advised Stanley Goritkov, president of the Recording Industry Association of America (RIAA) trade group: "You ought to do it [rate records] before somebody else does it for you." In fact, the RIAA had already reached a compromise with the PMRC, settling on a single-rating sticker that was quickly accepted by virtually all the major labels. EXPLICIT LYRICS: PARENTAL ADVISORY was a long way from the original Xs and Os, but this warning was claimed as a victory of sorts by the PMRC and had to be, at the very least, a headache for the record companies. Whether these stickers make much difference to the buying public or the artists themselves remains to be seen. "Yeah, we made their Top Ten hit list" shrugs Rob Halford, Judas Priest's leather-clad lead singer. "It was pure sensationalism." 'Eat Me Alive', from the Priest's million-selling *Defenders of the Faith*, was quoted countless times by PMRC supporters: *'I'm gonna force you at gunpoint/To eat me alive'*. Halford says the PMRC took a song that was "very much tongue-in-cheek, a total spoof", and "displayed it completely out of context". Judas Priest's rebuttal came on their next album, in the form of a song called 'Parental Guidance'. Naturally, they weren't having any, though this show of defiance, like the rest of *Turbo*, isn't remotely raunchy. "Had it warranted a sticker", Halford practically yawns, "it wouldn't have made any particular difference to me one way or another." Some metal bands even devised their own stickers, like the one appearing on Metallica's *Master of Puppets*: "THE ONLY TRACK YOU PROBABLY WON'T WANT TO PLAY IS 'DAMAGE, INC.' DUE TO MULTIPLE USE OF THE INFAMOUS 'F' WORD. OTHERWISE, THERE AREN'T ANY 'SHITS', 'FUCKS', 'PISSES', 'CUNTS', 'MOTHERFUCKERS' OR 'COCKSUCKERS' ANYWHERE ON THIS RECORD."

On a record called *Frank Zappa Meets the Mothers of Prevention*, the founding Mother of Invention sardonically tape-looped testimony from the Senate hearing throughout a computerised music-mash. However, Zappa still can't, or won't, laugh it off. "If there are 250 million people in the United States and the PMRC gets 10,000 letters supporting its point of view, why in the fuck do you think they're entitled to regulate the music industry?" he

● METALLICA

asks rhetorically. "Because there's money involved."

Around the same time the Senators were watching Twisted Sister videos, they were also considering the merits of a bill called H.R. 2911, better known as the blank tape tax. Prescribed as an antidote to the "home taping" that record companies feel is "killing the music industry", this proposed tax has been hotly contested for nearly five years now. In his statement to Congress, Zappa called it *a private tax, levied by an industry on consumers for the benefit of a select group within that industry*.

You certainly don't have to side with Zappa on the tape tax issue to follow his logic. "In order to distract people's attention from this tax, you need sex and lots of it. And two or three times during the hearing, various Senators were careful to say 'we've heard about some kind of tax and we claim there is no connection whatsoever.'" Nine months later Zappa still doesn't buy that, especially now that Senator Albert Gore has taken up his wife's interest in pop music. "His name now appears as a sponsor of the blank tape tax, then he turns around and announces he's going to do a payola investigation. He's playing good cop/bad cop.

"This is a man who does not like being a junior senator from Tennessee," Zappa says of Albert Gore. "He wants a bigger political career. Other examples of Albert Gore legislative expertise? Here's one: to declare 26 October National Mule Appreciation Day. That's an actual bill. His other great bill is to declare a certain week in May National Digestive Disorders Awareness Week. Imagine: during this week we will ponder the causes of flatulence."

On one hand, Zappa dismisses the agreed-upon ratings: "The record companies have agreed to something that is literally non-binding and can't be enforced. The agreement states that the parents' group will have no role in determining what's explicit – the record

● MÖTLEY CRÜE

● DEE SNIDER

companies will review and determine what's explicit. And artists who have control over their packaging are free to ignore the understanding. The PMRC went down from eight original demands to a plea for any kind of a sticker. They would have settled for a Happy Face."

At the same time, though, Zappa insists that some artists' freedom of speech has been seriously endangered. "What's wrong with a package warning, like you have on saccharine? Here's what's wrong with it. There are stores that refuse to rack or sell a record with any kind of sticker on it. There are chain-stores in shopping-malls that have been told by their landlords 'if you rack these records you lose your lease.' What to Tipper is a harmless little consumer guideline is a fucking economic disaster to a bunch of other people."

If nothing else, the labelling agreement may have spurred on more radical action. The state assembly of Maryland recently considered an amendment to local obscenity law that would stop 'rock porn' at the point of purchase. Any retailer caught selling a minor any record, tape or compact disc with lyrical content deemed pornographic by the state would get slapped with a $1000 fine and possible one-year jail sentence. Even as that bill was defeated in Maryland, similar legislation was under review in at least eight other states. And the debate over lyrics continued within the music industry itself, as well as on the political level. Prince's propensities were blasted by no less a wordsmith than Smokey Robinson, while leaders like Reverend Jesse Jackson drew a direct connection between libidinous dance tracks and the skyrocketing illegitimacy rate among black teenagers.

Zappa contends that the relationship between lyrics and behaviour can't be reduced to cause and effect. "There's no scientific documentation to prove that if you hear a certain lyric, you're going to perform any of the acts described in the lyric. By the PMRC's own count, not more than five per cent of all music that's released is objectionable. So ninety-five per cent of all the lyrics that you hear are dealing with suitable topics. You know, *love*. Everybody hears love songs. Do you see people loving each other? It's absurd.

"The problem is that the people who think that this is all stupid don't say anything. There are a lot of them, but they don't have access to the media. Or else they just think this will blow over and go away. The only people that call and write radio stations are these fanatic Christians."

And with an election year approaching, *they* certainly won't be silent for long. Perhaps it's time the opposition joined the fray.

● JUDAS PRIEST

POP SHOP

Was Michael Jackson responsible for new-formula Coke? Steve Taylor looks at the effectiveness of tour sponsorship by brand names

When the 'group' Sigue Sigue Sputnik announced in the early summer of 1986 that their debut album would be part-financed by the inclusion of advertisements in the gaps between the tracks, the response from the more radical sections of the music press and music-buying public was hardly one of outrage. Leaving aside the broad awareness that the band constituted little more than a marketing campaign masquerading as purveyors of pop music anyway, there remained an important reason for this indifference to what would have seemed a shocking commercial intrusion into the authenticity of rock/pop music ten years ago, let alone back in the halcyon days of the sixties.

The meaning of music has changed and the unsentimental recognition that it is merely another consumer leisure product like running shoes or posh Belgian lager has determined the attitude of a whole new generation of young record-buyers. Nobody expects Nik Kershaw to change the world or even pretend to be trying to. Charity shows like Live Aid are predicated on the commercial clout of artists like Sade, Spandau Ballet and Duran Duran rather than on any world-transforming ambitions that they themselves might harbour.

It is no surprise, then, that the advertising and marketing industries, ever ready to identify new groups of punters to flog things to and equally keen to establish new channels for reaching them, have begun to explore the possibilities for "targetting", as they say in the trade, young consumers who are ready enough to part with significant amounts of cash on a regular basis on the records themselves.

Products like certain kinds of make-up and alcohol, hi-fi equipment, blank tapes, sportswear, fashion goods, jeans, and soft drinks – these sell mostly to young buyers. Given that this broad age-band from 16 to 35 notoriously watches very little TV and doesn't read that many newspapers, it is easy to see how pop/rock music, freed of its ideological attachments, has begun to look like a powerful medium for reaching

● ROLLING STONES

● MARTIN GRIFFIN

those inaccessible millions.

In Britain this is not yet big business but a number of small companies have appeared with the intention of creating and identifying the opportunities. The model, inevitably, is the United States. Music sponsorship there is generally regarded as having taken off with the perfume company Jovan's backing of the 1981 Rolling Stones tour to the tune of $½ million, an enterprise which – in spite of the apparently unsuitable match between product and act – was seen as a success.

According to Martin Griffin, MD of the most prominent UK specialist music sponsorship company, Music Link Marketing: "The total British market for this kind of deal has probably not got above a million over the last twelve months. You can count the number of companies which have tried it on your fingers – Levis, Harp, Sony, Guinness, Boots, Malibu, Dr Pepper... a few more perhaps."

Griffin draws attention to the vast differences in scale between the US and UK touring scenes. Live tours are where the sponsorship money is aimed with the intention of hitting the fans when they are feeling closest to their idols. Cash to the band's management will buy on-stage banners and mentions on posters, badges, T-shirts. In Britain, however, Griffin says "a major tour only hits 100,000 people: in the States it's into millions. Here, we just don't have the venues."

The answer, again imported from America, is to tie the tour sponsorship into a complex package of related promotions organised by the product's below-the-line agency – the company which deals with all those activities that spread the good word about a product without declaring themselves explicitly as 'ads'.

Here the precedent is Pepsi-Cola who paid Michael Jackson an apocryphal sum – $5.5 million? $7 million? – in 1983: "Pepsi presents the Concert Tour America has been thirsting for". Just for good measure they got Jackson to re-record 'Beat It' with the lyric "You're the Pepsi Generation" on the TV ad campaign. The cumulative effect was that awareness of Pepsi overtook that of Coke for the first time; it is argued that this eventually led to the desperate attempts to market a new-formula Coca-Cola.

Rather more amusingly, it also led to Coke's stab at music sponsorship with smoothie-crooner Julio Iglesias, a move unsurprisingly regarded in the business as a joke. Such hiccups aside, the US market has grown steadily. In the words of Martin Griffin: "over there they're

● BARRY MANILOW

now saying that some tours couldn't happen at all without sponsorship. Here, it's just bunce, it's regarded as extra cash for nothing." It is reckoned – characters like Griffin will never discuss figures – that the sort of money changing hands for British rock sponsorship rarely represents more than ten per cent of the total tour budget and rarely exceeds £100,000. Often it is closer to half that sum.

So whatever might have been written by newspaper feature writers who have just discovered that rock tour sponsorship is big business – it isn't. Yet. Now that the marketing industry has established that the young buyers of rock and pop don't mind their products being piggybacked on their musical heroes' and heroines' successes, it is not going to let go.

The next move is to tie in the bigger below-the-line campaigns with tour promotion as one element in the marketing mix, which is why top PRs such as Lynne Franks, who married Feargal Sharkey and Swatch watches, are getting in on the act. The real growth area is in more carefully-engineered 'audio-based' offers and promotions, such as the one Persil engaged in with middle-of-the-market heart-throb Barry Manilow. He made a specially-commissioned album which Persil users were able to buy at £2.99 plus the requisite proof-of-purchase tokens. Free or knock-down-price albums, T-shirts, 'product placement' of the goods in videos and films featuring the act – these are the ways forward for music sponsorship.

Music sponsorship will probably continue its modest growth in this country and a small number of companies may find a living in it. A generation of music fans will grow up regarding it as just one more example of the penetration of marketing into every byway of our culture, and the mutterings of protest from older fans brought up on rock-as-socially-significant will be scarcely audible. Perhaps there will be a renewed demand for 'authenticity' in music – which I guess is where the likes of Billy Bragg come in – and the occasional hint of dissent from the ranks as when Max Headroom, hosting a Rock Week at London's ICA sponsored by Harp Lager, announced it as the drink "that looks the same in the bottom of the john as it does in the bottom of the glass."

● JULIO IGLESIAS

● MAX HEADROOM

THE YEAR IN
VIDEO

● THE WONDERFUL WORLD OF LEVI 501s

There's nothing like a TV retrospective to put the business in the biro; as this writer's deadline crept closer to give-up point, the Beeb's *Omnibus* arrived, avatar-like, with a six-and-a-half-hour history of the music video. *Video Jukebox* wasn't very good: the interviews meandered, the much-vaunted 'exhaustive research' proved to be selective and chart-oriented (no Cabs, no comment), and critical analysis seemed confined to shots of Ken Russell pursing his lips. Perhaps it was a mite London-based, too. But the woeful countenance of host John Peel said it all – 'all' being the fact that even as indie-oriented radio squonks manfully but almost inaudibly in the distance, television companies continue to produce programmes like ITV's *The Bizz* ("Kelly and Lisa look behind the scenes of new videos").

But in a glancing sort of way, *Jukebox* managed to refer to all that is fresh and profitable about present-day promotion, and the referee was Malcolm McLaren. Interestingly, McLaren received more air-time than all the 'punk videos' put together (the Class of '76 were on screen for precisely three minutes, proof positive that yesterday's DIY ethic is today's primetime poison). McLaren said "Pop video is now a medium to sell trousers in – it's full of *things*."

With this statement, McLaren was being his usual prescient self since the pop video of the year was not a promo at all but a lookalike commercial for Levis 501 jeans. This wildly successful hybrid won top prize at the 1986 British Television Advertising Awards; second prize went to the equally vid-like Brylcreem/Art of Noise spot. And while there have been promo-ish commercials before, none of them *arrived* in quite the full-blown way the Levis campaign did; the

press fuss was lavish and immediate. At the end of it all, commercial agencies of the old Mars Bar school of persuasion were forced to get the picture. Youthful spenders didn't want to hear 'work, rest, and play' – they wanted to hear 'play'.

And so 1985 was the year music video colonised the advertising world. If 1984's trend was the promo's upward drift to the movies, this last year saw a sharp drop to the realm of hair gel and stereo systems. It seemed you could sell anything as long as you had the requisite beat-conscious editing, air-of-menace sets, and that peculiar Ultravox-ish pomp endemic in car commercials. Even print adverts were not immune: over in America, Miller Beer offered a series of grainy spreads capturing the magic of musicians and video crews ("Shooting the Long Ryders video, Los Angeles, with the beer brewed in America"). Meanwhile, back at British Rail's Customer Care Service commercials, a porter gives directions to a lost kid as the strains of 'Every Breath You Take' sob in the background.

Music, of course, provides key 'audience identification'. Here is a partial list of singles used in television adverts 1985-6: 'I Want To Break Free' (Formula Shell); 'You Make Me Feel Brand New' (Bio-Tex Pre-Wash); 'A Whiter Shade Of Pale' (Dulux Silk Vinyl Emulsion); 'Baby Love' (Typhoo Tea); 'Good Golly Miss Molly' (Crown Roller Paint); 'La Bamba' (Vauxhall Nova); 'It's All Over Now' (Insignia Men's Toiletries); 'Ain't No Mountain High Enough' (DHL Deliveries); 'I Hear You Knocking' (Birds Eye Peas); 'Like A Natural Woman' (Nivea); and both 'I Heard It Through The Grapevine' and 'Wonderful World' for Levis. On the face of it, the enlistment of pop tunes would seem to make the corresponding use of video techniques quite reasonable – after all, if you're going to go for the song, why not nick the style as well? But this proposition almost always results in demonstrably naff adverts, for two reasons. The first is that most music videos are terrible. The second is that a tired, terrible video vocabulary in the hands of a tired, terrible commercials director equals snickers and jeers from the target market. Style eludes those who sweat after it – the diehard tryhards.

Youth cannot be fooled – if advertisers wish to crash the trend party, then their credentials must be absolutely and precisely correct, right down to the last stitch, eyelet, wink and nod. It is no good, for example, making a fifties-style advert permeated with eighties details – the canny yuppie knows the difference. It is no good hiring hairdressers, smoke machines and Steadicams. It is also no good studying perhaps three promo show-reels and emerging with the conviction that *this year it's designer violence*.

The misguided tactics of old-guard commercialism ruined many a viewing hour last year, with the apex of abuse being the advertising industry's treatment of Lou Reed. As millions of music fans tried not to watch, the ineffable 'Walk On The Wild Side' accompanied a consumer throwaway on screen together with a smug Leisure Man 'jiving' along in a sports suit. First you laughed, then you cried. Even fringe musicians weren't safe: Heineken provided a sort of ersatz Test Department and then asked them to behave with all the sick ferocity of management trainees on a bender. Someone, Somewhere, is very obviously getting it wrong.

But not for long. As the universal popularity of the Levis ads demonstrate, those few adverts that pass the hip test succeed beyond all reckoning. The rewards are increasingly enormous for the commercials director who understands the *Face* readership. It should be noted that when a promo-like television commercial becomes a hit, everything it contains makes heaps of money: the music, the clothes, and the stars. Levis' launderette advert not only sent jeans sales soaring but boosted Sam Cooke back into the charts and made an overnight sensation of model Nick Camen. When Camen appeared on the cover of *The Face* – a slot commonly occupied by pop stars – the marketing agency might have allowed themselves a thin smile, knowing that genuine style is . . . the right people saying the right things at the right time.

As it happens, the time is right to be a consumer again. Status has moved from the imagination to the pocket; today's icons no longer go in for leather, obscurity, and listening to *The Peel Show*, but for glossiness, ambition, and writing clear-eyed assessments of George Michael. Nothing could suit the hybrid promo-advert better than a youth market which regards owning things as absolutely crucial (money: don't leave home without it). The smarter advertisers took one look at music videos and realised that your average promo is full of sales potential; ie, attractively presented accessories – accessories like cosmetics, hair products, boots, shirts, dresses, string ties, black contact lenses, silver-topped walking-sticks, chaises-longues, chairs made of industrial scrap, pillars left over from *Legend*, fifties coffee tables, parrots, zebras, malevolent staircases, statuary, funny hats, power stations, cars, jewellery, bloody telephones and anything else the Americans might go for in a big way next spring. For the advertising houses, all it took was for someone to pitch this stuff to an audience beyond *Saturday Superstore*. In 1985, that someone was eager to make new friends.

Enter the fed-up promo director. By the time television commercials became an attractive alternative, the average video careerist had fairly burnt himself out as a result of dealing with the record business. Pop promos involve fractious stars, egotistical static from at least three different groups of businessmen, and such impossible scheduling that any affection for the nation's Top 30 is quickly diminished. Advertising seems like pastures green by comparison. And ads simply pay more.

Then, too, video directors are always being told that something dire is going to happen to production levels. When in February 1986 CBS Records America announced a more 'selective' promotional policy, spokesman Al Keller cited not only a feeling of staleness at MTV but that perennial chain-rattler, "spiralling video budgets". While it is true that production costs have risen by 40 per cent over the last two years, defendants of this expenditure argue that greater payouts yield greater rewards. A-ha's first video is a good example: 'Take On Me's' time- and cost-intensive animation was considered risky until the single broke massively in America. Above and beyond inflation squabbles, however, is the fact that exposure outlets in the UK are poised on the brink of substantial change.

First, the old 'pay for play' issue finally assembled itself into an ultimatum. The record companies – through their trade association The British Phonographic Industry – decreed that the BBC, the ITV networks and Channel 4 must pay fee increases for the broadcast of promotional clips. Unless the principle of payment is accepted (£500 per video by the close of 1986 as opposed to the BBC's customary £10), the record companies threaten to stop supplies altogether. Less glum news came from Virgin. As we go to press, the Virgin-backed *Music Box* is set to broadcast late hours on Yorkshire Television, beginning in July/August. Music video directors and their production companies looked at these developments and were unsure whether to celebrate or leave town; late night pop is a stroke of good luck, but the end of music videos as cheap programming means trouble.

Unlike the embattled pop clip, the new, improved promo-advert looks like the start of something big. It is unsurprising, then, that virtually every major video production house in the UK now has an advertising division. Some of these are doing better than others, but all face the same obstacles. In the world of commercials, the video director finds himself not the *wunderkind* of the record biz but just another freelancer scrambling after a limited number of jobs. The working environment can be trying since the nouveau pop person is unprepared for both staff deadwood and the pronounced dwindling of the director's role in the finished product. Another problem is the dismal track record of video directors in feature films. Everyone assumed that the senior video directors would vanish forthwith from the promo business, buoyed to Pinewood on the success of *Razorback* and *Electric Dreams* and *Absolute Beginners*. When this did not happen, the senior strata decided to try for advertising, an already crowded life-raft supporting between-jobs feature film directors. When Julien Temple competes for a beer advert, his rivals are not students and friends of the band but veterans like Ridley Scott.

However, what is truly exceptional about the pop world's infiltration of advertising is not a changing market-place but a changing aesthetic. It is one thing to borrow video's style – the smoke, the hair, the up-the-leg shots – but it is another, bigger, thing to absorb video's attitude. As anyone who watches MTV will testify, the prevailing emotion in pop promos is a sort of cornball isolation. Pop video accustoms us to the sight of preeners and pouters tripping disconsolately through a welter of *things*. And so too with promo-vert commercialism.

In their haste to imitate the allure of pop, the least imaginative advertisers have decided that commercials actors must look 'hip', the way musicians do in promos. Unfortunately, music video's notion of social superiority boils down to perhaps three facial expressions: farcical smugness, slit-eyed *ennui*, and (in the case of women) a sort of dominatrix's leer. Gerald Casale of Devo called the Promo Look 'puzzling evidence': why does everyone look so menacing? so unforgiving? so pissed off? Whatever the reason, the promo-vert has taken 'puzzling evidence' to risible extremes – after all, it isn't music that's causing all that gruesome *weltschmerz*, but a bottle of shampoo, or a 'new fragrance', or a compact disc player.

Aside from the Philips compact disc player ad – a promo-vert pinnacle since that quick-frozen yuppie male dying of boredom in his loft Simply Speaks Volumes – the most telling ad-vid of the year was for the Renault II. Handsomely executed but unbearably tacky, this one featured a lone Leisure Man caught in a traffic jam. Suddenly, inexplicably, a video-like editing shuffle allows him to escape three lanes of solid metal and swerve free, as a blast of youth music courses from the dashboard. Youthing away, Renault Man moves adroitly through the back streets, all thoughtfully cleared of traffic by a passing Renault II television crew. When at last he arrives at his unspecified destination, our hero pauses, jacket slung over his shoulder, and looks skyward in the certainty that he is an Individual, an Unruffled Guy, an Artist, even. In reality, of course, video techniques and video affectations make him the original road-to-nowhere man, coming from nowhere and going to nowhere with nothing but a sales pitch in between.

Dessa Fox

TOP TEN

Dessa Fox picks and praises her favourite videos of the year . . .

1 TALKING HEADS – The Movie (Palace)

Sense placed high in everyone else's honours list, and this one will be no exception. Directed by Jonathan Demme and conceived for the stage by David Byrne, this film-on-video sees New York's finest in a celebratory mood. A must, not least for Byrne's refrigerator-shaped jacket.

2 THE RESIDENTS – Whatever Happened To Vileness Fats? (Doublevision, dist IKON)

Produced by the Cryptic Corporation and written and produced by the Residents, *Fats* is part of the long-lost Residents video movie, this year re-edited by Doublevision and released on an unsuspecting public. Briefly, we have here an opus of space, time, and screaming mothers-in-law, all deliriously framed in some of the most brilliant set design ever seen on videotape. Also includes the live *Mole Show*.

3 THE CURE – Standing On A Beach (Palace)

Which sees the wiggly boys whooping it up with director Tim Pope. They were lucky to get him; virtually every one of these 15-odd promos is a joy to watch, from the charmed barm of 'Let's Go To Bed' to the magnificent 'Boys Don't Cry'. All in all, sixty minutes of dopey exhilaration.

4 CABARET VOLTAIRE – Gasoline In Your Eye (Virgin/Doublevision)

An unmissable release from the most visually adept band in the country. Includes the distressed allure of *Sensoria* (now in the video collection of the Museum of Modern Art in New York) and the groundbreaking *Crackdown*.

5 MOTOWN 25 – Yesterday, Today, Forever (MGM/UA)

Richard Pryor hosts Motown's twenty-fifth birthday celebrations live on television, with performances old and new elevating the proceedings to near-celestial level. "Look out baby," breathes first guest Smokey Robinson, words which see the expressway to your heart well started.

6 GOSPEL JOY – A Live Celebration (Hendring)

Featuring the ego-free fervour of the Spirit Of Watts, the Angelical Voice Choir, and the Trumpets Of Zion. Gospel star Shirley Fenty sums it up: *"Satan was shaking to the soles of his pointed shoes"*.

7 NEIL YOUNG – Berlin Live (PolyGram)

The Confederate moralist from Ontario is still packing 'em in: here, Young's stern stance and windy guitar playing enthral a stadium full of mesmerised eighteen-year-olds. Eleven songs, lucidly directed by Michael Lindsay-Hogg.

8 VARIOUS – Impact! (Auto Edit) (C&H Productions, distributed by Cartel)

Impact! is the indie success of the year, evincing much hard work, a flagrant disrespect for broadcast television, and fourteen adventures in post-industrial funk. Highlights include Hula, Portion Control, Severed Heads, Sonic Youth, and Boyd Rice and Frank Tovey blistering ears at the ICA. Ownership essential.

9 & 10 ONE NIGHT WITH BLUE NOTE – Preserved (Vols I & II) (PMI)

In which thirty major jazz artists – among them Herbie Hancock, McCoy Tyner, Cecil Taylor, and the spectacularly gifted Stanley Jordan – gather to pay tribute to the seminal jazz label. Both cassettes should be treasured for their dignity, generosity, and lack of cod camera angles.

REVIEWS

... and appraises with practised eye a selection of the rest

PHIL COLLINS. No Jacket Required EP
(Virgin Video, 30 *mins)*
This man was unconditionally brilliant in *Miami Vice*, which occasioned the first good review the *NME* has given Mr Collins in ten years. Still, it's lonely at the top, so let's return to normality with five vicious condemnations. This collection of promos is just middle class. Not being of the rollicking pub persuasion, I failed to see why everyone enjoyed themselves in 'Sussudio'; 'Who Said I Would' had all the mournful simplicity of a Wrigley's advert; 'One More Night' felt like it; 'Take Me Home' I abandoned; and 'Don't Lose My Number' contains an extremely unfunny parody of videos and video directors. Monitor those *Miami Vice* reruns instead.

STYX. Caught In The Act . . . Live
(A&M Sound Pictures, 87 *mins)*
The most scenic aspect of heavy metal is, of course, the bulging bits – the wallets, the codpieces, the overheated imaginations. *Caught In The Act* is plain blimpish all over, being a 'dramatisation' of a rockless future and consequently rife with repressive robots and Styx fans turned terrorist. This band has all the blue smoke money can buy, and after ninety-odd minutes of flat screaming and Orwellian air conditioners, the effects are quite magical: you feel you've turned into a giant thigh muscle, or inhaled a Mid-western shopping mall. Overall, it's the video least likely to be tinkling softly at yuppie dinner parties, so sneer not.

DEPECHE MODE. Some Great Videos
(Virgin Video, 46 *mins)*
A chronology of the Mode career, from the dewy 'Just Can't Get Enough' (with Vince Clarke) to 'It's Called A Heart'. Curiously, the clip that works best was shot live: 'Photographic' makes excellent use of the band's stage lighting. As to the rest, the good ones were directed by Peter Care and all others by Clive Richardson.

JIMI HENDRIX. Jimi Hendrix: The Documentary With Music
(Warner Home Video, 98 *mins)*
"The whole audience was on Owsley – that's acid, right," reminisces Eric Clapton, remembering the night Jimi Hendrix dragged 'Wild Thing' to its knees in front of Janis Joplin, Pete Townshend, Brian Jones and nobody at all from Simply Red, Animal Nightlife or Spelt Like This. Here is yet another archive tape that invites depressing comparisons between yesterday's geniuses and today's musical furniture.

This workmanlike biography follows Hendrix from Seattle to the army to Ike and Tina to leaving the USA and beyond. The stunning 'Purple Haze' at the Marquee Club in 1967 seems to have put the cat among the English pigeons quite nicely, and during 'Like A Rolling Stone' the crowd is almost ferociously ecstatic. Hendrix also had a million girlfriends, each of whom has something to contribute here. "He was a cutie pie with a guitar," says one, encapsulating the whole of rock mythology in one sentence. Highlights include 'Red House' at the Isle of Wight in 1970 and the plaintive 'Star Spangled Banner' at Woodstock.

NEW MODEL ARMY. Live 21-4-85
(PMI, 30 *mins)*
It Takes Talent Dept: how does a sensitive, angry young band maintain both *City Limits*-style credibility and macho rock appeal? One solution is to make music that is neither subversive nor sexy. As you will discover in 'Better Than Them', 'No Greater Love', 'Young, Gifted and Skint', 'Christian Militia', etc., etc.

JOHN COUGAR MELLENCAMP. Ain't That America
(Embassy, 90 mins)
"Ain't that America/for you and me/yeah" – this kind of sentiment stumps through approximately ten short videos, from the 'Jack And Diane' era to 'Pink Houses' and 'Hurts So Good'. Mellencamp is often accused of being the poor man's Springsteen, but he isn't – he's better looking and more fervent, like Sgt Rock with a guitar. His America is the kind of place where girls wear tight jeans, black people are gnarled and folksy, and all the wheatfields, trains, rodeos, and oil rigs conspire to produce an enormous number of male cliches. Thus there's the inevitable biker sequence, where the local chopper gang grooves to the freewheelin' sounds of JCM. There's also shots of beer joints, and little boys who dream of being boxers. An early girlfriend says, "He wanted to be tough, but I think he was rilly sensitive." Unfortunately for everyone, Americans are still voting on the former emotion and making terrible songs about the latter; thanks, but no thanks.

KID CREOLE AND THE COCONUTS. The Leisure Tour
(Embassy, 60 mins)
Montreal-born August Darnell looks like a man determined never to endure a cold winter again; all this unflagging tropicana obviously means something to him. Here, for about the fifth year running, the Kid Creole revue offers choreographed routines about suntans and cruise ships. But there's trouble up on the bandstand; Darnell looks bored and impatient, and the girls seem terrified of missing a dance step. All this and not much improvement in the tunes, of which the best is still 'Annie, I'm Not Your Daddy'.

DIRE STRAITS. Brothers In Arms: The Video Singles
(PolyGram, 20 mins)
Includes the award-winning 'Money For Nothing' and the equally esteemed 'Brothers In Arms'. While no one can fault these videos' technical inventiveness – we got your Quantel, your computer animation, your hand-tinted film, yeah – the rather parboiled social commentary rankles. *Brothers In Arms* is full of the stuff rock persons come up with when they become grandiose about war, which is to say shots of band members atop cliffs, stormy seas, and much insistence on the heroic beauty of guitar solos. Those who prefer more pungent views – and no glam posing – should refer to Madness' 'Uncle Sam'.

GENESIS. Live: The Mama Tour
(Virgin Video, 102 mins)
Recorded live at the NEC Birmingham before the Prince and Princess of Wales, and including 'Abacab', 'That's All, Mama', 'Illegal Alien', 'Home By The Sea', 'Keep It Dark' and countless others. At 102 minutes, no one can accuse Genesis of skimping, nor can they be called haughty: Phil Collins constantly regales Their Highnesses with thigh-slappers and zesty anecdotes. As to what Diana thought of jokes about nurses' outfits and being 'hard', we can only guess.

THE DOORS. Dance On Fire
(CIC, 60 mins)
One of the year's best, even though the archive clips are fleshed out with some mystifying 'free-form' footage. This video has everything – freeways, palm trees, Navajo children, flowers opening, even John Doe of X appearing in a slasher film. 'Moonlight Drive' shows clips of what looks like Columbia's gross national product circling Saturn.

Last year's dodgy, podgy *The Doors: A Tribute To Jim Morrison* was made unacceptable by a *Rolling Stone*-style commentary, in which rock critics spoke headily of Baudelaire while the *maudit male* in question barely got a chance to expose himself. Here, director Ray Manzarek has done three things right – remixed the sound, obtained the best material and abandoned voice-overs entirely. This band just doesn't need explanations, whether they're falling-down sloppy (a live 'Roadhouse Blues'), cold-blooded and immaculate ('Light My Fire', from a TV variety show), or just plain shriekworthy ('Touch Me'). And the ineffable rattle of 'The End' – once seen, never forgotten – should be studied by every would-be necromancer in the country.

JOHN LENNON. Live In New York City
(PMI, 55 mins)
In 1972 Lennon and Ono played a benefit concert at Madison Square Garden in aid of handicapped children; the set included 'Power To The People', 'Instant Karma', 'It's So Hard', 'Come Together' 'Imagine', and 'Give Peace A Chance'. As a measure of what has changed since then – and this is either the stuff of sniggers or evidence of complete freedom, I'm not sure which – the audience brought kids, dogs, and tambourines, and waved them all throughout. 'Imagine' works best, with Lennon undercutting its gravity by chewing gum throughout.

OZZY OSBOURNE. Bark At The Moon
(PolyGram, 75 mins)

The *Bark* set starts off with two geysers of fire, behind which the drummer hammers away atop a ziggurat. Seventy minutes pass, and during each one you notice that Ozzy looks exactly like Russell Grant – not so much 'Iron Man' or 'Paranoid' but a sweet-natured guy who likes the moon and worries about his big cheeks. He even let his wife produce the video. And there's a Travel Club bonus here: connoisseurs of spoken intros will treasure the words, "It's nice to be back in – huh? – Salt Lake City."

VISAGE. The Hits
(PolyGram, 60 mins)

Who can forget Steve Strange in 'The Damned Don't Cry'? This classic clip features Steve standing enigmatically on a thirties railway platform, a man haunted by his own achievements. We note Steve's enormous coat, which looks exactly like a military refrigerator-freezer. Smoke swirls around his ankles, but Steve dare not stir an inch, lest his coat bring him crashing to the ground. So there he stands – waiting, watching, slowly manufacturing ice cubes. Other points of interest in this tape include the birth of video surrealism – remember giant liquorice allsorts bounding down the stairs? chairs hanging from the ceiling? dolls-houses on fire? All this and more in 'Night Train', 'Fade To Grey', 'Mind Of A Toy', etc., etc.

THE ICICLE WORKS. Seven Horses Deep
(Channel 5, 58 mins)

The songs 'Birds Fly (Whisper To A Scream)', 'Conscience Of Kings', 'A Factory In The Desert', 'Nirvana', etc., etc. are here performed in concert, with aerial views of fjords and seashores to provide atmosphere. The music is a sort of Waterboys/China Crisis hybrid, with no real gifts or gaffes to lodge in the memory. All in all, a tape for naturalists who live in bedsits.

HÜSKER DÜ. Makes No Sense
(Hendring, 60 mins)

A delightfully plug-ugly performance, with the sticky core of the *Candy Apple Grey* album well in hand. The set ends with Bob Mould's sensitive interpretation of the theme from *The Mary Tyler Moore Show*, a definite plus.

VARIOUS. Electric Dreams: The Video Soundtrack
(Virgin Video, 29 mins)

Featuring seven short videos cobbled together from the film of the same name, with contributions from Culture Club, Jeff Lynne and Giorgio Moroder and Philip Oakey. If, as Julie Burchill has remarked, "Hell is other people's graphics", then we're fairly roasting in purgatory over here in the *Electric Dreams* editing room. The design of this movie is dismally coy – if you like smiley faces on computer screens, then this one's for you. Savour also the squiggles, fuzzy bits, teens falling in love, video display units proclaiming LOVE and ELECTRIC DREAMS, New Yorkers in joyous harmony and poor PP Arnold dunked in a vat of video gelatin. Sensibly, Phil Oakey is last seen leaving the city as quickly as possible.

DURAN DURAN. The Making Of Arena
(PMI, 50 mins)

A self-explanatory cassette, and really only worth it if you're (a) a wealthy Duran Duran fan, or (b) a jealous set designer. Best dialogue: "Trevor, see if you can get that flamethrower away from Simon."

DURAN DURAN. Arena
(PMI, 60 mins)

In which *Barbarella*'s evil Duran Duran (played once more by Milo O'Shea) returns to bother the lads and employ a few set builders. The Russell Mulcahy-directed *Arena* is a perfect example of the Designer Film, and as such can't be criticised for its plot – which no one cares about anyway – or its characters (who act as clothes hangers). The question is: does it look good? Or, rather, does it make the band look good? That they do – principally because of 'Wild Boys', a sort of elemental table of Designer Style. 'Boys'' direction is flawless, the editing suitably wired, and the choreography stunning; all the band have to do is look overwhelmed.

DIANA ROSS. The Visions Of Diana Ross EP
(PMI, 30 mins)
Featuring la Ross in five money-drenched but style-starved promos, with the distinct sixth being 'Chain Reaction'. The David Mallet-directed 'Reaction' gets its sixties details gloriously right, and for that deserves some sort of authenticity award. The others, however, are a pain.

JOHN LENNON. Imagine: The Film
(PMI, 60 mins)
Imagine is a collection of hand-made vignettes celebrating Yoko, home and hearth. But just as most love letters should remain private, so too should love films, even if they're touted as 'art' or 'the first rock video'. The seventies' answer to Edward and Mrs Simpson are here speaking to each other, not to an audience.

As the skits and costume dramas flow on, it becomes easy to see why Lennon was so entranced; the woman is absolutely fearless. She treats every piece of play-acting with stupendous gravity. Vamp, guerrrrilla, fantasy queen, none of these roles faze her, and none of them make her laugh. Lennon looks awed by her lack of selfconsciousness. Includes 'Imagine', 'Jealous Guy', 'It's So Hard', 'Power To The People' and Yoko's unclassifiable 'Mrs Lennon'.

TOM PETTY AND THE HEARTBREAKERS.
Pack Up The Plantation: Live!
(Virgin Video, 96 mins)
This one doesn't bring much to the live-in-concert genre, but since the Heartbreakers maintain a sort of deft professionalism for ninety minutes solid and there look to be few Portion Control fans present, I'll skip the art gripe. Sixteen hits, including a surprisingly spectral 'Breakdown'.

ALIEN SEX FIEND. Liquid Head In Tokyo
(Cherry Red Films, 60 mins)
Some tunes know exactly what they want to accomplish; 'Crazy', for example, waves its arms for a bit, scissors rapidly across the stage, and then comes back to vomit red liquid in your lap. Yes, it's that modern. Let's see, what else . . . during 'Back To The Egg' and 'Ignore The Machine' the Japanese audience go wild and discipline their nipples . . . and on the stage a post-apocalyptic clothesline signals a world in tatters, or perhaps poor video sales.

CARL PERKINS AND FRIENDS. A Rockabilly Session
(Virgin Video, 60 mins)
Carl looks a bit like Clayton Farlow from *Dallas*, except that Clayton doesn't greet Eric Clapton with a roaring "Lemme hear that guitar, boy". Perkins and pals George Harrison, Ringo Starr, Roseanne Cash, Dave Edmunds and two Stray Cats rip through all the classics, including 'Matchbox', 'Mean Woman Blues', and Perkins' first recording for Sun, 'Turn Around'. *Session* is a growing-old-gracefully tape with no unseemly star turns and seniorbilly Carl in fine shape.

THE CARS. Live 1984-5
(Vestron Video, 60 mins)
This live date suggests a sort of Beverly Hills version of 'new wave' – the musos have earrings and funny hair while all around them floats expensive video equipment and reedily sung angst. In other words, this is the cassette Coil make in their worst nightmares, and Mike Read makes in his dreams. With fourteen tracks, including 'Drive'.

JULIAN LENNON. Stand By Me
(Virgin Video, 59 mins)
Not so much a video, more a psychological casebook. As this tape testifies, the pressures on Lennon are weirdly unique, what with the name, the voice, and the older fans looking for glimpses of someone else. Still, the kid doesn't look too bothered, and 'Too Late For Goodbyes' is a good song by anyone's standards, famous nose or no famous nose. Almost all of the material is from *Valotte*.

PETE TOWNSHEND. White City: The Music Movie
(Vestron Video, 60 mins)
White City is a musical drama for *Guardian* readers; that's not to say it's bad, exactly, just that you have to be Forty And Concerned to really enjoy it.

In this self-penned story, Pete revisits the council estate of his youth and meets up with the slightly younger Jim, a divorced longhair shambling moodily from the DHSS office to the pub. The nattily dressed Pete sits with his chum and listens with the sort of facial expression that signals *Jim's fate is a metaphor for Thatcher's Britain.* According to the sleeve, Townshend eventually realises that the White City inhabitants "possess a strength and purpose that his own generation lacked," but this bit isn't too clear. Altogether, this cassette is for the sort of people who have parents like Pete, since neither the music nor the theme will mean much to Pete's juniors.

STRAY CATS. Stray Tracks
(Virgin, 60 mins)
Musicians will one day learn the power of video – it never forgets. The camera records embarrassing statements forever, till the end of time, eternally. Statements like "When I write a song, it's like climbing a huge mountain." Unfortunately, songs like 'Sexy and Seventeen' and 'Look At That Cadillac' are plainly not the Pyrenees of pop, and neither are the videos. Also, interviewers who say things like "It really is a bit mystical, isn't it?" don't help matters much.

Tracks has everything you'd expect: the romanticised, horrendously rewritten versions of the fifties ('Rock This Town', 'Stray Cat Strut'), unsolicited views of the American way of sex ('Sexy and Seventeen') and one very good bit which demonstrates what this band had in the first place ('The Race Is On' with Dave Edmunds). Still, Brian Setzer has that certain something – next year he should skip the video column and move to Hollywood.

STEWART COPELAND. The Rhythmatist
(A&M Sound Pictures, 58 mins)
On the face of it, the adventure looks promising: Police drummer Copeland undertakes a percussionist's tour of Tanzania, Kenya, Burundi, Zaire and the Congo. The sleeve makes it clear that our traveller is interested in the differences between Western music and African rhythms: no rockist dillydallying here, you think.

But no. *The Rhythmatist* turns out to be the most deranged sort of pop imperialism imaginable because it makes Copeland look cool and untouchable while everyone else becomes part of the wallpaper. This is the man who has a camera crew to cater to his every need but who has the nerve to express concern over local food supplies. This is the man whose patently uninteresting drumming supposedly wows 'em down in the villages. This is the man who chases a hapless giraffe across the plains because it Looks Good On Film. This is the man whose self-penned commentary is breathtakingly tacky: "Pygmies are a curious people," Copeland intones jokily, "Some of them even have guns." He's lucky they didn't see the script.

PAUL YOUNG AND THE Q-TIPS. Live
(Jettisoundz, 25 mins)
We are stageside at Nottingham's Theatre Royal one evening in 1981, and few know or care that the Tips contain a pearl of great price. The atmosphere reeks of last-ditch pub-ism, what with punks packing them in up the road and ruffled-shirt bands not garnering much press. There are only six songs, including 'You Are The Life', 'Empty Bed', and 'Some Kind Of Wonderful'.

Interestingly, few females look like they'd rather be somewhere else; nobody here is going to trade Paul for a night with the Gang Of Four. And who can blame them? There's the diehard romantic down on bended knee, imploring the ladies during 'A Man Can't Lose (What He Don't Have)'. The ladies – zing! go the strings of the future – scream for more. All the boy has to do is wait.

THE STYLE COUNCIL. Live!: Showbiz
(PolyGram, 53 mins)
With Dee C Lee, a string section, horns, congas, extra guitars, and Messrs Weller and Talbot live on stage at the Hammersmith Odeon. Directors Arnell and Benton have kept the editing crisp and the camera work incisive, aided by a well-organised stage set and clear, beautifully opulent lighting. Interestingly, there are almost no views of the audience – always a good modesty indicator. But as we all know from the records, the Council's problem is not gaudiness but a sort of needling my-sackcloth-is-angrier-than-yours attitude; Weller, as always, looks pissed off at his own success. His irritation is supposed to act as a call to arms but, lacking the humanism of a Dammers or a Wyatt, the battle cries bypass the heart entirely, and end up somewhere near the sleeve. Thus 'Internationalists' and 'Walls Come Tumbling Down' are less than good and the soul workouts plainly unbelievable. With the slower numbers, however, the band's humourlessness and misguided ire don't seem to matter – the lush 'Long Hot Summer' is always a treat, and '(When You) Call Me' is the one spark that ignites.

U2. The Unforgettable Fire Collection
(Island Video, 60 mins)
Great band, great video, and one question – if the Style Council can be slagged off for unsmileyness, then why not U2? The answer, of course, lies in the music: Weller is serious about ersatz 'soul' whereas Bono is serious about *wonder*; he has a battling incoherence about him, like a docker dumped on a cloud. Interestingly, U2 believe exactly the same thing soul artists do: namely, that the work doesn't come from them but through them.

The *Collection*'s first half is three performances – 'Bad', 'Pride', and 'A Sort Of Homecoming' – plus Meiert Avis' superb 'Unforgettable Fire' clip. The second part moves to Slane Castle and Dublin's Windwill Lane Studios for the usual making-the-album sequences. These are actually worth watching because the contrast between vocabularist Brian Eno and the shaggier approach of the band is a treat. In the studio, Eno will go on about 'wit' and 'brevity'; the band scratch themselves and respond "Er, dunno about the second chorus." All in all, one of the few videos containing likeable people, an eclipse of the moon, and fine, fine music.

FRANK ZAPPA. Does Humour Belong in Music?
(PMI, 57 mins)
Fourteen tracks and fifty-seven minutes of talking, vaudeville, panty jokes, Boy George imitations and intermittent noise. Carefully, my television set examined the humour vectors, pronounced them as funny as twenty copies of *Saturday Night Fever* wedged down the john, and conceded Frank few laughs. As usual with the things Californians think hilarious, you'll find terror here, and savagery: why does everyone but Frank look like an off-duty cop? Why do people with money hand it over to Frank? Fun-seekers may try their luck with 'Zoot Allures', 'Tinsel Town Rebellion', and Gregg Allman's 'Whippin' Post'.

OMD. Crush: The Movie
(Virgin Video, 70 mins)
Question: who can sit through seventy minutes of Orchestral Manoeuvres In The Dark, piecing together a new album? Answer: the band, the engineers, the camera people, airline executives, certain colourful residents of Spain and Mexico who featured in the location shots, the manufacturers of Ray-Bans and sports cars, and one video reviewer who is still *Organisation*'s biggest fan. The latter album was a combination of Presbyterian hymnal and the cartoon Archies, and therefore brilliant. Sadly, *Crush* – like *Dazzle Ships* – has left out the grandeur and retained the tiddleybonk plod. So too with the visuals: what is supposed to be a behind-the-scenes look has no scenes to look behind – it's not enough to take a camera crew to a picturesque village and then break into 'So In Love'. In other words, *Crush* is a bit on the uninteresting side.

FIAT LUX. Commercial Breakdown
(PolyGram, 45 mins)
"*Take no notice of me,*" cries the vocalist, calling down the very planets in his dark night of the soul. Oh, all right then.

Actually, if we prowl around these eleven video sets on little cat feet, the rewards are quite incomparable. There's a bonfire, a stately home – unfortunately not together – and some model girls gazing goatishly offscreen. The editing tricks are unsurpassed: at one point the band's bodies trail behind them in slices, which is like having a loaf of special-effects bread flung at your back.

USA FOR AFRICA: UNITED SUPPORT OF ARTISTS FOR AFRICA
We Are the World: the Video Event
(PMI, 60 mins)
With the brilliant Jagger-Bowie 'Dancing In The Street' clip, over forty contributing artists, and all profits helping to alleviate African hunger. In this context, a review seems like a pretty shabby enterprise, but some things just have to be said.

According to the *Sunday Times*, American market researchers have shown that the words 'poverty' and 'hunger' alienate the potential charity donor; instead, the emphasis is on 'caring' and 'community', terms which plainly do not convey horror and culpability. And that is exactly the problem with the USA For Africa artists – they're so busy celebrating they forget to be angry.

The 'Do They Know It's Christmas?' lot were issued with a styrofoam cup and a blast from Bob; here we find Jane Fonda and the plush rub of designer leathers. And unlike the British effort, the studio floor is a madhouse of hugging and kissing. Everyone sways and holds hands, joining in on a song that contains few distressing references to Band Aid's *dread, fear,* and *clanging chimes of doom*. Worse, the innumerable camera crews perform the weird task of busting any and all untearful faces – ie, anyone who won't visibly celebrate looks heartless next to Lionel Richie. What this project needs is the inimitable wrath of Geldof, or the chilling pitch of Bono.

Buy it anyway; just don't look at it.

DEAD OR ALIVE. Youthquake
(CBS Fox, 22 mins)
With six promos, including the three best-known hits 'That's The Way (I Like It)', 'You Spin Me Round (Like A Record)' and 'Lover Come Back To Me'. The Tim Pope-directed 'I'd Do Anything' still looks svelte, the others slightly less so.

VIOLENT FEMMES. No, Let's Start Over
(*PolyGram*, 45 mins)
Gordon Gano has eyes the colour of dirty windows, and because they barely move during 'Spiritual' (*"hack hack hack it apart"*) and seem to give up the ghost entirely during the brilliant, tubercular 'Country Death Song', the Femmes stand among the great close-up bands of our time. Tragedy strikes, however, when director Mike Mansfield leaves the Lyceum for the badlands of promo kitsch. Transmission is interrupted by duff inserts of hallways and graveyards, and – just as Gano sings *"take your lovely daughter/And throw her in the well"*, just as a ghastly scene is enacted in the privacy of your imagination – Mansfield cuts away to a dreadful advert child straight out of a Laura Ashley catalogue. Some people are just terrifyingly literal.

ROBYN HITCHCOCK AND THE EGYPTIANS. Gotta Let This Hen Out!
(*Jettisoundz*, 60 mins)
This excellent low-budget charmer contains not only a live set at the Marquee – with all the strangeness of Hitchcock's lyrics beamishly on target – but also a number of micro-dramas that show off the Sort Of Normal Man to good advantage. The best of these is 'The Fly', in which subtle special effects allow Hitchcock's eyes to wander from his face. The whimsy works because Hitchcock won't laugh, and because all his lyrical daffodils carry a sting in the tail (*"Please don't call me Reg/It's not my name/Not yet"*). Fourteen fowl tracks; get yourself in a flap.

KATE BUSH. The Hair Of The Hound EP
(*PMI*, 20 mins)
With four extended-length videos: 'Running Up That Hill', 'Hounds Of Love', 'Cloudbursting', and 'The Big Sky'. The latter has its moments, but it's a shame that this collection is so ordinary. Bush needs a director who understands her malice-in-wonderland appeal, and that director should at least have made 'Hounds Of Love'.

THE SHADOWS. Live
(*PMI*, 25 mins)
A very restrained video, with a craftsman's approach to the material and a touchingly unhip light display during 'Apache'. All the hits.

DAVID BOWIE. Ricochet
(*Virgin Video*, 59 mins)
This is positively the last, utmost, unconditionally final Entire-Warehouse-Must-Go free-salad-tongs-with-every-purchase tour video from the Serious Moonlight excursion; and never mind the location shots, feel the magic of this man's *hair*.

The much-touted exotic settings – Hong Kong, Bangkok, Singapore – are all right in their way, but Bowie's burnished barnet manages to shame all local colour. You can't tear your eyes away: when Bowie relaxes in the back of a Hong Kong limo, it's as if he's wearing frozen lemon ices combed to obedience on his scalp; later, awestruck locals watch their sunsets slink off and die when the buffed blond draws near.

Elsewhere, this video contains only four stage sequences: 'Heroes', 'Look Back In Anger', 'Ricochet' and 'Fame'. In between times, Bowie does his best to forget that he's a living legend, and through all the visits and dinner parties remains unflaggingly charming. Interestingly, he always asks the same questions Prince Charles does: how does this factory/housing development/musical instrument operate? And, Charles-like, he looks like he's dying for a good laugh.

FLIPSIDE VIDEO: Fanzine Number Five
(*Jettisoundz*, 60 mins)
Here we have a collection of US hardcore bands: Decry, Heart Attack, Red Cross, Bad Religion, Vagina Dentata, Pariah, etc., etc. and – the UK Subs. It has to be noted that when senior Eurogerms like the Subs are pitted against LA's finest, the Brits look merely tousled, like Alastair Cooke disturbed in his library. Everyone else looks brainless.

No matter who is on stage here – Crass clones, hoarse guys with gripes, hippies in bondage jammies – there are ten thousand others punching their way to the spotlight, trampling on the less wired and in general behaving like future Presidents (this tape was compiled in Richard Nixon's home town). Interestingly, these liberty-loving individuals go in for the same old repressive artcack everyone else is using: swastikas, World War II footage, mushroom clouds, etc. Once upon a time these images were an effective kiss-off letter to convention; now they're an asshole's idea of in-flight entertainment.

TUXEDOMOON. Ghost Sonata
(*Doublevision*, 60 mins)
Which sees the Belgian-based ensemble in a melancholic mood. 'Sonata' is a performance piece based on suicidal themes from the Strindberg play of the same name. Imagine a collaborative work from Laurie Anderson, Eugene Atget and Bela Lugosi, and then don't look at it – the music's better by itself. Directed by Tuxedomoon's Bruce Geduldig and Winston Tong, and including the shorts 'Time To Lose' and 'The Stranger'.

THOMPSON TWINS. Single Vision
(Virgin Video, 46 mins)
As the most ill-conceived, flat-footed band in recent history issues a promo retrospective, your first response is to try on a few metaphors. Watching the Thompson Twins is like watching three balls of cellophane with pretensions. Watching the Thompson Twins is like watching an Our Price advert furnish your living room. Watching the Thompson Twins is like watching music die before your very eyes.

Actually, if this video teaches us anything it's the fact that the camera is deeply suspicious of some people. Like a dog or a horse, a lens will sense the approach of raging smarm and act accordingly. Take Joe Leeway, for example. In 'Sister Of Mercy', 'Watching', 'We Are Detective' and 'Love On Your Side' he has nothing to do but pull agonising faces, and noodle a bit at the keyboards; impassively, the camera registers a man making a dope of himself. Or take some of the action sequences – in 'Lay Your Hands On Me' he's off in the left-hand corner, grappling with an upright bass like a spaceman strangling a garden hose. By the time we arrive at the anti-heroin song 'Don't Mess With Dr Dream' – a video so bad it makes Dr Dream look both right and necessary – you feel sorry for the entire bunch of them. Whither fingerless gloves, eh?

VARIOUS. Now That's What I Call Music 6
(Virgin Video, 60 mins)
This edition includes UB40 and Chrissie Hynde – 'I Got You Babe'; Arcadia – 'Election Day'; Kate Bush – 'Running Up That Hill'; Marillion – 'Lavender'; Feargal Sharkey – 'A Good Heart'; Simple Minds – 'Alive and Kicking'; Bryan Adams and Tina Turner – 'It's Only Love'; Gary Moore – 'Empty Rooms'; Queen – 'One Vision'; the Pet Shop Boys' excellent 'West End Girls'; something paisley from the Cult; and Madness' profoundly wonderful 'Uncle Sam'.

VIRGIN PRUNES. Sons Find Devils: A Live Retrospective 1981-83
(IKON, 60 mins)
If King Kurt were seminary students they'd resemble the Virgin Prunes, messy people who go in for angel outfits and candlelit dramatics. The music is so-so, but the interviews are brilliant. Thirteen tracks.

THE CLASH. This Is Video Clash
(CBS Fox, 40 mins)
Depressing. Of course they never got tough with the music business, rampant consumerism, or ugly politicos. The sackcloth fell to the fans – you remember, the ones who mistook style for content. The right jacket seemed to promise so much . . .

Winner of this year's Ozymandias Award.

VARIOUS. British Rock: The First Wave
(RCA Columbia Video, 62 mins)
Recommended, although it's best to retire the ears during Michael York's "battle cry of a generation"–type voice-over. 'The First Wave' is a compact chronology of the Beatles, the Rolling Stones, the Hollies, Brian Poole and the Tremeloes, the Kinks, the Animals and the Who. Bright spots include the sight of Roger Moore presenting Gerry Marsden with an award, Jagger inadvertently insulting the Animals and Eric Burdon's stumpy genius. Students of light shows will want to check out Cream's 'Tales Of Brave Ulysses'.

VARIOUS. Pirates Of The Panasoniks
(Jettisoundz, 60 mins)
The best thing about a Jettisoundz video is the camera work; never has shaky dismemberment looked so much like art.

This compilation contains two star turns from the ranting poet Attila The Stockbroker, and in both instances he's losing valuable humanity – most of his scalp in 'Airstrip One' and about three inches off the left side in 'Radio Rap' (which the manufacturers cruelly advertise as the 'complete' version). The Membranes, on the other hand, get the full free-form expressionist treatment: straight up the nose, back down the bum, and finally arriving at a sort of conceptual oasis of bulging leather. More anatomical contributions come from the Cardiacs, Suicidal Tendencies, Brian Brain, the Neurotics, Hagar the Womb, the Cult Maniax and the Toy Dolls, among others.

KING. From Steps In Time To Bitter Sweet: The Video Singles
(CBS Fox, 25 mins)
Featuring the soggy 'stylists' preening through 'Love And Pride', 'Won't You Hold My Hand Now' and three others too awful to mention. The cassette cover doubles as a lyric sheet in which the reviewer finds the apt instructions: *"take your hairdryer blow them all away"*. Consider them blown.

THE BEST AND WORST
ALBUM COVERS
OF THE YEAR

In which several persons involved in producing this book make their highly subjective and anonymous selection of what was finest and nastiest in sleeve design. A trend of the year seems to have been a move towards black-and-white portraits, striking images that stand out well from the madding crowd of colour. As this is a colour section, we obviously had to temper our natural enthusiasm for these. Elvis Costello, Prince and the Cure we felt deserved inclusion for their wit, subversion and elegance. Peter Gabriel and Robert Palmer, on the other hand, didn't even get into Worsts, so drillingly boring are their latest sleeves – enormous, healthy, AOR faces looming at you from everywhere.

This year there are two more Bests than Worsts. There's never a shortage of the latter, but we couldn't whittle down our selection of the former any further. You'll probably disagree with our choices, anyway . . . Well, one man's meat is another man's *poisson*, as they say.

THE BEST

PARADE – Prince and the Revolution

Photo by Jeff Katz/Art direction by Laura Lipuma and Jeffrey Kent Ayeroff

Pure sex. Well, pure sex 'n' religion: the devil's music brilliantly evoked. Would you buy a jar of hair cream from this man?

THE BEST

PSYCHO CANDY – Jesus And Mary Chain

Designed by the band/Still from video of 'Just Like Honey'

Difficult one, this. One said it was "the essence of rock 'n' roll"; another liked the not-quite-mirrored 'Candy'; yet another was drawn by the strategically placed figures and drum. So we shot those three and simply decided it was groovy.

153

THE BEST

THE WORST

LIVE FROM THE BASS CLEF LONDON – Various

Designed and illustrated by Sue Rentoul
A world of warmth and excitement conjured up with vibrant colours and simple graphics. Positively shouts at you to join in and promises the music will be just as lively.

RENDEZVOUS – Jean Michel Jarre

Designed by Michel Granger
Insupportable graphic buffoonery: laughable execution of world-view concept that was lamentably inappropriate in the first place.

STANDING ON A BEACH - The Singles - The Cure

Designed by Andy Vella and Porl Thompson of Parched Art
Peter Gabriel and Robert Palmer take note: this man is not Robert Smith. An evocative and atmospheric photo of a craggy and weatherbeaten face that invites you to investigate further. Hand-tinted background adds elegant contrast.

EASY PREY – Predator

Designer unknown
And long may he/she remain so. Although this is just so plainly *bad* it is almost a 'joke', the fact that sexist and violent (yes, sexist and violent) images like this are still being used to sell product is deeply offensive and not a little worrying.

154

THE BEST

THE WORST

PLEASE – Pet Shop Boys

Designed by Mark Farrow at 3 and PSB

Small is beautiful. Understatement is adorable. Creative use of white space estimable.

THE OTHER SIDE OF LIFE – The Moody Blues

Designed by Alwyn Clayden, Bruce Gill (Green Ink)

Is this a parody of a photocopier ad? What *on earth* is going on? Oh dear oh dear, thought we'd seen the last of this techno-acid nonsense.

A KIND OF MAGIC – Queen

Front cover illustration by Roger Chiasson/Sleeve design by Richard Gray

Satisfyingly, and surprisingly for this crew, self-deprecating. Has the cheap 'n' cheerful allure of cartoon figures and a child's paint-box, despite clearly being an expensive and professional production.

DIRTY WORK – The Rolling Stones

Art direction and package design by Janet Perr/Art direction and photography by Annie Leibovitz

Gordon Benetton, what a mess! And don't they look uncomfortable? The very 'trendy' and 'colourful' clothes cannot disguise the fact that these chaps have gathered some moss in their time; they ought to know better. So ought Annie Leibovitz.

THE BEST

THE WORST

A DATE WITH ELVIS – The Cramps

Cover layout and photos by the Cramps/Title lettering by Phil Smee at Waldo's Design

Has to be the tackiest cover around. Thank God it's not scratch 'n' sniff. Form and content in perfect harmony.

TIM – The Replacements

Cover by Robert Longo/Art direction by Deborah DeStaffan

What is this 'hallway' supposed to be? Why is that bloke's face upside down? Who is the guitarist? Is he any good? Who cares? Why are we here? Why is *this* here??

KING OF AMERICA – Elvis Costello

Photo by Terence Daniel Donovan/Design and typography by Michael Sören Krage/Consultant Matthew Patrick Declan MacManus

Demands to be taken at face value. Another lesson on the use of the mug shot for Messrs Gabriel and Palmer. Droll cove, this 'design consultant'.

THE COLOUR OF SPRING – Talk Talk

Cover illustration by James Marsh

Absolutely beguiling from a distance; absolutely revolting on closer inspection. Badly painted in the textbook-school of realism, but striving for surreal effect. (And it's a very parched spring that's this colour.)

THE BEST

THE WORST

MANIC POP THRILL – That Petrol Emotion

Photo and sleeve design by Hugh Cairns/Design and typography by Mike Krage

Full of mystery and imagination. Weird and enticing. That's right – we haven't a clue what it's all about, but it works.

STRENGTH – Alarm

Artwork conceived and designed by Lewis Evans
Strength!!!???

FLIP YOUR WIG – Hüsker Dü

Designed by Fake Name Communications/Photo by Bruce A Christianson

'Orrible marzipan things on a great big gooey cake. Nice enough to make yourself extremely ill on. Orgiastic possibilites.

FROM LUXURY TO HEARTACHE – Culture Club

Designed by Assorted iMaGes

Thoroughly unoriginal cover made worse by clever-clever graphic design touches. What are the mathematical symbols doing? The sum of these parts is at least = to the whole: lots of nothing always adds up to zero.

THE BEST

THE WORST

BEAT RUNS WILD – Various

Designed by P St John Nettleton/Globular Studios
Inspired rip-off – don't bother with the record, just feel the period insincerity.

THE SMALL PRICE OF A BICYCLE – The Icicle Works

Designed by Steve Hardstaff
A study in embarrassment: extras and group members caught in mid-concept. The former look slightly happier as they're being paid. Altogether humourless and meaningless.

KISSING HER & CRYING FOR YOU – Various

Sleeve and art by Ian Clark
Well-executed fifties pastiche, dreamy, romantic; the perfect housewife's choice. You just know you're going to *swoon* to this one.

WHO MADE WHO – AC/DC

Designed by AD Design
Looks like a bootleg T-shirt from Carnaby St. Angus Young's schoolboy humour is not worth one column inch. Cheap and anything but cheerful. Hard rock has always meant hard luck for sleeve design.

Tom Hibbert and Pete Clark say

THANKS . . .

PRINCE: Having been declared criminally insane, the Paisley Popinjay popped back with *Parade,* the most beguiling album of the eighties (so far).

CHEERS: For reminding us that situation comedy can actually be funny – and for Woody's mother's 'dream' (she wanted to see the drummer in a power trio, like her hero Ginger Baker) in particular.

MADONNA: For being consistently entertaining, for being the only pop person who can actually act on the 'silver' screen, and for driving the British daily press into apoplexisms of indignant rage by refusing to talk to them.

PARENTS MUSIC RESOURCE CENTRE: Thank you, Washington Wives, for your brave, albeit naive attempt to rid popular music of its gratuitously violent elements.

ROBERT CRAY: Woke up this morning to a better class of blues. The Robert Cray Band smoulder on record, burn on stage; you could do worse than check the RC Band-brand blues packet with extra added soul.

ABSOLUTE BEGINNERS: Er . . . not quite sure of the form here. Well, great musical, magnificent singing and dancing, social message, Tenpole Tudor, nice frocks. Okay?

RED WEDGE: A noble effort to get away from the mindless Page 3 pop and a timely reminder that not all lefties are whingeing bores.

NO. 73: Ghastly blokes with idiotic 'perms' – but the Sandwich Quiz is the most compulsive viewing EVER. Apparently it's for children.

B52s: RIP Ricky Wilson and farewell to one of America's finest exponents of dizzy dance pop. When will we see beehives behave like this again?

SARAH FERGUSON: At last a gal with a bit of staying power. Sarah looks like she's no stranger to the occasional all-nighter. Half princess, half biscuit.

CLINT EASTWOOD: Latest recruit to the chain gang. Probably the world's first thin mayor. See him terrorise the drainage sub-committee. Soon to be a major motion picture!

WHAM!: The two fastest tans in the West disappear into the sunset. The only group in the history of the world to have kept its word and gone out on top.

JOHN LYDON: Haw haw haw. What a wag.

. . . BUT NO THANKS

MR MISTER: Ancient, ugly and hopeless. But with singles sales going down the dumper, Richard Page and his talentless crew succeed in reintroducing non-film-linked AOR to the pop charts with some of the most horribly crass songs ever made.

JULIAN LENNON: Not content with producing music of appalling drabness, Julian also wants to assault people with it live. Europe says no thanks, matey.

STATUS QUO REFORM: Francis! Rick! Tell us it's not true! It was fine while it lasted, but twenty years is enough. Into the denim wheelchairs with you.

THE PERSON WHO INVENTED THE COMPACT DISC: A frightful phenomenon. No comment.

RAMBO: Making a film about a French poet and spelling his name wrong is inexcusable. Explanations are futile because we can't understand a word.

CLIFF RICHARD, ANDREW LLOYD WEBER, RICHARD STILGOE, TIM RICE, BJORN ULVAEUS, BENNY ANDERSSON, DAVID ESSEX: For clogging up the West End theatres with entirely atrocious so-called 'rock musicals' – *Time, Starlight Express, Chess, Mutiny, Phantom of the Opera etc.*

MICHAEL JACKSON: Wearing a Beatle wig is one thing, but buying the Beatles' song catalogue is wrong. A disco version of 'Yesterday' will not ease a writing block.

TODAY: Brand-new national newspaper, sparkling technology, the shape of things to come, doomed because the colour comes off on your fish and chips.

PARENTS MUSIC RESOURCE CENTRE: No thank you, Washington Wives, for your perverted, hysterical, sinister, Daughters-of-the-American-Revolution-type attempt to rid popular music of its (essential) gratuitously sexual elements.

ROGER DALTREY: The man who once bawled "Hope I die before I get old" down a microphone cropped up, twenty years later, wearing green wellingtons and advising television viewers to get hold of an American Express card. Bleeeeuuuuurrrgggghhhhhhhh!!!

LESS THAN ZERO: California's jeunesse dorée make heavy weather of fun and games in hip best-seller. Like having your nose pushed into someone's Filofax. Lockjaw boredom.

THE MONKEES: Why, oh why, oh *why*? Lined, grey at the gills, old enough to know much better (hem hem, haw haw), the human cartoon reformed and 'played' to millions of squealing middle-aged lunatics. (PS: Thanks to Mike Nesmith, who *did* know better than to trample on our memories.)

LOOK BACK AT ANGER

Tony Parsons applies a little spit 'n' polish to the tarnished memory of punk

● THE SEX PISTOLS

● THE CLASH

Everyone wore strange clothes and thought they were going to change the world. Everyone took mountains of drugs and fucked around a lot. Everyone thought that being thirty years old was something that only happened to other people. Yes – now you come to mention it – it *does* sound a lot like hippy, doesn't it?

But anyhow, happy anniversary, darling.

In 1976, times weren't tough. Jim Callaghan was hardly General Pinochet and, unless you were a complete no-hoper or one of Mother Nature's spongers, you could walk into work.

Hey, kid, know anything about nuclear physics?

That Class of '76, those punks, the No Future merchants – No Future! Is that the most glorious slice of self-pity you ever heard or what? – were the very last generation to come of age before Britain, in economic terms, became a Third World nation. The punks were the last generation who could afford the luxury of rebellion. Did they fail? I really don't think so. Punk looked at popular culture, saw how old and staid and intolerably dull almost all of it had become, and dragged that popular culture out of the stadia, the museums and the graveyard, dragged it kicking and screaming back to the young. Why shouldn't you be shaking your ass on a stage? Why shouldn't you be writing, designing, taking photographs, doing whatever you want? Doing whatever you want! What's stopping you? You, that's all . . . Punk's message to the nation's youth was: you ARE a swan.

Ten years since it began. Ten years since – stop me if you have heard this one – some rough beast slouched from a Finsbury Park council estate to a clothes shop in the King's Road, its moment to be born come at last.

Ah, I remember Johnny . . .

Bliss it was in that very dawn to stumble into the 100 Club or the Nashville or the Hope and Anchor or the Red Cow and come across the Sex Pistols, the Jam, the Clash, or the Buzzcocks for the very first time. Imagine how good that was: you knew immediately that you felt exactly the same as these people, that here were the greatest bands in the world. I hadn't been going to gigs for a couple of years, not since Bowie at Earl's Court in 1973 where I watched naked Australians throwing up over girls, where I decided I did not want my rock stars to *mince*, where I decided once and – I thought – for ever that I did not want to see any more live music. That feeling of being part of the huge herd, the contemptuous distance between performer and audience, the feeling that Bowie was the hottest action around but that he really wasn't all you could hope for. Rock music had become as banal as television.

I hadn't been going to rock gigs for two or three years and then suddenly I was going to at least one every night. The best bands in the world! Lonely and righteous young men dynamited into bliss by the Sex Pistols.

Those Sex Pistols – big babies they were; spoilt little bastards the lot of them; prone to temper tantrums and throwing around their food, spitting on the carpet in record company offices and saying rude words on TV, anything to get some attention.

So full of bullshit. The Sex Pistols were at least as hypocritical as the tabloids who sold papers by tut-tutting about their wicked ways. All that old tosh about being bored, no-future proles. Nonsense, the lot of it. For a start, punk in general and the Sex Pistols in particular would never have happened in the wonderful way it did without the benefit of a few middle-class minds which had been processed through some very good art schools. Without that influence (they just don't *teach* you things like 'Eddie Cochran was an anarchist' in comprehensive schools) punk and the Pistols would have been merely a premature ejaculation of Oy. Okay, not quite as bad as that, but you get my drift.

And that boredom line that everyone used as a calling card, taking their cue from the Pistols, which was par for the punk course, was never less than a total fib. Everyone was having the time of their lives, behaving like animals and getting paid for it.

"I'm so *bored*."

The grown ups loved it! They ate that stuff up! The reason why so many people behaved so badly from around 1976 to 1978 (it did not last long, best beloved) was because bad behaviour was actively encouraged. Punks were protected wildlife, as professional hoodlums with leather jackets and a career in show business always are, and for the pros punk was a good excuse for a second childhood.

Yes, the Sex Pistols only had one thing going for them, and that was that they were the greatest band in the history of the world. The Jam were younger, the Clash had better songs and the Stranglers had better looking groupies. But it was always the Pistols who counted most. Still is. Seeing them for the first time was musical Armageddon. Presence, edge, cute haircuts – everything a band should have, they had in spades.

● THE JAM

● THE BUZZCOCKS

You knew immediately that you felt exactly the same as these people – essentially, lapsed skinheads who liked Bowie but knew in their heart of hearts that he was not the hottest action they could hope for and who had been absolutely OVERWHELMED by the New York Dolls performing two songs, 'Looking For A Kiss' and 'Jet Boy', on the *Old Grey Whistle Test* a few years earlier – Bob Harris *sneered* at the Dolls! He said "Mock Rock"! Sid fixed *his* wagon good and proper a few years later. And the Pistols, they came on like

a scourge.

Everything that stank about rock music and the music business – its safeness, its mediocrity, its pretensions, its old age – they put in a cruel and withering spotlight because it was everything the Sex Pistols were not.

It wasn't just a line, it truly wasn't – they were taking on all those alleged rock 'n' roll heavyweights, all those 30-year-old self-made millionaires, all those Greatest Rock 'n' Roll Bands In The World, the Rolling Stones, the Who – and they wiped the floor with them.

They made it look easy. That was what was so liberating about the Pistols – they made the act of creating look like the most natural thing in the world. Musicians, writers, photographers, film producers, film directors, designers, managers – the finest minds of a generation were given a kick up the ass by the coming of the Sex Pistols. You can do it! You ARE a swan! Ah, it made for some unspeakable garbage – horrible bands, silly clothes, worthless writers, pompous managers – but it also made for a lot that was memorable and more than a little that was unforgettable. We're talking children's crusade here.

At the start there was a real sense of community. And punks were sweet characters; there's no getting around

● SID VICIOUS

● STING

the fact that they could be charming, the boys in these bands. I remember being on the Anarchy in the UK tour in late 1976, and while the mass media were discussing what it all meant – basically, the end of the world – Jones the Pistol and Jones the Clash were discussing what it was like to stay in a hotel for the first time. And I remember being at the Mont de Marsan festival on the French-Spanish border in 1977. I was chewing the fat with Weller when someone came up behind us, put his hands over our eyes and started sing-

ing – in that superlative voice that sounded just like a dentist's drill – a few mocking snatches of 'Away From The Numbers'. It was Strummer. Weller burst into spontaneous song himself – *"Away from Joe Strummer,"* he crooned, *"that's where I want to be,"* and we all laughed because – sweet moment of tender fraternity! – we knew we were in the right place.

By 1978 all feelings of brotherhood had gone. The Clash kicked the Jam off their tour; Rotten roamed the Round-house boasting "I just made Strummer cry"; the Pistols and the Jam got into a dispute about who a certain riff belonged to (the debate reached some kind of conclusion when Weller, after considerable provocation, pulped Sid in the Speakeasy); everybody bitched about everybody else, in public and in private and in print.

Punk was no longer controlled by the élite vanguard. You saw it most in the strange rehabilitation of punk's village idiots. Fat little Mr Ant, the ex-teacher Sting, that posturing piece of bodybait Billy Idol – the ugly runts of the litter all made their moves on the road to becoming top dogs.

It was out of our hands. Things went sour long before the dissolution of the Jam and the Pistols, and the slow sad decline of the Clash, long before Sid was taking his very last overdose and Rotten was becoming the world's for-gotten boy. It was the beginning of the end when punk turned professional. Suddenly, horribly, everyone had to get on with their jobs. What had once been pure teen venom was now a vocation. Our much vaunted rebellion was start-ing to look a little silly – oh, punk still frightened the record companies (we were going to turn everything upside down! They were *meant* to be fright-ened of us!) but only because the international sales figures of the bands were disappointingly low. (Luckily for the record industry, the good little niggers of New Wave – Costello, Blondie, the Police – were already on their way.)

Turning professional takes it out of you . . . the Pistols could not survive America; not the pre-MTV America where, to a certain extent, they had to play the game, touring around playing to cowboys and hippies like they were just some ordinary little guitar-based combo. The beat still had backbone in those days and nobody who had sunk lager in the upstairs bar of the Roxy was going to go around striving for what, in reference to Simple Minds (you said it), somebody called "stadium status". Everything that most bands aspire to in 1986 is exactly what, for all their crap and nonsense, the Sex Pistols feared becoming – and that is why I loved them so.

When they broke up in that hotel room in San Francisco they achieved what James Dean managed on the road to Salinas – death and glory com-bining in one perfectly timed moment. And no matter what a collection of tossers they seem in retrospect – Cook and Jones going cap in hand to the High Court for their belated redun-dancy money; Lydon making puerile records and living the life of Joni Mitchell; Sid long in the grave because he was too gutless to face prison for topping that overpainted porker; Malcolm with his film 'projects' and 'dates' and 'models' – there is still some-thing pure and good about the memory of the Sex Pistols. They gave music a heart transplant. The operation was successful. The current mood of dis-content that pervades the music business is thanks to the Pistols and those who followed them, God bless 'em all.

They shall not grow old, they will never disappoint. In the end, all the windy rhetoric and broken promises of punk, all the silliness and swastikas, none of it matters. Punk was exhilara-tion and sedition, fun and danger, speed and lager, punk was young and dumb. And those Sex Pistols, they were a gloriously reckless outfit; if they had kept their heads down and played their cards right, they could have had the bank balance of a Thompson Twin. They wanted to get rich and famous and laid as much as the next man but – and this is the mark of their greatness, this is why no one else has come close to them – they also wanted *more*. Ambition was offset with a certain churlish idealism, appetite tempered by a belief in the importance of attitude.

The Sex Pistols wanted to have their cake *and* eat it *and* throw it around the room. They wanted to have a laugh, and honour too. They did not fail.

And when I look at what has hap-pened since, how all you have to do to become successful is achieve 'stadium status'; how all you have to do to create a media blitz is upset Mike Read; how all you have to do to feel like a man of honour is throw a few crumbs to some starving African; when I see all that then I am glad that I was just getting started at the same time as the Sex Pistols. The Pistols, see, set their sights a little higher than that.

And when I see Rotten's bastard children on the King's Road on a Saturday afternoon; when I see the toy-punk mohican tribe playing animal for the small change and Japanese cameras of the tourists; when I see that it turns my stomach. They're so *tame*.

Forget what you heard. Punk did not target its sights on the gutter, punk targeted its sights on the stars.

163

BOOKS

A selection of the year's publications reviewed by sundry readers

● BIOGRAPHIES

AHA: THE STORY SO FAR
Tor Marcussen (*Zomba*)

Most of the A-ha books, poster magazines, fact files and so on that have flooded into the shops since their rapid rise to fame (if that's the word) have simply served to prove that it's very hard to cobble together anything but the flimsiest story about a group who've only been in the public for under a year. By their standards Tor Marcussen's book is a work of genius – he travelled the world with them for months as their success grew and they in return seem to have trusted him with surprisingly frank reflections about each other and their childhoods. It's a pity he scribbled it all down in such a slapdash way (perhaps its hurried translation from the Norwegian original text is partly to blame) but as a book which deftly caters for just about everything an A-ha fan would want to know it's excellent. If, however, you're of the opinion that they're just three dubiously-attractive Norwegians with meagre talents I doubt it will do much to change your mind . . . (CH)

AMERICAN FOOL – THE ROOTS AND IMPROBABLE RISE OF JOHN COUGAR MELLENCAMP
Martin Torgoff (*St Martins Press*)

This story is worth reading if only because Mr Mellencamp survived one of the most unpromising starts in the rockbiz that it is possible to conceive of. His first manager was Tony DeFries, one time Bowie mentor, who tried to turn the Indiana thug into an airbrushed teen idol for the midwest – Johnny Cougar, laughing stock. It took years of graft for the foul-mouthed boy with the self-confessed 'bad attitude' to wipe the smirk off the public's face with the type of simple, gutsy rock which eventually made his fortune. The full story is here in exhausting detail: naked ambition, covered in warts. (PC)

THE BEATLES
Hunter Davies (*Jonathan Cape*)

Anyone with any genuine interest in the Beatles will already have read either the original (Heinemann/Mayflower 1968), which is not infallible but a minor classic, or the so-called 'update' (Granada 1978), which claimed to deal with the solo years, but didn't in any depth. A further eight years on comes this new edition, containing exactly what the previous update claimed, and more. A major event in rock publishing, the original book is sandwiched between two seventy-page additions that contain a bevy of highly readable and often seemingly new information. The only drawback to this 'new' edition is that it costs about £8, which may put off those who already have the original, but anyone who cares even a bit about the events and circumstances surrounding the Beatles should investigate this. (JT)

BIG COUNTRY: A CERTAIN CHEMISTRY
John May (*Omnibus*)

As one of those bands who always want to 'let the music speak for itself', one imagines that Big Country rather recoiled in horror at the idea of an official biography. And, to be frank, they'd have done themselves a favour by following their first instincts and forgetting the idea altogether rather than shamefacedly taking their cut from this dull account. All it serves to do is confirm what Big Country have always screamed to anyone who'd listen – they're just four ordinary blokes doing what they're best at and aren't really worth writing about in themselves at all. The only lively moments in this book are when May collects together what *other* people have said about the band. "Tortuous mediocrity executed with the necessary precision," says Killing Joke's Jaz Coleman. "Given half the chance I would have them executed." "Put a pen in my hand and I'm a dangerous man," comments U2's Bono. "Either I'd write a thesis about Stuart Adamson, or end up writing something different altogher." I know which I'd advise. (CH)

THE CARS
Philip Kamin (*Sidgwick & Jackson*)

"The Cars", announces Philip Kamin in this book's very first sentence, "are among rock's leading riddles." From here on, I suspect, Kamin and most sane readers will part company – have the Cars (being the dull slightly arty American pop band that they are) actually really troubled the thoughts of more than about a dozen people ever? (And is Kamin even one of them?) One is sceptical as he boasts in the Author's Note that he has knocked out twenty-five pop books in the last four years.) Kamin plainly takes the task of unravelling one of "rock's leading riddles" very seriously indeed, actually enlisting the Cars' help and managing to spill the beans in his own "individual" style (sample: "The Cars are dining out. With a critic. The Cars are hungry. The critic is nervous. Sushi."). I sincerely doubt whether the Cars' *parents* take their children this seriously. (CH)

DAVID BOWIE: THE STARZONE INTERVIEWS
Ed. David Currie (*Omnibus*)

At first sniff this smells like a monstrous swizz indeed. Instead of a single fresh word from "Bowie" himself, Currie tries to palm us off with friends, associates, partners and people who once saw someone who looked a bit like him eating a cheese roll in a café. Surprisingly, it works quite well. Reading through these interviews from *Starzone* magazine (the best, most devoted David Bowie fanzine) – interviews with Angie Bowie (the ex-wife), Tony Visconti (the producer), Kenneth Pitt (the early manager), Lindsay Kemp (the dance 'guru'), Mick Ronson (the guitar 'sidekick') and so on – is a bit like eavesdropping on two people intently discussing a subject they're both obsessively interested in and, despite all the crazily unimportant trivia that is

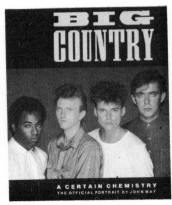

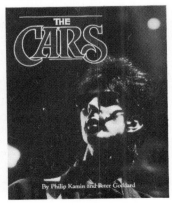

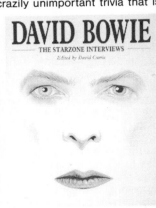

swapped, the cumulative effect is that the reader too gets drawn into the general fascination. And even if, at the end, Bowie remains 'a chameleon' and 'a mystery' (snore) his acquaintances still give away slightly more than he himself ever does in his own occasional pre-auditioned Sunday supplement interviews. (CH)

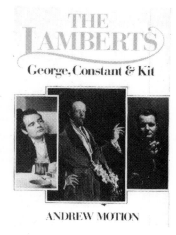

ELIMINATION: THE ZZ TOP STORY
David Thomas (Omnibus)

The one called Beard doesn't have one; the other two have very long ones; they play guitars of peculiar shapes and have a droll line in videos; it took years for the band to make it, then they took a long holiday, now they are mega. One of them shot himself in the abdomen. That's it. This is a boring book with dull pix and horrendous captions. I'd rather sit in on a jam session. (PC)

ELVIS: A KING FOREVER
Robert Gibson with Sid Shaw (Blandford Press)

Maybe the world really does need another Elvis Presley book but I somehow doubt it. We've had the fanatics' eulogies and the sceptics' Elvis-as-cheeseburger-guzzling-drug-sozzled-diaper-wearing-fat-man exposés. We've had the scrapbooks and the pop-up books. We've even had Elvis talking over the cosmic telephone to spiritual charlatans. *Elvis: A King Forever* purports to put right the muck-rakers, to set down the 'truth' and to stamp some authoritative 'finality' on the singer's life and memory. It does not, however, get off to a very convincing start when the authors, Gibson (the managing director of *Elvisly Yours*) and Shaw (a 'life-long Elvis fan' who even *looks* like Elvis, we are told), ask the question: "Who – or what – was Elvis Presley?" Their answer? "It is a question easy enough to pose, but *impossible* to answer." Oh. Well, that's really not good enough. The text that follows is a simple excursion through Elvis's career with the occasional reluctant admission – no, Elvis Presley's films were *not* terribly good ("Elvis was so nauseated by his films that they literally made him physically sick"), and, yes, Elvis Presley *was* known to take a drug or two – tossed in. This is nothing we did not already know. The book does, however, contain a jolly good photograph of Elvis eating a cake. (TH)

ELVIS COSTELLO: AN ILLUSTRATED BIOGRAPHY
Mick St Michael (Omnibus)

I suppose it would be fairly inconceivable for anyone to write a book on Elvis Costello that wasn't rather earnest, analytical and worthy, but it would be nice to see someone try. Mick St Michael unfortunately isn't that someone. He's fairly good on unearthing all the early trivia – the first bands, the first songs, the abortive pre-success marriage, the embarrassing photos – but unfortunately in 1977 Costello started releasing records and it's here that the account degenerates into a catalogue of song explanations, chart placings and record company or managerial wranglings. It may be all reeled off with compelling authority but to all save the keenest fans (who probably know all this already) it's simply not very interesting. And the cover – a disgusting drawing of Elvis Costello – is a disgrace. (CH)

FRANK SINATRA, MY FATHER
Nancy Sinatra (Hodder & Stoughton)

On the last page of this hefty and lavish hardback extravaganza, Nancy Sinatra presents a list of no less than 247 – count 'em! – of her father's famous and famously rich friends. Some of these are savoury – Doris Day, Marlene Dietrich, Trevor Howard, Orson Welles, Robert Mitchum. Some – Nancy Reagan, Hugh Hefner, Spiro T Agnew, Richard Nixon, Barry Goldwater… J. Edgar Hoover – are not. "These," says Nancy, "are the voices of the book." And indeed they are. On almost every page of text one or other of the 247 pipes up with some tribute to Sinatra… Sinatra the wondrously gifted, Sinatra the pro, Sinatra the saint of generosity, Frankie the razor wit, Sinatra the warm-hearted, humble, general all-round thoroughly good and ultimately flawless bloke whom only a jealous hypocrite would ever accuse of being connected with the 'Mob'. And there's a 248th voice in there, too – that of a doting daughter who gushes and puffs away about FS, her pop, until you feel like slapping her about the chops and screaming, "What do you *mean* when you say (*as she does in her introduction*) 'This is not a whitewash'??". Having said all *that*, if you ignore the tiresome text, this book is really rather splendid. Every photograph of Frank you could ever wish to see… Frank the sharpie, Frank the beaming 'family man', Frank with Presidents, Frank with goons, Frank advertising booze and fags and come what may – Frank the *legend*. Plus with stills from every film, and sleeves from every record he has ever made, this is nothing if not comprehensive. And when you get to the snaps of Nancy, *ravissante* queen of the kinky boot, in her radiant sixties prime, you can almost forgive her her overdose of creepy, cloying prose. (TH)

JANIS JOPLIN – PIECE OF MY HEART
David Dalton (Sidgwick & Jackson)

A positively infuriating tome which mixes brilliant reportage with truly tummy-bug exposition. Mr Dalton spent a considerable amount of time with Janis Joplin and appears to have recorded every word that was spoken during it. What emerges is a sharp picture of the tedious frenzy of life 'on the road' and an affectionate portrait of a lively, gutsy woman. However, between the zippy action scenes run rich seams of preposterous purple prose wherein nutty truisms are assailed by giant cod-philosophical sledgehammers. Muddle-headed blues belter or Kozmic Mama festooned with profound implications? I'll pass. (PC)

THE LAMBERTS – GEORGE, CONSTANT & KIT
Andrew Motion (Chatto & Windus)

This story of three generations of a brilliant but doomed family might not at first sight seem a tempting read for the crazed rock buff. But contained within its pages is a tale of success and excess which puts that of the average pop wildcat to shame. The grandfather, George, was an early example of transcontinental man, having been born in Russia of an American father, lived for a period in Britain and finally been acknowledged as Australia's leading painter. His devotion to art, studied wit and full-blown dandyism somewhat overshadowed his actual achievements. His son Constant was an extraordinarily successful composer and arranger, the first Englishman to be commissioned by the great Russian poove Diaghilev, an outspoken advocate of jazz and a founder of Sadler's Wells Ballet. He also had a razor tongue and a literally fatal attraction to alcohol which cost his friends in high places and blunted his talents. Nevertheless, his presence was such that he was the model for one of the central characters in Anthony Powell's *Dance to the Music of Time*, one of the great works of English fiction.

Constant's son and the last of the line was Kit. It was he that spotted the latent talent in the Who and reinvented them as one of the world's most compelling rock 'n' roll bands, while reinventing himself as their manager, producer and Pete Townshend's svengali (his was the inspiration behind 'Tommy'). He also founded Track Records, one of the country's first and most successful independent labels which numbered Jimi Hendrix among its artists. Tragically, in an age of conspicuous consumption of naughties, Kit was right in there with the front-runners and eventually the drugs and drink which had fuelled his creative madness turned him into a shambling, burnt-out wreck. His early death was both ignominious and utterly expected.

Mr Motion tells his tale briskly and competently, perhaps lacking the lightness of touch which would have better served his enormously witty cast. But the book has drama beyond the dreams of most rock biography. The only major blot is the editing of the third section which deals with Kit. To misspell The Blues Magoos is perhaps faintly excusable, but to do the same with Jimi Hendrix and Phil Spector in a book costing fourteen quid is appalling. (PC)

OZZY OSBOURNE – DIARY OF A MADMAN
Mick Wall (Zomba)

The official authorised biography of the Wild Man himself. With a couple of contributions from Gary Bushell, but with the majority written by the excellent Mick Wall, this makes a damn fine read. Ozzy's story is a great one, anyway, but Wall makes it even better with his pyrotechnic style. The pictures are excellent, too. I ought, I suppose, to own up here: I had a bash at writing this book but Ozzy and wife Sharon didn't like my version (which, of course, was entirely their privilege), so Zomba bought it for a most satisfactory sum and gave it to Wall to add to his own work. Message to Mick: you did a brilliant job. Message to Ozzy and Sharon: you finally picked the better writer. Hope this sells millions. Honest. (BH)

THE PHIL COLLINS STORY
Johnny Waller *(Zomba)*

Balding, plump, short . . . just what *is* the secret of Phil Collins? Why does he sell millions of smart MOR solo albums, millions more albums singing in Genesis, and still more for anyone else he chooses to drum with or produce? Not surprisingly Johnny Waller doesn't have the answers to any of these questions, just the usual guff about Phil's childhood acting career, a mini-book on the history of Genesis, Phil's marital crises and the inevitable mumbling about what-a-nice-normal-bloke-old-Phil-is-despite-it-all. And not much else really. Perfectly competently told if you're interested, but be warned – this is the sort of book where one of the chapters is actually titled "Production Work" . . . (CH)

QUINCY JONES
Raymond Horricks *(Omnibus)*

The excitement of discovering that Horricks, unlike most music biographers, not only *knows* his subject but has actually *corresponded* with him since 1953 sadly only lasts for about a page and a half. Fatigue quickly takes over as we read, in the remaining 100 odd pages, about the dull hard graft of Quincy's growth from a promising jazz musician to a world famous producer and arranger who actually *talks* to Michael Jackson. And there are precious few hints that their correspondence over the years ever discussed anything but musicians and recording studios. Whenever Horricks risks becoming dangerously interesting – revealing, for instance, that Jones, better than a saint for the rest of the book, has had three wives – he dismisses the issue with the swift determination of a man itching to get back to some serious dullness. And as for Michael Jackson, well one can only assume that Horricks' correspondence had all but dried up by the eighties – his clumsy attempts to get to grips with this odd singer from the bizarre world of pop fizzle away into the usual repertoire of 'wacko Jacko' rumours. A wasted opportunity. (CH)

SIMPLE MINDS: GLITTERING PRIZES
Dave Thomas *(Omnibus)*

It's a hard life being a Simple Minds fan. There you are with your complete set of albums just crying out for a book to explain all Jim Kerr's nonsensical tumbles of phrases and all you've got is Alfred Bos' truly dreadful official biography *The Race Is The Prize* prattling famously about how "hope is a fly's turd on an empty page. Simple Minds are that empty page." Unfortunately Dave Thomas' unofficial work is an absurd antidote, forsaking Bos' impenetrable pretentiousness for what is little more than a glorified trudge from recording studio to recording studio. (CH)

THE SMITHS
Mick Middles *(Omnibus)*

Oh dear. Smiths' fans will *almost* love this book and its impressionistic fan-like jog through the Smiths' past, but unfortunately Middles spoils everything by falling down on the most boring and unnecessary hurdle of all – his facts. The text is littered with errors – from wrong chart positions and spelling mistakes to badly-researched accounts of events – and I doubt whether serious bookish Smiths' fans will forgive him easily. And even if they did, I doubt whether they'd be fully satisfied with a book that neither does anything to lift the cloak of darkness from Morrissey's silent years and secret habits nor explores the fascinating plagiarism in his lyrics. (CH)

SPANDAU BALLET: THE AUTHORISED STORY
John Travis *(Sidgwick & Jackson)*

Apparently there's some debate over whether this story really is 'authorised' or not – if it *is* then it's an awful indictment of a band who care nothing for their fans. For £7 you get a few bearable studio photos of 'the Spands', lots more horrible live ones and a 20-minute slog through the band's history that must have taken at least a whole afternoon to write. A well thought-out sycophantic stroll through Spandau Ballet's past – the tablecloths, the loin-cloths, the oven gloves (or whatever) – could have been quite fascinating: this is junk. (CH)

THE SUPERTRAMP BOOK
Martin Melhuish *(Omnibus)*

One hundred and ninety-odd glossy pages devoted to the full biography (including zany antics) of Nick, Rick, Dick and Vic – or How The 'Tramp Came Up Trumps. Marvel at how the collected concepts of Damian, Luke, Zak, Darren and Julian came to fruition as a series of collected concepts. As the true story of Kev, Trev, Bev and Tone, this book is, er, crucial. (PC)

SURVIVOR: THE AUTHORIZED BIOGRAPHY OF ERIC CLAPTON
Ray Coleman *(Sidgwick & Jackson)*

The life and exceedingly troubled times of God, from extraordinary pre-eminence in the sixties, through the smack and brandy addled seventies, to the clean-living eighties. From the peevish cover shot to the somewhat cheapskate b/w illustrations, this is not an entirely satisfactory use of virgin forest. Although the author has spoken fully and frankly with God, he has seen fit to arrange his material in a manner which causes endless repetition, with chapters headed 'The Musician', 'The Lover' (!) covering the same ground from a different angle. The saddest fact of all is that God has not made an inordinate number of good records and that he finds it easier to choke his driveway with Ferraris than to remember his round in the pub. Unedifying stuff. (PC)

TALKING HEADS: THE BAND AND THEIR MUSIC
David Gans *(Omnibus)*

Another scissors-and-paste effort (yawn). The best bits of this book are when the so-called 'author' shuts up and simply lets the Talking Heads speak for themselves – Gans (obviously a dab hand with a photocopier) has put together an interesting compilation of quotes from four of the most intelligent, perceptive and articulate pop stars around. For which they (and not Gans) deserve some congratulation. But why are so many pop writers allowed to get away with dull third-hand accounts of their subjects from old interviews instead of teasing out a real story from behind their subject's backs like most other biographers have to? If it's facts you want they're here, but sadly you'll get a better idea of what David Byrne is actually *like* from listening to any Talking Heads record than from wasting time on this mediocrity. (CH)

TINA: THE TINA TURNER STORY
Ron Wynn *(Sidgwick & Jackson)*

The only redeeming feature in this £8-'worth' of garbage are the photos of Tina Turner throughout the ages, but even they are scattered willy-nilly, without explanation, throughout the text. Wynn's blatherings themselves are almost bearable for the book's first half as he skims through 'The Tina Turner Story' – Tina's discovery in a club by Ike Turner, the years together, the walk out, the fallow years

 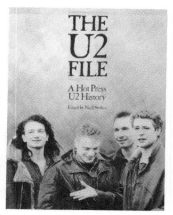  

and finally the success on her own – but then he shoots seriously off the rails. One whole chapter is spent dissecting 'What's Love Got To Do With It' (a song Tina didn't even write) and concluding that it's a parable of Tina's whole story and indeed, one suspects, of life itself. And there's another chapter on Tina's sexuality in which Wynn (once he's agonised over the personal ideological dilemmas he has faced in confronting his innate sexism – *poor* bloke) takes the 'novel' approach of methodically poring over Tina's anatomy bit by bit. "The vaunted Tina Turner legs," we are told, "are arguably her most attention-grabbing asset". One hopes Mr Wynn will write better books when he grows up . . . (CH)

ULTRA: SIGUE SIGUE SPUTNIK
Chris Salewicz, Peter-Paul Hartnett *(Virgin)*

Ah, the glorious joys of hindsight. Sigue Sigue Sputnik weren't very good, were they? Now that's not too much of a problem because *lots* of successful groups aren't very good either, but Sigue Sigue's particular stumbling block was that their only *raison d'être* was that they were going to change the, ahem, face of rock 'n' roll. The fact that they couldn't get to number one makes Tony James' introduction to the book ("The Sigue Sigue Sputnik is real horrorshow and it's going all the way to Number One") look a bit silly. We members of the press may have been taken in by all that, giving the Sputniks acres of coverage, but the buying public certainly weren't. Of course, if Tony James *had* succeeded this would have been a good book. The Fish Family's design tries but fails to capture the high-tech sophistication of Sputnik's Japanese video vision, but as a non-event's attempt at self-mytholgising it is really quite entertaining. Like this: "In the teeming heart of London's cosmopolitan Harrow Road, identifiable only by the steady stream of stretch limousines and women of indescribable beauty who arrive at its door, is the World Headquarters of the Sigue Sigue Sputnik Leisure Corporation." What a hoot, eh? (WS)

THE U2 FILE: A HOT PRESS HISTORY OF U2
Ed. Niall Stokes *(Omnibus)*

This book, claims Stokes in the introduction, tells the story of U2 "with innocence rather than hindsight, in the language of time rather than that of history". By and large, he's right. For the most part the fact that this is nothing but a collection of all the U2 articles to appear in Irish magazine *Hot Press* between 1978 and 1985 works to its advantage. The first jottings – like the introductory piece in April 1978 about this "promising new Dublin 4-piece" who've just won an Evening Press/Harp lager talent competition but are still "currently studying for their leaving certificates" – are refreshingly free of the pompous retrospective flourishes about "how the seeds of greatness are being sown" that one usually gets. It's a pity that as U2 (Bono especially) approach their current God-like status the *Hot Press* writers not only latch onto the rest of the world's hyperbolic fervour but lace it with some extra Irish pride for good measure; even then, at least *they* were getting interviews when U2 would only very occasionally deign to give other publications the time of day. And any book which gets U2 to admit that they started off playing 'Heart Of Gold', 'Jumpin' Jack Flash', 'Suffragette City', 'Nights In White Satin', '2-4-6-8 Motorway' and various "Bay City Rollers songs" isn't doing badly at all. (CH)

WILD ANIMALS: THE STORY OF THE ANIMALS
Andy Blackford *(Sidgwick & Jackson)*

The Animals were yet another sixties band who found the pop world to be a jungle. Despite massive live popularity and considerable chart success the group made peanuts. Andy Blackford charts the course of this familiar refrain with enough gusto and wit to elevate the story well above the average. (PC)

BOBCAT BOOKS
The Cure; Billy Idol; Dead Or Alive; Tears For Fears – all by Jo-Ann Green.
Marillion In Words And Pictures by Carol Clerk.
Paul Young by John Merill.
The Alarm by Rick Taylor.
Depeche Mode by Dave Thomas.
Gary Moore by Chris Welch.
Howard Jones by Helen Fitzgerald.

Bobcat Books know their corner, and stick rigorously to it. They have a production line for unofficial biogs: each one a 48-page "cuttings job". The formula is simple, efficient, and generally a bit dull – a brief history, a quick bit of picture research, a discography, and a well-designed cover that hides the fact that the inside pages have often been hurriedly thrown together, all sold at a price which is neither extortionate nor cheap.

Their problem is their complete one dimensionality. Firstly, they're based on a set of interviews which were probably pretty boring in the first place. And secondly they fall into the usual trap of sycophancy. Critical biographies they ain't. For instance when you're told by writer Rick Taylor that the Alarm are "rock's only future" you really do begin to wonder whether the man is operating on a full tank. Which is a pity, because these pages of often gooey prose show how much Bobcat's authors underestimate their readers. (WS)

ROBUS BOOKS
Howard Jones; Phil Collins; Wham!; Tina Turner; Tears For Fears; Bryan Adams – all by Phil Kamin.
Mötley Crüe; Twisted Sister; Billy Idol; Robert Plant – all by Phil S Tene.
Huey Lewis; Ratt – both by Jay Bird.
Springsteen by Marty Monroe.
Elvis; A Golden Tribute by Emory Glade.

Traditionally pop music is an industry dedicated to prising pocket-money from the undeserving hands of teenagers, and don't Robus Books just know it. Their jumped-up American poster mags cover every bankable pop star, and are compiled by people who certainly don't let the concept of quality interfere with their task of getting their own back on the young, spotty and gullible.

The sketchiest of texts are accompanied by the nastiest selection of photos ever assembled, usually from one or two concerts and the odd autograph session where pop stars grin through gritted teeth. The photo captions are the most hilarious bits. They range from ridiculously over-the-top to absolutely desperate: "Roland Orzabal," it says next to a dark and fuzzy picture of the man, "Dark, intense and committed to making the world a safer place." And hows about "Howard Jones and Jed: One of the most challenging performance duos in pop history"? That wins joint favourite with "Billy Idol: The Sinatra of our generation." No wonder half the authors use dodgy *noms de plume* like Phil S Tene (think about it) and Jay Bird. (WS)

●AUTOBIOGRAPHIES

DANA: AN AUTOBIOGRAPHY
(With Lucy Elphinstone) *(Hodder & Stoughton)*

Little Rosemary Brown had a passion for Walker's toffees and once squashed an earwig with a handbag. Then she changed her name to Dana ("an old Gaelic word meaning 'bold' or 'mischievous'") and won the 1970 Eurovision Song Contest against stiff competition from Mary Hopkins and – gasp! – Julio Iglesias. What else is there to say about this sheepish songstrel from Londonderry with the alluring gap in her front teeth? Not, it would seem, a great deal. For once Eurovision victory is hers, Dana gets on with the laborious (haw haw) task of having babies. The first is born after an emergency Caesarean, the next causes problems too (something about contractions and a tablecloth but I was overcome by the squeams and skipped that bit) – but everything turns out lovely in the end and mother's only 'ambition' for her offspring is that they grow up "with a personal relationship with the Lord". Yes, it is He who is the real star of the book; He hovers o'er every page cowing Dana into modesty and niceness which makes for one of the least riveting star stories ever committed to paper. (TH)

GOOD MORNING BLUES: THE AUTOBIOGRAPHY OF COUNT BASIE
(As told to Albert Murray) (Heinemann)

Reading about rock personalities is a dedicated calling. I must confess to a personal lack of drive in this department. However, Count Basie, the kid from Red Bank, holds a certain promise because, it has to be said, there must be more pound for pound enlightenment on musical and social history via a man like Basie than there ever can be from somebody whose career has lasted all of two minutes. If Basie's recollections fail to ignite, blame it on the boogie, probably. (DT)

IS THAT IT?
Bob Geldof (Sidgwick & Jackson)

Perhaps it's the Irish in him . . . Bob Geldof (KBE) doesn't half spin a good yarn. From childhood in Dublin, through "the greatest day of my life" (13 July 1985, ie Live Aid, as if you didn't know), to a brush with Margaret Thatcher and her "death-ray glare", his autobiography is sometimes hysterical, sometimes depressing, and always intensely readable. We are spared none of the gory details of what seems to have been, at times, a pretty sordid existence. Bob has his first sexual encounter at the age of 13 (grim). Bob "rips off" French tourists, selling them hot dogs at £10 a throw. Bob sets fire to his Dad's house during a bout of "spontaneous nobbing". Bob goes barmy on pot and tries to top himself. Bob gets a job in an abattoir (very grim). Bob becomes an international pop star and meets Paula who unzips his trousers in the back of a motor car. And then Bob sees a news report about famine in Ethiopia on his television . . .

The final 150 pages (of 350) are devoted to the Band Aid saga and, though he is obviously rather pleased with himself, Gelof does not get quite as saintly and pontificating as one might expect, enlivening his 'mission' narrative with anecdotes that offset the gloom. Like what the ghastly Prince William said when he spied Saint Bob in the corridors of Buckingham Palace. What did Wills say? "He's all dirty . . . He's got scruffy hair!" Correct! But, then, as Bob tells us, William's papa can't dance for toffee! . . .

Bob Geldof has a way with words, young man . . . even if most of them are 'fuck' . . . (TH)

JERRY HALL'S TALL TALES
(with Christopher Hemphill) (Elm Tree Books)

In which the lanky Texan takes us from her fairly unprepossessing childhood in Mesquite ("I used to lie on the ground there and think about being somewhere else . . . ") through high-life holidays with Bryan Ferry on Mustique ("It's a small island in the Caribbean where you see the same people at least ten times a day") and beyond to love and her first child with Mick. The First Lady of rock 'n' roll gives the impression of being ingenuous, straightforward and drily witty.

On family misfortune: "It really was a period of bad luck for us. First my grandmother had died and then my father died and then the dog died."

On her first sexual encounter: "And he just pulled down my jeans and pulled his jeans – we didn't even take our boots off – and the rain was dripping in on my face and the hay was stabbing me in the behind and this guy was . . . well, he was pretty quick. In an' out. And that was it."

On Mick as rock 'n' roll superstar: "They'll be all these tens of thousands of people wanting Mick and I'll think: That's my man! I'll just be bustin' with pride."

She's honest (or seems to be) about her relationship with Bryan Ferry, the reasons for her affair with Robert Sangster, her love of glamour. Then all of a sudden she seems vain, conceited and affected: "It's a little habit I still have" (having cucumber and smoked salmon sandwiches on brown bread for tea, a taste first acquired in London with Bryan); "I loved going shopping in London, like at Fortnum and Mason's" (where she got the staff to trail after her for an

hour or so while she bought one can of soup); "Often I think the main point of life is having something to talk about at dinner. Life is just so many dinners, you know" (yes, well . . . er . . thanks, Jerry).

Of course, it's hard to tell how much Mr Hemphill is responsible for the tone of the book. On the whole one feels he's done a good job (although he cannot be forgiven for spelling Pete Townshend's and Marianne Faithfull's names incorrectly): it reads easily and colloquially, like a long conversation, and as such is best read in short bursts. And on the whole Ms Hall comes out of it very well. She may be one of the world's top models, but she's also a champion leg wrestler (apparently a popular sport in Texas). Bryan didn't like this hobby. Mick loves it. I like her. (JC)

THEM OR US (THE BOOK)
Frank Zappa (Barfco-Swill)

"This cheesy little home-made book was prepared for the amusement of people who already enjoy Zappa Music. It is not for intellectuals or other dead people", spits Zappa in the foreword of this 351-page, filmscript-style (Z-rated) stream-of-consciousness.

The props are familiar: cheeseburgers, sofas, knackwurst etc; so, too, the cast who appear, perform, and troop by like the members of grisled 'family' in the receiving line at some nightmarish wedding: Groggary Peccary, Thing-Fish; there's even an Old Zircon – here a cloven-hoofed Byzantine devil. All Fade In, Dissolve To and Cut To each other in a bizarre series of unlikely encounters that only the most ardent of Zappaphiles will appreciate.

The concept is the concept of conceptual continuity – a long-serving Zappa cop-out dreamed up to rationalise the outpourings of his tortured, kalaidescopic, perverse and perverted mind. But it works. It's big. It's rubbish, but it's fun – though kind of expensive by the time you've paid $35 postage from Barking Pumpkin, Zappa's 'valley' HQ in California. (Julian Colbeck, who has actually handed over his $60.)

● GENERAL

THE FIRST ROCK & ROLL CONFIDENTIAL REPORT
Ed. Dave Marsh (Pantheon Books)

Musicians put people in such a tizz it's a wonder they haven't been banned. Take this little quote from The First Rock & Roll Confidential Report: "Boston Phoenix music editor Milo Miles has described Madonna as 'the kind of woman who comes into your room at three am and sucks your life out'." Milo, Milo, let's exchange rooms if it's really so bad.

The Rock & Roll etc. not to be confused with a similarly titled book of entirely dissimilar content and worth, is a compendium of material from the highly rated tip sheet and critical conscience that emerges from New Jersey. It is not a book that you open at the front and walk out the back. You dip in and you find such gems as the following portrait of boxing promoter and Jacksons' tour mastermind Don King: "He sat amid a 1.00 am audience in the lobby of a Kansas City Hotel, his gold watch and silver chains all aglitter. His porcupine hair, maturing with dignity, looking like that of a man who'd had a bag of powdered donuts detonate in his face." (DT)

LIKE PUNK NEVER HAPPENED: CULTURE CLUB AND THE NEW POP
Dave Rimmer (Faber & Faber)

The only really extraordinary thing is that anyone was at all taken aback when the punks went snuffling back to ground leaving a pride of pouting popinjays, who were more concerned with mastering convincing jacuzzi techniques than smashing any 'system', at the centre of the popular market place. Hadn't this happened *before* with Marc Bolan (and the Bay City Rollers (and David Cassidy (and Barry Blue)))? Yes, of course it had, in its own inevitable fashion, but no one had bothered to grumble and probe and wonder and thus produce a 'sociological' book such as this (you know it's 'sociological' because it's got no photos) *that* time around. *This* time we had *Smash Hits* 'reporter' Dave Rimmer 'on the spot' to chronicle the next decline of pop music civilisation as we perceived it. During 1983/4, he became the man 'who really knows the stars'; he flew, he ate, he drank, he tittered, he played 'Botticelli', he wore terrible pairs of shorts and T-shirts with great big words on, he tittered again – *with* the New Pop glitterati – Duran Duran, Culture Club, assorted people with streaks in their very sleek hair. At the end of a long day, he would ask the obligatory *Smash Hits* questions ("Has your mother ever grown parsnips in a plimsoll?" or whatever) and they'd answer in chuckling fashion ... and *then* he turned around and stabbed them in the back with this investigation of the vacuous, incestuous and ultimately crappy world of the New Pop music – an exposure (crushing by understatement) of eighties video froth and a 'scene' in which all participants look alarmingly beautiful and never get ill until the morning after and a morning-after isn't *proper* ill anyway, etc etc ... an insipid rainbow stretching forever and we're all going to be utterly, fabulously rich. There's no business like showbusiness and *Like Punk* goes far beyond *Hollywood Babylon* without even realising. (TH)

SWEET SOUL MUSIC
Peter Guralnick *(Virgin)*

Peter Guralnick is the man who changed my life and I'm not sure how grateful I am. Until I read *Lost Highway* my flat was full of records of most music except country. Post-*Lost Highway* and I'm now tripping over Merle Haggard and Kitty Wells albums, too. In that book Guralnick cut through the liberal prejudice of pinko-grey black-music fans. He does it again in *Sweet Soul Music* by showing that soul was a collaboration between blacks, Jews, Italians, Turks, poor-white-trash – American music in other words. Like most writers of his ilk he is lost in passion for the past and its rough intensity. Pity, because otherwise he would see that the same process continues in a different guise. Great book, however, and one that anyone who ever entered soul limbo should consider, yes, essential. (DT)

WHERE DID OUR LOVE GO? THE RISE AND FALL OF THE MOTOWN SOUND
Nelson George *(St Martins Press)*

As the title implies and subtitle confirms, this is very much an obituary for the golden age of Motown. Nelson George dedicates his book to James Jamerson and Benny Benjamin, deceased bassist and drummer of the legendary Funk Brothers, the Motown house band that propelled a copious stream of hits into the charts throughout the sixties and early seventies. The fact that both were disaffected, and finally discarded, elements of the Motown machine is strongly indicative of the author's stance.

The early days of the label are viewed in terms of an extended family. At the head was the benevolently despotic figure of Berry Gordy Jr, an aggressive hustler, talented songwriter, inspired talent-spotter and obsessive empire-builder. Below him was the imposing roster of talent, too familiar to relate, most of which seemed to have strolled in from the ghettos of Detroit on the off-chance. Then came the teams of producer/songwriters, charged with the daunting task of knocking off classics by the shift. At the bottom were the house musicians whose dramatic performances (and often arrangements) still repay closer listening. George describes this desperately competitive creative hot-house, where egos were ritually slaughtered on the altar of excellence, in loving and minute detail. But the rot set in early. Money, and in particular Gordy's reluctance to part with it, besets the story like toothache. Favouritism and nepotism intrude. The inevitable arrival of layers of middle-management (much of it white) occasion confusion and alienation. The eventual move from Detroit to the West Coast is viewed by George as a betrayal.

In the final analysis, this is a history in thrall to an argument. It is naive to think that a successful business can expand quantitatively without changing qualitatively. Yet, for the light it sheds on an explosion of creativity rarely equalled in pop music, *Where Did Our Love Go?* is worth more than casual perusal. (PC)

● PICTORIAL

BRUCE SPRINGSTEEN: BORN IN THE USA
Robert Hilburn *(Sidgwick & Jackson)*

You have to be careful what you say about Springsteen. Even if he is not actually divine and capable of visiting plagues of boils on unbelievers, he has millions of fanatically vengeful fans waiting to pounce on the hapless critic.

Robert Hilburn, author of the weighty *Bruce Springsteen: Born in the USA*, is, however, in no danger at all. Reverence is the name of his game as he lovingly gathers innumerable details of Bruce's early life (we see the house he grew up in), his career (we see his managers) and his music (we see lots of pictures of him on stage). All this is interspersed with scholarly musings on the development of the lyrics and frequent quotes from Hilburn's fellow critics about moments of revelation and how they discovered Brooce.

It is engaging in a serious sort of way and some of the photographs are good, if a bit repetitive. The problem is that it is too distant from the 'real' Bruce. The portrait that emerges is of a po-faced rock 'n' roll monk. Even when he talks about his songs it is all oddly abstract and we do not learn much of the emotions and experiences that give his lyrics their power. The few anecdotes that there are seem dry and impersonal – his relationships with women and his marriage are dealt with on the same half page.

What this book needs is a good dollop of gossip. But then gossip is not very reverential, is it? A book for the *serious* fan. (PR)

HM USA
Metal Age *(Omnibus)*

Heavy metal fans are weird. One: they like HM music. Two: they seem to like pictures of people drinking blood (it's a popular HM pose). Three: some of them will buy these books.

Of the three the last is the strangest. The books are almost identical (the biggest difference is that Metal Age is glossier), page after page of routine photos of long-haired men – and occasional women – in very tight trousers, snarling, pouting, grinding and thrusting, with blood, skulls and tattoos as optional extras. Most of the shots were taken on stage and show different practitioners going through the metal ritual. Guitarists in the fiery solo posture – grimace, legs apart, crotch out, back bent – or singers in mid-air with the upraised mike stand. All supposed to be very tough, macho and exciting but after a hundred or so pages it is just daft and very repetitious.

It does, however, demonstrate two things. Firstly, if you want to succeed in the HM world it is very important to have a long tongue because you are going to spend a lot of time sticking it out. They all do it, from Ozzy Osbourne to Dave Lee Roth. Secondly, WASP are the silliest looking group in the whole world. (PR)

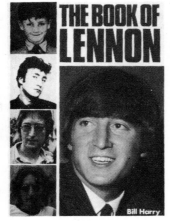

JOHN LENNON
Dezo Hoffmann *(Columbus Books)*
LISTEN TO THESE PICTURES
Bob Gruen *(Sidgwick & Jackson)*

Oh no! Not more John Lennon books! Six years after his death the Lennon industry still thrives. The demand is still there, but what is left to say or show?

In the case of Dezo Hoffmann's *John Lennon* sadly not a lot. Lennon described Hoffmann as the most inventive photographer he ever came across; from this collection of black-and-white pictures it is rather hard to see why.

Hoffmann worked extensively with the Beatles during the first years of their career. He fell from favour after an argument with Lennon over the publication of a picture Lennon did not like. Most of the photos come from the fab mop-top period culminating in the first US tour, though there are some from 1967 and '70. They run the gamut from posed publicity shots, some of which are very famous and very silly (ie, the bathing suit and boater session) to candids of the 'introspective, brooding' Lennon. Many of the pictures are both strong and memorable – and yet they are so predictable. Perhaps it is because both these versions of Lennon (and the pictures themselves) are so famous they have lost the element of surprise. You never feel you are getting behind the scenes. This probably will not deter Lennon's ardent fans but it is disappointing when a book like this fails to offer any new insight or angle.

The joy of Bob Gruen's *Listen to These Pictures* is that he manages to do just that. Admittedly he has the advantage of dealing with the reclusive seventies' Lennon living with Yoko in New York, but he also records expressions and emotions that other photographers did not reach. There are pictures of Lennon the proud father, clad in a kimono, hair tied back in a pony-tail, beaming joyfully at the week-old baby Sean. Or the careworn Lennon straightened up in suit and tie fighting deportation from the US. Or Lennon bashing at a piano, smiling and laughing with Mick Jagger while a seemingly bored Yoko looks on. You get a strong sense not only of his love for his wife and child but also of his passion for music and pleasure in the company of other musicians. Together with the gossipy readable text, it adds up to a sharp portrait of the last ten years of Lennon's work and home life. (PR)

REBEL ROCK
Dennis Morris *(Omnibus)*

Rebel Rock records the Sex Pistols' last tour and claims to capture the punk state of mind. But apart from the occasional strong picture – Johnny Rotten squeezing a spot, Sid's adoring stare at Nancy Spungen – the book is oddly flat and lifeless. Most of the shots of the band offstage are little more than snaps and don't really tell us much. And what they do tell us – that, for example, Steve Jones thought it was funny to have a banana sticking out of his flies – is not very interesting.

The best section deals with the gigs and the punters. There are some fine shots of the carnage that ensued when the Pistols played. Bouncers strain to maintain a little stage space as the strange motley audience surges forward. All very atmospheric; you can almost smell the sweat.

It is sad that Morris does not make more of the beginnings of punk style. It would have been good to see more pictures like the one of the rather straight young woman kitted out in Tesco bags and dog collar. It says far more than another shot of Sid snarling over his can of lager. (PR)

ROCK EXPLOSION
Harold Bronson *(Blandford Press)*

The sixties were the naive period of pop photography. The time when on sighting a camera ninety-nine per cent of pop groups would leap in the air, give a big thumbs aloft and grin. *Rock Explosion* (subtitle: The British Invasion of America in Photos 1962-67) lovingly catalogues the grins as they appear in hundreds of mainly black and white photographs of every British band that ever walked off a plane wearing elastic-sided boots. They range from the massively famous, Beatles, Stones et al, to the massively obscure. Remember Ian and the Zodiacs?

In the earlier pictures, wackiness is the order of the day. The Beatles push a Ford Popular, the fun-loving Animals iron their guitarist's leg, while those japesters Sounds Incorporated use one of their number as a battering ram. Even the Stones look quite cheerful. Only the Kink's Ray Davies manages to be surly throughout. As psychedelia looms, however, cheeks get sucked in and levity is harder to find – that is, if you ignore Dave Dee, Dozy, Beaky, Mick and Tich's paisley flares.

It is a fascinating collection, well and wittily captioned with intriguing bits of trivia and quotes from some of the artists, and only slightly marred by dull design and a very horrid cover. It is a perfect antidote for anyone who feels nostalgic about the sixties (I mean – some of those haircuts) and it poses some very serious questions. For example, did girls really fancy Peter and Gordon? Or could the Housemartins have existed if there had never been a Freddy and the Dreamers? (PR)

● JAZZ

LET'S JOIN HANDS AND CONTACT THE LIVING: RONNIE SCOTT AND HIS CLUB
John Fordham *(Elm Tree Books)*
JAZZWOMEN: 1900 TO THE PRESENT
Sally Placksin *(Pluto Press)*
UNFINISHED DREAM: THE MUSICAL WORLD OF RED CALLENDER
Red Callender and Elaine Cohen *(Quartet)*

Jazz is a wonderful medium for revealing and concealing, and jazz musicians are notorious for avoiding specifics. A born raconteur like Ronnie Scott has spent his life slipping nooses. Does biographer John Fordham get that rope in place? Sometimes, maybe, probably. *Let's Join Hands and Contact the Living* has its surprising moments and is valuable for the taste it gives of British bohemian nightlife between the war and the rock 'n' roll era. It is slightly disarming to find a photograph captioned "Faces of the 1950s" that could for all the world pass for Soho Brasserie faces of the 1980s (if you ignore the bottle of tomato ketchup).

Look out. There's a hackneyed old Andy Warhol edict coming up. Something about every Joe and Jane rising out of blissful obscurity for fifteen minutes. Is this the reason for a Red Callender biog? No question that *Unfinished Dream* has a great musician for its subject, but I would have thought a chapter about Red in a book on California jazz would have made more sense. More like Sally Placksin's *Jazzwomen*, in fact, which is absorbing enough to be deeper than worthy. You can dip, too, which is again preferable to this gruelling business of 'settling down with a good book'. Books. Love 'em. But music books . . . rather listen to the music, frankly. (DT)

● MISCELLANEOUS

ILLUSTRATED ROCK & POP BRAIN BUSTERS
John Tobler (Zomba)
ROCK AND POP MASTERMIND
Bob Harris (Orbis)

Not a lot to be said about quiz books really – if you know the answer then they're too easy and if you don't then they're heinously obscure. *Rock & Pop Brain Busters* is printed on extremely nasty cheap paper, dispenses with niceties like photographs in favour of some particularly repulsive cartoons ("illustrated") and belongs to the second category, being comprised of twenty-five sections ranging from major artistes to decades to musical categories, with a few general bits in between from the bottomless depths of the Tobler trivia pit (Q: what do Jimmy Cliff and the Tremoloes have in common? A: they both had UK hits with Cat Stevens cover versions. Of course!) Fascinating, no nonsense and an obscurantist's heaven.

Rock and Pop Mastermind, on the other hand, is a bigger, glossier Guinness-type paperback, has real photographs (albeit a very disappointing selection) and belongs to the first category, possibly with aspiring nursery-school entrants in mind, judging by the questions – "do you remember the original line-up?", "name as many of the other participating performers as you can" etc. Divided into sixteen categories, mostly chronological with a few conceptual bits at the end (charts, labels, writers etc) and a token nod to black music, it is, alas, written in the same doe-eyed, simpering style which made Harris such a tiresome *Old Grey Whistle Test* presenter – a gormless mixture of overawed fawning (Madonna as "the sensation of two hemispheres" – I mean, *really* . . .) and clichéd hyperbole ("brilliant debut album", "brightest new talents", "marvellous, much-missed Harry Chapin" etc etc etruddyc). According to the jacket, this book promises "hours of entertainment" (honest!). Hours of continual irritation, more like – its only entertainment value coming from such unwitting howlers as the 'fact' that Frankie Lyman (*sic*) died of a "heroine (*double sic*) overdose". This book adds new meaning to the phrase 'completely useless'. (IC)

BASIC GUITAR; ROCK GUITAR; ELECTRIC BASS GUITAR; SYNTHESISER BASICS; SYNTHESISER TECHNIQUE; SYNTHESISERS AND COMPUTERS
(Hal Leonard)

Wanna be a rock 'n' roll star? Well, start off by ignoring this six-set collection of instructional books, all of which have been cobbled together from a ten-year span of articles printed in a couple of worthy if wordy US muso mags called *Guitar Player* and *Keyboard*.

If, on the other hand, you wanna be a real muso, or more specifically a guitar player or keyboardist, then all the books' informed but ploddingly written pieces will provide you with the necessary qualifications for instant commercial oblivion, ie knowing all about the physics of sound and analog synthesiser programming (with such unmissable articles as 'Vibrato and Beyond'), being able to sight read, and learning the Circle of Fifths.

The editorial attitude is knowing and smug; the information accurate but boringly presented. While closet guitarists may get off on learning solos 'in the style of' Zappa, Clapton and Carl Perkins in the *Rock Guitar* volume, for synthesists, only the *Synthesiser and Computers* tome remains current enough for any practical use. (Julian Colbeck, who should know)

THE LANGUAGE OF ROCK 'N' ROLL
Bob Young and Micky Moody
(Sidgwick and Jackson)

Knowing who the authors are tells you a lot about this 'dictionary'. For many years Young was "tour manager/harmonica player and songwriter" for Status Quo. Moody is "still a muso at heart and a man of the road" who's put in a lot of time with the likes of Juicy Lucy and Whitesnake. That this supposedly humorous work is aimed exclusively at men (and a particular sort at that) is evidenced by two entries, 'Air Hostess' and 'Air Steward': the former is one who doesn't appreciate your attaching a mirror to your shoe the better to look up her skirt; the latter is one who *would* appreciate your doing the same the better to look up his trouser leg. A far better, more amusing, non-sexist volume, *Rockspeak*, was published by Omnibus a few years back. This is a useless addition to the genre. (JC)

ROCKUPS: THE BEATLES STORY, THE ELVIS STORY
(Orbis)

Extremely silly pop-ups giving the fan five spreads, each one encapsulating a phase in the stars' careers. The last contains a bit of high-tech magic in the shape of a microchip that plays a tune ('Hey Jude' and 'Love Me Tender' respectively). The accompanying text (50 or so words on each spread) is suitably tongue-in-cheek, if a little heavy on the word-play ('The parents of middle America were all shook up by the hound dog's pelvis, but their pony-tailed daughters sure loved him tender"), and there is the occasional visual joke, like the cell door in the 'Jailhouse Rock' scene which can be pulled back to reveal Colonel Parker smoking a fat cigar and throwing lots of lovely greenbacks in the air. Good fun, but at £9.95 probably short-lived novelties. (JC)

SO YOU WANT TO BE A ROCK 'N' ROLL STAR
Tom McGuinness (Javelin)

A slim volume with cartoons by Kipper Williams, which tells you that everyone in the record industry, the artiste aside, is a stupid, avaricious, coked-out squit. The artistes are all of the foregoing, minus the avaricious. This Cornish tin mine of information is topped off with a line in humour which has imaginary groups called The Lemmings, The Groins and Labia Minor. Ha! (PC)

● REFERENCE

THE BOOK OF LENNON
Billy Harry (Aurum)
THE McCARTNEY FILE
Bill Harry (Virgin)

Harry, erstwhile friend of the Beatles and the man behind *Mersey Beat*, certainly a milestone magazine of its time (sixties), has been writing books about the group collectively and the individuals thereof for some time now. Many of his past works have been interesting and informative (in particular his tome about the group's cinematic activities published by Virgin in their Beatles Library series). Here, however, he may be pushing his luck – very little, if anything, in either of these catchpenny books is original or even interesting to anyone with more than an average interest in the Fab

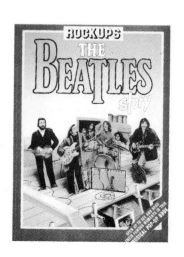

Four, although there may be a small passing tourist trade. If publishers are gullible enough to finance this sort of refried information, good luck to Harry, but surely this series cannot continue with George, Ringo and (deepbreath) Yoko? *Caveat emptor.* (JT)

THE BEATLES LIVE!
Mark Lewisohn *(Pavilion)*

While much of the available info about the biggest group in history has been written and rewritten in innumerable ways and in manners covering the entire spectrum from essential to utterly worthless, this book, for which Lewisohn deserves some kind of decoration for his research, contains a substantial quantity of new facts, more than it might be imagined any author could dredge up two decades after the event. While it is true that not too many of these new items are exactly world-shattering (possibly none of them can make that claim), Lewisohn here documents every live performance played by the chaps with a fine toothcomb-style scrutiny, and manages to deflate certain fairly interesting factoids, particularly relating to the dates of events. Also included is a flexi-disc of the group's first interview (hospital radio), making up an excellent package which will enhance even the most comprehensive Beatle library. Prolonged applause; what will he do next? (JT)

BILLBOARD'S TOP 1000 (1955-1984)
Joel Whitburn *(Record Research)*

Another of Whitburn's invaluable, if expensive, paperbacks. This time around he's programmed his computer to provide a list of the 1000 most successful singles ever to grace the American charts. His findings are based mainly on duration of stay in the Billboard charts and may not relate to actual sales – some records stay around for ever without selling more than a modicum each week, while others sell a million in a fortnight and are never heard of again. But the results make fascinating reading (surprisingly, Olivia Newton-John's 'Physical' is rated as the third most successful single of all-time, only topped by Elvis' 'Don't Be Cruel'/'Hound Dog' and Guy Mitchell's 'Singing The Blues') and the cross-referencing is of a high order, making it easy to trace any required info within a matter of seconds. (FD)

HM A-Z
Paul Suter *(Omnibus Press)*

Brief pause for personal announcement: I did the first one of these several years ago. Main programme: Paul Suter's is much better than mine. By no means as big entry-wise as Jasper and Oliver's effort (see below), nevertheless Suter scores by going into greater depth. He lists 120 bands, gives full personnel line-ups and changes, and (big plus for collectors) lists albums with catalogue numbers. Suter's writing style is attractive and sparky, too. (BH)

THE INTERNATIONAL ENCYCLOPEDIA OF HARD ROCK AND HEAVY METAL
Tony Jasper and Derek Oliver *(Sidgwick & Jackson)*

Highly and heavily recommended. Jasper and Oliver have done an awful lot of research to compile this trusty reference work. There are nearly 1500 entries covering the world of HM and hard rock both geographically and historically. The album listings in each entry are invaluable and anyone who says that Legs Diamond are "the best undiscovered major band in the world" is all right by me. Buy it. (BH)

LONDON'S ROCK LANDMARKS
Marcus Gray *(Omnibus)*

Do you *really* need to know the whereabouts of the social security office (now closed) where Mick Jones once worked or the location of Euston station, whence the Beatles caught the train to Bangor? If so you'll be interested in *my* next book which'll include a snap of the boys' bog at Wesley Road School, where Johnny Kidd once dangled his dongle and a colour shot of a dustbin into which *London's Rock Landmarks* was ditched. Truly awful. (FD)

ROCK ON – THE ILLUSTRATED ENCYCLOPEDIA OF ROCK 'N' ROLL
ROCK ON, VOL 2 – THE YEARS OF CHANGE 1964-1978
ROCK ON, VOL 3 – THE VIDEO REVOLUTION 1978-PRESENT
Norm N Nite *(Harper & Row)*

The original *Rock On* came out in 1974. A monumental affair in many ways, the book, authored by Cleveland DJ Nite, sought to be the all-embracing answer to all rock queries. Biogs on hundreds of artist were included, along with listings of every record they'd placed in the US charts. Packaged as a hardback, it seemed the ideal library item, the one destined to reside on every buff's main shelf. But familiarisation with the tome brought disappointments. The biogs proved sketchy, often worthless. Anyone checking out the achievements of the Spacemen, for instance, would merely discover that the group made one chart record, the A-side of which was stronger than the B-side. And 'rock *à la* Nite' proved merely a synonym for anyone having a chart record, with the result that such 'rockers' as Doris Day, Jack Jones, the Singing Nun and bandleader Art Mooney (renowned for such chunks of nitty-gritty as 'Hop-Scotch Polka') all grabbed their modicum of info-space. Now, twelve years on, Nite has not only updated his original – leaving in all the essential brouhaha on Mooney etc – but has added two further volumes, each of them following the original format. One-time Charlie's Angel Cheryl Ladd therefore receives her alloted brace of lines on the strength of a 1978 chart placing with 'Think It Over'; you can also learn something, albeit of minimal value, about the delights of Steve Carlisle, Continental Miniatures, Fred Knoblock, the Muppets, Streek and even George Burns (born 1896). But search for a line or two on such as Tom Waits, Van Dyke Parks, Ry Cooder or even the Sex Pistols and you're on to a loser. No US chart records, y'see. Therefore they just ain't rock. I knew we'd all been going wrong somewhere! (FD)

THE TOP TWENTY BOOK
Tony Jasper *(Javelin)*

The official British charts as documented by heavy-metal DJ, journalist and lay-preacher Jasper. Useful too, for Jasper's book complements the Guinness chart book rather than competing with it. If you wish to ascertain quickly the highest chart-rating achieved by any particularly act, then the Guinness publication is the one to turn to. But if you need to check the progress of any record on a week to week basis or merely wish to view a complete chart for any week between January 1955 and the end of December 1985, then there's nowhere to go but to Jasper's 450-page paperback. Invaluable to data freaks. (FD)

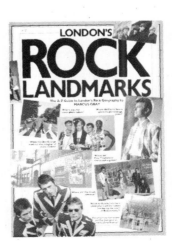

IN MEMORIAM

RICK NELSON
Died 31 December 1985, aged 45

Veteran rock star Rick (or Ricky) Nelson died in his private plane, which crashed between Dallas, Texas, and Guntersville, Alabama, and also killed Nelson's fiancée Helen Blair, the four members of his Stone Canyon Band (Bobby Neal, Patrick Woodward, Rick Intveld and Andy Chapin) and sound engineer Clark Russell. Subsequent rumours had it that the accident happened as a result of corner-cutting on routine plane maintenance or because Nelson (or A N Other) had been freebasing cocaine (naked flames in planes not being A Good Idea).

Nelson's long career began in his infancy when he appeared with his brother David on the nationally syndicated US TV show, *The Adventures of Ozzie and Harriet*, which starred his parents and ran for over twenty years – a promotional vehicle to be envied, indeed. He was able to plug his latest release at the end of the show for many years, the result being a string of pop hits in the late fifties and early sixties, including chart-toppers 'Poor Little Fool' and 'Travelin' Man', and many international hits besides.

An early boost to Nelson's recording career, which was launched in 1957 when he was 17, came in the shape of Elvis Presley's recruitment into the US army. To some extent he filled the void left by the absence of rock 'n' roll's first hero, although he was more easily digestible than the King; this, of course, recommended him to some girls and all parents, while alienating the mass of potential male teenagers.

One of the main ingredients of the successful Nelson hit formula was a very able backing band that starred ace guitarist James Burton, whose departure in the mid-sixties (he went on to work with Elvis Presley and many others) coincided with the end of Nelson's chart domination around 1964. In a bid to change his teen idol image he left the TV show in 1967, dropped the 'y' from his name and moved into what would later be known as country/rock music, releasing two pioneering albums *Bright Lights and Country Music* and *Country Fever* at almost exactly the same time as Gram Parsons was launching the International Submarine Band and a year before the Byrds released *Sweetheart of the Rodeo*. Later, he formed the Stone Canyon Band, with whom he enjoyed his last big hits, such as 'Garden Party' ('72), in which he voiced his complaints against the revival circuit, where his persona as a country/rock musician was not taken seriously. Despite such criticisms and flagging popularity, it was the revival circuit that kept Nelson going, and the boy who thrilled the girls with 'Hello Mary Lou' is the Nelson that will be best remembered.

GARY HOLTON
Died 25 October 1985, London, aged 32

Former vocalist with the Heavy Metal Kids, a minor-league London version of Slade who released two albums immediately before the punk rock phenomenon, Holton later became rather more celebrated as a member of the cast of hit TV series *Auf Wiedersehen, Pet*. It was widely assumed, and the coroner's report subsequently confirmed, that Holton's death was connected with drugs – he was young, apparently healthy and was enjoying what was probably the most successful period of his career at the time of his death.

MARK DINNING
Died 23 March 1986, aged 52

Dinning's chart career spanned little more than a year, from 1959 to early 1961. Born in 1933, he was the son of an Evangelist minister and the brother of eight other children, three of whom were the Dinning Sisters, a famous trio of the forties. In 1957 he signed to MGM Records, without much success until 1959 when 'Teen Angel' went to number one on the US national charts. Although subsequent songs, 'A Star Is Born', 'Lovin' Touch' and 'Top 40, News, Weather & Sport', also made the charts, Dinning's fifteen minutes undoubtedly came with his classic 'death' record. He died at home, of natural causes.

PHIL LYNOTT
Died 4 January 1986, Salisbury, aged 36

The hard-living streetwise leader of British hard rock chic, Phil Lynott, died of heart disease and pneumonia in a Salisbury hospital. As a black Irishman, Lynott combined the bluesy feel of half his parentage with the boozy bonhomie of the other half and formed the internationally celebrated group, Thin Lizzy, to present the results to the world.

While they enjoyed immense popularity and success in many countries, especially Britain, Thin Lizzy never seemed able to capture the imagination of the US, where they only achieved one Top 40 single during their thirteen-year career, compared to fourteen British Top 40 hits.

The group's purple period during the second half of the seventies saw them become an immense live attraction with frequent hits and a series of excellent Top Ten albums from *Jailbreak* ('76) to *Adventures of Thin Lizzy* ('81) via *Live and Dangerous* and *Black Rose (A Rock Legend)*. This last album cleverly exploited the band's Celtic roots, and many felt that if they had pursued this direction they might have been saved from their eventual stagnation, Lynott's 'rebel rocker' stance becoming a parody of what had been an exciting and inspiring image. He also made a handful of solo records (most notably 'Yellow Pearl', which was used as the theme music for *Top of the Pops)* and published several books of poetry; but his talent was ravaged by an interest in drugs, which probably hastened his premature demise as well as breaking up his marriage to the daughter of TV personality Leslie Crowther.

BENNY GOODMAN
Died on 13 June 1986, aged 77

Revered jazz clarinetist Benny Goodman, popularly known as the 'King of Swing', first won acclaim in the thirties and was supposedly the first bandleader to employ black musicians, such as Lionel Hampton and Teddy Wilson, in his orchestra. Other famous names who came to prominence during their time with Goodman include drummer Gene Krupa, Harry James and Peggy Lee. A measure of his fame was that a film biography, *The Benny Goodman Story*, was made in 1955, in which Goodman was portrayed by Steve Allen and numerous stars, such as Krupa, James and Sammy Davis Jr, made guest appearances. During a career which lasted more than half a century, Goodman recorded innumerable albums, and was certainly one of the finest musicians of the pre-rock 'n' roll era.

ALAN J LERNER
Died 14 June 1986, New York, aged 67

Eight-times-married Alan Jay Lerner, playwright and lyricist, will be remembered for such notable musicals as *Brigadoon, Paint Your Wagon, Camelot* and especially the immensely successful *My Fair Lady*. In 1962 he formed with tunesmith Frederick Loewe a successful writing team that was to last for twenty years, culminating in the adaptation of Shaw's *Pygmalion* as *My Fair Lady* and the well-loved *Gigi*. Lerner also worked with various collaborators, including André Prévin and Leonard Bernstein, although his last musical, *Dance a Little Closer*, apparently closed after only one night in 1983. A measure of his standing can be judged by a quote from *The Times*. "Since the death of Oscar Hammerstein in 1960, Lerner's position as America's leading lyric writer was virtually unchallenged."

RICHARD MANUEL
Died 4 March 1986, Florida, aged 41

Singer, songwriter and keyboard player with the Band, Richard Manuel was found dead, apparently having hanged himself, in a Florida hotel room during a tour by the then recently reunited group. He had reportedly been assailed by drug and alcohol problems, although these were not necessarily connected with his death.

Born in Ontario on 3 April 1944, Manuel, along with compatriots Robbie Robertson, Rick Danko and Garth Hudson and American Levon Helm, emerged as backing band to Canadian rock legend Ronnie Hawkins, before becoming Bob Dylan's semi-official regular band during the sixties, touring and recording with him for some years. Among the notable Dylan albums on which the group played were *The Basement Tapes* and *Before the Flood*; they also enjoyed great acclaim in their own right after changing their name from the Hawks (for the Hawkins era) to the Band. Their debut album, *Music from Big Pink*, was a revelation when it was released in 1968, and several subsequent works remain highly regarded.

The climax of their career came in 1976, when they hosted a superstar-studded event at the Winterland Ballroom, San Francisco, where performing guests included Eric Clapton, Bob Dylan, Van Morrison, Ringo Starr and Neil Young, under the title *The Last Waltz*. This concert, the group's final performance before disBanding, became a notable feature film and triple album.

RICKY WILSON
Died 13 October 1985, aged 32

Guitarist and founder member of the B52s, Ricky Wilson was largely responsible for the band's idiosyncratic sound. The quintet from Athens, Georgia, was formed in 1976 and attracted attention not only because of their knowing, witty and allusive music and lyrics but because of the equally humorous bouffant hair-dos of vocalists Cindy Wilson (Ricky's sister) and Kate Pierson (the southern slang expression for these beehives was the inspiration for the band's name).

Although their single releases never achieved much in the charts, the B52s' five albums (the fifth being *Party Mix*) sold consistently well and established a large and faithful following. Sadly, Ricky's untimely death from lymph cancer prevented him from enjoying the group's greatest commercial success, when a reissue of 'Rock Lobster', possibly the best 'silly' pop song ever, just failed to reach the Top Ten in the UK. His was an individual talent which will be sorely missed by all those who like a certain quirkiness and humour in their music.

LINDA CREED
Died 10 April 1986,
Ambler, Philadelphia

Notable lyricist Linda Creed, who collaborated with Thom Bell on many of the best compositions that characterised the 'Philly Sound', died of cancer. The Bell-Creed team's most famous compositions were recorded by the Stylistics in the seventies. Creed died only one month before 'The Greatest Love of All', which she co-wrote with Michael Masser, became her first US chart-topper with Whitney Houston.

D BOON
Died December 1985,
Arizona, aged 27

Singer/guitarist/founder member of Los Angeles hardcore band the Minutemen, Dennis Dale Boon was killed in a car crash in the Arizona Desert shortly before Xmas 1985. Boon and school friends from San Pedro, California, founded the group during the late seventies "as a vehicle for political comment".

SONNY TERRY
Died 12 March 1986,
New York, aged 74

Half the famous duo of Sonny Terry & Brownie McGhee finally capitulated after a lengthy illness. Born Saunders Terrill, Terry first came to prominence at the 1939 'Spirituals to Swing' concert in New York, teaming up with McGhee later that year. One of the last links with the authentic country blues, his vocals and harmonica-playing over McGhee's guitar were an inspiration to virtually every blues-influenced performer in Britain during the sixties, around when his fellow countrymen began to accord the duo some of the respect they had long deserved. Numerous albums by Terry & McGhee have been released on a wide variety of labels, despite the fact that rumour has it that they'd hardly had any personal contact with each other for many years. Their names, ironically, were rarely mentioned separately. Terry also appeared in several films, most recently *The Color Purple*.

O'KELLY ISLEY
Died 31 March 1986,
New Jersey, aged 48

The oldest of the Isley Brothers died of a heart attack in his sleep. Along with his brothers Ronald and Rudolph, O'Kelly was one of the original trio who started recording way back in 1958.

By 1977, several years after the group had been augmented by two more brothers, Marvin and Ernie, and by their cousin, Chris Jasper, the Isleys had taken over thirty hits into the US Top 100, as well as innumerable singles into the R&B charts. Among the most notable on which O'Kelly performed were 'Shout' (their first hit in 1959), 'Twist And Shout' (a Top Ten US hit for the Isleys before the Beatles' version), and such classics from the brothers' brief partnership with Motown during the mid-sixties as 'This Old Heart Of Mine', 'I Guess I'll Always Love You' and 'Behind A Painted Smile'.

Their Motown period often seems to have lasted longer than others, largely because in Britain the label released and re-released Isley material on several occasions. By 1969, however, the group were charting with 'It's Your Thing' (which became their biggest US hit) on their own T-Neck label, and by 1973 Epic Records had licensed their T-Neck material, charting a series of classics like 'That Lady', 'Summer Breeze' and 'Harvest For The World' throughout the mid-seventies.

In recent years, O'Kelly, Ronald and Rudolph left much of the action to the three younger members, who went under the name Isley, Jasper, Isley, although the original trio signed to Warner Bros in late '85 and were still active in the recording studio.

DICK JAMES
Died 1 February 1986, London, aged 65

Although recent years saw him surrounded by controversy, music publishing mogul Dick James, who began his career as a singer with London dance bands and orchestras led by the likes of Henry Hall and Geraldo, was a shrewd, powerful and well-respected member of the London music community. His death from a heart attack sadly coincided with a High Court judgement that did little to clarify claims made against him and his companies by Elton John and Bernie Taupin. These two had been signed to Dick James Music and its associated record label, DJM, for many years; the dispute was over copyrights of the John/Taupin songs and record royalties. The action had been going on for some time and at the end of the hearing, which lasted nearly two months during 1985, James was said to be "drained".

While Elton John was obviously his most significant discovery, James had first made his mark as a publisher when he signed the Beatles, before they had achieved international fame, and set up Northern Songs for them. He also enjoyed a certain celebrity during the fifties as vocalist on a hit single, the theme from the popular TV series, *Robin Hood*. Among other acts whose songs he published were Gerry and the Pacemakers and Billy J Kramer and the Dakotas (both signed, like the Beatles, to Brian Epstein's NEMS organisation).

ROBBIE BASHO
Died 2 March 1986, aged 45

Guitarist Robbie Basho, a player in the John Fahey/Leo Kottke mould, but who was never quite as famous as either of them, died of a stroke. He will probably be best remembered by posterity as the teacher of Will Ackerman, founder of Windham Hill Records, who released his final album, *The Art of the Acoustic Steel String Guitar*, in 1979.

PIANO RED
(William Perryman)
Died 25 July 1985, Atlanta, aged 73

Renowned R&B pioneer, Piano Red died after a protracted illness. Slightly predating the rock 'n' roll era, he scored hits with songs like 'The Right String But The Wrong Yoyo' and 'Rockin' With Red', recording for both CBS and RCA, and at one point, opening for the Rolling Stones on an American tour.

MERLE WATSON
Died 23 October 1985, North Carolina

The son and performing partner of the legendary blind folk blues guitarist Doc Watson was killed on a farm when a tractor he was driving overturned. Although not a mainstream performer in recent years, Merle's prowess on guitar and banjo, as well as his duties as 'eyes' and tour manager for his father, will leave a substantial gap in the progress of roots music as applied to traditional C&W.

LILY MAY LEDFORD
Died 14 July 1985, Lexington, Kentucky, aged 68

Primarily of note to fans of country and roots music, songwriter/banjo player and leader of country music's most acclaimed all-female string band, the Coon Creek Girls, Lily May died after a long illness. After commencing a musical career in 1936 while still a teenager, she continued to perform for almost all the remaining half-century of her life, cutting several albums over the years.

NELSON RIDDLE
Died 6 October 1985

Although his worst enemy would hardly have accused him of being a rock 'n' roller, arranger/composer/orchestra leader/producer Nelson Riddle, who died of cardiac and kidney failure, was notable as an innovator whose work was acceptable to a number of rock fans. During the fifties, he was responsible for the arrangements on several classic albums by Frank Sinatra, in particular the timeless *Songs for Swinging Lovers*, and in recent years had overseen an artistic change of direction in Linda Ronstadt, for whom he produced her three most recent albums; *What's New* and *Lush Life*, although not totally to the taste of her substantial following, were artistic successes; the third, almost completed at the time of Riddle's death, is due for release sometime in 1986. Riddle also orchestrated an album of popular material for Kiri Te Kanawa, *Blue Skies*, indicating a valuable ability to work with vocalists from different musical fields.

IAN STEWART
Died 12 December 1985, aged 47

Long-time auxiliary keyboard player/tour manager of the Rolling Stones, Ian Stewart, who died of a heart attack, would probably have enjoyed the wake thrown in his memory, and arranged in accordance with his family's wishes, at London's 100 Club. Among those who gathered to pay their respects were all the Stones, Jeff Beck, Pete Townshend, Eric Clapton and several others who had known 'Stu' since the sixties when he'd been a major enthusiast of the British R&B scene. Originally a founding member of the Stones, Stu was to take a subsidiary role allegedly because Andrew Loog Oldham felt that his looks did not blend in with the image presented by the slim hips and chic hairstyles of the rest of the band.

However, he remained closely involved with the group playing his trademark barrelhouse piano on many Stones' records over the years. He also led his own R&B group, Rocket 88, as a floating aggregation that recorded only occasionally but was well known around the London pub circuit. One of Stu's close friends was Ronnie Lane, who suffers from multiple sclerosis; Stu's experience of this illness inspired him to organise with producer Glyn Johns the now legendary 'ARMS' concerts. The Stones' latest album, *Dirty Work*, is dedicated to the man who was widely recognised as their sixth member.

JOE TURNER
Died 23 November 1985, Inglewood, California, aged 74

Big Joe Turner, whom many credit as the first person to cut a rock 'n' roll record ('Shake Rattle And Roll' in 1954 on Atlantic, his long-time label), had been hospitalised for some months, after suffering a heart attack. He started in music in the 1930s, working with pianist Peter Johnson in his birthplace, Kansas City, and first came to national prominence in 1938 when he was one of the stars of the celebrated 'Spirituals to Swing' (along with Sonny Terry) concert at New York's Carnegie Hall. He also worked during the late 1930s and most of the 1940s alongside such notables as Duke Ellington and Count Basie, but was only 'rediscovered' by a large audience when he began to make acclaimed albums such as *Boss of the Blues*, produced by Nesuhi Ertegun for Atlantic in the 1950s, after which he became a major attraction at jazz nightclubs and festivals. He supposedly recorded almost 200 albums during his career, most recently for the jazz oriented Pablo label, although his most acclaimed work was for Atlantic.

HUGO PERETTI
Died 1 May 1986, New Jersey, aged 68

Record producer and songwriter Hugo Peretti died in hospital in Englewood, New Jersey, after a long illness. He and his long-time partner Luigi Creatore, although not household names, in fact produced hits for, among others, Perry Como, Sam Cooke, the Isley Brothers and the Stylistics, as well as writing greats like 'Can't Help Falling in Love' (originally a hit for Elvis Presley, and recently revived in the UK charts by Lick The Tins) and 'The Lion Sleeps Tonight'. Known throughout the industry as Hugo & Luigi, the pair set up Avco Records (for which the Stylistics recorded) in the late sixties.

The year also saw the departure of journalist/publicist 'Waxie Maxie' Needham, journalist/broadcaster Derek Jewell, veteran rock photographer Dezo Hoffmann (whose estate includes a vast library of photographs of various stars, many of them as yet unseen) and jazz writer Rex Harris, all of whom made significant contributions to popular culture.

ALBERT GROSSMAN
Died 25 January 1986, mid-air, aged 59

Albert Grossman died of a heart attack aboard a flight to the MIDEM conference in Cannes. Although his influence had lessened in recent years, Grossman will be remembered as one of the key figures in folk music and associated rock during the fifties and sixties, managing such luminaries as Joan Baez, Bob Dylan, Peter, Paul & Mary, Richie Havens, Gordon Lightfoot, Janis Joplin and the Electric Flag, among many others. He was instrumental in launching the celebrated Newport Folk Festivals; during the early seventies he successfully floated the Bearsville record label, named after the upstate New York hamlet, most of which, including the restaurants, he owned. Bearsville was responsible for furthering the careers of Todd Rundgren and Jesse Winchester, among others. As a self-contained label with recording studios and other facilities all on its doorstep, Bearsville could be seen as the perfect location for artist-oriented music during the seventies, and although conflicts with artists were to cloud the later picture, Grossman remained the respected proprietor of both a notable label and a heritage in music which few, if any, entrepreneurs could match.

THE BPI CERTIFIED AWARDS

© British Phonographic Industry Ltd, reprinted with permission. The qualifying sales levels for BPI gold and platinum awards are, respectively, 500,000 units and one million units (singles); 100,000 and 300,000 units (albums). To qualify for double and triple platinum, a single or album must have been released since January 1985 or have appeared in the Gallup charts since then if it was released earlier.

● GOLD
Singles
AUGUST 1985

CARS
Drive (Warner Bros)
MADONNA
Into The Groove (Sire/Warner Bros)
MADONNA
Holiday (Sire/Warner Bros)

SEPTEMBER 1985

DAVID BOWIE and MICK JAGGER
Dancing In The Street (EMI America)
THE CROWD
You'll Never Walk Alone (Spartan)
MADONNA
Crazy For You (Sire/Warner Bros)

OCTOBER 1985

A-HA
Take On Me (Warner Bros)
COLONEL ABRAMS
Trapped (MCA)
JENNIFER RUSH
The Power Of Love (CBS)
FEARGAL SHARKEY
A Good Heart (Virgin)
WHAM!
I'm Your Man (CBS)

DECEMBER 1985

WHITNEY HOUSTON
Saving All My Love For You (Arista)
SHAKIN' STEVENS
Merry Christmas Everyone (CBS)
UB40
Red Red Wine (Dep International)
UB40
I Got You Babe (Dep International)

JANUARY 1986

PET SHOP BOYS
West End Girls (EMI)

FEBRUARY 1986

BILLY OCEAN
When The Going Gets Tough, The Tough Get Going (Zomba)

APRIL 1986

**CLIFF RICHARD
AND THE YOUNG ONES**
Livin' Doll (Warner Bros)
DIANA ROSS
Chain Reaction (EMI)

MAY 1986

FALCO
Rock Me Amadeus (A&M)
GEORGE MICHAEL
A Different Corner (CBS)

● GOLD
Albums
AUGUST 1985

CHINA CRISIS
Flaunt The Imperfection (Virgin)
BILLY JOEL
Greatest Hits Volumes 1/2 (CBS)
ALED JONES
All Through The Night (PRT)
U2
Boy (Island)
U2
October (Island)
VARIOUS
Soundtrack from Beverly Hills Cop (MCA)

SEPTEMBER 1985

CARS
Heartbeat City (Elektra)
BILLY IDOL
Vital Idol (Chrysalis)
MADONNA
The First Album (formerly Madonna) (Sire/Warner Bros)
BRUCE SPRINGSTEEN
Darkness On The Edge Of Town (Nice Price/CBS)
STING
The Dream Of The Blue Turtles (A&M)
THOMPSON TWINS
Here's To Future Days (Arista)
VARIOUS
West Side Story (Polygram)
VARIOUS
The Magic Of Torvill And Dean (Stylus)

OCTOBER 1985
GEORGE BENSON
The Love Songs (K-Tel)
MATT BIANCO
Whose Side Are You On? (Warner Bros)
KATE BUSH
Hounds Of Love (EMI)
CHICAGO
Chicago 17 (Warner Bros)
CHAS AND DAVE
Jamboree (Towerbell)
DEPECHE MODE
The Singles 81-85 (Spartan)
BARBARA DICKSON
Gold (K-Tel)
THE EAGLES
The Best Of The Eagles (Warner Bros)
IRON MAIDEN
Live After Death (EMI)
IRON MAIDEN
Killers (EMI)
SIMPLE MINDS
Once Upon A Time (Virgin)
MIDGE URE
The Gift (Chrysalis)
STEVIE WONDER
In Square Circle (RCA)
ZZ TOP
Afterburner (Warner Bros)

NOVEMBER 1985
**LLOYD COLE
AND THE COMMOTIONS**
Rattlesnakes (Polygram)
ECHO AND THE BUNNYMEN
Songs To Learn And Sing (Warner Bros)
THE FUREYS
At The End Of The Day (K-Tel)
BILLIE HOLIDAY
The Legend Of Billie Holiday (MCA)
ALED JONES
Aled Jones And The Welsh Choir
(Chrysalis)
KING
Bitter Sweet (CBS)
LEVEL 42
World Machine (Polygram)
ELAINE PAIGE
Love Hurts (Warner Bros)
JENNIFER RUSH
Jennifer Rush (CBS)
TALKING HEADS
Stop Making Sense (EMI)
TALKING HEADS
Little Creatures (EMI)
VARIOUS
Rock Anthems (K-Tel)

DECEMBER 1985
RUSS ABBOTT
I Love A Party (K-Tel)
BLACK LACE
Party Party II (Telstar)
EASTENDERS
The Cast Of EastEnders (PRT)
RICHARD CLAYDERMAN
The Classical Touch (Delphine)

**LLOYD COLE
AND THE COMMOTIONS**
Easy Pieces (Polygram)
THE COMMODORES
The Commodroes (Telstar)
THE CULT
Love (Beggars Banquet)
THE CURE
The Head Of The Door (Polygram)
WHITNEY HOUSTON
Whitney Houston (Arista)
ELTON JOHN
Ice On Fire (Phonogram)
HOWARD KEEL
The Howard Keel Collection (Telstar)
LONDON SYMPHONY ORCHESTRA
The Power of Classic Rock (CBS)
ELVIS PRESLEY
Elvis Presley Ballads (Telstar)
**TIM RICE AND ANDREW LLOYD
WEBBER**
The Very Best Of Tim Rice And Andrew
Lloyd Webber (Telstar)
FEARGAL SHARKEY
Feargal Sharkey (Virgin)
SLADE
The Slade Christmas Party Album
(Telstar)
VARIOUS
Greatest Hits Of '85 (Telstar)
VARIOUS
The Love Album (Telstar)
VARIOUS
The Prince's Trust Collection (Telstar)
VARIOUS
Telly Hits (Stylus)
VARIOUS
Ovation – A Tribute To
Andrew Lloyd Webber (K-Tel)
VARIOUS
Expressions (K-Tel)
VARIOUS
Miami Vice (PRT)

JANUARY 1986
A-HA
Hunting High And Low (Warner Bros)
FINE YOUNG CANNIBALS
Fine Young Cannibals (London)
KIRI TE KANAWA
Blue Skies (Polygram/Decca)
BARBRA STREISAND
The Broadway Album (CBS)
VARIOUS
Dance Hits Album (Towerbell)

FEBRUARY 1986
FIVE STAR
Luxury Of Life (RCA)
GRACE JONES
Island Life (Island)
MIKE OLDFIELD
The Complete Mike Oldfield (Virgin)
PREFAB SPROUT
Steve McQueen (CBS)
UB40
Baggariddim (Dep International)
VARIOUS
Jonathan King – Very Best Of Entertainment USA (Stylus)

MARCH 1986
HUEY LEWIS AND THE NEWS
Sports (Chrysalis)
VARIOUS
Soundtrack From Rocky IV (CBS)
VARIOUS
Hits For Lovers (CBS)
VARIOUS
Cinema Hits Album (Towerbell)

MAY 1986
EARTH, WIND AND FIRE
The Collection (K-tel)
BILLY OCEAN
Love Zone (Zomba)
PET SHOP BOYS
Please (EMI)
ROLLING STONES
Dirty Works (CBS)
SHAKIN' STEVENS
Lipstick, Powder And Paint (CBS)
SIMPLY RED
Picture Book (Warner Bros)
TALK TALK
The Colour Of Spring (EMI)
VARIOUS
Soundtrack From Absolute Beginners
(Virgin)
VARIOUS
Heart To Heart (K-Tel)

JUNE 1986
CLANNAD
Macalla (RCA)
SAM COOKE
Sam Cooke – The Man And His Music
(RCA)
THE CURE
Standing On A Beach (Polygram)
CHRIS DE BURGH
Into The Light (A&M)
PETER GABRIEL
So (Virgin)
GENESIS
Invisible Touch (Virgin)
QUEEN
A Kind Of Magic (EMI)
THE SHADOWS
Moonlight Shadows (Polygram)
THE SMITHS
The Queen Is Dead (Rough Trade)
SUZANNE VEGA
Suzanne Vega (A&M)

JULY 1986
EURYTHMICS
Revenge (RCA)
THE HOUSEMARTINS
Hull 4 London 0 (Chrysalis)
MADONNA
True Blue (Sire/Warner Bros)
LUCIANO PAVAROTTI
Greatest Hits (Polygram)
CHRIS REA
On The Beach (Magnet)
ROD STEWART
Every Beat Of My Heart (WEA)
WHAM!
The Final Wham! (CBS)

● PLATINUM
Albums
AUGUST 1985
EURYTHMICS
Be Yourself Tonight (RCA)
MADONNA
Like A Virgin (Sire/Warner Bros)
U2
War (Island)
VARIOUS
Now That's What I Call Music 5 (EMI)

OCTOBER 1985
KATE BUSH
Hounds Of Love (EMI)
DIRE STRAITS
Communique (Polygram)
● **BRYAN FERRY**
Boys And Girls (Polygram)
SPANDAU BALLET
The Singles Collection (Chrysalis)
VARIOUS
Out Now 2 (Chrysalis)

NOVEMBER 1985
GEORGE BENSON
The Love Songs (K-Tel)
MARILLION
Misplaced Childhood (EMI)
SADE
Promise (CBS)

DECEMBER 1985
BRYAN ADAMS
Reckless (A&M)
GO WEST
Go West (Chrysalis)
BILLY JOEL
Greatest Hits Volumes 1/2 (CBS)
JAMES LAST
Leave The Best To Last (Polydor)
ANDREW LLOYD WEBBER
Variations (MCA)
MADONNA
The First Album (formerly Madonna)
(Warner Bros)
ELAINE PAIGE
Love Hurts (Warner Bros)
KENNY ROGERS
The Kenny Rogers Story (EMI)
JENNIFER RUSH
Jennifer Rush (CBS)
SIMPLE MINDS
Once Upon A Time (Virgin)
VARIOUS
The Greatest Hits Of '85 (Telstar)
VARIOUS
Now – The Christmas Album (EMI)
VARIOUS
Now That's What I Call Music 6 (EMI)
VARIOUS
The Love Album (Telstar)

JANUARY 1986
BARBARA DICKSON
Gold (K-Tel)
ELTON JOHN
Ice On Fire (Phonogram)

LEVEL 42
World Machine (Polygram)
STING
The Dream Of The Blue Turtles (A&M)

FEBRUARY 1986
A-HA
Hunting High And Low (Warner Bros)
VARIOUS
West Side Story (Polygram)

APRIL 1986
● **BRYAN FERRY AND ROXY MUSIC**
Streetlife (Polydor)
WHITNEY HOUSTON
Whitney Houston (Arista)
VARIOUS
Hits 4 (Warner Bros)

JUNE 1986
GENESIS
Invisible Touch (Virgin)
U2
Unforgettable Fire (Island)

JULY 1986
PETER GABRIEL
So (Virgin)
MADONNA
True Blue (Sire/Warner Bros)
VARIOUS
Now – The Summer Album (EMI)

● DOUBLE PLATINUM
Albums
AUGUST 1985
DIRE STRAITS
Making Movies (Vertigo/Phonogram)
DIRE STRAITS
Love Over Gold (Vertigo/Phonogram)
JAMES LAST
Last The Whole Night Long (Polydor)

SEPTEMBER 1985
DIRE STRAITS
Brothers In Arms (Vertigo/Phonogram)
MADONNA
Like A Virgin (Sire/Warner Bros)
U2
Under A Blood Red Sky (Island)
VARIOUS
Now That's What I Call Music 3 (EMI)
VARIOUS
Now That's What I Call Music 5 (EMI)

DECEMBER 1985
GEORGE BENSON
The Love Songs (K-Tel)
SPANDAU BALLET
The Singles Collection (Chrysalis)
UB40
Labour Of Love (Dep International)
VARIOUS
Now That's What I Call Music 6 (EMI)

VARIOUS
Hits 3 (Warner Bros)
VARIOUS
Now – The Christmas Album (EMI)
PAUL YOUNG
The Secret Of Association (CBS)

JANUARY 1986
SADE
Promise (CBS)

FEBRUARY 1986
PHIL COLLINS
Hello, I Must Be Going (Virgin)
DIRE STRAITS
Dire Straits (Vertigo/Phonogram)
EURYTHMICS
Be Yourself Tonight (RCA)

MAY 1986
WHITNEY HOUSTON
Whitney Houston (Arista)

JUNE 1986
GO WEST
Go West (Chrysalis)

● TRIPLE PLATINUM
Albums
OCTOBER 1985
PHIL COLLINS
No Jacket Required (Virgin)

NOVEMBER 1985
MEAT LOAF
Bat Out Of Hell (CBS)
LIONEL RICHIE
Can't Slow Down (RCA)

DECEMBER 1985
DIRE STRAITS
Brothers In Arms (Vertigo/Phonogram)
JOHN LENNON
The John Lennon Collection (EMI)
MADONNA
Like A Virgin (Sire/Warner Bros)
VARIOUS
Now That's What I Call Music 1 (EMI)
VARIOUS
Now – The Christmas Album (EMI)
VARIOUS
Now That's What I Call Music 6 (EMI)

JANUARY 1986
● **TEARS FOR FEARS**
Songs From The Big Chair (Phonogram)

JUNE 1986
TINA TURNER
Private Dancer (Capitol)

THE RIAA CERTIFIED AWARDS

© Recording Industry Association of America Inc, reprinted with permission.

The qualifying sales levels for RIAA gold and platinum awards are, respectively, one million and two million units (singles); 500,000 and one million units (albums). To qualify for a multi-platinum award, which certifies successive million-level sales, an album or single must have been released on or after 1 January 1976. The figures at the end of the multi-platinum entries indicate the million level reached.

● GOLD
Singles
DECEMBER 1985
EDDIE MURPHY
Party All The Time (Columbia)

JANUARY 1986
DIONNE & FRIENDS
That's What Friends Are For (Arista)
LIONEL RICHIE
Say You, Say Me (Motown)

FEBRUARY 1986
THE CHICAGO BEARS SHUFFLIN' CREW
Superbowl Shuffle (Capitol)
DOUG E FRESH AND THE GET FRESH CREW
The Show (12") (Reality/Fantasy)

MARCH 1986
ELVIS PRESLEY
Crying In The Chapel (RCA)

MAY 1986
PATTI LABELLE & MICHAEL MCDONALD
On My Own (MCA)
PRINCE & THE REVOLUTION
Kiss (Warner Bros)

● GOLD
Albums
AUGUST 1985
AC/DC
Fly On The Wall (Atlantic)
DOKKEN
Tooth And Nail (Elektra)
ARETHA FRANKLIN
Who's Zooming Who? (Arista)
GLENN FREY
The Allnighter (MCA)
COREY HART
Boy In The Box (EMI America)
HEART
Heart (Capitol)
JESSE JOHNSON'S REVUE
Jesse Johnson's Revue (A&M)
MÖTLEY CRÜE
Theatre Of Pain (Elektra)
RAY PARKER JR
Chartbusters (Arista)
SCORPIONS
Worldwide Love (Mercury)
STING
The Dream Of The Blue Turtles (A&M)
TALKING HEADS
Little Creatures (Sire)
GEORGE THOROGOOD
Maverick (EMI America)
GEORGE THOROGOOD
Bad To The Bone (EMI America)
VANITY 6
Vanity 6 (Warner Bros)
PAUL YOUNG
The Secret Of Association (Columbia)

SEPTEMBER 1985
LAURA BRANIGAN
Branigan 2 (Atlantic)
AMY GRANT
Unguarded (Myrrh)
MEN AT WORK
Two Hearts (Columbia)
POINTER SISTERS
Contact (RCA)
SOUNDTRACK
Back To The Future (MCA)
TALKING HEADS
Remain In The Light (Sire)
TALKING HEADS
Fear Of Music (Sire)
TIL TUESDAY
Voices Carry (Epic)

OCTOBER 1985
A-HA
Hunting High And Low (Warner Bros)
BON JOVI
7800 Degree Fahrenheit (Mercury)
JOHN COUGAR MELLENCAMP
Scarecrow (Riva)
DIO
Sacred Heart (Warner Bros)
HALL & OATES
Live At The Appollo (RCA)
THE HOOTERS
Nervous Night (Columbia)
BILLY JOEL
Greatest Hits Vols I & II (Columbia)
HUEY LEWIS & THE NEWS
Picture This (Chrysalis)

RONNIE MILSAP
Greatest Hits Vol 2 (RCA)
READY FOR THE WORLD
Ready For The World (MCA)
SOUNDTRACK
St Elmo's Fire (Atlantic)
HANK WILLIAMS JR
Five-O (Warner Bros)

NOVEMBER 1985
ALABAMA
Alabama Christmas (RCA)
GEORGE BENSON
20/20 (Warner Bros)
CAMEO
Single Life (Atlanta Artists)
CHARLIE DANIELS BAND
A Decade Of Hits (Epic)
AMY GRANT
A Christmas Album (Myrrh)
LEE GREENWOOD
Greatest Hits (MCA)
KISS
Asylum (Mercury)
KLYMAXX
Meeting In The Ladies Room (MCA)
LOVERBOY
Lovin' Every Minute Of It (Columbia)
MR MISTER
Welcome To The Real World (RCA)
SOUNDTRACK
Music From Miami Vice (MCA)
STARSHIP
Knee Deep In The Hoopla (Grunt)
GEORGE STRAIT
Greatest Hits (MCA)
THOMPSON TWINS
Here's To Future Days (Arista)
STEVIE WONDER
In Square Circle (Motown)

DECEMBER 1985
MORRIS DAY
Color of Success (Warner Bros)
SHEENA EASTON
Do You? (EMI America)
IRON MAIDEN
Live After Death (Capitol)
EDDIE MURPHY
How Could It Be? (Columbia)
OLIVIA NEWTON-JOHN
Soul Kiss (MCA)
MAURICE ANDRE PAILLARD
The Pachelbel Choir (RCA)
BONNIE RAITT
Give It Up (Warner Bros)
RUSH
Power Windows (Mercury)
KENNY ROGERS
Heart of the Matter (RCA)
**SOUNDTRACK: ORIGINAL
BROADWAY CAST**
Cats (Geffen)
JAMES TAYLOR
That's Why I'm Here (Columbia)
S R VAUGHAN & DOUBLE TROUBLE
Couldn't Stand The Weather (Epic)
GEORGE WINSTON
Winter Into Spring (Windham Hill)

JANUARY 1986
ARCADIA
So Red The Rose (Capitol)
THE CARS
Greatest Hits (Elektra)
FAT BOYS
The Fat Boys Are Back (Sutra)
GLENN MILLER
Glenn Miller – A Memorial (RCA)
(1944-1969)
NEW EDITION
All For Love (MCA)
STEVIE NICKS
Rock A Little (Atlantic)
DIANA ROSS & THE SUPREMES
Anthology (Motown)
SADE
Promise (Portrait)
SHEILA E
Romance 1600 (Warner Bros)
SIMPLE MINDS
Once Upon A Time (A&M)
SOUNDTRACK
Rocky IV (Scotti Bros)
SOUNDTRACK
White Nights (Atlantic)
BARBRA STREISAND
The Broadway Album (Columbia)
PETE TOWNSHEND
White City – A Novel (Atlantic)
TWISTED SISTER
Come Out And Play (Atlantic)
DIONNE WARWICK
Friends (Arista)
WEIRD AL YANKOVIC
Dare To Be Stupid (Rock 'n' Roll)
HANK WILLIAMS JR
Strong Stuff (Warner Bros)
ZZ TOP
Afterburner (Warner Bros)

FEBRUARY 1986
ATLANTIC STARR
As The Band Turns (A&M)
BON JOVI
Bon Jovi (Mercury)
**CREEDENCE CLEARWATER
REVIVAL**
The Concert (Fantasy)
AL JARREAU
High Crime (Warner Bros)
**W JENNINGS, W NELSON, J CASH,
K KRISTOFFERSON**
Highwayman (Columbia)
THE JUDDS
Rockin' With The Rhythm (RCA)
SOUNDTRACK
Amadeus (Fantasy)
GEORGE STRAIT
Something Special (MCA)

MARCH 1986
ALABAMA
Greatest Hits (RCA)
PAT BENATAR
Seven The Hard Way (Chrysalis)
DOKKEN
Under Lock And Key (Elektra)
INXS
Listen Like Thieves (Atlantic)
NEW YORK PHILHARMONIC
Gershwin: An American In Paris (CBS)

APRIL 1986
THE BANGLES
Different Light (Columbia)
DIRE STRAITS
Love Over Gold (Warner Bros)
THE EVERLY BROTHERS
The Very Best Of . . . (Warner Bros)
FALCO
Falco 3 (A&M)
JANET JACKSON
Control (A&M)
LL COOL J
Radio (Def Jam/Columbia) .
LITTLE FEAT
Feats Don't Fail Me Now (Warner Bros)
MIAMI SOUND MACHINE
Primitive Love (Epic)
OZZY OSBOURNE
The Ultimate Sin (CBS Associated)
THE OUTFIELD
Play Deep (Columbia)
ROBERT PALMER
Riptide (Island/Atlantic)
SOUNDTRACK
Pretty In Pink (A&M)
WHITESNAKE
Slide It In (Geffen)
HANK WILLIAMS JR
High Notes (Warner Bros)

MAY 1986
BLACK SABBATH
Mob Rules (Warner Bros)
JULIAN LENNON
The Secret Value Of Daydreaming
(Atlantic)
MIKE & THE MECHANICS
Mike & the Mechanics (Atlantic)
PET SHOP BOYS
Please (EMI America/Capitol)
SCORPIONS
Lovedrive (Mercury/Polygram)
**BOB SEGER & THE
SILVER BULLET BAND**
Like A Rock (Capitol)
VAN HALEN
5150 (Warner Bros)
HANK WILLIAMS JR
Greatest Hits Vol 2 (Warner Bros)

JUNE 1986
ELTON JOHN
Ice On Fire (Geffen)
JOURNEY
Raised On Radio (Columbia)
JUDAS PRIEST
Turbo (Columbia)
PATTI LABELLE
Winner In Your (MCA)
BILLY OCEAN
Love Zone (Jive/Arista)
PRINCE AND THE REVOLUTION
Parade (Warner Bros)
ROLLING STONES
Dirty Work (Rolling Stones)
WHODINI
Back In Black (Jive/Arista)

JULY 1986
JACKSON BROWNE
Lives In The Balance (Asylum)

NEIL DIAMOND
Headed For The Future (Columbia)
FABULOUS THUNDERBIRDS
Tough Enough (CBS Associated)
JANE FONDA AND VARIOUS
Jane Fonda's Workout Record New & Improved (Columbia)
PETER GABRIEL
So (Geffen)
GTR
GTR (Arista)
MOODY BLUES
The Other Side Of Life (Polydor/Polygram)
RENE AND ANGELA
A Street Called Desire (Mercury)
RUN-DMC
Raising Hell (Profile)
SIMPLY RED
Picture Book (Elektra)
SOUNDTRACK
Top Gun (Columbia)
STARPOINT
Restless (Elektra)
.38 SPECIAL
Strength In Numbers (A&M)
UB40
Labour Of Love (A&M)

● PLATINUM
Albums
AUGUST 1985
DIRE STRAITS
Brothers In Arms (Warner Bros)
WHITNEY HOUSTON
Whitney Houston (Arista)
MÖTLEY CRÜE
Theatre Of Pain (Elektra)
THE POWER STATION
The Power Station (Capitol)
STING
The Dream Of The Blue Turtles (A&M)

SEPTEMBER 1985
PHIL COLLINS
Face Value (Atlantic)
EURYTHMICS
Be Yourself Tonight (RCA)
HEART
Heart (Capitol)
FREDDIE JACKSON
Rock Me Tonight (Capitol)
TOM PETTY AND THE HEARTBREAKERS
Southern Accents (MCA)
POINTER SISTERS
Contact (RCA)

OCTOBER 1985
JOHN COUGAR MELLENCAMP
Scarecrow (Riva)
BILLY JOEL
Greatest Hits Volumes 1/2 (Columbia)
LUCIANO PAVAROTTI
O Holy Night (London)

NOVEMBER 1985
ALABAMA
Alabama Christmas (RCA)
SAMMY HAGAR
VOA (Geffen)
KENNY LOGGINS
Keep The Fire (Columbia)
LOVERBOY
Lovin' Every Minute Of It (Columbia)
NIGHT RANGER
7 Wishes (MCA)
TALKING HEADS
Little Creatures (Sire)
VARIOUS
Miami Vice (MCA)
STEVIE WONDER
In Square Circle (Motown)

DECEMBER 1985
ARETHA FRANKLIN
Who's Zoomin' Who? (Arista)
STARSHIP
Knee Deep In The Hoopla (Grunt)
GEORGE WINSTON
December (Windham Hill)

JANUARY 1986
AEROSMITH
Aerosmith's Greatest Hits (Elektra)
ARCADIA
So Red The Rose (Capitol)
CARS
Cars Greatest Hits (EleKtra)
MR MISTER
Welcome To The Real World (RCA)
STEVIE NICKS
Rock A Little (Modern/Atlantic)
READY FOR THE WORLD
Ready For The World (MCA)
RUSH
Power Windows (Mercury)
SADE
Promise (Portrait)
BARBRA STREISAND
The Broadway Album (Columbia)
ZZ TOP
Afterburner (Warner Bros)

FEBRUARY 1986
CREEDENCE CLEARWATER REVIVAL
Chronicle (Fantasy)
VARIOUS
Soundtrack From Rocky IV (Scotti Bros)

MARCH 1986
A-HA
Hunting High And Low (Warner Bros)
ALABAMA
Alabama Greatest Hits (RCA)
THE HOOTERS
Nervous Night (Columbia)

APRIL 1986
BLACKFOOT
Strikes (Atco/Atlantic)
THE JUDDS
Why Not Me? (RCA)

OZZY OSBOURNE
The Ultimate Sin (CBS Associated)
VARIOUS
Children's Favourites Volume I (Disneyland/Vista)
HANK WILLIAMS JR
The Pressure Is On (Warner Bros)

MAY 1986
B-52s
The B-52s (Warner Bros)
BLACK SABBATH
Heaven And Hell (Warner Bros)
BLACK SABBATH
We Sold Our Soul To Rock 'N' Roll (Warner Bros)
DEVO
Freedom Of Choice (Warner Bros)
RICHARD PRYOR
Richard Pryor's Greatest Hits (Warner Bros)
BOB SEGER AND THE SILVER BULLET BAND
Like A Rock (Capitol)
SIMON AND GARFUNKEL
The Concert In Central Park (Warner Bros)
VAN HALEN
5150 (Warner Bros)

JUNE 1986
AMY GRANT
Unguarded (Myrrh)
JANET JACKSON
Control (A&M)
JOURNEY
Raised On Radio (Columbia)
PATTI LABELLE
Winner In You (MCA)
NEW EDITION
All For Love (MCA)
BILLY OCEAN
Love Zone (Jive/Arista)
THE OUTFIELD
Play Deep (Columbia)
PRINCE AND THE REVOLUTION
Parade (Warner Bros)
ROLLING STONES
Dirty Work (Rolling Stones)

JULY 1986
RUN-DMC
Raising Hell (Profile)
SOUNDTRACK
Top Gun (Columbia)
TALKING HEADS
Stop Making Sense (Sire)

● MULTI-PLATINUM
Albums
AUGUST 1985
PHIL COLLINS
No Jacket Required (Atlantic) (3m)
HUEY LEWIS AND THE NEWS
Sports (Chrysalis) (6m)
TEARS FOR FEARS
Songs From The Big Chair (Mercury) (3m)

SEPTEMBER 1985
DIRE STRAITS
Brothers In Arms *(Warner Bros)* (2m)
BILLY OCEAN
Suddenly *(Jive)* (2m)
BRUCE SPRINGSTEEN
Born In The USA *(Columbia)* (8m)
VARIOUS
Soundtrack from *The Big Chill (Motown)*
(2m)
VARIOUS
Soundtrack from *Beverly Hills Cop*
(MCA) (2m)

OCTOBER 1985
MADONNA
Madonna *(Sire)* (3m)
TEARS FOR FEARS
Songs From The Big Chair *(Mercury)* (3m)

NOVEMBER 1985
DIRE STRAITS
Brothers In Arms *(Warner Bros)* (3m)
WHITNEY HOUSTON
Whitney Houston *(Arista)* (2m)
MADONNA
Like A Virgin *(Sire)* (6m)
BRUCE SPRINGSTEEN
Born In The USA *(Columbia)* (10m)
VARIOUS
Miami Vice *(MCA)* (2m)

DECEMBER 1985
PHIL COLLINS
No Jacket Required *(Atlantic)* (4m)
JOHN COUGAR MELLENCAMP
Scarecrow *(Riva)* (2m)
HEART
Heart *(Capitol)* (2m)

POINTER SISTERS
Break Out *(Planet)* (3m)
LIONEL RICHIE
Can't Slow Down *(Motown)* (10m)
VARIOUS
Miami Vice *(MCA)* (3m)
WHAM!
Make It Big *(Columbia)* (4m)
STEVIE WONDER
In Square Circle *(Motown)* (2m)

JANUARY 1986
BRYAN ADAMS
Reckless *(A&M)* (4m)
PHIL COLLINS
Face Value *(Atlantic)* (2m)
DIRE STRAITS
Brothers In Arms *(Warner Bros)* (4m)
BILLY JOEL
Greatest Hits Volumes 1/2
(Columbia) (2m)
BARBRA STREISAND
The Broadway Album *(Columbia)* (2m)
TEARS FOR FEARS
Songs From The Big Chair *(Mercury)*
(4m)
ZZ TOP
Afterburner *(Warner Bros)* (2m)

FEBRUARY 1986
WHITNEY HOUSTON
Whitney Houston *(Arista)* (3m)
STING
The Dream Of The Blue Turtles *(A&M)*
(2m)
VARIOUS
Miami Vice *(MCA)* (4m)

MARCH 1986
HEART
Heart *(Capitol)* (3m)

WHITNEY HOUSTON
Whitney Houston *(Arista)* (4m)
KOOL AND THE GANG
Emergency *(De-Lite/Polygram)* (2m)
SADE
Promise *(Portrait/CBS)* (3m)

APRIL 1986
JOHN COUGAR MELLENCAMP
Scarecrow *(Riva)* (3m)
JOHN COUGAR MELLENCAMP
American Fool *(Riva)* (3m)
RONNIE MILSAP
Greatest Hits *(RCA)* (2m)
MÖTLEY CRÜE
Theatre of Pain *(Elektra)* (2m)
BARBRA STREISAND
The Broadway Album *(Columbia)* (3m)

MAY 1986
CHICAGO
Chicago 17 *(Full Moon/Warner Bros)*
(4m)
DIRE STRAITS
Brothers In Arms *(Warner Bros)* (5m)
WHITNEY HOUSTON
Whitney Houston *(Arista)* (5m)
VAN HALEN
5150 *(Warner Bros)* (2m)

JUNE 1986
PHIL COLLINS
No Jacket Required *(Atlantic)* (5m)
WHITNEY HOUSTON
Whitney Houston *(Arista)* (6m)
ZZ TOP
Afterburner *(Warner Bros)* (3m)

THE YEAR'S CHARTS

August 1985 – July 1986

United Kingdom record chart information
© Music Week/BBC/Gallup 1985 & 1986
Reprinted with permission

United States record chart information
© Billboard Publications Inc 1985 & 1986
Reprinted with permission

Featuring the *Billboard* and *Music Week* charts

S I N G L E S   UK   A L B U M S

#	Singles	Albums
1	INTO THE GROOVE — MADONNA (SIRE)	BROTHERS IN ARMS — DIRE STRAITS (VERTIGO)
2	THERE MUST BE AN ANGEL — EURYTHMICS (RCA)	BORN IN THE USA — BRUCE SPRINGSTEEN (CBS)
3	WE DON'T NEED ANOTHER HERO — TINA TURNER (CAPITOL)	BE YOURSELF TONIGHT — EURYTHMICS (RCA)
4	FRANKIE — SISTER SLEDGE (ATLANTIC)	SONGS FROM THE BIG CHAIR — TEARS FOR FEARS (MERCURY)
5	AXEL F — HAROLD FALTERMEYER (MCA)	THE SECRET OF ASSOCIATION — PAUL YOUNG (CBS)
6	LIVE IS LIFE — OPUS (POLYDOR)	THE KENNY ROGERS STORY — KENNY ROGERS (LIBERTY)
7	CHERISH — KOOL AND THE GANG (DE-LITE)	NO JACKET REQUIRED — PHIL COLLINS (VIRGIN)
8	MONEY FOR NOTHING — DIRE STRAITS (VERTIGO)	GREATEST HITS VOL 1 AND 2 — BILLY JOEL (CBS)
9	LIVING ON VIDEO — TRANS X (BOILING POINT)	ALL THROUGH THE NIGHT — ALED JONES (BBC)
10	ROUND AND AROUND — JAKI GRAHAM (EMI)	LIKE A VIRGIN — MADONNA (SIRE)
11	WHITE WEDDING — BILLY IDOL (CHRYSALIS)	THE DREAM OF THE BLUE TURTLES — STING (A&M)
12	CRAZY FOR YOU — MADONNA (GEFFEN)	THE UNFORGETTABLE FIRE — U2 (ISLAND)
13	MY TOOT TOOT — DENISE LASALLE (EPIC)	PHANTASMAGORIA — DAMNED (MCA)
14	IN YOUR CAR — COOL NOTES (ABSTRACT DANCE)	VOICES FROM THE HOLY LAND — BBC WELSH CHORUS (BBC)
15	SHE SELLS SANCTUARY — THE CULT (BEGGARS BANQUET)	UNDER A BLOOD RED SKY — U2 (ISLAND)
16	MONEY'S TOO TIGHT (TO MENTION) — SIMPLY RED (ELEKTRA)	MISPLACED CHILDHOOD — MARILLION (EMI)
17	DARE ME — POINTER SISTERS (RCA)	BOYS AND GIRLS — BRYAN FERRY (EG)
18	LET ME BE THE ONE — FIVE STAR (TENT)	OUT NOW — VARIOUS (CHRYSALIS/MCA)
19	I'M ON FIRE/BORN IN THE USA — BRUCE SPRINGSTEEN (CBS)	QUEEN GREATEST HITS — QUEEN (EMI)
20	IN BETWEEN DAYS — THE CURE (FICTION)	PRIVATE DANCER — TINA TURNER (CAPITOL)

S I N G L E S   US   A L B U M S

#	Singles	Albums
1	SHOUT — TEARS FOR FEARS (MERCURY)	SONGS FROM THE BIG CHAIR — TEARS FOR FEARS (MERCURY)
2	EVERYTIME YOU GO AWAY — PAUL YOUNG (COLUMBIA/CBS)	NO JACKET REQUIRED — PHIL COLLINS (ATLANTIC)
3	IF YOU LOVE SOMEBODY . . . — STING (A&M)	RECKLESS — BRYAN ADAMS (A&M)
4	YOU GIVE GOOD LOVE — WHITNEY HOUSTON (ARISTA)	BORN IN THE USA — BRUCE SPRINGSTEEN (COLUMBIA/CBS)
5	GLORY DAYS — BRUCE SPRINGSTEEN (COLUMBIA/CBS)	AROUND THE WORLD IN A DAY — PRINCE AND THE REVOLUTION (PAISLEY PARK)
6	NEVER SURRENDER — COREY HART (EMI AMERICA)	THE DREAM OF THE BLUE TURTLES — STING (A&M)
7	POWER OF LOVE — HUEY LEWIS AND THE NEWS (CHRYSALIS)	THE POWER STATION — POWER STATION (CAPITOL)
8	SENTIMENTAL STREET — NIGHT RANGER (CAMEL/MCA)	THEATRE OF PAIN — MOTLEY CRUE (ELEKTRA)
9	GET IT ON — POWER STATION (CAPITOL)	INVASION OF YOUR PRIVACY — RATT (ATLANTIC)
10	WHO'S HOLDING DONNA NOW? — DEBARGE (GORDY)	7 WISHES — NIGHT RANGER (CAMEL/MCA)
11	A VIEW TO A KILL — DURAN DURAN (CAPITOL)	LIKE A VIRGIN — MADONNA (SIRE)
12	FREEWAY OF LOVE — ARETHA FRANKLIN (ARISTA)	WHITNEY HOUSTON — WHITNEY HOUSTON (ARISTA)
13	PEOPLE ARE PEOPLE — DEPECHE MODE (SIRE)	BEVERLY HILLS COP — SOUNDTRACK (MCA)
14	RASPBERRY BERET — PRINCE AND THE REVOLUTION (PAISLEY PARK)	BE YOURSELF TONIGHT — EURYTHMICS (RCA)
15	SUMMER OF '69 — BRYAN ADAMS (A&M)	BROTHERS IN ARMS — DIRE STRAITS (WARNER BROS)
16	YOU SPIN ME ROUND — DEAD OR ALIVE (EPIC)	MAKE IT BIG — WHAM! (COLUMBIA/CBS)
17	WHAT ABOUT LOVE? — HEART (CAPITOL)	DREAM INTO ACTION — HOWARD JONES (ELEKTRA)
18	ST ELMO'S FIRE (MAN IN MOTION) — JOHN PARR (ATLANTIC)	GREATEST HITS VOL 1 AND 2 — BILLY JOEL (COLUMBIA/CBS)
19	19 — PAUL HARDCASTLE (CHRYSALIS)	VITAL SIGNS — SURVIVOR (SCOTTI BROS)
20	WE DON'T NEED ANOTHER HERO — TINA TURNER (CAPITOL)	LITTLE CREATURES — TALKING HEADS (SIRE)

S I N G L E S   UK   A L B U M S

#	Singles	Albums
1	INTO THE GROOVE — MADONNA (SIRE)	BROTHERS IN ARMS — DIRE STRAITS (VERTIGO)
2	THERE MUST BE AN ANGEL — EURYTHMICS (RCA)	BORN IN THE USA — BRUCE SPRINGSTEEN (CBS)
3	WE DON'T NEED ANOTHER HERO — TINA TURNER (CAPITOL)	BE YOURSELF TONIGHT — EURYTHMICS (RCA)
4	MONEY FOR NOTHING — DIRE STRAITS (VERTIGO)	SONGS FROM THE BIG CHAIR — TEARS FOR FEARS (MERCURY)
5	HOLIDAY — MADONNA (SIRE)	THE KENNY ROGERS STORY — KENNY ROGERS (LIBERTY)
6	WHITE WEDDING — BILLY IDOL (CHRYSALIS)	NO JACKET REQUIRED — PHIL COLLINS (VIRGIN)
7	I GOT YOU BABE — UB40/CHRISSIE HYNDE (DEP INTERNATIONAL)	THE SECRET OF ASSOCIATION — PAUL YOUNG (CBS)
8	CHERISH — KOOL AND THE GANG (DE-LITE)	GREATEST HITS VOL 1 AND 2 — BILLY JOEL (CBS)
9	LIVE IS LIFE — OPUS (POLYDOR)	THE UNFORGETTABLE FIRE — U2 (ISLAND)
10	FRANKIE — SISTER SLEDGE (ATLANTIC)	ALL THROUGH THE NIGHT — ALED JONES (BBC)
11	DON QUIXOTE — NIK KERSHAW (MCA)	PRIVATE DANCER — TINA TURNER (CAPITOL)
12	AXEL F — HAROLD FALTERMEYER (MCA)	UNDER A BLOOD RED SKY — U2 (ISLAND)
13	LIVING ON VIDEO — TRANS X (BOILING POINT)	THE DREAM OF THE BLUE TURTLES — STING (A&M)
14	ROUND AND AROUND — JAKI GRAHAM (EMI)	QUEEN GREATEST HITS — QUEEN (EMI)
15	CRAZY FOR YOU — MADONNA (GEFFEN)	MADONNA — MADONNA (WARNER BROS)
16	IN BETWEEN DAYS — THE CURE (FICTION)	MISPLACED CHILDHOOD — MARILLION (EMI)
17	GLORY DAYS — BRUCE SPRINGSTEEN (CBS)	LIKE A VIRGIN — MADONNA (SIRE)
18	MY TOOT TOOT — DENISE LASALLE (EPIC)	VOICES FROM THE HOLY LAND — BBC WELSH CHORUS (BBC)
19	SHE SELLS SANCTUARY — THE CULT (BEGGARS BANQUET)	PHANTASMAGORIA — DAMNED (MCA)
20	IN YOUR CAR — COOL NOTES (ABSTRACT DANCE)	GO WEST — GO WEST (CHRYSALIS)

S I N G L E S   US   A L B U M S

#	Singles	Albums
1	SHOUT — TEARS FOR FEARS (MERCURY)	RECKLESS — BRYAN ADAMS (A&M)
2	EVERYTIME YOU GO AWAY — PAUL YOUNG (COLUMBIA/CBS)	SONGS FROM THE BIG CHAIR — TEARS FOR FEARS (MERCURY)
3	IF YOU LOVE SOMEBODY . . . — STING (A&M)	NO JACKET REQUIRED — PHIL COLLINS (ATLANTIC)
4	NEVER SURRENDER — COREY HART (EMI AMERICA)	THE DREAM OF THE BLUE TURTLES — STING (A&M)
5	POWER OF LOVE — HUEY LEWIS AND THE NEWS (CHRYSALIS)	BORN IN THE USA — BRUCE SPRINGSTEEN (COLUMBIA/CBS)
6	WHO'S HOLDING DONNA NOW? — DEBARGE (GORDY)	THE POWER STATION — POWER STATION (CAPITOL)
7	GLORY DAYS — BRUCE SPRINGSTEEN (COLUMBIA/CBS)	THEATRE OF PAIN — MOTLEY CRUE (ELEKTRA)
8	FREEWAY OF LOVE — ARETHA FRANKLIN (ARISTA)	AROUND THE WORLD IN A DAY — PRINCE AND THE REVOLUTION (PAISLEY PARK)
9	GET IT ON — POWER STATION (CAPITOL)	INVASION OF YOUR PRIVACY — RATT (ATLANTIC)
10	YOU GIVE GOOD LOVE — WHITNEY HOUSTON (ARISTA)	BROTHERS IN ARMS — DIRE STRAITS (WARNER BROS)
11	ST ELMO'S FIRE (MAN IN MOTION) — JOHN PARR (ATLANTIC)	7 WISHES — NIGHT RANGER (CAMEL/MCA)
12	SUMMER OF '69 — BRYAN ADAMS (A&M)	WHITNEY HOUSTON — WHITNEY HOUSTON (ARISTA)
13	PEOPLE ARE PEOPLE — DEPECHE MODE (SIRE)	BE YOURSELF TONIGHT — EURYTHMICS (RCA)
14	WE DON'T NEED ANOTHER HERO — TINA TURNER (CAPITOL)	GREATEST HITS VOL 1 AND 2 — BILLY JOEL (COLUMBIA/CBS)
15	WHAT ABOUT LOVE? — HEART (CAPITOL)	LIKE A VIRGIN — MADONNA (SIRE)
16	YOU SPIN ME ROUND — DEAD OR ALIVE (EPIC)	MAKE IT BIG — WHAM! (COLUMBIA/CBS)
17	SENTIMENTAL STREET — NIGHT RANGER (CAMEL/MCA)	DREAM INTO ACTION — HOWARD JONES (ELEKTRA)
18	ROCK ME TONIGHT — FREDDIE JACKSON (CAPITOL)	BEVERLY HILLS COP — SOUNDTRACK (MCA)
19	A VIEW TO A KILL — DURAN DURAN (CAPITOL)	WORLD WIDE LIVE — SCORPIONS (MERCURY)
20	YOU'RE ONLY HUMAN — BILLY JOEL (COLUMBIA/CBS)	LITTLE CREATURES — TALKING HEADS (SIRE)

S I N G L E S UK A L B U M S

#	Singles	Albums
1	INTO THE GROOVE — MADONNA (SIRE)	NOW THAT'S WHAT I CALL MUSIC 5 — VARIOUS (EMI/VIRGIN)
2	HOLIDAY — MADONNA (SIRE)	LIKE A VIRGIN — MADONNA (SIRE)
3	I GOT YOU BABE — UB40/CHRISSIE HYNDE (DEP INTERNATIONAL)	BROTHERS IN ARMS — DIRE STRAITS (VERTIGO)
4	WE DON'T NEED ANOTHER HERO — TINA TURNER (CAPITOL)	BORN IN THE USA — BRUCE SPRINGSTEEN (CBS)
5	MONEY FOR NOTHING — DIRE STRAITS (VERTIGO)	BE YOURSELF TONIGHT — EURYTHMICS (RCA)
6	THERE MUST BE AN ANGEL — EURYTHMICS (RCA)	SONGS FROM THE BIG CHAIR — TEARS FOR FEARS (MERCURY)
7	WHITE WEDDING — BILLY IDOL (CHRYSALIS)	THE KENNY ROGERS STORY — KENNY ROGERS (LIBERTY)
8	DRIVE — CARS (ELEKTRA)	NO JACKET REQUIRED — PHIL COLLINS (VIRGIN)
9	RUNNING UP THAT HILL — KATE BUSH (EMI)	THE UNFORGETTABLE FIRE — U2 (ISLAND)
10	DON QUIXOTE — NIK KERSHAW (MCA)	MADONNA — MADONNA (WARNER BROS)
11	SAY I'M YOUR NUMBER ONE — PRINCESS (SUPREME)	UNDER A BLOOD RED SKY — U2 (ISLAND)
12	LIVE IS LIFE — OPUS (POLYDOR)	THE SECRET OF ASSOCIATION — PAUL YOUNG (CBS)
13	EXCITABLE — AMAZULU (ISLAND)	GO WEST — GO WEST (CHRYSALIS)
14	CHERISH — KOOL AND THE GANG (DE-LITE)	GREATEST HITS VOL 1 AND 2 — BILLY JOEL (CBS)
15	IN BETWEEN DAYS — THE CURE (FICTION)	QUEEN GREASTEST HITS — QUEEN (EMI)
16	AXEL F — HAROLD FALTERMEYER (MCA)	PRIVATE DANCER — TINA TURNER (CAPITOL)
17	FRANKIE — SISTER SLEDGE (ATLANTIC)	ALL THROUGH THE NIGHT — ALED JONES (BBC)
18	LIVING ON VIDEO — TRANS X (BOILING POINT)	RUM, SODOMY AND THE LASH — POGUES (STIFF)
19	CRAZY FOR YOU — MADONNA (GEFFEN)	STREET SOUNDS 13 — VARIOUS (STREETSOUNDS)
20	GLORY DAYS — BRUCE SPRINGSTEEN (CBS)	THE DREAM OF THE BLUE TURTLES — STING (A&M)

S I N G L E S US A L B U M S

#	Singles	Albums
1	SHOUT — TEARS FOR FEARS (MERCURY)	RECKLESS — BRYAN ADAMS (A&M)
2	POWER OF LOVE — HUEY LEWIS AND THE NEWS (CHRYSALIS)	SONGS FROM THE BIG CHAIR — TEARS FOR FEARS (MERCURY)
3	NEVER SURRENDER — COREY HART (EMI AMERICA)	NO JACKET REQUIRED — PHIL COLLINS (ATLANTIC)
4	IF YOU LOVE SOMEBODY . . . — STING (A&M)	THE DREAM OF THE BLUE TURTLES — STING (A&M)
5	FREEWAY OF LOVE — ARETHA FRANKLIN (ARISTA)	BORN IN THE USA — BRUCE SPRINGSTEEN (COLUMBIA/CBS)
6	EVERYTIME YOU GO AWAY — PAUL YOUNG (COLUMBIA/CBS)	THEATRE OF PAIN — MOTLEY CRUE (ELEKTRA)
7	ST ELMO'S FIRE (MAN IN MOTION) — JOHN PARR (ATLANTIC)	BROTHERS IN ARMS — DIRE STRAITS (WARNER BROS)
8	WHO'S HOLDING DONNA NOW? — DEBARGE (GORDY)	THE POWER STATION — POWER STATION (CAPITOL)
9	SUMMER OF '69 — BRYAN ADAMS (A&M)	AROUND THE WORLD IN A DAY — PRINCE AND THE REVOLUTION (PAISLEY PARK)
10	WE DON'T NEED ANOTHER HERO — TINA TURNER (CAPITOL)	7 WISHES — NIGHT RANGER (CAMEL/MCA)
11	YOU SPIN ME ROUND — DEAD OR ALIVE (EPIC)	INVASION OF YOUR PRIVACY — RATT (ATLANTIC)
12	WHAT ABOUT LOVE? — HEART (CAPITOL)	WHITNEY HOUSTON — WHITNEY HOUSTON (ARISTA)
13	GLORY DAYS — BRUCE SPRINGSTEEN (COLMBIA/CBS)	GREATEST HITS VOL 1 AND 2 — BILLY JOEL (COLUMBIA/CBS)
14	GET IT ON — POWER STATION (CAPITOL)	BE YOURSELF TONIGHT — EURYTHMICS (RCA)
15	CHERISH — KOOL AND THE GANG (DE-LITE)	DREAM INTO ACTION — HOWARD JONES (ELEKTRA)
16	PEOPLE ARE PEOPLE — DEPECHE MODE (SIRE)	LIKE A VIRGIN — MADONNA (SIRE)
17	INVINCIBLE — PAT BENATAR (MCA)	MAKE IT BIG — WHAM! (COLUMBIA/CBS)
18	YOU'RE ONLY HUMAN — BILLY JOEL (COLUMBIA/CBS)	WORLD WIDE LIVE — SCORPIONS (MERCURY)
19	DON'T LOSE MY NUMBER — PHIL COLLINS (ATLANTIC)	THE SECRET OF ASSOCIATION — PAUL YOUNG (COLUMBIA/CBS)
20	YOU GIVE GOOD LOVE — WHITNEY HOUSTON (ARISTA)	HEART — HEART (CAPITOL)

S I N G L E S UK A L B U M S

#	Singles	Albums
1	INTO THE GROOVE — MADONNA (SIRE)	NOW THAT'S WHAT I CALL MUSIC 5 — VARIOUS (EMI/VIRGIN)
2	I GOT YOU BABE — UB40/CHRISSIE HYNDE (DEP INTERNATIONAL)	LIKE A VIRGIN — MADONNA (SIRE)
3	HOLIDAY — MADONNA (SIRE)	BROTHERS IN ARMS — DIRE STRAITS (VERTIGO)
4	RUNNING UP THAT HILL — KATE BUSH (EMI)	NO JACKET REQUIRED — PHIL COLLINS (VIRGIN)
5	DRIVE — CARS (ELEKTRA)	BORN IN THE USA — BRUCE SPRINGSTEEN (CBS)
6	MONEY FOR NOTHING — DIRE STRAITS (VERTIGO)	MADONNA — MADONNA (WARNER BROS)
7	WE DON'T NEED ANOTHER HERO — TINA TURNER (CAPITOL)	SONGS FROM THE BIG CHAIR — TEARS FOR FEARS (MERCURY)
8	WHITE WEDDING — BILLY IDOL (CHRYSALIS)	BE YOURSELF TONIGHT — EURYTHMICS (RCA)
9	THERE MUST BE AN ANGEL — EURYTHMICS (RCA)	THE KENNY ROGERS STORY — KENNY ROGERS (LIBERTY)
10	SAY I'M YOUR NUMBER ONE — PRINCESS (SUPREME)	THE UNFORGETTABLE FIRE — U2 (ISLAND)
11	TARZAN BOY — BALTIMORA (COLUMBIA)	PRIVATE DANCER — TINA TURNER (CAPITOL)
12	EXCITABLE — AMAZULU (ISLAND)	GO WEST — GO WEST (CHRYSALIS)
13	ALONE WITHOUT YOU — KING (CBS)	RUM, SODOMY AND THE LASH — POGUES (STIFF)
14	DON QUIXOTE — NIK KERSHAW (MCA)	QUEEN GREATEST HITS — QUEEN (EMI)
15	I WONDER IF I TAKE YOU HOME — LISA LISA & CULT JAM & FULL FORCE (CBS)	UNDER A BLOOD RED SKY — U2 (ISLAND)
16	LIVE IS LIFE — OPUS (POLYDOR)	THE SECRET OF ASSOCIATION — PAUL YOUNG (CBS)
17	YOU'RE THE ONE FOR ME — D TRAIN (PRELUDE)	WIDE AWAKE IN AMERICA — U2 (ISLAND)
18	CHERISH — KOOL AND THE GANG (DE-LITE)	GREATEST HITS VOL 1 AND 2 — BILLY JOEL (CBS)
19	TAKE ME HOME — PHIL COLLINS (VIRGIN)	NIGHT BEAT — VARIOUS (STYLUS)
20	IN BETWEEN DAYS — THE CURE (FICTION)	THE DREAM OF THE BLUE TURTLES — STING (A&M)

S I N G L E S US A L B U M S

#	Singles	Albums
1	POWER OF LOVE — HUEY LEWIS AND THE NEWS (CHRYSALIS)	SONGS FROM THE BIG CHAIR — TEARS FOR FEARS (MERCURY)
2	SHOUT — TEARS FOR FEARS (MERCURY)	RECKLESS — BRYAN ADAMS (A&M)
3	NEVER SURRENDER — COREY HART (EMI AMERICA)	THE DREAM OF THE BLUE TURTLES — STING (A&M)
4	ST ELMO'S FIRE (MAN IN MOTION) — JOHN PARR (ATLANTIC)	NO JACKET REQUIRED — PHIL COLLINS (ATLANTIC)
5	FREEWAY OF LOVE — ARETHA FRANKLIN (ARISTA)	BROTHERS IN ARMS — DIRE STRAITS (WARNER BROS)
6	WE DON'T NEED ANOTHER HERO — TINA TURNER (CAPITOL)	1BORN IN THE USA — BRUCE SPRINGSTEEN (COLUMBIA/CBS)
7	SUMMER OF '69 — BRYAN ADAMS (A&M)	THEATRE OF PAIN — MOTLEY CRUE (ELEKTRA)
8	IF YOU LOVE SOMEBODY . . . — STING (A&M)	THE POWER STATION — POWER STATION (CAPITOL)
9	EVERYTIME YOU GO AWAY — PAUL YOUNG (COLUMBIA/CBS)	GREATEST HITS VOL 1 AND 2 — BILLY JOEL (COLUMBIA/CBS)
10	WHAT ABOUT LOVE? — HEART (CAPITOL)	INVASION OF YOUR PRIVACY — RATT (ATLANTIC)
11	WHO'S HOLDING DONNA NOW? — DEBARGE (GORDY)	WHITNEY HOUSTON — WHITNEY HOUSTON (ARISTA)
12	CHERISH — KOOL AND THE GANG (DE-LITE)	AROUND THE WORLD IN A DAY — PRINCE AND THE REVOLUTION (PAISLEY PARK)
13	DON'T LOSE MY NUMBER — PHIL COLLINS (ATLANTIC)	7 WISHES — NIGHT RANGER (CAMEL/MCA)
14	YOU'RE ONLY HUMAN — BILLY JOEL (COLUMBIA/CBS)	BE YOURSELF TONIGHT — EURYTHMICS (RCA)
15	INVINCIBLE — PAT BENATAR (MCA)	HEART — HEART (CAPITOL)
16	YOU SPIN ME ROUND — DEAD OR ALIVE (EPIC)	MAKE IT BIG — WHAM! (COLUMBIA/CBS)
17	MONEY FOR NOTHING — DIRE STRAITS (WARNER BROS)	LIKE A VIRGIN — MADONNA (SIRE)
18	POP LIFE — PRINCE AND THE REVOLUTION (WARNER BROS)	WORLD WIDE LIVE — SCORPIONS (MERCURY)
19	FREEDOM — WHAM! (COLUMBIA/CBS)	THE SECRET OF ASSOCIATION — PAUL YOUNG (COLUMBIA/CBS)
20	DARE ME — POINTER SISTERS (PLANET)	BOY IN THE BOX — COREY HART (EMI AMERICA)

WEEK ENDING AUGUST 31 1985
S I N G L E S UK A L B U M S

#	Singles	Albums
1	I GOT YOU BABE — UB40/CHRISSIE HYNDE (DEP INTERNATIONAL)	NOW THAT'S WHAT I CALL MUSIC 5 — VARIOUS (EMI/VIRGIN)
2	INTO THE GROOVE — MADONNA (SIRE)	LIKE A VIRGIN — MADONNA (SIRE)
3	RUNNING UP THAT HILL — KATE BUSH (EMI)	BROTHERS IN ARMS — DIRE STRAITS (VERTIGO)
4	DRIVE — CARS (ELEKTRA)	NO JACKET REQUIRED — PHIL COLLINS (VIRGIN)
5	TARZAN BOY — BALTIMORA (COLUMBIA)	BORN IN THE USA — BRUCE SPRINGSTEEN (CBS)
6	HOLIDAY — MADONNA (SIRE)	THE FIRST ALBUM — MADONNA (WARNER BROS)
7	SAY I'M YOUR NUMBER ONE — PRINCESS (SUPREME)	SONGS FROM THE BIG CHAIR — TEARS FOR FEARS (MERCURY)
8	MONEY FOR NOTHING — DIRE STRAITS (VERTIGO)	BE YOURSELF TONIGHT — EURYTHMICS (RCA)
9	ALONE WITHOUT YOU — KING (CBS)	THE KENNY ROGERS STORY — KENNY ROGERS (LIBERTY)
10	WE DON'T NEED ANOTHER HERO — TINA TURNER (CAPITOL)	PRIVATE DANCER — TINA TURNER (CAPITOL)
11	WHITE WEDDING — BILLY IDOL (CHRYSALIS)	WIDE AWAKE IN AMERICA — U2 (ISLAND)
12	I WONDER IF I TAKE YOU HOME — LISA LISA & CULT JAM & FULL FORCE (CBS)	THE UNFORGETTABLE FIRE — U2 (ISLAND)
13	EXCITABLE — AMAZULU (ISLAND)	GO WEST — GO WEST (CHRYSALIS)
14	THERE MUST BE AN ANGEL — EURYTHMICS (RCA)	UNDER A BLOOD RED SKY — U2 (ISLAND)
15	YOU'RE THE ONE FOR ME — D TRAIN (PRELUDE)	NIGHT BEAT — VARIOUS (STYLUS)
16	I CAN DREAM ABOUT YOU — DAN HARTMAN (MCA)	RUM, SODOMY AND THE LASH — POGUES (STIFF)
17	TAKES A LITTE TIME — TOTAL CONTRAST (LONDON)	GREATEST HITS VOL 1 AND 2 — BILLY JOEL (CBS)
18	BODY AND SOUL — MAI TAI (VIRGIN)	QUEEN GREATEST HITS — QUEEN (EMI)
19	TAKE ME HOME — PHIL COLLINS (VIRGIN)	THE DREAM OF THE BLUE TURTLES — STING (A&M)
20	CHERISH — KOOL AND THE GANG (DE-LITE)	THE SECRET OF ASSOCIATION — PAUL YOUNG (CBS)

S I N G L E S US A L B U M S

#	Singles	Albums
1	POWER OF LOVE — HUEY LEWIS AND THE NEWS (CHRYSALIS)	BROTHERS IN ARMS — DIRE STRAITS (WARNER BROS)
2	ST ELMO'S FIRE (MAN IN MOTION) — JOHN PARR (ATLANTIC)	SONGS FROM THE BIG CHAIR — TEARS FOR FEARS (MERCURY)
3	FREEWAY OF LOVE — ARETHA FRANKLIN (ARISTA)	THE DREAM OF THE BLUE TURTLES — STING (A&M)
4	WE DON'T NEED ANOTHER HERO — TINA TURNER (CAPITOL)	RECKLESS — BRYAN ADAMS (A&M)
5	SUMMER OF '69 — BRYAN ADAMS (A&M)	BORN IN THE USA — BRUCE SPRINGSTEEN (COLUMBIA/CBS)
6	SHOUT — TEARS FOR FEARS (MERCURY)	NO JACKET REQUIRED — PHIL COLLINS (ATLANTIC)
7	NEVER SURRENDER — COREY HART (EMI AMERICA)	THEATRE OF PAIN — MOTLEY CRUE (ELEKTRA)
8	CHERISH — KOOL AND THE GANG (DE-LITE)	GREATEST HITS VOL 1 & 2 — BILLY JOEL (COLUMBIA/CBS)
9	YOU'RE ONLY HUMAN — BILLY JOEL (COLUMBIA/CBS)	WHITNEY HOUSTON — WHITNEY HOUSTON (ARISTA)
10	MONEY FOR NOTHING — DIRE STRAITS (WARNER BROS)	INVASION OF YOUR PRIVACY — RATT (ATLANTIC)
11	DON'T LOSE MY NUMBER — PHIL COLLINS (ATLANTIC)	AROUND THE WORLD IN A DAY — PRINCE AND THE REVOLUTION (PAISLEY PARK)
12	INVINCIBLE — PAT BENATAR (MCA)	BE YOURSELF TONIGHT — EURYTHMICS (RCA)
13	POP LIFE — PRINCE AND THE REVOLUTION (WARNER BROS)	7 WISHES — NIGHT RANGER (CAMEL/MCA)
14	FREEDOM — WHAM! (COLUMBIA/CBS)	HEART — HEART (CAPITOL)
15	WHAT ABOUT LOVE? — HEART (CAPITOL)	THE POWER STATION — POWER STATION (CAPITOL)
16	DARE ME — POINTER SISTERS (PLANET)	LIKE A VIRGIN — MADONNA (SIRE)
17	SMOKIN' IN THE BOYS ROOM — MOTLEY CRUE (ELEKTRA)	MAKE IT BIG — WHAM! (COLUMBIA/CBS)
18	IF YOU LOVE SOMEBODY... — STING (A&M)	WORLD WIDE LIVE — SCORPIONS (MERCURY)
19	EVERYTIME YOU GO AWAY — PAUL YOUNG (COLUMBIA/CBS)	THE SECRET OF ASSOCIATION — PAUL YOUNG (COLUMBIA/CBS)
20	LIFE IN ONE DAY — HOWARD JONES (ELEKTRA)	BOY IN THE BOX — COREY HART (EMI AMERICA)

WEEK ENDING SEPTEMBER 7 1985
S I N G L E S UK A L B U M S

#	Singles	Albums
1	DANCING IN THE STREET — DAVID BOWIE/MICK JAGGER (EMI AMERICA)	NOW THAT'S WHAT I CALL MUSIC 5 — VARIOUS (EMI/VIRGIN)
2	I GOT YOU BABE — UB40/CHRISSIE HYNDE (DEP INTERNATIONAL)	LIKE A VIRGIN — MADONNA (SIRE)
3	TARZAN BOY — BALTIMORA (COLUMBIA)	BROTHERS IN ARMS — DIRE STRAITS (VERTIGO)
4	INTO THE GROOVE — MADONNA (SIRE)	SACRED HEART — DIO (VERTIGO)
5	RUNNING UP THAT HILL — KATE BUSH (EMI)	THE KENNY ROGERS STORY — KENNY ROGERS (LIBERTY)
6	DRIVE — CARS (ELEKTRA)	SONGS FROM THE BIG CHAIR — TEARS FOR FEARS (MERCURY)
7	SAY I'M YOUR NUMBER ONE — PRINCESS (SUPREME)	THE HEAD ON THE DOOR — THE CURE (FICTION)
8	ALONE WITHOUT YOU — KING (CBS)	NO JACKET REQUIRED — PHIL COLLINS (VIRGIN)
9	MONEY FOR NOTHING — DIRE STRAITS (VERTIGO)	THE FIRST ALBUM — MADONNA (SIRE)
10	HOLDING OUT FOR A HERO — BONNIE TYLER (CBS)	BORN IN THE USA — BRUCE SPRINGSTEEN (CBS)
11	BODY AND SOUL — MAI TAI (VIRGIN)	WORLD SERVICE — SPEAR OF DESTINY (EPIC/BURNING ROME)
12	I CAN DREAM ABOUT YOU — DAN HARTMAN (MCA)	THE UNFORGETTABLE FIRE — U2 (ISLAND)
13	I WONDER IF I TAKE YOU HOME — LISA LISA & CULT JAM & FULL FORCE (CBS)	BE YOURSELF TONIGHT — EURYTHMICS (RCA)
14	HOLIDAY — MADONNA (SIRE)	PRIVATE DANCER — TINA TURNER (CAPITOL)
15	DON'T MESS WITH DOCTOR DREAM — THOMPSON TWINS (ARISTA)	QUEEN GREATEST HITS — QUEEN (EMI)
16	KNOCK ON WOOD/LIGHT MY FIRE — AMII STEWART (SEDITION)	UNDER A BLOOD RED SKY — U2 (ISLAND)
17	WHITE WEDDING — BILLY IDOL (CHRYSALIS)	WIDE AWAKE IN AMERICA — U2 (ISLAND)
18	WE DON'T NEED ANOTHER HERO — TINA TURNER (CAPITOL)	RECKLESS — BRYAN ADAMS (A&M)
19	YOU'RE THE ONE FOR ME — D TRAIN (PRELUDE)	BOYS AND GIRLS — BRYAN FERRY (EG)
20	PART TIME LOVER — STEVIE WONDER (MOTOWN)	THE DREAM OF THE BLUE TURTLES — STING (A&M)

S I N G L E S US A L B U M S

#	Singles	Albums
1	ST ELMO'S FIRE (MAN IN MOTION) — JOHN PARR (ATLANTIC)	BROTHERS IN ARMS — DIRE STRAITS (WARNER BROS)
2	POWER OF LOVE — HUEY LEWIS AND THE NEWS (CHRYSALIS)	THE DREAM OF THE BLUE TURTLES — STING (A&M)
3	WE DON'T NEED ANOTHER HERO — TINA TURNER (CAPITOL)	SONGS FROM THE BIG CHAIR — TEARS FOR FEARS (MERCURY)
4	FREEWAY OF LOVE — ARETHA FRANKLIN (ARISTA)	RECKLESS — BRYAN ADAMS (A&M)
5	SUMMER OF '69 — BRYAN ADAMS (A&M)	BORN IN THE USA — BRUCE SPRINGSTEEN (COLUMBIA/CBS)
6	MONEY FOR NOTHING — DIRE STRAITS (WARNER BROS)	NO JACKET REQUIRED — PHIL COLLINS (ATLANTIC)
7	CHERISH — KOOL AND THE GANG (DE-LITE)	GREATEST HITS VOL 1 AND 2 — BILLY JOEL (COLUMBIA/CBS)
8	DON'T LOSE MY NUMBER — PHIL COLLINS (ATLANTIC)	THREATRE OF PAIN — MOTLEY CRUE (ELEKTRA)
9	YOU'RE ONLY HUMAN — BILLY JOEL (COLUMBIA/CBS)	WHITNEY HOUSTON — WHITNEY HOUSTON (ARISTA)
10	POP LIFE — PRINCE AND THE REVOLUTION (WARNER BROS)	HEART — HEART (CAPITOL)
11	INVINCIBLE — PAT BENATAR (CHRYSALIS)	AROUND THE WORLD IN A DAY — PRINCE AND THE REVOLUTION (PAISLEY PARK)
12	FREEDOM — WHAM! (COLUMBIA/CBS)	INVASION OF YOUR PRIVACY — RATT (ATLANTIC)
13	SHOUT — TEARS FOR FEARS (MERCURY)	7 WISHES — NIGHT RANGER (CAMEL/MCA)
14	NEVER SURRENDER — COREY HART (EMI AMERICA)	BE YOURSELF TONIGHT — EURYTHMICS (RCA)
15	DARE ME — POINTER SISTERS (PLANET)	MAKE IT BIG — WHAM! (COLUMBIA/CBS)
16	SMOKIN' IN THE BOYS ROOM — MOTLEY CRUE (ELEKTRA)	LIKE A VIRGIN — MADONNA (SIRE)
17	DRESS YOU UP — MADONNA (SIRE)	WORLD WIDE LIVE — SCORPIONS (MERCURY)
18	OH SHEILA — READY FOR THE WORLD (MCA)	BACK TO THE FUTURE — SOUNDTRACK (MCA)
19	LIFE IN ONE DAY — HOWARD JONES (ELEKTRA)	THE SECRET OF ASSOCIATION — PAUL YOUNG (COLUMBIA/CBS)
20	WHAT ABOUT LOVE? — HEART (CAPITOL)	BOY IN THE BOX — COREY HART (EMI AMERICA)

WEEK ENDING SEPTEMBER 14 1985

S I N G L E S UK A L B U M S

#	Singles	Albums
1	DANCING IN THE STREET — DAVID BOWIE/MICK JAGGER (EMI AMERICA)	NOW THAT'S WHAT I CALL MUSIC 5 — VARIOUS (EMI/VIRGIN)
2	HOLDING OUT FOR A HERO — BONNIE TYLER (CBS)	LIKE A VIRGIN — MADONNA (SIRE)
3	I GOT YOU BABE — UB40/CHRISSIE HYNDE (DEP INTERNATIONAL)	BROTHERS IN ARMS — DIRE STRAITS (VERTIGO)
4	TARZAN BOY — BALTIMORA (COLUMBIA)	THE KENNY ROGERS STORY — KENNY ROGERS (LIBERTY)
5	PART TIME LOVER — STEVIE WONDER (MOTOWN)	SONGS FROM THE BIG CHAIR — TEARS FOR FEARS (MERCURY)
6	DRIVE — CARS (ELEKTRA)	NO JACKET REQUIRED — PHIL COLLINS (VIRGIN)
7	INTO THE GROOVE — MADONNA (SIRE)	BORN IN THE USA — BRUCE SPRINGSTEEN (CBS)
8	RUNNING UP THAT HILL — KATE BUSH (EMI)	THE FIRST ALBUM — MADONNA (SIRE)
9	SAY I'M YOUR NUMBER ONE — PRINCESS (SUPREME)	THE HEAD ON THE DOOR — THE CURE (FICTION)
10	BODY AND SOUL — MAI TAI (VIRGIN)	BOYS AND GIRLS — BRYAN FERRY (EG)
11	ALONE WITHOUT YOU — KING (CBS)	SACRED HEART — DIO (VERTIGO)
12	KNOCK ON WOOD/LIGHT MY FIRE — AMII STEWART (SEDITION)	RUN FOR COVER — GARY MOORE (10 RECORDS)
13	LAVENDER BLUE — MARILLION (EMI)	UNDER A BLOOD RED SKY — U2 (ISLAND)
14	MONEY FOR NOTHING — DIRE STRAITS (VERTIGO)	PRIVATE DANCER — TINA TURNER (CAPITOL)
15	I CAN DREAM ABOUT YOU — DAN HARTMAN (MCA)	THE UNFORGETTABLE FIRE — U2 (ISLAND)
16	DON'T MESS WITH DOCTOR DREAM — THOMPSON TWINS (ARISTA)	MISPLACED CHILDHOOD — MARILLION (EMI)
17	I WONDER IF I TAKE YOU HOME — LISA LISA & CULT JAM & FULL FORCE (CBS)	VITAL IDOL — BILLY IDOL (CHRYSALIS)
18	YESTERDAY'S MEN — MADNESS (ZARJAZZ)	RECKLESS — BRYAN ADAMS (A&M)
19	THE POWER OF LOVE — HUEY LEWIS AND THE NEWS (CHRYSALIS)	BE YOURSELF TONIGHT — EURYTHMICS (RCA)
20	WHITE WEDDING — BILLY IDOL (CHRYSALIS)	BAGGARIDDIM — UB40 (DEP INTERNATIONAL)

S I N G L E S US A L B U M S

#	Singles	Albums
1	ST ELMO'S FIRE (MAN IN MOTION) — JOHN PARR (ATLANTIC)	BROTHERS IN ARMS — DIRE STRAITS (WARNER BROS)
2	WE DON'T NEED ANOTHER HERO — TINA TURNER (CAPITOL)	THE DREAM OF THE BLUE TURTLES — STING (A&M)
3	MONEY FOR NOTHING — DIRE STRAITS (WARNER BROS)	SONGS FROM THE BIG CHAIR — TEARS FOR FEARS (MERCURY)
4	CHERISH — KOOL AND THE GANG (DE-LITE)	RECKLESS — BRYAN ADAMS (A&M)
5	POWER OF LOVE — HUEY LEWIS AND THE NEWS (CHRYSALIS)	BORN IN THE USA — BRUCE SPRINGSTEEN (COLUMBIA/CBS)
6	DON'T LOSE MY NUMBER — PHIL COLLINS (ATLANTIC)	NO JACKET REQUIRED — PHIL COLLINS (ATLANTIC)
7	FREEWAY OF LOVE — ARETHA FRANKLIN (ARISTA)	GREATEST HITS VOL 1 AND 2 — BILLY JOEL (COLUMBIA/CBS)
8	FREEDOM — WHAM! (COLUMBIA/CBS)	WHITNEY HOUSTON — WHITNEY HOUSTON (ARISTA)
9	POP LIFE — PRINCE AND THE REVOLUTION (WARNER BROS)	THEATRE OF PAIN — MOTLEY CRUE (ELEKTRA)
10	INVINCIBLE — PAT BENATAR (CHRYSALIS)	HEART — HEART (CAPITOL)
11	SUMMER OF '69 — BRYAN ADAMS (A&M)	AROUND THE WORLD IN A DAY — PRINCE AND THE REVOLUTION (PAISLEY PARK)
12	YOU'RE ONLY HUMAN — BILLY JOEL (COLUMBIA/CBS)	INVASION OF YOUR PRIVACY — RATT (ATLANTIC)
13	DARE ME — POINTER SISTERS (PLANET)	BE YOURSELF TONIGHT — EURYTHMICS (RCA)
14	DRESS YOU UP — MADONNA (SIRE)	7 WISHES — NIGHT RANGER (CAMEL/MCA)
15	OH SHEILA — READY FOR THE WORLD (MCA)	MAKE IT BIG — WHAM! (COLUMBIA/CBS)
16	SMOKIN' IN THE BOYS ROOM — MOTLEY CRUE (ELEKTRA)	LIKE A VIRGIN — MADONNA (SIRE)
17	TAKE ON ME — A-HA (WARNER BROS)	WORLD WIDE LIVE — SCORPIONS (MERCURY)
18	SAVING ALL MY LOVE FOR YOU — WHITNEY HOUSTON (ARISTA)	BACK TO THE FUTURE — SOUNDTRACK (MCA)
19	LONELY OL' NIGHT — JOHN COUGAR MELLENCAMP (RIVA)	THE SECRET OF ASSOCIATION — PAUL YOUNG (COLUMBIA/CBS)
20	CRY — GODLEY AND CREME (POLYDOR)	BOY IN THE BOX — COREY HART (EMI AMERICA)

WEEK ENDING SEPTEMBER 21 1985

S I N G L E S UK A L B U M S

#	Singles	Albums
1	DANCING IN THE STREET — DAVID BOWIE/MICK JAGGER (EMI AMERICA)	LIKE A VIRGIN — MADONNA (SIRE)
2	HOLDING OUT FOR A HERO — BONNIE TYLER (CBS)	NOW THAT'S WHAT I CALL MUSIC 5 — VARIOUS (EMI/VIRGIN)
3	PART TIME LOVER — STEVIE WONDER (MOTOWN)	BROTHERS IN ARMS — DIRE STRAITS (VERTIGO)
4	TARZAN BOY — BALTIMORA (COLUMBIA)	THE KENNY ROGERS STORY — KENNY ROGERS (LIBERTY)
5	LAVENDER — MARILLION (EMI)	MISPLACED CHILDHOOD — MARILLION (EMI)
6	I GOT YOU BABE — UB40/CHRISSIE HYNDE (DEP INTERNATIONAL)	NO JACKET REQUIRED — PHIL COLLINS (VIRGIN)
7	KNOCK ON WOOD/LIGHT MY FIRE — AMII STEWART (SEDITION)	SONG FROM THE BIG CHAIR — TEARS FOR FEARS (MERCURY)
8	IF I WAS — MIDGE URE (CHRYSALIS)	THE FIRST ALBUM — MADONNA (SIRE)
9	BODY AND SOUL — MAI TAI (VIRGIN)	THE HEAD ON THE DOOR — THE CURE (FICTION)
10	ANGEL — MADONNA (SIRE)	BOYS AND GIRLS — BRYAN FERRY (EG)
11	THE POWER OF LOVE — HUEY LEWIS AND THE NEWS (CHRYSALIS)	BORN IN THE USA — BRUCE SPRINGSTEEN (CBS)
12	INTO THE GROOVE — MADONNA (SIRE)	RUN FOR COVER — GARY MOORE (10 RECORDS)
13	DRIVE — CARS (ELEKTRA)	OPEN TOP CARS & GIRLS IN T-SHIRTS — VARIOUS (TELSTAR)
14	SAY I'M YOUR NUMBER ONE — PRINCESS (SUPREME)	BAGGARIDDIM — UB40 (DEP INTERNATIONAL)
15	RUNNING UP THAT HILL — KATE BUSH (EMI)	UNDER A BLOOD RED SKY — U2 (ISLAND)
16	BODY ROCK — MARIA VIDAL (EMI AMERICA)	PRIVATE DANCER — TINA TURNER (CAPITOL)
17	SHE'S SO BEAUTIFUL — CLIFF RICHARD (EMI)	THE UNFORGETTABLE FIRE — U2 (ISLAND)
18	LEAN ON ME (AH-LI-AYO) — RED BOX (SIRE)	THE DREAM OF THE BLUE TURTLES — STING (A&M)
19	ALONE WITHOUT YOU — KING (CBS)	VITAL IDOL — BILLY IDOL (CHRYSALIS)
20	YESTERDAY'S MEN — MADNESS (ZARJAZZ)	BE YOURSELF TONIGHT — EURYTHMICS (RCA)

S I N G L E S US A L B U M S

#	Singles	Albums
1	MONEY FOR NOTHING — DIRE STRAITS (WARNER BROS)	BROTHERS IN ARMS — DIRE STRAITS (WARNER BROS)
2	CHERISH — KOOL AND THE GANG (DE-LITE)	THE DREAM OF THE BLUE TURTLES — STING (A&M)
3	ST ELMO'S FIRE (MAN IN MOTION) — JOHN PARR (ATLANTIC)	SONGS FROM THE BIG CHAIR — TEARS FOR FEARS (MERCURY)
4	WE DON'T NEED ANOTHER HERO — TINA TURNER (CAPITOL)	BORN IN THE USA — BRUCE SPRINGSTEEN (COLUMBIA/CBS)
5	DON'T LOSE MY NUMBER — PHIL COLLINS (ATLANTIC)	RECKLESS — BRYAN ADAMS (A&M)
6	FREEDOM — WHAM! (COLUMBIA/CBS)	NO JACKET REQUIRED — PHIL COLLINS (ATLANTIC)
7	POP LIFE — PRINCE AND THE REVOLUTION (WARNER BROS)	GREATEST HITS VOL 1 AND 2 — BILLY JOEL (COLUMBIA/CBS)
8	POWER OF LOVE — HUEY LEWIS AND THE NEWS (CHRYSALIS)	WHITNEY HOUSTON — WHITNEY HOUSTON (ARISTA)
9	OH SHIELA — READY FOR THE WORLD (MCA)	HEART — HEART (CAPITOL)
10	DRESS YOU UP — MADONNA (SIRE)	THEATRE OF PAIN — MOTLEY CRUE (ELEKTRA)
11	DARE ME — POINTER SISTERS (PLANET)	MAKE IT BIG — WHAM! (COLUMBIA/CBS)
12	INVINCIBLE — PAT BENATAR (MCA)	AROUND THE WORLD IN A DAY — PRINCE AND THE REVOLUTION (PAISLEY PARK)
13	TAKE ON ME — A-HA (WARNER BROS)	BACK TO THE FUTURE — SOUNDTRACK (MCA)
14	SAVING ALL MY LOVE FOR YOU — WHITNEY HOUSTON (ARISTA)	7 WISHES — NIGHT RANGER (CAMEL/MCA)
15	LONELY OL' NIGHT — JOHN COUGAR MELLENCAMP (RIVA)	LIKE A VIRGIN — MADONNA (SIRE)
16	FREEWAY OF LOVE — ARETHA FRANKLIN (ARISTA)	BE YOURSELF TONIGHT — EURYTHMICS (RCA)
17	DANCING IN THE STREET — MICK JAGGER/DAVID BOWIE (EMI AMERICA)	WORLD WIDE LIVE — SCORPIONS (MERCURY)
18	YOU'RE ONLY HUMAN — BILLY JOEL (COLUMBIA/CBS)	EMERGENCY — KOOL AND THE GANG (DE-LITE)
19	CRY — GODLEY AND CREME (POLYDOR)	THE SECRET OF ASSOCIATION — PAUL YOUNG (COLUMBIA/CBS)
20	SMOKIN' IN THE BOYS ROOM — MOTLEY CRUE (ELEKTRA)	BOY IN THE BOX — COREY HART (EMI AMERICA)

#	SINGLES UK	ALBUMS UK
1	DANCING IN THE STREET — DAVID BOWIE/MICK JAGGER (EMI AMERICA)	HOUNDS OF LOVE — KATE BUSH (EMI)
2	HOLDING OUT FOR A HERO — BONNIE TYLER (CBS)	LIKE A VIRGIN — MADONNA (SIRE)
3	PART TIME LOVER — STEVIE WONDER (MOTOWN)	NOW THAT'S WHAT I CALL MUSIC 5 — VARIOUS (EMI/VIRGIN)
4	IF I WAS — MIDGE URE (CHRYSALIS)	BROTHERS IN ARMS — DIRE STRAITS (VERTIGO)
5	ANGEL — MADONNA (SIRE)	IN SQUARE CIRCLE — STEVIE WONDER (MOTOWN)
6	LEAN ON ME (AH-LI-AYO) — RED BOX (SIRE)	HERE'S TO FUTURE DAYS — THOMPSON TWINS (ARISTA)
7	LAVENDER — MARILLION (EMI)	THE KENNY ROGERS STORY — KENNY ROGERS (LIBERTY)
8	KNOCK ON WOOD/LIGHT MY FIRE — AMII STEWART (SEDITION)	MISPLACED CHILDHOOD — MARILLION (EMI)
9	TARZAN BOY — BALTIMORA (COLUMBIA)	THE FIRST ALBUM — MADONNA (SIRE)
10	BODY AND SOUL — MAI TAI (VIRGIN)	NO JACKET REQUIRED — PHIL COLLINS (VIRGIN)
11	BODY ROCK — MARIA VIDAL (EMI AMERICA)	BOYS AND GIRLS — BRYAN FERRY (EG)
12	THE POWER OF LOVE — HUEY LEWIS AND THE NEWS (CHRYSALIS)	SONGS FROM THE BIG CHAIR — TEARS FOR FEARS (MERCURY)
13	REBEL YELL — BILLY IDOL (CHRYSALIS)	OPEN TOP CARS & GIRLS IN T-SHIRTS — VARIOUS (TELSTAR)
14	I GOT YOU BABE — UB40/CHRISSIE HYNDE (DEP INTERNATIONAL)	BORN IN THE USA — BRUCE SPRINGSTEEN (CBS)
15	THE POWER OF LOVE — JENNIFER RUSH (CBS)	VITAL IDOL — BILLY IDOL (CHRYSALIS)
16	TRAPPED — COLONEL ABRAMS (MCA)	THE HEAD ON THE DOOR — THE CURE (FICTION)
17	THE LODGERS — STYLE COUNCIL (POLYDOR)	THE UNFORGETTABLE FIRE — U2 (ISLAND)
18	SHE'S SO BEAUTIFUL — CLIFF RICHARDS (EMI)	UNDER A BLOOD RED SKY — U2 (ISLAND)
19	DRIVE — CARS (ELEKTRA)	QUEEN GREATEST HITS — QUEEN (EMI)
20	INTO THE GROOVE — MADONNA (SIRE)	PRIVATE DANCER — TINA TURNER (CAPITOL)

S I N G L E S US A L B U M S

#	SINGLES US	ALBUMS US
1	MONEY FOR NOTHING — DIRE STRAITS (WARNER BROS)	BROTHERS IN ARMS — DIRE STRAITS (WARNER BROS)
2	CHERISH — KOOL AND THE GANG (DE-LITE)	THE DREAM OF THE BLUE TURTLES — STING (A&M)
3	FREEDOM — WHAM! (COLUMBIA/CBS)	SONGS FROM THE BIG CHAIR — TEARS FOR FEARS (MERCURY)
4	DON'T LOSE MY NUMBER — PHIL COLLINS (ATLANTIC)	BORN IN THE USA — BRUCE SPRINGSTEEN (COLUMBIA/CBS)
5	OH SHEILA — READY FOR THE WORLD (MCA)	WHITNEY HOUSTON — WHITNEY HOUSTON (ARISTA)
6	DRESS YOU UP — MADONNA (SIRE)	GREATEST HITS VOL 1 AND 2 — BILLY JOEL (COLUMBIA/CBS)
7	TAKE ON ME — A-HA (WARNER BROS)	NO JACKET REQUIRED — PHIL COLLINS (ATLANTIC)
8	ST ELMO'S FIRE (MAN IN MOTION) — JOHN PARR (ATLANTIC)	RECKLESS — BRYAN ADAMS (A&M)
9	SAVING ALL MY LOVE FOR YOU — WHITNEY HOUSTON (ARISTA)	HEART — HEART (CAPITOL)
10	LONELY OL' NIGHT — JOHN COUGAR MELLENCAMP (RIVA)	THEATRE OF PAIN — MOTLEY CRUE (ELEKTRA)
11	DANCING IN THE STREET — DAVID BOWIE/MICK JAGGER (EMI AMERICA)	MAKE IT BIG — WHAM! (COLUMBIA/CBS)
12	WE DON'T NEED ANOTHER HERO — TINA TURNER (CAPITOL)	SCARECROW — JOHN COUGAR MELLENCAMP (RIVA)
13	POP LIFE — PRINCE AND THE REVOLUTION (WARNER BROS)	BACK TO THE FUTURE — SOUNDTRACK (MCA)
14	DARE ME — POINTER SISTERS (PLANET)	WORLD WIDE LIVE — SCORPIONS (MERCURY)
15	PART TIME LOVER — STEVIE WONDER (MOTOWN)	AROUND THE WORLD IN A DAY — PRINCE AND THE REVOLUTION (PAISLEY PARK)
16	FORTRESS AROUND YOUR HEART — STING (A&M)	7 WISHES — NIGHT RANGER (CAMEL/MCA)
17	POWER OF LOVE — HUEY LEWIS AND THE NEWS (CHRYSALIS)	EMERGENCY — KOOL AND THE GANG (DE-LITE)
18	CRY — GODLEY AND CREME (POLYDOR)	WHO'S ZOOMIN' WHO — ARETHA FRANKLIN (ARISTA)
19	C-I-T-Y — JOHN CAFFERTY/BEAVERBROWN BAND(SCOTTI BROS)	BE YOURSELF TONIGHT — EURYTHMICS (RCA)
20	I'M GOING DOWN — BRUCE SPRINGSTEEN (COLUMBIA/CBS)	INVASION OF YOUR PRIVACY — RATT (ATLANTIC)

#	SINGLES UK	ALBUMS UK
1	IF I WAS — MIDGE URE (CHRYSALIS)	HOUNDS OF LOVE — KATE BUSH (EMI)
2	THE POWER OF LOVE — JENNIFER RUSH (CBS)	LIKE A VIRGIN — MADONNA (SIRE)
3	DANCING IN THE STREET — DAVID BOWIE/MICK JAGGER (EMI AMERICA)	BROTHERS IN ARMS — DIRE STRAITS (VERTIGO)
4	LEAN ON ME (AH-LI-AYO) — RED BOX (SIRE)	NOW THAT'S WHAT I CALL MUSIC 5 — VARIOUS (EMI/VIRGIN)
5	PART TIME LOVER — STEVIE WONDER (MOTOWN)	MISPLACED CHILDHOOD — MARILLION (EMI)
6	ANGEL — MADONNA (SIRE)	IN SQUARE CIRCLE — STEVIE WONDER (MOTOWN)
7	HOLDING OUT FOR A HERO — BONNIE TYLER (CBS)	THE FIRST ALBUM — MADONNA (SIRE)
8	REBEL YELL — BILLY IDOL (CHRYSALIS)	THE KENNY ROGERS STORY — KENNY ROGERS (LIBERTY)
9	LAVENDER — MARILLION (EMI)	HERE'S TO FUTURE DAYS — THOMPSON TWINS (ARISTA)
10	TRAPPED — COLONEL ABRAMS (MCA)	VITAL IDOL — BILLY IDOL (CHRYSALIS)
11	THE POWER OF LOVE — HUEY LEWIS AND THE NEWS (CHRYSALIS)	NO JACKET REQUIRED — PHIL COLLINS (VIRGIN)
12	BODY ROCK — MARIA VIDAL (EMI AMERICA)	ASYLUM — KISS (VERTIGO)
13	THE LODGERS — STYLE COUNCIL (POLYDOR)	UNDER A BLOOD RED SKY — U2 (ISLAND)
14	KNOCK ON WOOD/LIGHT MY FIRE — AMII STEWART (SEDITION)	OPEN TOP CARS & GIRLS IN T-SHIRTS — VARIOUS (TELSTAR)
15	BODY AND SOUL — MAI TAI (VIRGIN)	THE HEAD ON THE DOOR — THE CURE (FICTION)
16	TARZAN BOY — BALTIMORA (COLUMBIA)	BOYS AND GIRLS — BRYAN FERRY (EG)
17	SHE'S SO BEAUTIFUL — CLIFF RICHARD (EMI)	SONGS FROM THE BIG CHAIR — TEARS FOR FEARS (MERCURY)
18	IT'S CALLED A HEART — DEPECHE MODE (MUTE)	STREET SOUNDS ELECTRO 9 — VARIOUS (STREETSOUNDS)
19	BRAND NEW FRIEND — LLOYD COLE AND THE COMMOTIONS (POLYDOR)	BORN IN THE USA — BRUCE SPRINGSTEEN (CBS)
20	RUNNING FREE — IRON MAIDEN (EMI)	PRIVATE DANCER — TINA TURNER (CAPITOL)

S I N G L E S US A L B U M S

#	SINGLES US	ALBUMS US
1	MONEY FOR NOTHING — DIRE STRAITS (WARNER BROS)	BROTHERS IN ARMS — DIRE STRAITS (WARNER BROS)
2	CHERISH — KOOL AND THE GANG (DE-LITE)	THE DREAM OF THE BLUE TURTLES — STING (A&M)
3	OH SHEILA — READY FOR THE WORLD (MCA)	SONGS FROM THE BIG CHAIR — TEARS FOR FEARS (MERCURY)
4	TAKE ON ME — A-HA (WARNER BROS)	BORN IN THE USA — BRUCE SPRINGSTEEN (COLUMBIA/CBS)
5	DRESS YOU UP — MADONNA (SIRE)	WHITNEY HOUSTON — WHITNEY HOUSTON (ARISTA)
6	SAVING ALL MY LOVE FOR YOU — WHITNEY HOUSTON (ARISTA)	GREATEST HITS VOL 1 AND 2 — BILLY JOEL (COLUMBIA/CBS)
7	FREEDOM — WHAM! (COLMBIA/CBS)	RECKLESS — BRYAN ADAMS (A&M)
8	LONELY OL' NIGHT — JOHN COUGAR MELLENCAMP (RIVA)	NO JACKET REQUIRED — PHIL COLLINS (ATLANTIC)
9	DANCING IN THE STREET — DAVID BOWIE/MICK JAGGER (EMI AMERICA)	SCARECROW — JOHN COUGAR MELLENCAMP (RIVA)
10	PART TIME LOVER — STEVIE WONDER (MOTOWN)	HEART — HEART (CAPITOL)
11	DON'T LOSE MY NUMBER — PHIL COLLINS (ATLANTIC)	MAKE IT BIG — WHAM! (COLUMBIA/CBS)
12	FORTRESS AROUND YOUR HEART — STING (A&M)	BACK TO THE FUTURE — SOUNDTRACK (MCA)
13	MIAMI VICE THEME — JAN HAMMER (MCA)	THEATRE OF PAIN — MOTLEY CRUE (ELEKTRA)
14	I'M GOING DOWN — BRUCE SPRINGSTEEN (COLUMBIA/CBS)	EMERGENCY — KOOL AND THE GANG (DE-LITE)
15	ST ELMO'S FIRE (MAN IN MOTION) — JOHN PARR (ATLANTIC)	AROUND THE WORLD IN A DAY — PRINCE AND THE REVOLUTION (PAISLEY PARK)
16	CRY — GODLEY AND CREME (POLYDOR)	7 WISHES — NIGHT RAGER (CAMEL/MCA)
17	DARE ME — POINTER SISTERS (PLANET)	WORLD WIDE — SCORPIONS (MERCURY)
18	C-I-T-Y — JOHN CAFFERTY/BEAVERBROWN BAND(SCOTTI BROS)	WHO'S ZOOMIN' WHO — ARETHA FRANKLIN (ARISTA)
19	LOVIN' EVERY MINUTE OF IT — LOVERBOY (COLUMBIA/CBS)	LIKE A VIRGIN — MADONNA (SIRE)
20	HEAD OVER HEELS — TEARS FOR FEARS (MERCURY)	BOY IN THE BOX — COREY HART (EMI AMERICA)

S I N G L E S UK A L B U M S

#	Singles	Albums
1	THE POWER OF LOVE — JENNIFER RUSH (CBS)	LIKE A VIRGIN — MADONNA (SIRE)
2	IF I WAS — MIDGE URE (CHRYSALIS)	HOUNDS OF LOVE — KATE BUSH (EMI)
3	LEAN ON ME (AH-LI-AYO) — RED BOX (SIRE)	BROTHERS IN ARMS — DIRE STRAITS (VERTIGO)
4	TRAPPED — COLONEL ABRAMS (MCA)	NOW THAT'S WHAT I CALL MUSIC 5 — VARIOUS (EMI/VIRGIN)
5	PART TIME LOVER — STEVIE WONDER (MOTOWN)	MISPLACED CHILDHOOD — MARILLION (EMI)
6	REBEL YELL — BILLY IDOL (CHRYSALIS)	IN SQUARE CIRCLE — STEVIE WONDER (MOTOWN)
7	DANCING IN THE STREET — DAVID BOWIE/MICK JAGGER (EMI AMERICA)	VITAL IDOL — BILLY IDOL (CHRYSALIS)
8	ANGEL — MADONNA (SIRE)	THE FIRST ALBUM — MADONNA (SIRE)
9	HOLDING OUT FOR A HERO — BONNIE TYLER (CBS)	BOYS AND GIRLS — BRYAN FERRY (EG)
10	ST ELMO'S FIRE (MAN IN MOTION) — JOHN PARR (LONDON)	THE KENNY ROGERS STORY — KENNY ROGERS (LIBERTY)
11	BODY ROCK — MARIA VIDAL (EMI AMERICA)	THE HEAD ON THE DOOR — THE CURE (FICTION)
12	ALIVE AND KICKING — SIMPLE MINDS (VIRGIN)	NO JACKET REQUIRED — PHIL COLLINS (VIRGIN)
13	LAVENDER — MARILLION (EMI)	HERE'S TO FUTURE DAYS — THOMPSON TWINS (ARISTA)
14	TAKE ON ME — A-HA (WARNER BROS)	EXPRESSIONS — VARIOUS (K-TEL)
15	THE POWER OF LOVE — HUEY LEWIS AND THE NEWS (CHRYSALIS)	SONGS FROM THE BIG CHAIR — TEARS FOR FEARS (MERCURY)
16	SINGLE LIFE — CAMEO (CLUB)	MAD NOT MAD — MADNESS (ZARJAZZ)
17	SHE'S SO BEAUTIFUL — CLIFF RICHARD (EMI)	UNDER A BLOOD RED SKY — U2 (ISLAND)
18	THE LODGERS — STYLE COUNCIL (POLYDOR)	BORN IN THE USA — BRUCE SPRINGSTEEN (CBS)
19	RUNNING FREE — IRON MAIDEN (EMI)	THE UNFORGETTABLE FIRE — U2 (ISLAND)
20	GAMBLER — MADONNA (GEFFEN)	PRIVATE DANCER — TINA TURNER (CAPITOL)

S I N G L E S US A L B U M S

#	Singles	Albums
1	OH SHEILA — READY FOR THE WORLD (MCA)	BROTHERS IN ARMS — DIRE STRAITS (WARNER BROS)
2	MONEY FOR NOTHING — DIRE STRAITS (WARNER BROS)	THE DREAM OF THE BLUE TURTLES — STING (A&M)
3	TAKE ON ME — A-HA (WARNER BROS)	SONGS FROM THE BIG CHAIR — TEARS FOR FEARS (MERCURY)
4	SAVING ALL MY LOVE FOR YOU — WHITNEY HOUSTON (ARISTA)	WHITNEY HOUSTON — WHITNEY HOUSTON (ARISTA)
5	PART TIME LOVER — STEVIE WONDER (MOTOWN)	BORN IN THE USA — BRUCE SPRINGSTEEN (COLUMBIA/CBS)
6	LONELY OL' NIGHT — JOHN COUGAR MELLENCAMP (RIVA)	SCARECROW — JOHN COUGAR MELLENCAMP (RIVA)
7	DANCING IN THE STREET — DAVID BOWIE/MICK JAGGER (EMI AMERICA)	RECKLESS — BRYAN ADAMS (A&M)
8	CHERISH — KOOL AND THE GANG (DE-LITE)	HEART — HEART (CAPITOL)
9	MIAMI VICE THEME — JAN HAMMER (MCA)	GREATEST HITS VOL 1 AND 2 — BILLY JOEL (COLUMBIA/CBS)
10	DRESS YOU UP — MADONNA (SIRE)	NO JACKET REQUIRED — PHIL COLLINS (ATLANTIC)
11	FORTRESS AROUND YOUR HEART — STING (A&M)	MAKE IT BIG — WHAM! (COLUMBIA/CBS)
12	I'M GOING DOWN — BRUCE SPRINGSTEEN (COLUMBIA/CBS)	BACK TO THE FUTURE — SOUNDTRACK (MCA)
13	HEAD OVER HEELS — TEARS FOR FEARS (MERCURY)	EMERGENCY — KOOL AND THE GANG (DE-LITE)
14	FREEDOM — WHAM! (COLUMBIA/CBS)	THEATRE OF PAIN — MOTLEY CRUE (ELEKTRA)
15	LOVIN' EVERY MINUTE OF IT — LOVERBOY (COLUMBIA/CBS)	LOVIN' EVERY MINUTE OF IT — LOVERBOY (COLUMBIA/CBS)
16	DON'T LOSE MY NUMBER — PHIL COLLINS (ATLANTIC)	LIKE A VIRGIN — MADONNA (SIRE)
17	CRY — GODLEY AND CREME (POLYDOR)	READY FOR THE WORLD — READY FOR THE WORLD (MCA)
18	. . . TEAR YOUR PLAYHOUSE DOWN — PAUL YOUNG (COLUMBIA/CBS)	WHO'S ZOOMIN' WHO — ARETHA FRANKLIN (ARISTA)
19	FOUR IN THE MORNING — NIGHT RANGER (CAMEL/MCA)	HUNTING HIGH AND LOW — A-HA (WARNER BROS)
20	. . . THE THINGS YOU DO/MY GIRL — DARYL HALL/JOHN OATES (RCA)	BOY IN THE BOX — COREY HART (EMI AMERICA)

S I N G L E S UK A L B U M S

#	Singles	Albums
1	THE POWER OF LOVE — JENNIFER RUSH (CBS)	HOUNDS OF LOVE — KATE BUSH (EMI)
2	IF I WAS — MIDGE URE (CHRYSALIS)	THE GIFT — MIDGE URE (CHRYSALIS)
3	TRAPPED — COLONEL ABRAMS (MCA)	LIKE A VIRGIN — MADONNA (SIRE)
4	LEAN ON ME (AH-LI-AYO) — RED BOX (SIRE)	BROTHERS IN ARMS — DIRE STRAITS (VERTIGO)
5	TAKE ON ME — A-HA (WARNER BROS)	LOVE SONGS — GEORGE BENSON (K-TEL)
6	ST ELMO'S FIRE (MAN IN MOTION) — JOHN PARR (LONDON)	NOW THAT'S WHAT I CALL MUSIC 5 — VARIOUS (EMI/VIRGIN)
7	GAMBLER — MADONNA (GEFFEN)	VITAL IDOL — BILLY IDOL (CHRYSALIS)
8	ALIVE AND KICKING — SIMPLE MINDS (VIRGIN)	MISPLACED CHILDHOOD — MARILLION (EMI)
9	REBEL YELL — BILLY IDOL (CHRYSALIS)	THE FIRST ALBUM — MADONNA (SIRE)
10	MIAMI VICE THEME — JAN HAMMER (MCA)	THE HEAD ON THE DOOR — THE CURE (FICTION)
11	PART TIME LOVER — STEVIE WONDER (MOTOWN)	EXPRESSIONS — VARIOUS (K-TEL)
12	HOLDING OUT FOR A HERO — BONNIE TYLER (CBS)	IN SQUARE CIRCLE — STEVIE WONDER (MOTOWN)
13	DANCING IN THE STREET — DAVID BOWIE/MICK JAGGER (EMI AMERICA)	BOYS AND GIRLS — BRYAN FERRY (EG)
14	SLAVE TO THE RHYTHM — GRACE JONES (ISLAND)	NO JACKET REQUIRED — PHIL COLLINS (VIRGIN)
15	SINGLE LIFE — CAMEO (CLUB)	THE KENNY ROGERS STORY — KENNY ROGERS (LIBERTY)
16	ANGEL — MADONNA (SIRE)	GREATEST HITS VOL 1 AND 2 — BILLY JOEL (CBS)
17	RAIN — THE CULT (BEGGARS BANQUET)	UNDER A BLOOD RED SKY — U2 (ISLAND)
18	LIPSTICK POWDER AND PAINT — SHAKIN' STEVENS (EPIC)	SONGS FROM THE BIG CHAIR — TEARS FOR FEARS (MERCURY)
19	NIKITA — ELTON JOHN (ROCKET)	HERE'S TO FUTURE DAYS — THOMPSON TWINS (ARISTA)
20	BODY ROCK — MARIA VIDAL (EMI AMERICA)	MAD NOT MAD — MADNESS (ZARJAZZ)

S I N G L E S US A L B U M S

#	Singles	Albums
1	TAKE ON ME — A-HA (WARNER BROS)	BROTHERS IN ARMS — DIRE STRAITS (WARNER BROS)
2	SAVING ALL MY LOVE FOR YOU — WHITNEY HOUSTON (ARISTA)	WHITNEY HOUSTON — WHITNEY HOUSTON (ARISTA)
3	PART TIME LOVER — STEVIE WONDER (MOWTOWN)	SONGS FROM THE BIG CHAIR — TEARS FOR FEARS (MERCURY)
4	OH SHEILA — READY FOR THE WORLD (MCA)	THE DREAM OF THE BLUE TURTLES — STING (A&M)
5	MIAMI VICE THEME — JAN HAMMER (MCA)	BORN IN THE USA — BRUCE SPRINGSTEEN (COLUMBIA/CBS)
6	LONELY OL' NIGHT — JOHN COUGAR MELLENCAMP (RIVA)	SCARECROW — JOHN COUGAR MELLENCAMP (RIVA)
7	MONEY FOR NOTHING — DIRE STRAITS (WARNER BROS)	MIAMI VICE — SOUNDTRACK (MCA)
8	DANCING IN THE STREET — DAVID BOWIE/MICK JAGGER (EMI AMERICA)	HEART — HEART (CAPITOL)
9	FORTRESS AROUND YOUR HEART — STING (A&M)	RECKLESS — BRYAN ADAMS (A&M)
10	HEAD OVER HEELS — TEARS FOR FEARS (MERCURY)	GREATEST HITS VOL 1 AND 2 — BILLY JOEL (COLUMBIA/CBS)
11	I'M GOING DOWN — BRUCE SPRINGSTEEN (COLUMBIA/CBS)	NO JACKET REQUIRED — PHIL COLLINS (ATLANTIC)
12	LOVIN' EVERY MINUTE OF IT — LOVERBOY (COLUMBIA/CBS)	IN SQUARE CIRCLE — STEVIE WONDER (MOTOWN)
13	CHERISH — KOOL AND THE GANG (DE-LITE)	LOVIN' EVERY MINUTE OF IT — LOVERBOY (COLUMBIA/CBS)
14	DRESS YOU UP — MADONNA (SIRE)	MAKE IT BIG — WHAM! (COLUMBIA/CBS)
15	YOU BELONG TO THE CITY — GLENN FREY (MCA)	EMERGENCY — KOOL AND THE GANG (DE-LITE)
16	. . . TEAR YOUR PLAYHOUSE DOWN — PAUL YOUNG (COLUMBIA/CBS)	ROCK ME TONIGHT — FREDDIE JACKSON (CAPITOL)
17	WE BUILT THIS CITY — STARSHIP (GRUNT)	READY FOR THE WORLD — READY FOR THE WORLD (MCA)
18	BE NEAR ME — ABC (MERCURY)	WHO'S ZOOMIN' WHO — ARETHA FRANKLIN (ARISTA)
19	ONE NIGHT LOVE AFFAIR — BRYAN ADAMS (A&M)	HUNTING HIGH AND LOW — A-HA (WARNER BROS)
20	FOUR IN THE MORNING . . . — NIGHT RANGER (CAMEL/MCA)	BACK TO THE FUTURE — SOUNDTRACK (MCA)

SINGLES UK ALBUMS (October 26 1985)

#	SINGLES	ALBUMS
1	THE POWER OF LOVE — JENNIFER RUSH (CBS)	LOVE SONGS — GEORGE BENSON (K-TEL)
2	TAKE ON ME — A-HA (WARNER BROS)	LIVE AFTER DEATH — IRON MAIDEN (EMI)
3	TRAPPED — COLONEL ABRAMS (MCA)	OUT NOW 2 — VARIOUS (CHRYSALIS)
4	GAMBLER — MADONNA (GEFFEN)	LOVE — THE CULT (BEGGARS BANQUET)
5	MIAMI VICE THEME — JAN HAMMER (MCA)	HOUNDS OF LOVE — KATE BUSH (EMI)
6	ST ELMO'S FIRE (MAN IN MOTION) — JOHN PARR (LONDON)	LIKE A VIRGIN — MADONNA (SIRE)
7	ALIVE AND KICKING — SIMPLE MINDS (VIRGIN)	THE GIFT — MIDGE URE (CHRYSALIS)
8	IF I WAS — MIDGE URE (CHRYSALIS)	THE SINGLES 81-85 — DEPECHE MODE (MUTE)
9	NIKITA — ELTON JOHN (ROCKET)	BROTHERS IN ARMS — DIRE STRAITS (VERTIGO)
10	LEAN ON ME (AH-LI-AYO) — RED BOX (SIRE)	WORLD MACHINE — LEVEL 42 (POLYDOR)
11	REBEL YELL — BILLY IDOL (CHRYSALIS)	WEST SIDE STORY — BERNSTEIN/TE KANAWA/CARRERAS (DEUTSCHE GRAM)
12	SLAVE TO THE RHYTHM — GRACE JONES (ISLAND)	GREATEST HITS VOL 1 AND 2 — BILLY JOEL (CBS)
13	SOMETHING ABOUT YOU — LEVEL 42 (POLYDOR)	VITAL IDOL — BILLY IDOL (CHRYSALIS)
14	ELECTION DAY — ARCADIA (PARLOPHONE)	MIAMI VICE — VARIOUS (BBC)
15	LIPSTICK POWDER AND PAINT — SHAKIN' STEVENS (EPIC)	EXPRESSIONS — VARIOUS (K-TEL)
16	PART TIME LOVER — STEVIE WONDER (MOTOWN)	NOW THAT'S WHAT I CALL MUSIC 5 — VARIOUS (EMI/VIRGIN)
17	RAIN — THE CULT (BEGGARS BANQUET)	MISPLACED CHILDHOOD — MARILLION (EMI)
18	HOLDING OUT FOR A HERO — BONNIE TYLER (CBS)	STRENGTH — ALARM (IRS)
19	SINGLE LIFE — CAMEO (CLUB)	THE FIRST ALBUM — MADONNA (SIRE)
20	THE TASTE OF YOUR TEARS — KING (CBS)	BOYS AND GIRLS — BRYAN FERRY (EG)

SINGLES US ALBUMS (October 26 1985)

#	SINGLES	ALBUMS
1	SAVING ALL MY LOVE FOR YOU — WHITNEY HOUSTON (ARISTA)	BROTHERS IN ARMS — DIRE STRAITS (WARNER BROS)
2	PART TIME LOVER — STEVIE WONDER (MOTOWN)	WHITNEY HOUSTON — WHITNEY HOUSTON (ARISTA)
3	TAKE ON ME — A-HA (WARNER BROS)	MIAMI VICE — SOUNDTRACK (MCA)
4	MIAMI VICE THEME — JAN HAMMER (MCA)	SCARECROW — JOHN COUGAR MELLENCAMP (RIVA)
5	HEAD OVER HEELS — TEARS FOR FEARS (MERCURY)	SONGS FROM THE BIG CHAIR — TEARS FOR FEARS (MERCURY)
6	OH SHEILA — READY FOR THE WORLD (MCA)	THE DREAM OF THE BLUE TURTLES — STING (A&M)
7	LONELY OL' NIGHT — JOHN COUGAR MELLENCAMP (RIVA)	BORN IN THE USA — BRUCE SPRINGSTEEN (COLUMBIA/CBS)
8	FORTRESS AROUND YOUR HEART — STING (A&M)	HEART — HEART (CAPITOL)
9	I'M GOING DOWN — BRUCE SPRINGSTEEN (COLUMBIA/CBS)	IN SQUARE CIRCLE — STEVIE WONDER (MOTOWN)
10	YOU BELONG TO THE CITY — GLENN FREY (MCA)	RECKLESS — BRYAN ADAMS (A&M)
11	LOVIN' EVERY MINUTE OF IT — LOVERBOY (COLUMBIA/CBS)	NO JACKET REQUIRED — PHIL COLLINS (ATLANTIC)
12	MONEY FOR NOTHING — DIRE STRAITS (WARNER BROS)	GREATEST HITS VOL 1 AND 2 — BILLY JOEL (COLUMBIA/CBS)
13	WE BUILT THIS CITY — STARSHIP (GRUNT)	LOVIN' EVERY MINUTE OF IT — LOVERBOY (COLUMBIA/CBS)
14	. . . TEAR YOUR PLAYHOUSE DOWN — PAUL YOUNG (COLUMBIA/CBS)	ROCK ME TONIGHT — FREDDIE JACKSON (CAPITOL)
15	DANCING IN THE STREET — DAVID BOWIE/MICK JAGGER (EMI AMERICA)	EMERGENCY — KOOL AND THE GANG (DE-LITE)
16	BE NEAR ME — ABC (MERCURY)	WHO'S ZOOMIN' WHO — ARETHA FRANKLIN (ARISTA)
17	ONE NIGHT LOVE AFFAIR — BRYAN ADAMS (A&M)	READY FOR THE WORLD — READY FOR THE WORLD (MCA)
18	YOU ARE MY LADY — FREDDIE JACKSON (CAPITOL)	MAKE IT BIG — WHAM! (COLUMBIA/CBS)
19	LAY YOUR HANDS ON ME — THOMPSON TWINS (ARISTA)	HUNTING HIGH AND LOW — A-HA (WARNER BROS)
20	SEPARATE LIVES — PHIL COLLINS/MARILYN MARTIN (ATLANTIC)	THE SECRET OF ASSOCIATION — PAUL YOUNG (COLUMBIA/CBS)

SINGLES UK ALBUMS (November 2 1985)

#	SINGLES	ALBUMS
1	THE POWER OF LOVE — JENNIFER RUSH (CBS)	ONCE UPON A TIME — SIMPLE MINDS (VIRGIN)
2	TAKE ON ME — A-HA (WARNER BROS)	LOVE SONGS — GEORGE BENSON (K-TEL)
3	TRAPPED — COLONEL ABRAMS (MCA)	OUT NOW 2 — VARIOUS (CHRYSALIS/MCA)
4	NIKITA — ELTON JOHN (ROCKET)	HOUNDS OF LOVE — KATE BUSH (EMI)
5	GAMBLER — MADONNA (GEFFEN)	LIKE A VIRGIN — MADONNA (SIRE)
6	ST ELMO'S FIRE (MAN IN MOTION) — JOHN PARR (LONDON)	THE SINGLES 81-85 — DEPECHE MODE (MUTE)
7	ELECTION DAY — ARCADIA (PARLOPHONE)	BROTHERS IN ARMS — DIRE STRAITS (VERTIGO)
8	MIAMI VICE THEME — JAN HAMMER (MCA)	LOVE — THE CULT (BEGGARS BANQUET)
9	SOMETHING ABOUT YOU — LEVEL 42 (POLYDOR)	LIVE AFTER DEATH — IRON MAIDEN (EMI)
10	ALIVE AND KICKING — SIMPLE MINDS (VIRGIN)	WORLD MACHINE — LEVEL 42 (POLYDOR)
11	LIPSTICK POWDER AND PAINT — SHAKIN' STEVENS (EPIC)	MIAMI VICE — VARIOUS (BBC)
12	A GOOD HEART — FEARGAL SHARKEY (VIRGIN)	THE GIFT — MIDGE URE (CHRYSALIS)
13	SLAVE TO THE RHYTHM — GRACE JONES (ISLAND)	WEST SIDE STORY — BERNSTEIN/TE KANAWA/CARRERAS (DEUTSCHE GRAM)
14	LEAN ON ME (AH-LI-AYO) — RED BOX (SIRE)	GREATEST HITS VOL 1 AND 2 — BILLY JOEL (CBS)
15	THE TASTE OF YOUR TEARS — KING (CBS)	VITAL IDOL — BILLY IDOL (CHRYSALIS)
16	IF I WAS — MIDGE URE (CHRYSALIS)	THE FIRST ALBUM — MADONNA (SIRE)
17	YEH YEH — MATT BIANCO (WEA)	NOW THAT'S WHAT I CALL MUSIC 5 — VARIOUS (EMI/VIRGIN)
18	REBEL YELL — BILLY IDOL (CHRYSALIS)	EXPRESSIONS — VARIOUS (K-TEL)
19	DON'T BREAK MY HEART — UB40 (DEP INTERNATIONAL/VIRGIN)	NO JACKET REQUIRED — PHIL COLLINS (VIRGIN)
20	CLOUDBUSTING — KATE BUSH (EMI)	MISPLACED CHILDHOOD — MARILLION (EMI)

SINGLES US ALBUMS (November 2 1985)

#	SINGLES	ALBUMS
1	PART TIME LOVER — STEVIE WONDER (MOTOWN)	MIAMI VICE — SOUNDTRACK (MCA)
2	MIAMI VICE THEME — JAN HAMMER (MCA)	BROTHERS IN ARMS — DIRE STRAITS (WARNER BROS)
3	SAVING ALL MY LOVE FOR YOU — WHITNEY HOUSTON (ARISTA)	WHITNEY HOUSTON — WHITNEY HOUSTON (ARISTA)
4	HEAD OVER HEELS — TEARS FOR FEARS (MERCURY)	SCARECROW — JOHN COUGAR MELLENCAMP (RIVA)
5	TAKE ON ME — A-HA (WARNER BROS)	SONGS FROM THE BIG CHAIR — TEARS FOR FEARS (MERCURY)
6	YOU BELONG TO THE CITY — GLENN FREY (MCA)	THE DREAM OF THE BLUE TURTLES — STING (A&M)
7	WE BUILT THIS CITY — STARSHIP (GRUNT)	IN SQUARE CIRCLE — STEVIE WONDER (MOTOWN)
8	FORTRESS AROUND YOUR HEART — STING (A&M)	HEART — HEART (CAPITOL)
9	LOVIN' EVERY MINUTE OF IT — LOVERBOY (COLUMBIA/CBS)	BORN IN THE USA — BRUCE SPRINGSTEEN (COLUMBIA/CBS)
10	BE NEAR ME — ABC (MERCURY)	RECKLESS — BRYAN ADAMS (A&M)
11	OH SHEILA — READY FOR THE WORLD (MCA)	NO JACKET REQUIRED — PHIL COLLINS (ATLANTIC)
12	LONELY OL' NIGHT — JOHN COUGAR MELLENCAMP (RIVA)	GREATEST HITS VOL 1 AND 2 — BILLY JOEL (COLUMBIA/CBS)
13	. . . TEAR YOUR PLAYHOUSE DOWN — PAUL YOUNG (COLUMBIA/CBS)	LOVIN' EVERY MINUTE OF IT — LOVERBOY (COLUMBIA/CBS)
14	ONE NIGHT LOVE AFFAIR — BRYAN ADAMS (A&M)	ROCK ME TONIGHT — FREDDIE JACKSON (CAPITOL)
15	SEPARATE LIVES — PHIL COLLINS/MARLYN MARTIN (ATLANTIC)	HUNTING HIGH AND LOW — A-HA (WARNER BROS)
16	YOU ARE MY LADY — FREDDIE JACKSON (CAPITOL)	WHO'S ZOOMIN' WHO — ARETHA FRANKLIN (ARISTA)
17	NEVER — HEART (CAPITOL)	READY FOR THE WORLD — READY FOR THE WORLD (MCA)
18	LAY YOUR HANDS ON ME — THOMPSON TWINS (ARISTA)	MAKE IT BIG — WHAM! (COLUMBIA/CBS)
19	I'M GOIN' DOWN — BRUCE SPRINGSTEEN (COLUMBIA/CBS)	EMERGENCY — KOOL AND THE GANG (DE-LITE)
20	BROKEN WING — MR MISTER (RCA)	THE SECRET OF ASSOCIATION — PAUL YOUNG (COLUMBIA/CBS)

SINGLES UK ALBUMS

#	Singles	Albums
1	THE POWER OF LOVE — JENNIFER RUSH (CBS)	LOVE SONGS — GEORGE BENSON (K-TEL)
2	TAKE ON ME — A-HA (WARNER BROS)	AFTERBURNER — ZZ TOP (WARNER BROS)
3	NIKITA — ELTON JOHN (ROCKET)	ONCE UPON A TIME — SIMPLE MINDS (VIRGIN)
4	A GOOD HEART — FEARGAL SHARKEY (VIRGIN)	OUT NOW 2 — VARIOUS (CHRYSALIS/MCA)
5	TRAPPED — COLONEL ABRAMS (MCA)	HOUNDS OF LOVE — KATE BUSH (EMI)
6	SOMETHING ABOUT YOU — LEVEL 42 (POLYDOR)	BROTHERS IN ARMS — DIRE STRAITS (WARNER BROS)
7	DON'T BREAK MY HEART — UB40 (DEP INTERNATIONAL/VIRGIN)	THE SINGLES 81-85 — DEPECHE MODE (MUTE)
8	GAMBLER — MADONNA (GEFFEN)	LIKE A VIRGIN — MADONNA (SIRE)
9	ST ELMO'S FIRE (MAN IN MOTION) — JOHN PARR (LONDON)	POWER WINDOWS — RUSH (VERTIGO)
10	ELECTION DAY — ARCADIA (PARLOPHONE)	LOVE — THE CULT (BEGGARS BANQUET)
11	ALIVE AND KICKING — SIMPLE MINDS (VIRGIN)	WORLD MACHINE — LEVEL 42 (POLYDOR)
12	THE TASTE OF YOUR TEARS — KING (CBS)	SLAVE TO THE RHYTHM — GRACE JONES (ISLAND)
13	YEH YEH — MATT BIANCO (WEA)	LIVE AFTER DEATH — IRON MAIDEN (EMI)
14	MIAMI VICE — JAN HAMMER (MCA)	MIAMI VICE — VARIOUS (BBC)
15	LIPSTICK POWDER AND PAINT — SHAKIN' STEVENS (EPIC)	THE GIFT — MIDGE URE (CHRYSALIS)
16	STAIRWAY TO HEAVEN — FAR CORPORATION (ARISTA)	WEST SIDE STORY — BERNSTEIN/TE KANAWA/CARRERAS(DEUTSCHE GRAM)
17	ROAD TO NOWHERE — TALKING HEADS (EMI)	GREATEST HITS VOL 1 AND 2 — BILLY JOEL (CBS)
18	SISTERS ARE DOIN' IT . . . — EURYTHMICS/ARETHA FRANKLIN (RCA)	NOW THAT'S WHAT I CALL MUSIC 5 — VARIOUS (EMI/VIRGIN)
19	SLAVE TO THE RHYTHM — GRACE JONES (ISLAND)	VITAL IDOL — BILLY IDOL (CHRYSALIS)
20	CLOUDBUSTING — KATE BUSH (EMI)	THE FIRST ALBUM — MADONNA (SIRE)

SINGLES US ALBUMS

#	Singles	Albums
1	MIAMI VICE THEME — JAN HAMMER (MCA)	MIAMI VICE — SOUNDTRACK (MCA)
2	PART TIME LOVER — STEVIE WONDER (MOTOWN)	BROTHERS IN ARMS — DIRE STRAITS (WARNER BROS)
3	HEAD OVER HEELS — TEARS FOR FEARS (MERCURY)	SCARECROW — JOHN COUGAR MELLENCAMP (RIVA)
4	YOU BELONG TO THE CITY — GLENN FREY (MCA)	WHITNEY HOUSTON — WHITNEY HOUSTON (ARISTA)
5	WE BUILT THIS CITY — STARSHIP (GRUNT)	SONGS FROM THE BIG CHAIR — TEARS FOR FEARS (MERCURY)
6	SAVING ALL MY LOVE FOR YOU — WHITNEY HOUSTON (ARISTA)	HEART — HEART (CAPITOL)
7	SEPARATE LIVES — PHIL COLLINS/MARILYN MARTIN (ATLANTIC)	IN SQUARE CIRCLE — STEVIE WONDER (MOTOWN)
8	TAKE ON ME — A-HA (WARNER BROS)	THE DREAM OF THE BLUE TURTLES — STING (A&M)
9	BE NEAR ME — ABC (MERCURY)	BORN IN THE USA — BRUCE SPRINGSTEEN (COLUMBIA/CBS)
10	LAY YOUR HANDS ON ME — THOMPSON TWINS (ARISTA)	RECKLESS — BRYAN ADAMS (A&M)
11	BROKEN WINGS — MR MISTER (RCA)	NO JACKET REQUIRED — PHIL COLLINS (ATLANTIC)
12	NEVER — HEART (CAPITOL)	GREATEST HITS VOL 1 AND 2 — BILLY JOEL (COLUMBIA/CBS)
13	ONE NIGHT LOVE AFFAIR — BRYAN ADAMS (A&M)	LOVIN' EVERY MINUTE OF IT — LOVERBOY (COLUMBIA/CBS)
14	YOU ARE MY LADY — FREDDIE JACKSON (CAPITOL)	ROCK ME TONIGHT — FREDDIE JACKSON (CAPITOL)
15	LOVIN' EVERY MINUTE OF IT — LOVERBOY (COLUMBIA/CBS)	HUNTING HIGH AND LOW — A-HA (WARNER BROS)
16	WHO'S ZOOMIN' WHO — ARETHA FRANKLIN (ARISTA)	WHO'S ZOOMIN' WHO — ARETHA FRANKLIN (ARISTA)
17	FORTRESS AROUND YOUR HEART — STING (A&M)	READY FOR THE WORLD — READY FOR THE WORLD (MCA)
18	. . . TEAR YOUR PLAYHOUSE DOWN — PAUL YOUNG (COLUMBIA/CBS)	MAKE IT BIG — WHAM! (COLUMBIA/CBS)
19	LOVE THEME FROM ST ELMO'S FIRE — DAVID FOSTER (ATLANTIC)	EMERGENCY — KOOL AND THE GANG (DE-LITE)
20	OH SHEILA — READY FOR THE WORLD (MCA)	THE SECRET OF ASSOCIATION — PAUL YOUNG (COLUMBIA/CBS)

SINGLES UK ALBUMS

#	Singles	Albums
1	A GOOD HEART — FEARGAL SHARKEY (VIRGIN)	PROMISE — SADE (EPIC)
2	THE POWER OF LOVE — JENNIFER RUSH (CBS)	LOVE SONGS — GEORGE BENSON (K-TEL)
3	TAKE ON ME — A-HA (WARNER BROS)	ICE ON FIRE — ELTON JOHN (ROCKET)
4	NIKITA — ELTON JOHN (ROCKET)	AFTERBURNER — ZZ TOP (WARNER BROS)
5	DON'T BREAK MY HEART — UB40 (DEP INTERNATIONAL/VIRGIN)	ONCE UPON A TIME — SIMPLE MINDS (VIRGIN)
6	SOMETHING ABOUT YOU — LEVEL 42 (POLYDOR)	BROTHERS IN ARMS — DIRE STRAITS (VERTIGO)
7	TRAPPED — COLONEL ABRAMS (MCA)	JENNIFER RUSH — JENNIFER RUSH (CBS)
8	STAIRWAY TO HEAVEN — FAR CORPORATION (ARISTA)	THE SINGLES COLLECTION — SPANDAU BALLET (CHRYSALIS)
9	ONE VISION — QUEEN (EMI)	HOUNDS OF LOVE — KATE BUSH (EMI)
10	SISTERS ARE DOIN' IT . . . — EURYTHMICS/ARETHA FRANKLIN (RCA)	OUT NOW 2 — VARIOUS (CHRYSALIS/MCA)
11	THE TASTE OF YOUR TEARS — KING (CBS)	WORLD MACHINE — LEVEL 42 (POLYDOR)
12	ROAD TO NOWHERE — TALKING HEADS (EMI)	LIKE A VIRGIN — MADONNA (SIRE)
13	THE SHOW — DOUG E FRESH (COOLTEMPO)	THE SINGLES 81-85 — DEPECHE MODE (MUTE)
14	GAMBLER — MADONNA (GEFFEN)	ROCK ANTHEMS — VARIOUS (K-TEL)
15	YEH YEH — MATT BIANCO (WEA)	SLAVE TO THE RHYTHM — GRACE JONES (ISLAND)
16	ELECTION DAY — ARCADIA (PARLOPHONE)	CUT THE CRAP — THE CLASH (CBS)
17	ST ELMO'S FIRE (MAN IN MOTION) — JOHN PARR (LONDON)	LOVE — THE CULT (BEGGARS BANQUET)
18	ALIVE AND KICKING — SIMPLE MINDS (VIRGIN)	SONGS FROM THE BIG CHAIR — TEARS FOR FEARS (MERCURY)
19	JUST FOR MONEY — PAUL HARDCASTLE (CHRYSALIS)	MIAMI VICE — VARIOUS (BBC)
20	LIPSTICK POWER AND PAINT — SHAKIN' STEVENS (EPIC)	LIVE AFTER DEATH — IRON MAIDEN (EMI)

SINGLES US ALBUMS

#	Singles	Albums
1	WE BUILT THIS CITY — STARSHIP (GRUNT)	MIAMI VICE — SOUNDTRACK (MCA)
2	YOU BELONG TO THE CITY — GLENN FREY (MCA)	SCARECROW — JOHN COUGAR MELLENCAMP (RIVA)
3	MIAMI VICE THEME — JAN HAMMER (MCA)	BROTHERS IN ARMS — DIRE STRAITS (WARNER BROS)
4	HEAD OVER HEELS — TEARS FOR FEARS (MERCURY)	WHITNEY HOUSTON — WHITNEY HOUSTON (ARISTA)
5	PART TIME LOVER — STEVIE WONDER (MOTOWN)	HEART — HEART (CAPITOL)
6	SEPARATE LIVES — PHIL COLLINS/MARILYN MARTIN (ATLANTIC)	IN SQUARE CIRCLE — STEVIE WONDER (MOTOWN)
7	BROKEN WINGS — MR MISTER (RCA)	SONGS FROM THE BIG CHAIR — TEARS FOR FEARS (MERCURY)
8	NEVER — HEART (CAPITOL)	THE DREAM OF THE BLUE TURTLES — STING (A&M)
9	BE NEAR ME — ABC (MERCURY)	BORN IN THE USA — BRUCE SPRINGSTEEN (COLUMBIA/CBS)
10	LAY YOUR HANDS ON ME — THOMPSON TWINS (ARISTA)	RECKLESS — BRYAN ADAMS (A&M)
11	WHO'S ZOOMIN' WHO — ARETHA FRANKLIN (ARISTA)	ROCK ME TONIGHT — FREDDIE JACKSON (CAPITOL)
12	YOU ARE MY LADY — FREDDIE JACKSON (CAPITOL)	NO JACKET REQUIRED — PHIL COLLINS (ATLANTIC)
13	TAKE ON ME — A-HA (WARNER BROS)	LOVIN' EVERY MINUTE OF IT — LOVERBOY (COLUMBIA/CBS)
14	SAVING ALL MY LOVE FOR YOU — WHITNEY HOUSTON (ARISTA)	GREATEST HITS VOL 1 AND 2 — BILLY JOEL (COLUMBIA/CBS)
15	LOVE THEME FROM ST ELMO'S FIRE — DAVID FOSTER (ATLANTIC)	POWER WINDOWS — RUSH (MERCURY)
16	ONE NIGHT LOVE AFFAIR — BRYAN ADAMS (A&M)	WHO'S ZOOMIN' WHO — ARETHA FRANKLIN (ARISTA)
17	ONE OF THE LIVING — TINA TURNER (CAPITOL)	HUNTING HIGH AND LOW — A-HA (WARNER BROS)
18	ELECTION DAY — ARCADIA (CAPITOL)	READY FOR THE WORLD — READY FOR THE WORLD (MCA)
19	SLEEPING BAG — ZZ TOP (WARNER BROS)	KNEE DEEP IN THE HOOPLA — STARSHIP (GRUNT)
20	LOVIN' EVERY MINUTE OF IT — LOVERBOY (COLUMBIA/CBS)	ASYLUM — KISS (MERCURY)

WEEK ENDING NOVEMBER 23 1985

S I N G L E S — UK — A L B U M S

#	SINGLES	ALBUMS
1	A GOOD HEART — FEARGAL SHARKEY (VIRGIN)	PROMISE — SADE (EPIC)
2	I'M YOUR MAN — WHAM! (EPIC)	LOVE SONGS — GEORGE BENSON (K-TEL)
3	DON'T BREAK MY HEART — UB40 (DEP INTERNATIONAL)	BROTHERS IN ARMS — DIRE STRAITS (VERTIGO)
4	THE POWER OF LOVE — JENNIFER RUSH (CBS)	ICE ON FIRE — ELTON JOHN (ROCKET)
5	TAKE ON ME — A-HA (WARNER BROS)	GREATEST HITS OF 1985 — VARIOUS (TELSTAR)
6	NIKITA — ELTON JOHN (ROCKET)	SONGS TO LEARN AND SING — ECHO AND THE BUNNYMEN (KOROVA)
7	ONE VISION — QUEEN (EMI)	JENNIFER RUSH — JENNIFER RUSH (CBS)
8	SOMETHING ABOUT YOU — LEVEL 42 (POLYDOR)	ONCE UPON A TIME — SIMPLE MINDS (VIRGIN)
9	SISTERS ARE DOIN' IT... — EURYTHMICS/ARETHA FRANKLIN (RCA)	THE SINGLES COLLECTION — SPANDAU BALLET (CHRYSALIS)
10	ROAD TO NOWHERE — TALKING HEADS (EMI)	ROCK ANTHEMS — VARIOUS (K-TEL)
11	STAIRWAY TO HEAVEN — FAR CORPORATION (ARISTA)	LIKE A VIRGIN — MADONNA (SIRE)
12	THE SHOW — DOUG E FRESH (COOLTEMPO)	FEARGAL SHARKEY — FEARGAL SHARKEY (VIRGIN)
13	TRAPPED — COLONEL ABRAMS (MCA)	LOVE HURTS — ELAINE PAGE (WEA)
14	SAY YOU SAY ME — LIONEL RICHIE (MOTOWN)	AFTERBURNER — ZZ TOP (WARNER BROS)
15	THE TASTE OF YOUR TEARS — KING (CBS)	WORLD MACHINE — LEVEL 42 (POLYDOR)
16	BROTHERS IN ARMS — DIRE STRAITS (VERTIGO)	BITTER SWEET — KING (CBS)
17	LOST WEEKEND — LLOYD COLE AND THE COMMOTIONS (POLYDOR)	THE POWER OF CLASSIC ROCK — LONDON SYMPHONY ORCHESTRA (PORTRAIT)
18	SEE THE DAY — DEE C LEE (CBS)	OUT NOW 2 — VARIOUS (CHRYSALIS/MCA)
19	THAT'S WHAT FRIENDS ARE FOR — DIONNE WARWICK AND FRIENDS (ARISTA)	THE SINGLES 81-85 — DEPECHE MODE (MUTE)
20	JUST FOR MONEY — PAUL HARDCASTLE (CHRYSALIS)	HOUNDS OF LOVE — KATE BUSH (EMI)

S I N G L E S — US — A L B U M S

#	SINGLES	ALBUMS
1	WE BUILT THIS CITY — STARSHIP (GRUNT)	MIAMI VICE — SOUNDTRACK (MCA)
2	YOU BELONG TO THE CITY — GLENN FREY (MCA)	SCARECROW — JOHN COUGAR MELLENCAMP (RIVA)
3	SEPARATE LIVES — PHIL COLLINS/MARILYN MARTIN (ATLANTIC)	BROTHERS IN ARMS — DIRE STRAITS (WARNER BROS)
4	BROKEN WINGS — MR MISTER (RCA)	HEART — HEART (CAPITOL)
5	NEVER — HEART (CAPITOL)	IN SQUARE CIRCLE — STEVIE WONDER (MOTOWN)
6	LAY YOUR HANDS ON ME — THOMPSON TWINS (ARISTA)	WHITNEY HOUSTON — WHITNEY HOUSTON (ARISTA)
7	HEAD OVER HEELS — TEARS FOR FEARS (MERCURY)	SONGS FROM THE BIG CHAIR — TEARS FOR FEARS (MERCURY)
8	MIAMI VICE THEME — JAN HAMMER (MCA)	THE DREAM OF THE BLUE TURTLES — STING (A&M)
9	WHO'S ZOOMIN' WHO — ARETHA FRANKLIN (ARISTA)	BORN IN THE USA — BRUCE SPRINGSTEEN (COLUMBIA/CBS)
10	PART TIME LOVER — STEVIE WONDER (MOTOWN)	AFTERBURNER — ZZ TOP (WARNER BROS)
11	BE NEAR ME — ABC (MERCURY)	ROCK ME TONIGHT — FREDDIE JACKSON (CAPITOL)
12	YOU ARE MY LADY — FREDDIE JACKSON (CAPITOL)	POWER WINDOWS — RUSH (MERCURY)
13	ELECTION DAY — ARCADIA (CAPITOL)	RECKLESS — BRYAN ADAMS (A&M)
14	SLEEPING BAG — ZZ TOP (WARNER BROS)	LOVIN' EVERY MINUTE OF IT — LOVERBOY (COLUMBIA/CBS)
15	ONE OF THE LIVING — TINA TURNER (CAPITOL)	NO JACKET REQUIRED — PHIL COLLINS (ATLANTIC)
16	LOVE THEME FROM ST ELMO'S FIRE — DAVID FOSTER (ATLANTIC)	WHO'S ZOOMIN' WHO — ARETHA FRANKLIN (ARISTA)
17	PARTY ALL THE TIME — EDDIE MURPHY (COLUMBIA/CBS)	GREATEST HITS VOL 1 AND 2 — BILLY JOEL (COLUMBIA/CBS)
18	ALIVE AND KICKING — SIMPLE MINDS (A&M)	KNEE DEEP IN THE HOOPLA — STARSHIP (GRUNT)
19	I MISS YOU — KLYMAXX (MCA)	HUNTING HIGH AND LOW — A-HA (WARNER BROS)
20	SOUL KISS — OLIVIA NEWTON-JOHN (MCA)	READY FOR THE WORLD — READY FOR THE WORLD (MCA)

WEEK ENDING NOVEMBER 30 1985

S I N G L E S — UK — A L B U M S

#	SINGLES	ALBUMS
1	I'M YOUR MAN — WHAM! (EPIC)	GREATEST HITS OF 1985 — VARIOUS (TELSTAR)
2	A GOOD HEART — FEARGAL SHARKEY (VIRGIN)	LOVE SONGS — GEORGE BENSON (K-TEL)
3	DON'T BREAK MY HEART — UB40 (DEP INTERNATIONAL/VIRGIN)	BROTHERS IN ARMS — DIRE STRAITS (VERTIGO)
4	SEE THE DAY — DEE C LEE (CBS)	PROMISE — SADE (EPIC)
5	THE POWER OF LOVE — JENNIFER RUSH (CBS)	EASY PIECES — LLOYD COLE AND THE COMMOTIONS (POLYDOR)
6	ROAD TO NOWHERE — TALKING HEADS (EMI)	THE SINGLES COLLECTION — SPANDAU BALLET (CHRYSALIS)
7	THE SHOW — DOUG E FRESH (COOLTEMPO)	THE LOVE ALBUM — VARIOUS (TELSTAR)
8	ONE VISION — QUEEN (EMI)	LOVE HURTS — ELAINE PAGE (WEA)
9	SAVING ALL MY LOVE FOR YOU — WHITNEY HOUSTON (ARISTA)	NOW THE CHRISTMAS ALBUM — VARIOUS (EMI/VIRGIN)
10	SEPARATE LIVES — PHIL COLLINS/MARILYN MARTIN (VIRGIN)	LIKE A VIRGIN — MADONNA (SIRE)
11	SAY YOU SAY ME — LIONEL RICHIE (MOTOWN)	ICE ON FIRE — ELTON JOHN (ROCKET)
12	TAKE ON ME — A-HA (WARNER BROS)	SONGS TO LEARN AND SING — ECHO AND THE BUNNYMEN (KOROVA)
13	SOMETHING ABOUT YOU — LEVEL 42 (POLYDOR)	THE POWER OF CLASSIC ROCK — LONDON SYMPHONY ORCHESTRA (PORTRAIT)
14	SISTERS ARE DOIN' IT... — EURYTHMICS/ARETHA FRANKLIN (RCA)	ROCK ANTHEMS — VARIOUS (K-TEL)
15	NIKITA — ELTON JOHN (ROCKET)	FEARGAL SHARKEY — FEARGAL SHARKEY (VIRGIN)
16	THAT'S WHAT FRIENDS ARE FOR — DIONNE WARWICK AND FRIENDS (ARISTA)	JENNIFER RUSH — JENNIFER RUSH (CBS)
17	STAIRWAY TO HEAVEN — FAR CORPORATION (ARISTA)	ONCE UPON A TIME — SIMPLE MINDS (VIRGIN)
18	BROTHERS IN ARMS — DIRE STRAITS (VERTIGO)	OUT NOW 2 — VARIOUS (CHRYSALIS/MCA)
19	LOST WEEKEND — LLOYD COLE AND THE COMMOTIONS (POLYDOR)	WORLD MACHINE — LEVEL 42 (POLYDOR)
20	TRAPPED — COLONEL ABRAMS (MCA)	AFTERBURNER — ZZ TOP (WARNER BROS)

S I N G L E S — US — A L B U M S

#	SINGLES	ALBUMS
1	SEPARATE LIVES — PHIL COLLINS/MARILYN MARTIN (ATLANTIC)	MIAMI VICE — SOUNDTRACK (MCA)
2	WE BUILT THIS CITY — STARSHIP (GRUNT)	SCARECROW — JOHN COUGAR MELLENCAMP (RIVA)
3	BROKEN WINGS — MR MISTER (RCA)	HEART — HEART (CAPITOL)
4	YOU BELONG TO THE CITY — GLENN FREY (MCA)	BROTHERS IN ARMS — DIRE STRAITS (WARNER BROS)
5	NEVER — HEART (CAPITOL)	IN SQUARE CIRCLE — STEVIE WONDER (MOTOWN)
6	LAY YOUR HANDS ON ME — THOMPSON TWINS (ARISTA)	AFTERBURNER — ZZ TOP (WARNER BROS)
7	WHO'S ZOOMIN' WHO — ARETHA FRANKLIN (ARISTA)	WHITNEY HOUSTON — WHITNEY HOUSTON (ARISTA)
8	ELECTION DAY — ARCADIA (CAPITOL)	THE DREAM OF THE BLUE TURTLES — STING (A&M)
9	PARTY ALL THE TIME — EDDIE MURPHY (COLUMBIA/CBS)	SONGS FROM THE BIG CHAIR — TEARS FOR FEARS (MERCURY)
10	SLEEPING BAG — ZZ TOP (WARNER BROS)	BORN IN THE USA — BRUCE SPRINGSTEEN (COLUMBIA/CBS)
11	ALIVE AND KICKING — SIMPLE MINDS (A&M)	POWER WINDOWS — RUSH (MERCURY)
12	SAY YOU, SAY ME — LIONEL RICHIE (MOTOWN)	ROCK ME TONIGHT — FREDDIE JACKSON (CAPITOL)
13	BE NEAR ME — ABC (MERCURY)	WHO'S ZOOMIN' WHO — ARETHA FRANKLIN (ARISTA)
14	MIAMI VICE THEME — JAN HAMMER (MCA)	KNEE DEEP IN THE HOOPLA — STARSHIP (GRUNT)
15	ONE OF THE LIVING — TINA TURNER (CAPITOL)	NO JACKET REQUIRED — PHIL COLLINS (ATLANTIC)
16	I MISS YOU — KLYMAXX (MCA)	RECKLESS — BRYAN ADAMS (A&M)
17	HEAD OVER HEELS — TEARS FOR FEARS (MERCURY)	LOVIN' EVERY MINUTE OF IT — LOVERBOY (COLUMBIA/CBS)
18	PART TIME LOVER — STEVIE WONDER (MOTOWN)	GREATEST HITS — CARS (ELEKTRA)
19	PERFECT WAY — SCRITTI POLITTI (WARNER BROS)	GREATEST HITS VOL 1 AND 2 — BILLY JOEL (COLUMBIA/CBS)
20	YOU ARE MY LADY — FREDDIE JACKSON (CAPITOL)	LIVE AFTER DEATH — IRON MAIDEN (CAPITOL)

SINGLES UK ALBUMS

#	Singles	Albums
1	I'M YOUR MAN — WHAM! (EPIC)	NOW THAT'S WHAT I CALL MUSIC 6 — VARIOUS (EMI/VIRGIN)
2	SAVING ALL MY LOVE FOR YOU — WHITNEY HOUSTON (ARISTA)	HITS 3 — VARIOUS (CBS/WEA)
3	SEE THE DAY — DEE C LEE (CBS)	THE SINGLES COLLECTION — SPANDAU BALLET (CHRYSALIS)
4	A GOOD HEART — FEARGAL SHARKEY (VIRGIN)	NOW THE CHRISTMAS ALBUM — VARIOUS (EMI/VIRGIN)
5	SEPARATE LIVES — PHIL COLLINS/MARILYN MARTIN (VIRGIN)	LOVE SONGS — GEORGE BENSON (K-TEL)
6	DON'T BREAK MY HEART — UB40 (DEP INTERNATIONAL)	GREATEST HITS OF 1985 — VARIOUS (TELSTAR)
7	THE SHOW — DOUG E FRESH (COOLTEMPO)	BROTHERS IN ARMS — DIRE STRAITS (VERTIGO)
8	ROAD TO NOWHERE — TALKING HEADS (EMI)	THE LOVE ALBUM — VARIOUS (TELSTAR)
9	SAY YOU SAY ME — LIONEL RICHIE (MOTOWN)	PROMISE — SADE (EPIC)
10	THE POWER OF LOVE — JENNIFER RUSH (CBS)	LOVE HURTS — ELAINE PAGE (WEA)
11	NIKITA — ELTON JOHN (ROCKET)	LIKE A VIRGIN — MADONNA (SIRE)
12	DRESS YOU UP — MADONNA (SIRE)	EASY PIECES — LLOYD COLE AND THE COMMOTIONS (POLYDOR)
13	DON'T LOOK DOWN — GO WEST (CHRYSALIS)	ICE ON FIRE — ELTON JOHN (ROCKET)
14	TAKE ON ME — A-HA (WARNER BROS)	WORLD MACHINE — LEVEL 42 (POLYDOR)
15	ONE VISION — QUEEN (EMI)	GOLD — BARBARA DICKSON (K-TEL)
16	THAT'S WHAT FRIENDS ARE FOR — DIONNE WARWICK AND FRIENDS (ARISTA)	LEAVE THE BEST TO LAST — JAMES LAST (PROTV)
17	SPIES LIKE US — PAUL McCARTNEY (PARLOPHONE)	ROCK ANTHEMS — VARIOUS (K-TEL)
18	SISTERS ARE DOIN' IT... — EURYTHMICS/ARETHA FRANKLIN (RCA)	JENNIFER RUSH — JENNIFER RUSH (CBS)
19	WE BUILT THIS CITY — STARSHIP (RCA)	I LOVE A PARTY — RUSS ABBOT (K-TEL)
20	MATED — DAVID GRANT AND JAKI GRAHAM (EMI)	GREATEST HITS VOL 1 AND 2 — BILLY JOEL (CBS)

SINGLES US ALBUMS

#	Singles	Albums
1	BROKEN WINGS — MR MISTER (RCA)	MIAMI VICE — SOUNDTRACK (MCA)
2	SEPARATE LIVES — PHIL COLLINS/MARILYN MARTIN (ATLANTIC)	HEART — HEART (CAPITOL)
3	WE BUILT THIS CITY — STARSHIP (GRUNT)	SCARECROW — JOHN COUGAR MELLENCAMP (RIVA)
4	NEVER — HEART (CAPITOL)	AFTERBURNER — ZZ TOP (WARNER BROS)
5	SAY YOU SAY ME — LIONEL RICHIE (MOTOWN)	BROTHERS IN ARMS — DIRE STRAITS (WARNER BROS)
6	YOU BELONG TO THE CITY — GLENN FREY (MCA)	IN SQUARE CIRCLE — STEVIE WONDER (MOTOWN)
7	ELECTION DAY — ARCADIA (CAPITOL)	WHITNEY HOUSTON — WHITNEY HOUSTON (ARISTA)
8	WHO'S ZOOMIN' WHO — ARETHA FRANKLIN (ARISTA)	SONGS FROM THE BIG CHAIR — TEARS FOR FEARS (MERCURY)
9	PARTY ALL THE TIME — EDDIE MURPHY (COLUMBIA/CBS)	BORN IN THE USA — BRUCE SPRINGSTEEN (COLUMBIA/CBS)
10	SLEEPING BAG — ZZ TOP (WARNER BROS)	ROCK ME TONIGHT — FREDDIE JACKSON (CAPITOL)
11	ALIVE AND KICKING — SIMPLE MINDS (A&M)	POWER WINDOWS — RUSH (MERCURY)
12	LAY YOUR HANDS ON ME — THOMPSON TWINS (ARISTA)	THE DREAM OF THE BLUE TURTLES — STING (A&M)
13	I MISS YOU — KLYMAXX (MCA)	THE BROADWAY ALBUM — BARBRA STREISAND (COLUMBIA)
14	SMALL TOWN — JOHN COUGAR MELLENCAMP (RIVA)	WHO'S ZOOMIN' WHO — ARETHA FRANKLIN (ARISTA)
15	PERFECT WAY — SCRITTI POLITTI (WARNER BROS)	KNEE DEEP IN THE HOOPLA — STARSHIP (GRUNT)
16	THAT'S WHAT FRIENDS ARE FOR — DIONNE WARWICK AND FRIENDS (ARISTA)	GREATEST HITS — CARS (ELEKTRA)
17	TONIGHT SHE COMES — CARS (ELEKTRA)	RECKLESS — BRYAN ADAMS (A&M)
18	SISTERS ARE DOIN' IT... — EURYTHMICS/ARETHA FRANKLIN (RCA)	NO JACKET REQUIRED — PHIL COLLINS (ATLANTIC)
19	WALK OF LIFE — DIRE STRAITS (WARNER BROS)	WELCOME TO THE REAL WORLD — MR MISTER (RCA)
20	WRAP HER UP — ELTON JOHN (GEFFEN)	LIVE AFTER DEATH — IRON MAIDEN (CAPITOL)

SINGLES UK ALBUMS

#	Singles	Albums
1	SAVING ALL MY LOVE FOR YOU — WHITNEY HOUSTON (ARISTA)	NOW THAT'S WHAT I CALL MUSIC 6 — VARIOUS (EMI/VIRGIN)
2	I'M YOUR MAN — WHAM! (EPIC)	NOW THE CHRISTMAS ALBUM — VARIOUS (EMI/VIRGIN)
3	SEE THE DAY — DEE C LEE (CBS)	HITS 3 — VARIOUS (CBS/WEA)
4	SEPARATE LIVES — PHIL COLLINS/MARILYN MARTIN (VIRGIN)	THE SINGLES COLLECTION — SPANDAU BALLET (CHRYSALIS)
5	DRESS YOU UP — MADONNA (SIRE)	BROTHERS IN ARMS — DIRE STRAITS (VERTIGO)
6	DO THEY KNOW IT'S CHRISTMAS? — BAND AID (MERCURY)	LOVE SONGS — GEORGE BENSON (K-TEL)
7	A GOOD HEART — FEARGAL SHARKEY (VIRGIN)	PROMISE — SADE (EPIC)
8	SAY YOU SAY ME — LIONEL RICHIE (MOTOWN)	GREATEST HITS OF 1985 — VARIOUS (TELSTAR)
9	WEST END GIRLS — PET SHOP BOYS (PARLOPHONE)	LIKE A VIRGIN — MADONNA (SIRE)
10	MERRY CHRISTMAS EVERYONE — SHAKIN' STEVENS (EPIC)	LOVE HURTS — ELAINE PAGE (WEA)
11	THE SHOW — DOUG E FRESH (COOLTEMPO)	THE LOVE ALBUM — VARIOUS (TELSTAR)
12	DON'T BREAK MY HEART — UB40 (DEP INTERNATIONAL)	I LOVE A PARTY — RUSS ABBOT (K-TEL)
13	DON'T LOOK DOWN — GO WEST (CHRYSALIS)	GOLD — BARBARA DICKSON (K-TEL)
14	WE BUILT THIS CITY — STARSHIP (RCA)	LEAVE THE BEST TO LAST — JAMES LAST (PROTV)
15	ROAD TO NOWHERE — TALKING HEADS (EMI)	ICE ON FIRE — ELTON JOHN (ROCKET)
16	SPIES LIKE US — PAUL McCARTNEY (PARLOPHONE)	JAMBOREE BAG NUMBER 3 — CHAS AND DAVE (ROCKNEY)
17	SANTA CLAUS IS COMIN' TO TOWN — BRUCE SPRINGSTEEN (CBS)	JENNIFER RUSH — JENNIFER RUSH (CBS)
18	NIKITA — ELTON JOHN (ROCKET)	PARTY PARTY 2 — BLACK LACE (TELSTAR)
19	DON'T YOU JUST KNOW IT — AMAZULU (ISLAND)	GREATEST HITS VOL 1 AND 2 — BILLY JOEL (CBS)
20	MATED — DAVID GRANT AND JAKI GRAHAM (EMI)	REMINISCING... — HOWARD KEEL (TELSTAR)

SINGLES US ALBUMS

#	Singles	Albums
1	BROKEN WINGS — MR MISTER (RCA)	MIAMI VICE — SOUNDTRACK (MCA)
2	SEPARATE LIVES — PHIL COLLINS/MARILYN MARTIN (ATLANTIC)	HEART — HEART (CAPITOL)
3	SAY YOU SAY ME — LIONEL RICHIE (MOTOWN)	SCARECROW — JOHN COUGAR MELLENCAMP (RIVA)
4	PARTY ALL THE TIME — EDDIE MURPHY (COLUMBIA/CBS)	AFTERBURNER — ZZ TOP (WARNER BROS)
5	NEVER — HEART (CAPITOL)	BROTHERS IN ARMS — DIRE STRAITS (WARNER BROS)
6	ELECTION DAY — ARCADIA (CAPITOL)	IN SQUARE CIRCLE — STEVIE WONDER (MOTOWN)
7	ALIVE AND KICKING — SIMPLE MINDS (A&M)	THE BROADWAY ALBUM — BARBRA STREISAND (COLUMBIA)
8	SLEEPING BAG — ZZ TOP (WARNER BROS)	BORN IN THE USA — BRUCE SPRINGSTEEN (COLUMBIA/CBS)
9	I MISS YOU — KLYMAXX (MCA/CONSTELLATION)	WHITNEY HOUSTON — WHITNEY HOUSTON (ARISTA)
10	WE BUILT THIS CITY — STARSHIP (GRUNT)	POWER WINDOWS — RUSH (MERCURY)
11	WHO'S ZOOMIN' WHO — ARETHA FRANKLIN (ARISTA)	SONGS FROM THE BIG CHAIR — TEARS FOR FEARS (MERCURY)
12	SMALL TOWN — JOHN COUGAR MELLENCAMP (RIVA)	ROCK ME TONIGHT — FREDDIE JACKSON (CAPITOL)
13	PERFECT WAY — SCRITTI POLITTI (WARNER BROS)	THE DREAM OF BLUE TURTLES — STING (A&M)
14	THAT'S WHAT FRIENDS ARE FOR — DIONNE WARWICK AND FRIENDS (ARISTA)	KNEE DEEP IN THE HOOPLA — STARSHIP (GRUNT)
15	LAY YOUR HANDS ON ME — THOMPSON TWINS (ARISTA)	GREATEST HITS — CARS (ELEKTRA)
16	TONIGHT SHE COMES — CARS (ELEKTRA)	WHO'S ZOOMIN' WHO — ARETHA FRANKLIN (ARISTA)
17	YOU BELONG TO THE CITY — GLENN FREY (MCA)	WELCOME TO THE REAL WORLD — MR MISTER (RCA)
18	WALK OF LIFE — DIRE STRAITS (WARNER BROS)	NO JACKET REQUIRED — PHIL COLLINS (ATLANTIC)
19	TALK TO ME — STEVIE NICKS (MODERN)	LIVE AFTER DEATH — IRON MAIDEN (CAPITOL)
20	WRAP HER UP — ELTON JOHN (GEFFEN)	RECKLESS — BRYAN ADAMS (A&M)

WEEK ENDING DECEMBER 21 1985

S I N G L E S — UK — A L B U M S

#	SINGLES	ALBUMS
1	SAVING ALL MY LOVE FOR YOU — WHITNEY HOUSTON (ARISTA)	NOW THE CHRISTMAS ALBUM — VARIOUS (EMI/VIRGIN)
2	MERRY CHRISTMAS EVERYONE — SHAKIN' STEVENS (EPIC)	NOW THAT'S WHAT I CALL MUSIC 6 — VARIOUS (EMI/VIRGIN)
3	DO THEY KNOW IT'S CHRISTMAS? — BAND AID (MERCURY)	HITS 3 — VARIOUS (CBS/WEA)
4	I'M YOUR MAN — WHAM! (EPIC)	BROTHERS IN ARMS — DIRE STRAITS (EPIC)
5	WEST END GIRLS — PET SHOP BOYS (PARLOPHONE)	PROMISE — SADE (EPIC)
6	SEE THE DAY — DEE C LEE (CBS)	THE SINGLES COLLECTION — SPANDAU BALLET (CHRYSALIS)
7	SEPARATE LIVES — PHIL COLLINS/MARILYN MARTIN (VIRGIN)	LOVE SONGS — GEORGE BENSON (K-TEL)
8	DRESS YOU UP — MADONNA (SIRE)	LIKE A VIRGIN — MADONNA (SIRE)
9	SANTA CLAUS IS COMING TO TOWN — BRUCE SPRINGSTEEN (CBS)	GREATEST HITS OF 1985 — VARIOUS (TELSTAR)
10	LAST CHRISTMAS — WHAM! (EPIC)	THE LOVE ALBUM — VARIOUS (TELSTAR)
11	SAY YOU SAY ME — LIONEL RICHIE (MOTOWN)	LEAVE THE BEST TO LAST — JAMES LAST (PROTV)
12	WE BUILT THIS CITY — STARSHIP (RCA)	GOLD — BARBARA DICKSON (K-TEL)
13	A GOOD HEART — FEARGAL SHARKEY (VIRGIN)	LOVE HURTS — ELAINE PAIGE (WEA)
14	WALKING IN THE AIR — ALED JONES (HMV)	I LOVE A PARTY — RUSS ABBOT (K-TEL)
15	DON'T LOOK DOWN — GO WEST (CHRYSALIS)	ICE ON FIRE — ELTON JOHN (ROCKET)
16	SPIES LIKE US — PAUL McCARTNEY (PARLOPHONE)	JAMBOREE BAG NUMBER 3 — CHAS AND DAVE (ROCKNEY)
17	HIT THAT PERFECT BEAT — BRONSKI BEAT (FORBIDDEN FRUIT)	ALED JONES/BBC WELSH CHORUS — ALED JONES/BBC WELSH CHORUS (10 RECORDS)
18	THE SHOW — DOUG E FRESH (COOLTEMPO)	THE CLASSIC TOUCH — RICHARD CLAYDERMAN/RPO (DELPHINE)
19	DON'T YOU JUST KNOW IT — AMAZULU (ISLAND)	JENNIFER RUSH — JENNIFER RUSH (CBS)
20	DON'T BREAK MY HEART — UB40 (DEP INTERNATIONAL)	REMINISCING — HOWARD KEEL (TELSTAR)

S I N G L E S — US — A L B U M S

#	SINGLES	ALBUMS
1	SAY YOU SAY ME — LIONEL RICHIE (MOTOWN)	HEART — HEART (CAPITOL)
2	BROKEN WINGS — MR MISTER (RCA)	MIAMI VICE — SOUNDTRACK (MCA)
3	PARTY ALL THE TIME — EDDIE MURPHY (COLUMBIA/CBS)	SCARECROW — JOHN COUGAR MELLENCAMP (RIVA)
4	ALIVE AND KICKING — SIMPLE MINDS (A&M)	AFTERBURNER — ZZ TOP (WARNER BROS)
5	SEPARATE LIVES — PHIL COLLINS/MARILYN MARTIN (ATLANTIC)	THE BROADWAY ALBUM — BARBRA STREISAND (COLUMBIA)
6	ELECTION DAY — ARCADIA (CAPITOL)	BROTHERS IN ARMS — DIRE STRAITS (WARNER BROS)
7	I MISS YOU — KLYMAXX (MCA/CONSTELLATION)	IN SQUARE CIRCLE — STEVIE WONDER (MOTOWN)
8	THAT'S WHAT FRIENDS ARE FOR — DIONNE WARWICK AND FRIENDS (ARISTA)	BORN IN THE USA — BRUCE SPRINGSTEEN (COLUMBIA/CBS)
9	SMALL TOWN — JOHN COUGAR MELLENCAMP (RIVA)	WHITNEY HOUSTON — WHITNEY HOUSTON (ARISTA)
10	SLEEPING BAG — ZZ TOP (WARNER BROS)	POWER WINDOWS — RUSH (MERCURY)
11	PERFECT WAY — SCRITTI POLITTI (WARNER BROS)	SONGS FROM THE BIG CHAIR — TEARS FOR FEARS (MERCURY)
12	TONIGHT SHE COMES — THE CARS (ELEKTRA)	GREATEST HITS — THE CARS (ELEKTRA)
13	NEVER — HEART (CAPITOL)	THE DREAM OF THE BLUE TURTLES — STING (A&M)
14	WALK OF LIFE — DIRE STRAITS (WARNER BROS)	NO JACKET REQUIRED — PHIL COLLINS (ATLANTIC)
15	WE BUILT THIS CITY — STARSHIP (GRUNT)	KNEE DEEP IN THE HOOPLA — STARSHIP (GRUNT)
16	TALK TO ME — STEVIE NICKS (MODERN)	WHO'S ZOOMIN' WHO — ARETHA FRANKLIN (ARISTA)
17	BURNING HEAT — SURVIVOR (SCOTTI BROS)	WELCOME TO THE REAL WORLD — MR MISTER (RCA)
18	WHO'S ZOOMIN' WHO — ARETHA FRANKLIN (ARISTA)	ONCE UPON A TIME — SIMPLE MINDS (A&M/VIRGIN)
19	EMERGENCY — KOOL AND THE GANG (DE-LITE)	RECKLESS — BRYAN ADAMS (A&M)
20	LOVE IS THE SEVENTH WAVE — STING (A&M)	ROCK A LITTLE — STEVIE NICKS (MODERN)

WEEK ENDING DECEMBER 28 1985

S I N G L E S — UK — A L B U M S

#	SINGLES	ALBUMS
1	MERRY CHRISTMAS EVERYONE — SHAKIN' STEVENS (EPIC)	NOW THE CHRISTMAS ALBUM — VARIOUS (EMI/VIRGIN)
2	SAVING ALL MY LOVE FOR YOU — WHITNEY HOUSTON (ARISTA)	NOW THAT'S WHAT I CALL MUSIC 6 — VARIOUS (EMI/VIRGIN)
3	DO THEY KNOW IT'S CHRISTMAS? — BAND AID (MERCURY)	HITS 3 — VARIOUS (CBS/WEA)
4	WEST END GIRLS — PET SHOP BOYS (PARLOPHONE)	BROTHERS IN ARMS — DIRE STRAITS (VERTIGO)
5	WALKING IN THE AIR — ALED JONES (HMV)	PROMISE — SADE (EPIC)
6	LAST CHRISTMAS — WHAM! (EPIC)	LOVE SONGS — GEORGE BENSON (K-TEL)
7	SEPARATE LIVES — PHIL COLLINS/MARILYN MARTIN (VIRGIN)	LIKE A VIRGIN — MADONNA (SIRE)
8	I'M YOUR MAN — WHAM! (EPIC)	THE SINGLES COLLECTION — SPANDAU BALLET (CHRYSALIS)
9	DRESS YOU UP — MADONNA (SIRE)	THE LOVE ALBUM — VARIOUS (TELSTAR)
10	SEE THE DAY — DEE C LEE (CBS)	GREATEST HITS OF 1985 — VARIOUS (TELSTAR)
11	SANTA CLAUS IS COMIN' TO TOWN — BRUCE SPRINGSTEEN (CBS)	GOLD — BARBRA DICKSON (K-TEL)
12	WE BUILT THIS CITY — STARSHIP (RCA)	ALED JONES/BBC WELSH CHORUS — ALED JONES/BBC WELSH CHORUS (10 RECORDS)
13	HIT THAT PERFECT BEAT — BRONSKI BEAT (FORBIDDEN FRUIT)	LOVE HURTS — ELAINE PAIGE (WEA)
14	SAY YOU SAY ME — LIONEL RICHIE (MOTOWN)	LEAVE THE BEST TO LAST — JAMES LAST (PROTV)
15	GIRLIE GIRLIE — SOPHIA GEORGE (WINNER)	JAMBOREE BAG NUMBER 3 — CHAS AND DAVE (ROCKNEY)
16	SPIES LIKE US — PAUL McCARTNEY (PARLOPHONE)	ICE ON FIRE — ELTON JOHN (ROCKET)
17	DON'T YOU JUST KNOW IT — AMAZULU (ISLAND)	I LOVE A PARTY — RUSS ABBOT (K-TEL)
18	A GOOD HEART — FEARGAL SHARKEY (VIRGIN)	GREATEST HITS VOL 1 AND 2 — BILLY JOEL (CBS)
19	DON'T LOOK DOWN — GO WEST (CHRYSALIS)	JENNIFER RUSH — JENNIFER RUSH (CBS)
20	WRAP HER UP — ELTON JOHN (ROCKET)	THE CLASSIC TOUCH — RICHARD CLAYDERMAN/RPO (DELPHINE)

S I N G L E S — US — A L B U M S

NO US CHARTS PUBLISHED

SINGLES UK

#	Single	Artist (Label)
1	MERRY CHRISTMAS EVERYONE	SHAKIN'STEVENS (EPIC)
2	SAVING ALL MY LOVE FOR YOU	WHITNEY HOUSTON (ARISTA)
3	WEST END GIRLS	PET SHOP BOYS (PARLOPHONE)
4	DO THEY KNOW IT'S CHRISTMAS?	BAND AID (MERCURY)
5	WALKING IN THE AIR	ALED JONES (HMV)
6	LAST CHRISTMAS	WHAM! (EPIC)
7	DRESS YOU UP	MADONNA (SIRE)
8	I'M YOUR MAN	WHAM! (EPIC)
9	SEPARATE LIVES	PHIL COLLINS/MARILYN MARTIN (VIRGIN)
10	SEE THE DAY	DEE C LEE (CBS)
11	HIT THAT PERFECT BEAT	BRONSKI BEAT (FORBIDDEN FRUIT)
12	WE BUILT THIS CITY	STARSHIP (RCA)
13	SPIES LIKE US	PAUL McCARTNEY (PARLOPHONE)
14	GIRLIE GIRLIE	SOPHIA GEORGE (WINNER)
15	DON'T YOU JUST KNOW IT	AMAZULU (ISLAND))
16	SAY YOU SAY ME	LIONEL RICHIE (MOTOWN)
17	A GOOD HEART	FEARGAL SHARKEY (VIRGIN)
18	DON'T LOOK DOWN	GO WEST (CHRYSALIS)
19	WRAP HER UP	ELTON JOHN (ROCKET)
20	SANTA CLAUS IS COMIN' TO TOWN	BRUCE SPRINGSTEEN (CBS)

ALBUMS

#	Album	Artist (Label)
1	NOW THAT'S WHAT I CALL MUSIC 6	VARIOUS (EMI/VIRGIN)
2	HITS 3	VARIOUS (CBS/WEA)
3	NOW THE CHRISTMAS ALBUM	VARIOUS (EMI/VIRGIN)
4	BROTHERS IN ARMS	DIRE STRAITS (VERTIGO)
5	LIKE A VIRGIN	MADONNA (SIRE)
6	PROMISE	SADE (EPIC)
7	LOVE SONGS	GEORGE BENSON (K-TEL)
8	THE SINGLES COLLECTION	SPANDAU BALLET (CHRYSALIS)
9	GREATEST HITS OF 1985	VARIOUS (TELSTAR)
10	THE LOVE ALBUM	VARIOUS (TELSTAR)
11	ALED JONES/BBC WELSH CHORUS	ALED JONES/BBC WELSH CHORUS (10 RECORDS)
12	JENNIFER RUSH	JENNIFER RUSH (CBS)
13	GREATEST HITS VOL 1 AND 2	BILLY JOEL (CBS)
14	GOLD	BARBARA DICKSON (K-TEL)
15	WORLD MACHINE	LEVEL 42 (POLYDOR)
16	ICE ON FIRE	ELTON JOHN (ROCKET)
17	WHITNEY HOUSTON	WHITNEY HOUSTON (ARISTA)
18	I LOVE A PARTY	RUSS ABBOT (K-TEL)
19	GO WEST	GO WEST (CHRYSALIS)
20	NO JACKET REQUIRED	PHIL COLLINS (VIRGIN)

SINGLES US / ALBUMS

NO US CHARTS PUBLISHED

SINGLES UK

#	Single	Artist (Label)
1	WEST END GIRLS	PET SHOP BOYS (PARLOPHONE)
2	SAVING ALL MY LOVE FOR YOU	WHITNEY HOUSTON (ARISTA)
3	MERRY CHRISTMAS EVERYONE	SHAKIN' STEVENS (EPIC)
4	HIT THAT PERFECT BEAT	BRONSKI BEAT (FORBBIDEN FRUIT)
5	THE SUN ALWAYS SHINES ON TV	A-HA (WARNER BROS)
6	DRESS YOU UP	MADONNA (SIRE)
7	GIRLIE GIRLIE	SOPHIA GEORGE (WINNER)
8	WALKING ON AIR	ALED JONES (HMV)
9	I'M YOUR MAN	WHAM! (EPIC)
10	SATURDAY LOVE	CHERRELLE/ALEXANDER O'NEAL (TABU)
11	SEPARATE LIVES	PHIL COLLINS/MARILYN MARTIN (VIRGIN)
12	WRAP HER UP	ELTON JOHN (ROCKET)
13	DO THEY KNOW IT'S CHRISTMAS?	BAND AID (MERCURY)
14	LAST CHRISTMAS	WHAM! (EPIC)
15	WE BUILT THIS CITY	STARSHIP (RCA)
16	SEE THE DAY	DEE C LEE (CBS)
17	DON'T YOU JUST KNOW IT	AMAZULU (ISLAND)
18	SPIES LIKE US	PAUL McCARTNEY (PARLOPHONE)
19	DON'T LOOK DOWN	GO WEST (CHRYSALIS)
20	RUSSIANS	STING (A&M)

ALBUMS

#	Album	Artist (Label)
1	NOW THAT'S WHAT I CALL MUSIC 6	VARIOUS (EMI/VIRGIN)
2	BROTHERS IN ARMS	DIRE STRAITS (VERTIGO)
3	LIKE A VIRGIN	MADONNA (SIRE)
4	HITS 3	VARIOUS (CBS/WEA)
5	THE SINGLES COLLECTION	SPANDAU BALLET (CHRYSALIS)
6	PROMISE	SADE (EPIC)
7	WORLD MACHINE	LEVEL 42 (POLYDOR)
8	GREATEST HITS OF 1985	VARIOUS (TELSTAR)
9	ISLAND LIFE	GRACE JONES (ISLAND)
10	SONGS FROM THE BIG CHAIR	TEARS FOR FEARS (MERCURY)
11	WHITNEY HOUSTON	WHITNEY HOUSTON (ARISTA)
12	THE LOVE ALBUM	VARIOUS (TELSTAR)
13	JENNIFER RUSH	JENNIFER RUSH (CBS)
14	HUNTING HIGH AND LOW	A-HA (WARNER BROS)
15	GO WEST	GO WEST (CHRYSALIS)
16	LOVE SONGS	GEORGE BENSON (K-TEL)
17	THE CLASSIC TOUCH	RICHARD CLAYDERMAN/RPO. (DELPHINE)
18	NO JACKET REQUIRED	PHIL COLLINS (VIRGIN)
19	ICE ON FIRE	ELTON JOHN (ROCKET)
20	ONCE UPON A TIME	SIMPLE MINDS (VIRGIN)

SINGLES US

#	Single	Artist (Label)
1	SAY YOU, SAY ME	LIONEL RICHIE (MOTOWN)
2	PARTY ALL THE TIME	EDDIE MURPHY (COLUMBIA/CBS)
3	THAT'S WHAT FRIENDS ARE FOR	DIONNE WARWICK AND FRIENDS (ARISTA)
4	ALIVE AND KICKING	SIMPLE MINDS (A&M/VIRGIN)
5	I MISS YOU	KLYMAXX (MCA/CONSTELLATION)
6	SMALL TOWN	JOHN COUGAR MELLENCAMP (RIVA)
7	TONIGHT SHE COMES	CARS (ELEKTRA)
8	TALK TO ME	STEVIE NICKS (MODERN)
9	BROKEN WINGS	MR MISTER (RCA)
10	WALK OF LIFE	DIRE STRAITS (WARNER BROS)
11	SEPARATE LIVES	PHIL COLLINS/MARILYN MARTIN (ATLANTIC)
12	BURNING HEAT	SURVIVOR (SCOTTI BROS)
13	MY HOMETOWN	BRUCE SPRINGSTEEN (COLUMBIA/CBS)
14	I'M YOUR MAN	WHAM! (COLUMBIA/CBS)
15	ELECTION DAY	ARCADIA (CAPITOL)
16	IT'S ONLY LOVE	BRYAN ADAMS AND TINA TURNER (A&M)
17	LOVE IS THE SEVENTH WAVE	STING (A&M)
18	GO HOME	STEVIE WONDER (MOTOWN)
19	SPIES LIKE US	PAUL McCARTNEY (CAPITOL)
20	CONGA	MIAMI SOUND MACHINE (EPIC)

ALBUMS

#	Album	Artist (Label)
1	MIAMI VICE	SOUNDTRACK (MCA)
2	THE BROADWAY ALBUM	BARBRA STREISAND (COLUMBIA/CBS)
3	HEART	HEART (CAPITOL)
4	SCARECROW	JOHN COUGAR MELLENCAMP (RIVA)
5	AFTERBURNER	ZZ TOP (WARNER BROS)
6	BROTHERS IN ARMS	DIRE STRAITS (WARNER BROS)
7	IN SQUARE CIRCLE	STEVIE WONDER (MOTOWN)
8	BORN IN THE USA	BRUCE SPRINGSTEEN (COLUMBIA/CBS)
9	KNEE DEEP IN THE HOOPLA	STARSHIP (GRUNT)
10	SONGS FROM THE BIG CHAIR	TEARS FOR FEARS (MERCURY)
11	PROMISE	SADE (PORTRAIT)
12	GREATEST HITS	CARS (ELEKTRA)
13	WELCOME TO THE REAL WORLD	MR MISTER (ARISTA)
14	ROCK A LITTLE	STEVIE NICKS (MODERN)
15	WHITNEY HOUSTON	WHITNEY HOUSTON (ARISTA)
16	THE DREAM OF THE BLUE TURTLES	STING (A&M)
17	POWER WINDOWS	RUSH (MERCURY)
18	ONCE UPON A TIME	SIMPLE MINDS (A&M/VIRGIN)
19	RECKLESS	BRYAN ADAMS (A&M)
20	NO JACKET REQUIRED	PHIL COLLINS (ATLANTIC)

WEEK ENDING JANUARY 18 1986
S I N G L E S UK A L B U M S

WEST END GIRLS PET SHOP BOYS (PARLOPHONE)	**1**	**BROTHERS IN ARMS** DIRE STRAITS (VERTIGO)	
THE SUN ALWAYS SHINES ON TV A-HA (WARNER BROS)	**2**	**HUNTING HIGH AND LOW** A-HA (WARNER BROS)	
HIT THAT PERFECT BEAT BRONSKI BEAT (FORBIDDEN FRUIT)	**3**	**NOW THAT'S WHAT I CALL MUSIC 6** VARIOUS (EMI/VIRGIN)	
WALK OF LIFE DIRE STRAITS (VERTIGO)	**4**	**THE BROADWAY ALBUM** BARBRA STREISAND (CBS)	
YOU LITTLE THIEF FEARGAL SHARKEY (VIRGIN)	**5**	**LIKE A VIRGIN** MADONNA (SIRE)	
SATURDAY LOVE CHERRELLE/ALEXANDER O'NEAL (TABU)	**6**	**WORLD MACHINE** LEVEL 42 (POLYDOR)	
GIRLIE GIRLIE SOPHIA GEORGE (WINNER)	**7**	**ISLAND LIFE** GRACE JONES (ISLAND)	
BROKEN WINGS MR MISTER (RCA)	**8**	**THE DREAM OF THE BLUE TURTLES** STING (A&M)	
SAVING ALL MY LOVE FOR YOU WHITNEY HOUSTON (ARISTA)	**9**	**WHITNEY HOUSTON** WHITNEY HOUSTON (ARISTA)	
ALICE, I WANT YOU JUST FOR ME FULL FORCE (CBS)	**10**	**PROMISE** SADE (EPIC)	
WHO'S ZOOMIN' WHO ARETHA FRANKLIN (ARISTA)	**11**	**HITS 3** VARIOUS (CBS/WEA)	
RUSSIANS STING (A&M)	**12**	**JENNIFER RUSH** JENNIFER RUSH (CBS)	
IT'S ALRIGHT (BABY'S COMING BACK) EURYTHMICS (RCA)	**13**	**GO WEST** GO WEST (CHRYSALIS)	
RING OF ICE JENNIFER RUSH (CBS)	**14**	**THE SINGLES COLLECTION** SPANDAU BALLET (CHRYSALIS)	
LEAVING ME NOW LEVEL 42 (POLYDOR)	**15**	**FEARGAL SHARKEY** FEARGAL SHARKEY (VIRGIN)	
WRAP HER UP ELTON JOHN (ROCKET)	**16**	**NO JACKET REQUIRED** PHIL COLLINS (VIRGIN)	
SUSPICIOUS MINDS FINE YOUNG CANNIBALS (LONDON)	**17**	**SONGS FROM THE BIG CHAIR** TEARS FOR FEARS (MERCURY)	
WALKING IN THE AIR ALED JONES (HMV)	**18**	**THE LOVE ALBUM** VARIOUS (TELSTAR)	
SEPARATE LIVES PHIL COLLINS/MARILYN MARTIN (VIRGIN)	**19**	**FINE YOUNG CANNIBALS** FINE YOUNG CANNIBALS (LONDON)	
MERRY CHRISTMAS EVERYONE SHAKIN' STEVENS (EPIC)	**20**	**LOVE SONGS** GEORGE BENSON (K-TEL)	

S I N G L E S US A L B U M S

THAT'S WHAT FRIENDS ARE FOR DIONNE WARWICK AND FRIENDS (ARISTA)	**1**	**MIAMI VICE** SOUNDTRACK (MCA)	
SAY YOU, SAY ME LIONEL RICHIE (MOTOWN)	**2**	**THE BROADWAY ALBUM** BARBRA STREISAND (COLUMBIA/CBS)	
PARTY ALL THE TIME EDDIE MURPHY (COLUMBIA/CBS)	**3**	**SCARECROW** JOHN COUGAR MELLENCAMP (RIVA)	
ALIVE AND KICKING SIMPLE MINDS (A&M/VIRGIN)	**4**	**HEART** HEART (CAPITOL)	
I MISS YOU KLYMAXX (MCA/CONSTELLATION)	**5**	**AFTERBURNER** ZZ TOP (WARNER BROS)	
SMALL TOWN JOHN COUGAR MELLENCAMP (RIVA)	**6**	**BROTHERS IN ARMS** DIRE STRAITS (WARNER BROS)	
TALK TO ME STEVIE NICKS (MODERN)	**7**	**PROMISE** SADE (PORTRAIT)	
BURNING HEART SURVIVOR (SCOTTI BROS)	**8**	**BORN IN THE USA** BRUCE SPRINGSTEEN (COLUMBIA/CBS)	
WALK OF LIFE DIRE STRAITS (WARNER BROS)	**9**	**KNEE DEEP IN THE HOOPLA** STARSHIP (GRUNT)	
TONIGHT SHE COMES THE CARS (ELEKTRA)	**10**	**IN SQUARE CIRCLE** STEVIE WONDER (MOTOWN)	
MY HOMETOWN BRUCE SPRINGSTEEN (COLUMBIA/CBS)	**11**	**SONGS FROM THE BIG CHAIR** TEARS FOR FEARS (MERCURY)	
I'M YOUR MAN WHAM! (COLUMBIA/CBS)	**12**	**WHITNEY HOUSTON** WHITNEY HOUSTON (ARISTA)	
SPIES LIKE US PAUL McCARTNEY (CAPITOL)	**13**	**WELCOME TO THE REAL WORLD** MR MISTER (ARISTA)	
GO HOME STEVIE WONDER (MOTOWN)	**14**	**ROCK A LITTLE** STEVIE NICKS (MODERN)	
IT'S ONLY LOVE BRYAN ADAMS AND TINA TURNER (A&M)	**15**	**GREATEST HITS** THE CARS (ELEKTRA)	
WHEN THE GOING GETS TOUGH BILLY OCEAN (JIVE)	**16**	**ONCE UPON A TIME** SIMPLE MINDS (A&M/VIRGIN)	
CONGA MIAMI SOUND MACHINE (EPIC)	**17**	**POWER WINDOWS** RUSH (MERCURY)	
YOU'RE A FRIEND OF MINE C. CLEMONS/J. BROWNE (COLUMBIA/CBS)	**18**	**THE DREAM OF THE BLUE TURTLES** STING (A&M)	
SEPARATE LIVES PHIL COLLINS/MARILYN MARTIN (ATLANTIC)	**19**	**NO JACKET REQUIRED** PHIL COLLINS (ATLANTIC)	
GOODBYE NIGHT RANGER (CAMEL/MCA)	**20**	**WHITE NIGHTS** SOUNDTRACK (ATLANTIC)	

WEEK ENDING JANUARY 25 1986
S I N G L E S UK A L B U M S

THE SUN ALWAYS SHINES ON TV A-HA (WARNER BROS)	**1**	**BROTHERS IN ARMS** DIRE STRAITS (VERTIGO)	
WALK OF LIFE DIRE STRAITS (VERTIGO)	**2**	**HUNTING HIGH AND LOW** A-HA (WARNER BROS)	
WEST END GIRLS PET SHOP BOYS (PARLOPHONE)	**3**	**THE BROADWAY ALBUM** BARBRA STREISAND (CBS)	
BROKEN WINGS MR MISTER (RCA)	**4**	**WORLD MACHINE** LEVEL 42 (POLYDOR)	
YOU LITTLE THIEF FEARGAL SHARKEY (VIRGIN)	**5**	**THE DREAM OF THE BLUE TURTLES** STING (A&M)	
SATURDAY LOVE CHERRELLE/ALEXANDER O'NEAL (TABU)	**6**	**LIKE A VIRGIN** MADONNA (SIRE)	
HIT THAT PERFECT BEAT BRONSKI BEAT (FORBIDDEN FRUIT)	**7**	**ISLAND LIFE** GRACE JONES (ISLAND)	
ONLY LOVE NANA MOUSKOURI (CARRERE/PHILLIPS)	**8**	**NOW THAT'S WHAT I CALL MUSIC 6** VARIOUS (EMI/VIRGIN)	
ALICE, I WANT YOU JUST FOR ME FULL FORCE (CBS)	**9**	**GO WEST** GO WEST (CHRYSALIS)	
SUSPICIOUS MINDS FINE YOUNG CANNIBALS (LONDON)	**10**	**WHITNEY HOUSTON** WHITNEY HOUSTON (ARISTA)	
WHO'S ZOOMIN' WHO ARETHA FRANKLIN (ARISTA)	**11**	**PROMISE** SADE (EPIC)	
IT'S ALRIGHT (BABY'S COMING BACK) EURYTHMICS (RCA)	**12**	**BE YOURSELF TONIGHT** EURYTHMICS (RCA)	
SYSTEM ADDICT FIVE STAR (TENT)	**13**	**FEARGAL SHARKEY** FEARGAL SHARKEY (VIRGIN)	
RUSSIANS STING (A&M)	**14**	**JENNIFER RUSH** JENNIFER RUSH (CBS)	
BORDERLINE MADONNA (SIRE)	**15**	**FINE YOUNG CANNIBALS** FINE YOUNG CANNIBALS (LONDON)	
GIRLIE GIRLIE SOPHIA GEORGE (WINNER)	**16**	**ONCE UPON A TIME** SIMPLE MINDS (VIRGIN)	
LEAVING ME NOW LEVEL 42 (POLYDOR)	**17**	**HIGH PRIORITY** CHERRELLE (TABU)	
RING OF ICE JENNIFER RUSH (CBS)	**18**	**HITS 3** VARIOUS (CBS/WEA)	
SAVING ALL MY LOVE FOR YOU WHITNEY HOUSTON (ARISTA)	**19**	**THE SINGLES COLLECTION** SPANDAU BALLET (CHRYSALIS)	
PULL UP TO THE BUMPER GRACE JONES (ISLAND)	**20**	**NO JACKET REQUIRED** PHIL COLLINS (VIRGIN)	

S I N G L E S US A L B U M S

THAT'S WHAT FRIENDS ARE FOR DIONNE WARWICK AND FRIENDS (ARISTA)	**1**	**SCARECROW** JOHN COUGAR MELLENCAMP (RIVA)	
SAY YOU, SAY ME LIONEL RICHIE (MOTOWN)	**2**	**MIAMI VICE** SOUNDTRACK (MCA)	
BURNING HEART SURVIVOR (SCOTTI BROS)	**3**	**HEART** HEART (CAPITOL)	
TALK TO ME STEVIE NICKS (MODERN)	**4**	**THE BROADWAY ALBUM** BARBRA STREISAND (COLUMBIA/CBS)	
I'M YOUR MAN WHAM! (COLUMBIA/CBS)	**5**	**PROMISE** SADE (PORTRAIT)	
MY HOMETOWN BRUCE SPRINGSTEEN (COLUMBIA/CBS)	**6**	**BROTHERS IN ARMS** DIRE STRAITS (WARNER BROS)	
WALK OF LIFE DIRE STRAITS (WARNER BROS)	**7**	**AFTERBURNER** ZZ TOP (WARNER BROS)	
I MISS YOU KLYMAXX (MCA/CONSTELLATION)	**8**	**KNEE DEEP IN THE HOOPLA** STARSHIP (GRUNT)	
PARTY ALL THE TIME EDDIE MURPHY (COLUMBIA/CBS)	**9**	**WELCOME TO THE REAL WORLD** MR MISTER (RCA)	
SPIES LIKE US PAUL McCARTNEY (CAPITOL)	**10**	**BORN IN THE USA** BRUCE SPRINGSTEEN (COLUMBIA/CBS)	
WHEN THE GOING GETS TOUGH BILLY OCEAN (JIVE)	**11**	**WHITNEY HOUSTON** WHITNEY HOUSTON (ARISTA)	
ALIVE AND KICKING SIMPLE MINDS (A&M/VIRGIN)	**12**	**IN SQUARE CIRCLE** STEVIE WONDER (MOTOWN)	
GO HOME STEVIE WONDER (MOTOWN)	**13**	**SONGS FROM THE BIG CHAIR** TEARS FOR FEARS (MERCURY)	
SMALL TOWN JOHN COUGAR MELLENCAMP (RIVA)	**14**	**ROCK A LITTLE** STEVIE NICKS (MODERN)	
TONIGHT SHE COMES THE CARS (ELEKTRA)	**15**	**ONCE UPON A TIME** SIMPLE MINDS (A&M/VIRGIN)	
CONGA MIAMI SOUND MACHINE (EPIC)	**16**	**GREATEST HITS** THE CARS (ELEKTRA)	
HOW WILL I KNOW WHITNEY HOUSTON (ARISTA)	**17**	**THE DREAM OF THE BLUE TURTLES** STING (A&M)	
IT'S ONLY LOVE BRYAN ADAMS/TINA TURNER (A&M)	**18**	**WHITE NIGHTS** SOUNDTRACK (ATLANTIC)	
GOODBYE NIGHT RANGER (CAMEL/MCA)	**19**	**ROCKY IV** SOUNDTRACK (SCOTTI BROS)	
SIDEWALK TALK JELLYBEAN (EMI AMERICA)	**20**	**NO JACKET REQUIRED** PHIL COLLINS (ATLANTIC)	

S I N G L E S — UK A L B U M S

#	Singles	Albums
1	THE SUN ALWAYS SHINES ON TV — A-HA (WARNER BROS)	BROTHERS IN ARMS — DIRE STRAITS (VERTIGO)
2	ONLY LOVE — NANA MOUSKOURI (CARRERE/PHILIPS)	HUNTING HIGH AND LOW — A-HA (WARNER BROS)
3	WALK OF LIFE — DIRE STRAITS (VERTIGO)	THE BROADWAY ALBUM — BARBARA STREISAND (CBS)
4	BORDERLINE — MADONNA (SIRE)	WORLD MACHINE — LEVEL 42 (POLYDOR)
5	BROKEN WINGS — MR MISTER (RCA)	THE DREAM OF THE BLUE TURTLES — STING (A&M)
6	WHEN THE GOING GETS TOUGH — BILLY OCEAN (JIVE)	ISLAND LIFE — GRACE JONES (ISLAND)
7	WEST END GIRLS — PET SHOP BOYS (PARLOPHONE)	BE YOURSELF TONIGHT — EURYTHMICS (RCA)
8	SUSPICIOUS MINDS — FINE YOUNG CANNIBALS (LONDON)	LIKE A VIRGIN — MADONNA (SIRE)
9	SATURDAY LOVE — CHERRELLE/ALEXANDER O'NEAL (TABU)	WHITNEY HOUSTON — WHITNEY HOUSTON (ARISTA)
10	SYSTEM ADDICT — FIVE STAR (TENT)	GO WEST — GO WEST (CHRYSALIS)
11	YOU LITTLE THIEF — FEARGAL SHARKEY (VIRGIN)	NOW THAT'S WHAT I CALL MUSIC 6 — VARIOUS (EMI/VIRGIN)
12	THE PHANTOM OF THE OPERA — SARAH BRIGHTMAN/STEVE HARLEY (POLYDOR)	FEARGAL SHARKEY — FEARGAL SHARKEY (VIRGIN)
13	ALICE, I WANT YOU JUST FOR ME — FULL FORCE (CBS)	FINE YOUNG CANNIBALS — FINE YOUNG CANNIBALS (LONDON)
14	IT'S ALRIGHT (BABY'S COMING BACK) — EURYTHMICS (RCA)	THE FIRST ALBUM — MADONNA (SIRE)
15	PULL UP TO THE BUMPER — GRACE JONES (ISLAND)	ONCE UPON A TIME — SIMPLE MINDS (VIRGIN)
16	HIT THAT PERFECT BEAT — BRONSKI BEAT (FORBIDDEN FRUIT)	PROMISE — SADE (EPIC)
17	SANCTIFY YOURSELF — SIMPLE MINDS (VIRGIN)	THE SINGLES COLLECTION — SPANDAU BALLET (CHRYSALIS)
18	WHO'S ZOOMIN' WHO — ARETHA FRANKLIN (ARISTA)	LUXURY OF LIFE — FIVE STAR (TENT)
19	LIVING IN AMERICA — JAMES BROWN (SCOTTI BROS)	JENNIFER RUSH — JENNIFER RUSH (CBS)
20	IN A LIFETIME — CLANNAD/BONO (RCS)	HITS 3 — VARIOUS (CBS/WEA)

S I N G L E S — US A L B U M S

#	Singles	Albums
1	THAT'S WHAT FRIENDS ARE FOR — DIONNE WARWICK AND FRIENDS (ARISTA)	THE BROADWAY ALBUM — BARBRA STREISAND (CBS)
2	BURNING HEART — SURVIVOR (SCOTTI BROS)	PROMISE — SADE (EPIC)
3	I'M YOUR MAN — WHAM! (COLUMBIA/CBS)	MIAMI VICE — SOUNDTRACK (MCA)
4	TALK TO ME — STEVIE NICKS (MODERN)	HEART — HEART (CAPITOL)
5	SAY YOU, SAY ME — LIONEL RICHIE (MOTOWN)	SCARECROW — JOHN COUGAR MELLENCAMP (RIVA)
6	MY HOMETOWN — BRUCE SPRINGSTEEN (COLUMBIA/CBS)	BROTHERS IN ARMS — DIRE STRAITS (WARNER BROS)
7	WHEN THE GOING GETS TOUGH — BILLY OCEAN (JIVE)	AFTERBURNER — ZZ TOP (WARNER BROS)
8	SPIES LIKE US — PAUL McCARTNEY (CAPITOL)	WELCOME TO THE REAL WORLD — MR MISTER (RCA)
9	WALK OF LIFE — DIRE STRAITS (WARNER BROS)	WHITNEY HOUSTON — WHITNEY HOUSTON (ARISTA)
10	GO HOME — STEVIE WONDER (MOTOWN)	KNEE DEEP IN THE HOOPLA — STARSHIP (GRUNT)
11	HOW WILL I KNOW — WHITNEY HOUSTON (ARISTA)	BORN IN THE USA — BRUCE SPRINGSTEEN (COLUMBIA/CBS)
12	CONGA — MIAMI SOUND MACHINE (EPIC)	IN SQUARE CIRCLE — STEVIE WONDER (MOTOWN)
13	KYRIE — MR MISTER (RCA)	ROCK A LITTLE — STEVIE NICKS (MODERN)
14	I MISS YOU — KLYMAXX (MCA/CONSTELLATION)	ONCE UPON A TIME — SIMPLE MINDS (A&M/VIRGIN)
15	LIVING IN AMERICA — JAMES BROWN (SCOTTI BROS)	SONGS FROM THE BIG CHAIR — TEARS FOR FEARS (MERCURY)
16	THE SWEETEST TABOO — SADE (PORTRAIT)	ROCKY IV — SOUNDTRACK (ATLANTIC)
17	GOODBYE — NIGHT RANGER (CAMEL/MCA)	WHITE NIGHTS — SOUNDTRACK (ATLANTIC)
18	SIDEWALK TALK — JELLYBEAN (EMI AMERICA)	FRIENDS — DIONNE WARWICK (ARISTA)
19	PARTY ALL THE TIME — EDDIE MURPHY (COLUMBIA/CBS)	THE DREAM OF THE BLUE TURTLES — STING (A&M)
20	LIFE IN A NORTHERN TOWN — DREAM ACADEMY (WARNER BROS)	GREATEST HITS — THE CARS (ELEKTRA)

S I N G L E S — UK A L B U M S

#	Singles	Albums
1	WHEN THE GOING GETS TOUGH — BILLY OCEAN (JIVE)	BROTHERS IN ARMS — DIRE STRAITS (VERTIGO)
2	THE SUN ALWAYS SHINES ON TV — A-HA (WARNER BROS)	HUNTING HIGH AND LOW — A-HA (WARNER BROS)
3	BORDERLINE — MADONNA (SIRE)	WORLD MACHINE — LEVEL 42 (POLYDOR)
4	ONLY LOVE — NANA MOUSKOURI (CARRERE/PHILIPS)	THE BROADWAY ALBUM — BARBRA STREISAND (CBS)
5	WALK OF LIFE — DIRE STRAITS (VERTIGO)	ISLAND LIFE — GRACE JONES (ISLAND)
6	SYSTEM ADDICT — FIVE STAR (TENT)	THE DREAM OF THE BLUE TURTLES — STING (A&M)
7	THE PHANTOM OF THE OPERA — SARAH BRIGHTMAN/STEVE HARLEY (POLYDOR)	BE YOURSELF TONIGHT — EURYTHMICS (RCA)
8	LIVING IN AMERICA — JAMES BROWN (SCOTTI BROS)	WHITNEY HOUSTON — WHITNEY HOUSTON (ARISTA)
9	SUSPICIOUS MINDS — FINE YOUNG CANNIBALS (LONDON)	LIKE A VIRGIN — MADONNA (SIRE)
10	SANCTIFY YOURSELF — SIMPLE MINDS (VIRGIN)	ONCE UPON A TIME — SIMPLE MINDS (VIRGIN)
11	BROKEN WINGS — MR MISTERS (RCA)	FINE YOUNG CANNIBALS — FINE YOUNG CANNIBALS (LONDON)
12	PULL UP TO THE BUMPER — GRACE JONES (ISLAND)	FEARGAL SHARKEY — FEARGAL SHARKEY (VIRGIN)
13	SATURDAY LOVE — CHERRELLE/ALEXANDER O'NEAL (TABU)	GO WEST — GO WEST (CHRYSALIS)
14	THE CAPTAIN OF HER HEART — DOUBLE (POLYDOR)	THE FIRST ALBUM — MADONNA (SIRE)
15	YOU LITTLE THIEF — FEARGAL SHARKEY (VIRGIN)	LUXURY OF LIFE — FIVE STAR (TENT)
16	LIFE'S WHAT YOU MAKE IT — TALK TALK (EMI)	NOW THAT'S WHAT I CALL MUSIC 6 — VARIOUS (EMI/VIRGIN)
17	IT'S ALRIGHT (BABY'S COMING BACK) — EURYTHMICS (RCA)	PROMISE — SADE (EPIC)
18	ELOISE — DAMNED (MCA)	ROCKY IV — ORIGINAL SOUNDTRACK (SCOTTI BROS)
19	HOW WILL I KNOW — WHITNEY HOUSTON (ARISTA)	EASY PIECES — LLOYD COLE AND THE COMMOTIONS (POLYDOR)
20	RISE — PUBLIC IMAGE LIMITED (VIRGIN)	HITS 3 — VARIOUS (CBS/WEA)

S I N G L E S — US A L B U M S

#	Singles	Albums
1	THAT'S WHAT FRIENDS ARE FOR — DIONNE WARWICK AND FRIENDS (ARISTA)	THE BROADWAY ALBUM — BARBRA STREISAND (COLUMBIA/CBS)
2	BURNING HEART — SURVIVOR (SCOTTI BROS)	PROMISE — SADE (PORTRAIT)
3	I'M YOUR MAN — WHAM! (COLUMBIA/CBS)	HEART — HEART (CAPITOL)
4	WHEN THE GOING GETS TOUGH — BILLY OCEAN (JIVE)	SCARECROW — JOHN COUGAR MELLENCAMP (RIVA)
5	HOW WILL I KNOW — WHITNEY HOUSTON (ARISTA)	BROTHERS IN ARMS — DIRE STRAITS (WARNER BROS)
6	KYRIE — MR MISTER (RCA)	WELCOME TO THE REAL WORLD — MR MISTER (RCA)
7	SPIES LIKE US — PAUL McCARTNEY (CAPITOL)	WHITNEY HOUSTON — WHITNEY HOUSTON (ARISTA)
8	TALK TO ME — STEVIE NICKS (MODERN)	AFTERBURNER — ZZ TOP (WARNER BROS)
9	LIVING IN AMERICA — JAMES BROWN (SCOTTI BROS)	KNEE DEEP IN THE HOOPLA — STARSHIP (GRUNT)
10	CONGA — MIAMI SOUND MACHINE (EPIC)	ROCKY IV — SOUNDTRACK (ATLANTIC)
11	GO HOME — STEVIE WONDER (MOTOWN)	ROCK A LITTLE — STEVIE NICKS (MODERN)
12	THE SWEETEST TABOO — SADE (PORTRAIT)	ONCE UPON A TIME — SIMPLE MINDS (A&M/VIRGIN)
13	MY HOMETOWN — BRUCE SPRINGSTEEN (COLUMBIA/CBS)	IN SQUARE CIRCLE — STEVIE WONDER (MOTOWN)
14	SAY YOU SAY ME — LIONEL RICHIE (MOTOWN)	BORN IN THE USA — BRUCE SPRINGSTEEN (COLUMBIA/CBS)
15	SARA — STARSHIP (GRUNT)	FRIENDS — DIONNE WARWICK (ARISTA)
16	LIFE IN A NORTHERN TOWN — DREAM ACADEMY (WARNER BROS)	WHITE NIGHTS — SOUNDTRACK (ATLANTIC)
17	WALK OF LIFE — DIRE STRAITS (WARNER BROS)	SONGS FROM THE BIG CHAIR — TEARS FOR FEARS (MERCURY)
18	SILENT RUNNING — MIKE AND THE MECHANICS (ATLANTIC)	THE DREAM OF THE BLUE TURTLES — STING (A&M)
19	A LOVE BIZARRE — SHEILA E. (PAISLEY PARK)	GREATEST HITS — THE CARS (ELEKTRA)
20	SIDEWALK TALK — JELLYBEAN (EMI AMERICA)	ROCKY IV — SOUNDTRACK (SCOTTI BROS)

S I N G L E S — UK — A L B U M S

#	Singles	Albums
1	WHEN THE GOING GETS TOUGH — BILLY OCEAN (JIVE)	BROTHERS IN ARMS — DIRE STRAITS (VERTIGO)
2	BORDERLINE — MADONNA (SIRE)	HUNTING HIGH AND LOW — A-HA (WARNER BROS)
3	SYSTEM ADDICT — FIVE STAR (TENT)	WORLD MACHINE — LEVEL 42 (POLYDOR)
4	ELOISE — THE DAMNED (MCA)	ISLAND LIFE — GRACE JONES (ISLAND)
5	LIVING IN AMERICA — JAMES BROWN (SCOTTI BROS)	THE BROADWAY ALBUM — BARBRA STREISAND (CBS)
6	THE SUN ALWAYS SHINES ON TV — A-HA (WARNER BROS)	WHITNEY HOUSTON — WHITNEY HOUSTON (ARISTA)
7	ONLY LOVE — NANA MOUSKOURI (CARRERE/PHILIPS)	BE YOURSELF TONIGHT — EURYTHMICS (RCA)
8	THE CAPTAIN OF HER HEART — DOUBLE (POLYDOR)	ROCKY IV — ORIGINAL SOUNDTRACK (SCOTTI BROS)
9	STARTING TOGETHER — SU POLLARD (RAINBOW)	LIKE A VIRGIN — MADONNA (SIRE)
10	HOW WILL I KNOW — WHITNEY HOUSTON (ARISTA)	THE DANCE HITS ALBUM — VARIOUS (TOWERBELL)
11	THE PHANTOM OF THE OPERA — SARAH BRIGHTMAN/STEVE HARLEY (POLYDOR)	THE DREAM OF THE BLUE TURTLES — STING (A&M)
12	RISE — PUBLIC IMAGE LIMITED (VIRGIN)	ONCE UPON A TIME — SIMPLE MINDS (VIRGIN)
13	WALK OF LIFE — DIRE STRAITS (VERTIGO)	LUXURY OF LIFE — FIVE STAR (TENT)
14	CHAIN REACTION — DIANA ROSS (CAPITOL)	ALBUM — PUBLIC IMAGE LIMITED (VIRGIN)
15	BURNING HEART — SURVIVOR (SCOTTI BROS)	THE FIRST ALBUM — MADONNA (SIRE)
16	PULL UP TO THE BUMPER — GRACE JONES (ISLAND)	GO WEST — GO WEST (CHRYSALIS)
17	SUSPICIOUS MINDS — FINE YOUNG CANNIBALS (LONDON)	FEARGAL SHARKEY — FEARGAL SHARKEY (VIRGIN)
18	SANCTIFY YOURSELF — SIMPLE MINDS (VIRGIN)	FINE YOUNG CANNIBALS — FINE YOUNG CANNIBALS (LONDON)
19	LIFE'S WHAT YOU MAKE IT — TALK TALK (EMI)	PROMISE — SADE (EPIC)
20	SHOT IN THE DARK — OZZY OSBOURNE (EPIC)	LITTLE CREATURES — TALKING HEADS (EMI)

S I N G L E S — US — A L B U M S

#	Singles	Albums
1	HOW WILL I KNOW — WHITNEY HOUSTON (ARISTA)	PROMISE — SADE (PORTRAIT)
2	WHEN THE GOING GETS TOUGH — BILLY OCEAN (JIVE)	THE BROADWAY ALBUM — BARBRA STREISAND (COLUMBIA/CBS)
3	BURNING HEAT — SURVIVOR (SCOTTI BROS)	WELCOME TO THE REAL WORLD — MR MISTER (RCA)
4	KYRIE — MR MISTER (RCA)	HEART — HEART (CAPITOL)
5	THAT'S WHAT FRIENDS ARE FOR — DIONNE WARWICK AND FRIENDS (ARISTA)	WHITNEY HOUSTON — WHITNEY HOUSTON (ARISTA)
6	I'M YOUR MAN — WHAM! (COLUMBIA/CBS)	SCARECROW — JOHN COUGAR MELLENCAMP (RIVA)
7	LIVING IN AMERICA — JAMES BROWN (SCOTTI BROS)	BROTHERS IN ARMS — DIRE STRAITS (WARNER BROS)
8	THE SWEETEST TABOO — SADE (PORTRAIT)	KNEE DEEP IN THE HOOPLA — STARSHIP (GRUNT)
9	SARA — STARSHIP (GRUNT)	MIAMI VICE — SOUNDTRACK (MCS)
10	CONGA — MIAMI SOUND MACHINE (EPIC)	AFTERBURNER — ZZ TOP (WARNER BROS)
11	LIFE IN A NORTHERN TOWN — DREAM ACADEMY (WARNER BROS)	ROCKY IV — SOUNDTRACK (SCOTTI BROS)
12	SILENT RUNNING — MIKE AND THE MECHANICS (ATLANTIC)	ONCE UPON A TIME — SIMPLE MINDS (A&M/VIRGIN)
13	A LOVE BIZARRE — SHEILA E (PAISLEY PARK)	ROCK A LITTLE — STEVIE NICKS (MODERN)
14	SPIES LIKE US — PAUL McCARTNEY (CAPITOL)	FRIENDS — DIONNE WARWICK (ARISTA)
15	SECRET LOVERS — ATLANTIC STARR (A&M)	BORN IN THE USA — BRUCE SPRINGSTEEN (COLUMBIA/CBS)
16	GO HOME — STEVIE WONDER (MOTOWN)	IN SQUARE CIRCLE — STEVIE WONDER (MOTOWN)
17	TARZAN BOY — BALTIMORA (MANHATTAN)	SONGS FROM THE BIG CHAIR — TEARS FOR FEARS (MERCURY)
18	TALK TO ME — STEVIE NICKS (MODERN)	THE DREAM OF THE BLUE TURTLES — STING (A&M)
19	THESE DREAMS — HEART (CAPITOL)	MEETING IN THE LADIES ROOM — KLYMAXX (MCA/CONSTELLATION)
20	SAY YOU, SAY ME — LIONEL RICHIE (MOTOWN)	WHITE NIGHTS — SOUNDTRACK (ATLANTIC)

S I N G L E S — UK — A L B U M S

#	Singles	Albums
1	WHEN THE GOING GETS TOUGH — BILLY OCEAN (JIVE)	BROTHERS IN ARMS — DIRE STRAITS (VERTIGO)
2	STARTING TOGETHER — SU POLLARD (RAINBOW)	NO JACKET REQUIRED — PHIL COLLINS (VIRGIN)
3	ELOISE — THE DAMNED (MCA)	BE YOURSELF TONIGHT — EURYTHMICS (RCA)
4	CHAIN REACTION — DIANA ROSS (CAPITOL)	WHITNEY HOUSTON — WHITNEY HOUSTON (ARISTA)
5	HOW WILL I KNOW — WHITNEY HOUSTON (ARISTA)	HUNTING HIGH AND LOW — A-HA (WARNER BROS)
6	BORDERLINE — MADONNA (SIRE)	THE BROADWAY ALBUM — BARBRA STREISAND (CBS)
7	SYSTEM ADDICT — FIVE STAR (TENT)	ROCKY IV — ORIGINAL SOUNDTRACK (SCOTTI BROS)
8	BURNING HEART — SURVIVOR (SCOTTI BROS)	THE ULTIMATE SIN — OZZY OSBOURNE (EPIC)
9	LIVING IN AMERICA — JAMES BROWN (SCOTTI BROS)	ISLAND LIFE — GRACE JONES (ISLAND)
10	THE CAPTAIN OF HER HEART — DOUBLE (POLYDOR)	THE DANCE HITS ALBUM — VARIOUS (TOWERBELL)
11	RISE — PUBLIC IMAGE LIMITED (VIRGIN)	WORLD MACHINE — LEVEL 42 (POLYDOR)
12	ONLY LOVE — NANA MOUSKOURI (CARRERE/PHILIPS)	LUXURY OF LIFE — FIVE STAR (TENT)
13	DON'T WASTE MY TIME — PAUL HARDCASTLE (CHRYSALIS)	ENTERTAINMENT FROM THE USA — VARIOUS (STYLUS)
14	WALK OF LIFE — DIRE STRAITS (VERTIGO)	LIKE A VIRGIN — MADONNA (SIRE)
15	TURNING AWAY — SHAKIN' STEVENS (EPIC)	ONCE UPON A TIME — SIMPLE MINDS (VIRGIN)
16	THE SUN ALWAYS SHINES ON TV — A-HA (WARNER BROS)	THE DREAM OF THE BLUE TURTLES — STING (A&M)
17	IMAGINATION — BELOUIS SOME (PARLOPHONE)	GO WEST — GO WEST (CHRYSALIS)
18	THE PHANTOM OF THE OPERA — SARAH BRIGHTMAN/STEVE HARLEY (POLYDOR)	THE FIRST ALBUM — MADONNA (SIRE)
19	RADIO AFRICA — LATIN QUARTER (ROCKIN' HORSE/ARISTA)	HOUNDS OF LOVE — KATE BUSH (EMI)
20	AS SHE WAS — TALKING HEADS (EMI)	LITTLE CREATURES — TALKING HEADS (EMI)

S I N G L E S — US — A L B U M S

#	Singles	Albums
1	HOW WILL I KNOW — WHITNEY HOUSTON (ARISTA)	PROMISE — SADE (PORTRAIT)
2	KYRIE — MR MISTER (RCA)	WELCOME TO THE REAL WORLD — MR MISTER (RCA)
3	WHEN THE GOING GETS TOUGH — BILLY OCEAN (JIVE)	THE BROADWAY ALBUM — BARBRA STREISAND (COLUMBIA/CBS)
4	SARA — STARSHIP (GRUNT)	WHITNEY HOUSTON — WHITNEY HOUSTON (ARISTA)
5	LIVING IN AMERICA — JAMES BROWN (SCOTTI BROS)	HEART — HEART (CAPITOL)
6	THE SWEETEST TABOO — SADE (PORTRAIT)	SCARECROW — JOHN COUGAR MELLENCAMP (RIVA)
7	LIFE IN A NORTHERN TOWN — DREAM ACADEMY (WARNER BROS)	BROTHERS IN ARMS — DIRE STRAITS (WARNER BROS)
8	SILENT RUNNING — MIKE AND THE MECHANICS (ATLANTIC)	KNEE DEEP IN THE HOOPLA — STARSHIP (GRUNT)
9	BURNING HEART — SURVIVOR (SCOTTI BROS)	AFTERBURNER — ZZ TOP (WARNER BROS)
10	THAT'S WHAT FRIENDS ARE FOR — DIONNE WARWICK AND FRIENDS (ARISTA)	ROCKY IV — SOUNDTRACK (ATLANTIC)
11	SECRET LOVERS — ATLANTIC STARR (A&M)	ONCE UPON A TIME — SIMPLE MINDS (A&M/VIRGIN)
12	A LOVE BIZARRE — SHEILA E (PAISLEY PARK)	MIAMI VICE — SOUNDTRACK (SCOTTI BROS)
13	I'M YOUR MAN — WHAM! (COLUMBIA/CBS)	FRIENDS — DIONNE WARWICK (ARISTA)
14	THESE DREAMS — HEART (CAPITOL)	ROCK A LITTLE — STEVIE NICKS (MODERN)
15	CONGA — MIAMI SOUND MACHINE (EPIC)	BORN IN THE USA — BRUCE SPRINGSTEEN (COLUMBIA/CBS)
16	TARZAN BOY — BALTIMORA (MANHATTAN)	IN SQUARE CIRCLE — STEVIE WONDER (MOTOWN)
17	KING FOR A DAY — THOMPSON TWINS (ARISTA)	SONGS FROM THE BIG CHAIR — TEARS FOR FEARS (MERCURY)
18	DAY BY DAY — THE HOOTERS (COLUMBIA/CBS)	MEETING IN THE LADIES ROOM — KLYMAXX (MCA/CONSTELLATION)
19	RUSSIANS — STING (A&M)	THE ULTIMATE SIN — OZZY OSBOURNE (CBS ASSOCIATED)
20	THE SUN ALWAYS SHINES ON TV — A-HA (WARNER BROS)	HERE'S TO FUTURE DAYS — THOMPSON TWINS (ARISTA)

WEEK ENDING MARCH 1 1986

SINGLES UK ALBUMS

#	SINGLES	#	ALBUMS
1	WHEN THE GOING GETS TOUGH — BILLY OCEAN (JIVE)	1	BROTHERS IN ARMS — DIRE STRAITS (VERTIGO)
2	CHAIN REACTION — DIANA ROSS (CAPITOL)	2	WHITNEY HOUSTON — WHITNEY HOUSTON (ARISTA)
3	STARTING TOGETHER — SU POLLARD (RAINBOW)	3	ROCKY IV — ORIGINAL SOUNDTRACK (SCOTTI BROS)
4	ELOISE — THE DAMNED (MCA)	4	NO JACKET REQUIRED — PHIL COLLINS (VIRGIN)
5	BURNING HEART — SURVIVOR (SCOTTI BROS)	5	BE YOURSELF TONIGHT — EURYTHMICS (RCA)
6	HOW WILL I KNOW — WHITNEY HOUSTON (ARISTA)	6	HUNTING HIGH AND LOW — A-HA (WARNER BROS)
7	LOVE MISSILE F1-11 — SIGUE SIGUE SPUTNIK (PARLOPHONE)	7	ENTERTAINMENT FROM THE USA — VARIOUS (STYLUS)
8	DON'T WASTE MY TIME — PAUL HARDCASTLE (CHRYSALIS)	8	THE COLOUR OF SPRING — TALK TALK (EMI)
9	SYSTEM ADDICT — FIVE STAR (TENT)	9	GO WEST — GO WEST (CHRYSALIS)
10	MANIC MONDAY — THE BANGLES (CBS)	10	THE BROADWAY ALBUM — BARBRA STREISAND (CBS)
11	BORDERLINE — MADONNA (SIRE)	11	KING OF AMERICA — ELVIS COSTELLO (F BEAT)
12	RISE — PUBLIC IMAGE LIMITED (VIRGIN)	12	ISLAND LIFE — GRACE JONES (ISLAND)
13	LIVING IN AMERICA — JAMES BROWN (SCOTTI BROS)	13	ONCE UPON A TIME — SIMPLE MINDS (VIRGIN)
14	ONLY LOVE — NANA MOUSKOURI (CARRERE/PHILIPS)	14	HOUNDS OF LOVE — KATE BUSH (EMI)
15	STRIPPED — DEPECHE MODE (MUTE)	15	LUXURY OF LIFE — FIVE STAR (TENT)
16	TURNING AWAY — SHAKIN' STEVENS (EPIC)	16	THE DREAM OF THE BLUE TURTLES — STING (A&M)
17	THE CAPTAIN OF HER HEART — DOUBLE (POLYDOR)	17	WORLD MACHINE — LEVEL 42 (POLYDOR)
18	THE POWER OF LOVE — HUEY LEWIS AND THE NEWS (CHRYSALIS)	18	THE DANCE HITS ALBUMS — VARIOUS (TOWERBELL)
19	AND SHE WAS — TALKING HEADS (EMI)	19	LIKE A VIRGIN — MADONNA (SIRE)
20	IMAGINATION — BELOUIS SOME (PARLOPHONE)	20	LITTLE CREATURES — TALKING HEADS (EMI)

SINGLES US ALBUMS

#	SINGLES	#	ALBUMS
1	KYRIE — MR MISTER (RCA)	1	WELCOME TO THE REAL WORLD — MR MISTER (RCA)
2	HOW WILL I KNOW — WHITNEY HOUSTON (ARISTA)	2	PROMISE — SADE (PORTRAIT)
3	SARA — STARSHIP (GRUNT)	3	WHITNEY HOUSTON — WHITNEY HOUSTON (ARISTA)
4	LIVING IN AMERICA — JAMES BROWN (SCOTTI BROS)	4	THE BROADWAY ALBUM — BARBRA STREISAND (COLUMBIA/CBS)
5	THE SWEETEST TABOO — SADE (PORTRAIT)	5	SCARECROW — JOHN COUGAR MELLENCAMP (RIVA)
6	WHEN THE GOING GETS TOUGH — BILLY OCEAN (JIVE)	6	HEART — HEART (CAPITOL)
7	LIFE IN A NORTHERN TOWN — DREAM ACADEMY (WARNER BROS)	7	KNEE DEEP IN THE HOOPLA — STARSHIP (GRUNT)
8	SILENT RUNNING — MIKE AND THE MECHANICS (ATLANTIC)	8	BROTHERS IN ARMS — DIRE STRAITS (WARNER BROS)
9	SECRET LOVERS — ATLANTIC STARR (A&M)	9	AFTERBURNER — ZZ TOP (WARNER BROS)
10	THESE DREAMS — HEART (CAPITOL)	10	ONCE UPON A TIME — SIMPLE MINDS (A&M/VIRGIN)
11	A LOVE BIZARRE — SHEILA E (PAISLEY PARK)	11	ROCKY IV — SOUNDTRACK (SCOTTI BROS)
12	KING FOR A DAY — THOMPSON TWINS (ARISTA)	12	FRIENDS — DIONNE WARWICK (ARISTA)
13	TARZAN BOY — BALTIMORA (MANHATTAN)	13	THE ULTIMATE SIN — OZZY OSBOURNE (CBS ASSOCIATED)
14	BURNING HEART — SURVIVOR (SCOTTI BROS)	14	ROCK A LITTLE — STEVIE NICKS (MODERN)
15	CONGA — MIAMI SOUND MACHINE (EPIC)	15	BORN IN THE USA — BRUCE SPRINGSTEEN (COLUMBIA/CBS)
16	RUSSIANS — STING (A&M)	16	IN SQUARE CIRCLE — STEVIE WONDER (MOTOWN)
17	ROCK IN THE USA — JOHN COUGAR MELLENCAMP (RIVA)	17	SONGS FROM THE BIG CHAIR — TEARS FOR FEARS (MERCURY)
18	DAY BY DAY — THE HOOTERS (COLUMBIA/CBS)	18	MEETING IN THE LADIES ROOM — KLYMAXX (MCA/CONSTELLATION)
19	NIKITA — ELTON JOHN (GEFFEN)	19	MIAMI VICE — SOUNDTRACK (MCA)
20	THAT'S WHAT FRIENDS ARE FOR — DIONNE WARWICK AND FRIENDS (ARISTA)	20	NERVOUS NIGHT — THE HOOTERS (COLUMBIA)

WEEK ENDING MARCH 8 1986

SINGLES UK ALBUMS

#	SINGLES	#	ALBUMS
1	CHAIN REACTION — DIANA ROSS (CAPITOL)	1	BROTHERS IN ARMS — DIRE STRAITS (VERTIGO)
2	WHEN THE GOING GETS TOUGH — BILLY OCEAN (JIVE)	2	WHITNEY HOUSTON — WHITNEY HOUSTON (ARISTA)
3	LOVE MISSILE F1-11 — SIGUE SIGUE SPUTNIK (PARLOPHONE)	3	NO JACKET REQUIRED — PHIL COLLINS (VIRGIN)
4	MANIC MONDAY — THE BANGLES (CBS)	4	ROCKY IV — ORIGINAL SOUNDTRACK (SCOTTI BROS)
5	STARTING TOGETHER — SU POLLARD (RAINBOW)	5	BE YOURSELF TONIGHT — EURYTHMICS (RCS)
6	BURNING HEART — SURVIVOR (SCOTTI BROS)	6	ENTERTAINMENT FROM THE USA — VARIOUS (STYLUS)
7	HOW WILL I KNOW — WHITNEY HOUSTON (ARISTA)	7	HITS FOR LOVERS — VARIOUS (EPIC)
8	ELOISE — DAMNED (MCA)	8	GO WEST — GO WEST (CHRYSALIS)
9	DON'T WASTE MY TIME — PAUL HARDCASTLE (CHRYSALIS)	9	HOUNDS OF LOVE — KATE BUSH (EMI)
10	THEME FROM NEW YORK NEW YORK — FRANK SINATRA (REPRISE)	10	HUNTING HIGH AND LOW — A-HA (WARNER BROS)
11	THE POWER OF LOVE — HUEY LEWIS AND THE NEWS (CHRYSALIS)	11	KING OF AMERICA — ELVIS COSTELLO (F BEAT)
12	HEAVEN MUST BE MISSING AN ANGEL — TAVARES (CAPITOL)	12	ONCE UPON A TIME — SIMPLE MINDS (VIRGIN)
13	IF YOU WERE HERE TONIGHT — ALEXANDER O'NEAL (TABU)	13	THE COLOUR OF SPRING — TALK TALK (EMI)
14	(NOTHING SERIOUS) JUST BUGGIN' — WHISTLE (CHAMPION)	14	LITTLE CREATURES — TALKING HEAD (EMI)
15	RISE — PUBLIC IMAGE LIMITED (VIRGIN)	15	ISLAND LIFE — GRACE JONES (ISLAND)
16	HI HO SILVER (THEME FROM BOON) — JIM DIAMOND (A&M)	16	THE DREAM OF THE BLUE TURTLES — STING (A&M)
17	AND SHE WAS — TALKING HEADS (EMI)	17	THE DANCE HITS ALBUM — VARIOUS (TOWERBELL)
18	HOUNDS OF LOVE — KATE BUSH (EMI)	18	THE BROADWAY ALBUM — BARBRA STREISAND (CBS)
19	LIVING IN AMERICA — JAMES BROWN (SCOTTI BROS)	19	WORLD MACHINE — LEVEL 42 (POLYDORE)
20	ONE DANCE WON'T DO — AUDREY HALL (REVOLUTIONARY SOUNDS/GERMAIN)	20	LIKE A VIRGIN — MADONNA (SIRE)

SINGLES US ALBUMS

#	SINGLES	#	ALBUMS
1	KYRIE — MR MISTER (RCA)	1	WHITNEY HOUSTON — WHITNEY HOUSTON (ARISTA)
2	SARA — STARSHIP (GRUNT)	2	PROMISE — SADE (PORTRAIT)
3	HOW WILL I KNOW — WHITNEY HOUSTON (ARISTA)	3	WELCOME TO THE REAL WORLD — MR MISTER (RCA)
4	THESE DREAMS — HEART (CAPITOL)	4	THE BROADWAY ALBUM — BARBRA STREISAND (COLUMBIA/CBS)
5	SECRET LOVERS — ATLANTIC STARR (A&M)	5	HEART — HEART (CAPITOL)
6	SILENT RUNNING — MIKE AND THE MECHANICS (ATLANTIC)	6	SCARECROW — JOHN COUGAR MELLENCAMP (RIVA)
7	THE SWEETEST TABOO — SADE (PORTRAIT)	7	KNEE DEEP IN THE HOOPLA — STARSHIP (GRUNT)
8	LIVING IN AMERICA — JAMES BROWN (SCOTTI BROS)	8	BROTHERS IN ARMS — DIRE STRAITS (WARNER BROS)
9	LIFE IN A NORTHERN TOWN — DREAM ACADEMY (WARNER BROS)	9	THE ULTIMATE SIN — OZZY OSBOURNE (CBS ASSOCIATED)
10	KING FOR A DAY — THOMPSON TWINS (ARISTA)	10	ONCE UPON A TIME — SIMPLE MINDS (A&M/VIRGINee02)
11	ROCK IN THE USA — JOHN COUGAR MELLENCAMP (RIVA)	11	ROCKY IV — SOUNDTRACK (SCOTTI BROS)
12	WHEN THE GOING GETS TOUGH — BILLY OCEAN (JIVE)	12	FRIENDS — DIONNE WARWICK (ARISTA)
13	NIKITA — ELTON JOHN (GEFFEN)	13	AFTERBURNER — ZZ TOP (WARNER BROS)
14	ROCK ME AMADEUS — FALCO (A&M)	14	ROCK A LITTLE — STEVIE NICKS (MODERN)
15	TARZAN BOY — BALTIMORA (MANHATTAN)	15	BORN IN THE USA — BRUCE SPRINGSTEEN (COLUMBIA/CBS)
16	RUSSIANS — STING (A&M)	16	NERVOUS NIGHT — THE HOOTERS (COLUMBIA)
17	WHAT YOU NEED — INXS (ATLANTIC)	17	IN SQUARE CIRCLE — STEVIE WONDER (MOTOWN)
18	DAY BY DAY — THE HOOTERS (COLUMBIA/CBS)	18	MEETING IN THE LADIES ROOM — KLYMAXX (MCA/CONSTELLATION)
19	THIS COULD BE THE NIGHT — LOVERBOY (COLUMBIA/CBS)	19	SONGS FROM THE BIG CHAIR — TEARS FOR FEARS (MERCURY)
20	SANCTIFY YOURSELF — SIMPLE MINDS (A&M/VIRGIN)	20	THE DREAM ACADEMY — DREAM ACADEMY (WARNER BROS)

WEEK ENDING MARCH 15 1986

SINGLES UK

#	Single
1	CHAIN REACTION — DIANA ROSS (CAPITOL)
2	MANIC MONDAY — THE BANGLES (CBS)
3	LOVE MISSILE F1-11 — SIGUE SIGUE SPUTNIK (PARLOPHONE)
4	THEME FROM NEW YORK NEW YORK — FRANK SINATRA (REPRISE)
5	WHEN THE GOING GETS TOUGH — BILLY OCEAN (JIVE)
6	HI HO SILVER (THEME FROM BOON) — JIM DIAMOND (A&M)
7	(NOTHING SERIOUS) JUST BUGGIN' — WHISTLE (CHAMPION)
8	ABSOLUTE BEGINNERS — DAVID BOWIE (VIRGIN)
9	DO YOU BELIEVE IN LOVE — HUEY LEWIS AND THE NEWS (CHRYSALIS)
10	BURNING HEART — SURVIVOR (SCOTTI BROS)
11	STARTING TOGETHER — SU POLLARD (RAINBOW)
12	HOW WILL I KNOW — WHITNEY HOUSTON (ARISTA)
13	KISS — PRINCE AND THE REVOLUTION (PAISLEY PARK)
14	IF YOU WERE HERE TONIGHT — ALEXANDER O'NEAL (TABU)
15	DON'T WASTE MY TIME — PAUL HARDCASTLE (CHRYSALIS)
16	HEAVEN MUST BE MISSING AN ANGEL — TAVARES (CAPITOL)
17	MOVE AWAY — CULTURE CLUB (VIRGIN)
18	KYRIE — MR MISTER (RCA)
19	ELOISE — DAMNED (MCA)
20	DIGGING YOUR SCENE — BLOW MONKEYS (RCA)

ALBUMS UK

#	Album
1	BROTHERS IN ARMS — DIRE STRAITS (VERTIGO)
2	WHITNEY HOUSTON — WHITNEY HOUSTON (ARISTA)
3	HITS FOR LOVERS — VARIOUS (EPIC)
4	NO JACKET REQUIRED — PHIL COLLINS (VIRGIN)
5	ROCKY IV — ORIGINAL SOUNDTRACK (SCOTTI BROS)
6	HOUNDS OF LOVE — KATE BUSH (EMI)
7	BE YOURSELF TONIGHT — EURYTHMICS (RCA)
8	ENTERTAINMENT FROM THE USA — VARIOUS (STYLUS)
9	THE BROADWAY ALBUM — BARBRA STREISAND (CBS)
10	LITTLE CREATURES — TALKING HEADS (EMI)
11	GO WEST — GO WEST (CHRYSALIS)
12	BALANCE OF POWER — ELECTRIC LIGHT ORCHESTRA (EPIC)
13	THE COLOUR OF SPRING — TALK TALK (EMI)
14	NIGHT BEAT — VARIOUS (STYLUS)
15	ONCE UPON A TIME — SIMPLE MINDS (VIRGIN)
16	PRECIOUS MEMORIES — ANN WILLIAMSON (EMERALD GREEN)
17	HUNTING HIGH AND LOW — A-HA (WARNER BROS)
18	ISLAND LIFE — GRACE JONES (ISLAND)
19	ALONE — NANA MOUSKOURI (CARRERE/PHILIPS)
20	WELCOME TO THE REAL WORLD — MR MISTEER (RCA)

SINGLES US

#	Single
1	SARA — STARSHIP (GRUNT)
2	THESE DREAMS — HEART (CAPITOL)
3	KYRIE — MR MISTER (RCA)
4	SECRET LOVERS — ATLANTIC STARR (A&M)
5	HOW WILL I KNOW — WHITNEY HOUSTON (ARISTA)
6	ROCK IN THE USA — JOHN COUGAR MELLENCAMP (RIVA)
7	ROCK ME AMADEUS — FALCO (A&M)
8	SILENT RUNNING — MIKE AND THE MECHANICS (ATLANTIC)
9	KING FOR A DAY — THOMPSON TWINS (ARISTA)
10	NIKITA — ELTON JOHN (GEFFEN)
11	WHAT YOU NEED — INXS (ATLANTIC)
12	THIS COULD BE THE NIGHT — LOVERBOY (COLUMBIA/CBS)
13	THE SWEETEST TABOO — SADE (PORTRAIT)
14	SANCTIFY YOURSELF — SIMPLE MINDS (A&M)
15	KISS — PRINCE AND THE REVOLUTION (PAISLEY PARK)
16	LET'S GO ALL THE WAY — SLY FOX (CAPITOL)
17	LIVING IN AMERICA — JAMES BROWN (SCOTTI BROS)
18	LIFE IN A NORTHERN TOWN — DREAM ACADEMY (WARNER BROS)
19	MANIC MONDAY — THE BANGLES (COLUMBIA/CBS)
20	BEAT'S SO LONELY — CHARLIE SEXTON (MCA)

ALBUMS US

#	Album
1	WHITNEY HOUSTON — WHITNEY HOUSTON (ARISTA)
2	PROMISE — SADE (PORTRAIT)
3	WELCOME TO THE REAL WORLD — MR MISTER (RCA)
4	HEART — HEART (CAPITOL)
5	THE BROADWAY ALBUM — BARBRA STREISAND (COLUMBIA/CBS)
6	SCARECROW — JOHN COUGAR MELLENCAMP (RIVA)
7	KNEE DEEP IN THE HOOPLA — STARSHIP (GRUNT)
8	BROTHERS IN ARMS — DIRE STRAITS (WARNER BROS)
9	THE ULTIMATE SIN — OZZY OSBOURNE (CBS ASSOCIATED)
10	ONCE UPON A TIME — SIMPLE MINDS (A&M/VIRGIN)
11	AFTERBURNER — ZZ TOP (WARNER BROS)
12	ROCKY IV — SOUNDTRACK (SCOTTI BROS)
13	FRIENDS — DIONNE WARWICK (ARISTA)
14	IN SQUARE CIRCLE — STEVIE WONDER (MOWTOWN)
15	NERVOUS NIGHT — THE HOOTERS (COLUMBIA)
16	ROCK A LITTLE — STEVIE NICKS (MODERN)
17	PICTURES FOR PLEASURE — CHARLIE SEXTON (MCA)
18	LISTEN LIKE THIEVES — INXS (ATLANTIC)
19	BORN IN THE USA — BRUCE SPRINGSTEEN (COLUMBIA/CBS)
20	MEETING IN THE LADIES ROOM — KLYMAXX (MCS/CONSTELLATION)

WEEK ENDING MARCH 22 1986

SINGLES UK

#	Single
1	CHAIN REACTION — DIANA ROSS (CAPITOL)
2	ABSOLUTE BEGINNERS — DIANA ROSS (CAPITOL)
3	MANIC MONDAY — THE BANGLES (CBS)
4	LIVING DOLL — CLIFF RICHARD AND THE YOUNG ONES (WEA)
5	HI HO SILVER (THEME FROM BOON) — JIM DIAMOND (A&M)
6	KISS — PRINCE AND THE REVOLUTION (PAISLEY PARK)
7	MOVE AWAY — CULTURE CLUB (VIRGIN)
8	(NOTHING SERIOUS) JUST BUGGIN' — WHISTLE (CHAMPION)
9	THEME FROM NEW YORK NEW YORK — FRANK SINATRA (REPRISE)
10	LOVE MISSILE F1-11 — SIGUE SIGUE SPUTNIK (PARLOPHONE)
11	DO YOU BELIEVE IN LOVE — HUEY LEWIS AND THE NEWS (CHRYSALIS)
12	DIGGING IN YOUR SCENE — BLOW MONKEYS (RCA)
13	HARLEM SHUFFLE — ROLLING STONES (ROLLING STONES)
14	WHEN THE GOING GETS TOUGH — BILLY OCEAN (JIVE)
15	KYRIE — MR MISTER (RCA)
16	NO ONE IS TO BLAME — HOWARD JONES (WEA)
17	THE HONEYTHIEF — HIPSWAY (MERCURY)
18	ROCK ME TONIGHT — FREDDIE JACKSON (CAPITOL)
19	YOU TO ME ARE EVERYTHING — REAL THING (PRT)
20	IF YOU WERE HERE TONIGHT — ALEXANDER O'NEAL (TABU)

ALBUMS UK

#	Album
1	BROTHERS IN ARMS — DIRE STRAITS (VERTIGO)
2	HITS FOR LOVERS — VARIOUS (EPIC)
3	WHITNEY HOUSTON — WHITNEY HOUSTON (ARISTA)
4	NO JACKET REQUIRED — PHIL COLLINS (VIRGIN)
5	ROCKY IV — ORIGINAL SOUNDTRACK (SCOTTI BROS)
6	HOUNDS OF LOVE — KATE BUSH (EMI)
7	NIGHT BEAT — VARIOUS (STYLUS)
8	BE YOURSELF TONIGHT — EURYTHMICS (RCA)
9	BALANCE OF POWER — ELECTRIC LIGHT ORCHESTRA (EPIC)
10	THE HYMNS ALBUM — HUDDERSFIELD CHORAL SOCIETY (HMV)
11	WELCOME TO THE REAL WORLD — MR MISTER (RCA)
12	THE COLOUR OF SPRING — TALK TALK (EMI)
13	ENTERTAINMENT FROM THE USA — VARIOUS (STYLUS)
14	HIS GREATEST HITS — FRANK SINATRA (REPRISE)
15	EATEN ALIVE — DIANA ROSS (CAPITOL)
16	ONCE UPON A TIME — SIMPLE MINDS (A&M/VIRGIN)
17	LITTLE CREATURES — TALKING HEADS (EMI)
18	HUNTING HIGH AND LOW — A-HA (WARNER BROS)
19	ALEXANDER O'NEAL — ALEXANDER O'NEAL (TABU)
20	ISLAND LIFE — GRACE JONES (ISLAND)

SINGLES US

#	Single
1	THESE DREAMS — HEART (CAPITOL)
2	SARA — STARSHIP (GRUNT)
3	SECRET LOVERS — ATLANTIC STARR (A&M)
4	ROCK ME AMADEUS — FALCO (A&M)
5	ROCK IN THE USA — JOHN COUGAR MELLENCAMP (RIVA)
6	KYRIE — MR MISTER (RCA)
7	NIKITA — ELTON JOHN (GEFFEN)
8	KING FOR A DAY — THOMPSON TWINS (ARISTA)
9	WHAT YOU NEED — INXS (ATLANTIC)
10	KISS — PRINCE AND REVOLUTION (PAISLEY PARK)
11	THIS COULD BE THE NIGHT — LOVERBOY (COLUMBIA/CBS)
12	HOW WILL I KNOW — WHITNEY HOUSTON (ARISTA)
13	LET'S GO ALL THE WAY — SLY FOX (CAPITOL)
14	SANCTIFY YOURSELF — SIMPLE MINDS (A&M)
15	MANIC MONDAY — THE BANGLES (COLUMBIA/CBS)
16	SILENT RUNNING — MIKE AND THE MECHANICS (ATLANTIC)
17	BEAT'S SO LONELY — CHARLIE SEXTON (MCA)
18	ADDICTED TO LOVE — ROBERT PALMER (ISLAND)
19	TENDER LOVE — FORCE MDs (WARNER BROS/TOMMY BOY)
20	(HOW TO BE) A MILLIONAIRE — ABC (MERCURY)

ALBUMS US

#	Album
1	WHITNEY HOUSTON — WHITNEY HOUSTON (ARISTA)
2	PROMISE — SADE (PORTRAIT)
3	HEART — HEART (CAPITOL)
4	SCARECROW — JOHN COUGAR MELLENCAMP (RIVA)
5	WELCOME TO THE REAL WORLD — MR MISTER (RCA)
6	THE BROADWAY ALBUM — BARBRA STREISAND (COLUMBIA/CBS)
7	BROTHERS IN ARMS — DIRE STRAITS (WARNER BROS)
8	THE ULTIMATE SIN — OZZY OSBOURNE (CBS ASSOCIATED)
9	KNEE DEEP IN HOOPLA — STARSHIP (GRUNTS)
10	ONCE UPON A TIME — SIMPLE MINDS (A&M/VIRGINee02)
11	AFTERBURNER — ZZ TOP (WARNER BROS)
12	NERVOUS NIGHT — THE HOOTERS (COLUMBIA)
13	ROCKY IV — SOUNDTRACK (SCOTTI BROS)
14	LISTEN LIKE THIEVES — INXS (ATLANTIC)
15	PICTURES FOR PLEASURE — CHARLIE SEXTON (MCA)
16	FRIENDS — DIONNE WARWICK (ARISTA)
17	IN SQUARE CIRCLE — STEVIE WONDER (MOTOWN)
18	FALCO 3 — FALCO (A&M)
19	DIFFERENT LIGHT — THE BANGLES (COLUMBIA/CBS)
20	AS THE BAND TURNS — ATLANTIC STARR (A&M)

UK SINGLES / ALBUMS — Week Ending March 29 1986

#	Singles	Albums
1	LIVING DOLL — CLIFF RICHARD AND THE YOUNG ONES (WEA)	HITS 4 — VARIOUS (CBS/WEA/RCA)
2	CHAIN REACTION — DIANA ROSS (CAPITOL)	BROTHERS IN ARMS — DIRE STRAITS (VERTIGO)
3	ABSOLUTE BEGINNERS — DAVID BOWIE (VIRGIN)	WHITNEY HOUSTON — WHITNEY HOUSTON (ARISTA)
4	TOUCH ME (I WANT YOUR BODY) — SAMANTHA FOX (JIVE)	BLACK CELEBRATION — DEPECHE MODE (MUTE)
5	WONDERFUL WORLD — SAM COOKE (RCA)	HITS FOR LOVERS — VARIOUS (EPIC)
6	YOU TO ME ARE EVERYTHING — REAL THING (PRT)	WELCOME TO THE REAL WORLD — MR MISTER (RCA)
7	HI HO SILVER (THEME FROM BOON) — JIM DIAMOND (A&M)	NO JACKET REQUIRED — PHIL COLLINS (VIRGIN)
8	MANIC MONDAY — THE BANGLES (CBS)	ROCKY IV — ORIGINAL SOUNDTRACK (SCOTTI BROS)
9	KISS — PRINCE AND THE REVOLUTION (PAISLEY PARK)	THE HYMNS ALBUM — HUDDERSFIELD CHORAL SOCIETY (HMV)
10	MOVE AWAY — CULTURE CLUB (VIRGIN)	BE YOURSELF TONIGHT — EURYTHMICS (RCA)
11	KYRIE — MR MISTER (RCA)	EATEN ALIVE — DIANA ROSS (CAPITOL)
12	PETER GUNN — ART OF NOISE AND DUANE EDDY (CHINA)	THE COLOUR OF SPRING — TALK TALK (EMI)
13	DIGGING YOUR SCENE — BLOW MONKEYS (RCA)	HOUNDS OF LOVE — KATE BUSH (EMI)
14	HARLEM SHUFFLE — ROLLING STONES (ROLLING STONES)	BALANCE OF POWER — ELECTRIC LIGHT ORCHESTRA (EPIC)
15	(NOTHING SERIOUS) JUST BUGGIN' — WHISTLE (CHAMPION)	HUNTING HIGH AND LOW — A-HA (WARNER BROS)
16	A KIND OF MAGIC — QUEEN (EMI)	HIS GREATEST HITS — FRANK SINATRA (REPRISE)
17	LOVE MISSILE F1-11 — SIGUE SIGUE SPUTNIK (PARLOPHONE)	ONCE UPON A TIME — SIMPLE MINDS (VIRGIN)
18	DO YOU BELIEVE IN LOVE — HUEY LEWIS AND THE NEWS (CHRYSALIS)	LITTLE CREATURES — TALKING HEADS (EMI)
19	LOVE COMES QUICKLY — PET SHOP BOYS (PARLOPHONE)	STREETSOUNDS HIP HOP ELECTRO II — VARIOUS (STREETSOUNDS)
20	NO ONE IS TO BLAME — HOWARD JONES (WEA)	ALEXANDER O'NEAL — ALEXANDER O'NEAL (TABU)

UK SINGLES / ALBUMS — Week Ending April 5 1986

#	Singles	Albums
1	LIVING DOLL — CLIFF RICHARD AND THE YOUNG ONES (WEA)	HITS 4 — VARIOUS (CBS/WEA/RCA)
2	WONDERFUL WORLD — SAM COOKE (RCA)	BROTHERS IN ARMS — DIRE STRAITS (VERTIGO)
3	TOUCH ME (I WANT YOUR BODY) — SAMANTHA FOX (JIVE)	PLEASE — PET SHOP BOYS (PARLOPHONE)
4	A DIFFERENT CORNER — GEORGE MICHAEL (EPIC)	DIRTY WORK — ROLLING STONES (ROLLING STONES)
5	YOU TO ME ARE EVERYTHING — REAL THING (PRT)	WHITNEY HOUSTON — WHITNEY HOUSTON (ARISTA)
6	CHAIN REACTION — DIANA ROSS (CAPITOL)	WELCOME TO THE REAL WORLD — MR MISTER (RCA)
7	A KIND OF MAGIC — QUEEN (EMI)	NO JACKET REQUIRED — PHIL COLLINS (VIRGIN)
8	ABSOLUTE BEGINNERS — DAVID BOWIE (VIRGIN)	THE HYMNS ALBUM — HUDDERSFIELD CHORAL SOCIETY (HMV)
9	PETER GUNN — ART OF NOISE AND DUANE EDDY (CHINA)	HITS FOR LOVERS — VARIOUS (EPIC)
10	ROCK ME AMADEUS — FALCO (A&M)	ROCKY IV — ORIGINAL SOUNDTRACK (SCOTTI BROS)
11	HI HO SILVER (THEME FROM BOON) — JIM DIAMOND (A&M)	HUNTING HIGH AND LOW — A-HA (WARNER BROS)
12	MANIC MONDAY — THE BANGLES (CBS)	BE YOURSELF TONIGHT — EURYTHMICS (RCA)
13	KYRIE — MR MISTER (RCA)	HIS GREATEST HITS — FRANK SINATRA (REPRISE)
14	SECRET LOVERS — ATLANTIC STARR (A&M)	BLACK CELEBRATION — DEPECHE MODE (MUTE)
15	KISS — PRINCE AND THE REVOLUTION (PAISLEY PARK)	EATEN ALIVE — DIANA ROSS (CAPITOL)
16	MOVE AWAY — CULTURE CLUB (VIRGIN)	ONCE UPON A TIME — SIMPLE MINDS (VIRGIN)
17	OVERJOYED — STEVIE WONDER (MOTOWN)	STREET SOUND 16 — VARIOUS (STREETSOUNDS)
18	DIGGING YOUR SCENE — BLOW MONKEYS (RCA)	5150 — VAN HALEN (WARNER BROS)
19	LOVE COMES QUICKLY — PET SHOP BOYS (PARLOPHONE)	HOUNDS OF LOVE — KATE BUSH (EMI)
20	$E = MC^2$ — BIG AUDIO DYNAMITE (CBS)	THE COLOUR OF SPRING — TALK TALK (EMI)

S I N G L E S US A L B U M S

US SINGLES / ALBUMS — Week Ending March 29 1986

#	Singles	Albums
1	ROCK ME AMADEUS — FALCO (A&M)	WHITNEY HOUSTON — WHITNEY HOUSTON (ARISTA)
2	THESE DREAMS — HEART (CAPITOL)	PROMISE — SADE (PORTRAIT)
3	SECRET LOVERS — ATLANTIC STARR (A&M)	HEART — HEART (CAPITOL)
4	ROCK IN THE USA — JOHN COUGAR MELLENCAMP (RIVA)	SCARECROW — JOHN COUGAR MELLENCAMP (RIVA)
5	KISS — PRINCE AND THE REVOLUTION (PAISLEY PARK)	WELCOME TO THE REAL WORLD — MR MISTER (RCA)
6	WHAT YOU NEED — INXS (ATLANTIC)	THE BROADWAY ALBUM — BARBRA STREISAND (COLUMBIA/CBS)
7	NIKITA — ELTON JOHN (GEFFEN)	BROTHERS IN ARMS — DIRE STRAITS (WARNER BROS)
8	SARA — STARSHIP (GRUNT)	THE ULTIMATE SIN — OZZY OSBOURNE (CBS ASSOCIATED)
9	LET'S GO ALL THE WAY — SLY FOX (CAPITOL)	KNEE DEEP IN THE HOOPLA — STARSHIP (GRUNT)
10	THIS COULD BE THE NIGHT — LOVERBOY (COLUMBIA/CBS)	ONCE UPON A TIME — SIMPLE MINDS (A&M/VIRGIN)
11	MANIC MONDAY — THE BANGLES (CBS)	FALCO 3 — FALCO (A&M)
12	KING FOR A DAY — THOMPSON TWINS (ARISTA)	LISTEN LIKE THIEVES — INXS (ATLANTIC)
13	ADDICTED TO LOVE — ROBERT PALMER (ISLAND)	AFTERBURNER — ZZ TOP (WARNER BROS)
14	SANCTIFY YOURSELF — SIMPLE MINDS (A&M)	NERVOUS NIGHT — THE HOOTERS (COLUMBIA)
15	KYRIE — MR MISTER (RCA)	PICTURES FOR PLEASURE — CHARLIE SEXTON (MCA)
16	TENDER LOVE — FORCE MDs (WARNER BROS/TOMMY BOY)	PRETTY IN PINK — SOUNDTRACK (A&M)
17	BEAT'S SO LONELY — CHARLIE SEXTON (MCA)	AS THE BAND TURNS — ATLANTIC STARR (A&M)
18	HOW WILL I KNOW — WHITNEY HOUSTON (ARISTA)	DIFFERENT LIGHT — THE BANGLES (COLUMBIA/CBS)
19	WEST END GIRLS — PET SHOP BOYS (EMI AMERICA)	IN SQUARE CIRCLE — STEVIE WONDER (MOTOWN)
20	HARLEM SHUFFLE — ROLLING STONES (ROLLING STONES/COLUMBIA)	ROCKY IV — SOUNDTRACK (SCOTTI BROS)

US SINGLES / ALBUMS — Week Ending April 5 1986

#	Singles	Albums
1	ROCK ME AMADEUS — FALCO (A&M)	WHITNEY HOUSTON — WHITNEY HOUSTON (ARISTA)
2	ROCK IN THE USA — JOHN COUGAR MELLENCAMP (RIVA)	HEART — HEART (CAPITOL)
3	KISS — PRINCE AND THE REVOLUTION (PAISLEY PARK)	PROMISE — SADE (PORTRAIT)
4	SECRET LOVERS — ATLANTIC STARR (A&M)	SCARECROW — JOHN COUGAR MELLENCAMP (RIVA)
5	THESE DREAMS — HEART (CAPITOL)	WELCOME TO THE REAL WORLD — MR MISTER (RCA)
6	WHAT YOU NEED — INXS (ATLANTIC)	THE ULTIMATE SIN — OZZY OSBOURNE (CBS ASSOCIATED)
7	MANIC MONDAY — THE BANGLES (COLUMBIA/CBS)	BROTHERS IN ARMS — DIRE STRAITS (WARNER BROS)
8	LET'S GO ALL THE WAY — SLY FOX (CAPITOL)	FALCO 3 — FALCO (A&M)
9	ADDICTED TO LOVE — ROBERT PALMER (ISLAND)	THE BROADWAY ALBUM — BARBRA STREISAND (COLUMBIA/CBS)
10	NIKITA — ELTON JOHN (GEFFEN)	KNEE DEEP IN THE HOOPLA — STARSHIP (GRUNT)
11	TENDER LOVE — FORCE MDs (WARNER BROS/TOMMY BOY)	PRETTY IN PINK — SOUNDTRACK (A&M)
12	WEST END GIRLS — PET SHOP BOYS (EMI AMERICA)	LISTEN LIKE THIEVES — INXS (ATLANTIC)
13	THIS COULD BE THE NIGHT — LOVERBOY (COLUMBIA/CBS)	ONCE UPON A TIME — SIMPLE MINDS (A&M/VIRGIN)
14	HARLEM SHUFFLE — ROLLING STONES (ROLLING STONES)	AFTERBURNER — ZZ TOP (WARNER BROS)
15	SARA — STARSHIP (GRUNT)	PICTURES FOR PLEASURE — CHARLIE SEXTON (MCA)
16	WHY CAN'T THIS BE LOVE — VAN HALEN (WARNER BROS)	NERVOUS NIGHTS — THE HOOTERS (COLUMBIA)
17	BEAT'S SO LONELY — CHARLIE SEXTON (MCA)	AS THE BAND TURNS — ATLANTIC STARR (A&M)
18	CALLING AMERICA — ELECTRIC LIGHT ORCHESTRA (CBS ASSOCIATED)	DIFFERENT LIGHT — THE BANGLES (COLUMBIA/CBS)
19	I CAN'T WAIT — STEVIE NICKS (MODERN)	NO JACKET REQUIRED — PHIL COLLINS (ATLANTIC)
20	KING FOR A DAY — THOMPSON TWINS (ARISTA)	IN SQUARE CIRCLE — STEVIE WONDER (MOTOWN)

WEEK ENDING APRIL 12 1986

S I N G L E S — UK — A L B U M S

#	Singles	Albums
1	LIVING DOLL — CLIFF RICHARD AND THE YOUNG ONES (WEA)	HITS 4 — VARIOUS (CBS/WEA/RCA)
2	A DIFFERENT CORNER — GEORGE MICHAEL (EPIC)	BROTHERS IN ARMS — DIRE STRAITS (VERTIGO)
3	WONDERFUL WORLD — SAM COOKE (RCA)	PLEASE — PET SHOP BOYS (PARLOPHONE)
4	TOUCH ME (I WANT YOUR BODY) — SAMANTHA FOX (JIVE)	PARADE — PRINCE AND THE REVOLUTION (WARNER BROS)
5	ROCK ME AMADEUS — FALCO (A&M)	WHITNEY HOUSTON — WHITNEY HOUSTON (ARISTA)
6	YOU TO ME ARE EVERYTHING — REAL THING (PRT)	HUNTING HIGH AND LOW — A-HA (WARNER BROS)
7	A KIND OF MAGIC — QUEEN (EMI)	WELCOME TO THE REAL WORLD — MR MISTER (RCA)
8	PETER GUNN — ART OF NOISE AND DUANE EDDY (CHINA)	DIRTY WORK — ROLLING STONES (ROLLING STONES/CBS)
9	TRAIN OF THOUGHT — A-HA (WARNER BROS)	NO JACKET REQUIRED — PHIL COLLINS (VIRGIN)
10	SECRET LOVERS — ATLANTIC STARR (A&M)	FROM LUXURY TO HEARTACHE — CULTURE CLUB (VIRGIN)
11	E = MC² — BIG AUDIO DYNAMITE (CBS)	HITS FOR LOVERS — VARIOUS (EPIC)
12	CHAIN REACTION — DIANA ROSS (CAPITOL)	ROCKY IV — ORIGINAL SOUNDTRACK (SCOTTI BROS)
13	ABSOLUTE BEGINNERS — DAVID BOWIE (VIRGIN)	ONCE UPON A TIME — SIMPLE MINDS (VIRGIN)
14	HAVE YOU EVER HAD IT BLUE — STYLE COUNCIL (POLYDOR)	BE YOURSELF TONIGHT — EURYTHMICS (RCA)
15	ALL THE THINGS SHE SAID — SIMPLE MINDS (VIRGIN)	BLACK CELEBRATION — DEPECHE MODE (MUTE)
16	KYRIE — MR MISTER (RCA)	RENDEZVOUS — JEAN MICHEL JARRE (POLYDOR)
17	HI HO SILVER (THEME FROM BOON) — JIM DIAMOND (A&M)	THE HYMNS ALBUM — HUDDERSFIELD CHORAL SOCIETY (HMV)
18	LOOK AWAY — BIG COUNTRY (MERCURY)	5150 — VAN HALEN (WARNER BROS)
19	OVERJOYED — STEVIE WONDER (MOTOWN)	HIS GREATEST HITS — FRANK SINATRA (REPRISE)
20	MANIC MONDAY — THE BANGLES (CBS)	STREET SOUNDS 16 — VARIOUS (STREETSOUNDS)

S I N G L E S — US — A L B U M S

#	Singles	Albums
1	ROCK ME AMADEUS — FALCO (A&M)	WHITNEY HOUSTON — WHITNEY HOUSTON (ARISTA)
2	KISS — PRINCE AND THE REVOLUTION (PAISLEY PARK)	HEART — HEART (CAPITOL)
3	MANIC MONDAY — THE BANGLES (COLUMBIA/CBS)	PROMISE — SADE (PORTRAIT)
4	ROCK IN THE USA — JOHN COUGAR MELLENCAMP (RIVA)	SCARECROW — JOHN COUGAR MELLENCAMP (RIVA)
5	WHAT YOU NEED — INXS (ATLANTIC)	FALCO 3 — FALCO (A&M)
6	ADDICTED TO LOVE — ROBERT PALMER (ISLAND)	THE ULTIMATE SIN — OZZY OSBOURNE (CBS ASSOCIATED)
7	LET'S GO ALL THE WAY — SLY FOX (CAPITOL)	BROTHERS IN ARMS — DIRE STRAITS (WARNER BROS)
8	WEST END GIRLS — PET SHOP BOYS (EMI AMERICA)	PRETTY IN PINK — SOUNDTRACK (A&M)
9	HARLEM SHUFFLE — ROLLING STONES (ROLLING STONES)	WELCOME TO THE REAL WORLD — MR MISTER (RCA)
10	TENDER LOVE — FORCE MDS (WARNER BROS/TOMMY BOY)	THE BROADWAY ALBUM — BARBRA STREISAND (COLUMBIA/CBS)
11	SECRET LOVERS — ATLANTIC STARR (A&M)	LISTEN LIKE THIEVES — INXS (ATLANTIC)
12	WHY CAN'T THIS BE LOVE — VAN HALEN (WARNER BROS)	KNEE DEEP IN THE HOOPLA — STARSHIP (GRUNT)
13	THESE DREAMS — HEART (CAPITOL)	5150 — VAN HALEN (WARNER BROS)
14	WHAT HAVE YOU DONE FOR ME . . . — JANET JACKSON (A&M)	DIFFERENT LIGHT — THE BANGLES (COLUMBIA/CBS)
15	YOUR LOVE — OUTFIELD (COLUMBIA/CBS)	NO JACKET REQUIRED — PHIL COLLINS (ATLANTIC)
16	I CAN'T WAIT — STEVIE NICKS (MODERN)	PICTURES FOR PLEASURE — CHARLIE SEXTON (MCA)
17	NIKITA — ELTON JOHN (GEFFEN)	AFTERBURNER — ZZ TOP (WARNER BROS)
18	I THINK IT'S LOVE — JERMAINE JACKSON (ARISTA)	RIPTIDE — ROBERT PALMER (ISLAND)
19	TAKE ME HOME — PHIL COLLINS (ATLANTIC)	AS THE BAND TURNS — ATLANTIC STARR (A&M)
20	AMERICAN STORM — BOB SEGER/SILVER BULLET BAND (CAPITOL)	NERVOUS NIGHT — THE HOOTERS (COLUMBIA/CBS)

WEEK ENDING APRIL 19 1986

S I N G L E S — UK — A L B U M S

#	Singles	Albums
1	A DIFFERENT CORNER — GEORGE MICHAEL (EPIC)	HITS 4 — VARIOUS (CBS/WEA/RCA)
2	LIVING DOLL — CLIFF RICHARD AND THE YOUNG ONES (WEA)	BROTHERS IN ARMS — DIRE STRAITS (VERTIGO)
3	ROCK ME AMADEUS — FALCO (A&M)	HUNTING HIGH AND LOW — A-HA (WARNER BROS)
4	A KIND OF MAGIC — QUEEN (EMI)	PLEASE — PET SHOP BOYS (PARLOPHONE)
5	TOUCH ME (I WANT YOUR BODY) — SAMANTHA FOX (JIVE)	WHITNEY HOUSTON — WHITNEY HOUSTON (ARISTA)
6	WONDERFUL WORLD — SAM COOKE (RCA)	PARADE — PRINCE AND THE REVOLUTION (WARNER BROS)
7	YOU TO ME ARE EVERYTHING — REAL THING (PRT)	HITS FOR LOVERS — VARIOUS (EPIC)
8	TRAIN OF THOUGHT — A-HA (WARNER BROS)	NO JACKET REQUIRED — PHIL COLLINS (VIRGIN)
9	ALL THE THINGS SHE SAID — SIMPLE MINDS (VIRGIN)	ONCE UPON A TIME — SIMPLE MINDS (VIRGIN)
10	LOOK AWAY — BIG COUNTRY (MERCURY)	WELCOME TO THE REAL WORLD — MR MISTER (RCA)
11	SECRET LOVERS — ATLANTIC STARR (A&M)	RENDEZVOUS — JEAN MICHEL JARRE (POLYDOR)
12	PETER GUNN — ART OF NOISE AND DUANE EDDY (CHINA)	THE GREATEST HITS — SHALAMAR (STYLUS)
13	E = MC² — BIG AUDIO DYNAMITE (CBS)	HEART TO HEART — VARIOUS (K-TEL)
14	CAN'T WAIT ANOTHER MINUTE — FIVE STAR (TENT)	DIRTY WORK — ROLLING STONES (ROLLING STONES/CBS)
15	HAVE YOU EVER HAD IT BLUE — STYLE COUNCIL (POLYDOR)	ROCKY IV — ORIGINAL SOUNDTRACK (SCOTTI BROS)
16	WHAT HAVE YOU DONE FOR ME . . . — JANET JACKSON (A&M)	5150 — VAN HALEN (WARNER BROS)
17	THE FINEST — SOS BAND (TABU)	BE YOURSELF TONIGHT — EURYTHMICS (RCA)
18	CHAIN REACTION — DIANA ROSS (CAPITOL)	BLACK CELEBRATION — DEPECHE MODE (MUTE)
19	HI HO SILVER (THEME FROM BOON) — JIM DIAMOND (A&M)	THE TV HITS ALBUM VOL 2 — VARIOUS (TOWERBELL)
20	C'MON C'MON — BRONSKI BEAT (FORBIDDEN FRUIT)	ABSOLUTE BEGINNERS — SOUNDTRACK (VIRGIN)

S I N G L E S — US — A L B U M S

#	Singles	Albums
1	KISS — PRINCE AND THE REVOLUTION (PAISLEY PARK)	WHITNEY HOUSTON — WHITNEY HOUSTON (ARISTA)
2	MANIC MONDAY — THE BANGLES (COLUMBIA/CBS)	HEART — HEART (CAPITOL)
3	ADDICTED TO LOVE — ROBERT PALMER (ISLAND)	5150 — VAN HALEN (WARNER BROS)
4	ROCK ME AMADEUS — FALCO (A&M)	PROMISE — SADE (PORTRAIT)
5	WEST END GIRLS — PET SHOP BOYS (EMI AMERICA)	FALCO 3 — FALCO (A&M)
6	WHAT YOU NEED — INXS (ATLANTIC)	PRETTY IN PINK — SOUNDTRACK (A&M)
7	LET'S GO ALL THE WAY — SLY FOX (CAPITOL)	THE ULTIMATE SIN — OZZY OSBOURNE (CBS ASSOCIATED)
8	HARLEM SHUFFLE — ROLLING STONES (ROLLING STONES)	SCARECROW — JOHN COUGAR MELLENCAMP (RIVA)
9	WHY CAN'T THIS BE LOVE — VAN HALEN (WARNER BROS)	DIRTY WORK — ROLLING STONES (COLUMBIA/CBS)
10	TENDER LOVE — FORCE MDs (WARNER BROS/TOMMY BOY)	BROTHERS IN ARMS — DIRE STRAITS (WARNER BROS)
11	ROCK IN THE USA — JOHN COUGAR MELLENCAMP (RIVA)	WELCOME TO THE REAL WORLD — MR MISTER (RCA)
12	WHAT HAVE YOU DONE FOR ME . . . — JANET JACKSON (A&M)	DIFFERENT LIGHT — THE BANGLES (COLUMBIA/CBS)
13	YOUR LOVE — THE OUTFIELD (COLUMBIA/CBS)	LISTEN LIKE THIEVES — INXS (ATLANTIC)
14	TAKE ME HOME — PHIL COLLINS (ATLANTIC)	PARADE — PRINCE AND THE REVOLUTION (PAISLEY PARK)
15	AMERICAN STORM — BOB SEGER/SILVER BULLET BAND (CAPITOL)	RIPTIDE — ROBERT PALMER (ISLAND)
16	I CAN'T WAIT — STEVIE NICKS (MODERN)	THE BROADWAY ALBUM — BARBRA STREISAND (COLUMBIA/CBS)
17	I THINK IT'S LOVE — JERMAINE JACKSON (ARISTA)	NO JACKET REQUIRED — PHIL COLLINS (ATLANTIC)
18	BAD BOY — MIAMI SOUND MACHINE (EPIC)	KNEE DEEP IN THE HOOPLA — STARSHIP (GRUNT)
19	SECRET LOVERS — ATLANTIC STARR (A&M)	PLAY DEEP — THE OUTFIELD (COLUMBIA/CBS)
20	IF YOU LEAVE — OMD (A&M)	TURBO — JUDAS PRIEST (COLUMBIA)

S I N G L E S — UK — A L B U M S

#	SINGLES	ALBUMS
1	A DIFFERENT CORNER — GEORGE MICHAEL (EPIC)	STREET LIFE – 20 GREAT HITS — BRYAN FERRY/ROXY MUSIC (EG)
2	ROCK ME AMADEUS — FALCO (A&M)	HITS 4 — VARIOUS (CBS/WEA/RCA)
3	A KIND OF MAGIC — QUEEN (EMI)	BROTHERS IN ARMS — DIRE STRAITS (VERTIGO)
4	LIVING DOLL — CLIFF RICHARD AND THE YOUNG ONES (WEA)	WHITNEY HOUSTON — WHITNEY HOUSTON (ARISTA)
5	JUST SAY NO — CAST OF GRANGE HILL (BBC)	HUNTING HIGH AND LOW — A-HA (WARNER BROS)
6	WHAT HAVE YOU DONE FOR ME . . . — JANET JACKSON (A&M)	ONCE UPON A TIME — SIMPLE MINDS (VIRGIN)
7	LOOK AWAY — BIG COUNTRY (MERCURY)	PLEASE — PET SHOP BOYS (PARLOPHONE)
8	CAN'T WAIT ANOTHER MINUTE — FIVE STAR (TENT)	HEART TO HEART — VARIOUS (K-TEL)
9	TOUCH ME (I WANT YOUR BODY) — SAMANTHA FOX (JIVE)	THE GREATEST HITS — SHALAMAR (STYLUS)
10	LIVE TO TELL — MADONNA (SIRE)	VICTORIALAND — COCTEAU TWINS (4AD)
11	ALL THE THINGS SHE SAID — SIMPLE MINDS (VIRGIN)	ON THE BEACH — CHRIS REA (MAGNET)
12	WONDERFUL WORLD — SAM COOKE (RCA)	NO JACKET REQUIRED — PHIL COLLINS (VIRGIN)
13	TRAIN OF THOUGHT — A-HA (WARNER BROS)	TINDERBOX — SIOUXSIE AND THE BANSHEES (WONDERLAND)
14	YOU TO ME ARE EVERYTHING — REAL THING (PRT)	PARADE — PRINCE AND THE REVOLUTION (WARNER BROS)
15	SECRET LOVERS — ATLANTIC STARR (A&M)	THE MAN AND HIS MUSIC — SAM COOKE (RCA)
16	GREATEST LOVE OF ALL — WHITNEY HOUSTON (ARISTA)	HITS FOR LOVERS — VARIOUS (EPIC)
17	THE FINEST — SOS BAND (TABU)	RENDEZVOUS — JEAN MICHEL JARRE (POLYDOR)
18	DRIVING AWAY FROM HOME — IT'S IMMATERIAL (SIREN)	INVISIBLE SILENCE — ART OF NOISE (CHINA)
19	$E = MC^2$ — BIG AUDIO DYNAMITE (CBS)	WELCOME TO THE REAL WORLD — MR MISTER (RCA)
20	YOU AND ME TONIGHT — AURRA (10 RECORDS)	ABSOLUTE BEGINNERS — SOUNDTRACK (VIRGIN)

S I N G L E S — US — A L B U M S

#	SINGLES	ALBUMS
1	KISS — PRINCE AND THE REVOLUTION (PAISLEY PARK)	5150 — VAN HALEN (WARNER BROS)
2	ADDICTED TO LOVE — ROBERT PALMER (ISLAND)	WHITNEY HOUSTON — WHITNEY HOUSTON (ARISTA)
3	WEST END GIRLS — PET SHOP BOYS (EMI AMERICA)	FALCO 3 — FALCO (A&M)
4	MANIC MONDAY — THE BANGLES (COLUMBIA/CBS)	HEART — HEART (CAPITOL)
5	WHY CAN'T THIS BE LOVE — VAN HALEN (WARNER BROS)	DIRTY WORK — ROLLING STONES (COLUMBIA/CBS)
6	HARLEM SHUFFLE — ROLLING STONES (ROLLING STONES)	PARADE — PRINCE AND THE REVOLUTION (PAISLEY PARK)
7	ROCK ME AMADEUS — FALCO (A&M)	PRETTY IN PINK — SOUNDTRACK (A&M)
8	WHAT HAVE YOU DONE FOR ME . . . — JANET JACKSON (A&M)	PROMISE — SADE (PORTRAIT)
9	YOUR LOVE — THE OUTFIELD (COLUMBIA/CBS)	LIKE A ROCK — BOB SEGER/SILVER BULLET BAND (CAPITOL)
10	TAKE ME HOME — PHIL COLLINS (ATLANTIC)	THE ULTIMATE SIN — OZZY OSBOURNE (CBS ASSOCIATED)
11	WHAT YOU NEED — INXS (ATLANTIC)	SCARECROW — JOHN COUGAR MELLENCAMP (RIVA)
12	GREATEST LOVE OF ALL — WHITNEY HOUSTON (ARISTA)	DIFFERENT LIGHT — THE BANGLES (COLUMBIA/CBS)
13	BAD BOY — MIAMI SOUND MACHINE (EPIC)	RIPTIDE — ROBERT PALMER (ISLAND)
14	AMERICAN STORM — BOB SEGER/SILVER BULLET BAND (CAPITOL)	BROTHERS IN ARMS — DIRE STRAITS (WARNER BROS)
15	LET'S GO ALL THE WAY — SLY FOX (CAPITOL)	WELCOME TO THE REAL WORLD — MR MISTER (RCA)
16	I THINK IT'S LOVE — JERMAINE JACKSON (ARISTA)	PLAY DEEP — THE OUTFIELD (COLUMBIA/CBS)
17	TENDER LOVE — FORCE MDs (WARNER BROS/TOMMY BOY)	TURBO — JUDAS PRIEST (COLUMBIA/CBS)
18	IF YOU LEAVE — OMD (A&M)	NO JACKET REQUIRED — PHIL COLLINS (ATLANTIC)
19	SO FAR AWAY — DIRE STRAITS (WARNER BROS)	CONTROL — JANET JACKSON (A&M)
20	SOMETHING ABOUT YOU — LEVEL 42 (POLYDOR)	LISTEN LIKE THIEVES — INXS (ATLANTIC)

S I N G L E S — UK — A L B U M S

#	SINGLES	ALBUMS
1	A DIFFERENT CORNER — GEORGE MICHAEL (EPIC)	STREET LIFE – 20 GREAT HITS — BRYAN FERRY/ROXY MUSIC (EG)
2	ROCK ME AMADEUS — FALCO (A&M)	HITS 4 — VARIOUS (CBS/WEA/RCA)
3	WHAT HAVE YOU DONE FOR ME . . . — JANET JACKSON (A&M)	WHITNEY HOUSTON — WHITNEY HOUSTON (ARISTA)
4	LIVE TO TELL — MADONNA (SIRE)	BROTHERS IN ARMS — DIRE STRAITS (VERTIGO)
5	JUST SAY NO — CAST OF GRANGE HILL (BBC)	HUNTING HIGH AND LOW — A-HA (WARNER BROS)
6	A KIND OF MAGIC — QUEEN (EMI)	ONCE UPON A TIME — SIMPLE MINDS (VIRGIN)
7	CAN'T WAIT ANOTHER MINUTE — FIVE STAR (TENT)	THE GREATEST HITS — SHALAMAR (STYLUS)
8	LOOK AWAY — BIG COUNTRY (MERCURY)	HEART TO HEART — VARIOUS (K-TEL)
9	LESSONS IN LOVE — LEVEL 42 (POLYDOR)	THE MAN AND HIS MUSIC — SAM COOKE (RCA)
10	GREATEST LOVE OF ALL — WHITNEY HOUSTON (ARISTA)	RENDEZVOUS — JEAN MICHEL JARRE (POLYDOR)
11	I HEARD IT THROUGH THE GRAPEVINE — MARVIN GAYE (MOTOWN)	PLEASE — PET SHOP BOYS (PARLOPHONE)
12	YOU AND ME TONIGHT — AURRA (10 RECORDS)	NO JACKET REQUIRED — PHIL COLLINS (VIRGIN)
13	LIVING DOLL — CLIFF RICHARD AND THE YOUNG ONES (WEA)	ON THE BEACH — CHRIS REA (MAGNET)
14	TOUCH ME (I WANT YOUR BODY) — SAMANTHA FOX (JIVE)	WORLD MACHINE — LEVEL 42 (POLYDOR)
15	ALL THE THINGS SHE SAID — SIMPLE MINDS (VIRGIN)	PARADE — PRINCE AND THE REVOLUTION (WARNER BROS)
16	SECRET LOVERS — ATLANTIC STARR (A&M)	SUZANNE VEGA — SUZANNE VEGA (A&M)
17	THE FINEST — SOS BAND (TABU)	WELCOME TO THE REAL WORLD — MR MISTER (RCA)
18	WONDERFUL WORLD — SAM COOKE (RCA)	LUXURY OF LIFE — FIVE STAR (TENT)
19	ON MY OWN — PATTI LABELLE/MICHAEL MCDONALD (MCA)	ABSOLUTE BEGINNERS — SOUNDTRACK (VIRGIN)
20	YOU TO ME ARE EVERYTHING — REAL THING (PRT)	HITS FOR LOVERS — VARIOUS (EPIC)

S I N G L E S — US — A L B U M S

#	SINGLES	ALBUMS
1	ADDICTED TO LOVE — ROBERT PALMER (ISLAND)	5150 — VAN HALEN (WARNER BROS)
2	WEST END GIRLS — PET SHOP BOYS (EMI AMERICA)	WHITNEY HOUSTON — WHITNEY HOUSTON (ARISTA)
3	KISS — PRINCE AND THE REVOLUTION (PAISLEY PARK)	PARADE — PRINCE AND THE REVOLUTION (PAISLEY PARK)
4	WHY CAN'T THIS BE LOVE — VAN HALEN (WARNER BROS)	DIRTY WORK — ROLLING STONES (COLUMBIA/CBS)
5	HARLEM SHUFFLE — ROLLING STONES (ROLLING STONES)	PRETTY IN PINK — SOUNDTRACK (A&M)
6	WHAT HAVE YOU DONE FOR ME . . . — JANET JACKSON (A&M)	LIKE A ROCK — BOB SEGER/SILVER BULLET BAND (CAPITOL)
7	GREATEST LOVE ALL — WHITNEY HOUSTON (ARISTA)	FALCO 3 — FALCO (A&M)
8	YOUR LOVE — THE OUTFIELD (COLUMBIA/CBS)	HEART — HEART (CAPITOL)
9	TAKE ME HOME — PHIL COLLINS (ATLANTIC)	RIPTIDE — ROBERT PALMER (ISLAND)
10	MANIC MONDAY — THE BANGLES (COLUMBIA/CBS)	PROMISE — SADE (PORTRAIT)
11	BAD BOY — MIAMI SOUND MACHINE (EPIC)	THE ULTIMATE SIN — OZZY OSBOURNE (CBS ASSOCIATED)
12	IF YOU LEAVE — OMD (A&M)	CONTROL — JANET JACKSON (A&M)
13	AMERICAN STORM — BOB SEGER/SILVER BULLET BAND (CAPITOL)	SCARECROW — JOHN COUGAR MELLENCAMP (RIVA)
14	LIVE TO TELL — MADONNA (SIRE)	PLAY DEEP — THE OUTFIELD (COLUMBIA/CBS)
15	ROCK ME AMADEUS — FALCO (A&M)	DIFFERENT LIGHT — THE BANGLES (COLUMBIA/CBS)
16	ON MY OWN — PATTI LABELLE/MICHAEL MCDONALD (MCA)	PLEASE — PET SHOP BOYS (EMI AMERICA)
17	I CAN'T WAIT — NU SHOOZ (ATLANTIC)	TURBO — JUDAS PRIEST (COLUMBIA/CBS)
18	SOMETHING ABOUT YOU — LEVEL 42 (POLYDOR)	NO JACKET REQUIRED — PHIL COLLINS (COLUMBIA/CBS)
19	LET'S GO ALL THE WAY — SLY FOX (CAPITOL)	BROTHERS IN ARMS — DIRE STRAITS (WARNER BROS)
20	WHAT YOU NEED — INXS (ATLANTIC)	WELCOME TO THE REAL WORLD — MR MISTER (RCA)

WEEK ENDING MAY 10 1986

SINGLES UK

#	Title	Artist
1	ROCK ME AMADEUS	FALCO (A&M)
2	LIVE TO TELL	MADONNA (SIRE)
3	LESSONS IN LOVE	LEVEL 42 (POLYDOR)
4	ON MY OWN	PATTI LABELLE/MICHAEL McDONALD (MCA)
5	WHAT HAVE YOU DONE FOR ME . . .	JANET JACKSON (A&M)
6	A DIFFERENT CORNER	GEORGE MICHAEL (EPIC)
7	CAN'T WAIT ANOTHER MINUTE	FIVE STAR (TENT)
8	I HEARD IT THROUGH THE GRAPEVINE	MARVIN GAYE (MOTOWN)
9	A KIND OF MAGIC	QUEEN (EMI)
10	GREATEST LOVE OF ALL	WHITNEY HOUSTON (ARISTA)
11	THE CHICKEN SONG	SPITTING IMAGE (VIRGIN)
12	JUST SAY NO	CAST OF GRANGE HILL (BBC)
13	YOU AND ME TONIGHT	AURRA (10 RECORDS)
14	LOOK AWAY	BIG COUNTRY (MERCURY)
15	SLEDGEHAMMER	PETER GABRIEL (VIRGIN)
16	I'LL KEEP ON LOVING YOU	PRINCESS (SUPREME)
17	SECRET LOVERS	ATLANTIC STARR (A&M)
18	ALL AND ALL	JOYCE SIMS (LONDON)
19	THE FINEST	SOS BAND (TABU)
20	ALL THE THINGS SHE SAID	SIMPLE MINDS (VIRGIN)

ALBUMS UK

#	Title	Artist
1	STREET LIFE — 20 GREAT HITS	BRYAN FERRY/ROXY MUSIC (EG)
2	BROTHERS IN ARMS	DIRE STRAITS (VERTIGO)
3	WHITNEY HOUSTON	WHITNEY HOUSTON (ARISTA)
4	HITS 4	VARIOUS (CBS/WEA/RCA)
5	THE GREATEST HITS	SHALAMAR (STYLUS)
6	HUNTING HIGH AND LOW	A-HA (WARNER BROS)
7	ONCE UPON A TIME	SIMPLE MINDS (VIRGIN)
8	THE COLLECTION	EARTH WIND AND FIRE (K-TEL)
9	WORLD MACHINE	LEVEL 42 (POLYDOR)
10	COMIC RELIEF: UTTERLY UTTERLY LIVE	ORIGINAL TV SOUNDTRACK (WEA)
11	HEART TO HEART	VARIOUS (K-TEL)
12	THE MAN AND HIS MUSIC	SAM COOKE (RCA)
13	NO JACKET REQUIRED	PHIL COLLINS (VIRGIN)
14	PLEASE	PET SHOP BOYS (PARLOPHONE)
15	RENDEZVOUS	JEAN MICHEL JARRE (POLYDOR)
16	ON THE BEACH	CHRIS REA (MAGNET)
17	SUZANNE VEGA	SUZANNE VEGA (A&M)
18	TRUTHDARE DOUBLEDARE	BRONSKI BEAT (FORBIDDEN FRUIT)
19	LUXURY OF LIFE	FIVE STAR (TENT)
20	5150	VAN HALEN (WARNER BROS)

SINGLES US

#	Title	Artist
1	WEST END GIRLS	PET SHOP BOYS (EMI AMERICA)
2	ADDICTED TO LOVE	ROBERT PALMER (ISLAND)
3	GREATEST LOVE OF ALL	WHITNEY HOUSTON (ARISTA)
4	WHY CAN'T THIS BE LOVE	VAN HALEN (WARNER BROS)
5	WHAT HAVE YOU DONE FOR ME . . .	JANET JACKSON (A&M)
6	YOUR LOVE	THE OUTFIELD (COLUMBIA/CBS)
7	TAKE ME HOME	PHIL COLLINS (ATLANTIC)
8	BAD BOY	MIAMI SOUND MACHINE (EPIC)
9	HARLEM SHUFFLE	ROLLING STONES (ROLLING STONES/CBS)
10	IF YOU LEAVE	OMD (A&M)
11	LIVE TO TELL	MADONNA (SIRE)
12	KISS	PRINCE AND THE REVOLUTION (PAISLEY PARK)
13	ON MY OWN	PATTI LABELLE/MICHAEL McDONALD (MCA)
14	I CAN'T WAIT	NU SHOOZ (ATLANTIC)
15	SOMETHING ABOUT YOU	LEVEL 42 (POLYDOR)
16	AMERICAN STORM	BOB SEGER/SILVER BULLET BAND (CAPITOL)
17	ALL I NEED IS A MIRACLE	MIKE AND THE MECHANICS (ATLANTIC)
18	MANIC MONDAY	THE BANGLES (COLUMBIA/CBS)
19	IS IT LOVE	FORCE MDs (WARNER BROS/TOMMY BOY)
20	BE GOOD TO YOURSELF	JOURNEY (COLUMBIA/CBS)

ALBUMS US

#	Title	Artist
1	5150	VAN HALEN (WARNER BROS)
2	WHITNEY HOUSTON	WHITNEY HOUSTON (ARISTA)
3	PARADE	PRINCE AND THE REVOLUTION (PAISLEY PARK)
4	DIRTY WORK	ROLLING STONES (COLUMBIA/CBS)
5	PRETTY IN PINK	SOUNDTRACK (A&M)
6	LIKE A ROCK	BOB SEGER/SILVER BULLET BAND (CAPITOL)
7	HEART	HEART (CAPITOL)
8	FALCO 3	FALCO (A&M)
9	RIPTIDE	ROBERT PALMER (ISLAND)
10	PLAY DEEP	THE OUTFIELD (COLUMBIA/CBS)
11	CONTROL	JANET JACKSON (A&M)
12	PLEASE	PET SHOP BOYS (EMI AMERICA)
13	PROMISE	SADE (PORTRAIT)
14	THE ULTIMATE SIN	OZZY OSBOURNE (CBS ASSOCIATED)
15	BROTHERS IN ARMS	DIRE STRAITS (WARNER BROS)
16	DIFFERENT LIGHT	THE BANGLES (COLUMBIA/CBS)
17	NO JACKET REQUIRED	PHIL COLLINS (ATLANTIC)
18	SCARECROW	JOHN COUGAR MELLENCAMP (RIVA)
19	TURBO	JUDAS PRIEST (COLUMBIA/CBS)
20	WELCOME TO THE REAL WORLD	MR MISTER (RCA)

WEEK ENDING MAY 17 1986

SINGLES UK

#	Title	Artist
1	THE CHICKEN SONG	SPITTING IMAGE (VIRGIN)
2	ON MY OWN	PATTI LABELLE/MICHAEL McDONALD (MCA)
3	LESSONS IN LOVE	LEVEL 42 (POLYDOR)
4	ROCK ME AMADEUS	FALCO (A&M)
5	LIVE TO TELL	MADONNA (SIRE)
6	WHAT HAVE YOU DONE FOR ME . . .	JANET JACKSON (A&M)
7	SLEDGEHAMMER	PETER GABRIEL (VIRGIN)
8	GREATEST LOVE OF ALL	WHITNEY HOUSTON (ARISTA)
9	I HEARD IT THROUGH THE GRAPEVINE	MARVIN GAYE (MOTOWN)
10	CAN'T WAIT ANOTHER MINUTE	FIVE STAR (TENT)
11	SNOOKER LOOPY	MATCHROOM MOB/CHAS AND DAVE (ROCKNEY)
12	A DIFFERENT CORNER	GEORGE MICHAEL (EPIC)
13	WHY CAN'T THIS BE LOVE	VAN HALEN (WARNER BROS)
14	THERE'LL BE SAD SONGS	BILLY OCEAN (JIVE)
15	A KIND OF MAGIC	QUEEN (EMI)
16	ALL AND ALL	JOYCE SIMS (LONDON)
17	SPIRIT IN THE SKY	DOCTOR AND THE MEDICS (IRS)
18	YOU AND ME TONIGHT	AURRA (10 RECORDS)
19	I'LL KEEP ON LOVING YOU	PRINCESS (SUPREME)
20	ROCK LOBSTER	B52s (ISLAND)

ALBUMS UK

#	Title	Artist
1	STREET LIFE — 20 GREAT HITS	BRYAN FERRY/ROXY MUSIC (EG)
2	LOVE ZONE	BILLY OCEAN (JIVE)
3	WHITNEY HOUSTON	WHITNEY HOUSTON (ARISTA)
4	BROTHERS IN ARMS	DIRE STRAITS (VERTIGO)
5	THE COLLECTION	EARTH WIND AND FIRE (K-TEL)
6	THE GREATEST HITS	SHALAMAR (STYLUS)
7	HITS 4	VARIOUS (CBS/WEA/RCA)
8	HOME AND ABROAD	STYLE COUNCIL (POLYDOR)
9	ONCE UPON A TIME	SIMPLE MINDS (VIRGIN)
10	WORLD MACHINE	LEVEL 42 (POLYDOR)
11	HUNTING HIGH AND LOW	A-HA (WARNER BROS)
12	COMIC RELIEF: UTTERLY UTTERLY LIVE	ORIGINAL TV SOUNDTRACK (WEA)
13	THE MAN AND HIS MUSIC	SAM COOKE (RCA)
14	NO JACKET REQUIRED	PHIL COLLINS (VIRGIN)
15	SANDS OF TIME	SOS BAND (TABU)
16	HEART TO HEART	VARIOUS (K-TEL)
17	PRINCESS	PRINCESS (SUPREME)
18	PLEASE	PET SHOP BOYS (PARLOPHONE)
19	SUZANNE VEGA	SUZANNE VEGA (A&M)
20	RENDEZVOUS	JEAN MICHEL JARRE (POLYDOR)

SINGLES US

#	Title	Artist
1	GREATEST LOVE OF ALL	WHITNEY HOUSTON (ARISTA)
2	WEST END GIRLS	PET SHOP BOYS (EMI AMERICA)
3	WHY CAN'T THIS BE LOVE	VAN HALEN (WARNER BROS)
4	WHAT HAVE YOU DONE FOR ME . . .	JANET JACKSON (A&M)
5	LIVE TO TELL	MADONNA (SIRE)
6	YOUR LOVE	THE OUTFIELD (COLUMBIA/CBS)
7	TAKE ME HOME	PHIL COLLINS (ATLANTIC)
8	BAD BOY	MIAMI SOUND MACHINE (EPIC)
9	IF YOU LEAVE	OMD (A&M)
10	ADDICTED TO LOVE	ROBERT PALMER (ISLAND)
11	ON MY OWN	PATTI LABELLE/MICHAEL McDONALD (MCA)
12	I CAN'T WAIT	NU SHOOZ (ATLANTIC)
13	SOMETHING ABOUT YOU	LEVEL 42 (POLYDOR)
14	ALL I NEED IS A MIRACLE	MIKE AND THE MECHANICS (ATLANTIC)
15	IS IT LOVE	FORCE MDs (WARNER BROS/TOMMY BOY)
16	BE GOOD TO YOURSELF	JOURNEY (COLUMBIA/CBS)
17	KISS	PRINCE AND THE REVOLUTION (PAISLEY PARK)
18	MOVE AWAY	CULTURE CLUB (VIRGIN/EPIC)
19	HARLEM SHUFFLE	ROLLING STONES (ROLLING STONES)
20	NEVER AS GOOD AS THE FIRST TIME	SADE (PORTRAIT)

ALBUMS US

#	Title	Artist
1	WHITNEY HOUSTON	WHITNEY HOUSTON (ARISTA)
2	5150	VAN HALEN (WARNER BROS)
3	PARADE	PRINCE AND THE REVOLUTION (PAISLEY PARK)
4	LIKE A ROCK	BOB SEGER/SILVER BULLET BAND (CAPITOL)
5	PRETTY IN PINK	SOUNDTRACK (A&M)
6	DIRTY WORK	ROLLING STONES (COLUMBIA/CBS)
7	CONTROL	JANET JACKSON (A&M)
8	RIPTIDE	ROBERT PALMER (ISLAND)
9	RAISED ON RADIO	JOURNEY (COLUMBIA)
10	PLAY DEEP	THE OUTFIELD (COLUMBIA/CBS)
11	HEART	HEART (CAPITOL)
12	PLEASE	PET SHOP BOYS (EMI AMERICA)
13	FALCO 3	FALCO (A&M)
14	PROMISE	SADE (PORTRAIT)
15	BROTHERS IN ARMS	DIRE STRAITS (WARNER BROS)
16	SCARECROW	JOHN COUGAR MELLENCAMP (RIVA)
17	THE ULTIMATE SIN	OZZY OSBOURNE (CBS ASSOCIATED)
18	TURBO	JUDAS PRIEST (COLUMBIA/CBS)
19	DIFFERENT LIGHT	THE BANGLES (COLUMBIA/CBS)
20	NO JACKET REQUIRED	PHIL COLLINS (ATLANTIC)

WEEK ENDING MAY 24 1986

SINGLES UK

#	Title	Artist (Label)
1	THE CHICKEN SONG	SPITTING IMAGE (VIRGIN)
2	ON MY OWN	PATTI LABELLE/MICHAEL MCDONALD (MCA)
3	LESSONS IN LOVE	LEVEL 42 (POLYDOR)
4	SLEDGEHAMMER	PETER GABRIEL (VIRGIN)
5	SPIRIT IN THE SKY	DOCTOR AND THE MEDICS (IRS)
6	SNOOKER LOOPY	MATCHROOM MOB/CHAS AND DAVE (ROCKNEY)
7	ROCK ME AMADEUS	FALCO (A&M)
8	WHY CAN'T THIS BE LOVE	VAN HALEN (WARNER BROS)
9	ROLLIN' HOME	STATUS QUO (VERTIGO)
10	LIVE TO TELL	MADONNA (SIRE)
11	GREATEST LOVE OF ALL	WHITNEY HOUSTON (ARISTA)
12	ROCK LOBSTER	B52s (ISLAND)
13	THERE'LL BE SAD SONGS	BILLY OCEAN (JIVE)
14	CAN'T WAIT ANOTHER MINUTE	FIVE STAR (TENT)
15	WHAT HAVE YOU DONE FOR ME . . .	JANET JACKSON (A&M)
16	ADDICTED TO LOVE	ROBERT PALMER (ISLAND)
17	ALL AND ALL	JOYCE SIMS (LONDON)
18	I HEARD IT THROUGH THE GRAPEVINE	MARVIN GAYE (MOTOWN)
19	HOLDING BACK THE YEARS	SIMPLY RED (ELEKTRA)
20	SET ME FREE	JAKI GRAHAM (EMI)

ALBUMS

#	Title	Artist (Label)
1	STREET LIFE – 20 GREAT HITS	BRYAN FERRY/ROXY MUSIC (EG)
2	LOVE ZONE	BILLY OCEAN (JIVE)
3	BROTHERS IN ARMS	DIRE STRAITS (VERTIGO)
4	WHITNEY HOUSTON	WHITNEY HOUSTON (ARISTA)
5	THE COLLECTION	EARTH WIND AND FIRE (K-TEL)
6	WORLD MACHINE	LEVEL 42 (POLYDOR)
7	HITS 4	VARIOUS (CBS/WEA/RCA)
8	HUNTING HIGH AND LOW	A-HA (WARNER BROS)
9	THE MAN AND HIS MUSIC	SAM COOKE (RCA)
10	COMIC RELIEF: UTTERLY UTTERLY LIVE	ORIGINAL TV SOUNDTRACK (WEA)
11	ONCE UPON A TIME	SIMPLE MINDS (VIRGIN)
12	THE GREATEST HITS	SHALAMAR (STYLUS)
13	HOME AND ABROAD	STYLE COUNCIL (POLYDOR)
14	PICTURE BOOK	SIMPLY RED (ELEKTRA)
15	PRINCESS	PRINCESS (SUPREME)
16	ON THE BEACH	CHRIS REA (MAGNET)
17	LET'S HEAR IT FROM THE GIRLS	VARIOUS (STYLUS)
18	MOONLIGHT SHADOWS	SHADOWS (PROTV)
19	LUXURY OF LIFE	FIVE STAR (TENT)
20	SANDS OF TIME	SOS BAND (TABU)

SINGLES US

#	Title	Artist (Label)
1	GREATEST LOVE OF ALL	WHITNEY HOUSTON (ARISTA)
2	LIVE TO TELL	MADONNA (SIRE)
3	ON MY OWN	PATTI LABELLE/MICHAEL MCDONALD (MCA)
4	WEST END GIRLS	PET SHOP BOYS (EMI AMERICA)
5	IF YOU LEAVE	OMD (A&M)
6	WHAT HAVE YOU DONE FOR ME . . .	JANET JACKSON (A&M)
7	TAKE ME HOME	PHIL COLLINS (ATLANTIC)
8	BAD BOY	MIAMI SOUND MACHINE (EPIC)
9	I CAN'T WAIT	NU SHOOZ (ATLANTIC)
10	ALL I NEED IS A MIRACLE	MIKE AND THE MECHANICS (ATLANTIC)
11	WHY CAN'T THIS BE LOVE	VAN HALEN (WARNER BROS)
12	SOMETHING ABOUT YOU	LEVEL 42 (POLYDOR)
13	BE GOOD TO YOURSELF	JOURNEY (COLUMBIA/CBS)
14	IS IT LOVE	FORCE MDs (WARNER BROS/TOMMY BOY)
15	YOUR LOVE	THE OUTFIELD (COLUMBIA/CBS)
16	MOVE AWAY	CULTURE CLUB (VIRGIN/EPIC)
17	ADDICTED TO LOVE	ROBERT PALMER (ISLAND)
18	CRUSH ON YOU	THE JETS (MCA)
19	THERE'LL BE SAD SONGS	BILLY OCEAN (JIVE)
20	NOTHIN' AT ALL	HEART (CAPITOL)

ALBUMS

#	Title	Artist (Label)
1	WHITNEY HOUSTON	WHITNEY HOUSTON (ARISTA)
2	5150	VAN HALEN (WARNER BROS)
3	LIKE A ROCK	BOB SEGER/SILVER BULLET BAND (CAPITOL)
4	PARADE	PRINCE AND THE REVOLUTION (PAISLEY PARK)
5	PRETTY IN PINK	SOUNDTRACK (A&M)
6	RAISED ON RADIO	JOURNEY (COLUMBIA)
7	CONTROL	JANET JACKSON (A&M)
8	DIRTY WORK	ROLLING STONES (COLUMBIA/CBS)
9	PLEASE	PET SHOP BOYS (EMI AMERICA)
10	RIPTIDE	ROBERT PALMER (ISLAND)
11	PLAY DEEP	THE OUTFIELD (COLUMBIA/CBS)
12	HEART	HEART (CAPITOL)
13	FALCO 3	FALCO (A&M)
14	WINNER IN YOU	PATTI LABELLE (MCA)
15	SCARECROW	JOHN COUGAR MELLENCAMP (RIVA)
16	BROTHERS IN ARMS	DIRE STRAITS (WARNER BROS)
17	PROMISE	SADE (PORTRAIT)
18	NO JACKET REQUIRED	PHIL COLLINS (ATLANTIC)
19	DIFFERENT LIGHT	THE BANGLES (COLUMBIA/CBS)
20	TURBO	JUDAS PRIEST (COLUMBIA/CBS)

WEEK ENDING MAY 31 1986

SINGLES UK

#	Title	Artist (Label)
1	THE CHICKEN SONG	SPITTING IMAGE (VIRGIN)
2	ON MY OWN	PATTI LABELLE/MICHAEL MCDONALD (MCA)
3	SPIRIT IN THE SKY	DOCTOR AND THE MEDICS (IRS)
4	SLEDGEHAMMER	PETER GABRIEL (VIRGIN)
5	LESSONS IN LOVE	LEVEL 42 (POLYDOR)
6	HOLDING BACK THE YEARS	SIMPLY RED (ELEKTRA)
7	SNOOKER LOOPY	MATCHROOM MOB/CHAS AND DAVE (ROCKNEY)
8	WHY CAN'T THIS BE LOVE	VAN HALEN (WARNER BROS)
9	SET ME FREE	JACKI GRAHAM (EMI)
10	ADDICTED TO LOVE	ROBERT PALMER (ISLAND)
11	ROLLIN' HOME	STATUS QUO (VERTIGO)
12	THERE'LL BE SAD SONGS	BILLY OCEAN (JIVE)
13	EVERYBODY WANTS TO RUN THE WORLD	TEARS FOR FEARS (MERCURY)
14	ROCK LOBSTER	B52s (ISLAND)
15	ROCK ME AMADEUS	FALCO (A&M)
16	WHO MADE WHO	AC/DC (ATLANTIC)
17	LIVE TO TELL	MADONNA (SIRE)
18	MINE ALL MINE/PARTY FREAK	CASHFLOW (CLUB)
19	CAN'T WAIT ANOTHER MINUTE	FIVE STAR (TENT)
20	SINFUL	PETE WYLIE (MDM)

ALBUMS

#	Title	Artist (Label)
1	SO	PETER GABRIEL (VIRGIN)
2	STREET LIFE – 20 GREAT HITS	BRYAN FERRY/ROXY MUSIC (EG)
3	LOVE ZONE	BILLY OCEAN (JIVE)
4	STANDING ON A BEACH: THE SINGLES	THE CURE (FICTION)
5	PICTURE BOOK	SIMPLY RED (ELEKTRA)
6	BROTHERS IN ARMS	DIRE STRAITS (VERTIGO)
7	WHITNEY HOUSTON	WHITNEY HOUSTON (ARISTA)
8	GO WEST/BANGS AND CRASHES	GO WEST (CHRYSALIS)
9	WORLD MACHINE	LEVEL 42 (POLYDOR)
10	THE COLLECTION	EARTH WIND AND FIRE (K-TEL)
11	MOONLIGHT SHADOWS	SHADOWS (PROTV)
12	THE MAN AND HIS MUSIC	SAM COOKE (RCA)
13	HITS 4	VARIOUS (CBS/WEA/RCA)
14	HUNTING HIGH AND LOW	A-HA (WARNER BROS)
15	THE GREATEST HITS	SHALAMAR (STYLUS)
16	ONCE UPON A TIME	SIMPLE MINDS (VIRGIN)
17	PLEASE	PET SHOP BOYS (PARLOPHONE)
18	ON THE BEACH	CHRIS REA (MAGNET)
19	LET'S HEAR IT FROM THE GIRLS	VARIOUS (STYLUS)
20	5150	VAN HALEN (WARNER BROS)

SINGLES US

#	Title	Artist (Label)
1	GREATEST LOVE OF ALL	WHITNEY HOUSTON (ARISTA)
2	LIVE TO TELL	MADONNA (SIRE)
3	ON MY OWN	PATTI LABELLE/MICHAEL MCDONALD (MCA)
4	IF YOU LEAVE	OMD (A&M)
5	I CAN'T WAIT	NU SHOOZ (ATLANTIC)
6	ALL I NEED IS A MIRACLE	MIKE AND THE MECHANICS (ATLANTIC)
7	SOMETHING ABOUT YOU	LEVEL 42 (POLYDOR)
8	IS IT LOVE	MR MISTER (RCA)
9	BE GOOD TO YOURSELF	JOURNEY (COLUMBIA/CBS)
10	WHAT HAVE YOU DONE FOR ME . . .	JANET JACKSON (A&M)
11	CRUSH ON YOU	THE JETS (MCA)
12	MOVE AWAY	CULTURE CLUB (VIRGIN/EPIC)
13	THERE'LL BE SAD SONGS	BILLY OCEAN (JIVE)
14	WEST END GIRLS	PET SHOP BOYS (EMI AMERICA)
15	A DIFFERENT CORNER	GEORGE MICHAEL (COLUMBIA/CBS)
16	BAD BOY	MIAMI SOUND MACHINE (EPIC)
17	NOTHIN' AT ALL	HEART (CAPITOL)
18	TAKE ME HOME	PHIL COLLINS (ATLANTIC)
19	NO ONE IS TO BLAME	HOWARD JONES (ELEKTRA)
20	YOUR LOVE	THE OUTFIELD (COLUMBIA/CBS)

ALBUMS

#	Title	Artist (Label)
1	WHITNEY HOUSTON	WHITNEY HOUSTON (ARISTA)
2	5150	VAN HALEN (WARNER BROS)
3	LIKE A ROCK	BOB SEGER/SILVER BULLET BAND (CAPITOL)
4	RAISED ON RADIO	JOURNEY (COLUMBIA)
5	PARADE	PRINCE AND THE REVOLUTION (PAISLEY PARK)
6	CONTROL	JANET JACKSON (A&M)
7	PRETTY IN PINK	SOUNDTRACK (A&M)
8	WINNER IN YOU	PATTI LABELLE (MCA)
9	PLEASE	PET SHOP BOYS (EMI AMERICA)
10	PLAY DEEP	THE OUTFIELD (COLUMBIA/CBS)
11	DIRTY WORK	ROLLING STONES (COLUMBIA/CBS)
12	RIPTIDE	ROBERT PALMER (ISLAND)
13	HEART	HEART (CAPITOL)
14	SCARECROW	JOHN COUGAR MELLENCAMP (RIVA)
15	FALCO 3	FALCO (A&M)
16	LOVE ZONE	BILLY OCEAN (JIVE)
17	BROTHERS IN ARMS	DIRE STRAITS (WARNER BROS)
18	PROMISE	SADE (PORTRAIT)
19	THE OTHER SIDE OF LIFE	THE MOODY BLUES (POLYDOR)
20	TURBO	JUDAS PRIEST (COLUMBIA/CBS)

WEEK ENDING JUNE 7 1986

SINGLES — UK

#	Title / Artist (Label)
1	SPIRIT IN THE SKY — DOCTOR AND THE MEDICS (IRS)
2	HOLDING BACK THE YEARS — SIMPLY RED (ELEKTRA)
3	THE CHICKEN SONG — SPITTING IMAGE (VIRGIN)
4	SLEDGEHAMMER — PETER GABRIEL (VIRGIN)
5	EVERYBODY WANTS TO RUN THE WORLD — TEARS FOR FEARS (MERCURY)
6	ON MY OWN — PATTI LABELLE/MICHAEL MCDONALD (MCA)
7	LESSONS IN LOVE — LEVEL 42 (POLYDOR)
8	ADDICTED TO LOVE — ROBERT PALMER (ISLAND)
9	SET ME FREE — JAKI GRAHAM (EMI)
10	I CAN'T WAIT — NU SHOOZ (ATLANTIC)
11	CAN'T GET BY WITHOUT YOU — REAL THING (PRT)
12	SNOOKER LOOPY — MATCHROOM MOB/CHAS AND DAVE (ROCKNEY)
13	SINFUL — PETE WYLIE (MDM)
14	WHY CAN'T THIS BE LOVE — VAN HALEN (WARNER BROS)
15	MINE ALL MINE/PARTY FREAK — CASHFLOW (CLUB)
16	INVISIBLE TOUCH — GENESIS (VIRGIN)
17	OPPORTUNITIES — PET SHOP BOYS (PARLOPHONE)
18	THERE'LL BE SAD SONGS — BILLY OCEAN (JIVE)
19	VIENNA CALLING — FALCO (A&M)
20	ROLLIN' HOME — STATUS QUO (VERTIGO)

ALBUMS — UK

#	Title / Artist (Label)
1	SO — PETER GABRIEL (VIRGIN)
2	PICTURE BOOK — SIMPLY RED (ELEKTRA)
3	BROTHERS IN ARMS — DIRE STRAITS (VERTIGO)
4	STREET LIFE – 20 GREAT HITS — BRYAN FERRY/ROXY MUSIC (EG)
5	LOVE ZONE — BILLY OCEAN (JIVE)
6	STANDING ON A BEACH – THE SINGLES — THE CURE (FICTION)
7	WHITNEY HOUSTON — WHITNEY HOUSTON (ARISTA)
8	INTO THE LIGHT — CHRIS DE BURGH (A&M)
9	WORLD MACHINE — LEVEL 42 (POLYDOR)
10	GO WEST/BANGS AND CRASHES — GO WEST (CHRYSALIS)
11	WHO MADE WHO — AC/DC (ATLANTIC)
12	MOONLIGHT SHADOWS — SHADOWS (PROTV)
13	HUNTING HIGH AND LOW — A-HA (WARNER BROS)
14	THE COLLECTION — EARTH WIND AND FIRE (K-TEL)
15	PLEASE — PET SHOP BOYS (PARLOPHONE)
16	THE MAN AND HIS MUSIC — SAM COOKE (RCA)
17	ONCE UPON A TIME — SIMPLE MINDS (VIRGIN)
18	HITS 4 — VARIOUS (CBS/WEA/RCA)
19	LUXURY OF LIFE — FIVE STAR (TENT)
20	NO JACKET REQUIRED — PHIL COLLINS (VIRGIN)

SINGLES — US

#	Title / Artist (Label)
1	LIVE TO TELL — MADONNA (SIRE)
2	ON MY OWN — PATTI LABELLE/MICHAEL MCDONALD (MCA)
3	GREATEST LOVE OF ALL — WHITNEY HOUSTON (ARISTA)
4	I CAN'T WAIT — NU SHOOZ (ATLANTIC)
5	ALL I NEED IS A MIRACLE — MIKE AND THE MECHANICS (ATLANTIC)
6	IF YOU LEAVE — OMD (A&M)
7	SOMETHING ABOUT YOU — LEVEL 42 (POLYDOR)
8	CRUSH ON YOU — THE JETS (MCA)
9	THERE'LL BE SAD SONGS — BILLY OCEAN (JIVE)
10	A DIFFERENT CORNER — GEORGE MICHAEL (COLUMBIA/CBS)
11	BE GOOD TO YOURSELF — JOURNEY (COLUMBIA/CBS)
12	MOVE AWAY — CULTURE CLUE (VIRGIN/EPIC)
13	IS IT LOVE — MR MISTER (RCA)
14	NO ONE IS TO BLAME — HOWARD JONES (ELEKTRA)
15	NOTHIN' AT ALL — HEART (CAPITOL)
16	HOLDING BACK THE YEARS — SIMPLY RED (ELEKTRA)
17	I WANNA BE A COWBOY — BOYS DON'T CRY (PROFILE)
18	WHO'S JOHNNY — EL DEBARGE (GORDY)
19	WHAT HAVE YOU DONE FOR ME… — JANET JACKSON (A&M)
20	WEST END GIRLS — PET SHOP BOYS (EMI AMERICA)

ALBUMS — US

#	Title / Artist (Label)
1	WHITNEY HOUSTON — WHITNEY HOUSTON (ARISTA)
2	5150 — VAN HALEN (WARNER BROS)
3	LIKE A ROCK — BOB SEGER/SILVER BULLET BAND (CAPITOL)
4	RAISED ON RADIO — JOURNEY (COLUMBIA)
5	WINNER IN YOU — PATTI LABELLE (MCA)
6	CONTROL — JANET JACKSON (A&M)
7	PARADE — PRINCE AND THE REVOLUTION (PAISLEY PARK)
8	PLEASE — PET SHOP BOYS (EMI AMERICA)
9	PRETTY IN PINK — SOUNDTRACK (A&M)
10	PLAY DEEP — THE OUTFIELD (COLUMBIA/CBS)
11	HEART — HEART (CAPITOL)
12	RIPTIDE — ROBERT PALMER (ISLAND)
13	DIRTY WORK — ROLLING STONES (COLUMBIA/CBS)
14	LOVE ZONE — BILLY OCEAN (JIVE)
15	THE OTHER SIDE OF LIFE — THE MOODY BLUES (POLYDOR)
16	FALCO 3 — FALCO (A&M)
17	SCARECROW — JOHN COUGAR MELLENCAMP (RIVA)
18	TUFF ENUFF — FABULOUS THUNDERBIRDS (CBS ASSOCIATED)
19	BROTHERS IN ARMS — DIRE STRAITS (WARNER BROS)
20	TURBO — JUDAS PRIEST (COLUMBIA/CBS)

WEEK ENDING JUNE 14 1986

SINGLES — UK

#	Title / Artist (Label)
1	SPIRIT IN THE SKY — DOCTOR AND THE MEDICS (IRS)
2	HOLDING BACK THE YEARS — SIMPLY RED (ELEKTRA)
3	I CAN'T WAIT — NU SHOOZ (ATLANTIC)
4	SLEDGEHAMMER — PETER GABRIEL (VIRGIN)
5	ADDICTED TO LOVE — ROBERT PALMER (ISLAND)
6	CAN'T GET BY WITHOUT YOU — REAL THING (PRT)
7	SET ME FREE — JAKI GRAHAM (EMI)
8	EVERYBODY WANTS TO RUN THE WORLD — TEARS FOR FEARS (MERCURY)
9	ON MY OWN — PATTI LABELLE/MICHAEL MCDONALD (MCA)
10	VIENNA CALLING — FALCO (A&M)
11	OPPORTUNITIES — PET SHOP BOYS (PARLOPHONE)
12	THE CHICKEN SONG — SPITTING IMAGE (VIRGIN)
13	LESSONS IN LOVE — LEVEL 42 (POLYDOR)
14	SINFUL — PETE WYLIE (MDM)
15	INVISIBLE TOUCH — GENESIS (VIRGIN)
16	HUNTING HIGH AND LOW — A-HA (WARNER BROS)
17	MINE ALL MINE/PARTY FREAK — CASHFLOW (CLUB)
18	BAD BOY — MIAMI SOUND MACHINE (EPIC)
19	AMITYVILLE — LOVE BUG STARSKI (EPIC)
20	21st CENTURY BOY — SIGUE SIGUE SPUTNIK (PARLOPHONE)

ALBUMS — UK

#	Title / Artist (Label)
1	A KIND OF MAGIC — QUEEN (EMI)
2	SO — PETER GABRIEL (VIRGIN)
3	PICTURE BOOK — SIMPLY RED (ELEKTRA)
4	BROTHERS IN ARMS — DIRE STRAITS (VERTIGO)
5	STREET LIFE – 20 GREAT HITS — BRYAN FERRY/ROXY MUSIC (EG)
6	LOVE ZONE — BILLY OCEAN (JIVE)
7	STANDING ON A BEACH – THE SINGLES — THE CURE (FICTION)
8	THE MAN AND HIS MUSIC — SAM COOKE (RCA)
9	INTO THE LIGHT — CHRIS DE BURGH (A&M)
10	WORLD MACHINE — LEVEL 42 (POLYDOR)
11	MOONLIGHT SHADOWS — SHADOWS (PROTV)
12	HUNTING HIGH AND LOW — A-HA (WARNER BROS)
13	WHITNEY HOUSTON — WHITNEY HOUSTON (ARISTA)
14	WHO MADE WHO — AC/DC (ATLANTIC)
15	PLEASE — PET SHOP BOYS (PARLOPHONE)
16	GO WEST/BANGS AND CRASHES — GO WEST (CHRYSALIS)
17	UP FRONT 1 — VARIOUS (SERIOUS)
18	SUZANNE VEGA — SUZANNE VEGA (A&M)
19	ONCE UPON A TIME — SIMPLE MINDS (VIRGIN)
20	NO JACKET REQUIRED — PHIL COLLINS (VIRGIN)

SINGLES — US

#	Title / Artist (Label)
1	ON MY OWN — PATTI LABELLE/MICHAEL MCDONALD (MCA)
2	LIVE TO TELL — MADONNA (SIRE)
3	I CAN'T WAIT — NU SHOOZ (ATLANTIC)
4	THERE'LL BE SAD SONGS — BILLY OCEAN (JIVE)
5	CRUSH ON YOU — THE JETS (MCA)
6	GREATEST LOVE OF ALL — WHITNEY HOUSTON (ARISTA)
7	A DIFFERENT CORNER — GEORGE MICHAEL (COLUMBIA/CBS)
8	NO ONE IS TO BLAME — HOWARD JONES (ELEKTRA)
9	ALL I NEED IS A MIRACLE — MIKE AND THE MECHANICS (ATLANTIC)
10	SOMETHING ABOUT YOU — LEVEL 42 (POLYDOR)
11	HOLDING BACK THE YEARS — SIMPLY RED (ELEKTRA)
12	NOTHIN' AT ALL — HEART (CAPITOL)
13	IF YOU LEAVE — OMD (A&M)
14	WHO'S JOHNNY — EL DEBARGE (GORDY)
15	I WANNA BE A COWBOY — BOYS DON'T CRY (PROFILE)
16	IS IT LOVE — MR MISTER (RCA)
17	BE GOOD TO YOURSELF — JOURNEY (COLUMBIA/CBS)
18	MOVE AWAY — CULTURE CLUE (VIRGIN/EPIC)
19	VIENNA CALLING — FALCO (A&M)
20	TUFF ENUFF — FABULOUS THUNDERBIRDS (CBS ASSOCIATED)

ALBUMS — US

#	Title / Artist (Label)
1	WHITNEY HOUSTON — WHITNEY HOUSTON (ARISTA)
2	5150 — VAN HALEN (WARNER BROS)
3	LIKE A ROCK — BOB SEGER/SILVER BULLET BAND (CAPITOL)
4	WINNER IN YOU — PATTI LABELLE (MCA)
5	CONTROL — JANET JACKSON (A&M)
6	RAISED ON RADIO — JOURNEY (COLUMBIA)
7	PARADE — PRINCE AND THE REVOLUTION (PAISLEY PARK)
8	PLEASE — PET SHOP BOYS (EMI AMERICA)
9	PLAY DEEP — THE OUTFIELD (COLUMBIA/CBS)
10	HEART — HEART (CAPITOL)
11	PRETTY IN PINK — SOUNDTRACK (A&M)
12	LOVE ZONE — BILLY OCEAN (JIVE)
13	RIPTIDE — ROBERT PALMER (ISLAND)
14	THE OTHER SIDE OF LIFE — THE MOODY BLUES (POLYDOR)
15	DIRTY WORK — ROLLING STONES (COLUMBIA/CBS)
16	TUFF ENUFF — FABULOUS THUNDERBIRDS (CBS ASSOCIATED)
17	FALCO 3 — FALCO (A&M)
18	SCARECROW — JOHN COUGAR MELLENCAMP (RIVA)
19	BROTHERS IN ARMS — DIRE STRAITS (WARNER BROS)
20	TURBO — JUDAS PRIEST (COLUMBIA/CBS)

WEEK ENDING JUNE 21 1986

SINGLES UK

#	Title	Artist (Label)
1	SPIRIT IN THE SKY	DOCTOR AND THE MEDICS (IRS)
2	THE EDGE OF HEAVEN	WHAM! (EPIC)
3	I CAN'T WAIT	NU SHOOZ (ATLANTIC)
4	HOLDING BACK THE YEARS	SIMPLY RED (ELEKTRA)
5	HUNTING HIGH AND LOW	A-HA (WARNER BROS)
6	ADDICTED TO LOVE	ROBERT PALMER (ISLAND)
7	CAN'T GET BY WITHOUT YOU	REAL THING (PRT)
8	SLEDGEHAMMER	PETER GABRIEL (VIRGIN)
9	TOO GOOD TO BE FORGOTTEN	AMAZULU (ISLAND)
10	VIENNA CALLING	FALCO (A&M)
11	NEW BEGINNING (MAMBA SEYRA)	BUCKS FIZZ (POLYDOR)
12	HAPPY HOUR	HOUSEMARTINS (GO! DISCS)
13	AMITYVILLE	LOVEBUG STARSKI (EPIC)
14	MY FAVOURITE WASTE OF TIME	OWEN PAUL (EPIC)
15	OPPORTUNITIES	PET SHOP BOYS (PARLOPHONE)
16	SET ME FREE	JAKI GRAHAM (EMI)
17	INVISIBLE TOUCH	GENESIS (VIRGIN)
18	BAD BOY	MIAMI SOUND MACHINE (EPIC)
19	NASTY	JANET JACKSON (A&M)
20	ON MY OWN	PATTI LABELLE/MICHAEL MCDONALD (MCA)

ALBUMS UK

#	Title	Artist (Label)
1	INVISIBLE TOUCH	GENESIS (VIRGIN)
2	A KIND OF MAGIC	QUEEN (EMI)
3	SO	PETER GABRIEL (VIRGIN)
4	PICTURE BOOK	SIMPLY RED (ELEKTRA)
5	BROTHERS IN ARMS	DIRE STRAITS (VERTIGO)
6	MOONLIGHT SHADOWS	SHADOWS (PROTV)
7	STREET LIFE — 20 GREAT HITS	BRYAN FERRY/ROXY MUSIC (EG)
8	THE MAN AND HIS MUSIC	SAM COOKE (RCA)
9	HUNTING HIGH AND LOW	A-HA (WARNER BROS)
10	WHITNEY HOUSTON	WHITNEY HOUSTON (ARISTA)
11	LOVE ZONE	BILLY OCEAN (JIVE)
12	PLEASE	PET SHOP BOYS (PARLOPHONE)
13	STANDING ON A BEACH — THE SINGLES	THE CURE (FICTION)
14	INTO THE LIGHT	CHRIS DE BURGH (A&M)
15	WORLD MACHINE	LEVEL 42 (POLYDOR)
16	ONCE UPON A TIME	SIMPLE MINDS (VIRGIN)
17	GO WEST/BANGS AND CRASHES	GO WEST (CHRYSALIS)
18	WHO MADE WHO	AC/DC (ATLANTIC)
19	QUEEN GREATEST HITS	QUEEN (EMI)
20	SUZANNE VEGA	SUZANNE VEGA (A&M)

SINGLES US

#	Title	Artist (Label)
1	ON MY OWN	PATTI LABELLE/MICHAEL MCDONALD (MCA)
2	THERE'LL BE SAD SONGS	BILLY OCEAN (JIVE)
3	CRUSH ON YOU	THE JETS (MCA)
4	LIVE TO TELL	MADONNA (SIRE)
5	I CAN'T WAIT	NU SHOOZ (ATLANTIC)
6	NO ONE IS TO BLAME	HOWARD JONES (ELEKTRA)
7	A DIFFERENT CORNER	GEORGE MICHAEL (COLUMBIA/CBS)
8	HOLDING BACK THE YEARS	SIMPLY RED (ELEKTRA)
9	WHO'S JOHNNY	EL DEBARGE (GORDY)
10	NOTHIN' AT ALL	HEART (CAPITOL)
11	GREATEST LOVE OF ALL	WHITNEY HOUSTON (ARISTA)
12	I WANNA BE A COWBOY	BOYS DON'T CRY (PROFILE)
13	SOMETHING ABOUT YOU	LEVEL 42 (POLYDOR)
14	NASTY	JANET JACKSON (A&M)
15	SLEDGEHAMMER	PETER GABRIEL (GEFFEN)
16	TUFF ENUFF	FABULOUS THUNDERBIRDS (CBS ASSOCIATED)
17	INVISIBLE TOUCH	GENESIS (ATLANTIC)
18	VIENNA CALLING	FALCO (A&M)
19	ALL I NEED IS A MIRACLE	MIKE AND THE MECHANICS (ATLANTIC)
20	LIKE A ROCK	BOB SEGER/SILVER BULLET BAND (CAPITOL)

ALBUMS US

#	Title	Artist (Label)
1	WHITNEY HOUSTON	WHITNEY HOUSTON (ARISTA)
2	WINNER IN YOU	PATTI LABELLE (MCA)
3	CONTROL	JANET JACKSON (A&M)
4	LIKE A ROCK	BOB SEGER/SILVER BULLET BAND (CAPITOL)
5	5150	VAN HALEN (WARNER BROS)
6	RAISED ON RADIO	JOURNEY (COLUMBIA/CBS)
7	PLEASE	PET SHOP BOYS (EMI AMERICA)
8	LOVE ZONE	BILLY OCEAN (JIVE)
9	PARADE	PRINCE AND THE REVOLUTION (PAISLEY PARK)
10	PLAY DEEP	THE OUTFIELD (COLMBIA/CBS)
11	THE OTHER SIDE OF LIFE	THE MOODY BLUES (POLYDOR)
12	HEART	HEART (CAPITOL)
13	SO	PETER GABRIEL (GEFFEN)
14	PRETTY IN PINK	SOUNDTRACK (A&M)
15	TUFF ENUFF	FABULOUS THUNDERBIRDS (CBS ASSOCIATED)
16	RIPTIDE	ROBERT PALMER (ISLAND)
17	DIRTY WORK	ROLLING STONES (COLUMBIA/CBS)
18	WORLD MACHINE	LEVEL 42 (POLYDOR)
19	TOP GUN	SOUNDTRACK (COLUMBIA)
20	PICTURE BOOK	SIMPLY RED (ELEKTRA)

WEEK ENDING JUNE 28 1986

SINGLES UK

#	Title	Artist (Label)
1	THE EDGE OF HEAVEN	WHAM! (EPIC)
2	I CAN'T WAIT	NU SHOOZ (ATLANTIC)
3	HAPPY HOUR	HOUSEMARTINS (GO! DISCS)
4	SPIRIT IN THE SKY	DOCTOR AND THE MEDICS (IRS)
5	TOO GOOD TO BE FORGOTTEN	AMAZULU (ISLAND)
6	HUNTING HIGH AND LOW	A-HA (WARNER BROS)
7	MY FAVOURITE WASTE OF TIME	OWEN PAUL (EPIC)
8	NEW BEGINNING (MAMBA SEYRA)	BUCKS FIZZ (POLYDOR)
9	HOLDING BACK THE YEARS	SIMPLY RED (ELEKTRA)
10	ADDICTED TO LOVE	ROBERT PALMER (ISLAND)
11	CAN'T BET BY WITHOUT YOU	REAL THING (PRT)
12	AMITYVILLE	LOVEBUG STARSKI (EPIC)
13	PAPA DON'T PREACH	MADONNA (SIRE)
14	FRIENDS WILL BE FRIENDS	QUEEN (EMI)
15	VENUS	BANANARAMA (LONDON)
16	BAD BOY	MIAMI SOUND MACHINE (EPIC)
17	VIENNA CALLING	FALCO (A&M)
18	SLEDGEHAMMER	PETER GABRIEL (VIRGIN)
19	NASTY	JANET JACKSON (A&M)
20	OPPORTUNITIES	PET SHOP BOYS (PARLOPHONE)

ALBUMS UK

#	Title	Artist (Label)
1	INVISIBLE TOUCH	GENESIS (VIRGIN)
2	THE QUEEN IS DEAD	SMITHS (ROUGH TRADE)
3	A KIND OF MAGIC	QUEEN (EMI)
4	SO	PETER GABRIEL (VIRGIN)
5	PICTURE BOOK	SIMPLY RED (ELEKTRA)
6	HUNTING HIGH AND LOW	A-HA (WARNER BROS)
7	BROTHERS IN ARMS	DIRE STRAITS (VERTIGO)
8	STREET LIFE — 20 GREAT HITS	BRYAN FERRY/ROXY MUSIC (EG)
9	MOONLIGHT SHADOWS	SHADOWS (PROTV)
10	PLEASE	PET SHOP BOYS (PARLOPHONE)
11	WHITNEY HOUSTON	WHITNEY HOUSTON (ARISTA)
12	LOVE ZONE	BILLY OCEAN (JIVE)
13	INTO THE LIGHT	CHRIS DE BURGH (A&M)
14	THE MAN AND HIS MUSIC	SAM COOKE (RCA)
15	STANDING ON A BEACH — THE SINGLES	THE CURE (FICTION)
16	BRING ON THE NIGHT	STING (A&M)
17	WORLD MACHINE	LEVEL 42 (POLYDOR)
18	ONCE UPON A TIME	SIMPLE MINDS (VIRGIN)
19	SUZANNE VEGA	SUZANNE VEGA (A&M)
20	RIPTIDE	ROBERT PALMER (ISLAND)

SINGLES US

#	Title	Artist (Label)
1	ON MY OWN	PATTI LABELLE/MICHAEL MCDONALD (MCA)
2	THERE'LL BE SAD SONGS	BILLY OCEAN (JIVE)
3	CRUSH ON YOU	THE JETS (MCA)
4	HOLDING BACK THE YEARS	SIMPLY RED (ELEKTRA)
5	NO ONE IS TO BLAME	HOWARD JONES (ELEKTRA)
6	WHO'S JOHNNY	EL DEBARGE (GORDY)
7	A DIFFERENT CORNER	GEORGE MICHAEL (COLUMBIA/CBS)
8	INVISIBLE TOUCH	GENESIS (ATLANTIC)
9	NASTY	JANET JACKSON (A&M)
10	SLEDGEHAMMER	PETER GABRIEL (GEFFEN)
11	LIVE TO TELL	MADONNA (SIRE)
12	I CAN'T WAIT	NU SHOOZ (ATLANTIC)
13	I WANNA BE A COWBOY	BOYS DON'T CRY (PROFILE)
14	DANGER ZONE	KENNY LOGGINS (COLUMBIA/CBS)
15	TUFF ENUFF	FABULOUS THUNDERBIRDS (CBS ASSOCIATED)
16	NOTHIN' AT ALL	WHITNEY HOUSTON (ARISTA)
17	LIKE A ROCK	BOB SEGER/THE SILVER BULLET BAND (CAPITOL)
18	YOUR WILDEST DREAMS	THE MOODY BLUES (POLYDOR)
19	LIKE NO OTHER NIGHT	.38 SPECIAL (A&M)
20	VIENNA CALLING	FALCO (A&M)

ALBUMS US

#	Title	Artist (Label)
1	WHITNEY HOUSTON	WHITNEY HOUSTON (ARISTA)
2	WINNER IN YOU	PATTI LABELLE (MCA)
3	CONTROL	JANET JACKSON (A&M)
4	LIKE A ROCK	BOB SEGER/SILVER BULLET BAND (CAPITOL)
5	5150	VAN HALEN (WARNER BROS)
6	LOVE ZONE	BILLY OCEAN (JIVE)
7	RAISED ON RADIO	JOURNEY (COLUMBIA/CBS)
8	PLEASE	PET SHOP BOYS (EMI AMERICA)
9	THE OTHER SIDE OF LIFE	THE MOODY BLUES (POLYDOR)
10	SO	PETER GABRIEL (GEFFEN)
11	TOP GUN	SOUNDTRACK (COLUMBIA/CBS)
12	HEART	HEART (CAPITOL)
13	PLAY DEEP	THE OUTFIELD (COLUMBIA/CBS)
14	PARADE	PRINCE AND THE REVOLUTION (PAISLEY PARK)
15	TUFF ENUFF	FABULOUS THUNDERBIRDS (CBS ASSOCIATED)
16	GTR	GTR (ARISTA)
17	STRENGTH IN NUMBERS	.38 SPECIAL (A&M)
18	WORLD MACHINE	LEVEL 42 (POLYDOR)
19	PICTURE BOOK	SIMPLY RED (ELEKTRA)
20	PRETTY IN PINK	SOUNDTRACK (A&M)

WEEK ENDING JULY 5 1986

S I N G L E S — UK — A L B U M S

#	UK Singles	UK Albums
1	THE EDGE OF HEAVEN — WHAM! (EPIC)	INVISIBLE TOUCH — GENESIS (VIRGIN)
2	PAPA DON'T PREACH — MADONNA (SIRE)	A KIND OF MAGIC — QUEEN (EMI)
3	HAPPY HOUR — HOUSEMARTINS (GO! DISCS)	LONDON 0 HULL 4 — HOUSEMARTINS (GO! DISCS)
4	MY FAVOURITE WASTE OF TIME — OWEN PAUL (EPIC)	PICTURE BOOK — SIMPLY RED (ELEKTRA)
5	I CAN'T WAIT — NU SHOOZ (ATLANTIC)	SO — PETER GABRIEL (VIRGIN)
6	TOO GOOD TO BE FORGOTTEN — AMAZULU (ISLAND)	THE QUEEN IS DEAD — SMITHS (ROUGH TRADE)
7	HUNTING HIGH AND LOW — A-HA (WARNER BROS)	EVERY BEAT OF MY HEART — ROD STEWART (WARNER BROS)
8	NEW BEGINNING (MAMBA SEYRA) — BUCKS FIZZ (POLYDOR)	BROTHERS IN ARMS — DIRE STRAITS (VERTIGO)
9	VENUS — BANANARAMA (LONDON)	HUNTING HIGH AND LOW — A-HA (WARNER BROS)
10	SPIRIT IN THE SKY — DOCTOR AND THE MEDICS (IRS)	STREET LIFE — 20 GREAT HITS — BRYAN FERRY/ROXY MUSIC (EG)
11	CAN'T GET BY WITHOUT YOU — REAL THING (PRT)	SUZANNE VEGA — SUZANNE VEGA (A&M)
12	DO YA DO YA (WANNA PLEASE ME) — SAMANTHA FOX (JIVE)	WHITNEY HOUSTON — WHITNEY HOUSTON (ARISTA)
13	AMITYVILLE — LOVEBUG STARSKI (EPIC)	MOONLIGHT SHADOWS — SHADOWS (PROTV)
14	FRIENDS WILL BE FRIENDS — QUEEN (EMI)	INTO THE LIGHT — CHRIS DE BURGH (A&M)
15	HOLDING BACK THE YEARS — SIMPLY RED (ELEKTRA)	PLEASE — PET SHOP BOYS (PARLOPHONE)
16	ADDICTED TO LOVE — ROBERT PALMER (ISLAND)	LOVE ZONE — BILLY OCEAN (JIVE)
17	HEADLINES — MIDNIGHT STAR (SOLAR)	ONCE UPON A TIME — SIMPLE MINDS (VIRGIN)
18	(BANG ZOOM) LET'S GO GO — REAL ROXANNE/HITMAN HOWIE TEE (COOLTEMPO)	WORLD MACHINE — LEVEL 42 (POLYDOR)
19	IT'S 'ORRIBLE BEING IN LOVE — CLAIRE AND FRIENDS (BBC)	BRING ON THE NIGHT — STING (A&M)
20	BAD BOY — MIAMI SOUND MACHINE (EPIC)	STANDING ON A BEACH — THE SINGLES — THE CURE (FICTION)

S I N G L E S — US — A L B U M S

#	US Singles	US Albums
1	THERE'LL BE SAD SONGS — BILLY OCEAN (JIVE)	CONTROL — JANET JACKSON (A&M)
2	HOLDING BACK THE YEARS — SIMPLY RED (ELEKTRA)	WINNER IN YOU — PATTI LABELLE (MCA)
3	WHO'S JOHNNY — EL DEBARGE (GORDY)	WHITNEY HOUSTON — WHITNEY HOUSTON (ARISTA)
4	NO ONE IS TO BLAME — HOWARD JONES (ELEKTRA)	LIKE A ROCK — BOB SEGER/SILVER BULLET BAND (CAPITOL)
5	NASTY — JANET JACKSON (A&M)	SO — PETER GABRIEL (GEFFEN)
6	INVISIBLE TOUCH — GENESIS (ATLANTIC)	LOVE ZONE — BILLY OCEAN (JIVE)
7	CRUSH ON YOU — THE JETS (MCA)	5150 — VAN HALEN (WARNER BROS)
8	ON MY OWN — PATTI LABELLE/MICHAEL MCDONALD (MCA)	TOP GUN — SOUNDTRACK (COLUMBIA/CBS)
9	SLEDGEHAMMER — PETER GABRIEL (GEFFEN)	THE OTHER SIDE OF LIFE — THE MOODY BLUES (POLYDOR)
10	DANGER ZONE — KENNY LOGGINS (COLUMBIA/CBS)	INVISIBLE TOUCH — GENESIS (ATLANTIC)
11	TUFF ENUFF — FABULOUS THUNDERBIRDS (CBS ASSOCIATED)	RAISED ON RADIO — JOURNEY (COLUMBIA/CBS)
12	YOUR WILDEST DREAMS — THE MOODY BLUES (POLYDOR)	PLEASE — PET SHOP BOYS (EMI AMERICA)
13	LIKE A ROCK — BOB SEGER/SILVER BULLET BAND (CAPITOL)	TUFF ENUFF — FABULOUS THUNDERBIRDS (CBS ASSOCIATED)
14	LIKE NO OTHER NIGHT — .38 SPECIAL (A&M)	RAISING HELL — RUN DMC (PROFILE)
15	WHEN THE HEART RULES THE MIND — GTR (ARISTA)	GTR — GTR (ARISTA)
16	A DIFFERENT CORNER — GEORGE MICHAEL (COLUMBIA/CBS)	PLAY DEEP — THE OUTFIELD (COLUMBIA/CBS)
17	I WANNA BE A COWBOY — BOYS DON'T CRY (PROFILE)	PICTURE BOOK — SIMPLY RED (ELEKTRA)
18	OPPORTUNITIES — PET SHOP BOYS (EMI AMERICA)	HEART — HEART (CAPITOL)
19	GLORY OF LOVE — PETER CETERA (WARNER BROS)	PARADE — PRINCE AND THE REVOLUTION (PAISLEY PARK)
20	LIVE TO TELL — MADONNA (SIRE)	STRENGTH IN NUMBERS — .38 SPECIAL (A&M)

WEEK ENDING JULY 12 1986

S I N G L E S — UK — A L B U M S

#	UK Singles	UK Albums
1	PAPA DON'T PREACH — MADONNA (SIRE)	TRUE BLUE — MADONNA (SIRE)
2	THE EDGE OF HEAVEN — WHAM! (EPIC)	THE SEER — BIG COUNTRY (MERCURY)
3	MY FAVOURITE WASTE OF TIME — OWEN PAUL (EPIC)	REVENGE — EURYTHMICS (RCA)
4	HAPPY HOUR — HOUSEMARTINS (GO! DISCS)	INVISIBLE TOUCH — GENESIS (VIRGIN)
5	TOO GOOD TO BE FORGOTTEN — AMAZULU (ISLAND)	A KIND OF MAGIC — QUEEN (EMI)
6	LET'S GO ALL THE WAY — SLY FOX (CAPITOL)	LONDON 0 HULL 4 — HOUSEMARTINS (GO! DISCS)
7	I CAN'T WAIT — NU SHOOZ (ATLANTIC)	EVERY BEAT OF MY HEART — ROD STEWART (WARNER BROS)
8	VENUS — BANANARAMA (LONDON)	PICTURE BOOK — SIMPLY RED (ELEKTRA)
9	NEW BEGINNING (MAMBA SEYRA) — BUCKS FIZZ (POLYDOR)	BROTHERS IN ARMS — DIRE STRAITS (VERTIGO)
10	DO YA DO YA (WANNA PLEASE ME) — SAMANTHA FOX (JIVE)	BACK IN THE HIGH LIFE — STEVE WINWOOD (ISLAND)
11	HUNTING HIGH AND LOW — A-HA (WARNER BROS)	HUNTING HIGH AND LOW — A-HA (WARNER BROS)
12	(BANG ZOOM) LET'S GO GO — REAL ROXANNE/HITMAN HOWIE TEE (COOLTEMPO)	SO — PETER GABRIEL (VIRGIN)
13	IT'S 'ORRIBLE BEING IN LOVE — CLAIRE AND FRIENDS (BBC)	SUZANNE VEGA — SUZANNE VEGA (A&M)
14	PARANOIMIA — ART OF NOISE WITH MAX HEADROOM (CHINA)	THE QUEEN IS DEAD — SMITHS (ROUGH TRADE)
15	SPIRIT IN THE SKY — DOCTOR AND THE MEDICS (IRS)	INTO THE LIGHT — CHRIS DE BURGH (A&M)
16	HEADLINES — MIDNIGHT STAR (SOLAR)	STREET LIFE — 20 GREAT HITS — BRYAN FERRY/ROXY MUSIC (EG)
17	EVERY BEAT OF MY HEART — ROD STEWART (WARNER BROS)	MOONLIGHT SHADOWS — SHADOWS (PROTV)
18	CAN'T GET BY WITHOUT YOU — REAL THING (PRT)	WHITNEY HOUSTON — WHITNEY HOUSTON (ARISTA)
19	HOLDING BACK THE YEARS — SIMPLY RED (ELEKTRA)	WORLD MACHINE — LEVEL 42 (POLYDOR)
20	FRIENDS WILL BE FRIENDS — QUEEN (EMI)	ONCE UPON A TIME — SIMPLE MINDS (VIRGIN)

S I N G L E S — US — A L B U M S

#	US Singles	US Albums
1	HOLDING BACK THE YEARS — SIMPLY RED (ELEKTRA)	CONTROL — JANET JACKSON (A&M)
2	INVISIBLE TOUCH — GENESIS (ATLANTIC)	WINNER IN YOU — PATTI LABELLE (MCA)
3	THERE'LL BE SAD SONGS — BILLY OCEAN (JIVE)	WHITNEY HOUSTON — WHITNEY HOUSTON (ARISTA)
4	NASTY — JANET JACKSON (A&M)	SO — PETER GABRIEL (GEFFEN)
5	WHO'S JOHNNY — EL DEBARGE (GORDY)	INVISIBLE TOUCH — GENESIS (ATLANTIC)
6	SLEDGEHAMMER — PETER GABRIEL (GEFFEN)	LOVE ZONE — BILLY OCEAN (JIVE)
7	DANGER ZONE — KENNY LOGGINS (COLUMBIA)	LIKE A ROCK — BOB SEGER/SILVER BULLET BAND (CAPITOL)
8	NO ONE IS TO BLAME — HOWARD JONES (ELEKTRA)	TOP GUN — SOUNDTRACK (COLUMBIA/CBS)
9	YOUR WILDEST DREAMS — THE MOODY BLUES (POLYDOR)	THE OTHER SIDE OF LIFE — THE MOODY BLUES (POLYDOR)
10	TUFF ENUFF — FABULOUS THUNDERBIRDS (CBS ASSOCIATED)	5150 — VAN HALEN (WARNER BROS)
11	GLORY OF LOVE — PETER CETERA (WARNER BROS)	GTR — GTR (ARISTA)
12	LIKE A ROCK — BOB SEGER/SILVER BULLET BAND (CAPITOL)	PLEASE — PET SHOP BOYS (EMI AMERICA)
13	ON MY OWN — PATTI LABELLE/MICHAEL MCDONALD (MCA)	TUFF ENUFF — FABULOUS THUNDERBIRDS (CBS ASSOCIATED)
14	WHEN THE HEART RULES THE MIND — GTR (ARISTA)	RAISING HELL — RUN DMC (PROFILE)
15	CRUSH ON YOU — THE JETS (MCA)	RAISED ON RADIO — JOURNEY (COLUMBIA)
16	OPPORTUNITIES — PET SHOP BOYS (EMI AMERICA)	PICTURE BOOK — SIMPLY RED (ELEKTRA)
17	LOVE TOUCH — ROD STEWART (WARNER BROS)	PLAY DEEP — THE OUTFIELD (COLUMBIA)
18	MAD ABOUT YOU — BELINDA CARLISLE (IRS)	HEART — HEART (CAPITOL)
19	MODERN WOMAN — BILLY JOEL (EPIC)	STRENGTH IN NUMBERS — .38 SPECIAL (A&M)
20	LIKE NO OTHER NIGHT — .38 SPECIAL (A&M)	PARADE — PRINCE AND THE REVOLUTION (PAISLEY PARK)

WEEK ENDING JULY 19 1986

SINGLES UK / ALBUMS

#	SINGLES	ALBUMS
1	PAPA DON'T PREACH — MADONNA (SIRE)	TRUE BLUE — MADONNA (SIRE)
2	EVERY BEAT OF MY HEART — ROD STEWART (WARNER BROS)	THE FINAL — WHAM! (EPIC)
3	LET'S GO ALL THE WAY — SLY FOX (CAPITOL)	REVENGE — EURYTHMICS (RCA)
4	MY FAVOURITE WASTE OF TIME — OWEN PAUL (EPIC)	A KIND OF MAGIC — QUEEN (EMI)
5	THE EDGE OF HEAVEN — WHAM! (EPIC)	EVERY BEAT OF MY HEART — ROD STEWART (WARNER BROS)
6	SING OUR OWN SONG — UB40 (DEP INTERNATIONAL/VIRGIN)	INVISIBLE TOUCH — GENESIS (VIRGIN)
7	HAPPY HOUR — HOUSEMARTINS (GO! DISCS)	NOW – THE SUMMER ALBUM — VARIOUS (EMI/VIRGIN)
8	VENUS — BANANARAMA (LONDON)	BACK IN THE HIGH LIFE — STEVE WINWOOD (ISLAND)
9	TOO GOOD TO BE FORGOTTEN — AMAZULU (ISLAND)	THE SEER — BIG COUNTRY (MERCURY)
10	THE LADY IN RED — CHRIS DE BURGH (A&M)	LONDON 0 HULL 4 — HOUSEMARTINS (GO! DISCS)
11	(BANG ZOOM) LET'S GO GO — REAL ROXANNE/HITMAN HOWIE TEE (COOLTEMPO)	HUNTING HIGH AND LOW — A-HA (WARNER BROS)
12	PARANOIMIA — ART OF NOISE WITH MAX HEADROOM (CHINA)	PICTURE BOOK — SIMPLY RED (ELEKTRA)
13	I CAN'T WAIT — NU SHOOZ (ATLANTIC)	BROTHERS IN ARMS — DIRE STRAITS (VERTIGO)
14	HIGHER LOVE — STEVE WINWOOD (ISLAND)	INTO THE LIGHT — CHRIS DE BURGH (A&M)
15	IT'S 'ORRIBLE BEING IN LOVE — CLARE AND FRIENDS (BBC)	SO — PETER GABRIEL (VIRGIN)
16	DO YA DO YA (WANNA PLEASE ME) — SAMANTHA FOX (JIVE)	RIPTIDE — ROBERT PALMER (ISLAND)
17	CAMOUFLAGE — STAN RIDGWAY (IRS)	SUZANNE VEGA — SUZANNE VEGA (A&M)
18	NEW BEGINNING (MAMBA SEYRA) — BUCKS FIZZ (POLYDOR)	THE QUEEN IS DEAD — SMITHS (ROUGH TRADE)
19	ROSES — HAYWOODE (CBS)	ONCE UPON A TIME — SIMPLE MINDS (VIRGIN)
20	HEADLINES — MIDNIGHT STAR (SOLAR)	STREET LIFE – 20 GREAT HITS — BRYAN FERRY/ROXY MUSIC (EG)

SINGLES US / ALBUMS

#	SINGLES	ALBUMS
1	INVISIBLE TOUCH — GENESIS (ATLANTIC)	WINNER IN YOU — PATTI LABELLE (MCA)
2	SLEDGEHAMMER — PETER GABRIEL (GEFFEN)	CONTROL — JANET JACKSON (A&M)
3	NASTY — JANET JACKSON (A&M)	SO — PETER GABRIEL (GEFFEN)
4	DANGER ZONE — KENNY LOGGINS (COLUMBIA)	TOP GUN — SOUNDTRACK (COLUMBIA/CBS)
5	HOLDING BACK THE YEARS — SIMPLY RED (ELEKTRA)	INVISIBLE TOUCH — GENESIS (ATLANTIC)
6	WHO'S JOHNNY — EL DEBARGE (GORDY)	LOVE ZONE — BILLY OCEAN (JIVE)
7	GLORY OF LOVE — PETER CETERA (WARNER BROS)	WHITNEY HOUSTON — WHITNEY HOUSTON (ARISTA)
8	THERE'LL BE SAD SONGS — BILLY OCEAN (JIVE)	LIKE A ROCK — BOB SEGER/SILVER BULLET BAND (CAPITOL)
9	YOUR WILDEST DREAMS — THE MOODY BLUES (POLYDOR)	THE OTHER SIDE OF LIFE — THE MOODY BLUES (POLYDOR)
10	LOVE TOUCH — ROD STEWART (WARNER BROS)	5150 — VAN HALEN (WARNER BROS)
11	MAD ABOUT YOU — BELINDA CARLISLE (IRS)	GTR — GTR (ARISTA)
12	PAPA DON'T PREACH — MADONNA (SIRE)	RAISING HELL — RUN DMC (PROFILE)
13	OPPORTUNITIES — PET SHOP BOYS (EMI AMERICA)	TUFF ENUFF — FABULOUS THUNDERBIRDS (CBS ASSOCIATED)
14	WHEN THE HEART RULES THE MIND — GTR (ARISTA)	PLEASE — PET SHOP BOYS (EMI AMERICA)
15	MODERN WOMAN — BILLY JOEL (EPIC)	RAISED ON RADIO — JOURNEY (COLUMBIA)
16	LIKE A ROCK — BOB SEGER/SILVER BULLET BAND (CAPITOL)	PICTURE BOOK — SIMPLY RED (ELEKTRA)
17	WE DON'T HAVE TO . . . — JERMAINE STEWART (ARISTA)	PLAY DEEP — THE OUTFIELD (COLUMBIA)
18	DIGGING YOUR SCENE — THE BLOW MONKEYS (RCA)	STRENGTH IN NUMBERS — .38 SPECIAL (A&M)
19	NO ONE IS TO BLAME — HOWARD JONES (ELEKTRA)	HEART — HEART (CAPITOL)
20	TUFF ENUFF — FABULOUS THUNDERBIRDS (CBS ASSOCIATED)	HEADED FOR THE FUTURE — NEIL DIAMOND (COLUMBIA/CBS)

WEEK ENDING JULY 26 1986

SINGLES UK / ALBUMS

#	SINGLES	ALBUMS
1	PAPA DON'T PREACH — MADONNA (SIRE)	TRUE BLUE — MADONNA (SIRE)
2	THE LADY IN RED — CHRIS DE BURGH (A&M)	THE FINAL — WHAM! (EPIC)
3	EVERY BEAT OF MY HEART — ROD STEWART (WARNER BROS)	A KIND OF MAGIC — QUEEN (EMI)
4	LET'S GO ALL THE WAY — SLY FOX (CAPITOL)	REVENGE — EURYTHMICS (RCA)
5	SING OUR OWN SONG — UB40 (DEP INTERNATIONAL/VIRGIN)	INTO THE LIGHT — CHRIS DE BURGH (A&M)
6	MY FAVOURITE WASTE OF TIME — OWEN PAUL (EPIC)	EVERY BEAT OF MY HEART — ROD STEWART (WARNER BROS)
7	CAMOUFLAGE — STAN RIDGWAY (IRS)	NOW – THE SUMMER ALBUM — VARIOUS (EMI/VIRGIN)
8	WHAT'S THE COLOUR OF MONEY? — HOLLYWOOD BEYOND (WEA)	BACK IN THE HIGH LIFE — STEVE WINWOOD (ISLAND)
9	VENUS — BANANARAMA (LONDON)	BROTHERS IN ARMS — DIRE STRAITS (VERTIGO)
10	HAPPY HOUR — HOUSEMARTINS (GO! DISCS)	INVISIBLE TOUCH — GENESIS (VIRGIN)
11	I DIDN'T MEAN TO TURN YOU ON — ROBERT PALMER (ISLAND)	HUNTING HIGH AND LOW — A-HA (WARNER BROS)
12	THE EDGE OF HEAVEN — WHAM! (EPIC)	RIPTIDE — ROBERT PALMER (ISLAND)
13	HIGHER LOVE — STEVE WINWOOD (ISLAND)	PICTURE BOOK — SIMPLY RED (ELEKTRA)
14	ROSES — HAYWOODE (CBS)	THE SEER — BIG COUNTRY (MERCURY)
15	(BANG ZOOM) LET'S GO GO — REAL ROXANNE/HITMAN HOWIE TEE (COOLTEMPO)	LONDON 0 HULL 4 — HOUSEMARTINS (GO! DISCS)
16	SO MACHO — SINITTA (FANFARE)	SO — PETER GABRIEL (VIRGIN)
17	PARANOIMIA — ART OF NOISE WITH MAX HEADROOM (CHINA)	TOUCH ME — SAMANTHA FOX (JIVE)
18	TOO GOOD TO BE FORGOTTEN — AMAZULU (ISLAND)	SUZANNE VEGA — SUZANNE VEGA (A&M)
19	SMILE — AUDREY HALL (GERMAIN)	STREET LIFE – 20 GREAT HITS — BRYAN FERRY/ROXY MUSIC (EG)
20	SOME CANDY — JESUS AND MARY CHAIN (BLANCO Y NEGRO)	QUEEN GREATEST HITS — QUEEN (EMI)

SINGLES US / ALBUMS

#	SINGLES	ALBUMS
1	SLEDGEHAMMER — PETER GABRIEL (GEFFEN)	TOP GUN — SOUNDTRACK (COLUMBIA/CBS)
2	DANGER ZONE — KENNY LOGGINS (COLUMBIA)	SO — PETER GABRIEL (GEFFEN)
3	INVISIBLE TOUCH — GENESIS (ATLANTIC)	CONTROL — JANET JACKSON (A&M)
4	NASTY — JANET JACKSON (A&M)	INVISIBLE TOUCH — GENESIS (ATLANTIC)
5	GLORY OF LOVE — PETER CETERA (WARNER BROS)	WINNER IN YOU — PATTI LABELLE (MCA)
6	PAPA DON'T PREACH — MADONNA (SIRE)	LOVE ZONE — BILLY OCEAN (JIVE)
7	LOVE TOUCH — ROD STEWART (WARNER BROS)	WHITNEY HOUSTON — WHITNEY HOUSTON (ARISTA)
8	MAD ABOUT YOU — BELINDA CARLISLE (IRS)	LIKE A ROCK — BOB SEGER/SILVER BULLET BAND (CAPITOL)
9	HOLDING BACK THE YEARS — SIMPLY RED (ELEKTRA)	TRUE BLUE — MADONNA (SIRE)
10	MODERN WOMAN — BILLY JOEL (EPIC)	THE OTHER SIDE OF LIFE — THE MOODY BLUES (POLYDOR)
11	OPPORTUNITIES — PET SHOP BOYS (EMI AMERICA)	5150 — VAN HALEN (WARNER BROS)
12	WE DON'T HAVE TO . . . — JERMAINE STEWART (ARISTA)	GTR — GTR (ARISTA)
13	YOUR WILDEST DREAMS — THE MOODY BLUES (POLYDOR)	RAISING HELL — RUN DMC (PROFILE)
14	WHO'S JOHNNY — EL DEBARGE (GORDY)	TUFF ENUFF — FABULOUS THUNDERBIRDS (CBS ASSOCIATED)
15	DIGGING YOUR SCENE — THE BLOW MONKEYS (RCA)	PLEASE — PET SHOP BOYS (EMI AMERICA)
16	THERE'LL BE SAD SONGS — BILLY OCEAN (JIVE)	PICTURE BOOK — SIMPLY RED (ELEKTRA)
17	WHEN THE HEART RULES THE MIND — GTR (ARISTA)	PLAY DEEP — THE OUTFIELD (COLUMBIA)
18	HIGHER LOVE — STEVE WINWOOD (ISLAND)	STRENGTH IN NUMBERS — .38 SPECIAL (A&M)
19	SECRET SEPARATION — THE FIXX (MCA)	RAISED ON RADIO — JOURNEY (COLUMBIA)
20	RUMOURS — TIMEX SOCIAL CLUB (JAY)	MUSIC FROM THE EDGE OF HEAVEN — WHAM! (EPIC)

ROCK REFERENCE UK

● RECORD COMPANIES

● **A&M Records**
136-140 New Kings Road, London
SW6 4LZ. Tel: (01) 736 3311 Tx: 916342
Labels: A&M, Windham Hill

● **Abstract Sounds**
10 Tiverton Road, London NW10 3HL
Tel: (01) 969 4018
Labels: Abstract Dance, Abstract Records

● **Ace Records**
48-50 Steele Road, London NW10
Tel: (01) 453 1311 Tx: 893805 Acerec
Labels: Ace, Big Beat, Boplicity, Cascade,
Contemporary, Crown, Del Rio, Globe
Style, Impact, Kent, Off Beat

● **Arista Records**
3 Cavendish Square, London W1
Tel: (01) 580 5566 Tx: 298933
Labels: Arista

● **Backs Cartel**
St Mary's Works, St Mary's Plain,
Norwich NR3 3AF. Tel: (0603) 626221
Labels: Backs, Criminal Damage, Empire,
Grunt-Grunt-A-Go-Go, Vinyl Drip

● **Bam-Caruso Records**
9 Ridgemont Road, St Albans, Herts
Tel: (0727) 32109
Labels: Bam-Caruso

● **BBC Records**
Woodlands, 80 Wood Lane, London W12
0TT. Tel: (01) 576 0202 Tx: 934678
Labels: Artium, BBC Records

● **Beggar's Banquet**
17-19 Alma Road, London SW18
Tel: (01) 870 9912 Tx: 915733
Labels: Beggar's Banquet, Coda, 4AD

● **BGS Productions**
Newtown Street, Kilsyth, Glasgow
G65 0JX. Tel: (0236) 821081
Labels: Country House, Scotdiscs

● **Big Bear Records**
190 Monument Road, Birmingham
B16 8UU. Tel: (021) 454 7020
Labels: Big Bear

● **Bright Records**
34-36 Maddox Street, London W1R 9PD
Tel: (01) 408 0288
Labels: Bright Records

● **Carrere Records**
3rd Floor, Mutual House, 193-197 Regent
Street, London W1. Tel: (01) 437 7581
Tx: 8953657
Labels: Carrere

● **Castle Communications**
Unit 7, 271 Merton Road, London SW18
Tel: (01) 871 1419 Tx: 911515
Labels: Castle Classics, Dojo, Raw Power,
Showcase

● **CBS Records**
17-19 Soho Square, London W1
Tel: (01) 734 8181 Tx: 24203
Labels: Blue Sky, Cameo, Caribou, CBS,
Diamond, Epic, Geffen, Monument,
Philadelphia International, Portrait,
Scotti Bros, Tabu, Unlimited Gold

● **Charly Records**
156-166 Ilderton Road, London SE15
1NT. Tel: (01) 639 8603/6 Tx: 8953184
Labels: Affinity, Charly, Directional, Sun

● **Cherry Red Records**
53 Kensington Gardens Square, London W2
4BA. Tel: (01) 229 8854 Tx: 943763 Chr
Labels: Anagram, Baad! Be-Bop-&-Fresh,
Cherry Red, El, Time Stood Still, Zebra

● **Chrysalis**
12 Stratford Place, London W1N 9AF
Tel: (01) 408 2355 Tx: 21753
Labels: Big Top, China, Chrysalis, Cool
Tempo, MAM, Music Fest, Reformation,
Two Tone, Ultravox

● **Circus Records**
156 Kennington Park Road, London SE11
4DJ. Tel: (01) 735 1194 Tx: 946240
Cweasy G Ref. 19017005
Labels: Circus

● **Cocteau Records**
10 King's Drive, Thames Ditton, Surrey
Tel: (01) 398 6413 Tx: 912881
Labels: Cocteau Records

● **Compact Organisation**
Compact House, 31 Riding House Street,
London W1P 7PG. Tel: (01) 580 1617
Labels: Compact, Easy Listeners

● **Conifer Records**
Horton Road, West Drayton, Middlesex
UB7 8JL. Tel: (0895) 447707 Tx: 27492
Labels: Conifer, Happy Days, Saville
Starjazz

● **Creole Records**
91-93 High Street, Harlesden, London
NW10. Tel: (01) 965 9223 Tx: 28905
Labels: Blast From The Past, Cactus,
Creole, Dynamic, Ecstasy, Replay, Review,
Winner

● **Decca International**
1 Rockley Road, London W14 0DL
Tel: (01) 743 9111 Tx: 23533
Labels: Decca, Deram, Threshold

● **Demon Records**
928 Great West Road, Brentford,
Middlesex TW8 9EW. Tel: (01) 847 2481
Tx: 894666
Labels: Demon, Edsel, HDH, Hi, Imp,
Vervals, Zippo

● **DEP International**
92 Fazeley Street, Digbeth, Birmingham
B5 5RD. Tel: (021) 643 1321 Tx: 339447
Depint
Labels: Dep International

● **DJM Records**
James House, Salisbury Place, Upper
Montagu Street, London W1H 1FJ
Tel: (01) 486 5838 Tx: 27135
Labels: DJM

● **EG Records**
63 King's Raod, London SW3 4NT
Tel: (01) 730 2162 Tx: 919205
Labels: Editions EG, EG Records

● **EMI Records**
20 Manchester Square, London W1A 1ES
Tel: (01) 486 4488 Tx: 22643
Labels: Blue Note, Capitol, Columbia, EMI,
Harvest, HMV, Manhattan, Parlophone,
Zonophone

● **Ensign Records**
3 Monmouth Place, London W2 5SH
Tel: (01) 727 0527
Labels: Ensign

● **Factory Communications**
86 Palatine Road, Manchester 20
Tel: (061) 434 3876 Tx: 669009 Facman
Labels: Factory Records

● **Fast Forward**
21a Alva Street, Edinburgh EH2 4PS
Tel: (031) 226 4616
Labels: Disposable, 53rd and 3rd

● **Flicknife**
1st Floor, The Metrostore, 5/10 Eastman
Road, The Vale, London W3 7YG
Tel: (01) 743 9412
Labels: Flicknife

● **FM Revolver**
152 Goldthorn Hill, Penn, Wolverhampton
WV2 3JA. Tel: (0902) 345345 Tx: 335419
Rokson G
Labels: FM, Heavy Metal Records,
Revolver

● **Go! Discs**
Go! Mansions, 8 Wendell Road, London
W12. Tel: (01) 743 3845/3919
Labels: Go! Discs

● **Greensleeves Records**
Unit 7, Goldhawk Industrial Estate,
2a Brackenbury Road, London W6
Tel: (01) 749 3277/8 Tx: 8955504
Labels: Greensleeves, Ras, UK Bubblers,
Unit 7

● **Hannibal Records**
36 Berwick Street, London W1
Tel: (01) 439 0808 Tx: 266982
Labels: Hannibal

● **Illuminated Productions**
46 Carter Lane, London EC4
Tel: (01) 236 6668
Labels: Illuminated Records

● **(IRS) International Recording
Syndicate**
5 Sherwood Street, London W1B 7RA
Tel: (01) 437 9797 Tx: 299338 Mcarec G
Labels: Illegal, IRS

● **Island Records**
22 St Peter's Square, London W6 9NW
Tel: (01) 741 1511 Tx: 934541
Labels: Ensign, Fourth & Broadway, Mango,
Mother, Taxi, Tommy Boy, TTED, ZTT

● **Jet Records**
35 Portland Place, London W1N 3AG
Tel: (01) 637 2111 Tx: 25929
Labels: Jet

● **Jungle Records**
24 Gaskin Street, London N1 2RY
Tel: (01) 359 8444 Tx: 896559 Gecoms G
(Attn. Jungle)
Labels: Fallout, Jungle

● **K-Tel International**
K-Tel House, 620 Western Avenue, London
W3 0TU. Tel: (01) 992 8055 Tx: 934195
Labels: K-Tel, Lotus

● **London Records**
15 St George Street, London W1. Tel: (01)
491 4600 Tx: 261583 Polygn G
Labels: London, Slash

● **Magnet Records,**
Magnet House, 22 York Street, London
W1H 1ED. Tel: (01) 486 8151 Tx: 25537
Labels: Magnet, Rodent

● **MCA Records**
72-74 Brewer Street, London W1
Tel: (01) 437 9797 Tx: 23158
Labels: MCA

● **Magnum Music Group**
Magnum House, Drake Avenue, Staines,
Middlesex TW18 2AW. Tel: (0784) 62426
Tx: 936689 Esjay G
Labels: Blue Moon, Magnum Force,
Meteor, Sundown, Thunderbolt

● **Making Waves**
6-8 Alie Street, London E1 8DE
Tel: (01) 481 9917 Tx: 884555 M Waves
Labels: Making Waves

● **Music For Nations**
8 Carnaby Street, London W1 1PG
Tel: (01) 437 4688 Tx: 296217
Labels: Food For Thought, Fun After All,
Music For Nations, Rough Justice, Under
One Flag

● **Music For Pleasure**
1-3 Uxbridge Road, Hayes, Middlesex
UB4 0SY. Tel: (01) 561 8722 Tx: 934614
Labels: Classics For Pleasure, Eminence,
Fame, Golden Age, Hour Of, Listen For
Pleasure, Music For Pleasure

● **Mute Records**
49-53 Kensington Gardens Square,
London W2. Tel: (01) 221 4840 Tx: 268623
Labels: Mute

● **Neat Records**
71 High Street, East Wallsend, Tyne and
Wear NE28 7RJ. Tel: (091) 262 4999
Tx: 537681 Alwrld
Labels: Completely Different, Floating
World, Neat

● **Old Gold Records**
Unit 1, Langhedge Lane Industrial Estate,
Edmonton N18 2TQ. Tel: (01) 884 2220
Tx: 264597 OldGol G
Labels: Decades, Old Gold

● **Oval Records**
11 Liston Road, London SW4. Tel: (01) 622
0111 Tx: 946240 Cweasy G Ref. 19017005
Labels: Oval

● **People Unite**
50.52 King Street, Southall, Middlesex.
Tel: (01) 574 1718
Labels: People Unite

● **Phonogram Ltd**
50 New Bond Street, London W1Y 9HA
Tel: (01) 491 4600 Tx: 261583
Labels: Club, Mercury, Phillips,
Phonogram, Rockets, Vertigo

● **Pickwick International**
The Hyde Industrial Estate, The Hyde,
London NW9 6JU. Tel: (01) 200 7000
Tx: 922170
Labels: Camden, Contour, Ditto, Hallmark,
IMP Red, Pickwick, Spot

● **Polydor**
13-14 St George Street, London W1R
9DE. Tel: (01) 499 8686 Tx: 261583
Labels: Boiling Point, Capricorn, MGM,
Polydor, RSO, Verve, Wonderland

● **President Records**
Broadmead House, 21 Panton Street,
London SW1 4DR. Tel: (01) 839 4672/5
Tx: 24158 Kassmu G
Labels: Bulldog, Energy, Enterprise, Joy,
Max's Kansas City, New World, President,
Rhapsody, Seville, Spiral, TBG

● **Probe Records**
8-12 Rainford Gardens, Liverpool 2
Tel: (051) 236 6591
Labels: Probe Plus

● **PRT Records**
ACC House, 17 Great Cumberland Place,
London W1A 1AG. Tel: (01) 262 8040
Tx: 261807
Labels: PRT

● **Quiet Records**
The Metrostore, 231 The Vale, London W3
7QS. Tel: (01) 740 0680
Labels: Quiet

● **RAK Records**
42 Charlbert Street, London NW8
Tel: (01) 568 2012 Tx: 299501
Labels: RAK

● **RCA/Ariola Records**
1 Bedford Avenue, London WC1
Tel: (01) 580 5566 Tx: 21349
Labels: Gordy, Ice, Inevitable, Morocco,
Motown, Planet, Prelude, RCA, Victor,
Salsoul, Tent, Total Experience

● **Red Flame**
PO Box 927, London W3 6YB
Tel: (01) 993 8634
Labels: Ink, Red Flame

● **Red Lightnin' Records**
The White House, North Lopham, Diss,
Norfolk. Tel: (0379) 88693 Tx: 97203
Blues G
Labels: Daddy Kool, Red Lightnin',
Syndicate Chapter, Union Pacific

● **Rocket Record Company**
51 Holland Street, London W8 7JB
Tel: (01) 938 1741 Tx: 265870
Labels: Rocket

● **Rough Trade Records**
61-71 Collier Street, London N1
Tel: (01) 833 2133/2561/3 Tx: 299579
Labels: Rough Trade

● **Sabril Records**
444 Finchley Road, London NW2
Tel: (01) 435 8065 Tx: 8954958 Ref. 219
Labels: Big Red, Crash, Sabril

● **Siren Records**
61-63 Portobello Road, London W11 3DD.
Tel: (01) 221 7535 Tx: 295417 Siren G
Labels: Siren

● **Some Bizarre**
166 New Cavendish Street, London W1M
7LJ. Tel: (01) 631 3140 Tx: 8951182
Gecoms G
Labels: Some Bizarre

● **Sonet Records**
121 Ledbury Road, London W11
Tel: (01) 229 7267 Tx: 25793
Labels: Alligator, Kicking Mule, Red Stripe, Sonet, Stone, Titanic

● **Spotlite Records**
103 London Road, Sawbridgeworth, Herts CMI 9JJ. Tel: (0279) 724572
Labels: Spotlite

● **Statik Records**
1a Normand Gardens, Greyhound Road, London W14. Tel: (01) 381 0116/385 0567 Tx: 943763 Crocom G
Labels: Statik

● **Stiff Records**
45 Coronet Street, London N1 6HD
Tel: (01) 729 5777 Tx: 299894
Labels: Gates Of Heaven, Stiff

● **Towerbell Records**
1 Ilverson Road, London NW6 2QT
Tel: (01) 328 1787 Tx: 297558 Towrec G
Labels: Important, Rockney, Towerbell

● **Unamerican Activities**
26 Melville Place, Leeds 6, Yorkshire
Tel: (0532) 742106
Labels: Unamerican Activities

● **Upright Records**
61-71 Collier Street, London N1 9BE
Tel: (01) 833 3456
Labels: Alternative Tentacles, Upright

● **Virgin Records**
Kensal House, 533-579 Harrow Road, London W10. Tel: (01) 968 6688
Tx: 22542
Labels: Bluebird, Charisma, Foundry, Inner Vision, MDM, Red Eye, 10, Virgin, Zarjazz

● **WEA Records**
20 Broadwick Street, London W1V 2BH.
Tel: (01) 434 3232 Tx: 261425
Labels: Asylum, Atlantic, blanco y negro, Cotillion, Elektra, Korova, Nonesuch, Quest, Reprise, Sire, Vindaloo, Warner Brothers, WEA UK

● **Zomba Productions**
Zomba House, 165-167 Willesden High Road, London NW10 2SG
Tel: (01) 459 8899 Tx: 237316 Zomba
Labels: Jive, Jive Afrika, Jive Electro, Lifestyle

● **ZTT Records**
111 Talbot Road, London W11
Tel: (01) 221 5012 Tx: 297314 Sarm G
Labels: ZTT

● LABELS

Affinity – Charly
Alligator – Sonet
Alternative Tentacles – Upright
Anagram – Cherry Red
Artium – BBC
Asylum – WEA
Atlantic – WEA
Baad! – Cherry Red
Be-Bop-&-Fresh – Cherry Red
Big Beat – Ace
Big Red – Satril
Big Top – Chrysalis
blanco y negro – WEA
Blast From The Past – Creole
Blue Moon – Magnum
Blue Note – EMI
Blue Sky – CBS
Bluebird – Virgin
Boiling Point – Polydor
Boplicity – Ace
Bulldog – President
Cactus – Creole
Camden – Pickwick
Cameo – CBS
Capitol – EMI
Capricorn – Polydor
Caribou – CBS
Cascade – Ace
Charisma – Virgin
China – Chrysalis
Classics For Pleasure – Music For Pleasure
Club – Phonogram
Coda – Beggar's Banquet
Columbia – EMI
Completely Different – Neat
Contemporary – Ace
Contour – Pickwick
Cool Tempo – Chrysalis
Cotillion – WEA
Country House – BGS
Crash – Satril
Criminal Damage – Backs
Crown – Ace
DaddyKool – Red Lightnin'
Decades – Old Gold
Del Rio – Ace
Deram – Decca
Diamond – CBS
Directional – Charly
Disposable – Fast Forward
Ditto – Pickwick
Dojo – Castle

Dynamic – Creole
Easy Listeners – Compact
Ecstasy – Creole
Edsel – Demon
El – Cherry Red
Elektra – WEA
Eminence – Music For Pleasure
Empire – Backs
Energy – President
Ensign – Island
Enterprise – President
Epic – CBS
Fallout – Jungle
Fame – Music For Pleasure
53rd and 3rd – Fast Forward
Floating World – Neat
Food For Thought – Music For Nations
Foundry – Virgin
4AD – Beggar's Banquet
Fourth and Broadway – Island
Fun After All – Music For Nations
Gates Of Heaven – Stiff
Geffen – CBS
Globe Style – Ace
Golden Age – Music For Pleasure
Gordy – RCA/Ariola
Grunt-Grunt-A-Go-Go – Backs
Hallmark – Pickwick
Happy Days – Conifer
Harvest – EMI
HDH – Demon
Heavy Metal – FM Revolver
Hi – Demon
HMV – EMI
Hour Of – Music For Pleasure
Ice – RCA/Ariola
Illegal – IRS
Imp – Demon
IMP Red – Pickwick
Impact – Ace
Important – Towerbell
Inevitable – RCA/Ariola
Ink – Red Flame
Inner Vision – Virgin
Jive – Zomba
Joy – President
Kent – Ace
Kicking Mule – Sonet
Korova – WEA
Lifestyle – Zomba
Listen For Pleasure – Music For Pleasure
Lotus – K-Tel
MAM – Chrysalis
Mango – Island

Manhattan – EMI
Max's Kansas City – President
MDM – Virgin
Mercury – Phonogram
Meteor – Magnum
MGM – Polydor
Monument – CBS
Morocco – RCA/Ariola
Mother – Island
Motown – RCA/Ariola
Music Fest – Chrysalis
New World – President
Nonesuch – WEA
Off Beat – Ace
Parlophone – EMI
Philadelphia International – CBS
Phillips – Phonogram
Planet – RCA/Ariola
Portrait – CBS
Prelude – RCA/Ariola
Quest – WEA
Ras – Greensleeves
Raw Power – Castle
Red Eye – Virgin
Red Stripe – Sonet
Reformation – Chrysalis
Replay – Creole
Reprise – WEA
Review – Creole
Revolver – FM Revolver
Rhapsody – President
Rockets – Phonogram
Rockney – Towerbell
Rodent – Magnet
Rough Justice – Music For Nations
RSO – Polydor
Salsoul – RCA/Ariola
Saville – Conifer
Scotdiscs – BGS
Scotti Bros – CBS
Seville – President
Showcase – Castle
Sire – WEA
Slash – London
Spiral – President
Spot – Pickwick
Starjazz – Conifer
Stone – Sonet
Sun – Charly
Sundown – Magnum
Syndicate Chapter – Red Lightnin'
Tabu – CBS
Taxi – Island
TBG – President

10 – Virgin
Tent – RCA/Ariola
Threshold – Decca
Thunderbolt – Magnum
Time Stood Still – Cherry Red
Titanic – Sonic
Tommy Boy – Island
Total Experience – RCA/Ariola
TTED – Island
Two Tone – Chrysalis

UK Bubblers – Greensleeves
Ultravox – Chrysalis
Under One Flag – Music For Nations
Union Pacific – Red Lightnin'
Unit 7 – Greensleeves
Unlimited Gold – CBS
Verbals – Demon
Vertigo – Phonogram
Verve – Polydor
Vindaloo – WEA

Vinyl Drip – Backs
Warner Bros – WEA
Windham Hill – A&M
Winner – Creole
Wonderland – Polydor
Zarjazz – Virgin
Zebra – Cherry Red
Zippo – Demon
Zonophone – EMI
ZTT – Island

● MUSIC PUBLISHERS

● **Albion Music**
119-121 Freston Road, London W11 4BD
Tel: (01) 243 0011 Tel: 8954780

● **Ambassador Music**
22 Denmark Street, London WC2
Tel: (01) 836 5996

● **Ash Music Publishers**
Cropwell House, Salmon Lane, Kirkby-in-Ashfield Notts. Tel: (0623) 752448

● **Barn Publishing**
12 Thayer Street, London W1
Tel: (01) 935 8323 Tx: 22787 Thayer G

● **Belsize Music**
2nd Floor, 24 Baker Street, London W1.
Tel: (01) 935 2076 Tx: 23840

● **Big Secret Music**
Havoc House, Cods Hill, Beenham,
Berkshire. Tel: (0734) 713623 Tx: 848507
Attn. BSM

● **Black Sheep Music**
Fulmer Gardens House, Fulmer, Bucks
Tel: (02816) 2143/2109 Tx: 849208

● **Blue Mountain Music**
334-336 King Street, London W6 0RA
Tel: (01) 846 9566 Tx: 934541

● **Bocu Music**
1 Wyndham Yard, Wyndham Place, London
W1H 1AR. Tel: (01) 402 7433/5
Tx: 298976

● **Bourne Music**
34-36 Maddox Street, London W1R 9PD
Tel: (01) 493 6412

● **Margaret Brace Copyright Bureau**
4a Newman Passage, London W1A 4QD
Tel: (01) 580 7118

● **BTW Music**
125 Myddleton Road, Wood Green,
London N22 4NG. Tel: (01) 888 6655

● **Bullseye Music**
Air House, Spennymoor, Co Durham
DL16 7SE. Tel: (0388) 814632 Tx: 587513

● **Burlington Music**
129 Park Street, London W1. Tel: (01) 499
0067 Tx: 268403

● **Carlin Music**
14 New Burlington Street, London W1X
2LR. Tel: (01) 734 3251 Tx: 267488

● **Castle Hill Music**
2 Laurel Bank, Golcar, Huddersfield,
Yorkshire HD7 4ER. Tel: (0484) 846333

● **CBS Songs**
3-5 Rathbone Place, London W1V SDG
Tel: (01) 637 5831 Tx: 28963 CBSong G

● **Chappell Music**
129 Park Street, London W1Y 3FA
Tel: (01) 629 7600 Tx: 268403

● **Charly Publishing**
156-166 Ilderton Road, London SE15
Tel: (01) 732 5647 Tx: 8953184

● **Chelsea Music Publishing**
184-186 Regent Street, London W1R
5DR. Tel: (01) 439 7731 Tx: 27557

● **Cherry Music**
49 Greek Street, London W1
Tel: (01) 437 7418/9

● **Chevron Music Publishing**
Yorkshire Television Centre, Leeds LS3
1JS. Tel: (0532) 438283 Tx: 557232

● **Chrysalis Music**
12 Stratford Place, London W1N 9AF
Tel: (01) 408 2355 Tx: 21753

● **Barry Collings Music**
15 Claremont Road, Westcliffe-on-sea,
Essex. Tel: (0702) 347343 Tx: 24224
Ref. 181

● **Collins Music**
38 Kendal Street, London W2
Tel: (01) 262 2639 Tx: 261507

● **Copyright Control**
60 Lillie Road, London SW6
Tel: (01) 644 5207

● **Creole Music**
91-93 High Street, Harlesden, London
NW10. Tel: (01) 965 9223 Tx: 296133

● **Eaton Music**
8 West Eaton Place, London SW1X 8LS.
Tel: (01) 235 9046 Tx: 296133

● **John Edward Music**
38-40 Upper Clapton Road, London E5
8BQ. Tel: (01) 806 0071 Tx: 261697
Holrec

● **Edwardson Music**
106 Bickenhall Mansions, London W1H
3LB. Tel: (01) 935 7615

● **EG Music**
63a King's Road, London SW3 4NT
Tel: (01) 730 2162 Tx: 919205

● **EMI Music Publishing**
138-140 Charing Cross Road, London
WC2H 0LD. Tel: (01) 836 6699
Tx: 269189 Emi Pub G

● **E&S Music**
20-24 Beaumont Road, London W4 5AP.
Tel: (01) 995 5432 Tx: 265871 Monres G
Ref. Mag 10366

● **Faber Music**
3 Queen Square, London WC1N 3AU
Tel: (01) 278 6881 Tx: 299633

● **Fentone Music**
Fleming Road, Earlstrees, Corby,
Northants. Tel: (0536) 60981

● **Filmtrax**
4 Mornington Place, London NW1 7RP.
Tel: (01) 388 0141/2037 Tx: 946240
Cweasy G

● **Noel Gay Music**
24 Denmark Street, London WC2H 8NJ
Tel: (01) 836 3941 Tx: 21760

● **GES Music**
30 Bridstow Place, London W2 5AE
Tel: (01) 221 2999 Tx: 295834 Ges G

● **Handle Music**
1 Derby Street, London W1. Tel: (01) 493
9637 Tx: 892756

● **Happy Face Music**
The Old Smithy, Post Office Lane,
Kempsey, Worcs. Tel: (0905) 820659
Tx: 334142 Ssp G

● **Heisenberg Music**
18 Crofton Road, London SE5 8NB
Tel: (01) 703 7677

● **Hensley Music Publishing**
4 Rushton Mews, London W11 4JB
Tel: (01) 727 5118

● **Hollywood Music**
38-40 Upper Clapton Road, London E5
Tel: (01) 806 0071 Tx: 261697 Holrec

● **Hub Music**
4-10 Queen's Road, Twickenham
TW1 4ES. Tel: (01) 891 3146

● **Intersong Music**
129 Park Street, London W1Y 3FA
Tel: (01) 499 0067 Tx: 268403

● **Island Music**
Media House, 334-336 King Street,
London W6 0RA. Tel: (01) 846 9141
Tx: 934541

● **Jackson Music**
The Studios, Rickmansworth, Herts
WD3 2XD. Tel: (0923) 772351 Tx: 262284
Ref. 1728

● **Jess Music**
Beachwood, Beech Grove, Amersham,
Bucks. Tel: (02403) 4990 Tx: 268048

● **Jobete Music**
Tudor House, 35 Gresse Street, London
W1P 1PN. Tel: (01) 631 0380
Tx: 8811658 G

● **Kassner Associated Publishers**
21 Panton Street, London SW1
Tel: (01) 839 4672 Tx: 24158

● **Kennick Music**
Flat 3, 50 Cadogan Square, London SW1X
0JW. Tel: (01) 589 7711/8861

● **Lantern Music Publishing**
66 Roebuck House, Palace Street, London
SW1. Tel: (01) 828 4595

● **Leosong Copyright Service**
4a Newman Passage, London W1
Tel: (01) 580 7118 Tx: 268048

● **Lionheart Music**
29 Maddox Street, London W1R 9LD
Tel: (01) 499 0567 Tx: 8953097

● **Lip Service Enterprises**
2 Unwin Mansions, Queens Club Gardens,
London W14 9TH. Tel: (01) 385 3759

● **Logorhythm Music**
6-10 Lexington Street, London W1
Tel: (01) 734 7443/4

● **Magnet Music**
22 York Street, London W1H 1FD
Tel: (01) 486 8151 Tx: 25537

● **Bill Martin Music**
11th Floor, Alembic House, 93 Albert
Embankment, London SE1 7TY
Tel: (01) 582 7622

● **MCA Music**
139 Piccadilly, London W1V 9FH
Tel: (01) 629 7211 Tx: 22219

● **Mercury Music**
1-3 Upper James Street, London W1R
4BP. Tel: (01) 734 8080 Tx: 27937

● **Minder Music**
22 Bristol Gardens, London W9 2JQ
Tel: (01) 289 7281 Tx: 923421 Wemsec G

● **Morrison Leahy Music**
Flat 3, 1 Hyde Park Place, London W2
2LH. Tel: (01) 402 9238 Tx: 266589 Mlm G

● **MPL Communications**
1 Soho Square, London W1V 6BQ
Tel: (01) 439 6621 Tx: 21294

● **Neptune Music**
31 Old Burlington Street, London W1X
1LB. Tel: (01) 437 2066/7 Tx: 8954748

● **Oval Music**
11 Liston Road, London SW4
Tel: (01) 622 0111 Tx: 946240 Cweasy G
Ref. 19017005

● **Page One Music**
29 Rushton Mews, London W11 1RB
Tel: (01) 221 7179/7381 Tx: 8954665 Ref.
Pensong

● **Palace Music**
129 Park Street, London W1Y 3FA
Tel: (01) 499 0067 Tx: 268403

● **Paragon Music**
Park House, 22 Park Street, Croydon,
Surrey. Tel: (01) 681 6663

● **Patch Music**
Harley House South, Portsmouth Road,
Esher, Surrey KT10 9BH. Tel: (0372)
67752 Tx: 946240 Cweasy G Ref.
19018800

● **Pattern Music**
22 Denmark Street, London WC2
Tel: (01) 836 5996

● **Pink Floyd Music Publishers**
27 Noel Street, London W1V 3RD
Tel: (01) 734 6892 Tx: 28905 Ref. 907

● **Plangent Visions**
27 Noel Street, London W1V 3RD
Tel: (01) 734 6892

● **Point Music**
Studio 5, The Royal Victoria Patriotic
Building, Trinity Road, London SW18
Tel: (01) 871 4155 Tx: 265871 Monres G
Attn. DGS1483

● **Polar Union Music**
119-121 Freston Road, London W11 4BD
Tel: (01) 243 0011 Tx: 8954780

● **RAK Publishing**
42-48 Charlbert Street, London NW8 7BU
Tel: (01) 586 2012 Tx: 299501

● **RCA Music**
3 Cavendish Square, London W1
Tel: (01) 580 5566 Tx: 298933

● **The Really Useful Company**
20 Greek Street, London W1V 5LF
Tel: (01) 734 2114 Tx: 8953151

● **Red Bus Music**
Red Bus House, 48 Broadley Terrace,
London NW1. Tel: (01) 258 0324/8 Telex:
25873 Red Bus

● **Riva Music**
114 Wardour Street, London W1
Tel: (01) 734 3481 Tx: 28781 Gass G

● **Rock City Music**
Shepperton Studio Centre, Shepperton,
Middlesex. Tel: (09328) 66531/2

● **Rock Music**
27 Noel Street, London W1V 3RD
Tel: (01) 734 6892

● **Rondor Music**
Rondor House, 10a Parsons Green,
London SW6 4TW. Tel: (01) 731 4161/5

● **St Anne's Music**
Kennedy House, 31 Stamford Street,
Altrincham, Cheshire WA14 1ES
Tel: (061) 941 5151 Tx: 666255

● **Satril Music**
444 Finchley Road, London NW2 2HT
Tel: (01) 435 8063/5

● **Sonet Music Publishing**
121 Ledbury Road, London W11 2AQ
Tel: (01) 229 7267 Tx: 25793

● **Songs For Today**
PO Box 130, Hove, East Sussex BN3 6QU
Tel: (0273) 550088 Tx: 877050 Kruger G

● **Sound Diagrams**
21 Atholl Crescent, Edinburgh, EH3 8HQ.
Tel: (031) 229 8946 Tx: 265871 Monref G

● **Southern Music Publishing**
8 Denmark Street, London WC2H 8LT
Tel: (01) 836 4524 Tx: 23557

● **State Music**
26-27 Castlereagh Street, London W1H
5YR. Tel: (01) 402 2191 Tx: 25740 State G

● **Storm Music**
25 Rossall Road, Cleveleys, Blackpool FY5
1DX. Tel: (0253) 864598

● **Street Music**
Zomba House, 165-167 Willesden High
Road, London NW10. Tel: (01) 459 8899

● **Tabitha Music**
39 Cordery Road, St Thomas, Exeter,
Devon EX2 9DJ. Tel: (0392) 79914

● **Tactik Music**
1a Normand Gardens, Greyhound Road,
London W14. Tel: (01) 381 0116/
385 0567 Tx: 943763

● **Tembo Music**
2 Dorset Square, London NW1 6PU
Tel: (01) 586 5591/2 Tx: 299220 Tembo G

● **10 Music**
Advance House, 101-109 Ladbroke Grove,
London W11 1PG. Tel: (01) 221 8585

● **Thames Music**
117 Church Road, London SW13 9HL
Tel: (01) 741 2406

● **Tristan Music**
22 Denmark Street, London WC2
Tel: (01) 836 5996

● **United Music Publishers**
42 Rivington Street, London EC2A 3BN
Tel: (01) 729 4700

● **Valentine Music Group**
7 Garrick Street, London WC2E 9AR
Tel: (01) 240 1628/9 Tx: 268630 Valmus

● **Virgin Music Publishers**
Advance House, 101-109 Ladbroke Grove,
London W11 1PG. Tel: (01) 229 1282

● **Warner Brothers Music**
17 Berners Street, London W1P 3DD
Tel: (01) 637 3771 Tx: 25522

● **Watteau Music**
Oak House, 13 Parson Street, London
NW4. Tel: (01) 740 0680

● **Bruce Welch Music**
64 Stirling Court, Marshall Street, London
W1V 1LG. Tel: (01) 434 1839

● **Westminster Music**
19-20 Poland Street, London W1V 3DD
Tel: 734 8121 Tx: 22701

● **Zebra Publishing**
Greyhound House, 23-24 George Street,
Richmond, Surrey TW9 1JY. Tel: (01) 948
5771 Tx: 928940 Richbig

INDEPENDENT RECORD DISTRIBUTORS

● **Arabesque Ltd**
Swan Centre, Fisher's Lane, London W4
1RX. Tel: (01) 747 0365 Tx: 291908

● **Backs Cartel**
St Mary's Works, St Mary's Plain, Norwich.
Tel: (0603) 626221

● **Caroline Exports**
56 Standard Road, London NW10
Tel: (01) 961 2919 Tx: 22164

● **Conifer Records**
Horton Road, West Drayton, Middlesex
UB7 8LJ. Tel: (0895) 447707 Tx: 27492

● **Counterpoint Distribution**
Wharf Road, London E15 2SU
Tel: (01) 555 4321 Tx: 8951427

● **Discovery Records**
107 Broad Street, Beechingstoke, Pewsey,
Wilts. Tel: (067285) 406

● **Electronic Synthesizer Sound Projects (ESSP)**
The Sound House, PO Box 37B, East
Molesey, Surrey. Tel: (01) 979 9997/
577 5818

● **Fast Forward**
21a Alva Road, Edinburgh EH2 4PS
Tel: (031) 226 4616

● **S. Gold and Son**
Gold House, 69 Flempton Road, Leyton,
London E10 7NL. Tel: (01) 539 3600
Tx: 894793

● **Greensleeves Records**
Unit 7, Goldhawk Industrial Estate, 2a
Brackenbury Road, London W6
Tel: (01) 749 3277/8 Tx: 8955504

● **Hotshot Records**
29 St Michael's Road, Headingley, Leeds,
Yorkshire. Tel: (0532) 742106

● **Jazz Horizons**
103 London Road, Sawbridgeworth, Herts
CM1 9JJ. Tel: (0279) 724572

● **Jazz Music**
7 Kildare Road, Swinton, Manchester M27
3AB. Tel: (061) 794 3525

● **Jungle Records**
24 Gaskin Street, London N1 2RY
Tel: (01) 359 8444/9161 Tx: 896559
Gecoms G Attn. Jungle

● **Lasgo Exports**
Unit 2, Chapman's Park Industrial Estate,
378-388 High Road, Willesden, London
NW10 2DY. Tel: (01) 459 8800 Tx: 22111
Lasgo G

● **Lightning Distribution**
Bashley Road, London NW10 6SD.
Tel: (01) 965 5555 Tx: 927813 Larrec

● **Making Waves**
6-8 Alie Street, London E1 8DE
Tel: (01) 481 9917 Tx: 884555

● **9-Mile Distribution**
3 Lower Avenue, Leamington Spa,
Warwickshire. Tel: (0926) 881292

● **Oldies Unlimited**
Dukes Way, St George's, Telford,
Shropshire. Tel: (0952) 616911 Tx: 35493

● **Pickwick International**
The Hyde Industrial Estate, The Hyde,
London NW9 6JU. Tel: (01) 200 7000
Tx: 922170

● **Pinnacle Records**
Unit 2, Orpington Trading Estate,
Sevenoaks Way, Orpington, Kent BR5
3FR. Tel: (0689) 70622 Tx: 929053

● **Pizza Express Music Distribution**
29 Romilly Street, London W1
Tel: (01) 734 6112 Tx: 27950 Ref. 3396

● **Probe Records**
8-12 Rainford Gardens, Liverpool 2
Tel: (051) 236 6591

● **PRT Distribution**
105 Bond Road, Mitcham, Surrey CR4
3UT. Tel: (01) 648 7000

● **Recommended Distribution**
387 Wandsworth Road, London SW8
Tel: (01) 622 8834 Tx: 8813271 Gecoms G

● **Red Lightnin' Records**
The White House, North Lopham, Diss,
Norfolk. Tel: (0379) 88693

● **Red Rhino Distribution**
The Coach House, Fetter Lane, York YO1
1EM. Tel: (0904) 641415 or 27828

● **Revolver Distribution**
The Old Malt House, Little Ann Street,
Bristol 2. Tel: (0272) 541291/4

● **Rose Records**
3 Ellington Street, London N7 8PP
Tel: (01) 609 8288 Tx: 268048

● **Ross Record Distribution**
29 Main Street, Turriff, Aberdeenshire
Tel: (0888) 62403

● **Rough Trade Distribution**
61-71 Collier Street, London N1
Tel: (01) 833 2133 Tx: 299579

● **Spartan Records**
London Road, Wembley, Middlesex HA9
7HQ. Tel: (01) 903 4753 Tx: 923175

● **Stage One Records**
Parshire House, 2 King's Road, Haslemere,
Surrey. Tel: (0428) 4001 Tx: 858226

● **Wynd-up Records**
Turntable House, Guinness Road Trading
Estate, Trafford Park, Manchester
Tel: (061) 872 0170 Tx: 635363

MUSIC MAGAZINES

● **Beatles Monthly**
43 St Mary's Road, Ealing, London W5
5RQ. Tel: (01) 579 1082

Beatlemania resurrected; monthly, 48pp;
£1.10; circ. n/a

● **Blitz**
1 Lower James Street, London W1
Tel: (01) 734 8311/3

A stylish multi-media extravaganza;
monthly; 116pp; £1.00; circ. 60,000

● **Blue and Rhythm**
18 Maxwelton Close, London NW7 3NA
Tel: (01) 906 0986

Blues, R&B, gospel, vintage, soul, cajun,
tex-mex, news, updates, and latest albums;
monthly (except January and August) in
first fortnight; 36pp; £1.25; circ. 2,000

● **Blues and Soul**
153 Praed Street, London W2
Tel: (01) 402 6869

Covers all black music and dance music
(except reggae); fortnightly; 48pp; £0.80;
circ. 41,600

● **Brum Beat**
190 Monument Road, Birmingham B16
8UU. Tel: (021) 454 7020

The Birmingham and West Midlands
scene; monthly; 16pp; free; circ. 40,000

● **Country Music People**
78 Grovelands Road, St Paul's Cray,
Orpington, Kent. Tel: (01) 309 7606

Covers all country music; monthly; 42pp;
£0.90; circ. 12,000 worldwide

● **Disco and Club Trade International**
410 St John Street, London EC1
Tel: (01) 278 3591/6 Tx: 24637 Wigmor

Trade magazine for discos, clubs, pubs etc;
monthly; 86pp; £1.00; circ. 25,000

● **Echoes**
Rococo House, 283 City Road, London
EC1 1LA. Tel: (01) 253 6662/4

Covers all black music, especially funk,
soul and reggae; every Wednesday; 24pp;
£0.50; circ. 25,000

● **Electronics and Music Maker**
Alexander House, 1 Milton Road,
Cambridge CB4 1UY. Tel: (0223) 313722

Interviews and reviews of new equipment,
for musicians and studio technicians;
monthly; 112pp; £1.20; circ. 20,500

● **Elvis Monthly**
41-47 Derby Road, Heanor, Derbyshire
DE7 7QH. Tel: (0773) 712460

Elvis, Elvis . . . and more Elvis; monthly, last
Tuesday; 56pp; £0.95; circ. 25,000

● **Elvisly Yours**
107 Shoreditch High Street, London E1
Tel: (01) 739 2001

As above; bi-monthly; 32pp; £1.50; circ. n/a

● **The Face**
The Old Laundry, Ossington Buildings,
Off Moxon Street, London W1. Tel: (01)
935 8232

The magazine by which others are judged
– the gazette of style in the UK; monthly,
third Thursday; 116pp; 90p; circ. 92,000
worldwide

● **Folk Roots**
PO Box 73, Farnham, Surrey GU9 7UN.
Tel: (0252) 724638

Across the board, traditional and modern
folk from the UK, US, and around the
world, plus blues, tex-mex, African, etc;
monthly, third Thursday; 60pp; £1.20; circ.
12,000

● **Guitarist**
Alexander House, 1 Milton Road,
Cambridge CB4 1UY. Tel: (0223) 313722

For guitarists! Lots of interviews, reviews
of new equipment; monthly, second
Thursday; 72pp; £1.20; circ. 21,000

● **History of Rock**
Griffin House, 159 Hammersmith Road,
London W6. Tel: (01) 846 9977

Illustrated encyclopedia of rock history,
with features on prominent artists and
major trends plus matching set of LPs;
every, Thursday; 32pp; £1.00; circ. 20,000

● **Home and Studio Recording**
Alexander House, 1 Milton Road,
Cambridge CB4 1UY. Tel: (0223) 313722

For anyone interested in music recording
and how to do it; monthly, third Thursday;
80pp; £1.20; circ. 18,500

● **Home Keyboard Review**
Alexander House, 1 Milton Road,
Cambridge CB4 1UY. Tel: (0223) 313722

For the domestic keyboard player;
monthly, 3rd Thursday; 64pp; £0.90; circ.
16,000

● **i-D**
27-29 Macklin Street, London WC2
Tel: (01) 430 0871

Music of all descriptions, as well as fashion
and features; monthly, third Tuesday;
100pp; £1.00; circ. 47,000

● **In The City**
c/o Compendium Books, 234 Camden
High Street, London NW1. Tel: (01) 267
1525/450 4506

Long-running fanzine covering alternative
music; irregular quarterly; 32pp; £0.80;
circ. 11,000

● **International Country Music News**
18 Burley Rise, Kegworth, Derby DE8 2DZ
Tel: (05097) 3224

British and American country music;
monthly, fourth Thursday; 24pp; £0.50,
circ. 25,000

● **International Musician and
Recording World**
PO Box 381, Mill Harbour, London E14
Tel: (01) 987 5090 Tx: 24676 Norshl G

Everything the modern musician needs to
know about equipment, recordings,
production, etc; monthly, in the last week;
148pp; £1.95; circ. 24,000

● **Jazz Journal International**
35 Great Russell Street, London WC1 3PP
Tel: (01) 580 7244

Jazz enthusiasts' and record collectors'
magazine; monthly, last Friday; 40pp;
£1.20; circ. 11,500

● **Kerrang!**
Greater London House, Hampstead Road,
London NW1. Tel: (01) 387 6611

Heavy metal and heavy rock; fortnightly,
Thursdays; 56pp; £0.85; circ. 90,000
worldwide

● **Mega Metal Kerrang!**
Greater London House, Hampstead Road,
London NW1. Tel: (01) 387 6611

Heavy heavy metal; quarterly; 52pp;
£1.25; circ. 45,000

● **Melody Maker**
Berkshire House, 168-173 High Holborn,
London WC1. Tel: (01) 379 3581

Music, trouble, and fun for the older
'teenager'; every Wednesday, 52pp;
£0.50; circ. 61,000

● **Music Week**
Greater London House, Hampstead Road,
London NW1. Tel: (01) 387 6611

Music trade magazine for record
companies and retailers; every
Wednesday; 36pp; £1.50; circ. 13,500

● **New Kommotion**
3 Bowrons Avenue, Wembley, Middlesex
Tel: (01) 902 6417

Fifties rockabilly and rock 'n' roll for record
collectors; quarterly; 50pp; £1.20;
circ. 3,000

● **NME (New Musical Express)**
Commonwealth House, 1-19 New Oxford
Street, London WC1.
Tel: (01) 404 0700

"What? You'll only give us twelve words to
describe NME? It's *outrageous*!!!" – the
editor; every Wednesday; 56pp; £0.50;
circ. 105,000

● **No. 1**
Commonwealth House, 1-19 New Oxford
Street, London WC1. Tel: (01) 404 0700

Teenage magazine covering the whole
range of pop music; every Wednesday;
48pp; £0.45; circ. 171,000

● **Now Dig This**
69 Quarry Lane, Simonside, South Shields,
Tyne and Wear. Tel: (0632) 563213

Fifties US rock 'n' roll, roots; monthly, first
week; 40pp; £1.25; circ. 2,000

● **One Two Testing**
PO Box 381, Mill Harbour, London E14
Tel: (01) 987 5090 Tx: 24676 Norshl G

Instrument reviews, interviews, and
features for the younger musician;
monthly, third week; 100pp; £1.40;
circ. 12,000

● **Outlet**
33 Aintree Crescent, Barkingside, Ilford,
Essex. Tel: (01) 551 3346

Bands on independent labels; quarterly;
30pp; £1.00; circ. 800

● **Pop Puzzler**
26-28 Addison Road, Bromley, Kent BR2
9RR. Tel: (01) 464 8058

Pop reviews and puzzles for teenagers;
monthly, second Thursday; 46pp; £0.65;
circ. 75,000

● **Pop, Rock, and Puzzles**
Alexander House, 1 Milton Road,
Cambridge CB4 1UY. Tel: (0223) 313722

Pin-ups, interviews, features, music-related
puzzles for the teenypop market; monthly,
third Thursday; 48pp; £0.60; circ. 125,000

● **Q**
42 Great Portland Street, London W1N
5AH. Tel: (01) 637 9181

A modern guide to music and more with
features and reviews of albums, CDs,
videos, books, films, etc; monthly; 100pp;
£1.10; circ. n/a

● **Record Collector**
43 St Mary's Road, London W5
Tel: (01) 579 1082

All kinds of music from the fifties to the
present, with discographies of major
artists, features etc for the serious record
collector; monthly; 116pp; £1.20; circ.
25,000

● **Rhythm**
Alexander House, 1 Milton Road,
Cambridge CB4 1UY. Tel: (0223) 313722

For drummers and drummer programmers.
Interviews, and reviews of new equipment;
monthly; 72pp; £1.00; circ. 18,000

● **RM (Record Mirror)**
Greater London House, Hampstead Road,
London NW1. Tel: (01) 387 6611

Concentrates on up-and-coming bands,
all types of music for the younger person;
every Thursday; 48pp; £0.55; circ. 63,000

● **Rock This Town**
c/o Reliable Promotions, 132 Chase Way,
London N14 5DH. Tel: (01) 368 2921

Reviews and features of rock 'n' roll,
rockabilly; monthly, third week; 30pp;
£1.00; circ. 25,000

● **Smash Hits**
Lisa House, 52-55 Carnaby Street, London
W1. Tel: (01) 437 8050

Chart hits, news and features for
teenagers; "the biggest-selling music
magazine in the world"; fortnightly,
Wednesdays, 68pp; £0.45; circ. 515,000

● **Sounds**
Greater London House, Hampstead Road,
London NW1. Tel: (01) 387 6611

Broad-based rock magazine for the under-
25's; every Wednesday; 52pp; £0.55; circ.
77,000

● **Stick It In Your Ear**
5 Sunvale Close, Sholing, Southampton
SO2 8GU. Tel: (0703) 448617

Reviews independently released
cassettes; bi-monthly; 8pp; £0.50; circ. 300

● **Studio Sound and Broadcast
Engineering**
Link House, Dingwall Avenue, Croydon
CR9 2TA. Tel: (01) 686 2599

Trade magazine for recording engineers,
record producers, etc; monthly, second
Friday; 140pp; £1.50 (free for
professionals);
circ. 16,000 worldwide

● **Swing 51**
41 Bushey Road, Sutton, Surrey SM1 1QR

Roots, rock and beyond . . . reviews of folk,
ethnic, and rock music worldwide; every
six months; 60pp; £1.50; circ. 1,500

● **The Wire**
Unit G/H 115 Cleveland Street, London
W1P 5PN. Tel: (01) 580 7522

Jazz, improvised and new music etc;
monthly, first week; 56pp; £1.20;
circ. 15,000

● MUSIC RELATED ASSOCIATIONS

● **American Society of Composers,
Authors, and Publishers (ASCAP)**
Suite 9, 52 Haymarket, London SW1Y
4RP. Tel: (01) 930 1121 Tx: 25833

● **Association of Professional
Recording Studios**
23 Chestnut Avenue, Chorleywood, Herts
WD3 4HA. Tel: (0923) 772907

● **British Academy of Songwriters,
Composers, and Authors**
148 Charing Cross Road, London WC2H
0LB. Tel: (01) 240 2823/4

● **The British Library National Sound
Archive**
29 Exhibition Road, London SW7 2AS
Tel: (01) 589 6603/4

● **British Music Information Centre**
10 Stratford Place, London W1N 9AE. Tel:
(01) 499 8567

● **British Phonographic Industry**
4th Floor, Roxburghe House, 273/287
Regent Street, London W1R 7PB
Tel: (01) 629 8642

● **British Tape Industry Association**
7-15 Lansdowne Road, Croydon CR9 2PL.
Tel: (01) 688 4422 Tx: 917857 Binder G

● **Composers Guild of Great Britain**
10 Stratford Place, London W1N 9AE
Tel: (01) 499 4795

● **Country Music Association**
Suite 3, 52 Haymarket, London SW1Y
4RP. Tel: (01) 930 2445/6 Tx: 25833

● **International Federation of
Phonogram and Videogram Producers**
54 Regent Street, London W1R 5PJ
Tel: (01) 434 3521 Tx: 919044 IFPI G

● **International Jazz Federation**
13 Foulser Road, London SW17 8UE
Tel: (01) 767 2213

● **Jazz Centre Society**
5 Dryden Street, London WC2E 9NW
Tel: (01) 240 2430

● **London Musicians' Collective**
42a Gloucester Avenue, London NW1
Tel: (01) 722 0456

● **Mechanical Copyright Protection
Society**
Elgar House, 41 Streatham High Road,
London SW16 1ER. Tel: (01) 769 4400

● **Media Research and Information
Bureau (MRIB)**
12 Manchester Mews, London W1M 5PJ
Tel: (01) 935 0346 Tx: 946240 Cweasy G

● **Music Publishers' Association**
7th Floor, 103 Kingsway, London WC2B
6QX. Tel: (01) 831 7591

● **Musicians Benevolent Fund**
16 Ogle Street, London W1P 7LG
Tel: (01) 636 4481

● **Musicians Union**
60-62 Clapham Road, London SW9 0JJ
Tel: (01) 582 5566 Tx: 8814691

● **Performing Rights Society**
29-33 Berners Street, London W1P 4AA.
Tel: (01) 580 5544 Tx: 892678

● **Record Labels Register**
202 Finchley Road, London NW3 6BL
Tel: (01) 794 0461 Tx: 261712

● **Royal Society of Musicians of Great
Britain**
10 Stratford Place, London W1N 9AE
Tel: (01) 629 6137

● **Society for the Promotion of New
Music**
10 Stratford Place, London W1N 9AE
Tel: (01) 491 8111

● **Variety Club of Great Britain**
32 Welbeck Street, London W1M 7PG
Tel: (01) 935 4466

ROCK REFERENCE US

● RECORD COMPANIES

● A&M Records
1416 North LaBrea Avenue, Hollywood, CA 90068. Tel: (213) 469 2411 Tx: 691282

and

New York office:
595 Madison Avenue, New York, NY 10022. Tel: (212) 826 0477 Tx: 961105
Labels: A&M

● Airwave Records
6430 Sunset Boulevard, Penthouse 1502, Hollywood, CA 90028. Tel: (213) 463 9500
Labels: Airwave, Dance-it, East River, Flamingo

● Arista Records
6 West 57th Street, New York, NY 10019
Tel: (212) 489 7400 Tx: 666282
Labels: Arista

● Atlantic Recording Corp
75 Rockerfeller Plaza, New York, NY 10019. Tel: (212) 484 6000 Tx: 424602
and
LA office:
9229 Sunset Boulevard, Los Angeles, CA 90069. Tel: (213) 205 7450 Tx: 4720852
Labels: Atco, Atlantic, Cotillion, Electra, 21

● Bearsville Records
P.O. Box 135, Bearsville, NY 12409
Tel: (914) 679 7303 Tx: 5102470848
Bearson G
Labels: Bearsville

● The Benson Co
365 Great Circle Road, Nashville, TN 37228. Tel: (615) 259 9111
Labels: !Alarma!, Greentree, Heartwarming, Impact, Lifeline, NewPax, Onyx, Paragon

● Biograph Records
16 River Street, Chatham, NY 12037
Tel: (518) 392 3400/1
Labels: Biograph, Center, Dawn, Historical, Melodeon, Waterfall

● Bomp Records
2702 San Fernando Road, Los Angeles, CA 99065. Tel: (213) 227 4141
Labels: Bomp, Voxx

● Buddha Records
1790 Broadway, New York, NY 10019
Tel: (212) 582 6900 Tx: 422573
Labels: Buddha, Roulette, Streetwise, Sunnyview, Sutra

● Capitol/EMI Records
1750 Vine Street, Hollywood, CA 90028
Tel: (213) 462 6252 Tx: 674051

and

New York office:

1370 Avenue of the Americas, New York, NY 10019. Tel: (212) 757 7470
Labels: Blue Note, Capitol, EMI-America, Manhattan

● CBS Records
51 West 52nd Street, New York, NY 10019
Tel: (212) 975 4321 Tx: 220561
and
LA office:
1801 Century Park West, Los Angeles, CA 90067. Tel: (213) 556 4700
Labels: CBS, Columbia, Epic

● Chrysalis Records
645 Madison Avenue, New York, NY 10022. Tel: (212) 758 3555 Tx: 971860
Labels: China, Chrysalis

● Cream Records
13107 Ventura Boulevard, Suite 102, Studio City, CA 91604. Tel: (818) 905 6344 Tx: 182693 Shelby
Labels: Cream, Hi

● Enigma Records
1750 East Holly Avenue, P.O. Box 2428, El Segundo, CA 90245. Tel: (213) 640 6869 Tx: 503809
Labels: Attune, Enigma, Metal Blade, Pink Dust, Restless

● Fantasy Records
2600 10th Street, Berkeley, CA 94710
Tel: (415) 549 2500 Tx: 171312 Universal Berk
Labels: Contemporary, Fantasy, Galaxy, Goodtime Jazz, Milestone, Prestige, Riverside, Stax

● Flying Fish Records
1304 West Schubert Street, Chicago, IL 60614. Tel: (312) 528 5455 Tx: 297175
Labels: Flying Fish

● Folkways Records
632 Broadway, New York, NY 10012
Tel: (212) 777 6606 Tx: 220883 Tour
Labels: Folkways

● 415 Records
P.O. Box 14563, San Francisco, CA 94114
Tel: (415) 621 3415
Labels: 415

● Geffen Records
9130 Sunset Boulevard, Los Angeles, CA 90069. Tel: (213) 278 9010 Tx: 295854

and

New York office:
75 Rockerfeller Plaza, New York, NY 10019. Tel: (212) 474 7170 Tx: 424602
Labels: Geffen

● Gold Mountain Records
120 West 44th Street, Suite 608, New York, NY 10036. Tel: (212) 840 6011
Labels: Gold Mountain

● Hannibal Records
3575 Cahuenga Boulevard West, Suite 470, Los Angeles, CA 90068
Tel: (213) 850 5660
Labels: Hannibal

● Intrepid Records
4520 Bellevue, Suite 210, P.O. Box 8033, Kansas City, MO 64119
Tel: (816) 923 5741
Labels: Gillum, Intrepid, Koko

● Island Records
14 East 4th Street, New York, NY 10012
Tel: (212) 477 8000 Tx: 7105815292
Labels: Antilles, 4th and Broadway, Island, Mango

● Jem Records
3619 Kennedy Road, South Plainfield, NJ 07080. Tel: (201) 753 6100 Tx: 275297 Jemur

and

West Coast office:
18629 Topham Street, Reseda, CA 91335.
Tel: (213) 996 6754 Tx: 674851 Jemrec wstreda
Labels: Audion, Coda, Editions EG, EG, EG Classics, Jem, Landscape, Ode, Passport, PVC, Visa

● **Landslide Records**
450 14th Street NW, Atlanta, GA 30318
Tel: (404) 873 3918
Labels: DB, Landslide

● **MCA Records**
100 Universal City Plaza, Universal City, CA 91608. Tel: (818) 777 1000
and

New York office:
445 Park Avenue, 6th Floor, New York, NY 10022. Tel: (212) 759 7500
Labels: Chess, Dot, Impulse, MCA, Zebra

● **Mobile Fidelity Sound Lab**
1260 Holm Road, Petaluma, CA 94952
Tel: (707) 778 0134
Labels: Cafe

● **Motown Records**
6255 Sunset Boulevard, Los Angeles, CA 90028. Tel: (213) 468 3500 Tx: 4720916
Labels: Gordy, Motown, Tamla

● **PolyGram Records**
810 Seventh Avenue, New York, NY 10019. Tel: (212) 333 8000 Tx: 620985
and

LA office:
8335 Sunset Boulevard, Los Angeles, CA 90069. Tel: (213) 656 3003
Labels: Casablanca, Mercury, Polydor

● **Ralph Records**
109 Minna Street, Suite 391, San Francisco, CA 94105. Tel: (415) 543 4085
Labels: Ralph

● **RCA/Ariola Records**
1133 Avenue of the Americas, New York, NY 10036. Tel: (212) 930 4000
and

LA office:
6363 Sunset Boulevard, Hollywood, CA 90028. Tel: (213) 468 4000 Tx: 234367 Attn. Hollywood
Labels: RCA

● **Reachout International Records**
611 Broadway, Suite 725, New York, NY 10012. Tel: (212) 477 0563
Labels: Reachout

● **Ralph Records**
109 Minna Street, Suite 391, San Francisco, CA 94105. Tel: (415) 543 4085
Labels: Ralph

● **RCA/Ariola Records**
1133 Avenue of the Americas, New York, NY 10036. Tel: (212) 930 4000
Tx: 234367

and

LA office:
6363 Sunset Boulevard, Hollywood, CA 90028. Tel: (213) 468 4000
Tx: 234367 Attn. Hollywood
Labels: RCA

● **Reachout International Records**
611 Broadway, Suite 725, New York, NY 10012. Tel: (212) 477 0563
Labels: Reachout

● **Rhino Records**
1201 Olympic Boulevard, Santa Monica, CA 90404. Tel: (213) 450 6323
Tx: 4972305
Labels: Rhino

● **Rough Trade Inc**
326 Sixth Street, San Francisco, CA 94103. Tel: (415) 621 4045
Tx: 6771141
Labels: Factory-US, Pitch Attempt, Rough Trade, Silo

● **Rounder Records**
1 Camp Street, Cambridge, MA 02142
Tel: (617) 354 0700 Tx: 921724
Labels: Daring, Fretless, Heartbeat, Philo, Rounder, Varrick

● **Rykodisc**
Pickering Wharf, Building C-3G, Salem, MA 01970. Tel: (617) 744 7678
Tx: 4996804 Eatrecs
Labels: Rykodisc

● **Shanachie Records**
1 Hollywood Avenue, Ho-Ho-Kus, NJ 07423. Tel: (201) 445 5561
Tx: 247352
Labels: Herwin, Meadow Lark, Morning Star, Shanachie

● **Slash Records**
7381 Beverly Boulevard, Los Angeles, CA 90036. Tel: (213) 937 4660
Labels: Slash

● **Sugar Hill Records**
96 West Street, Englewood, NJ 07631. Tel: (201) 569 5170
Tx: 429762
Labels: Sugar Hill

● **Survivor Records**
349 South Lafayette Park Place, Suite 323, Los Angeles, CA 90057
Tel: (213) 650 6800
Labels: Birthright, Public, Revelation, Rough Diamond, Survivor

● **TNA Records**
10 George Street, Wallingford, CT 06492
Tel: (203) 269 4465
Labels: TNA

● **Tommy Boy Records**
1747 First Avenue, New York, NY 10128
Tel: (212) 722 2211
Tx: 6971684 Funk
Labels: Tommy Boy

● **Twin Tone Records**
2541 Nicolette Avenue South, Minneapolis, MN 55404
Tel: (612) 872 0646 Tx: 6502881571
Labels: Twin Tone

● **Upstart Records**
2210 Rapier Boulevard, Arlington, TX 76013. Tel: (817) 461 8481
Labels: Marquee, Upstart

● **Vanguard Records**
71 West 23rd Street, New York, NY 10010
Tel: (212) 255 7732 Tx: 469150
Labels: Terra, Vanguard

● **Warner Brothers Records**
3300 Warner Boulevard, Burbank, CA 91510. Tel: (818) 846 9090
Tx: 698512
and

New York office:
3 East 54th Street, New York, NY 10022
Tel: (212) 702 0318 Tx: 7105815718
Labels: Warner Brothers, Warner Nashville

● **Windham Hill Records**
P.O. Box 9388, Stanford, CA 94305
Tel: (415) 329 0647
Labels: Windham Hill

● RECORD LABELS

!Alarma! – Benson
Antilles – Island
Atco – Atlantic
Attune – Enigma
Audion – Jem
Birthright – Survivor
Blue Note – Capitol/EMI
Cafe – Mobile Fidelity
Casablanca – PolyGram
Center – Biograph
Chess – MCA
China – Chrysalis
Coda – Jem
Columbia – CBS

Contemporary – Fantasy
Cotillion – Atlantic
Dance-it – Airwave
Daring – Rounder
Dawn – Biograph
DB – Landslide
Dot – MCA
East River – Airwave
Editions EG – Jem
EG – Jem
Electra – Atlantic
EMI America – Capitol/EMI
Epic – CBS
Factory US – Rough Trade

Flamingo – Airwave
4th and Broadway – Island
Fretless – Rounder
Galaxy – Fantasy
Gillum – Intrepid
Goodtime Jazz – Fantasy
Gordy – Motown
Greentree – Benson
Heartbeat – Rounder
Heartwarming – Benson
Herwin – Shanachie
Hi – Cream
Historical – Biograph
Impact – Benson

Impulse – MCA
Koko – Intrepid
Landscape – Jem
Lifeline – Benson
Mango – Island
Manhattan – Capitol/EMI
Marquee – Upstart
Meadow Lark – Shanachie
Melodeon – Biograph
Mercury – PolyGram
Metal Blade – Enigma
Milestone – Fantasy
Morning Star – Shanachie
NewPax – Benson
Ode – Jem

Onyx – Benson
Paragon – Benson
Passport – Jem
Philo – Rounder
Pink Dust – Enigma
Pitch Attempt – Rough Trade
Polydor – PolyGram
Prestige – Fantasy
Public – Survivor
PVC – Jem
Restless – Enigma
Revelation – Survivor
Riverside – Fantasy
Rough Diamond – Survivor
Roulette – Buddha

Silo – Rough Trade
Stax – Fantasy
Streetwise – Buddha
Sunnyview – Buddha
Sutra – Buddha
Tamla – Motown
Terra – Vanguard
21 – Atlantic
Varrick – Rounder
Visa – Jem
Voxx – Bomp
Waterfall – Biograph
Zebra – MCA

● MUSIC PUBLISHERS

● **Abkco Music**
1700 Broadway, 41st Floor, New York, NY 10019. Tel: (212) 399 0300 Tx: 234874

● **Acuff-Rose Publications**
2510 Franklin Road, Nashville, TN 37204 Tel: (615) 385 3031 Tx: 554366

● **April/Blackwood Music**
49 East 52nd Street, New York, NY 10022 Tel: (212) 975 4886 Tx: 220561

● **Augsburg Publishing**
426 South Fifth Street, Minneapolis, MN 55415. Tel: (612) 330 3300

● **Beserkley**
2054 University Avenue, Suite 400, Berkeley, CA 94704. Tel: (415) 848 6701

● **Big Music**
10 George Street, Wallingford, CT 06492 Tel: (203) 269 4465

● **Big Seven Music**
1790 Broadway, 18th Floor, New York, NY 10019. Tel: (212) 582 4267 Tx: 422573

● **Bourne Co**
437 Fifth Avenue, New York, NY 10016 Tel: (212) 679 3700

● **Buddha Music**
1790 Broadway, New York, NY 10019 Tel: (212) 582 6900 Tx: 422573

● **Bug Music**
6777 Hollywood Boulevard, 9th Floor, Hollywood, CA 90028. Tel: (213) 466 4352 Tx: 9103213926

● **Cameron Organisation**
822 Hillgrove Avenue, Western Springs, IL 60558. Tel: (312) 246 8222

● **CBS Songs**
49 East 52nd Street, New York, NY 10022 Tel: (212) 975 4886 Tx: 960213

● **Chappell/Intersong Music**
810 Seventh Avenue, 32nd Floor, New York, NY 10019. Tel: (212) 399 6910 Tx: 421749

● **Chrysalis Music Group**
645 Madison Avenue, New York, NY 10022. Tel: (212) 758 3555 Tx: 971860

● **Cotillion Music**
75 Rockerfeller Plaza, New York, NY 10019. Tel: (212) 484 8132 Tx: 424602

● **Crazy Cajun Music**
5626 Brock Street, Houston, TX 77023 Tel: (713) 926 4431

● **Cream Publishing**
13107 Ventura Boulevard, Suite 102, Studio City, CA 91604. Tel: (818) 905 6344

● **Entertainment Company Music**
1700 Broadway, 41st Floor, New York, NY 10019. Tel: (212) 265 2600 Tx: 6972989

● **Evansongs**
1790 Broadway, New York, NY 10019 Tel: (212) 765 8450 Tx: 125609 Espnyk

● **Famous Music**
1 Gulf and Western Plaza, New York, NY 10023. Tel: (212) 333 3433 Tx: 235260

● **Carl Fisher Inc**
62 Cooper Square, New York, NY 10003 Tel: (212) 777 0900 Tx: 4774129

● **Flying Fish Music**
1304 West Schubert Street, Chicago IL 60614. Tel: (312) 528 5455 Tx: 297175

● **Al Gallico Music**
344 East 49th Street, New York, NY 10017. Tel: (212) 355 5980

● **Garrett Music**
4121½ Radford Avenue, Studio City, CA 91604. Tel: (818) 506 8964

● **Glad Music**
3409 Brinkman Street, Houston, TX 77018 Tel: (713) 861 3630

● **Graph Music**
34 Ratterman Road, Woodstock, New York, NY 12498. Tel: (914) 679 2458

● **Al Green Music**
P.O. Box 456, Millington, TN 38053 Tel: (901) 794 6220

● **Hilaria Music**
315 West Gorham Street, Madison, WI 53703. Tel: (608) 251 2644

● **Home Grown Music**
4412 Whitsett Avenue, Studio City, CA 91604. Tel: (818) 763 6323

● **House of Cash**
700 Johnny Cash Parkway, Hendersonville, TN 37075 Tel: (615) 824 5110

● **Hudson Bay Music**
1619 Broadway 11th Floor, New York, NY 10019. Tel: (212) 489 8170 Tx: 62932

● **Intersong Music**
6255 Sunset Boulevard, Suite 1904, Hollywood, CA 90028. Tel: (213) 469 5141 Tx: 4991128

● **Island Music**
6525 Sunset Boulevard, 2nd Floor, Hollywood, CA 90028. Tel: (213) 469 1285 Tx: 691223 Ackeelsa

● **Jobete Music**
6255 Sunset Boulevard, Hollywood, CA 90028. Tel: (213) 468 3500

● **Largo Music**
425 Park Avenue, New York, NY 10022 Tel: (212) 371 9400 Tx: 8389487

● **Laurie Publishing**
450 Livingston Street, Norwood, NJ 07648. Tel: (201) 767 5551

● **Hal Leonard Publishing**
P.O. Box 13809, Milwaukee WI 53213 Tel: (414) 774 3630 Tx: 26668

● **Marsaint Music**
3809 Clematis Avenue, New Orleans, LA 70122. Tel: (504) 949 8386

● **MCA Music**
70 Universal City Plaza, Suite 425, Universal City CA 91608. Tel: (818) 777 4550 Tx: 677053 Universal City

● **Ivan Mogull Music**
625 Madison Avenue, New York, NY 10022. Tel: (212) 355 5636 Tx: 236973

● **Neil Music**
8400 Sunset Boulevard, Suite 4a, Los Angeles, CA 90069. Tel: (213) 656 2614 Tx: 5106000877

● **Pale Pachyderm Publishing**
566 Folsom Street, San Francisco, CA 94105. Tel: (415) 543 8248

● **Peer-Southern Organisation**
1740 Broadway, New York, NY 10019
Tel: (212) 265 3910 Tx: 424361

● **The Richmond Organisation (TRO)**
10 Columbus Circle, New York, NY 10019
Tel: (212) 765 9889 Tx: 429359

● **Rough Trade**
326 Sixth Avenue, San Francisco, CA 94103. Tel: (415) 621 4045
Tx: 6771141

● **Screen Gems – EMI Music**
6920 Sunset Boulevard, Hollywood, CA 90028. Tel: (213) 469 8371

● **Paul Simon Music**
1619 Broadway, Room 500, New York, NY 10019. Tel: (212) 541 7571 Tx: 645491

● **Special Rider Music**
PO Box 860, Cooper Station, New York, NY 10276. Tel: (212) 473 5900 Tx: 661139

● **TRO**
See the Richmond Organisation

● **20th Century-Fox Music**
PO Box 900, Beverly Hills, CA 90213
Tel: (213) 203 1487 Tx: 674895

● **Warner Brothers Music**
9000 Sunset Boulevard, The Penthouse Suite, Los Angeles, CA 90069. Tel: (213) 273 3323 Tx: 9104902598

● **Welk Music**
1299 Ocean Avenue, Suite 800, Santa Monica, CA 90401. Tel: (213) 870 1582

● **Word Music**
P.O. Box 2790, Waco, TX 76796. Tel: (817) 772 7650 Tx: 530642

● **WPN Music**
10 Swirl Lane, Levittown, NY 11756
Tel: (516) 796 3698

● DISTRIBUTORS/IMPORTERS

● **Abbey Road Record Distributors**
1721 Newport Circle, Santa Ana, CA 92705. Tel: (714) 546 7177

● **All South Distribution**
1037 Broadway, New Orleans, LA 70118
Tel: (504) 861 2906

● **ARC Distributing Corp**
580 Reading Road, Cincinnati, OH 45202
Tel: (513) 381 4237

● **Associated Distributors**
3803 North 36th Avenue, Phoenix, AZ 85019. Tel: (602) 278 5584

● **Rick Ballard Imports**
P.O. Box 24854, Oakland, CA 94623
Tel: (415) 832 1277

● **Bayside Record Distribution**
10341 San Pablo Avenue, El Cerrito, CA 94530. Tel: (415) 525 4996

● **California Record Distributors**
1242 Los Angeles Street, Glendale, CA 91204. Tel: (818) 246 8228

● **Dutch East India Trading**
81 North Forest Avenue, Rockville Center, NY 11570 Tel: (516) 764 6200

● **Goldenrod Distribution**
5505 Delta River Drive, Lansing, MI 48906
Tel: (517) 323 4325

● **Greenworld Distribution**
20445 Gramercy Place, Torrance, CA 90501. Tel: (213) 533 8075 Tx: 4720103

● **Important Record Distribution**
149-03 Guy R. Brewer Boulevard, Jamaica, NY 11434. Tel: (718) 995 9200

● **Jem Record Distribution**
3619 Kennedy Road, South Plainfield, NJ 07080 Tel: (201) 753 6100
and
West Coast office:
18629 Topham Street, Reseda, CA 91335.
Tel: (213) 996 6754

● **MS Distributing Co**
1050 Arthur Avenue, Elk Grove Village, IL 60007. Tel: (312) 364 2888

● **Music Town Record Distributors**
830 Glastonbury Road, Suite 614, Nashville, TN 37217. Tel: (615) 327 4538

● **Rough Trade**
326 Sixth Street, San Francisco, CA 94103. Tel: (415) 621 4045 Tx: 6771141

● **Rounder Distribution**
1 Camp Street, Cambridge, MA 02142 Tel: (617) 345 0700 Tx: 921724

● **SDA Distribution**
1109 Xerxes Avenue South, Minneapolis, MN 55405. Tel: (612) 377 0590

● **Sounds Good Import Co**
3355 West El Segundo Avenue, Hawthorne, CA 90250. Tel: (213) 973 8800 Tx: 4990518

● **Southern Cross Record Distributors**
1200 Newell Hill Place, Suite 302, Walnut Creek, CA 94596. Tel: (415) 945 1855

● **Spring Arbor Distribution**
10885 Textile Road, Belleville, MI 48111
Tel: (313) 481 0900

● **Systematic Record Distributors**
1331 Fulsom Street, San Francisco, CA 94103. Tel: (415) 431 9377

● **Twin Cities Imports**
1451 University Avenue, St Paul, MN 55104. Tel: (612) 645 0227 Tx: 4940057

● **Universal Record Distribution**
919 North Broad Street, Philadelphia, PA 19123. Tel: (215) 232 3333

● MUSIC RELATED ASSOCIATIONS

● **Academy of Country Music**
6255 Sunset Boulevard, Suite 915, Hollywood, CA 90028. Tel: (213) 462 2351

● **American Federation of Musicians**
1501 Broadway, Suite 600, New York, NY 10036. Tel: (212) 869 1330

● **ASCAP**
1 Lincoln Plaza, New York, NY 10023
Tel: (212) 585 3050. Tx: 7105812084

● **Association of Independent Music Publishers**
c/o Harrison Music, 6253 Hollywood Boulevard, Hollywood, CA 90028
Tel: (213) 466 3834

● **Black Music Association**
1500 Locust Street, Suite 1905, Philadelphia, PA 19102
Tel: (215) 545 8600

● **BMI**
320 West 57th Street, New York, NY 10019. Tel: (212) 586 2000 Tx: 127823

● **Country Music Association**
7 Music Circle North, Nashville, TN 37202
Tel: (615) 244 2840 Tx: 786528

● **Jazz Composers' Orchestra Association**
500 Broadway, New York, NY 10012
Tel: (212) 925 2121 Tx: 291524

● **National Academy of Recording Arts and Sciences**
303 North Gen Oaks Boulevard, Suite 140. Burbank, CA 91502. Tel: (818) 843 8233

● **National Association of Independent Record Distributors**
c/o Richman Brothers Records, 6935 Airport Highway Lane, Pennsauken, NJ 08109. Tel: (609) 665 8085

● **National Association of Music Merchants**
5140 Avenida Encinas, Carlsbad, CA 92008. Tel: (619) 438 8001

● **Recording Industry Association of America**
888 Seventh Avenue, New York, NY 10106. Tel: (212) 765 4330

● **SESAC**
10 Columbus Circle, 13th Floor, New York, NY 10019. Tel: (212) 586 3450

● **Songwriters Guild of America**
276 5th Avenue, Room 306, New York, NY 10001 Tel: (212) 686 6820

● MUSIC MAGAZINES

● **American Songwriter**
5065 Lebanon Road, Old Hickory,
Tennessee 37138. Tel: (615) 754 5200
Pop, R&B, country music, geared to the professional and
amateur songwriter; bi-monthly; 32pp; $2.25 circ: 5,000
subscription only

● **BAM**
5951 Canning Street, Oakland, CA 94609
Tel: (415) 652 3810
and
1800 North Highland, Suite 220,
Hollywood CA 90028. Tel: (213) 467 7878
Covers US and international bands with the emphasis of
commercial successes from mainstream rock to pop and
progressive; also has features on up-and-coming bands
(California edition covers mainly Californian artists);
national ed. bi-monthly, California ed. fortnightly; 64pp;
national ed. $1.95; California ed. free; circ: 125,000
(each)

● **Billboard**
1515 Broadway, New York, NY 10036
Tel: (212) 764 7300
Trade magazine covering most areas of rock music, also
sells to the punter on the street; every Tuesday; 80pp;
$3.50; circ: 48,000

● **Boston Rock**
1318 Beacon Street, Suite 7, Brooklyme,
MA 02146. Tel: (617) 734 7043
Alternative arts and lifestyle magazine, covering local and
national underground acts, as well as imports; monthly;
32pp; free in MA, $1.50 outside MA; circ: 30,000

● **Cash Box**
330 West 58th Street, New York,
NY 10019 Tel: (212) 586 2640
Trade Magazine covering rock, pop, jazz, black
contemporary and dance music; every Monday; 50pp;
$3.50; circ: n/a

● **Circus**
419 Park Avenue South, New York,
NY 10016. Tel: (212) 685 5050
Hard rock and heavy metal superstars; monthly, last
week; 90pp; $1.95/£1.50; circ: n/a

● **CMJ New Music Report**
834 Willis Avenue, Albertson, NY 11507
Tel: (516) 248 9600
Magazine covering progressive rock, jazz, folk, country,
reggae, selling primarily to younger musicians and record
industry execs; 50% charts, 50% features; fortnightly;
60pp; $6.00; circ: 14,000

● **Country News**
5065 Lebanon Road, Old Hickory,
Tennessee 37138. Tel: (615) 754 5200
The latest country industry news for fans as well as
record executives; monthly; 24pp; $1.50; circ: 160,000
subscription only

● **Country Rhythms**
5065 Lebanon Road, Old Hickory,
Tennessee 37138 Tel: (615) 754 5200
Features and interviews with prominent country artists;
monthly; 56 pp; $2.50; circ: 120,000

● **Country Songs Round-up**
Charlton Buildings, Division Street, Derby,
CT 06418. Tel: (203) 735 3381
Lyrics of country music Top 40, reviews, features;
monthly; 58pp; $1.75; circ: n/a

● **Country Sounds**
700 East State Street, Iola, WI 54990
Tel: (715) 445 2214
Country record collectors' Magazine; monthly; 60pp;
$1.95; circ: n/a

● **CREEM**
210 South Woodward Avenue,
Birmingham, MI 48011
Tel: (313) 642 8833
Eclectic magazine that credits its readers with a sense of
humour and the second longest-running US music
magazine after Rolling Stone ; monthly; 66pp; $2.25; circ:
c. 100,000

● **Down Beat**
180 West Park Avenue, Elmhurst,
IL 60126 Tel: (312) 941 2030
Jazz magazine for contemporary musicians, also
covering rock, blues, and contemporary classical
instrumentalists; monthly; 62pp; $1.75/£2.00; circ:
95,000

● **Flipside**
PO Box 363, Whittier, CA 90608
Hardcore punk fanzine; irregular monthly; nothing else
known

● **Frets**
20605 Lazaneo, Cupertino, CA 95014
Tel: (408) 446 1105
Folk, classical, and bluegrass for acoustic stringed
instrument players; monthly; 68pp; $1.95; circ: 70,000

● **Goldmine**
700 East State Street, Iola, WI 54990
Tel: (715) 445 2214
Eclectic record collectors' magazine from hard rock to
folk and country; fortnightly; 90pp; $1.95; circ: 15,000

● **Guitar Player**
20605 Lazaneo, Cupertino, CA 95014
Tel: (408) 446 1105
Guitar magazine written by musicians for musicians, rock,
jazz, classical; monthly; 156pp; $2.95; circ: 170,000
worldwide

● **Guitar World**
1115 Broadway, 8th Floor, New York,
NY 10010. Tel: (212) 807 7100
Covers all kinds of guitar-based music, rock, jazz, blues,
etc, except classical; bi-monthly; 102pp; $2.95; circ:
160,000

● **Hard Rock**
475 Park Avenue South, New York,
NY 10016. Tel: (212) 689 2830
Mainstream hard rock, hardcore and metal; lots of
interviews and regular features; monthly; 80pp; $2.25/
£1.45; circ: 200,000 worldwide

● **High Fidelity**
825 Seventh Avenue, New York,
NY 10019. Tel: (212) 887 8337
Reviews of the latest hi-fi equipment, along with some
features on pop and classical releases; monthly; 86pp;
$2.25;
circ: 350,000

● **Hit Parader**
Charlton Building, Division Street, Derby
CT 06418. Tel: (203) 735 3381
and
New York office:
441 Lexington Avenue, Suite 808,
New York, NY 10017. Tel: (212) 370 0986
Looks at hard rock and heavy metal superstars,
interviews, features, etc. for the teenager; monthly; 82pp;
$2.25/£1.50; circ: 100,000

● **Illinois Entertainer**
P.O. Box 356, Mount Prospect, IL 60056
Tel: (312) 298 9333
Entertainment magazine covering the music scene
(among other things) in Illinois; monthly; 90pp; free in
record stores, etc; circ: 80,000

● **International Musician and
Recording World**
1075 Easton Avenue, Suite 1, Tower 2,
Somerset, NJ 08873. Tel: (201) 249 1600
Spans all types of contemporary music from pop, rock to
avant-garde ethnic. Reviews latest equipment and
releases primarily for musicians and recording
executives, but also for the listener; monthly; 64pp;
$2.50; circ: 65,000

● **Jazz Times**
8055 13th Street, Silver Springs,
MD 20910. Tel: (301) 588 4114
Straight-ahead traditional jazz, trade and fan magazine;
news, reviews, artist profiles, listings of radio airplay;
monthly; 28pp; $1.50; circ: 58,000

● **Keyboard**
20605 Lazaneo, Cupertino, CA 95014
Tel: (408) 446 1105
Features on equipment, techniques and artists, for
keyboard players; monthly; 140pp; $2.50/£2.00; circ:
85,000

● **Living Blues**
The Center for the Study of Southern
Culture, University of Mississippi,
University, MS 38677. Tel: (601) 232 5993
Blues news, interviews, and record reviews; bi-monthly;
48pp; $3.00; circ: 5,000

● **Musician**
31 Commercial Street, Gloucester,
MA 01930. Tel: (617) 281 3110
and
New York office:
1515 Broadway, New York, NY 10036
Tel: (212) 764 7300
Up-market serious magazine covering the entire
spectrum of the music-making process, creative and
technological, for the professional and dedicated
amateur; monthly; 116pp; $2.50/£1.50; circ: 116,000

● **Radio and Records**
1930 Century Park West, Los Angeles,
CA 90067. Tel: (213) 553 4330
Radio and record industry magazine with lots of charts,
regular features on US radio, news, etc; every Friday;
96pp; $5.00;
circ: n/a

● **Rock & Soul**
Charlton Building, Division Street, Derby,
CT 06418. Tel: (203) 735 3381
and
New York Office:
441 Lexington Avenue, Suite 808,
New York, NY 10017. Tel: (212) 370 0986
Glossy magazine covering commercial black music, with
news hotline, profiles, reviews; monthly; 50pp; $1.75; circ:
80,000

● **Rocket**
Charlton Building, Division Street, Derby,
CT 06418. Tel: (203) 735 3381
New superstar magazine; monthly; 50pp $1.95; circ: n/a

● **The Rocket**
2322 Second Avenue, Seattle, WA 98121
Tel: (206) 587 4001
Sardonic entertainments magazine covering local and
national acts, music, arts, politics, cartoons and gossip
columns; monthly; 38pp; $2.00; circ: 65,000

● **Rockpool Newsletter**
83 Leonard Street, 2nd Floor, New York,
NY 10013. Tel: (212) 219 0777
An alternative look at hip black music and new wave
dance, playlists and charts from club DJs and US college
radio scene; fortnightly; 30pp; $1.75; circ: 2,000

● **Rolling Stone**
745 Fifth Avenue, New York, NY 10151
Tel: (212) 758 3800
The magazine for young American adults; much more
than just a music magazine: looks at politics, popular
culture, etc etc;
a national institution; fortnightly; 100pp; $1.95/£1.90;
circ: 1,000,000 world wide

● **Song Hits**
Charlton Building, Division Street, Derby
CT 06418. Tel: (203) 735 3381
Song lyrics, concert and album reviews of Top 40 rock,
soul and country musicians; for teenage girls; monthly;
66pp; $1.95; circ: 160,000

● **Spin**
1965 Broadway, New York, NY 10023
Tel: (212) 496 6100
A zany, humorous look at established, new, and
underground acts; news and reviews from mainstream
rock to ethnic sounds; also looks at topical issues of
youth culture; monthly; 82pp; $2.00; circ: 15,000

● **Star Hits**
150 East 58th Street, New York, NY
10022 Tel: (212) 302 2626
Glossy teenage girl's magazine styled after the British
Smash Hits; interviews and features on commercial
successes; monthly; 64pp; $1.95; circ: 163,000

● **WAM**
P.O. Box 356, Mount Prospect, IL 60056
Tel: (312) 298 9333
Entertainment magazine covering the music scene in
Wisconsin; monthly; 60pp; free at record stores, etc; circ:
30,000

● **WAVELENGTH**
P.O. Box 15667, New Orleans, LA 70175
Tel: (504) 895 2342
New Orleans jazz, R&B, blues, cajun, etc and local
culture; reviews independently released records;
monthly; 40pp; free in LA, $1.50 outside LA; circ: 30,000